TRANSPORTATION

SIXTH EDITION

John J. Coyle

Edward J. Bardi

Robert A. Novack

THOMSON
SOUTH-WESTERN

Australia · Canada · Mexico · Singapore · Spain · United Kingdom · United States

THOMSON
SOUTH-WESTERN

Transportation, 6e

John C. Coyle, Edward J. Bardi, Robert A. Novack

VP/Editorial Director:
Jack W. Calhoun

Publisher:
Rob Dewey

Senior Acquisitions Editor:
Charles E. McCormick, Jr.

Developmental Editor:
Taney Wilkins

Senior Marketing Manager:
Larry Qualls

Production Editor:
Lora Arduser

Manager of Technology, Editorial:
Vicky True

Technology Project Editor:
Christine A. Wittmer

Manufacturing Coordinator:
Diane Lohman

Art Director:
Chris Miller

Production House:
GEX Publishing Services

Cover and Internal Designer:
Justin Klefeker

Cover Illustration:
©GettyImages/PhotoDisc, Inc.

Printer:
Courier
Westford, MA

Printed in the United States of America
1 2 3 4 5 07 06 05 04

ISBN: 0-324-20214-8

Library of Congress Control Number:
2004112065

For more information contact South-Western, 5191 Natorp Boulevard, Mason, Ohio, 45040.
Or you can visit our Internet site at: http://www.swlearning.com

To our wives, Barbara, Carol, and Judith, and our children,
John and Susan; Susan and Pamela; and Tom, Elizabeth, and Alex,
for all their support and sacrifice

About the Authors

John J. Coyle was the first person to teach a course at Penn State under the label "Business Logistics." After joining the faculty in 1961, he played an active role in developing the logistics and transportation program at Penn State. Dr. Coyle served as executive director of the Center for Supply Chain Research (CSCR) from 1989 until 2000. He currently is the director of corporate relations for CSCR and professor emeritus of business administration. His many career highlights include 12 college and university awards for outstanding teaching and advising. In 2001 he received the Distinguished Lions Paw Award for outstanding service to the University. He received the Council of Logistics Management's highest honor, the Distinguished Service Award, in 1991. For 30 years Dr. Coyle served as the faculty athletic representative to the NCAA and the Big Ten for Penn State (1970–2000). He served as special assistant for strategic planning to the president of Penn State University from 1983 to 1986 and from 1989 to 1991. During 1982 to 1987 he served as assistant dean and director of the undergraduate program and from 1987 to 1989 as associate dean in The Smeal College of Business Administration at Penn State. Coyle has also chaired many University-wide committees and served as chairman of the faculty senate. Dr. Coyle has written more than 100 publications and provided in-house educational programs for more than 300 companies. Coyle is president of CLSA Associates, a supply chain and logistics consulting company. He is a member of the boards of Sears Logistics Services Company, ChemLogix, and Avicon.

Dr. Edward J. Bardi is principal of Bardi Consulting and professor emeritus of logistics and transportation at the University of Toledo. Dr. Bardi held faculty positions at Pennsylvania State University, the University of Toledo, and Iowa State University. Dr. Bardi has served as a consultant to numerous businesses and public agencies in the areas of transportation, distribution, reverse logistics, private trucking, warehouse location and operation, marketing, business organization, and economic development. He is a popular seminar leader of transportation and logistics/supply chain management development programs. Dr. Bardi is a co-author of two textbooks, *The Management of Business Logistics* and *Transportation*. He has published numerous articles dealing with business logistics, transportation management, carrier selection, economic development, and employee household goods movement in various academic and professional journals. Dr. Bardi is married to the former Carol Ann Pearson and has two grown children, Susan Renee and Pamela Lynn, and five grandchildren.

Robert A. Novack is an associate professor of supply chain management at Penn State. He received his B.S. and M.B.A. degrees from Penn State with majors in business logistics and earned his Ph.D. from the University of Tennessee with a major in business logistics. Before coming to Penn State, he taught logistics and transportation courses at both the University of Cincinnati and the University of Tennessee. He currently teaches courses in introduction to supply chain management, transportation, fulfillment and operations management, and strategic supply chain management. He received the Fred Brand, Jr. Outstanding Undergraduate Teaching Award as well as the Fred Brand, Jr. Outstanding Undergraduate Advising Award in the Smeal College at Penn State.

His research has been published in *The Journal of Business Logistics*, *Transportation Journal*, *International Journal of Physical Distribution and Logistics Management*, and *International Journal of Operations and Production Management*. Dr. Novack also authored a chapter entitled, "Introduction to Supply Chain management" in the *Strategic Purchasing Handbook*. Dr. Novack is also a co-author on a textbook entitled *Transportation* and a co-author on a research based book entitled *Creating Logistics Value: Themes for the Future*. Dr. Novack has professional experience in both carrier management and logistics management. He has worked for Yellow Freight, Inc. as an operations planning analyst and for the Drackett Company (formerly a division of Bristol Myers/Squibb) as manager of logistics planning and control. He has done consulting work for a variety of companies dealing with topics such as strategic planning, information systems, customer satisfaction measurement, distribution management, transportation management, and inventory management.

Preface

Since the first edition of *Transportation* was published in 1982, much has changed in the world of transportation and much has remained the same. This paradox can be explained by first exploring what has remained the same during the intervening 23 years since the first edition. The common trait during these years is change. The preface to the first edition cites dramatic changes in deregulation, fuel costs, and technology as major forces impacting the transportation sector. These same change factors are present today but with different characteristics.

However, the major constant in transportation is the value it creates in the economy. Transportation enables citizens throughout the world to enjoy the goods and services produced in different countries as well as to travel and interact with different peoples and cultures. Without an efficient transportation system, the level of social and economic advancement we enjoy today would not be possible. The level of industrial development depends on a sound transportation system to bridge the temporal and spatial gaps associated with mass production and geographically fixed raw materials. Transportation remains the glue that binds supply sources and markets.

The world and the transportation environment are much different today compared to what existed during the previous editions. We are operating in a global economy requiring transportation to extend its reach over great distances. Shippers have adopted supply chain management that focuses managerial attention on the total cost of and time required to lay down a product at a given market. Transportation management systems are becoming more widely used by shippers seeking to consolidate shipments, optimize carrier loading, and reduce transportation costs. The Internet has changed the way shippers/passengers and carriers communicate, with freight loads being tendered via Internet and passengers booking their own flights on carrier websites. The advancement of global positioning systems (GPS) software enables the carrier to track a shipment from pickup to delivery. The cost of petroleum fuels reached an all-time high during this writing and is causing tremendous inflationary pressures on freight rates, passenger travel costs, and the world economy. The escalating cost of fuel is forcing carriers to modify operating procedures, shippers to optimize freight shipments, and citizen to modify travel patterns and automobile usage in an attempt to reduce fuel costs. Considerable effort is underway to develop alternative energy sources and engines to power our automobiles, trucks, planes, and boats with goals of lower fuel costs and less environmental impact.

Probably the most significant change was the September 11, 2001 terrorist attack on the United States. The U.S. air transportation system was grounded in a matter of hours, and rail, water, and truck shipments to the East Coast were suspended. But in a matter of days the transportation system was functioning. The flow of vital food and other necessities continued to the major metropolitan areas of the East Coast. The resilience of the U.S. transportation providers kept the U.S. supply chains functioning during this crisis. Today, we see increased regulations aimed at protecting the United States from future attacks using the transportation system. Inspections of global shipments entering the United States has increased transit times for global supply chains, while the increased security attention to domestic transportation operations is increasing domestic supply chain transit times.

The text is organized into three parts. Part I contains two chapters, "Transportation, the Supply Chain and the Economy" and "Transportation Regulation and Public Policy." In these two chapters the role and importance of transportation in the supply chain management and the economy are explored, along with an overview of transportation regulation and public policy. Part II addresses the traditional modes of transportation, including special carriers and global transportation. There are six chapters that examine the fundamental economic and operating characteristics of each mode, along with special carriers and global transportation. Part III discusses transportation management from both the shipper and carrier perspective. The five chapters give attention to transportation costing and pricing, carrier strategy, information management and technology, and shipper transportation management strategy and process.

Changes in the Sixth Edition

This edition of *Transportation* contains three new chapters in addition to significant revisions of the overview, modal, and transportation management chapters. The new chapters are:

- Chapter 10, Carrier Strategies: This chapter begins with an examination of the operating conditions—networks, operations, labor, and performance metrics—of today's carriers and the operations, marketing, and financial strategies utilized by today's carriers. A managerial approach is employed in the discussion of such carrier strategies as consolidation, technology, pricing, labor, infrastructure and congestion, finance, equipment, and third-party subsidiaries.
- Chapter 12, Shipper Strategies: The first of two shipper-oriented transportation management chapters, this chapter provides an overview of the transportation management function, general strategies relating to management, small and bulk shipments, as well as outbound and inbound transportation and outsourcing. Attention is given to the strategic approaches used in carrier selection, negotiations, contracting, and bidding, with consideration given to relationship management and contingency planning.
- Chapter 13, Shipper Process: The second transportation management chapter focuses on the shipper process. Both the domestic and global transportation processes are discussed with the attendant managerial functions. Topics given consideration include shipment analysis, carrier scheduling, load tendering, shipment monitoring INCOTERMS, and documentation. The tactical aspects of transportation management will give the reader a good grasp of what is involved in managing a shipper's transportation function.

The "Information and Management and Technology" chapter is not a new chapter, but it has been revised to give consideration to transportation management systems (TMS) software and new technologies such as the Internet and Global Positioning Systems (GPS) utilized by carriers and shippers for communication and shipment tracking.

Features

Although there have been many changes in this edition of *Transportation*, the student orientation and managerial approach remain the focal points. The authors have endeavored to use an easy-to-read writing style supplemented with examples from today's transportation system to help the student understand transportation management issues. We concentrate on the fundamentals of transportation management and temper these fundamentals with the conditions confronting today's managers such as the supply chain management approach utilized by shippers and carriers. Given the authors' combined teaching experience, the text attempts to anticipate many student questions and proffer explanations. We retained features of the book that made previous editions successful: "Stop Offs" that expand chapter material by providing real-life examples that deepen students' understanding; thorough chapter outlines and bullet summaries; suggested readings and cases; and key terms at the end of the chapter will help the student become more familiar with transportation terminology and focus on key concepts.

Ancillaries

The text contains a number of ancillaries that will aid the student and instructor.

- **Instructor Resource CD with Instructor's Manual and Test Bank** (ISBN 0-324-20215-6), prepared by Wally Weart of the Institute of Logistical Management, includes chapter outlines, answers to end-of-chapter study questions, commentary on end-of-chapter cases, teaching tips, and transparency masters. The test bank contains multiple choice, true/false, and essay questions for each chapter.
- **A PowerPoint** presentation, prepared by Gary Gittings of Pennsylvania State University, is included in the Instructor Resource CD, and contains slides that cover the major chapter topics and figures from the text.
- **The Book Support Website**, http://coyle.swlearning.com, provides additional resources. The instructor's manual and PowerPoint files are downloadable from the website so instructors can easily customize class presentations.

Acknowledgements

Many people have helped us complete this edition of *Transportation*. The authors are indebted to the numerous academic colleagues and transportation professionals who have helped us sharpen our focus on the major transportation issues to be included in the text. The many students at our respective academic institutions and the executive education programs have served as sounding boards to help us sharpen our presentation of today's complex and interrelated transportation topics. Some individuals deserve special consideration: Michael Levans, Editor of *Logistics Management* magazine, Jean Beierlein, LuAnn Jaworski, Teresa Lehman, and Tracy Shannon.

We extend our appreciation to the members of our South-Western team, who have provided support throughout the completion of this revision: Charles McCormick, Senior Acquisitions Editor; Taney Wilkins, Developmental Editor; Lora Arduser, Production Editor; and, Larry Qualls, Senior Marketing Manager.

We continue to owe a debt to our many colleagues for their beneficial comments and suggestions in the development of earlier editions of our text. These colleagues include:

Jim Bander	University of Florida
Richard Barsness	Lehigh University
William A. Cunningham	University of South Alabama
Michael Demetsky	University of Virginia

Kathryn Dobie	North Carolina A & T State University
Martin Dresner	University of Maryland
Phil Evers	University of Maryland
Jerry Foster	University of Colorado
Kent N. Gourdin	College of Charleston
Mary Holcomb	Iowa State University
Kevin Horn	University of North Florida
Lester Howel	University of Virginia
Jim Kling	Niagara University
Eric Mohr	Golden Gate University
Paul Murphy	John Carroll University
Edwin P. Patton	University of Tennessee
Clyde Walter	Iowa State University
Walter L. Weart	Oakton College
Philip A. Weatherford	Embry-Riddle Aeronautical University
Ken Williamson	James Madison College

Brief Contents

Contents

Part I

The Role and Importance of Transportation

Chapter 1

Transportation, the Supply Chain, and the Economy

Transportation is a vital activity in moving both freight and passengers around the world. The management of transportation is concerned with the overall purchase and control of this movement service used by a firm in achieving its logistics objectives. **Business logistics** is the process of planning, implementing, and controlling the efficient and effective flow and storage of goods, services, and related information from the point of origin to the point of consumption for the purpose of conforming to customer requirements.[1] This definition specifically includes the importance of transportation in business logistics. A new term is being used to describe this flow and movement in an organizational environment: supply chain management. **Supply chain management** is an expanded version of the logistics process. Whereas logistics has traditionally focused on coordinating the product, the information movement, and the flow activities of an individual firm, supply chain management coordinates the product, information, cash movement, and flow activities in a **logistics channel environment**. The effective and efficient management of transportation has a significant impact on all three types of interfirm flows (product, information, and cash) and is critical in achieving supply chain integration and objectives.[2]

The objective of this chapter is to emphasize the importance of transportation to the individual firm as well as to the economy. Attention is given to how transportation functions within the realm of supply chain management and business logistics. Finally, the nature of transportation demand is discussed.

THE 2000s: A DECADE OF CHALLENGE

During the 1990s, many businesses throughout the United States were compelled to reevaluate their approach to doing business and to focus their attention upon some fundamentals of successful business operations, such as customer service, quality, and the value added by service and/or productivity. The external factors that resulted in this reexamination of business practices included intensified global competition and increased involvement in international markets, deregulation of transportation, mergers and acquisitions, and shrinking profit margins.[3]

Business practices in the 2000s have been dramatically influenced by the Internet's facilitation of electronic transactions. Information available through the Internet has exponentially increased customer expectations for the basics that companies focused on in the 1990s: customer service, quality, and value-added services. For example, order cycle time, which was measured in weeks or days, today is called "click to receipt" and is measured in days or hours. These customer demands have increased the importance of the "backroom" operations of an organization (i.e., transportation and logistics). Advances in technology have allowed companies to provide full supply chain visibility of inventory, whether in motion or at rest. These changes have challenged companies to focus more on the concept of supply chain than ever before.

The focus of attention on basics, such as the **value added** by customer service, has increased management's interest in logistics as a potential contribution to revitalizing organizations and making them more competitive again. Companies have realized the importance of logistics execution to supply chain excellence. Although logistics has been a growing area of responsibility in many companies since the 1960s, it is fair to say that the profile of logistics managers in corporate America was not as high in most companies prior to 1980 as it is today. Logistics managers tended to be regarded as hard-working individuals who played primarily a supporting role to marketing and manufacturing. However, the "back-to-basics" movement helped to change the profile level of logistics in the 1980s, particularly because a growing number of companies recognized the role that logistics can play *at the margin* in their strategic efforts to gain or regain a sustainable competitive edge.[4] Efficient transportation systems support logistics practices such as "just-in-time" inventory and manufacturing; vendor managed inventory (VMI); and collaborative planning, forecasting, and replenishment (CPFR). Companies such as Pfizer and Wal*Mart have used these concepts to lower costs and gain significant market share.

The beginning of the 21st century actually saw a continuation of the evolution of logistics that began during the decades following World War II; however, since then, several variables have introduced new challenges:

1. The Internet and e-business
2. Continued globalization
3. Business alliances
4. Rapidly changing technology[5]

Because the influence of these factors will continue to be felt throughout the 2000s, a brief explanation is in order here.

The late 1990s saw an explosion of Internet sites offering customers the convenience of shopping from home and promising the reliable and swift delivery of their purchases. Many of these sites, however, were "front ends" (only a website) and relied on other organizations for the "back end" (fulfillment) operations. This proved disastrous for many sites during the Christmas of 1999, as delivery date promises were missed and the quality of customer service declined because of a lack of coordination between order taking and order fulfillment. Today, however, many of these firms have gained control of fulfillment operations through the use of private operations or third party logistics providers (3PLs). **E-business** over the **Internet** has quickly developed into a powerful medium for firms to reach customers through information, products, and services. This has put pressure on the logistics and transportation networks of shippers. Firms such as UPS and FedEx Ground have seen an explosion of small package deliveries to both business and residential addresses. Shipment sizes have decreased and frequency of shipments have increased. Real-time inventory tracking has allowed companies in the supply chain to eliminate inventories. Reliable transportation networks have also allowed firms to eliminate unnecessary safety stock inventories. With all of these challenges, the use of the Internet for e-business is still in the developmental stage. The decade of the 2000s will provide many more opportunities and challenges for companies to use this powerful method of information exchange to shape their supply chains and logistics networks.

The globalization of business has had a tremendous impact on the way companies operate today. The scope of **globalization** runs the gamut from foreign sourcing in the procurement area and/or selective sales in other countries to multifaceted international distribution, manufacturing, and marketing strategies that encompass international production sites, multiple staging of inventory, countertrading in the sale of products, and so on. Whatever the situation, the cost of logistics as a percentage of total cost is greater for international ventures, and the complexity of logistics operations usually increases at a geometric rate in the international arena. Often if procurement is included, logistics is the single-most important factor for successful international ventures.[6] Transportation, in particular, has been affected because of the distances involved both inbound to manufacturing from foreign sourcing and outbound for additional manufacturing or delivery to customers. Transportation might account for as much as 50 percent of the total logistics costs.

The 1990s saw a dramatic growth in the use of 3PLs for basic transportation and distribution processes. This growth continues in the 2000s with 3PLs expanding their services to include inventory management, order management, and inventory ownership. These relationships allow 3PLs to gain a larger "share of wallet" of their clients business. This is one example of the change in the nature of **business alliances** that are being developed in industry. The beginning of this decade has seen Amazon.com performing fulfillment for Toys "Я" Us.com, Wal*Mart.com outsourcing their Internet fulfillment operations, US Airways and United Airlines joining forces to share flights, fares, and frequent traveler programs, and food manufacturers sharing capacity in transportation vehicles for customer deliveries. The 2000s have brought a new type of alliance among companies, which are sometimes competitors. These alliances focus on eliminating duplication of assets and processes so that both parties can benefit. The remainder of the 2000s will more than likely see more innovative types of business alliances.

Another factor is rapidly changing **technology** and, in particular, changes in computer hardware and software. The significant price reductions for powerful computer equipment have helped bring about better inventory control, better equipment scheduling, more efficient rating of transportation movements, and so on. Technological changes in communications (such as satellite global positioning systems to maintain contact with motor carrier fleets) have helped to improve service quality to the extent that motor carrier companies now are able to meet narrowly defined time windows for pickups and deliveries. The continued development of radio frequency identification (RFID) is allowing companies to track freight to the individual package level. The interface between communication technology and computers is another area that has tremendous potential for logistics. These changes are just the tip of the iceberg; many other developments could be included in this area, such as bar coding and robotics.[7]

All of these challenges have provided opportunities for logistics and transportation processes to add value to product movement throughout the globe. They have also given the logistics and transportation processes more responsibility for the management of information and cash flows throughout the supply chain.

THE LOGISTICS CONCEPT

Logistics, as we know it today, began to develop after World War II in response to internal cost pressures associated with expanding product lines and increased product value, as well as external pressures from more competitive market conditions. All of these factors led to activities being revamped in companies on the physical distribution side of logistics. In many cases the result was an **integration** of outbound transportation and field warehousing to more systematically examine trade-offs that would result in overall lower costs (see Figure 1.1). Integration was a key element even during this very early period of logistics development (i.e., an integration of outbound transportation and field warehousing and the application of a systems perspective that emphasized total cost).

The cost and market pressures continued to mount in the 1960s and 1970s with more global competition in U.S. domestic markets, rising labor costs, and shortages of some essential raw materials and supplies, which resulted in additional activities being added to the logistics function in many organizations (see Figure 1.2). These activities usually included **inbound** transportation, production scheduling, customer service, and packaging, which were integrated into the logistics function for

FIGURE 1.1 Typical Logistics Network—Physical Distribution

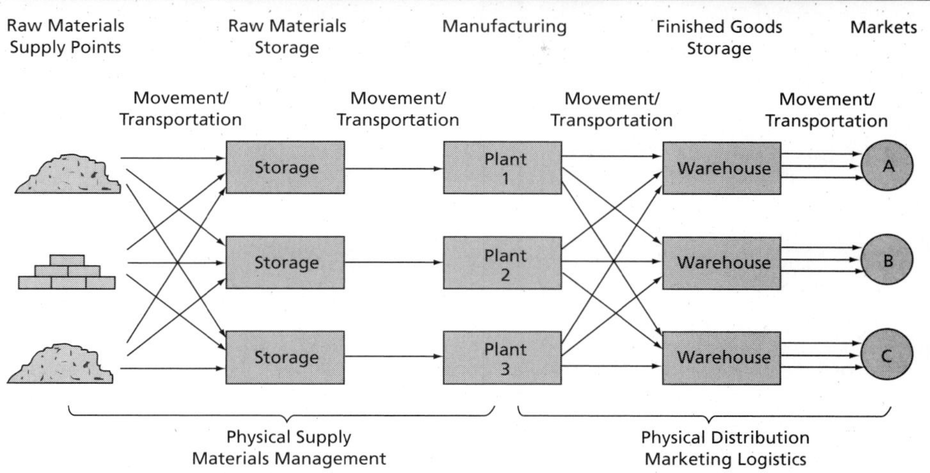

FIGURE 1.2 Typical Logistics Network—Materials Management

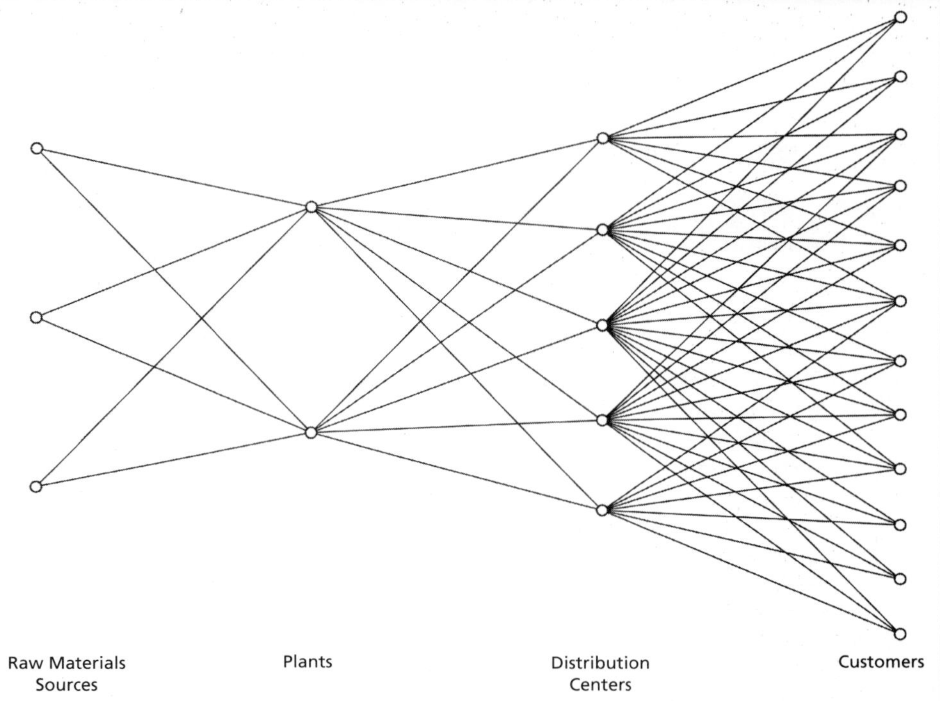

Source: Center for Supply Chain Research, Penn State University, 2004

additional cost control and evaluation of trade-offs. Therefore, it again can be stated that integration and the systems concept played a key role in the development of successful logistics organizations in the 1960s and 1970s. The 1980s were a period of rapid or revolutionary change, with the addition of more activities—that is, further integration of the logistics function and a more comprehensive package of line and staff activities to manage (see Figure 1.3).

The modern era has seen the importance of logistics to the U.S. military effort during the Persian Gulf war in the early 1990s. In fact, the Persian Gulf effort has been referred to as the "logistics war," and the importance of the integrated logistics pipeline supporting the fighting effort was acknowledged repeatedly by the military and civilian leadership. The *integrated* logistics concept was obviously critical to the military's success in the Gulf War. Today, the U.S. military is revolutionizing the processes they use for logistics. The Marines have formed the Integrated Logistics Concept (ILC) to reengineer how they perform the maintenance and supply processes for their land-based weapon systems. They are adopting commercial best practices (such as the use of 3PLs) to eliminate waste and duplication of assets while improving the readiness of their weapon systems.

One of the most widely used and cited definitions of logistics is as follows:

> Logistics is the process of planning, implementing, and controlling the efficient, effective flow and storage of raw materials, in-process inventory, finished goods, services, and related information from point of origin to point of consumption (including inbound, outbound, internal, and external movements) for the purpose of conforming to customer requirements.[8]

Implied in the definition is that the logistics process *provides a systems framework for decision making* that integrates transportation, inventory levels, warehousing space, materials-handling systems, packaging, and other related activities that encompass appropriate trade-offs involving cost and service. Another widely used definition states that logistics involves the efficient and effective management of inventory, whether in motion or at rest, to satisfy customer requirements and organizational objectives.[9] The important aspect of the latter definition is that transportation service is recognized as inventory in motion; therefore, the true cost is more than the actual rate charged by the transportation company.

FIGURE 1.3 The Logistics Evolution

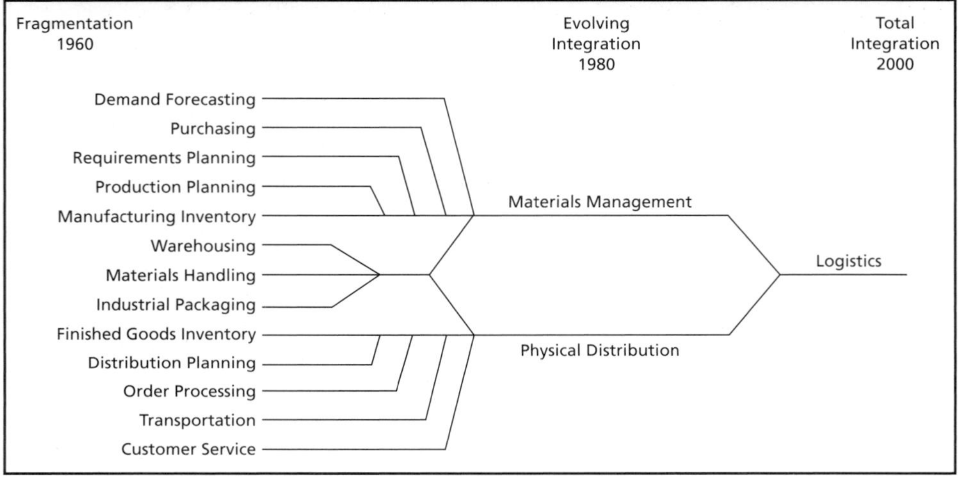

To gain some additional perspective on the importance of the integrated logistics concept and how it has affected business organizations, let's use Dow Chemical Company as an illustrative example.[10] Dow Chemical Company is a diversified manufacturer of chemicals and plastics, and produces and sells more than 1,800 products that can be categorized into four major product groups: basic chemicals, basic plastics, industrial specialties, and consumer specialties. There are many different formulations of these products, which are packaged in many different containers at 28 manufacturing locations in the United States. These products can be distributed through any one or a combination of 350 stocking points.

Because Dow is highly integrated, the supplier for raw materials for one manufacturing process is often another Dow plant. Managing work-in-process inventories is not difficult, but managing finished goods inventories is complex and challenging.

Many of the finished products must be in inventory when customer orders are received without incurring excess carrying costs. Just the size and complexity of the logistics network makes managing it extremely difficult, but other factors add to the problem as well. Traditionally, for example, the product supply chain links of manufacturing, distribution, and suppliers worked independently of one another, trying to anticipate demand but without any real insight into the future demand from the other links in the chain. Inventory was used to buffer uncertainty at each step, which resulted in large inventories at plant and field warehouses.[11]

Computer systems are now being used to substitute information for inventory all along the supply chain. Each link works with the same demand information, properly offset by time and rounding qualities. The result is that each link in the supply chain provides a time-phased schedule of the demand it expects to place on the next link.

Demand forecasting is used to anticipate customer demand. Some customers might provide estimates of demand, leaving forecasting to anticipate the rest. Distribution requirements planning (DRP) considers inventory position and translates forecasts into realistic shipping quantities and schedules, and then consolidates that demand at each shipping point in the distribution network and, ultimately, to the plants. Master production scheduling (MPS) systems are used to translate schedules of DRP demand into feasible master schedules of when finished goods will be produced. The master schedule puts demand on raw materials, so MRP translates master schedules into a schedule of when raw materials need to arrive from the suppliers.[12]

Computer systems also support the flow of materials and products along the supply chain. Purchasing and transportation systems supported by electronic data interchange (EDI), and more recently the Internet, manage the flow of material from vendors. Numerous technologies, such as CAD/CAM and automatic materials-handling systems, support the manufacturing process. Deployment planning, vehicle load management, and vehicle routing and scheduling systems plan the movement of products from plants to warehouses to customers. The benefits of using an integrated systems approach to supply and demand have allowed Dow to reduce its logistics costs on a relative basis and improve its customer service.

Much more could be included here in relation to integrated logistics at companies like Dow, but enough perspective has been provided to show that companies want to attain high levels of customer service while reducing inventory levels and transportation costs. The improvement of service and the reduction of cost would have been described as contradictory 10 years ago, but not today. Logistics and transportation systems in the leading organizations are achieving these seemingly contradictory goals by strategic management of their logistics systems.[13]

As indicated, modal choice decisions are now made using a selection framework based on an integrated set of logistics-related factors. Decisions are no longer based simply on transportation cost (rates). Other logistics factors can significantly influence the decision.

THE SUPPLY CHAIN CONCEPT

The concept of supply chain management is the newest thrust for many organizations attempting to integrate business processes between their channel partners. Many companies and authors are using the terms *logistics* and *supply chain* interchangeably. This is not correct. Supply chain management integrates **product**, **information**, and **cash flows** among organizations from the point of origin to the point of consumption, with the goal of maximizing consumption satisfaction and minimizing organization costs.[14] Figure 1.4 is an attempt to depict this integration.

Logistics has traditionally been responsible for managing the physical flow of products among organizations. Activities such as transportation and warehousing were used to ensure that the movement of goods was continuous and reliable. Marketing and sales have been responsible for providing information to customers before and after the transaction. Information technology has allowed logistics to take on additional responsibility for managing information flow among organizations. Bar coding and EDI (discussed in Chapter 11, "Information Management and Technology") have allowed logistics to provide information on **product flows** before they occur, during movement, and after delivery. Finally, finance and accounting have been responsible for cash flows among organizations in a channel by controlling invoicing and collections. Some logistics organizations, like Welch's Foods, have taken on these additional cash-flow activities. Even if logistics does not have control over a firm's cash flow, it certainly has influence over it. For example, many firms will invoice a customer upon receipt of an order. The customer will not process payment until proof of delivery is received, so faster and more reliable transportation

FIGURE 1.4 Logistics Evolution to Supply Chain Management

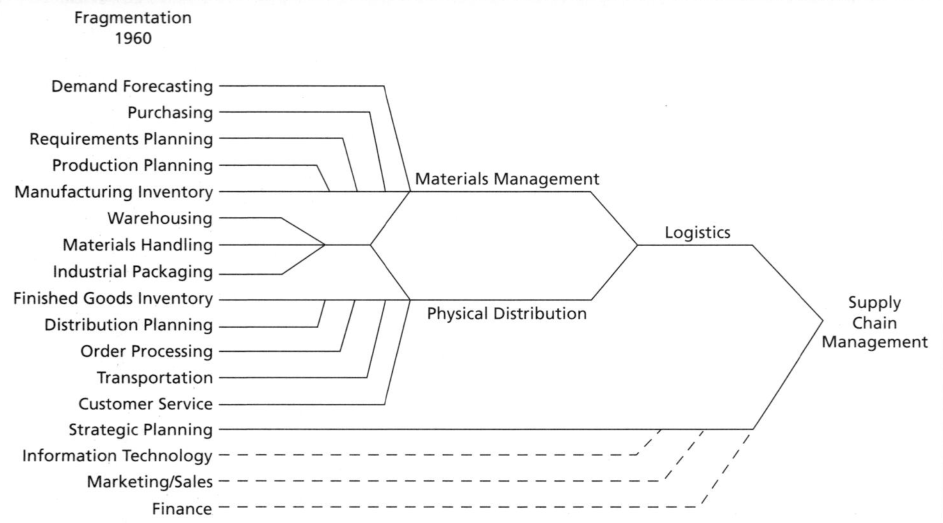

can begin this customer payment process sooner as well as offer the ability to generate a proof of delivery document through EDI. Thus, logistics management is part of supply chain management. In some organizations logistics controls all three flows: product, information, and cash. In other organizations logistics controls product flow, manages additional information flows, and influences cash flows. This integral involvement of logistics in supply chain management might be one explanation for the two terms being used interchangeably.

As is the case for logistics, transportation plays a significant role in integrating these flows among channel partners. The concept of flows has traditionally been a part of how transportation is managed—a continuous movement of product and its related information between suppliers and customers. Along with its impact on cash flows, it is easy to realize the importance of transportation to the supply chain. Satellite technology and EDI have allowed the transportation activity to reduce inventories, improve service, and generate positive financial results for supply chain partners. These technologies allow firms in the supply chain to "see" inventory while it is moving, thus improving the predictability of delivery time.

The concept of supply chain management is the next stage in logistics evolution. Logistics has proven to be an enabling process for firms in their attempts to integrate product, information, and cash flows into a true enterprise model. Many firms have found that logistics has provided the impetus for this integration.[15]

TOTAL-COST ANALYSIS

An inherent characteristic of the business logistics approach is the **total-cost analysis.** Logistics managers must consider three levels of optimality when making decisions. The first level of optimality in the decision-making process must consider the interrelationship between transportation, warehousing, inventory, and customer service. No one area of logistics operates independently. The decisions made in the transportation area, for example, have an impact on the cost of warehousing and inventory, product marketability, and the cost of lost sales or productivity.

In the absence of a total-cost approach to transportation decision making, a company might use a mode of transportation that has a low transportation rate. The use of a low-cost transportation method of movement might minimize total transportation costs, but it does not guarantee the minimization of total movement and storage costs. Low-cost transportation is usually associated with slow service, which means higher warehousing and inventory costs and lower customer service.

The second level of optimality for logistics is the impact a logistics decision has on other areas within the firm, such as marketing and manufacturing. The use of a slower mode of transportation might save transportation expense but might also negatively impact customer service or production efficiencies.

The third level of optimality concerns the impact of a logistics decision on supply chain partners. A warehouse might decide that a 32 x 40-inch pallet fits their slotting strategies, whereas their customer requires a 40 x 48-inch pallet. This would cause a transfer of cost from the shipper's warehouse to the customer. This decision might not be in the best interest of the supply chain.

The total-cost analysis also requires the decision maker to consider **cost trade-offs** within the system. A decision to use air rather than motor carrier transportation would trade the higher costs of transportation for possible savings in warehousing, inventory, and increased sales. Cost trade-offs might result in lower overall logistics costs or higher total costs. The significance of the cost trade-off, and the total-cost analysis, is the recognition of the interrelationship of the logistics variables.

Without a business logistics approach within a company, the total-cost approach might be difficult to implement. For example, total costs might be lowered by the switch to higher-cost air transportation because the higher transportation costs are traded for lower costs of warehousing and inventory. From the viewpoint of the total firm, such a decision would be desirable. However, from the transportation manager's viewpoint (performance is measured upon transportation costs incurred), the decision to use air carriage is not desirable. In the absence of an integrated, business logistics approach, the switch to air carriers probably would not be made.

As previously mentioned, the total-cost approach to business logistics emphasizes the interrelationship of logistics to other areas of the firm. The two functions most directly affected by logistics are marketing and production. Physical distribution activities are sometimes considered part of the marketing function because the movement of the finished goods to the customer completes the sales transaction. The quality of the logistics service provided to the customer can be used as a marketing tool to enhance sales, or, if the service is unacceptable, logistics service can cause a loss in sales. Firms that are capable of offering logistics service levels that reduce a buyer's cost will have a competitive edge in the marketplace.

This logistics impact upon sales is considered in a total-cost context by examining decisions in terms of cost of lost sales (profits). The level of inventory, the number and location of warehouses, and the carrier used to deliver goods determines the level of service provided and the resultant impact upon sales and profits. When changes are considered in any of these areas, the total cost of the proposed change must reflect the benefit of increased profits as well as the added cost of lost profits due to the service level changes.

STOP OFF

The True Meaning of Supply Chain Management

There has been much discussion in recent years of the differences between the terms "distribution," "logistics," and "supply chain management." To many people, those terms are synonymous. Yet they *are* different, and I think it's important to distinguish between them, not only to ensure clarity of communication, but also as a way to understand the progressive levels of capabilities that companies need to develop to successfully compete today.

Here are some definitions I find useful:

- ***Distribution*** involves the outbound flow of materials from the supplier or manufacturer to customers. It naturally includes warehousing, transportation, and inventory management activities.
- ***Logistics***, according to the Council of Logistics Management, is "that part of the supply chain that plans, implements, and controls the efficient forward and reverse flow and storage of goods, services, and related information between the point of origin and the point of consumption in order to meet customer requirements."
- ***Supply chain management***, in my mind, is broader than logistics and includes all activities involved in the sourcing, manufacturing or conversion, storage, distribution, and delivery of goods to customers. It involves integration with channel partners, including suppliers, distributors, and customers, to create a linked channel.

That's a lot of words. But supply chain management is more that just words or a concept. In the real world, I find that companies that practice supply chain management use their operations not only to reduce costs and inventories, but also drive up revenues. For example:

- ***Seven-Eleven Japan*** replenishes stores up to eight times a day to provide high in-stock levels, fresh products, and a varying assortment to meet customer needs at different times of the day. Its supply chain capabilities have helped Seven-Eleven Japan become the largest and most profitable convenience store in that country.
- ***Zara Corporation***, a Spanish apparel retailer, has built an operating model that allows it to bring new products to market as well as to replenish stores three times faster than its competitors. The company has effectively used postponement strategies to hold uncut fabrics in inventory, then cut, dye, and sew to fill electronically transmitted orders. This supply chain capability allows Zara to bring hot fashion styles to market very quickly, rapidly replenish hot sellers, and maintain a high level of in-stock availability. This capability also has allowed Zara to grow its revenues at a 20-percent annual rate—far above the industry average.
- ***Dell Computers'*** "direct-to-customer" operating model is famous for its efficiency, driving down costs, and enabling Dell to maintain the lowest inventories in the computer industry. It is also a powerful revenue generator because it allows Dell to configure products that are tailored for specific customer needs.

Companies like Seven-Eleven Japan, Zara, Dell, and many others have discovered the true meaning of supply chain management in low costs, high asset productivity, and increased revenues. My advice is to follow their lead: Forget about wordy definitions, but be sure your company is using supply chain management to grow its top line.

William C. Copacino is group chief executive of the Business Consulting Group of Accenture. A frequent speaker before business and professional groups, Mr. Copacino has a number of publications to his credit, including the book *Supply Chain Management: The Basics and Beyond* (The St. Lucie Press, 1997). He is based in Accenture's Boston office, 100 William St., Wellesley, MA 02181. Phone (617) 454-4480.

The relationship between production and logistics stems from the physical supply activities that support the production process. More specifically, the production department is the customer for the raw materials required for manufacturing. The movement and storage functions establish a quality of service that will impact the cost of production. If goods are late or not available for use, the production line might be forced to stop. Most firms recognize that the cost of stopping the production line is extremely high and that the potential total cost associated with low supply levels is also very high. Accordingly, the logistics decisions are made to ensure high service levels and virtually no shortages.

Another total-cost impact of logistics and production deals with the length of the production run and the amount of inventory generated. Cost trade-offs exist between long production runs that result in low production costs and the corresponding high inventory and inventory carrying costs. The length of the production run is determined by examining the total cost of the average production costs and the inventory holding costs at various levels of production.

The total-cost concept of logistics provides an analytical framework for considering the impact of logistics decisions. Decisions in one area of logistics, such as transportation, have a cost trade-off effect with other areas of logistics and of the firm. The minimization of total logistics costs is the objective of logistics.

BUSINESS LOGISTICS ACTIVITIES

The business logistics function recognizes the movement–storage interaction in the provision of time, place, and quantity utilities in goods. That is, a positive and direct relationship exists between the movement and storage elements of the logistics system. This relationship enables the transportation manager to make decisions that are beneficial to the total logistics system, the company as a whole, and the supply chain, rather than to the transportation area exclusively.

Transportation decisions have an impact on the functional costs of finance, production, and marketing. The decision regarding the mode of transportation used affects the level of **inventories** to be held, the size of raw material orders, and the quality of **service** provided to the customer. For example, water transportation is slow, requires large-sized shipments, and is discontinuous during the winter months, causing increased inventory levels and costs. The purchasing department must purchase in lot sizes approximating 1,000 to 1,500 tons, causing large inventories to be held. In addition, large inventories are required to prevent business stoppage during the winter months, a definite customer service disadvantage.

The above example illustrates how the transportation decision affects other functional areas in a company. Figure 1.5 shows the interrelationship of the logistics functional areas and of logistics and other functions of the firm. For simplicity, company functions in Figure 1.5 are based on **utility creation**, that is, form utility created by production, time, place, and quantity utilities created by logistics, as well as possession utility created by marketing. Other functional areas are required for the viable operation of any business, but these three functions permit examination of the role of transportation in business logistics and in the operation of a company.

A number of functions included in logistics also are included under production and/or marketing. For example, purchasing is included under the auspices of production and the materials management portion of logistics, pricing is included in

FIGURE 1.5 Business Logistics Functions

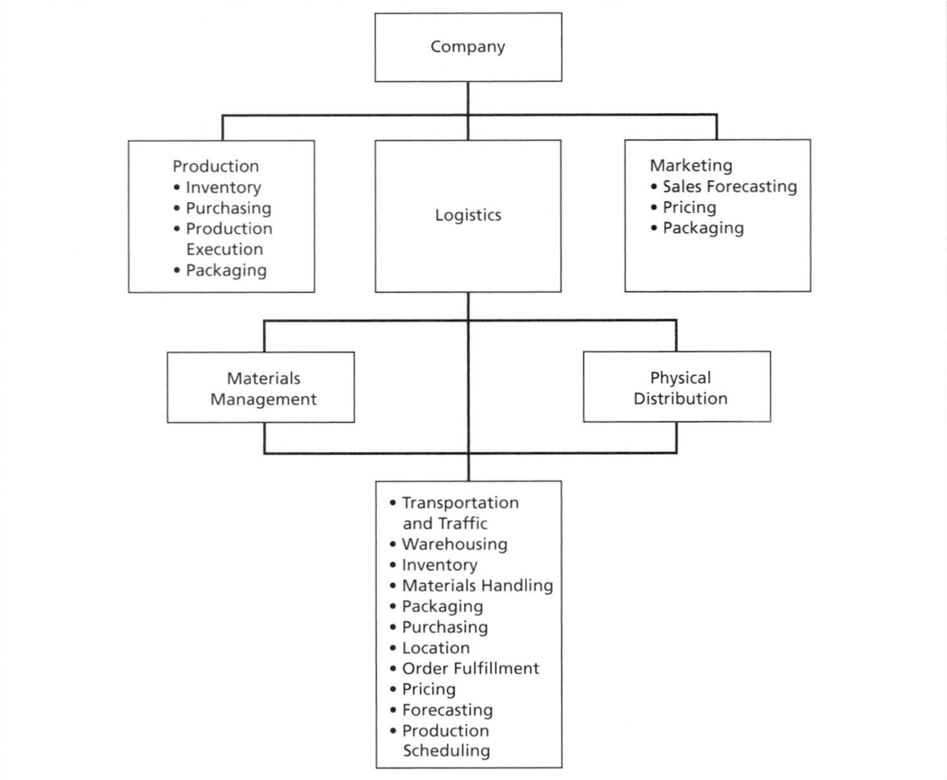

both marketing and logistics, and packaging is contained in all three functions. The reason for this duplication is the multifunctional consideration that must be given to these areas. Packaging decisions, for example, must consider the efficiency of the production process, consumer acceptance (marketing), and the need to protect the product while it is in storage and transit, while making efficient use of the carrier's vehicles (logistics).

The conclusion to be drawn is that the logistics function does not operate in a vacuum; the decisions made in the logistics area impact other areas of the company. In addition, a number of logistics functions also can be included in production or marketing because of the impact these functions have on all these areas.

Further examination of Figure 1.5 shows the dichotomy of the business logistics function into **materials management** and **physical distribution**. The materials management function is concerned with the inbound movement and storage of raw materials, whereas physical distribution is directed toward the outbound movement and storage of finished products. However, the activities performed are basically the same in both logistics areas; that is, transportation activities are conducted in both inbound and outbound product moves.

TRANSPORTATION AND THE ECONOMY

The previous discussion attempted to show the importance of transportation to the firm in implementing both the logistics and supply chain concepts. This portion of the chapter will present a discussion on the importance of transportation to the economy. Transportation is one of the tools that civilized societies need to bring order out of chaos. It reaches into every phase and facet of our existence. Viewed in historical, economic, environmental, social, and political terms, it is unquestionably the most important industry in the world. Without transportation, we could not operate a grocery store or win a war. The more complex life becomes, the more indispensable are the elements of transportation systems.[16]

Transportation systems are so well developed that most citizens rarely stop to think about their benefits. Americans, though, use transportation every day in one form or another. It provides the thoroughfare for the nation's products, it provides a means for traveling to and from work, and it supports our communication networks. Seldom do individuals stop and wonder how restricted their life-styles would be if the U.S. Post Office lost its right to use any of the common modes of transportation.

At this early stage, it might be helpful to define the transportation product. **Transportation** is the creation of place and time utility. When goods are moved to places where they have higher value than they had at the places from which they originated, they have place utility. Time utility means that this service occurs when it is needed. Time and place utility are provided to passengers when they are moved from where they don't want to be to places where they do want to be, and at the demanded time.

Some individuals find it difficult to understand the nature of transportation because it is a service and not a physical, tangible product. Transportation is a service to the user, but it has basic characteristics that make purchasing this service similar to buying goods.

One aspect of transportation is the movement service. This includes speed (whether it is door to door or terminal to terminal), reliability, and the frequency of the service. Another factor is the equipment used, which is a major factor for both passengers and freight. For passengers, the equipment affects comfort and safety. For freight, equipment affects shipment preparation, the size of the shipment, and loading and unloading costs.

The third factor is the cost of the transportation service. Cost includes a charge or rate quoted by the primary carrier as well as any peripheral costs borne by the user. The latter might include pickup and delivery costs, packaging requirements, damage or detention charges, and special service charges such as refrigeration or heat.

Transportation should not be viewed as the simple movement of persons or things through space. The user is actually purchasing a **bundle of services** from a carrier at a certain cost. The bundle of services varies among carriers and modes of transportation, with different prices frequently in effect from the different services. If the user focuses on the simplistic version of transportation, that is, movement through space, the lowest-priced service will be selected. However, the higher-priced carrier might be the best choice because of superior service, which will result in lower costs in other areas, such as inventory.

Transportation is also one of the economic factors in the production of goods and services. The basic function of transportation is to provide the market with access to the resultant products. Transportation plays a major role in the spatial relations between geographic points, and it also affects temporal relationships.

The following discussion will investigate the historical, economic, environmental, social, and political effects of a well-designed transportation system.

HISTORICAL SIGNIFICANCE

The importance of transportation becomes more apparent when one understands its history-making role. The growth of civilizations is directly associated with the development of transportation systems. The strength of ancient Egypt demonstrated how one form of transportation, water, could become the foundation for a great society. The Nile River held Egypt together. It provided a means to transport Egyptian goods, a way to communicate, and a way in which Egyptian soldiers could move to defend the country. The Nile River, like all transportation systems, also affected the society's political and cultural development. The Roman Empire was successful due in part to its vast system of roads, which linked distant areas and made communication, trade, and military conquest possible. This continues today in the United States with our interstate highway system.

A transportation system can also help create a social structure. People traveling or living within the bounds of a particular transportation network share ideas and experiences. Eventually a society develops with unified political opinions, cultural ideals, and educational methods.

Yet, methods of transportation also can tear societies apart when people are alienated from the common systems. For example, America's secession from Great Britain can be partly attributed to the localized systems developing in the 13 colonies. Transportation to and from Great Britain was slow and inefficient, and Americans found that they could economically lead more efficient lives trading among themselves without having to pay dues to the government of King George III. As the colonies grew into a separate economic nation, political and cultural attitudes that were unique to America took hold.

The United States continued to grow in tandem with its transportation network. Few families thought to move west without first knowing that explorers had blazed trails or found rivers suitable for travel. The Erie Canal, steamboats, early turnpikes, and the rail system developed to meet the economic and social needs of the growing nation. See Table 1.1 for an overview of transport developments in the United States.

Transportation also plays a major role in national defense. This role has long been recognized by governments. The Roman Empire built its great system of roads primarily for military reasons. Sir Winston Churchill once wrote, "Victory is the beautiful, bright-colored flower. Transport is the stem without which it could never have blossomed."[17] In the United States, the requirements of national defense have been advanced as a major reason for the construction of a system of nationwide, interconnected superhighways. Similarly, the large expenditures on air transport are based more on military and political considerations than on economic ones.

ECONOMIC SIGNIFICANCE

Transportation systems have a great impact on population patterns and economic development. Consider Table 1.2, which indicates that New York City needs more than 5334 tons of foodstuffs per day. The approximately 353 trailers that this figure represents are not all inclusive of products that would be used. For example, it does not include all foods nor does it include newsprint, clothing, books, cigarettes, gasoline, cars, appliances, furniture, and so on. It does not take much imagination to understand why transportation is sometimes referred to as the lifeline of cities.

Value of Goods

Transportation systems help determine the economic value of products. A simple model will serve to illustrate this point. Consider a certain commodity that is desired in one location, provided it is offered below a certain price. In Figure 1.6,

Table 1.1 U.S. Transport Developments

Year	Development	Year	Development
1774	Lancaster Turnpike: first toll road—Pennsylvania	1927	Lindbergh solo flight—New York to Paris
1804	Fulton's steamboat—Hudson River, New York	1961	Manned space flights begin
1825	Erie Canal: first canal—New York	1970	Amtrak established
1838	Steamship service—Atlantic Ocean	1976	Contrail established
1865	First pipeline—Pennsylvania	1978	Act to deregulate airlines passed
1866	Completion of transcontinental rail link	1980	Act to deregulate motor carriers and Staggers Rail act
1869	Bicycles introduced—United States	1982	Double Stack Rail container service initiated
1887	First daily rail service coast to coast	1986	Conrail profitable and sold by government
1887	Federal regulation of transportation begins	1986	Norfolk Southern initiates roadrailer service
1903	First successful airplane flight—Wright Brothers	1990	National Transportation Policy Statement
1904	Panama Canal opens	1995	ICC Abolished
1919	Transcontinental airmail service by U.S. Post Office begins	1998	Internet applications widely used in transportation
1925	Kelly Act: airmail contract to private companies	2002	Airline industry suffers after 9/11 terrorist attacks

Table 1.2 Foodstuffs Required Daily in New York City

Product	Quantity (in lbs)
Butter	36.80
Milk and Cream	92.00
Cheese	239.20
Eggs	1,997.60
Meat, Poultry, Fish	1,565.60
Fruits	2,235.20
Fats and Oils	281.60
Flour and Cereal	1,599.20
Potatoes	1,109.60
Sugar and Other Sweeteners	1,219.20
Coffee, Tea, Cocoa	133.92
Rice and Grains	157.60
Total	**10,667.52**

Source: Based on U.S. Department of Agriculture estimates (2000) of daily average per capita consumption of these products for New York City's population of 8 million (2000).

this commodity is produced at point A and costs OC at the point of production. The community desiring the commodity, located at point B, is the distance AB from A. The maximum price that people will pay for the commodity is shown on the vertical axis as OE, at community B.

If the original, inefficient transport system is used, moving the commodity from A to B will cost CH. The CD portion of the cost line is known as the fixed cost, and the DH portion of the line is the cost per mile or slope. With this inefficient system, the total cost at B is OH, a price greater than the maximum cost limit (OE) in the community B.

FIGURE 1.6 Landed Cost with Old and New Transport Systems

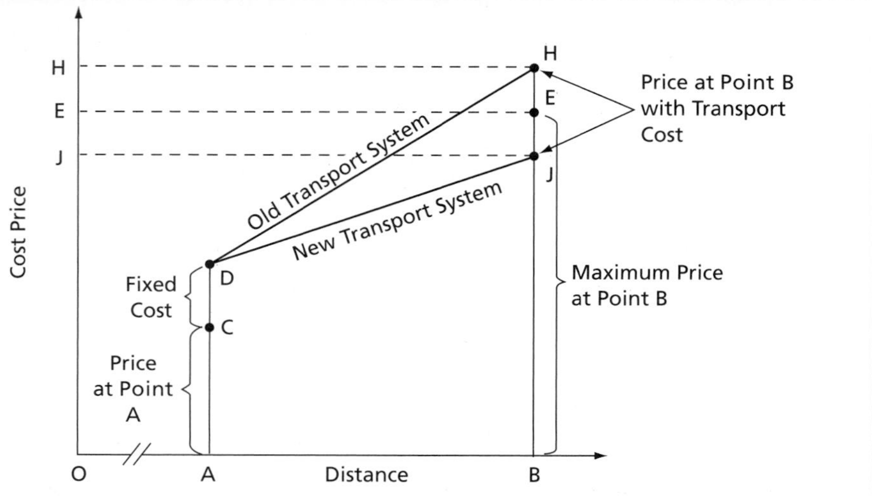

Source: Adapted from Morlok, Edward, *Introduction to Transportation, Engineering, and Planning,* New York: McGraw-Hill, 1978, p. 33.

Now assume the transport system is improved. The cost per mile or slope is reduced, and the transportation variable cost line becomes DJ. The cost at the community now becomes OJ, well below the maximum cost of OE. The market for the commodity would be expanded to community B, while production continues at A.

PLACE UTILITY

The reduction in transportation costs between points A and B gives the commodity **place utility**. In the less efficient system, the goods will have no value because they would not be sold at the market. The more efficient method of transportation creates utility; the goods now have value at point B.

Reductions in transportation costs will encourage market areas to purchase products from distant suppliers that might otherwise be produced locally. The reduction in transportation cost is actually much greater for long distances than for short ones because of the fixed charges alluded to in Figure 1.6. If a supplier can cover the transportation cost of a certain amount in his or her price range, an increase in the distance over which this given amount will cover the transport of goods will increase the market area of the product in an even greater ratio.

Dionysius Lardner, an early transportation economist, referred to this phenomenon as the Law of Squares in Transportation and Trade (also known as **Lardner's Law**). As shown in Figure 1.7, a producer at Point A can afford to transport a product 100 miles and meet competitive laid-down costs. The boundary of the relevant market area is shown by the circumference of the smaller circle. If transportation cost is cut in half, the same sum will now transport the supplier goods for twice the distance, that is, 200 miles. Now the market boundary is shown by the circumference of the larger circle. The relevant market area increased four times in size when the radius doubled from 100 to 200 miles.

TIME UTILITY

The concept of **time utility** is closely aligned to that of place utility. The demand for a particular commodity can only exist during certain periods of time. If a product is at a market in a time when there is no demand for it, then it possesses no value. For example, the demand for Halloween costumes only exists during a specific time of the year. After Halloween passes, these goods have little value to the holder. Efficient transportation creates time utility by ensuring that products are at

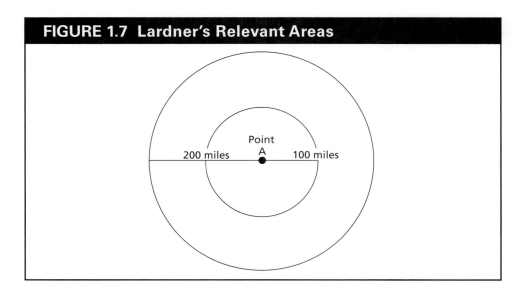

FIGURE 1.7 Lardner's Relevant Areas

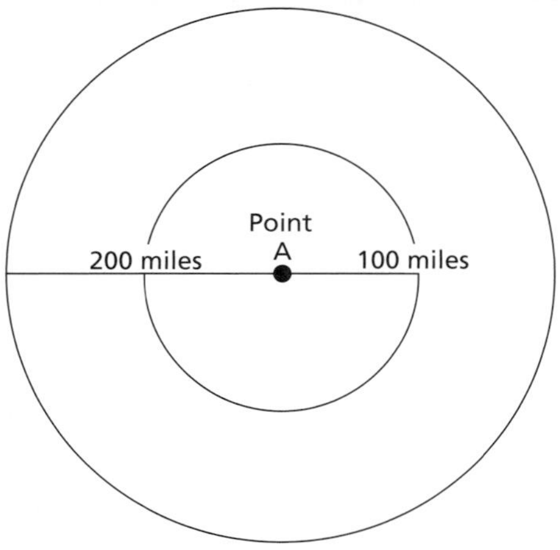

the proper locations when needed. For example, raw materials for production, fruit, and Christmas toys all need to arrive at certain locations during specific times, or their value will be limited.

Lardner's Law can also be related to time utility. For example, the speed of transportation might be a governing factor for the transportation of certain perishable products that have a limited shelf life. Suppose the small circle in Figure 1.7 represents the current market area based on a specific transportation speed. If the speed were doubled, the potential service area would quadruple.

QUANTITY UTILITY

In addition, transportation gives goods **quantity utility** through the assurance that the goods will arrive without damage. This helps assure that the quantity demanded is the same as the quantity delivered. This utility has increased in importance in recent years with the high level of importance placed on minimizing safety stock inventories for both shippers and receivers. Shippers might alter the form of the product to ensure safe transportation. Carriers can use special bracing, blocking, and/or strapping, along with temperature control, to help ensure damage-free delivery.

Utility of Goods

Transportation adds utility to goods. Efficient highway systems and modern modes of transportation allow geographic specialization, large-scale production, increased competition, and increased land values.

GEOGRAPHIC SPECIALIZATION

The concept of geographic specialization assumes that each nation, state, or city produces products and services for which its capital, labor, and raw materials are best suited. Because any one area can't produce all needed goods, transportation is needed to send the goods that might be most efficiently produced at point A to point B in return for different goods efficiently produced at point B. The concept is closely aligned to the principle of **comparative advantage**. This principle assumes that an area will specialize in the production of goods for which it has the greatest advantage or the least comparative disadvantage. Gain from the specialization of goods will be mutually advantageous when the cost ratios of producing two commodities are different in different areas. Hence, Pennsylvania can concentrate on the production of coal, California on citrus fruit, and the Greek Islands on olives.

LARGE-SCALE PRODUCTION

Geographic specialization is complemented by large-scale production, but, without the use of effective and efficient transportation networks, the advantages of scale economies, production efficiencies, and cheaper manufacturing facilities would be destroyed. The raw materials for production need to be transported to the manufacturing facility, and the finished products must be transported out of an area at reasonable costs. Geographic specialization assumes that the large-scale production of efficiently produced goods is demanded at distances far from the production site. Obviously, one area cannot rely upon its comparative advantage and large-scale production without the use of systems to transport the goods efficiently to the distant areas requiring them.

INCREASED COMPETITION

Efficient transportation also provides the consumer with the benefit of increased competition. Without transportation, local entrepreneurs could produce inefficient goods and charge high prices for their consumption. Transportation increases the market area for a product; thus, goods must be produced in the most efficient fashion, or distant competitors will enter the market and legitimately capture its attention.

LAND VALUES

Transportation improvements are also credited with enhancing an area's economy by increasing the value of land that is adjacent to or served by the improvements. Thus, the land becomes more accessible and more useful. Today the suburban centers provide excellent examples of land areas that have increased in value due to the accessibility that results from efficient transportation systems. Suburbanites can take advantage of nearby city life for work and pleasure and then retire to rural areas via public transportation networks to avoid crowded conditions. Commuters from Greenwich, Connecticut, to New York City and from Cherry Hill, New Jersey, to Philadelphia all reap both city and suburban benefits as the result of reliable train systems. Hence, the value of the land in these areas has increased to reflect the advantageous life-styles that the new or improved transportation systems have made possible.

However, transportation does not always have a positive effect on land values. Noise and air pollution accompanying some networks decrease adjacent land values. The homeowners who have to bear this pollution also suffer from overaccessibility.

Transportation Patterns

Transportation patterns reflect the flow of people and commerce. Transportation has a catalytic effect on a society in that it stimulates commerce and movement. The reverse is true also. That is, the demand for commerce and movement will cause transportation to be developed.

The world's major water routes for transporting merchandise are shown in Figure 1.8. The merchandise includes finished and semifinished goods but does not include heavy bulk goods such as ores and petroleum. These routes traditionally go to and from Europe, the United States, and the Far East (Japan, Korea, Hong Kong, and Taiwan). These routes have an east–west pattern between the developed nations

FIGURE 1.8 Major World Water Routes—Merchandise Traffic

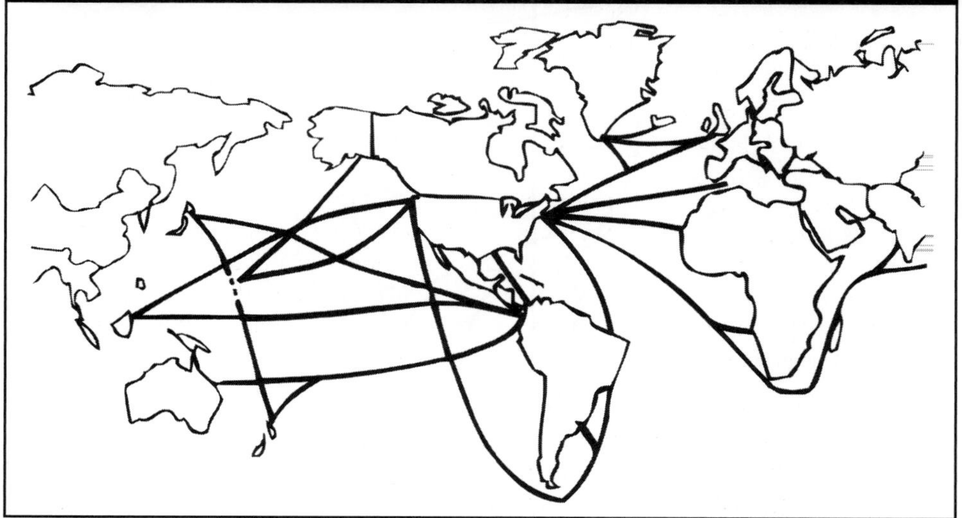

and a north–south pattern between the developed nations primarily in the Northern Hemisphere and developing nations in Africa and South America. These routes closely resemble major air cargo and passenger routes of the world.

Major North American routes of commerce are shown in Figure 1.9. In the United States, these routes link the major metropolitan areas and represent the existing rail trunk line, interstate highway, and inland waterway patterns. The Canadian pattern links the major cities that are in a narrow population band along the border with the United States. This route connects Halifax, Montreal, Toronto, and the industrial sectors of southern Ontario, Edmonton, Calgary, and Vancouver. Here the route follows the Trans-Canada Highway as well as the mainlines of the Canadian Pacific and the Canadian National Railroads. The Great Lakes and St. Lawrence River water system is also important because it is an outlet for grain and other products from Canada to the rest of the world.

Mexico's major commerce routes are strongly tied to its economic center, represented by Mexico City. Here again the railroad mainlines and early highway development created an economic and social orientation in this pattern.

FIGURE 1.9 Major Commerce Routes of North America

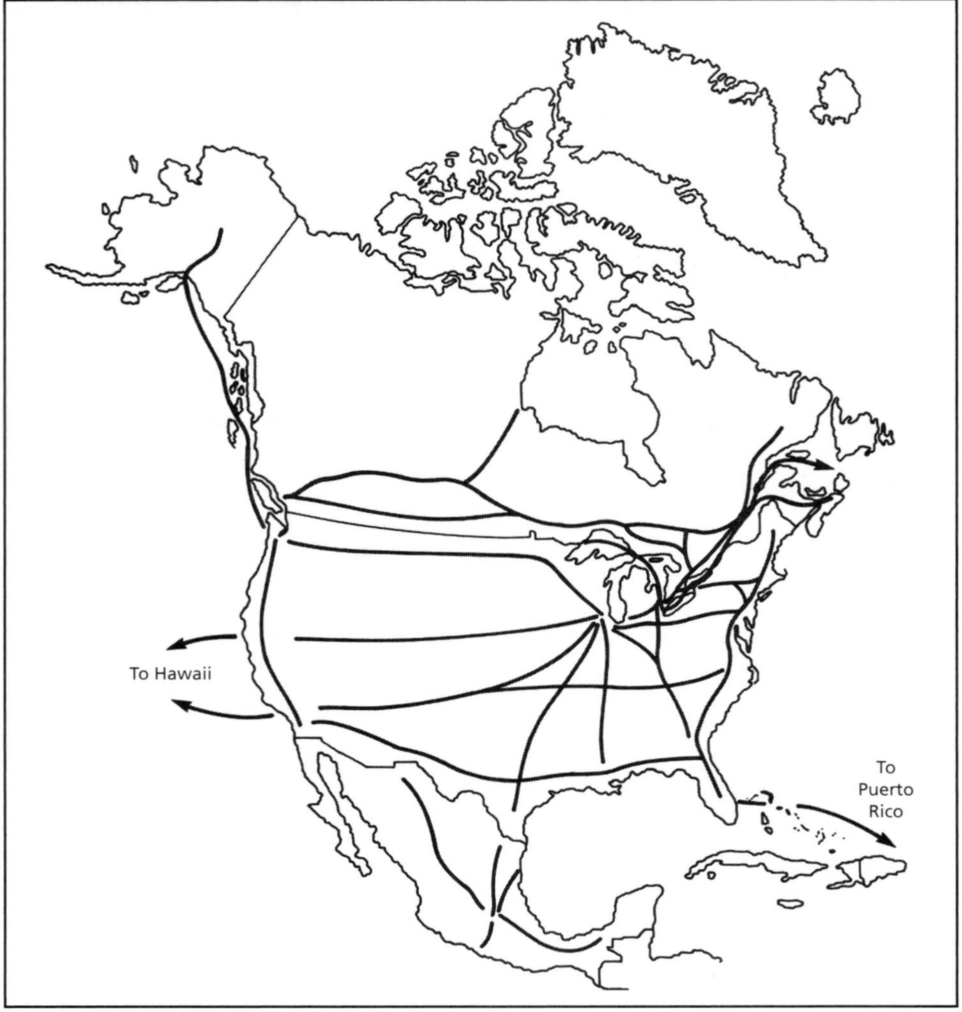

The airline industry, however, does not require specific geographic routes to move passengers or freight from origins to destinations. Unlike rail, highway, and water transportation, which must traverse specific routes, airlines only require the end points. In recent years, the creation of airline hub and spoke systems has created travel through cities that heretofore were not significant in that traffic. For example, in years past, a person traveling from New York to Roanoke, Virginia, would use a multi-stop airplane that would stop in Philadelphia, Baltimore, and Washington. Today that same person would probably travel on US Airways to Pittsburgh and change to a commuter flight to Roanoke. This is an out-of-the-way route, but it is much faster than in the past. Major airline hubs in the United States and Canada are shown in Figure 1.10. These represent central connecting points for long-distance and feeder routes.

Gross Domestic Product

Transportation plays a major role in the overall economy of the United States (see Table 1.3). On the average, transportation now accounts for less than 16 percent of this nation's gross domestic product (GDP).

Passenger transportation has been growing in relation to the GDP until recently. Much of this increase was due to the greater use of automobiles and the energy costs associated with operating them. Air travel also accounts for a large part of transportation expenditures in the economy. The U.S. Department of Transportation (DOT) reports that in 1980 airlines generated 204.4 billion passenger miles; by 2001, this had grown to more than 487 billion passenger miles, an increase of 138 percent in 21 years. Travel for business, personal, and vacation purposes are an important activity in the economy.

Freight transportation has traditionally accounted for between eight and nine percent of the GDP. In 2001, this has decreased to 5.7 percent, as shown in Table 1.3. Much of this decrease is due to the more efficient use of transportation resulting from less regulation. Although the economy is expanding, productivity increases in,

FIGURE 1.10 Major U.S. and Canadian Air Hub Points

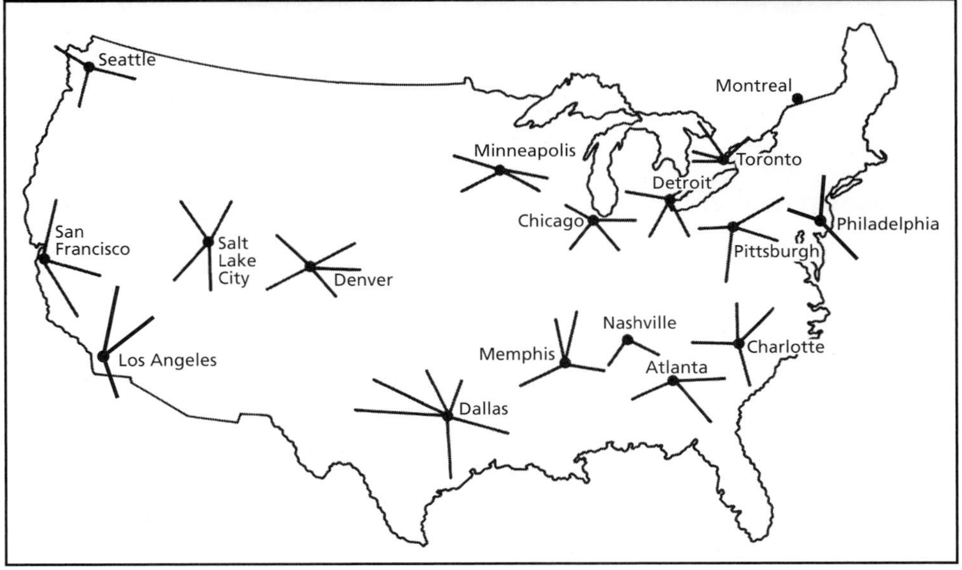

Table 1.3 Transportation as a Percent of Gross Domestic Product (GDP)

	Percent of GDP		
	1980	1990	2001
Freight Expenditures	7.6	6.0	5.7
Passenger Expenditures	12.7	11.1	10.0
Total Freight and Passenger Expenditures	20.3	17.1	15.7

Source: Eno Transportation Foundation, Washington DC, "Transportation in America," 19th ed., 2002.

and better use of, existing transportation systems have enabled this growth to take place without proportionate increases in freight expenditures.

Modal split is a useful analytical tool in the study of transportation. This concept divides the entire transportation passenger or freight market according to the major modes of transportation. Table 1.4 shows the relative splits of intercity passenger travel. The two major categories are for-hire forms of transportation versus private automobile and private aircraft. The automobile dominates, representing more than 77 percent of this travel in the U.S. economy. The proportion has been decreasing slightly over the past two decades due to growth in airline travel. Deregulation of airline service in the late 1970s has brought about a great increase in travel options and services for the traveling public. During this period, the relative level of airfares did not keep pace with the overall inflation level. As a result, air travel became more convenient and relatively cheaper for long-distance travel.

The freight intercity modal split is dominated by railroads, with 41.7 percent of the ton-miles in 2001 (see Table 1.5). Railroads have declined in relative share since World War II, with motor carriers, rivers, and oil pipelines increasing relative shares of the total ton-mile market in that time. Railroads typically move bulk, low-value commodities such as grain, coal, ore, and chemicals. In recent years, rail traffic by container, which transports relatively high-value finished goods, has increased. The air mode, while highly visible, still handles less than one percent of the total ton-miles in the United States.

The economy has expanded at a faster rate than the demand for freight transportation. The total ton-miles of all modes have increased between 1965 and 2001, as

Table 1.4 Modal Split of For-Hire Passenger Miles (%)

Year	Railroads	Buses	Air	For Hire* (% of Total Passengers)	Automobile (% of Total Passengers)
1980	0.7	1.9	13.9	16.5	82.5
1990	0.7	1.2	18.7	20.6	78.6
2001	0.6	1.7	19.5	21.8	77.6

*The difference between the total of for-hire plus auto and 100% is private air.

Source: Eno Transportation Foundation, Washington DC, "Transportation in America," 19th ed., 2002.

Table 1.5 Percent Volume of Intercity Freight Expressed as Percent of Total

Year	Railroads	Trucks	Great Lakes	Rivers	Oil Pipelines	Air	Total Ton-Miles (Millions-100%)
1965	43.3	21.9	6.7	9.3	18.7	0.12	1,638,000
1975	36.7	22.0	4.8	11.8	24.5	0.18	2,066,000
1985	36.4	24.8	3.1	12.5	22.9	0.27	2,458,000
1995	40.4	27.1	2.7	11.9	17.6	0.37	3,407,000
2001	41.7	28.1	2.5	10.7	16.5	0.41	3,733,000

Source: Eno Transportation Foundation, Washington DC, "Transportation in America," 19th ed., 2002.

shown in Table 1.5. One simple explanation gives some insight into this phenomenon. In the past, a domestic steel firm purchased transportation of raw materials (ore, lime, coal) and the movement of the outbound finished goods to the customer. At the very minimum, this involved four different movements. Today the steel might be imported, requiring one domestic movement between the port and the customer. Thus, steel is being used in the economy, but fewer transportation moves are involved in making it available to the customer.

Good transportation spurs economic development by giving mobility to production factors, which permits scale economies and increased efficiency. Good transportation enlarges the area that consumers and industries can draw on for resources and products. Good transportation expands the area to which a given plant might distribute its products economically, and the resulting specialization and scale economies provide a wider choice of products for consumers at a lower cost.

ENVIRONMENTAL SIGNIFICANCE

Although transportation provides the economy with numerous benefits, these positive aspects are not without associated costs. Transportation sometimes pollutes the environment and exploits natural resources, although most citizens feel that the benefits provided by transportation far exceed these costs. The environmental challenge of the future will be to accurately assess the relationship between industrial benefits and their external societal costs.

The Environment

There has been growing concern over the impact of transportation on the environment, with particular emphasis on air quality (pollution), noise, and water quality. The synergy between the transportation system and the environment is increasingly being investigated by both environmentalists and by transportation planners at all governmental levels. In fact, increasing pressure from the environmentalists has resulted in legal restrictions that help govern the balance between a sound and efficient transportation system and a safe and clean environment.

There will be a growing challenge in the 21st century to ensure efficient transportation facilities and mobility by maintaining our present system and developing new facilities to meet the growing needs of individuals and organizations. There will be even more trade-offs between competing objectives. Highway and air planners will be particularly challenged to develop innovative design solutions because of the more than 30 federal statutes and executive orders governing the environment.

AIR QUALITY

Pollution is an external side effect of transportation because of the widespread use of internal combustion engines. In fact, the internal combustion engine emissions are a concern not only for their effect on urban air quality (pollution) but also their involvement in acid rain and potential global climate changes.

Transportation is a major contributor to air pollution, accounting for about 57 percent of carbon monoxide, 33 percent of volatile organic compounds, about 43 percent of nitrogen oxides, and 50 percent of suspended particles.[18] Dramatic reductions have taken place in motor vehicle emission rates because of governmental requirements, but economic and population growth will result in persisting problems with pollution. Table 1.6 summarizes current motor vehicle emission standards.

ACID RAIN

Essentially, acid rain is a pollution-related phenomenon that causes falling rain to be much more acidic than normal. The addition of sulfur dioxide, nitrogen oxides, and volatile organic compounds to the atmosphere causes acid rain. The pollutants result from industrial and commercial processes and combustion, as well as vehicle emissions. The acid deposits have an adverse impact on aquatic systems, crops, forests, human health, and visibility. It is difficult to reliably measure transportation's contribution to acid rain, but it is likely that this area will be a source of growing concern and increased regulation on transportation emissions in the future.

Table 1.6 2003 Motor Vehicle Emission Standards

Autos (Light-Duty Vehicles)	**(Grams per Mile)**
Hydrocarbons	0.41
Carbon Monoxide	3.40
Oxides of Nitrogen (Gasoline)	0.40
Particulates	0.08
Light-Duty Trucks	**(Grams per Mile)**
Hydrocarbons	0.80
Carbon monoxide	3.40
Oxides of Nitrogen (Gasoline)	0.40
(Diesel)	1.00
Particulates	0.08
Heavy-Duty Trucks	**(Grams per Brake Horsepower-Hour)**
Hydrocarbons	1.90 (Gasoline-Powered) 1.30 (Diesel-Powered)
Carbon Monoxide	37.10 (Gasoline-Powered) 15.50 (Diesel-Powered)
Oxides of nitrogen	4.00 (Gasoline- and Diesel-Powered)
Particulates	0.10 (Diesel-Powered)

Source: U.S. DOT Bureau of Transportation Statistics, *National Transportation Statistics*, Washington, DC, 2003.

GLOBAL CLIMATE CHANGES

An important issue facing the United States and the rest of the world is the so-called "greenhouse effect" and the related climate changes. Basically, the greenhouse effect is the physical process by which energy from the sun passes through the atmosphere relatively free, while heat radiating from the earth is partially blocked or absorbed by particular gases in the atmosphere released by human activities such as transportation.

Ozone reduction in the stratosphere is a big concern because ozone reduces the amount of ultraviolet radiation reaching the earth's surface from the sun. The hole in the ozone layer has been the focus of much concern and investigation because of health-related problems and increased risk of skin cancer. A particular concern in this area is the CFC (chlorofluorocarbons) compound used as the refrigerant for recharging and servicing air conditioning units in homes and vehicles. Again, we can expect worldwide concern and the development of protocols to reduce the risks in this area.

MARITIME AND WATER QUALITY

The protection of the marine environment from the adverse effects of oil spills, garbage dumping from ships, hazardous material losses, and so on is a growing concern shared by many federal and state agencies. One of the largest oil spills occurred in 1989 near Valdez, Alaska, from a tanker ship carrying crude oil from Alaska for the Exxon Oil Company. Almost 11 million gallons of crude oil were spilled; this environmental disaster raised awareness for controls and better contingency preparedness to respond to such accidents.

In recent years, there has been a growing concern about the damage that plastic items and other ship-generated garbage can cause to the marine environment. Birds, marine mammals, and sea turtles are susceptible to this type of refuse because they can ingest the materials and die as a result. It is estimated that more than one million birds die each year from ingesting these materials.

Water quality, both for surface water and drinking water sources, is an area of risk and concern. Both surface water and drinking water sources are highly susceptible to many types of potential pollutants. Again, there will be continuing pressure to protect water quality by governmental controls and standards.

NOISE

Another type of pollution is noise, which can emit from many sources, including transportation. There is an annoyance factor, but also a health concern involved. Airplanes and motor vehicles are the major causes of noise. The U.S. DOT and the Federal Aviation Administration have been particularly active in this area, helping to guide land-use planning for compatibility with transportation facilities and conducting research to help solve the problem. Noise emissions are governed by the Noise Control Act of 1972, which allows the setting of operational standards for aircraft and trucks and even rail equipment operated by interstate carriers.

Safety

One of the most disturbing by-products of transportation is injury and loss of life. In 2000, a total of 44,186 persons lost their lives in the United States while engaged in transport. Approximately 95 percent of those fatalities occurred in highway vehicles. However, as Table 1.7 shows, the number of deaths has remained stable in relation to the ever-growing demand for transportation. This positive statistic is the result of increased licensing regulations and more reliable vehicle designs. Unfortunately, trends in the area of safety for freight transportation aren't as

Table 1.7 Transportation Fatalities

	1985	1995	2000
Motor Vehicles	43,825	41,798	41,800
Passenger Car Occupants	23,212	22,358	20,455
Truck Occupants	7,666	10,183	11,439
Motorcycle Riders	4,564	2,221	2,680
Pedestrian/Others	7,782	6,524	5,711
Railroad	454	567	770
Aircraft	1,594	961	777
Large-Scheduled	526	168	92
Commuter	37	9	5
Air Taxi	76	52	71
General Aviation	955	732	592
Water Vessels	1,247	882	801
Commercial	131	46	64
Recreational	1,116	836	701
Pipeline	33	21	38
Gas	28	18	37
Liquid	5	3	1
Total Transportation Fatalities	**47,153**	**44,229**	**44,186**

Source: U.S. DOT Bureau of Transportation Statistics, *National Transportation Statistics*, Washington, D.C., 2001.

promising. Train accidents, oil spills, and the threat of gaseous explosions while in transit have increased. With an increasing variety of products being shipped and an increasing volume of transportation, these problems require greater attention. We can hope that safety in freight transportation will soon parallel the progress made in passenger transportation; however, much work remains to be done.

The nation's increasing demand for transportation services has imposed social costs in addition to monetary costs. Over the past 25 years, great strides have been made, particularly at the national level, in mitigating those negative social costs. Overall, the benefits far outweigh the costs to society, but vigilance is necessary. Table 1.8 indicates some of the actions taken to constrain the negative impacts of transportation.

Table 1.8 Actions to Mitigate the Negative Impact of Transportation

Impact	Action
Noise	Vehicle and equipment standards; researching the impact of noise and developing solutions; improved aviation operating procedures; environmental impact statements.
Air Pollution	Emission standards; transportation control plans; environmental impact statements.
Water Pollution	Compulsory oil spill insurance; improved regulations concerning waste and hazardous materials handling; environmental impact statements.
Marred Vision	Billboard standards in interstate system.
Safety	Increased safety regulations; safer design standards.
Petroleum Dependence	Auto fuel consumption standards; more realistic petroleum fuel costs.
Alcohol and Substance Abuse	Tighter laws and greater enforcement.

Substance Abuse

Abuse of alcohol and drugs is an issue in transportation. Railroad, motor carrier, and aircrews are involved in public safety when they help move passengers or when they operate freight vehicles on the highways and through towns. Success has been achieved as recent studies have shown that less than one percent of drivers tested were positive for alcohol and less than two percent tested positive for drugs. Much has been achieved by joint industry–carrier partnerships that changed attitudes from adversarial to cooperative. The federal government has also played a significant role by drafting regulations that focus not only on detection but assistance as well.

SOCIAL SIGNIFICANCE

Transportation provides employment and enhances travel. Transportation employs approximately 4.7 million persons (see Table 1.9). This has increased since the 1990s, which indicates the increasing service intensity of the industry.

A good transportation system also can enhance the health and welfare of a population. One of the major problems that faced the famine relief efforts in the eastern region of Africa in the middle 1980s was the lack of sufficient and effective transportation networks to move needed food and farm supplies from the ports inland to the population centers. Insufficient railroads, roads, vehicles, storage, and related distribution facilities hampered effective delivery of the needed food and supplies. In addition, one of the problems facing the region in normal times is insufficient transportation, which hinders inbound and outbound product flows.[19]

POLITICAL SIGNIFICANCE

The origin and maintenance of transportation systems are dependent on the government. Government intervention is needed to design feasible routes, cover the expense of building public highways, and develop harbors and waterways. Adequate transportation is needed to create national unity; the transportation network must permit the leaders of government to travel rapidly to and communicate with the people they govern.

Governmental Responsibility

The government is responsible for aiding all passenger and freight transportation systems in which the costs cannot be covered reasonably by a central group of users. The government has also created regulations that offer consumers the opportunity to transact in a competitive free-market environment.

One outgrowth of regulation is the **common carrier**. The common carrier has a duty to render service without discrimination based upon set rates for specific commodities.

The government's role as a regulator of transportation services does mean certain drawbacks for the public. For example, the right of **eminent domain** often forces individuals to move and sell their land, even though they might not wish to do so. The government's power of eminent domain gives it the right to acquire land for public use. Hence, the construction of many highways displaces families because

Table 1.9 U.S. Employment in Transportation and Related Industries

	Number of Persons Employed (In Thousands)		
	1990	**1995**	**2000**
Total Workers, 16 Years and Over	118,793	124,900	135,208
Total Workers in Transportation Occupations	4,039	4,308	4,684
Motor Vehicle Operators			
Supervisors	76	87	77
Truck Drivers	2,627	2,860	3,088
Driver-Sales Workers	201	158	167
Bus Drivers	443	526	539
Taxicab Drivers and Chauffeurs	213	211	280
Parking Lot Attendants	53	50	60
Motor Transportation Occupations, NEC*	5	8	11
Total	**3,618**	**3,900**	**4,222**
Rail Transportation			
Railroad Conductors and Yardmasters	36	33	48
Locomotive Operating Occupations	46	51	63
Railroad Brake, Signal, and Switch Operators	28	17	11
Rail Vehicle Operators, NEC	8	3	5
Total	**118**	**104**	**127**
Water Transportation			
Ship Captains and Mates, Except Fishing Boats	27	33	38
Sailors and Deckhands	18	26	14
Marine Engineers	2	3	2
Bridge, Lock, and Lighthouse Tenders	6	4	3
Total	**53**	**66**	**56**
Air Transportation			
Airplane Pilots and Navigators	114	114	129
Air Traffic Controllers	36	30	23
Total	**150**	**144**	**152**
Public Transportation Attendants	**100**	**94**	**127**

*NEC = not elsewhere classified.

NOTE: Beginning in January 2000, data are not comparable with data for earlier years due to new composite estimations.

SOURCE: U.S. Department of Transportation, http://www.bts.gov/publications/national_transportation_statistics/.

All data except total workers, 16 years and over:

U.S. Department of Labor, Bureau of Labor Statistics, *Employment and Earnings*, Washington, DC: Annual January issues.

Ibid., Personal communications: unpublished revisions: Aug. 6, 2001.

Total workers, 16 years and over:

Ibid., *Employment and Earnings*, Washington, DC: January, 2001 revised Table 1.

governmental intervention has opened the right-of-way for certain transportation routes. Although families might be displaced, the government's role is to act in the best interest of the public by designing routes that help the citizens of the nation efficiently conduct their business.

Closely connected with transportation's political role is its function as a provider for national defense. Today our transportation system enhances our life-styles and protects us from outsiders. The ability to transport troops acts as both a weapon and a deterrent in this age of energy shortages and global conflicts. The conflicts in Central America and the Middle East place even greater emphasis on the importance of transportation in protecting our distant vital interests.

Although it is accurate to say that the American transportation system has been shaped by economic factors, political and military developments have also played important roles. Transportation policy incorporates more than economics—the expected benefits of the system extend beyond the economic realm.

OVERVIEW OF MODERN TRANSPORTATION

The significance of our transportation system touches all aspects of life. For example, the location of transportation facilities has effects on the surrounding communities. Railroads and superhighways divide towns and neighborhoods, and the location of highway interchanges can determine the location of manufacturing, retailing, and distribution operations. The character of a neighborhood or a city is often determined by its ability to act as a transportation center. The port city of New Orleans, the rail city of Altoona, Pennsylvania, and St. Louis's role as the "Gateway to the West" are examples of towns that have become known for their ability to provide transportation services.

Factors can be identified correlating network changes to changes in neighborhood characteristics. However, transportation factors in connection with a whole series of other factors cause sociological change that extends beyond transportation factors alone. According to sociologists and urbanologists, regional shopping centers, higher-income commuter enclaves, and resort, vacation, and amusement districts grow as the result of available transportation networks, as well as the relative expense of maintaining these areas.

The consumer makes decisions based on transportation services, availability, cost, and adequacy. Product decisions (what products or product to produce or distribute) are closely related to this availability of transportation and adequacy of the transporter to move the goods. Market area decisions are dominated by the ability of the transporter to get the product to market at a low cost. Decisions about whether to purchase parts, raw materials, supplies, or finished goods for resale must reflect transport costs. Location decisions, too, are influenced by many transportation factors. The decisions about where plants, warehouses, offices, and stores should be located all take transportation requirements into consideration. Last, pricing decisions are strongly affected by the transportation operation. The logistics area of the firm is often considered a cost center; therefore, changes in the price of transportation will often have a serious effect on the prices of products in general.

Overall, **transportation interacts** with three groups of our society: users, providers, and the government. Thus, transportation decisions makers are expected to consider all aspects of society in one form or another.

The role of the user is to make decisions that will maximize the relevant consumer-oriented goals. The power of the user lies in the ability to demand and pay (or not pay if the wrong service is offered) for certain forms of transportation.

The providers, both public and private, including agencies such as freight forwarders and brokers, must determine the demands of the system and services to be offered. These decisions are made in light of total modal use, the importance of each mode to the economy, profits, and the way in which each company views itself in relation to its competitors.

OVERVIEW OF TRANSPORTATION TRENDS

The transportation industry is in a constant state of flux. It is intertwined with the social, political, and economic forces in a society and economy. The industry as a whole has undergone a tremendous change since deregulation in the late 1970s. This has affected how carriers have organized, priced, sold their services, and managed operations. Table 1.10 presents many of the key forces in transportation during the 1990s and the early 2000s and the impact they might have for the remainder of this decade. These points set the stage for the remaining chapters of this book, which deal with individual modes of transportation, cost and rate making, the buying and selling of transportation service, government regulation and policies, and carrier management.

Table 1.10 Transportation Trends
The Transportation Market
Tailoring of services and equipment for specific shipper/receiver needs
Freight transportation provided for just-in-time, sequenced movements
User cost for international transportation declining
International transactions easier
Sale of transportation service being done more by parties other than the sales and marketing group of the carriers
Shift from heavy industrial, production-oriented transportation to fast, service-demanding finished goods transportation
Users of transportation are seeing transportation less as a distinct operation and more in the context of total production, overhead, sourcing, labor, distribution, and marketing factors
Greater marketing orientation by carriers
More travel
More discretionary travel
More international transportation
Transportation Supply
Increased use of third-party services
Consolidation in air, rail, and motor modes
Integration of modes via joint ownership or special arrangements
Strength and health of feeder firms (commuters, regional motor carriers)
Continued technological advances in most modes
Less private carriage use for reasons of cost savings; still present where special services are involved
More international alliances of carrier
Operations and Management
Operations in closer link with marketing and sales of the carrier
Leasing of containers, aircraft, terminal facilities, and other assets on increase
Information-driven organization and structures
Decision making and accountability being pushed lower in the organization
More substitution of communication of transportation
Government Policies and Regulation
Deregulation spreading from the United States to Canada and Europe
Less economic regulation (rates, routes, services, finance)
Increased noneconomic regulation (environmental, substance abuse, safety)
Government funding not keeping up with the deterioration of transportation infrastructure

In the 21st century, our transportation system faces significant challenges and problems because of global competition, governmental budget constraints, and increased demand from special interest groups such as senior citizens. The patterns of trade that help to drive transportation are changing more quickly and becoming more complex because of the dynamic global environment that we now live in and the changing economic base in the United States.

Transportation touches the lives of all U.S. citizens and affects their economic well-being, their safety, their access to people and places, and the quality of their environment. When the transportation system does not function well, it is a source of great personal frustration and, perhaps, economic loss, but when the transportation system performs well, it provides opportunity and economic rewards for everyone.

DEMAND FOR TRANSPORTATION

Transportation is an important and pervasive element in our society, affecting every person, either directly or indirectly. The goods we consume, our economic livelihood, our mobility, and our entertainment are in some way affected by transportation.

The growth of the U.S. economy, as well as the economy of most industrialized countries, is attributable in part to the benefits derived from mass production and the division of labor. This specialization of labor and production results in an oversupply of goods at one location and an undersupply, or demand, for these goods at another place. Transportation bridges the supply-and-demand gap inherent in mass production.

The interrelationship between transportation and mass production points out the dependency of our society on transportation. As each of us specializes in the production of a particular good or service, we are relying upon someone else to produce the goods and services that we need to survive. Also, we depend upon transportation to move these goods and services to our location in an efficient and economical manner. Like the citizens of most industrialized countries, U.S. citizens, as individuals, are not self-sufficient.

On a global scale, countries recognize international dependencies. The United States supplies many countries with manufactured goods, while other countries provide the United States with raw materials and agricultural products. For example, the United States is dependent on the Arab oil-producing nations for oil, and these countries rely on the United States to provide a vast array of manufactured goods such as aircraft, clothing, and computers. Again, transportation plays a key role in this international dependency, or trade, by permitting the equalization of supply and demand on a global basis.

Likewise, people must move from areas where they are currently situated to areas where they desire to be. Within the supply–demand context, the origin of a passenger is an area of oversupply and the destination is an area of undersupply. Transportation performs the bridging function between the supply–demand gap for people, such as the movement of people from their homes to their work locations.

As with freight, people depend on transportation for their **mobility**. The more mobile a society, the more critical and efficient an economical passenger transportation system is to its citizens. With today's technology, an executive in Chicago leaves home at 6:00 a.m. on Monday to catch an 8:00 a.m. flight to Los Angeles to attend a 1:00 p.m. meeting. At 5:00 p.m. (Pacific Coast time) that afternoon, the executive boards a flight to Australia with a continuation to London later in the week. This global workweek is possible because of the speed of air transportation.

Transportation has a definite and identifiable effect upon a person's life-style. An individual's decisions about where to work, live, and play are influenced by transportation. Cultural differences among geographic regions in the United States, as well as among countries and regions of the world, are lessened by the ability of residents to travel outside the confines of their region (or country).

The automobile has been the form of transportation that most affects U.S. lifestyles. The convenience, flexibility, and relatively low cost of automobile travel have permitted individuals to live in locations different from where they work. The growth of suburbs can be attributed to the automobile because people can drive 20 to 60 miles or more one way to work. The automobile also enables people to seek medical, dental, and recreational services at varying locations throughout a region.

A prime ingredient in increased passenger travel is economical transportation. Unfortunately, the rising cost of automobile and air travel, a result of escalating energy, labor, and equipment costs, is beginning to cause a change in life-styles. Instead of traveling long distances for a vacation, many people now stay closer to home or do not travel at all. Areas of the country that are highly dependent on tourists have experienced economic difficulties.

Flight from the cities to the suburbs has been somewhat stalled by the rising costs of automobile travel. The 50- to 100-mile round trip per day is becoming quite expensive for many commuters. Some recent developments indicate that families are returning to the cities to live so that they can reduce travel-to-work expenses. This trend is not overwhelming yet, but the next few years might see a stronger growth in the demand for city rather than suburban dwellings.

The remainder of this chapter will focus on the demand for freight and passenger transportation. Attention is directed to the economic characteristics of freight and passenger transportation demand as well as the traits unique to each. Initially, consideration is given to transportation demand measurement units and the level of aggregation.

DEMAND MEASUREMENT UNITS

Transportation demand is essentially a request to move a given amount of cargo or people a specific distance. Therefore, the demand for transportation is measured in weight/passenger-distance units. For freight, the demand unit is the ton-mile and for people it is the passenger-mile.

The **ton-mile** is not a homogenous unit. The demand for 200 ton-miles of freight transportation could be for moving 200 tons one mile, 100 tons two miles, one ton 200 miles, or any other combination of weight and distance that equals 200 ton-miles. In addition, the unique transportation requirements for direction, equipment, and service will vary among customers with a 200 ton-mile demand. For example, the demand for 200 ton-miles of ice cream from Pittsburgh might require movement in all directions and a refrigerated vehicle with same-day delivery, whereas the demand for 200 ton-miles of gasoline from Philadelphia might be for movement north, south, and west in a tank vehicle with next-day delivery.

The above examples are aimed at delineating the heterogeneous nature of the transportation demand unit. The same unit demand might have a different cost of producing and different user service requirements. However, no other measurement unit reflects the basic weight and distance components of freight transportation demand.

Similarly, the **passenger-mile** is a heterogeneous unit. A 500 passenger-mile demand could be one passenger moving 500 miles or 500 passengers moving one mile. The demand of 500 passenger-miles could be via automobile, railroad, or airplane, as well as first class or coach, luxury or basic, and quick or slow. The demand attributes of the passenger-mile vary from passenger to passenger.

LEVEL OF AGGREGATION

The demand for transportation can be examined at different levels of aggregation. **Aggregate demand** for transportation is the sum of the individual demands for freight and passenger transportation. In addition, aggregate demand is the sum of the demand for transportation via different modes, and the aggregate demand for a particular mode is the sum of the demand for specific carriers in that mode. Table 1.4 shows the allocation of aggregate passenger-miles and Table 1.5 shows the allocation of aggregate ton-miles.

DEMAND ELASTICITY

Demand elasticity refers to the sensitivity of customers to changes in the price. If customers are sensitive to price, a price reduction will increase the demand for the item and total revenue received. If customers are insensitive to price, that is, demand is inelastic, a price reduction will result in a small relative change in quantity demanded and total revenue will fall slightly. In traditional terms, demand elasticity is the ratio of the percentage change in quantity demanded to percentage change in price, or,

$$\text{elasticity} = \%\text{ change in quantity} / \%\text{ change in price}$$

If demand is elastic, the quantity demanded changes more than the change in price and the elasticity coefficient (E) is greater than one. Conversely, a product or service is said to be **price inelastic**, or insensitive to price change, if the quantity demanded changes less than the change in price (E is less than one).

In general, the demand for freight transportation is inelastic. Freight rate reductions will not dramatically increase the demand for freight transportation because transportation costs represent, in the aggregate, less than four percent of a product's landed cost. Substantial rate reductions would be required for a meaningful increase in the demand for the product and consequently demand for transportation of the product.

On a modal and specific carrier basis, demand is price-sensitive. The relative modal share of aggregate demand is in part determined by the rates charged. Reductions in rates charged by a particular mode will result in increases in volume of freight handled by that mode. This assumes that the mode that reduced the rate is physically capable of transporting the freight.

For example, the long-haul transportation of new automobiles was dominated by motor carrier transportation in the 1960s. In the 1970s, the railroads developed a new railcar specifically designed to transport new automobiles. This new railcar enabled the railroads to improve efficiency and reduce the rates charged for hauling new automobiles. The percentage of new automobiles hauled by railroads increased after the introduction of the new railcar, whereas lower rates and the share of intercity ton-miles of new automobiles transported by motor carrier decreased. Today, motor carriers are used primarily to transport new automobiles short distances, from rail yards to dealerships.

Modal and specific carrier demand is also **service elastic**. Assuming no price changes, the modal or specific carrier demand is much more sensitive to changes in service levels provided. Many air passengers monitor the "on-time" service levels of the various air carriers and, when possible, will select the air carrier that provides the best on-time service. For example, if two air carriers are available and one is on time 100 percent of the time and the other only 60 percent of the time, the air passenger is more likely to use the carrier that has a 100-percent on-time performance record.

FREIGHT TRANSPORTATION

The demand for freight transportation is based upon the demand for a product in a given location. Because of the specialization of labor and mass production, specific areas have an oversupply of product while other geographic areas face a deficit. This geographic imbalance in the supply of a product gives rise to the demand for freight transportation. In this section, attention is given to the characteristics of freight transportation demand.

Derived Demand

The demand to transport a product to a given location depends on the existence of a demand to consume (use) the product at that location. Freight is generally not transported to a location unless a need for the product exists at the location. Thus, the demand for freight transportation is derived from the customer demand for the product.

For example, Figure 1.11 illustrates the derived demand nature of freight transportation. The oversupply of widgets at the production site, City A, will not be transported to City C because no demand for widgets exists at City C. However, there is a demand for 100 widgets at City B and, consequently, a demand for the transportation of 100 widgets to City B. Because of the demand for 100 widgets at City B, there is a demand for the transportation of widgets from City A to City B.

The derived demand characteristics imply that freight transportation demand cannot be affected by freight carrier actions. As noted above, this assumption is true for the aggregate demand for transportation. For example, if a freight carrier lowers the rate to zero for moving high-tech personal computers from the United States to a developing nation, this "free" transportation will not materially change the demand for personal computers in the developing nation. The demand for personal

FIGURE 1.11 Derived Demand for Freight Transportation

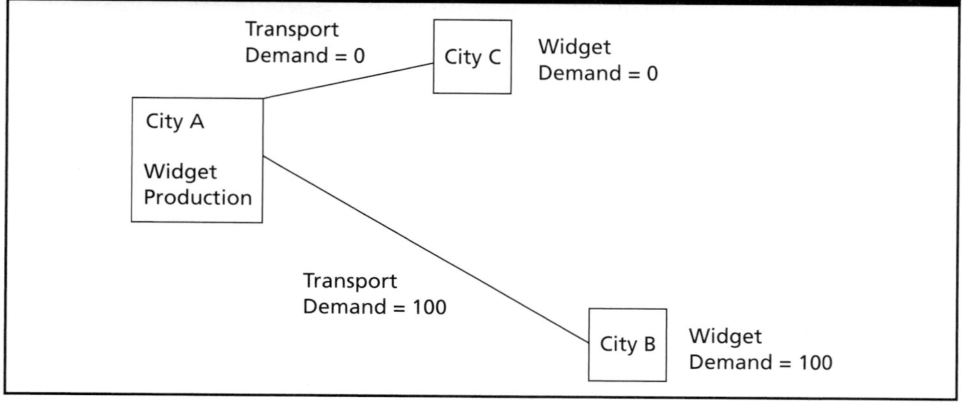

computers is dependent on educational levels of the citizens, electrical power availability, and so on, not price alone.

However, at the disaggregate level (i.e. modal, carrier, or specific traffic lane), the rates charged or service level provided can influence the demand for the product and the demand to transport the product. This impact on product demand considers the value of the service provided to the user of the product and is discussed next.

VALUE OF SERVICE

Value of service considers the impact of the transportation cost and service on the demand for the product. Lower transportation cost will cause a shift in demand for transportation among the modes and specific carriers. It can also affect the demand to transport freight over a specific traffic lane.

The impact of transportation cost on the demand for a product at a given location focuses on the **landed cost** of the product. The landed cost of a product includes the cost of the product at the source plus the cost to transport the product to its destination. If the landed cost of a product is lower than that of other sources, there will be a demand for that product and for transportation of that product.

For example, in Figure 1.12, a manufacturer of bicycle tires located in Chicago is competing in the Boston market with local producers. For the Chicago bicycle tire manufacturer to be competitive, the landed cost of its tire must be lower than the cost of the local manufacturers' tires. The Boston manufacturers have a manufacturing cost of $4 per tire, whereas the Chicago manufacturer's cost is $3. As long as the transportation cost per tire from Chicago to Boston is less than $1, the Chicago tire will have a **landed cost advantage** and a demand for the Chicago tire will exist in Boston (assuming the quality is equal to that of the locally produced tires). Conversely, if the transportation cost exceeds $1 per tire, Boston consumers will purchase tires from local manufacturers and there will be no demand for, as well as no demand to transport, the Chicago tire.

The landed cost also determines the extent of the market for a business. The greater the distance the product is shipped, the greater the landed cost. At some distance from the product source, the landed cost becomes prohibitive to the buyer, and there is no demand for the product. Also, the landed cost can determine the **extent of the market** between two competing companies.

The works of Fetter and Losch suggest that the extent of the market area for two competing firms is the point at which the lowest price (or landed cost) is equal for the products of the two firms.[20] The market area for a seller will be the area where the seller has a landed cost advantage over its competitor because the buyer is assumed to select the seller that offers the lowest price.

To illustrate this concept, Figure 1.13 presents an example of two producers located 200 miles apart. Producer P has a production cost of $50 per unit and a transportation

FIGURE 1.12 Demand and Landed Cost

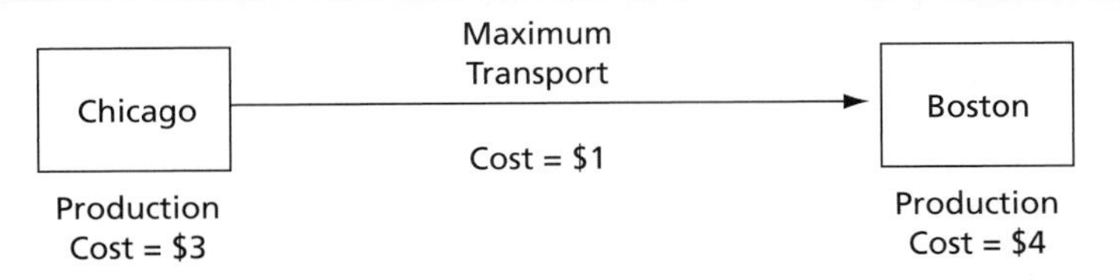

FIGURE 1.13 Extent of Market Area

200 Miles

P ———————————————— S

Production = \$50/unit	Production = \$50/unit
Transportation = \$0.60/unit/mile	Transportation = \$0.50/unit/mile

cost of \$0.60 per unit per mile. Producer S has a production cost of \$50 per unit and a transportation cost of \$0.50 per unit per mile. The extent of the market between the two producers is the point at which the landed cost (LC) of P is equal to that of S, or where x is the distance from P's plant to the limit of the market area and $(200 — x)$ is the distance from S's plant to the market area.

$$\text{LC (P)} = \text{LC (S)}$$
$$\text{Production (P)} + \text{Transportation (P)} = \text{Production (S)} + \text{Transportation (S)}$$
$$\$50 + \$0.60\,(x) = \$50 + \$0.50\,(200 - x)$$
$$\$0.60\,(x) + \$0.50\,(x) = \$50 + \$100 - \$50$$
$$\$1.10 = \$100$$
$$x = 90.9 \text{ miles from P}$$

Solving the equation for x shows that P has a market area that extends 90.9 miles from its plant and S has a market area that extends 109.1 miles from its facility. The company with the lower transportation cost (S) has a greater market area than the firm with the higher transportation cost (P).

Service Components of Freight Demand

Shippers of freight have varying service requirements of transport providers. These service requirements range from specific pickup times to equipment and communication.

The service demands are related to the cost implications of the transportation service provided. The transportation service characteristics of freight shippers include transit time, reliability, accessibility, capability, and security.[21]

Transit time affects the level of inventory held by both the shipper and receiver and the cost of holding inventory. The longer the transit time, the higher the inventory levels and inventory carrying cost. Also, transit times impact the cost of inventory in the supply chain. For example, the supply of clothing produced in the Pacific Rim might require 45 days transit time from manufacturer to retail store. While the clothes are in transit for 45 days, someone, either buyer or seller, incurs the cost of financing the shipment for 45 days. If the transit time is reduced to 15 days by use of air transportation, this in-transit inventory financing cost would be reduced by 30 days.

The longer the transit time, the greater the potential cost of stockouts. Using the Pacific Rim example above, a stockout of clothing at the retail store could mean a maximum of 45 days, during which sales are lost and the profits from these potential sales are foregone. Shorter transit times reduce the potential stockout cost.

Reliability refers to the consistency of transit time. Meeting pickup and delivery schedules enables shippers and receivers to optimize inventory levels and minimize stockout costs. Unreliable transit time requires the freight receiver to either increase inventory levels to guard against stockout conditions or incur stockouts. Reliable service directly affects the level of modal and specific carrier demand; that is, a shipper will shift from an unreliable carrier (mode) to one that is reliable. And the customer might switch from a supplier who provides unreliable delivery service to one that is reliable, thereby impacting the transportation demand for specific carriers on specific traffic lanes.

Accessibility is the ability of the transportation provider to move the freight between a specific origin and destination. The inability of a carrier to provide direct service between an origin and destination results in added costs and transit time for the shipper. For example, an air carrier does not move freight from Lansing, Michigan, directly to Angers, France. First, the freight is moved by motor carrier from Lansing to Detroit; it is then flown to Paris, and last, it is moved from Paris to Angers by either motor carrier or rail. The inability of the air carrier to provide direct service requires additional transportation by motor carrier and rail and adds to the transit time. Similar conditions exist for rail and water carriers. Motor carriers have a distinct advantage in accessibility in most countries.

The ability of the carrier to provide such "special" service requirements is the essence of **capability**. Based on the physical and marketing characteristics of the freight, shippers have unique demands for equipment, facilities, and communication. Products requiring controlled temperature necessitate the use of refrigerated vehicles. Time-sensitive shipments demand state-of-the-art communication systems to monitor their exact location and arrival time. Marketing considerations might dictate the demand for carriers to provide freight consolidation and break-bulk facilities to lower total freight costs and transit times so as to maintain or increase the demand for the product. These are just a few of the many and varied demands placed on transportation service providers.

Finally, **security** is concerned with the safety of the goods in transit. Shipments that are damaged or lost in transit cause increased costs in the areas of inventory and/or stockouts. A damaged shipment cannot be used (sold), and the buyer faces the possibility of losing a sale or stopping the production process. Increasing inventory levels to guard against the stockout cost resulting from a damaged shipment causes increased inventory carrying costs. Table 1.11 provides a summary of the service components of freight demand.

Location of Economic Activity

Transportation has been a major determinant in the location of industrial facilities since the Industrial Revolution. The cost of transporting raw materials into a facility and the cost of transporting finished goods to markets directly affect the profitability of the plant or warehouse. In addition, the quality of the transport service, such as the time required to traverse the spatial gap between sources of supply, plants, warehouses, and markets, affects inventory, stockout, and other costs as identified below.

Table 1.11 Service Components of Freight Demand

Service Component	User Implication
Transit Time	Inventory, Stockout Costs
Reliability	Inventory, Stockout Costs
Accessibility	Transit Time, Transportation Cost
Capability	Meets Products' Unique Physical and Marketing Requirements
Security	Inventory, Stockout Costs

Water transportation has played an important role in the location of many major cities. Early settlers to the United States relied on water transportation to tie European markets and supply sources to the developing country. Thus, cities that are major population centers such as New York, Philadelphia, and Boston are port cities. As the U.S. frontier was settled, it became tied to these port cities that provided a source of supplies and markets for the western region. Other cities—Pittsburgh, Cincinnati, and St. Louis—developed along the internal waterways. As railroad transportation developed, however, cities and industrial facilities grew at locations that were not adjacent to waterways. Later, the automobile and motor carrier enabled the development of cities and industrial facilities at virtually any location.

As the U.S. market grew, firms had to decide where new facilities should be located. Today many companies are faced with the question of where to locate plants and warehouses in light of changing markets, especially the exodus of people and many industries to the Sun Belt states, as well as changing raw material supply locations. As markets and supply locations change and transit times become longer, firms experience higher costs for transportation, inventory, and warehousing.

As the location of economic activity changes, so does the demand for transportation. The aging of the U.S. population has seen a shifting of population to, for example, the southern states of Florida, North and South Carolina, and Arizona. This shift in population requires businesses supplying consumer products to demand more transportation services into these states, and some companies have responded to this population shift by locating production facilities in these states.

PASSENGER TRANSPORTATION

Passenger transportation is the movement of people. Passenger movement accounts for about 10 percent of the annual GDP. In addition, there are many related industries, including hotels/motels, parks and recreation facilities, restaurants, and travel agencies. The study of passenger transportation demand requires an examination of people's motives for travel and movement. Attention is directed initially at long-distance, intercity passenger demand and finally urban, short-distance, travel demand.

Business Travel

Business travel is one of the major passenger markets. This is employment-related travel, and it is often travel in which the person is reimbursed or otherwise compensated in some way. This is a major market segment of the airline industry. Business travel is a much smaller part of the bus and water passenger markets.

The air-travel business market is highly **sensitive to schedules** rather than to price. The strength of a carrier's business is often based on this market segment. Airlines find that it is important to offer many flights throughout the day between two points to become a dominant carrier in a market. Further, it is a travel demand that usually consists of "out in the morning and back in the evening" scheduling. Traffic is typically heaviest Monday through Friday. Travel convenience, schedules, in-flight amenities, and special services are important to business travelers.

A low fare is generally not as important in this market as it is with personal or vacation travel. Business travel is derived from the need for a meeting at another location, and the cost of travel is usually not a major factor in the decision to go or not to go. For this reason, the airlines find that they can charge higher full coach fares, rather than resorting to discount fares in this market. Business travelers are the first-class passengers or the full-fare coach passengers.

Vacation Travel

Vacation travel, or pleasure travel, represents another major passenger market. These travelers often view transportation as a means of getting to a vacation destination point. In some cases, carriers have been able to include the transportation leg itself as part of the vacation experience; that is, the transportation leg can be both part of the derived demand for the trip to a destination as well as part of the vacation experience. This is the case with cruise ship travel and long-distance rail movement.

Vacation travel is typically **price-sensitive** and often concerned with the particular time of day or day of week schedules. Vacation travel has been heavily promoted by the airlines for Saturday and Sunday travel, when their transport capacity is not heavily used by business travelers. Further, the vacation travel market is where the airlines often offer lower fares. These tickets often have many restrictions designed to prevent regular business travelers from switching to the lower fares. For example, the super-saver fare requires the passenger to stay at the destination over a Saturday night. Such fares are not good during certain heavy holiday periods or Monday and Friday flights, or they constitute only a small number of seats on flights that normally would not be filled by full-fare business passengers.

The vacation market is important to Florida, the Caribbean, Colorado, and Vermont during the winter months for sun and ski vacations. The United States to Europe and the United States coast to coast are strong vacation markets in the summer. Travel agents and tour operators are heavily involved in the vacation market. Charter bus trips and tours are also major parts of the vacation market.

The vacation travel market is also splintering into "boutique" travel niches as well. These are specialty vacations in which recreation and/or rest at a hotel or on a cruise ship are not the major elements of the trip. Trips in this category that have become increasingly popular in recent years include viewing rare animal life at the Galápagos Islands, whale watching in Baja California, hiking in Nepal, photographic expeditions in the wilds of Alaska or the Northwest Territories, safaris in Africa, and nature cruises up the Amazon River. These trips typically are educational; they often employ naturalists who give speeches and show films relating to the site on the trip.

Personal Travel

Personal travel is the other major long-distance passenger market; this is travel that is motivated by visits to home, travel to school, and emergency trips. People in this market segment might be attracted to the fastest possible means of travel, but low price can also be a significant demand characteristic.

The dominant demand characteristic for emergency trips, such as visiting an ill relative, is speed. The traveler is interested in arriving at the destination as quickly as possible, and, depending on the type of emergency, without regard to the cost. Alternatively, the college student traveling between home and college is more concerned with the cost of the trip and will wait hours or days to get a "free" ride with a friend or relative. The traveler going home to visit family is usually concerned with the departure and arrival times. These trips are scheduled around work, usually over the weekend or during holidays.

Urban Transit

Urban-related trip demands fall into three broad categories that provide insights into origin–destination density patterns or **primary trip markets**. The first is the work or school trip. The need for this type of trip is the most consistent and repetitive because it has one origin and one destination. The work point is often a concentrated employment stop (office, factory, etc.). The second major trip needed in a household is the trip to shop for food and other necessities. This, too, can be repetitive in pattern. The third type of trip, miscellaneous, includes recreational and medical trips. Miscellaneous trips are the least repetitive and are not always conducive to transit service attraction.

The automobile has often been referred to as the "fifth freedom" held by Americans. It has pervaded life-styles to the extent that it is often used even in the face of alternative lower-cost transportation options. The personal convenience and privacy of the auto has created, in many cases, an intolerance of the waiting, walking, and crowding often associated with public forms of transportation. The convenience and privacy factors, accompanied by the relatively inexpensive availability of gas and oil for several decades, created a dramatic diversion to the auto and away from public transport. This diversion was felt mostly in shopping and recreational intra-city trips and to a lesser extent in commuting trips.

Urban sprawl has been accompanied by the growth of suburban shopping centers. This has caused retail stores, theaters, and restaurants to be concentrated in suburban locations, rather than downtown. Thus, shopping trips to downtown areas during the day or in the evening via public transit systems have tended to disappear.

The drop in the use of public transit systems for shopping and recreation has meant that these systems are not fully used during the day. Formerly, they were intensively used by commuters in the morning, shoppers during the day, commuters in the evening, and people attending theater, cultural events, and restaurants in the evening. Transit equipment was often used 12 to 15 hours per day, and employees operated public transit for full-shift periods.

When only commuting demand remains, a transit system experiences a travel demand similar to that shown in Figure 1.14. The peak situation calls for greater demand than before, but the demand is largely concentrated in two, two-hour periods per day for only five days per week; roughly only six percent of the week is represented by full utilization. It is not uncommon for a city like Washington, DC, to require 2,000 buses in service during rush hours, only to have half of them in service during the day, a quarter of them in the evening, and only five percent during

FIGURE 1.14 Urban Travel Peaking Problem

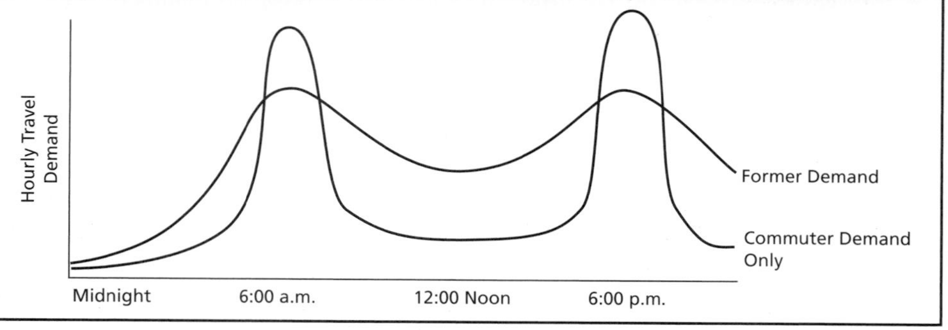

the night and early morning. This **peak–valley demand** problem means that capital investments are largely underutilized and many operating employees who are paid full eight-hour shifts are only required to work runs that take one-half to three-quarters of that time. In many cities, some bus drivers and train crews are paid for a full day for one trip into the city in the morning and one trip at night.

Gradually over a two-decade period, the industry found it could not survive under private ownership. Whereas public urban transportation was viewed in the late 1960s and early 1970s as a *desirable* service for cities to retain, many public agencies began to subsidize urban transportation operations, to invest in them, or to purchase them outright for public agency operation. Since the beginning of the energy crunch in the 1970s, urban transportation services have been viewed as a necessary component to the viable function of cities and their environments.

Passenger Demand Characteristics

The demand characteristics of passenger transportation consist of many individual components. These range from very objective and tangible items to some that are very intangible.

DESTINATION

The destination is where the traveler seeks to go. It can be important, such as a business destination (Chicago, Detroit, or Los Angeles) or it can have a vacation appeal (the Virgin Islands or Stowe, Vermont). Most locations represent a blend of these two destination segments, such as New York, which attracts many business as well as vacation travelers. In some situations, a destination is a means of getting to somewhere else. For example, Atlanta is an airline hub through which a person must transfer to get to his or her ultimate destination. In today's cruise travel, the destination is the origin and the important demand aspect of the cruise is the quality of the trip.

SCHEDULES AND SPEED

Often a means of travel is selected because it is the only one with a convenient departure or arrival time. The consistency with which a carrier meets schedules is also an important factor, and many air travelers consult the U.S. DOT's on-time record of air carriers over a given origin–destination. Further, the speed of travel can be an advantage or disadvantage. The speed of the airplane allows travelers more productive time on the ground at the origin and destination. However, the arrival or destination time is of less importance and slow speed is an advantage when touring the Rocky Mountains via Amtrak.

COST

Cost is one objective measure of the transportation product. It comprises the actual fare and several other costs. These other costs include access, parking, overnight lodging, food, and, in some cases, ability or opportunity to perform work or make sales calls.

EQUIPMENT

This factor can be part of the advertised appeal of travel. It was a key element in the airline industry when new jets were being built and many of the older and slower propeller airplanes were still in service. In other modes, equipment can make a difference if it represents cleanliness and the avoidance of maintenance delays. This was a travel problem with Amtrak when it first started and had to operate with equipment that was old and often broke down. In the cruise industry, the ship is the item that is advertised. It is a major component of the entire vacation.

ENTERTAINMENT AND ATTENTION

These amenities are often important in vacation travel. This is the case with onboard entertainment, food, and available diversions on ships. Some airlines recognize the nature of business travel and promote their services as providing close in-flight attention only if the passenger wants it. Some airlines are now offering meals in coach class for a fee in an attempt to reduce operating expenses, while first class still receives free meals.

TERMINALS

These are the points from which persons board and depart the transportation vehicles. To be attractive to the traveling public, terminals must be accessible, clean, and safe. They should be designed to move baggage efficiently and to give easy access to other modes of transport.

COMPLAINTS AND EXPERIENCES

Passenger travel is a highly visible service industry. Unlike industrial buying where many objective elements come into the buying decision, passenger travel can be subject to sudden shifts resulting from intangible perceptions.

ROLE OF THE TRAVEL AGENT

The travel agent is a valuable but often overlooked and misunderstood facilitator of passenger travel. Though not providing movement service themselves, travel agents provide a wide range of informational and arrangement services.

The travel agent is a link between the passenger, on the one hand, and carriers and hotels on the other. Their services include explaining the lowest cost and most direct transportation services, as well as making reservations for and issuing tickets to the passenger. Agents also arrange for car rentals, hotels, and complete tour services. The cost of using a travel agent has increased to the passenger. The cost of a ticket purchased directly from an airline, Amtrak, or steamship company, for example, is lower than if arranged and purchased through a travel agent. The travel agent is no longer compensated through a commission paid by the carrier. Travel agents must now assess a fee to the passenger for the use of their services. This has had a dramatic impact on the structure and size of the travel agent industry. Carriers now have Internet sites that allow passengers to choose their flight, pick their seat, and pay for the ticket. The same can be said for major hotel chains. Along with ticketing and hotel reservation services, travel agents can also offer travel advice to passengers seeking this type of help. This is especially helpful to vacation passengers.

Summary

- The decade of the 2000s will bring many challenges to logistics and transportation activities through the Internet, globalization, business alliances, and technology.
- Transportation is an integral activity in a firm's implementation of logistics and supply chain concepts.
- Total-cost analysis is an important part of the logistics system perspective because of the interactions of logistics decisions with the firm and other channel partners' decisions.
- Transportation is a necessary activity for a modern society, and it influences almost every aspect of our lives.

- Transportation helps to determine the value of goods by adding time, place, and quantity utilities to them.
- Transportation is an important part of the U.S. economy, contributing 16 percent to the GDP.
- Transportation has a significant impact on the environment because of its potential consequences to air and water quality, as well as its influence on noise levels.
- Freight demand is measured in ton-miles, a combination of weight and distance; the ton-mile is a heterogeneous unit. The passenger-mile is a heterogeneous unit of measure for passenger demand.
- The service components of freight demand include transit time, reliability, accessibility, capability, and security.

Key Terms

accessibility, 39
aggregate demand, 35
bundle of services, 16
business alliance, 6
business logistics, 4
capability, 39
cash flows, 10
common carrier, 29
comparative advantage, 20
cost trade-offs, 11
demand elasticity, 35
deregulation, 32
e-business, 5
eminent domain, 29
environmental concern, 25
extent of the market, 37
freight transportation, 23
globalization, 5
inbound, 6
inelastic, 35
information flows, 10
integration, 6
Internet, 5
inventories, 14
landed cost, 37
landed cost advantage, 37
Lardner's Law,19
logistics channel environment, 4
materials management, 15
mobility, 33
modal split, 24
passenger service, 40
passenger transportation, 23
passenger-mile, 35
peak demand, 43
physical distribution, 15
place utility, 19
price inelastic, 35
price-sensitive, 41
primary trip markets, 42
product flows, 10
quantity utility, 20
reliability, 38
security, 39
sensitive to schedules, 40
service, 14
service elastic, 36
supply chain management, 4
technology, 6
time utility, 19
ton-mile, 34
total-cost analysis, 11
transit time, 38
transportation, 15
utility creation, 14
value added, 4

Study Questions

1. The decade of the 2000s will see significant challenges occurring in logistics and transportation. Discuss the factors that helped introduce these challenges.
2. What is the nature of total-cost analysis? Why is it so important to the logistics systems approach?
3. Why are the three levels of optimality in total-cost analysis important to consider when making logistics decisions?
4. What role did transportation play in the economic development of the United States? Is this role of transportation still important today?
5. How does transportation add value for manufacturing or distribution firms?
6. How does transportation contribute to geographic specialization and large-scale production? Is there a relationship between the two?

7. Describe the economic role of transportation in an economy and relate this role to the demand for transportation services. How has the movement toward a global economy impacted the demand for transportation?
8. The ton-mile is a heterogeneous measure of transportation demand. Explain.
9. Distinguish between aggregate, modal, and specific demand.
10. Aggregate demand for freight is price and service inelastic, whereas modal and specific freight demand is price and service elastic. What is the rationale for this?
11. What is meant by *derived demand* and how does this demand characteristic impact freight demand?

Notes

1. Council of Supply Chain Management Professionals, Oak Brook, IL.
2. For a more detailed discussion of logistics and supply chain management, see John J. Coyle, Edward J. Bardi, and C. John Langley, Jr., *The Management of Business Logistics,* 7th ed. (Mason, OH: Southwestern, 2003), Ch. 1.
3. Donald J. Bowersox, Patricia J. Daugherty, Cornelia L. Droge, Dale S. Rogers, and Daniel L. Wardlow, *Leading Edge Logistics: Competitive Positioning for the 1990s*, Oakbrook, IL: CLM, 1989, pp. 7-10.
4. Ibid.
5. Ibid., pp. 15-20.
6. Ibid., pp. 20-25.
7. Ibid.
8. John J. Coyle, Edward J. Bardi, and C. John Langley, *Management of Business Logistics,* 7th ed. Mason, OH: Southwestern, 2003, p. 38.
9. Ibid.
10. C.J. Smith, "Integrating Logistics in a Major Chemical Company," *Proceedings of Council of Logistics Management,* Vol. 2 1990, pp. 173-176.
11. Ibid.
12. Ibid.
13. Coyle, et. al., *op. cit.,* pp. 23-26.
14. Allen W. Kiefer and Robert A. Novack, "An Empirical Analysis of Warehouse Measurement Systems in the Context of Supply Chain Implementation," *Transportation Journal,* Vol. 38, No. 3, 1999, pp. 18-27.
15. See, for example, Robert A. Novack, C. John Langley, Jr., and Lloyd M. Rinehart, *Creating Logistics Value: Themes for the Future* Oak Brook, IL: Council of Logistics Management, 1995, pp. 176-189.
16. U.S. Senate, Committee on Interstate and Foreign Commerce, *National Transportation Policy,* December 1960, p. 29.
17. Sang Youn Kim, "The Role of Transportation to African Famine Relief Operations," *Journal of Transportation Management,* Vol. 1, No. 1, 1988, pp. 369-377.
18. U.S. Department of Transportation, Bureau of Transportation Statistics, *National Transportation Statistics, 2002,* Washington, DC, December 2002.
19. Donald Harper, *Transportation in America,* Englewood Cliffs, NJ: Prentice-Hall, 1978, p. 8.
20. See Robert B. Fetter and Winston C. Dalleck, *Decision Models for Inventory Management,* Homewood, IL: Richard D. Irwin, 1961.
21. John J. Coyle, Edward J. Bardi, and C. John Langley, Jr., *The Management of Business Logistics,* 7th ed., Mason, OH: Southwestern, 2003, Ch. 10.

Suggested Readings

Bowersox, Donald J., David J. Closs, and Theodore P. Stank. "Ten Mega-Trends that will Revolutionize Supply Chain Logistics," *Journal of Business Logistics,* Vol. 21, No. 2, 2000, pp. 1-16.

Burr, John T. "A New Name for a Not-So-New Concept," *Quality Progress*, March 1993, pp. 87-88.

Coyle, John J. "Future Manufacturing, Markets and Logistics Needs," *Proceedings of International Symposium on Motor Carrier Transportation*, Summer 1993, pp. 1-55.

Coyle, John J., Edward J. Bardi, and C. John Langley, Jr. *The Management of Business Logistics*, 7th ed., Cincinnati, OH: Southwestern Publishing, 2003.

Gammelgaard, Britta and Paul D. Larson. "Logistics Skills and Competencies for Supply Chain Management," *Journal of Business Logistics*, Vol. 22, No. 2, 2001, pp. 27-50.

Mentzer, John T., William DeWitt, James S. Keebler, Soonhong Min, Nancy W. Nix, Carlo D. Smith, and Zach G. Zacharia. "Defining Supply Chain Management," *Journal of Business Logistics*, Vol. 22, No. 2, 2001, pp. 1-26.

Poole, Kevin. "Seizing the Potential of the Service Supply Chain," *Supply Chain Management Review*, July/August 2003, pp. 54-61.

Regan, Amelia C., and Thomas F. Golob. "Freight Operators' Perceptions of Congestion Problems and the Application of Advanced Technologies: Results from a 1998 Survey of 1200 Companies Operating in California," *Transportation Journal*, Vol. 38, No. 3, 1999, pp. 57-67.

Scannell, Thomas V., Shawnee K. Vickery, and Cornelia L. Droge. "Upstream Supply Chain Management and Competitive Performance in the Automotive Supply Industry," *Journal of Business Logistics*, Vol. 21, No. 1, 2000, pp. 23-48.

Shanahan, John. "Making It Easier on the Customer," *Logistics Management*, September 2003, pp. 26-31.

Case 1-1

Hardee Transportation

Jim O'Brien, operations manager for Hardee Transportation (a Class I truckload carrier), received a phone call from Stacey Holmgren, the vice president of logistics of one of Hardee's largest customers.

"Jim, we've been involved with our largest retail customer in a number of new initiatives involving inventories, forecasting, and planning. We've come to realize that we are missing a critical link in making our initiatives work: our carrier base. We have shared forecasts, invested in technology, and formed joint planning teams to help us maximize our manufacturing capacity while minimizing stock-outs at retail. However, we realized that all of these efforts are not going to work unless we coordinate this inventory with its movements between our facilities and our customer's distribution centers. We are going to need you to start moving in this direction with us. It will require a change in the way you do business with us. And, by the way, it's probably going to require some investment on your part."

Jim wasn't sure exactly what this meant for Hardee. Hardee Transportation is a major truckload motor carrier servicing the North American market. It has 12 dispatch centers in the United States and has partnerships with truckload carriers in Mexico and Canada. For certain customers, like Stacey, Hardee maintains trailer pools at their distribution centers based on contract agreements. Their dispatch operations rely on customer requests for product movement. This reactive position is not optimum for Hardee, but it is how they have done business for 75 years. Their tractors use Qualcomm satellite technology and they are linked to their large customers through electronic data interchange. They currently are not using the Internet for transaction management.

Over the past few years, Jim has noticed that customers have required even higher service levels than in the past. Adding to this is the customers' constant pressure on prices. Hardee's operating ratio overall is currently 96%, so they don't have a lot of room for future price reductions. In fact, this is not in agreement with Hardee's operating strategy. They pride themselves as a high-service carrier, which is why they maintain excess rolling stock in trailer pools at major customer locations. Their trailer-to-power ratio is 3.1 to 1, one of the highest in the industry. They bobtail tractors from their dispatch locations when customers have a trailer to move, adding to their operating costs. Therefore, the notion of additional investment on their part is not an attractive option to Hardee, given their operating profit margin and high-service strategy. However, Jim knows that he has to do something if he wants to retain his largest customer.

Jim has read about some of the new trends in carrier/shipper operations and relationships. He can easily see that these trends will require Hardee to change the way it does business. He really isn't sure what this means, but he knows that some major changes are on the horizon. Hardee's current operating model is not in line with these new trends.

Case Questions

1. Using the information presented in this chapter, what changes would you suggest to Jim?
2. How would you suggest he present this scenario to the president of Hardee?

Case 1-2

Soup to Nuts, Inc.

Soup to Nuts, Inc. (STN) is a wholesaler of various types of sundry items used to supply the electronics manufacturing industry. These items include everything from color monitors' control knobs to sophisticated computer chips. Chip N. Dale, STN's founder and president, felt that offering this broad product line to these manufacturers would give STN a market niche as a one-stop supplier. Coupled with its broad product line, STN prides itself on fast and accurate delivery to customers because of the critical nature of STN's products in the manufacture of electronic devices.

Through the efforts of STN's logistics manager, Skip Grenoble, STN has established a long and successful relationship with an overnight, small package delivery company called Century Express. STN is one of Century's largest customers, with shipments originating at multiple origins to destinations all over the world. Century is not the lowest-priced carrier in the market, but it is certainly one of the best for service. The relationship between the two companies is mutually beneficial.

Because STN places a high priority on correct and prompt delivery to customers, it places a great deal of emphasis on a carrier's ability to trace and expedite shipments. Historically, Century had used a manual phone system for tracing where the customer would call in to a local terminal with a bill of lading number or pro number. Century's tracing clerk would then begin the process to locate the shipment by using an internal computer system and, many times, through phone calls to other terminals. As far as STN was concerned, this process was acceptable for its service requirements.

Century decided to implement a fully web-based tracing system using bar codes and scanners, allowing the customer to perform the tracing function. This system can also be used to enter customer orders, generate bills of lading and freight bills, and transmit documents electronically. Each customer has to learn Century's tracing system and has to fill out a customer profile including such information as shipping locations, freight classifications, freight terms, and the like. With this information, Century feels it can speed up the tracing process.

The first shipment to be made under the new system by STN was an extremely time-sensitive part to a manufacturer who needed it to keep a production line running. With all of the appropriate documents generated and information input to the system, the shipment was picked up by Century with a scheduled delivery time the next morning to the customer. The following afternoon, Skip received a call from his customer, who was not in a very good mood. "Skip, I thought you said that part would be here this morning. I am really close to having to shut down my line. I am really in a difficult position with the plant manager. She wants that part now." Skip replied, "Century was supposed to have delivered it this morning. I'm not sure what the problem is, but I plan to find out." After he hung up the phone, Skip attempted to get into Century's system to trace the shipment. After several attempts to log on to a system that was busy, he gave up and decided to try the old tracing method. He called his contact at the local Century terminal and explained his dilemma. His contact told him that tracing was no longer a local terminal activity but was centralized at Century's headquarters. Placing a call to Century's HQ got him in touch with the Customer Service department. He once again explained how important it was to find his customer's shipment immediately.

The Customer Service representative reminded Skip that he could trace his own shipments using the website. Skip informed the agent that the system had been busy when he tried to get into it. Reluctantly, the Customer Service representative took down the pertinent information concerning STN's shipment and informed Skip that he would look into it and call Skip back. In the meantime, STN's customer had also called Chip N. Dale to complain about the nondelivery. Chip in turn called the regional manager for Century to voice his concerns. As in Skip's case, Chip was reminded that he could use the website to trace his own shipments.

About 12 hours after Skip's initial call to Century, the Customer Service representative returned his call. He told Skip that the shipment was not in the system at all, so he doubted that Century had even picked up the shipment. Skip argued that this was impossible because he had a bill of lading number and a pro number. The representative responded by stating that it could be a number for another carrier. Because neither number showed up in the system, Century obviously never had the shipment. Skip had other problems on his hands because his customer's line had to be shut down and he was threatening to cut off all business ties with STN.

Skip and Chip N. Dale both made numerous calls to Century executives demanding an explanation for the situation. Both also demanded full compensation for the shipment from Century and that Century make full restitution to STN's customer for the costs of shutting down its production line. Plus, STN wanted an apology from Century management for the embarrassment they suffered in the eyes of their customers. If they did not receive their requests, they were going to take their small package delivery business to a competitor.

Case Questions

1. If you were Century's management, what would you do?
2. Are some customers not worth keeping? In other words, are STN's requests too costly for Century?
3. How would you rate the effectiveness of the new system? Would you have instituted this new system in the same manner as Century?

Case 1-3

Fly-By-Night Helicopter Service

In mid-July 2002, the Youngstown, Ohio, community was shocked by an announcement from Crow Airline that it would discontinue flights to and from the Youngstown airport by the end of the year. Crow provides commuter airline service to major hub airports in Cleveland, Pittsburgh, and Chicago, as well as direct service to such cities as Buffalo, Rochester, Toledo, and Indianapolis. Although a number of very small air carriers provide service, Crow is the only major air carrier serving Youngstown.

The business community leaders became quite concerned with the possibility of two-hour drives to airports in Cleveland and Pittsburgh to catch flights. The Youngstown Port Authority met with the business leaders to ascertain suggestions that could alleviate this blow to air travelers. A number of alternatives were suggested, including recruitment of a new commuter airline, establishment of an airport bus service, and formation of a joint-venture air commuter to connect Youngstown to Cleveland and Pittsburgh.

After the announcement of the Port Authority's meeting in the local newspaper, Darrin Yugg, President of Fly-By-Night Helicopter Service (FBN), contacted the Port Authority executive director with the idea of providing helicopter service between Youngstown and the Cleveland and Pittsburgh airports. The initial discussion was positive, and Mr. Yugg felt that enough interest existed to develop and present a formal proposal to the Port Authority.

Mr. Yugg was a seasoned helicopter pilot who had served with distinction in the Vietnam War. He had successfully built a helicopter service in the Youngstown area and currently had a fleet of 10 choppers. FBN's primary market was providing service to construction, agriculture, and pipeline companies. FBN would fly client personnel to construction job sites, spray farm fields, and provide surveillance of pipelines. FBN's service was highly regarded in the business community, and it enjoyed a reputation as a well-managed and financially strong company.

The shift from FBN's current type of business into shuttling passengers between airports was a new business venture, one with which Mr. Yugg did not have experience. He was somewhat concerned about the marketability of a helicopter shuttle service and, in particular, the acceptance of such a service by passengers not accustomed to flying in a helicopter. The helicopter flight would save passengers about 75 minutes on the commute to either Cleveland or Pittsburgh, but the cost of operating a helicopter would result in a round-trip charge approximately 2.5 times greater than a bus fare and 1.5 times greater than the current Crow fare.

Case Questions

1. What additional demand factors should Mr. Yugg consider as he develops his proposal?
2. As executive director of the Youngstown Port Authority, what areas would you want to see addressed in the proposal presented by FBN?
3. Given the information presented, would you recommend that FBN establish a helicopter shuttle service? Why or why not?

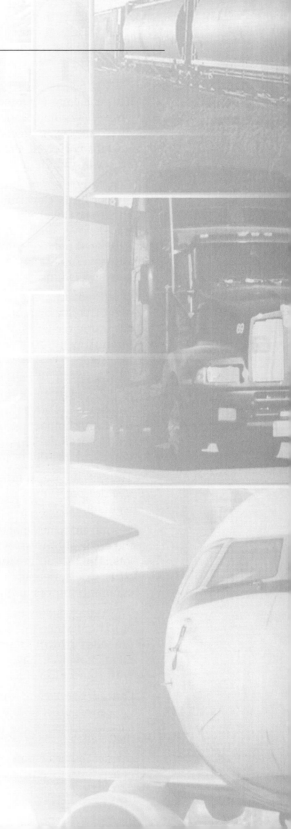

Chapter 2

Transportation Regulation and Public Policy

Why Doesn't Someone Do Something?

Regulation of Transportation

Development of Regulation

Current Economic Regulations

Antitrust Laws in Transportation

Transportation Policy

Stop Off: "Play By the Rules"

Why Do We Need a Transportation Policy?

Declaration of National Transportation Policy

Public Promotion

Transportation Promotion in Perspective

Transportation Safety

Summary

Key Terms

Study Questions

Notes

Suggested Readings

Cases

Appendix 2-A: Department of Transportation

WHY DOESN'T SOMEONE DO SOMETHING?

After sitting in a traffic jam for over an hour, your blood pressure begins to rise and your temper is off the scale. You can't understand why all these drivers are on this highway at this time. They should be at home, shopping, or anywhere else except here on this roadway at this time. Finally, you ask yourself, why doesn't someone do something about this traffic situation?

This is a common lament that we have all used when faced with one of life's many problems or irritations. Usually, the person lamenting is frustrated with his or her own inability to fix the problem and doesn't understand why those in power haven't corrected the situation. The lamenter does not specifically identify the *someone* and the *something*.

Generally, the *someone* referred to in the lament is the government—federal, state, and/or local. Government may be the only entity that has the power to correct the situation. Government could pass laws to ease the highway congestion; the frustrated driver does not have this power. And the *something* to be done is what the frustrated person wants. In the case of the traffic jam, the frustrated person would like government to legislate all drivers, except you, to refrain from using this highway at this time or to expand the existing highway system.

Often, government has been the cause of the frustrating issue. First, the government's policy regarding promotion of highway transportation is in part the cause of the traffic congestion. As some argue, the trucking industry has received favorable tax treatment for payment of highway construction and maintenance, thereby giving trucks a cost advantage over railroads and increasing truck freight shipments and, consequently, truck traffic on today's highways.

In the case of transportation, the *someone* referred to in the lament often is the federal and state government. The *something* is federal and state economic and safety regulation impacting the operation of all modes of transportation and the public policies fostered to promote and regulate them. Local government also passes laws that either restrict or promote the modes of transportation.

Thus, in the transportation field the *someone* in the question, "Why doesn't someone do something?", is the government, through economic and safety policies and regulations.

Resources in the United States are allocated through two main processes. The first is the political process, wherein the public or its elected representatives vote with ballots. The second is the market process, where the people vote with their dollars. In other words, people buy certain products or services and not others and, therefore, commit resources or inputs to the products or services purchased in the marketplace.

The United States has traditionally relied on the market process to provide transportation. Since the early part of the century, however, Congress has created and funded a growing number of transportation programs. All three levels of government, however, have been reluctant to abandon the market process, particularly with respect to vehicle ownership and **operation**.

Overall, the current **allocation of resources** to transportation reflects both a market allocation process and a political allocation process. Ideally, the political process should recognize the potential inadequacies of an unrestrained market that provides for each individual's basic necessities and that acts to prevent or mitigate market imperfections. Furthermore, the market process should operate within such constraints to efficiently provide what the transportation society wants and for which it is willing and able to pay. This blend of government and marketplace interaction in the transportation area is important to understand.

All facets of government's roles are important in this discussion. A convenient starting point for developing an understanding of this role is to discuss transportation regulation. Transportation regulation influences and constrains carrier operations and user services.

This chapter examines the basis of regulation, along with the role of the regulatory commissions and the courts. A discussion of the development of transportation regulation from its inception in 1887 to its role today is presented, along with the national transportation policies directing and promoting transportation and national security.

REGULATION OF TRANSPORTATION

Nature of Regulation

In the United States, the government influences the activities of business in many different ways. The amount of influence in business activity varies from providing the legal foundation and framework in which business operates to governmental ownership and control. There has been a long history of governmental regulation and control, but even today there is still some opposition on the part of managers to the governmental activity that influences their operations.

The amount of governmental control and regulation has increased as the United States has grown and prospered. If one compared the controls exercised by the government 150 years ago with those in existence today, the former would probably seem insignificant. The expansion of governmental influence, however, has been necessitated to some extent by the increase in the scope of activity, complexity, and the size of individual firms.

In the United States, we tend to view our economic activity as one of private enterprise. Competition is a necessary requirement to a free-enterprise economy. The allocation of scarce resources can be decided in the competitive market. The case for free-market enterprise and competition has been developed by economists for more than 150 years.

The definitions of *pure competition* and *free market* involve a number of conditions that may not exist in reality. Products are justified only by people's willingness to buy them. A product should not be sold at a price below the marginal cost of the last unit. The theory also assumes that people are able to assess whether a given economic act will make them better off—either as producers or consumers—and that people will use personal resources to achieve a more positive life-style.

Our belief that competition is most conducive to the betterment of all is joined by a feeling that **monopoly** or monopolistic practices are undesirable. The problem would be simple if our market structures took the form of either perfect competition or monopoly. Most individuals would not quarrel with governmental regulation of monopoly, and a valid case would be made for little or no governmental interference in an economy characterized by perfect competition. However, the prevailing situation is not this simple. The market structures usually take some form between the extremes of perfect competition and monopoly.

The imperfections in the marketplace in a free-enterprise economy provide the rationale for governmental control. The control exercised by the government can take one of several forms. One form is that of maintaining or enforcing competition—for example, the antitrust actions of the government. Second, the government can substitute regulation for competition, as it did in transportation. Third, the government can assume ownership and direct control, as it has done with the U.S. Post Office.

The basic problem of regulation in our society is that of establishing or maintaining the conditions necessary for the economical use of resources under a system of private enterprise. Regulation should seek to maintain a competitive framework and rely on the competitive forces whenever possible. The institutional framework for regulating transportation is provided by federal statute. A perspective on the overall legal basis for regulation is important to the student of transportation, and we will examine this topic in the next section.

Common Law

The legal system of the United States is based upon **common law** and civil or statutory law. The former is a system basic to most English-speaking countries because it was developed in England. Common law relies upon judicial precedent, or principles of law developed from former court decisions. Therefore, if one wants to find out what the law is on a particular topic, one must search out the court decisions to see what was originally decided about the topic. When a court decision establishes a rule for a situation, then that rule becomes part of the law of the land. As conditions change, the law sometimes needs further interpretation. Therefore, an important feature of the common law system is that it changes and evolves as society changes. We have many examples of such change in the interpretation of the areas of federal and state control or responsibility for regulating transportation.[1] Common law involves a continuous process of court interpretation.

The common law approach fits well with a free-market enterprise system because the individual is the focus of attention and can engage in any business that is not prohibited. Each individual is essentially regarded as possessing equal power and responsibility before the law.[2] The early regulation of transportation developed under common law. The obvious connection is with the concept of common carriage. Common law rules were developed for those common carriers because they serve all shippers on a similar basis, at reasonable rates, and without discrimination.

Statutory law or civil law is based upon the Roman legal system and is characteristic of continental Europe and the parts of the world colonized by European countries. Statutory law is enacted by legislative bodies, but it is a specific enactment. It is, in a sense, a written law that is more apparent and easier to check. A large part of the laws pertaining to business control, in general, and to transportation in particular, are based upon statutory law. However, two points are important to note in this regard. First, common law rules are still very important in the transportation area because many statutes were, in effect, copied from common law principles. Second, statutes are usually general and need to be interpreted by the courts. Thus, in the United States, there is a very close relationship between common law and statutory law.

The regulation of transportation began at the state level under the common law system when a number of important rules for regulation were developed, as well as the basic issue of whether business could even be regulated at all. In the latter regard, a concept of "business affected with the public interest" was developed under the common law. **State regulation** also included use of charters for some of the early turnpike companies and canal operations. The development of the railroad necessitated a move to statutory regulation, which was in effect by 1870 with the passage of **granger laws** in various states. These granger laws were the product of the granger movement, which began about 1867 in states such as Illinois, Iowa, Minnesota, and Wisconsin. Granges were organizations formed by farmers in various states and functioned as political action groups where farmers could discuss problems. The granger movement was started by the farmers through their grange organizations because of their dissatisfaction with railroad rates and service. The development of state laws, and later federal laws, also gave rise to independent regulatory commissions, which are discussed next.

Role of the Independent Regulatory Commission

Our federal government is set up under a system of checks and balances in three separate branches—the executive, judicial, and legislative. The independent regulatory commission is an administrative body created by the legislative authority operating within the framework of the Constitution. The members of the commission are appointed by the president and approved by the Senate for a fixed term of office.

The Interstate Commerce Commission (ICC) was the first independent regulatory commission to be established in the United States at the federal level. It was set up under the Act to Regulate Commerce in 1887. Originally, the ICC had somewhat limited powers. However, over the years it evolved as the most comprehensive and powerful commission in the country. The independent regulatory commission is somewhat peculiar to the United States.

The ICC served as an expert body, providing a continuity to regulation that neither the courts nor the legislature could provide. The ICC exercised legislative, judicial, and executive powers. As a consequence, it was often labeled as a quasi-legislative, quasi-executive, and quasi-judicial body. Regulatory agencies can be regarded as a fourth branch of the government. When the ICC enforced statutes, it served in the executive capacity. When it ruled upon the reasonableness of a rate, it served in its judicial capacity. When it filled out legislation by promulgating rules or prescribing rules or prescribing rates, it exercised its legislative powers.

On December 31, 1995, the ICC was abolished. The ICC Termination Act of 1995 (ICCTA) ended the 108-year-old ICC and replaced it with the **Surface Transportation Board** (STB), which implements a greatly reduced body of economic regulation exercised over the modes of transportation. The STB is housed in the **U.S. Department of Transportation** (DOT), but it is constituted as an independent regulatory agency, immune from DOT direction and supervision. The three-member STB is appointed by the president with approval of the Senate.

The role of the STB in the economic operations of carriers has been greatly reduced from that of the ICC. Congress intended for the marketplace, not the STB, to be the primary control mechanism for rates and services. The STB exercises economic controls over railroads, motor carriers, motor carrier freight brokers, water carriers, freight forwarders, and pipelines. (See "Current Economic Regulations," later in this chapter, for more details on the ICCTA regulations.)

In addition to the ICC and STB, other independent regulatory commissions have been established for transportation. In 1938 the **Civil Aeronautics Board** (CAB) was established to administer the economic regulations imposed upon airlines. The CAB was abolished in 1985 under the provisions of the Airline Deregulation Act of 1978, and the remaining regulatory jurisdictions (safety issues) were transferred to the DOT.

The **Federal Maritime Commission** (FMC) was created in 1961 to administer the regulations imposed on international water carriers. The FMC exercises control over the rates, practices, agreements, and services of common water carriers operating in international trade and domestic trade to points beyond the continental United States. The laws under which the FMC operates saw great change in 1998. This will be discussed in more detail in Chapter 9.

The **Federal Energy Regulatory Commission** (FERC) was created to administer the regulations governing rates and practices of oil and natural gas pipelines. However, the FERC is not an independent regulatory commission that reports to Congress, such as the ICC or FMC. Rather, it is a semi-independent regulatory commission that reports to the Department of Energy.

Our regulatory laws are often stated in vague terms, such as reasonable rates, inherent advantages, and unjust discrimination. Therefore, in administering and interpreting the law, the regulatory commission exercises broad discretionary powers over the regulated transport firms. We must not, however, lose sight of the fact that the commission is still limited by the regulatory laws. It can only carry out the law to the best of its ability and is subject to the opinions of the courts.

Role of the Courts

Even though the independent commission plays a powerful role in regulating transportation, it is still subject to judicial review. The courts are the sole judges of the law, and only court decisions can serve as legal precedent under common law. The courts make the final ruling on the constitutionality of regulatory statutes and the interpretation of the legislation. The review of the courts acts as a check on arbitrary or capricious actions, actions that do not conform to statutory standards or authority, or actions that are not in accordance with fair procedure or substantial evidence. The parties involved in a commission decision have the right, therefore, to appeal the decision to the courts.

Over the years, the courts had come to recognize the ICC as an expert body on policy and the authority on matters of fact and, to some extent, the STB. Therefore, the courts limited their restrictions on ICC and STB authority. The courts would not substitute their judgment for that of the ICC and STB on matters such as what constitutes a reasonable rate or whether a discrimination is unjust because such judgments would usurp the administrative function of the commission.

Safety Regulations

As will be noted in this chapter's appendix, which describes the DOT functions, various federal agencies administer transportation safety regulations. Some of these regulations are enacted into law by Congress, whereas others are promulgated by the respective agencies. A thorough discussion of the specific regulations pertaining to each type of transportation is beyond our scope, but a general description of safety regulations is presented below.

Safety regulations have been established to control the operations, personnel qualifications, vehicles, equipment, hours of service for vehicle operators, etc. The **Federal Aviation Administration** (FAA) enforces and promulgates safety regulations governing the operation of air carriers and airports. The **Federal Motor Carrier Safety Administration** administers motor carrier safety regulations, and the **National Highway Traffic Safety Administration** has jurisdiction over safety features and the performance of motor vehicles and motor vehicle equipment. The **Federal Railroad Administration** exercises railroad safety regulations, and the Coast Guard is responsible for marine safety standards for vessels and ports. The **Office of Hazardous Materials Transportation** develops hazardous materials transportation safety regulations for all modes. The **National Transportation Safety Board** is charged with investigating and reporting the causes, facts, and circumstances relating to transportation accidents.

In addition, the states, through the **police powers** contained in the Constitution, exercise various controls over the safe operation of vehicles. These safety regulations set standards for speed, vehicle size, operating practices, operator licensing, etc. The purpose of the state safety regulations is to protect the health and welfare of the citizens of that state.

Often, the federal and state safety regulations conflict. For example, the federal government restricted the automobile speed limit to 55 miles per hour during the energy crisis of the 1970s. Some states did not agree with the mandate but followed the requirement to qualify for federal money to construct and maintain the highway system. In 1982 the Surface Transportation Act established federal standards for vehicle weight and length of trucks operating on the interstate highway system. The states complied with the standards for the interstate highways but not for the state highways.

After the September 11, 2001, terrorist attack on the United States, transportation safety has taken on a new dimension of national security. Securing the nation's transportation system from terrorism became a major governmental focus because of the massive geographic expanse of the U.S. border and the millions of tons of foreign cargo entering the country. In addition, the free flow of commerce within the 50 states makes it very difficult to increase security measures without curtailing commerce.

The responsibility for transportation security has been given to the Department of Transportation and the Department of Homeland Security. Within the Department of Transportation, national transportation security interests are of primary concern to such agencies as the Federal Aviation Administration, Federal Railroad Administration, and Federal Motor Carrier Safety Administration. The Transportation Security Administration, Customs Service, and the U.S. Coast Guard are the agencies within the Department of Homeland Security addressing national transportation security issues.

State Regulations

The states establish various transportation safety regulations to protect the health and welfare of their citizens. In addition, the states exercise limited economic regulation over the transportation of commodities and passengers wholly within the state. The states' powers were greatly limited under various federal laws. States generally cannot impose stricter regulation than that imposed on that mode at the federal level. States can still regulate safety, provided it does not impose an undue burden on interstate commerce. This type of transportation is known as **intrastate commerce**, and most states had a regulatory commission that was charged with enforcing these intrastate controls. The agencies may still exist to regulate utilities, such as telephone or electric companies.

The intrastate economic regulations vary from state to state, but they are generally patterned after federal economic regulations.

In 1994 the federal government eliminated the intrastate economic regulation of motor carriers with the passage of the FAA Reauthorization Act of 1994. The law, which applies to all motor carriers of property except household good carriers, prohibits the states from requiring operating authority or regulating intrastate trucking rates, routes, and services. The states have the option to regulate the uniform business practices, cargo liability, and credit rules of intrastate motor carriers.

The determination as to what constitutes commerce subject to state economic regulations is generally based on whether the shipment crosses a state line. If the shipment has an origin in one state and a destination in another state, it is an interstate shipment and is subject to federal regulations, if any. However, for shipments that are moved into a distribution center from a point outside the state and then moved from the distribution center to a destination in the same state, the distinction is not that clear. The move within the state from the distribution center to the final destination can be considered interstate commerce and subject to federal regulations.

DEVELOPMENT OF REGULATION

As has been seen in this chapter, transportation does not operate in a completely free-market environment. Government has controlled the economic operations of transportation since the 1860s. Regulatory constraints to entry, pricing, and customer relations have dictated the management practices of carriers and transportation users even after the deregulation laws of the late 1970s, 1980s, and 1990s. Transportation regulation has been a major force shaping the transportation industry.

Transportation has long been considered an industry that impacts public interest. In fact, transportation is so vital to the economic viability of the country that it has been argued that government should provide the service, rather than private enterprise. Without a sound transportation system, the level of economic activity, the exchange and movement of goods and services, would be greatly limited and the well-being of the citizens reduced. Thus, government involvement has been directed toward ensuring that the public has equal access to an economically viable transportation system.

Table 2.1 provides a a chronology of transportation regulation. The regulatory history is broken down into four areas. First, the initiation era from 1887 to 1920 saw the establishment of federal transportation regulation and the ICC. Second, the era of positive regulation from 1920 to 1935 was oriented toward promoting transportation. The third era, intermodal regulation from 1935 to 1960, witnessed the expansion of regulation to motor carriers, air carriers, water carriers, and freight forwarders. Finally, the deregulation era from 1976 to 1996 was the period of gradual lessening and elimination of economic regulation, culminating in the elimination of the ICC and most truck regulations in 1995.

In the next section, a summary of the current regulation applied to railroads and motor carriers is given.

CURRENT ECONOMIC REGULATIONS

As stated above, the air carrier industry is deregulated. Cargo and passenger rates are not controlled, and domestic air carriers are permitted to serve any locale as long as the carrier meets safety regulations and landing slots are available.

The majority of the economic regulation over pipelines has been transferred to the Federal Energy Regulatory Commission. Because most water carrier operations are exempt from economic regulation, domestic water carrier economic regulation is a moot issue.

Table 2.1 Chronology of Major Transportation Regulation*

Date	Act	Nature of Regulation
Initiation Era		
1887	Act to Regulate Commerce	Regulated railroads and established ICC; rates must be reasonable; discrimination prohibited
1903	Elkins Act	Prohibited rebates and filed rate doctrine
1906	Hepburn Act	Established maximum and joint rate controls
1910	Mann-Elkins Act	Gave shipper right to route shipment
1912	Panama Canal Act	Prohibited railroads from owning water carriers
Positive Era		
1920	Transportation Act of 1920	Established a rule of ratemaking; pooling and joint use of terminals permitted; began recapture clause
1933	Emergency Transportation Act	Financial assistance to railroads
Intermodal Era		
1935	Motor Carrier Act	Federal regulation of trucking, similar to rail
1938	Civil Aeronautics Act	Federal regulation of air carriers established Civil Aeronautics Board (CAB)
1940	Transportation Act	Provided for federal regulation of water carriers, declaration of national transportation policy
1942	Freight Forwarder Act	Federal regulation of surface freight forwarders
1948	Reed-Bulwinkle Act	Antitrust immunity for joint rate making
1958	Transportation Act	Eliminated umbrella (protective) rate making and provided financial aid to railroads
1966	Department of Transportation Act	Established the U.S. Department of Transportation
1970	Rail Passenger Service Act	Established Amtrak
1973	Regional Rail Reorganization Act	Established Consolidated Rail Corporation (Conrail)
Deregulation Era		
1976	Railroad Revitalization and Regulatory Reform Act	Rate freedom; ICC could exempt rail operations; abandonment and merger controls began
1977	Airline Deregulation Act	Deregulated air transportation, sunset CAB (1985)
1980	Motor Carrier Act	Eased entry restrictions and permitted rate negotiation
1980	Rail Staggers Act	Permitted railroads to negotiate contracts, allowed rate flexibility, and defined maximum rates
1993	Negotiated Rates Act	Provided for settlement options for motor carrier undercharges
1994	Trucking Industry Regulatory Reform Act	Eliminated motor carrier filing of individual tariffs; ICC given power to deregulate categories of traffic
1994	FAA Reauthorization Act	Prohibited states from regulating (economic) intrastate trucking
1995	ICC Termination Act	Abolished ICC, established STB, and eliminated most truck economic regulation

*For a detailed description of these acts, see John J. Coyle, Edward J. Bardi, and Robert A. Novack, *Transportation*, 4th ed., St. Paul, MN: West Publishing, 1994, pp. 58–83.

Effective January 1, 1996, the ICC Termination Act of 1995 abolished the Interstate Commerce Commission, further deregulated transportation, and transferred the remaining ICC functions to the three-person **Surface Transportation Board** located within the DOT. The STB now administers the remaining economic regulations exercised over railroads, motor carriers, freight forwarders, freight brokers, water carriers, and pipelines. The key provisions of the ICCTA are summarized below:

Railroad Regulations

- Rail economic regulation is basically unchanged by the ICCTA.
- The STB has jurisdiction over rates, classifications, rules, practices, routes, services, facilities, acquisitions, and abandonments.
- Railroads continue to be subject to the common carrier obligations (to serve, not discriminate, charge reasonable rates, and deliver).
- Rail tariff filling is eliminated; railroads must provide 20 days advance notice before changing a rate.
- Rail contract filing is eliminated except for agricultural contracts.

Motor Carriers

- All tariff filing and rate regulation is eliminated, except for household goods and noncontiguous trade (trade between the continental United States and Hawaii, for example).
- Motor carriers are required to provide tariffs to shippers upon request.
- Motor carriers are held liable for damage according to the conditions of the Carmack Act, (i.e., the full value of the product at destination). However, motor carriers can use released value rates that set limits on liability.
- The Negotiated Rates Act undercharge resolution procedures are retained and the unreasonable practices defense is extended indefinitely for pending undercharge cases.
- Undercharge/overcharge claims must be filed within 180 days from receipt of the freight bill.
- The STB has broad powers to exempt operations from regulation with the existing exemptions remaining.
- Antitrust immunity for collective rate making (publishing the national motor freight classification, for example) is retained.
- The motor carrier is required to disclose to the person directly paying the freight bill whether and to whom discounts or allowances are given.
- The concept of common and contract carrier authority is eliminated; all regulated carriers can contract with shippers.
- The STB will develop a single registration system without the common or contract authority.
- Regulated carriers are to provide safe and adequate service, equipment, and facilities upon reasonable request; thus, the common carrier obligations are eliminated.

Freight Forwarders and Brokers

- Both are required to register with the STB.
- The freight forward is regulated as a carrier and is liable for freight damage.

- The broker is not a carrier and is not held liable for freight damage.
- The STB can impose insurance requirements for both.

In summary, the ICCTA has eliminated the ICC and substituted the STB as the administrator of remaining economic regulations. Railroads are no longer required to file tariffs and nonagricultural contracts. The historical railroad economic regulation remains in force, including the common carrier obligations.

Motor carrier economic regulation has been drastically altered by the ICCTA. While the common carrier concept still exists, the requirements to file tariffs and the controls over rates have been removed, making this almost a moot point. Carriers are liable for the full value of damaged freight but are permitted to use release value rates that limit their liability value. Finally, any motor carriers can contract with shippers.

ANTITRUST LAWS IN TRANSPORTATION

The deregulatory movement has exposed many practices to be in violation of antitrust laws. Antitrust regulations were first established in 1890 with passage of the **Sherman Antitrust Act**. The key points of this act are as follows:

> Trusts, etc., in restraint of trade illegal; penalty. Every contract, combination in the form of trust or otherwise, or conspiracy, in restraint of trade or commerce among the several States, or with foreign nations, is declared to be illegal. Every person who shall make any contract or engage in any combination or conspiracy declared by Sections 1 to 7 of this title to be illegal shall be deemed guilty of a felony, and, on conviction thereof, shall be punished by fine not exceeding one million dollars if a corporation, or if any other person, one hundred thousand dollars, or by imprisonment not exceeding three years, or both said punishments, in the discretion of the court.
>
> Monopolizing trade a felony; penalty. Every person who shall monopolize, or attempt to monopolize, or combine or conspire with any other person or persons, to monopolize any part of the trade or commerce among the several States, or with foreign nations, shall be deemed guilty of a felony. . . .[3]

The thrust of the Sherman Act was intended to outlaw price fixing among competing firms, eliminate business practices that tended toward monopolization, and prevent any firm or combination of firms from refusing to sell or deal with certain firms or avoiding geographic market allocations.

The law was strengthened in 1914 by the **Clayton Act**. This act specifically described some other practices that would be interpreted as attempts to monopolize, or as actual monopolization. These include exclusive dealing arrangements whereby a buyer and/or seller agree to deal only with the other party for a period of time. Another is a tying contract. This is where a seller agrees to sell goods only if the buyer also buys another product.

Also in 1914 legislation was passed that created the **Federal Trade Commission** (FTC). This agency was the primary overseer and enforcement agency in this business practice area.

Collective rate making by carriers was made exempt from antitrust laws by the **Reed-Bulwinkle Act of 1948**, which empowered the ICC to oversee carrier rate making. As such, it limited traditional jurisdiction by the FTC and Department of

Justice in this area. A repeal of those parts of the Interstate Commerce Act that traditionally allowed collective rate making by carriers in rate bureaus caused this practice to become subject to the antitrust laws.

Collective rate making over single-line rates of rail, motor, air, and household goods carriers is not allowed by law, as mandated by the regulatory changes. This means that any such practices would come under the jurisdiction and penalties of the Sherman Act and those that follow.

Another major law that might apply to the recent deregulation of transportation is the Robinson-Patman Act of 1936. This law prohibits sellers from practicing price discrimination among buyers unless the differences in price can be justified by true differences in manufacturing and marketing (distribution). Defenses against such a practice are: (1) differences in cost, (2) the need to meet competition, and (3) changing market conditions. Although this law was created for application to the buying and selling of goods, many observers of transportation state that it might be applied in carrier contracting (a service and not a physical good). Whether this law might be applied in carrier pricing will only be determined as deregulation evolves further and cases based on this theory are brought to the courts.

In the selling and purchase of transportation services, two types of antitrust violations can occur. The first is called a **per se violation**. This type of violation is illegal, regardless if any economic harm is done to competitors or other parties. Types of per se violations include price fixing, division of markets, boycotts, and tying agreements.

The second type of antitrust violation is called **rule of reason**. In this type of violation, economic harm must be shown to have been caused to competitors or other parties because these activities can be undertaken by firms with no antitrust implications. Rule of reason violations include exclusive deals, requirements contracts, joint bargaining, and joint action among affiliates.

Carriers, in the selling of transportation services, are normally thought to be the party to which antitrust regulations apply. However, in buying these services, shippers are also subject to these same laws and are at an equal risk of committing an antitrust violation. Because transportation has been subject to antitrust laws only since around 1980, these laws, as they relate to transportation, have not yet been fully tested in the courts.

TRANSPORTATION POLICY

The federal government has played an important role in molding the transportation system that exists in the United States today. The federal government's role has been defined through various laws, rules, and funding programs directed toward collecting and promoting the different modes of transportation. The federal government's policy toward transportation is a composite of these federal laws, rules, funding programs, and regulatory agencies; however, there is no unified federal transportation policy statement or goal that guides the federal government's actions.

In addition to the Congress and the president, more than 60 federal agencies and 30 congressional committees are involved in setting transportation policy. Two independent regulatory agencies interpret transport law, establish operating rules, and set policy. Lastly, the Justice Department interprets statutes involving transportation and reconciles differences between the carriers and the public. Each of these groups has made decisions that have affected the DOT.

The purpose of this section is to examine the national transportation policy, both explicit and implicit, that has molded the present U.S. transportation system. Although the national transportation policy is constantly evolving and changing, there are some major underpinnings upon which the basic policy is built. These basic policy issues will be examined, as well as the declared statement of national transportation policy contained in the ICC Termination Act of 1995.

STOP OFF

Play By the Rules

How you package your airfreight shipment isn't always left entirely up to you. For some products, federal and international regulations make that decision for you.

If, for example, you ship products that are classified as hazardous materials, International Air Transport Association (IATA) regulations will specify the inner packaging and outer packing that's required. They also restrict which commodities and how much volume can be packed together. Those rules are intended to protect potentially dangerous shipments and minimize the chance of leaks, spills, fires, or explosions. If you fail to match a hazardous product with the specified packaging and your product leaks, you not only subject your company to huge fines but also put peoples' lives at risk, says Steven Goldberg, vice president of operations at Seko Worldwide.

Some perishable products fall under packaging rules that were developed to ensure food safety. One federal program, for example, requires seafood shippers to guarantee that specified temperatures were maintained at all times during transportation and storage. Many air carriers, moreover, have their own packaging rules for perishables.

Even the packing materials themselves can be subject to restrictions. Australia, China, Japan, and the European Union are among the governments that prohibit the use of untreated wood to pack ocean and airfreight shipments. Attempting to prevent the further spread of insect pests, those and other countries require wooden crates and pallets to be treated by approved methods and be marked to that effect with specified symbols.

Source: "Play By The Rules," *Logistics Management*, April 2004, p. 51. Reprinted with permission.

WHY DO WE NEED A TRANSPORTATION POLICY?

A good starting point for examining the nature of our national transportation policy is the consideration of our need for such a policy. The answer to the question of need lies in the significance of transportation to the very life of the country. Transportation permeates every aspect of a community and touches the life of every member. The transportation system ties together the various communities of a country, making possible the movement of people, goods, and services. The physical connection that transportation gives to spatially separated communities permits a sense of unity to exist.

In addition, transportation is fundamental to the economic activity of a country. Transportation furthers economic activity—the exchange of goods that are mass-produced in one location to locations deficient in these goods. The carry-over benefits of economic activity—jobs, improved goods and services, and so on—would not be reaped by a country's citizens without a good transportation system.

An efficient transportation system is fundamental to national defense. In times of emergencies, people and materials must be deployed quickly to various trouble spots within the United States or throughout the world to protect American interests. Without an efficient transportation system, more resources would have to be dedicated to defense purposes in many more locations. Thus, an efficient transportation system reduces the amount of resources consumed for national defense.

Many of our transportation facilities could not be developed by private enterprise. For example, the capital required to build a transcontinental highway is very likely beyond the resources of the private sector. Efficient and economical rail and highway routes require governmental assistance in securing land from private owners; if the government did not assert its power of eminent domain, routes would be quite circuitous and inefficient. Furthermore, public ownership and the operation of certain transportation facilities, such as highways or waterways, is necessary to ensure access to all who desire to use the facilities.

The purpose of transportation policy is to provide direction for determining the amount of national resources that will be dedicated to transportation and for determining the quality of service that is essential for economic activity and national defense. National policy provides guidelines to the many agencies that exercise transportation decision-making powers and to Congress, the president, and the courts that make and interpret the laws affecting transportation. Thus, transportation policy provides the framework for the allocation of resources to the transportation modes.

The federal government has been a major factor in the development of transportation facilities—highways, waterways, ports, and airports. It also has assumed the responsibility to:

- Ensure the safety of travelers
- Protect the public from the abuse of monopoly power
- Promote fair competition
- Develop or continue vital transport services
- Balance environmental, energy, and social requirements in transportation
- Plan and make decisions[4]

This statement of the federal government's transportation responsibility indicates the diversity of public need that transportation policy must serve. The conflicts inherent in such a diverse set of responsibilities will be discussed in a later section.

DECLARATION OF NATIONAL TRANSPORTATION POLICY

The ICC Termination Act of 1995 included statements of national transportation policy. Congress made these statements to provide direction to the STB in administering transportation regulation over railroads, motor carriers, water carriers, and pipelines.

The declaration of national rail transportation policy is stated in Public Law 104-88:

> In regulating the railroad industry, it is the policy of the United States Government:
>
> (1) to allow, to the maximum extent possible, competition and the demand for services to establish reasonable rates for transportation by rail;
>
> (2) to minimize the need for Federal regulatory control over the rail transportation system and to require fair and expeditious regulatory decisions when regulation is required;

(3) to promote a safe and efficient rail transportation system by allowing rail carriers to earn adequate revenues, as determined by the Board;
(4) to ensure the development and continuation of a sound rail transportation system with effective competition among rail carriers and with other modes, to meet the needs of the public and the national defense;
(5) to foster sound economic conditions in transportation and to ensure effective competition and coordination between rail carriers and other modes;
(6) to maintain reasonable rates where there is an absence of effective competition and where rail rates provide revenues which exceed the amount necessary to maintain the rail system and to attract capital;
(7) to reduce regulatory barriers to entry into and exit from the industry;
(8) to operate transportation facilities and equipment without detriment to the public health and safety;
(9) to encourage honest and efficient management of railroads;
(10) to require rail carriers, to the maximum extent practicable, to rely on individual rate increases, and to limit the use of increases of general applicability;
(11) to encourage fair wages and safe and suitable working conditions in the railroad industry;
(12) to prohibit predatory pricing and practices, to avoid undue concentrations of market power, and to prohibit unlawful discrimination;
(13) to ensure the availability of accurate cost information in regulatory proceedings, while minimizing the burden on the rail carriers of developing and maintaining the capability of providing such information;
(14) to encourage and promote energy conservation; and
(15) to provide for the expeditious handling and resolution of all proceedings required or permitted to be brought this part.

The declaration of national transportation policy for motor carriers, water carriers, brokers, and freight forwarders is stated in the same document:

In General. To ensure the development, coordination, and preservation of a transportation system that meets the transportation needs of the United States Postal Service and national defense, it is the policy of the United States Government to oversee the modes of transportation and:

(1) in overseeing these modes:
(A) to recognize and preserve the inherent advantage of each mode of transportation
(B) to promote safe, adequate, economical, and efficient transportation;
(C) to encourage sound economic conditions in transportation, including sound economic conditions among carriers;
(D) to encourage the establishment and maintenance of reasonable rates of transportation, without unreasonable discrimination or unfair or destructive competitive practices;
(E) to cooperate with each State and the officials of each State on transportation matters; and
(F) to encourage fair wages and working conditions in the transportation industry;

(2) in overseeing transportation by motor carrier, to promote competitive and efficient transportation in order to:
(A) encourage fair competition, and reasonable rates for transportation by motor carriers of property;
(B) promote efficiency in the motor carrier transportation system and to require fair and expeditious decisions when required;

(C) meet the needs of shippers, receivers, passengers, and consumers;
(D) allow a variety of quality and price options to meet changing market demands and the diverse requirements of the shipping and traveling public;
(E) allow the most productive use of equipment and energy resources;
(F) enable efficient and well-managed carriers to earn adequate profits, attract capital and maintain fair wages and working conditions;
(G) provide and maintain service to small communities and small shippers and intrastate bus services;
(H) provide and maintain commuter bus operations;
(I) improve and maintain a sound, safe, and competitive privately owned motor carrier system;
(J) promote greater participation by minorities in the motor carrier system;
(K) promote intermodal transportation;

(3) in overseeing transportation by motor carriers of passengers:
(A) to cooperate with the States on transportation matters for the purpose of encouraging the States to exercise intrastate regulatory jurisdiction in accordance with the objectives of this part;
(B) to provide Federal procedures which ensure the intrastate regulation is exercised in accordance with this part; and
(C) to ensure that Federal reform initiatives enacted by section 31138 and the Bus Regulatory Reform Act of 1982 are not nullified by State regulatory actions; and

(4) in overseeing transportation by water carrier, to encourage and promote service and price competition in the noncontiguous domestic trade.

The declaration of pipeline national transportation policy is as follows:

> In General. To ensure the development, coordination, and preservation of a transportation system that meets the transportation needs of the United States, including the national defense, it is the policy of the United States Government to oversee of the modes of transportation and in overseeing those modes:
> (1) to recognize and preserve the inherent advantage of each mode of transportation;
> (2) to promote safe, adequate, economical, and efficient transportation;
> (3) to encourage sound economic conditions in transportation; including sound economic conditions among carriers;
> (4) to encourage the establishment and maintenance of reasonable rates for transportation without unreasonable discrimination or unfair or destructive competitive practices;
> (5) to cooperate with each State and the officials of each State on transportation matters; and
> (6) to encourage fair wages and working conditions in the transportation industry.

Policy Interpretations

Although the declarations of national transportation policy are general and somewhat vague, the statements do provide a guide to the factors that should be considered in transportation decision making. However, the statements contain numerous conflicting provisions. This section analyzes the incompatibility of the various provisions.

PROVISIONS

First, the declarations are statements of policy for those modes regulated by the STB. Therefore, only railroads, oil pipelines, motor carriers, and water carriers are considered. **Air carriers** are excluded from consideration.

The requirement of "fair and impartial regulation" also overlooks the **exempt carriers** in motor and water transportation. The exempt carriers are eliminated from the economic controls administered by the STB and therefore are not included in the stated policy provisions.

Congress requested the STB administer the transportation regulation in such a manner as to recognize and preserve the inherent advantage of each mode. An inherent advantage is the innate superiority one mode possesses in the form of cost or service characteristics. Such modal characteristics change over time as technology and infrastructure change.

It has been recognized that railroads have an inherent advantage of lower cost in transporting freight long distances and that motor carriers have the advantage for moving freight short distances, less than 300 miles. If the preservation of inherent advantage were the only concern, the STB would not permit trucks to haul freight long distances, more than 300 miles, nor railroads to haul freight short distances. However, the shippers demand long-distance moves from motor carriers and short-distance moves from railroads, and the STB permits these services to be provided.

Safe, adequate, economical, and efficient service is not totally attainable. An emphasis on safety may mean an uneconomical or inefficient service. Added safety features on equipment and added safety procedures for employees will increase total costs and cost per unit of output and may reduce the productivity of employees. However, when lives are involved, safety takes precedence over economical and efficient service.

Providing adequate service has been construed to mean meeting normal demand. If carriers were forced to have capacity that is sufficient to meet peak demand, considerable excess capacity would exist, resulting in uneconomical and inefficient operations. Fostering sound economic conditions among the carriers does not mean ensuring an acceptable profit for all carriers. Nor does it imply that the STB should guarantee the survival of all carriers. The STB must consider the economic condition of carriers in rate rulings so as to foster stability of transportation supply.

The policy statement regarding reasonable charges, unjust discrimination, undue preference, and unfair competitive practices is merely a reiteration of the **common carrier** obligations. Congress made no attempt to define these concepts. The STB was given the task of interpreting them as it hears and decides individual cases.

A number of laws provided some degree of definition for these common carrier policy statements. For example, the Staggers Rail Act of 1980 defined a **reasonable rail rate** as one that is not more than 160 percent of variable costs. The Motor Carrier Act of 1980 defined a zone of rate freedom in which a rate change of 610 percent in one year is presumed to be reasonable. Both acts defined the normal business entertainment of shippers as acceptable practice and not an instance of underpreference.

The cooperative efforts between the federal and state governments have not always been smooth. The very foundation for federal regulation of transportation was the judicial decision that only the federal government could regulate interstate transportation. Through police powers, the states have the right to establish laws regarding transportation safety. Thus, for example, states have enacted laws governing the height, length, weight, and speed of motor carrier trucks. However, the federal government has standardized weight and speed laws on interstate highways. One approach the federal government has taken has been to threaten to withhold federal highway money from states that do not comply.

Finally, the STB was charged with the responsibility of encouraging fair wages and working conditions. No attempt was made to interpret the terms *fair wage* and *working conditions.* A wage that is deemed fair by an employee may be unfair to an employer. An air-conditioned cab may be equitable working conditions to a driver, but it is merely an added cost to the employer. In addition, both of the above examples may conflict with the policy statement regarding the promotion of economical and efficient service.

The stated goals of the national transportation policy are to provide a system of transportation that meets the needs of commerce, the U.S. Postal Service, *and* national defense. It is possible that a system that meets the needs of commerce may be insufficient to meet the needs of national defense during an emergency situation. In addition, a system that has the capacity to meet national defense needs will have excess capacity for commerce and postal service needs during peace times and will be inefficient and uneconomical.

For example, the United States maintains a merchant marine fleet that can be called into service to haul defense material during a national defense emergency. However, this fleet may be twice the size of that needed for commerce. Many government critics claim a fleet with such excess capacity is a waste of resources. Defense advocates argue that national defense needs dictate that such a fleet be operated to preclude dependency on a foreign country for water transportation during defense emergencies. As the arguments rage on, one can see the conflict that exists in the stated national policy goals.

The ICCTA provides specific direction regarding the railroads and motor carriers. For the railroads, the STB is directed to minimize the need for federal regulatory control, reduce regulatory barriers to entry and exit, prohibit predatory pricing, and promote energy conservation. For motor carriers, the STB is to allow pricing variety, serve small communities, promote greater participation by minorities, and promote transportation.

Who Establishes Policy?

National transportation policies are developed at various levels of government and by many different agencies. The specifics of a particular policy may reflect the persuasion of a group of individuals (for example, a consumer group) or of a single individual (for example, an elected official). The purpose of this section is to examine the basic institutional framework that aids in the development of national transportation policy.

EXECUTIVE BRANCH[5]

Many departments within the executive branch of government influence (establish) transportation policy. At the top of the list is the office of the president. The president has authority over international air transportation and foreign air carriers operating into the United States. The president also appoints individuals to head the various agencies that influence transportation and to head the two regulatory agencies—the STB and Federal Maritime Commission (FMC).

The Department of State is directly involved in developing policy regarding international transportation by air and water. The policies and programs designed to encourage foreign visitors to the United States are implemented by the U.S. Travel Service. The Maritime Administration is involved with ocean (international) transportation policy. It determines ship requirements, service, and routes essential to foreign commerce. In addition, international transportation policies and programs are shaped by the Military Sealift Command, Military Airlift Command, and Military Traffic Management and Terminal Service—agencies responsible for the movement of military goods and personnel.

On the domestic level, the Department of Energy develops policies regarding energy availability and distribution (fuel and rationing). The U.S. Postal Service contracts for the transportation of the mail; such contracts have been used to promote air transportation as well as motor and rail transportation at other times. The Department of Housing and Urban Development (HUD) consults with the DOT regarding the compatibility of urban transportation systems within the HUD-administered housing and community development programs. The Army Corps of Engineers is responsible for constructing and maintaining rivers and harbors and for protecting the navigable waterways.

The DOT, however, is the most pervasive influence of policy at the domestic level. The secretary of transportation is responsible for assisting the president in all transportation matters, including public investment, safety, and research. (See Appendix A at the end of this chapter for a list of agencies within the DOT.)

CONGRESSIONAL COMMITTEES[6]

The laws that are formulated by Congress are the formal method by which Congress influences national transportation. The congressional committee structure is the forum in which Congress develops policy, programs, and funding for transportation.

Within the Senate, the two standing committees that influence transportation are the Commerce, Science, and Transportation Committee and the Environment and Public Works Committee. The Commerce, Science, and Transportation Committee is concerned with the regulations of the modes, the promotion of air transportation (subsidies and construction funding), and the promotion of water transportation (Maritime Administration programs). The Environment and Public Works Committee is concerned with internal waterway and harbor projects, highway construction and maintenance projects, and air and water pollution regulations.

The House of Representatives' standing committees relating to transportation include the Energy and Commerce Committee, Public Works and Transportation Committee, and Merchant Marine and Fisheries Committee. The Interstate and Foreign Commerce Committee has jurisdiction over railroads, the Railroad Labor Act, and air pollution. The Merchant Marine and Fisheries Committee is concerned with international water transportation and Maritime Administration programs. The Public Works and Transportation Committee is concerned with internal waterway and harbor projects, the regulation of all modes, and urban mass transportation.

In addition to the above standing committees, numerous other congressional committees have an impact on transportation. Federal funding can be decided in the Appropriations Committee, Senate Banking Committee, Housing and Urban Affairs Committee, House Ways and Means Committee, or Senate Finance Committee.

REGULATORY AGENCIES

The STB and FMC are independent agencies charged with implementing the laws regulating transportation. The agencies have quasi-judicial and quasi-legislative powers, and when they decide on a case (for example, reasonableness of rates), the agencies are exercising quasi-judicial powers. The courts enforce agency decisions.

JUDICIAL SYSTEM

The courts have been called upon to interpret laws or reconcile conflicts. In doing so, the courts have an impact upon transportation policies. Carriers, shippers, and the general public may call upon the courts to change existing policy through interpretation of statutes. As the regulatory commissions exercise quasi-legislative and quasi-judicial powers, the affected parties seek recourse to the courts to determine the legality of the decisions. The role of the courts is basically to interpret the meaning of policy as stated in laws, regulations, and executive orders.

INDUSTRY ASSOCIATIONS

One facet of national policy development that is often overlooked in the study of transportation is the role of industry associations in shaping national, state, and local promotion, regulation, and policy. These associations exist in most industries, and many of the transportation industry associations are based in Washington, DC.

Industry associations in transportation serve two basic purposes: establishment of industry standards, and policy formulation and influence. The organizations are nonprofit entities that derive their powers and resources from individual member firms. They act on the charges given to them by their members. In transportation, the railroads in the Association of American Railroads (AAR) and the motor carriers in the American Trucking Associations (ATA) often meet to resolve matters of equipment conformity and loss and damage prevention. On the policy side, these associations develop legislative and administrative ruling concepts that favor the collective membership, or they serve as a united front against proposals that are perceived to be harmful to the group.

The major industry associations in the transportation field have evolved from specific modes. The AAR represents the larger railroads in the United States; it was instrumental in the passage of the Staggers Rail Act of 1980. The ATA is divided into subconferences including regular common carriers, household goods carriers, local and short-haul carriers, bulk tank firms, and automobile transporters. The Air Transport Association of America (ATAA) represents the airline industry in the United States. The American Waterways Operators (AWO) consists of barge operators on the inland waterway system. The Freight Forwarders' Institute (FFI) serves member carriers in that mode. The American Bus Association (ABA) represents common and charter bus firms.

Two major associations exist for the interests of large shippers. One is the National Industrial Traffic League (NITL), and the other is the National Small Shipment Transportation Conference (NASSTRAC). Both are active before congressional bodies, regulator agencies, and carrier groups.

The Transportation Association of America (TAA) (which ceased operation in 1982) had as its concern the health and vitality of the entire U.S. transportation system. It became involved in policy issues relating to two or more modes, or between modes and shippers, as well as investors. The TAA was largely instrumental in the passage of the act that created the DOT, as well as the passage of the Uniform Time Standards Act, which caused all areas of the United States electing to recognize daylight savings time to do so at the same time in April. Previously, each state did so on different dates, which caused major confusion in railroad and airline scheduling systems and timetable publication. At one point, United Airlines had to publish 27 different timetables during the spring as various states recognized daylight savings time on different dates. Since it was enacted in 1967, the Uniform Time Standards Act has simplified these facets of transportation management.

Other groups and associations are involved in transportation policy, including non-transportation special interest groups such as the grange and labor unions. Various governmental agencies such as the Department of Agriculture and the Department of Defense influence existing and proposed transportation legislation, rules, and policies on their behalf, or on behalf of the groups within them.

One of the most important governmental policy issues has been the public promotion of transportation. All of the above groups and associations have been involved over the years in this important area. The topic is of such importance as a policy issue that it is considered in detail in the next section.

PUBLIC PROMOTION

This section presents an overview of the major transportation planning and promotion activities conducted in the U.S. public sector. Promotion connotes encouragement or provision of aid or assistance so transportation can grow or survive. *Planning* and *promotion* are general terms used to refer to programs, policies, and actual planning. Programs involve actual public cash investments into or funding for transportation activities both privately and publicly owned. Agencies make policies to encourage beneficial actions or impacts for transportation. Planning determines future transportation needs and then establishes policies or programs to bring about certain goals through the public or private sector. All three activities promote transportation and cause it to grow or survive in instances in which pure market forces would not have done so.

Transportation Project Planning in the Public Sector

Transportation project planning is the process whereby federal, state, or local groups review the movement needs or demands of a region or population segment, develop transport alternatives, and usually propose or implement one of them. It enables the development of new movement functions or allows an existing one to continue in the face of adverse trends or change.

Transportation project planning is a public activity; purely financial returns and other concerns are not the overriding benefits sought. It is a major part of the public activity in the U.S. economy for several reasons. Public transportation processes can open trade or movement where private actions have not or would not have been enticed to do so for financial gain alone. Various cultural and political benefits often come from projects and programs provided publicly. Transportation planning also lowers the cost of living or reduces the social costs of delay or congestion. Finally, it provides services that are not remunerative but are deemed socially necessary or desirable.

Transportation planning has been a critical factor in the last quarter of the 20th century and continues to be today. There are many areas of transportation from which private firms have withdrawn. Many forms of carriage today are no longer economically profitable or compensatory. Urban bus systems, commuter railroads, rail and urban research and development, and many rail services are examples of transportation forms that would not now exist without public sector involvement.

Many forms of transportation require large capital investments that contain cost lumpiness that would normally discourage or basically prohibit private investment. Port dredging and development, as well as airport construction, are examples of capital items that are not affordable by the carriers using them. Instead, the ability of a public authority to attract capital enables the asset to be built; cost is recovered through user charges.

Public planning of transportation is generally found in situations where environmental or social needs override financial ones. A major argument used in modern subway construction is that, although the system might not recover its full costs from the fare box, the city as a whole will gain by increased access to already existing downtown facilities, including buildings, offices, stores, and water utility systems. Constructing other facilities in developing suburban areas will not be necessary. Also, commuters save money because the subway eliminates the need for a second family auto, long driving, excess fuel consumption, costly parking in downtown areas, and so on. It is apparent that public planning of transportation involves a different viewpoint and set of objectives than does capital investment analysis in private firms.

AN APPROACH TO PUBLIC PLANNING PROJECT ANALYSIS

Whereas the private firm is seeking a financial return to the firm itself, public planning agencies compare the initial costs of a project to the financial, environmental, and measurable social benefits to everyone affected by the project. Thus, it compares total societal cost to total societal benefits, whether they be monetary or nonmonetary in nature.

The specific analytical tool typically used in public planning is the **benefit/cost ratio** (BCR). In essence, it is a measure of total measurable benefits to society divided by the initial capital cost. The formula for it in basic form is as follows:

$$BCR = \frac{\textit{Sum of yearly benefits to society}}{\textit{Sum of costs to agencies and those in society initially impacted}}$$

$$= \frac{\textit{Sum of benefits}}{\textit{Sum of initial costs}} = \frac{\textit{Year 1 benefit} + \textit{Year 2 benefit} + \ldots}{\textit{Sum of all initial costs}}$$

If the resulting answer is greater than one, the project is said to produce a "profit" for society. A BCR of one indicates the break-even point; less than one indicates that the agency will spend more on the project than society will ever reap in long-term benefits.

The major costs of a project include those expenses typically involved in private projects. Planning, engineering, constructing, and financing costs are critical. Other costs include delay or congestion measured in terms of dollars per hour and in terms of everyone in society who will be inconvenienced during the construction phase of a transportation project. This is certainly the case in new lock and dam construction with regard to barge operations. Project costs also can include a cost of lost sales to downtown businesses; for example, stores are more difficult to access during several years of subway construction. The costs of bond financing incurred to construct the system are pertinent also. All costs are monetarily measured or translated into monetary measures and listed according to the year in which they will occur. Typically, the major expenses arise in the initial years of construction; financing is a major cost carried through the project's life.

The benefits of a project include any measurable benefit to the agency, other agencies, and the public at large. Benefits include increased employment, decreased prices for products, lowered costs of commuting or freight transfer, reduced maintenance, improved health due to lessened pollution, less travel time due to faster commuting or travel, increased travel, and often increased recreational benefits. Many benefit measures are easily quantified, though others pose analytical difficulties in the form of forecasting volumes and cost relationships in future periods.

Three analytical steps or checks must be undertaken to compute the actual benefit/cost ratio:

1. Both costs and benefits must be assessed in such a way that *all costs* and *benefits* to both agencies and the general public are included. It is wise to be analytically conservative about costs, assuming they will be incurred by everyone in society and assuming they may be higher than what current

estimates show them to be. Similarly, benefits should only be limited to actual benefits that are sound and quantifiable in logical ways.

2. The individual costs and benefits should be summed for each year of occurrence and presented in the respective position of numerator or denominator as shown earlier.
3. A yearly discount rate should be used against each cost and benefit because most costs and benefits will not be incurred until the future.

The timing and **time value of funds** are important parts of any capital project analysis. Political controversy exists about the choice of the specific discount rate and its application. Several analytical points can be examined that will shed light on this task. One, the discount rate should reflect the interest cost and impact to the public agency that borrows the initial funds. Second, the rate should become higher in later years to reflect increasing risk, inflation, uncertainty, and forecasting difficulties. This is a conservative practice of private project financial managers, and the logic of it can be applied soundly in a public setting. Third, the counting of benefits should cease in some future period, even though the project might last longer. This is another practice that is an implicit way of conservatively considering only those benefits within the intermediate term, unless a logical case can be made for an extended period of time. These points are made so as to ensure that benefit overcounting is minimized, especially for those items such as recreation, which are generally not central to the main project need or justification. By including benefits for 25 years or more, it is easy to inflate the ratio or cause it to be above the break-even point when it would not be otherwise. Conservative risk analysis states that costs should be analytically considered higher and benefits lower than what a first-glance measure indicates.

An example of a benefit/cost ratio application to a proposed subway line will show how public planning processes are employed. Costs include those of organization development, design, engineering, initial financing, land purchases, relocation, and disruption to the public. Costs projected into the future include operations, lost property taxes, interest costs, and any other costs directly tied to the project. Benefits to the agencies include lowered operational costs of city buses; alternative application of funds released from the bus operation (reduced street and highway requirements); decreased need to expand highways or downtown parking; increased property, sales, and wage taxes from higher economic activity downtown; avoidance of federal penalties for not reducing citywide auto emissions; and many others. Benefits to society include the income multiplier effect from the initial project investment in the form of employment, reduced unemployment, and general dollar spending and circulation from construction. The general public also gains from savings in direct commuting costs and greater area-wide mobility. The system will improve society in the form of time savings, less pollution, and reduced commuting stress. The subway will generally cause the downtown to become more fully utilized. Thus, industry and retail stores might not leave the downtown for the suburbs, and the overall region benefits from the reduced need to expand streets, fire protection, water, electricity, and so on. In this manner, the unit tax base of the city itself remains low.

As we have seen, public planning involves many of the basic concepts inherent in private project planning, but the application is different. The public agency is concerned about costs and benefits to all parties affected by the project. Thus, costs, benefits, and "profits" are measured for society as a whole in tangible and intangible ways. The following discussion presents those forms of modal promotion found in the United States.

Air

The domestic air system received the benefits of several government programs. Foremost is the Federal Aviation Administration's (FAA) **air traffic control system**. It is the right-of-way system for the airlines. The navigation and traffic-flow control system is used by every aircraft in flight. It is a necessary standardized safety system, which is provided at little direct fee cost to the airlines. The FAA is part of the U.S. DOT.

Another direct air system benefit is the subsidy system. These subsidies generally apply to short and medium nonjet flights to cities that are unable to support high traffic volumes. The subsidy has been a significant support mechanism for regional airlines. In recent years, the growth of air commuter lines has enabled regional airlines to discontinue service to small cities. The Air Deregulation Act of 1978 accelerated this trend, which resulted in a lessened need for regional airline subsidies. This act might also cause increased political pressure for subsidies for commuter lines serving very small cities.

The U.S. Postal Service also provides substantial support to airlines. In the airline industry's early years, its prime earnings came from this subsidy system. In recent years, mail income has not been as significant, but this subsidy still is a major revenue source for the industry.

State and local agencies help promote the airline industry through air terminal development and construction. Terminals represent substantial capital investments and would be difficult for the industry to finance and construct. State and local bodies are able to raise the necessary large construction funds at reasonable municipal bond interest rates, often backed by the taxing power of the community. The airlines then rent terminal and hangar facilities and pay landing fees for each flight. This system reduces the problem of capital investment cost for the airlines.

Many aircraft safety matters are handled by the federal government. The FAA provides aircraft construction and safety rules as well as pilot certification. This relieves the industry of many research, development, and information tasks related to safety of the system. In another capacity, the National Transportation Safety Board investigates accidents so that many can be avoided or reduced through aircraft specification or flight procedures.

Another indirect form of promotion to this industry comes from the military. Defense contracts for military airplane development often provide spillover benefits to commercial aviation in the form of mechanical or navigational aircraft improvements. Without military-related research and development activity, advancements in this area would no doubt occur at a slower pace.

A last form of airline promotion, which is not found in the U.S. system, is direct government ownership, operation, or subsidy of air service. This is common with foreign airlines that serve the United States and other routes. In these instances, African, Asian, Latin American, and many European lines are subsidized so the countries can operate their airlines for purposes of national pride, have some degree of control over traffic to and from their nations, and gain balance of payment benefits and hard currencies through ticket sales and revenues.

A related form of such **home-flag airline** promotion exists here in the United States and in most foreign nations. In the United States, there is a requirement that only American flag carriers with domestically owned aircraft and domestic crews may originate and terminate domestic passengers and freight. Many foreign lines serve both New York and San Francisco, for example, with a flight originating abroad, but these flights are limited to international passengers. The only way in which a foreign line can originate and terminate a passenger in two U.S. cities is when that passenger is exercising stopover privileges as part of a tour or through movement. This home-flag requirement serves to protect the domestic lines.

Several forms of **user charges** are essentially designed, in whole or part, to have the modes pay for many of the public benefits they receive. As mentioned before, landing fees are charged to repay investments or incur revenue for specific airports. A major user charge is levied against passenger movements through ticket taxes. An international per-head tax is also part of this user tax, as are some aircraft registration fees. Many of these funds go into the **Airport and Airway Trust Fund**, which is used for airport facility projects on a shared basis with local agencies.

Motor and Highway

With regard to public promotion, the highway system and motor carrier firms have a joint relationship. There is no direct promotion to motor carriers themselves, but indirect benefit comes to the industry through **highway development** because most highway projects are done with government funds.

The Federal Highway Administration branch of the DOT is responsible for federal highway construction and safety. A predecessor agency, the Bureau of Public Roads, carried out the mandate to build the Interstate Highway System, which was paid for on a 90 percent/10 percent federal/state sharing basis. Today the agency is largely devoted to highway research, development, and safety. It also is charged with certain repair projects on critical parts of the Federal and Interstate Highway System. Motor carriers benefit from the increased access, speed, and safety of this system because without it they would have to travel more congested routes, presenting safety hazards.

The National Highway Traffic Safety Administration is responsible for highway and auto safety. It also conducts major research into vehicle safety, accidents, and highway design related to safety. This agency provides administrative regulations for certain minimum automobile safety features.

The Federal Motor Carrier Safety Administration is a noneconomic regulatory body whose main purpose is truck safety. Though this agency imposes strict standards on truck safety, the long-term benefit is increased safety for everyone on the highways.

Highway development also comes from states and various regional planning commissions. One example is the Appalachian Development Commission, which is charged with improving the infrastructure and economy of that region. Many highway building and improvement projects are funded by this agency.

User charges are present in the highway systems in several forms. A major form is the gas and fuel tax. States look to this per-gallon tax as a major revenue source for highway construction and upkeep. The federal government's fuel taxes go to the **Federal Highway Trust Fund**, which is the financing source of the Interstate Highway System. Some states are switching from a per-gallon to a percent-of-sales-price method of fuel-based taxation because in recent years the number of gallons of fuel sold has decreased, leaving state agencies with less revenue in times that demand greater highway maintenance. The percent-of-sales-price approach can avoid much of this decline. Another public revenue source is the federal excise tax on road tires. States also obtain revenues through vehicle registration fees. These mostly are assessed on a vehicle weight basis so as to recoup, somewhat, a proportionate share of construction costs related to heavier versus light vehicles. Further, some states assess a ton-mile tax. Finally, tolls are a form of user taxes on many turnpikes and bridges.

Two major controversies are currently taking place with regard to highway user charges. One concerns the Federal Highway Trust Fund. The tax money that goes into this fund is collected primarily for interstate highway construction. Approximately 96 percent of the interstate system has been built, but doubt exists over whether the remaining portions, mostly very costly urban sections, will ever be built. Meanwhile, the fuel tax continues to be collected and accumulated in the fund.

A second problem with user taxes is on the state level. Most states collecting vehicle fees and vehicle taxes only return a portion of them for highway purposes. Some states have earmarked some of these funds for education and other uses. In addition, industry groups continue to seek a greater share of these funds for highway development and improvement.

Rail

The railroads currently can avail themselves of direct assistance from the Regional Railroad Reorganization Act of 1973, the Railroad Revitalization and Regulatory Reform Act of 1976, and the Staggers Rail Act of 1980. Most of the assistance is in the form of track repair and motive power acquisition financing. These provisions are attempts to overcome the problem of poor equipment and facilities, which lead to poorer service and blighted financial conditions, which usually perpetuate into a further downward spiral.

Another form of funding has been available as a subsidy to lines that are abandoned by railroads but that states and other groups continue to operate. This assistance was designed to make rail line abandonment easier by railroads while still allowing service to be continued.

The Consolidated Rail Corporation (Conrail) had been the subject of special federal funding and promotion. It has received special appropriations for operations and capital improvements, mainly through provisions of the Regional Railroad Reorganization Act of 1973. Recently, after a successful transformation, Conrail was purchased by the Norfolk Southern and CSX Railroads. Conrail's routes were integrated into those companies.

Research and development in this mode essentially disappeared in the late 1950s. Financial problems in most railroads caused cutbacks in the research and development area, thereby stagnating the technology. In response to this situation, the Federal Railroad Administration (FRA) was created as part of the DOT in 1966. The FRA has become a major source of gains in railroad technology as well as safety. A test facility at Pueblo, Colorado, originally owned by the FRA, is used to test improvements in existing power and rolling equipment and to develop advanced high-speed rail technologies for the future. This facility, now known as the Transportation Technology Center, has been privatized and is managed by the AAR.

Another form of help to the rail industry is **Amtrak**. In 1969, the industry's intercity passenger deficit reached more than $500 million. Because the ICC, the DOT, and the public deemed many of these services essential to the public need, the railroads could only discontinue them slowly after major procedural steps were taken. Amtrak was created to relieve this burden from the railroads, while at the same time providing some of the needed services to the public. Thus, much of the passenger train deficit was shifted from the railroads and their shippers and stockholders to the federal taxpayer.

Domestic Waterway Operations

The inland barge industry receives two major forms of federal promotion. The first is from the **Army Corps of Engineers**, which is responsible for river and port channel **dredging** and clearances, as well as lock and dam **construction**. Operation and maintenance of these facilities rest with the corps as well. The second is provided by the **Coast Guard**, which is responsible for navigation aids and systems on the inland waterway system.

Historically, the barge industry paid no user charges except what could be interpreted as a very indirect form through general income taxes. A major controversy over a critical lock and dam on the upper Mississippi River in Alton, Illinois, brought the free-use issue to a head. The competing railroad industry lobbied to prevent this lock from being improved and enlarged. The resulting legislation and appropriation provided for improvement of that lock and initiated a fuel tax user charge for that industry.

International Water Carriage

The American flag overseas steamship industry receives major assistance from the federal government through the Maritime Administration (**MARAD**). The Merchant Marine Act of 1936 was designed to prevent economic decline of the U.S. steamship industry. One major facet of this act is construction differential subsidies (CDS). These are paid by the Maritime Administration to U.S. steamship yards that are constructing subsidized lines' ships. A ship that might only cost $20 million to build in Asia might cost $30 million to build in a U.S. yard. Without CDS, U.S. lines would build their ships abroad and American ship-building capacity would cease to exist. Instead, the steamship line pays, say, $20 million and MARAD pays the other $10 million to construct the ship in the United States. The survival of the U.S. shipyard also is viewed as essential to U.S. military capability. The Merchant Marine Act of 1936 also provides for operating differential subsidies (ODS), which cover the higher-cost increment resulting from having higher-paid American crews on ships, rather than less costly foreign labor.

Several **indirect** forms of **promotion** exist in this industry as well. The U.S. cabotage laws state that freight or passengers originating and terminating in two U.S. points can only be transported in ships constructed in the United States and owned and manned by U.S. citizens. The United States also has a **cargo preference** law that assists the U.S. fleet. Enacted in 1954, it stipulates that at least 50 percent of the gross tonnage of certain U.S. government-owned and -sponsored cargoes must be carried by U.S. flagships. This law extends to Department of Defense military goods, foreign aid by the State Department, surplus food movements by the Department of Agriculture, and products whose financing is sponsored by the Export-Import Bank.

Several planning and facilitating promotional efforts also assist the American flag ocean fleet. MARAD continually studies and develops plans for port improvements and ways in which export–import movements can be made more efficient. The Department of Commerce has a subagency whose prime purpose is to stimulate export sales that also benefit the U.S. fleet.

Two points should be brought out here with regard to the major funding and support roles played by MARAD. One deals with the control MARAD has over the lines it subsidizes. The agency exercises decision powers over the design and construction of each ship. It also plays a major role in the routes taken by each one. In this manner, the agency makes certain decisions that are normally within the discretion of carrier managements. This form of control is unique to the transportation industry in the United States.

The other point relates to the rationale for such extensive assistance to this one industry. A strong home shipping fleet is a vital part of national defense sealift capacity in the event of war. Also, existence of the fleet tends to exert some influence on services and rates on various trade routes to the benefit of the United States and its interests. Further, export and import movements on U.S. flagships help retain U.S. dollars to accumulate certain other strong foreign currencies.

The **Shipping Act of 1984** is a further example of the U.S. policy toward supporting a strong U.S. ocean fleet. The act was designed to reduce the regulation on foreign ocean shipping with the following goals:

- Establishing a nondiscriminatory regulatory process for common ocean carriers with a minimum of government intervention and regulatory costs
- Providing an efficient and economic transportation system in the ocean commerce of the United States that is in harmony and responsive to international shipping practices
- Encouraging the development of an economically sound and efficient U.S. flag liner fleet capable of meeting national security needs

The St. Lawrence Seaway Development Corporation within the DOT functions as the U.S. financing and operating arm of the joint U.S./Canada venture to upgrade the Great Lakes waterway and lock system to accommodate oceangoing ships. This waterway opened a fourth seacoast for the United States, enabling oceangoing ships to call at Buffalo, Cleveland, Toledo, Detroit, Chicago, Duluth, and other inland ports.

A final, and major, positive role in the water carrier industry is played by various port authorities. These agencies provide financing, major construction, and leasing of facilities in much the same way that the airport authorities provide facilities to the air industry.

Pipeline

The pipeline industry receives no public financial support, but it has benefited in a legal sense from the right of eminent domain permitted to oil, gas, and petroleum product lines. Typically, a pipeline will negotiate for land acquisition or rental. If the landowner will not negotiate at all or in good faith, the law of eminent domain will uphold the use of the land for a pipeline right-of-way in a court of law.

Miscellaneous Forms of Promotion

Various other activities directly or indirectly benefit the transportation industry. The DOT conducts planning and research activities in several ways. The Office of Assistant Secretary for Policy Plans and International Affairs is involved with improving international goods flow and conducting studies about the transportation systems and data coordination. The assistant secretary for the Systems Development and Technology Department is responsible for research and development into improved transport vehicles and methods.

Other research and development studies of benefit to transportation are conducted by the Transportation Research Board and the National Science Foundation. A small but effective group within the Department of Agriculture is concerned with improving loading, unloading, packaging, and carriage methods of food products on all modes. Many of these efforts result in equipment design changes that make transportation equipment more efficient for food movements. The Department of Defense continually examines methods to improve shipping, and many improvements spill over into the commercial area.

TRANSPORTATION PROMOTION IN PERSPECTIVE

Two major concepts override the entire topic of transportation promotion: user charges and nationalization. User charges often are created and assessed to pay for some or all of the services used by the carrier or mode. Nationalization represents an extreme form of public assistance or provision of transportation.

User Charges

User charges are assessments or fees charged by public bodies against carriers. They are created for a variety of reasons. One is to pay back the public for assistance during modal conception and encouragement. Some user charges are assessed to finance construction. The federal fuel tax on gasoline is an example, as is the barge fuel tax. Coverage of operating costs is often a reason for the origin of user charges. Examples here are airport landing fees, road tolls, and state fuel tax when it is applied to road maintenance. In addition, a user charge also can serve to equalize intermodal competitive conditions. The barge fuel tax, while paying for some lock construction, also makes barge operators bear some of the full cost of providing their service. This lessens, to a degree, some of the advantage that existed when right-of-way costs were borne by the public and not the barge firm.

FORMS

User charges are present in three basic forms. The first is an **existence charge**, a charge related to existence. This is similar to driver's license and auto registration fees. A charge is made against the person or unit regardless of the extent of use made of the services.

A second user charge is a **unit charge**. This is a fee assessed for use of a facility or resource. This fee is variable according to use, but it does not distinguish between passengers or freight within each unit. Tolls and gas mileage taxes are examples. Thus, a bus with two passengers pays the same as does a bus with 40 passengers. An empty truck or one with scrap is charged the same as a truck carrying calculators and cameras. This form of fee assessment does not take into account the economic value of the service being performed.

A third user fee is based upon **relative use**. This form assesses fees according to the investment of cost incurred by the agency to provide the service. An increased truck registration fee for heavier vehicles is an example here. Deeper road bases are required for heavier trucks. Road and bridge wear and damage is believed to be experienced on the basis of vehicle weight. Another example of relative use charge is a commuter route bridge toll. In the San Francisco area, bridge tolls are assessed for each vehicle. However, cars and vans having four or more passengers can cross the bridge toll-free. In this instance, the user charge becomes a behavior inducement. A form of *nonuser fee* also has arisen in recent years. Atlanta and San Francisco and area counties are partially paying for their shares of rapid transit development through a one-cent additional sales tax on all retail transactions within those areas. Here, many persons do not, or might not, ever use the rapid transit system, but they do bear some of its costs. A major rationale behind this nonuser charge is that all persons in a community benefit at least indirectly from the improved infrastructure provided by the system.

Nationalization

Nationalization is an extreme form of public promotion. It basically consists of public ownership, financing, and operation of a business entity. No true forms of nationalization exist in the U.S. transportation system except the Alaska Railroad, which was owned by the DOT and is now owned by the state of Alaska. Nationalization is a method of providing transportation service where neither financing, ownership, nor operation is possible in a private manner. Railroads and airlines in foreign countries are examples of nationalization, but many countries, such as Mexico, New Zealand, and Great Britain, are privatizing their railroads. Transportation service in many lands probably would not exist in a desirable form, or at all, without such government intervention. Advantages of nationalization that are often cited are that services can be provided that would not exist under private ownership, and capital can be attracted at favorable rates. But nationalized organizations have been criticized as being slow to innovate, unresponsive to the general public, subject to the same labor reduction as private enterprise, dependent on large management staffs, and subject to political influence.

TRANSPORTATION SAFETY

As noted earlier, the federal government has assumed the responsibility of ensuring the safety of travelers. It has promulgated numerous safety regulations for all modes and has centralized safety enforcement in the DOT. Protection of the traveler and the general public is an increasing government concern in light of the reduced economic regulation of transportation and the resultant concerns that carriers will sacrifice safety matters for profitability or economic viability.

Since **economic deregulation**, greater attention has been given to the establishment and enforcement of safety regulations to ensure that the transportation providers do not defer required vehicle and operating safety requirements in the heat of competition. Critics of economic deregulation cite that the marketplace pressures carriers to increase productivity and improve efficiency at the expense of safety. The deregulation experience in the airline and motor-carrier industries has resulted in economic strains on the carriers and a deleterious effect on safety, whereas the opposite is true for the railroads, which have been able to increase profitability and safety.[7]

Federal safety regulations cover all aspects of transportation operations from labor qualifications and operating procedures to equipment specifications. The primary objective of the safety regulations is to establish a **minimum level of safety** for transportation providers to maintain. Many transportation companies establish higher safety levels than those required by law, and these companies have their own enforcement personnel to ensure compliance.

Labor safety regulations have established minimum qualifications for operating personnel, including such factors as age, health, training, licensing, and experience. Minimum age requirements were established for driving a tractor-trailer in interstate commerce, and a nationwide commercial driver-licensing program was initiated in 1988. Pilots are required to pass a physical examination, to have training and experience on specific types of aircraft, and to be certified for various types of flying conditions. Similar regulations govern rail engineers and ship captains.

The policy of safe transportation has been extended to the specification of **standards** for transportation **vehicles**. These standards range from design specifications for aircraft to required safety equipment for automobiles. The vehicle manufacturer is obligated to adhere to the safety specifications, and the vehicle operator is required to maintain the vehicle and equipment in good operating condition and to use the safety equipment. For example, the automobile manufacturer must equip the vehicle with seat belts, a minimum number of headlights and taillights, a horn, etc. The auto owner then is required by state law to use the seat belt and to ensure proper functioning of the lights, horn, etc.

Of all the commodities moved within the boundaries of the United States, **hazardous materials** pose the greatest threat to public safety. Consequently, the movement of hazardous materials and hazardous wastes has been subjected to considerable regulations. A hazardous material is a substance that poses more than a reasonable risk to the health and safety of individuals and includes products such as explosives, flammables, corrosives, oxidizers, and radioactive materials. The safety regulations govern the movement of hazardous wastes as well.

A plethora of hazardous material and hazardous waste safety regulations have been imposed upon the transportation of such commodities. The regulations govern loading and unloading practices, packaging, routing, commodity identification, and documentation. Transportation personnel must be trained to properly handle hazardous cargoes and to respond to emergencies.

These regulations overlap somewhat because of the overlapping jurisdiction of the regulatory agencies originating and enforcing the rules. For example, the DOT promulgates and enforces hazardous material regulations, while the Environmental Protection Agency regulates the movement of hazardous wastes. In addition, the various states and municipalities within the states establish various laws impacting the movement of hazardous commodities through their jurisdiction.

As indicated above, the states are involved in regulating the safe operation of transportation vehicles. The police powers of the Constitution grant the states the right to protect the health and welfare of their citizens. The states have used this power to establish safety regulations governing the safe operations of trains through a state, and to limit the maximum speed, height, length, and weight of trucks, etc. These regulations are not standard from state to state because of the differing political, economical, sociological, and geographical conditions. However, the common denominator in state safety regulations is that all states regulate transportation safety matters.

Transportation safety matters have been extended to include environmental safety. Auto emission standards are designed to protect air quality; flight take-off procedures and patterns are designed to reduce noise levels for the citizens living near airports; and tanker loading and unloading procedures for petroleum products are meant to protect the animals, sea life, and the landscape from the degradative effects of an oil spill.

One effect of these myriad safety regulations is an increase in the cost of transporting people and goods. The safety controls exercised by government usually add a direct cost to a transportation operation, making its service more costly to consumers. However, when the indirect social costs are considered, society feels that the benefits of safety regulations, including fewer deaths and injuries and a cleaner environment, more than offset the direct cost. In the future, the number and scope of safety regulations will increase as government expands its safety regulating authority into additional transportation areas.

Transportation Security

After the September 11, 2001, terrorist attack on the United States, the Department of Homeland Security (DHS) was established with the goal of mobilizing and organizing the nation to secure the homeland from terrorist attacks. Its mission is to lead a unified national effort to secure America; to prevent and deter terrorist attacks and protect against and respond to threats and hazards to the nation; and to ensure safe and secure borders, welcome lawful immigrants and visitors, and promote the free flow of commerce.

DHS is charged with protecting the security of the transportation system encompassing approximately 700 million air passengers, 11 million trucks, and 2 million railcars crossing the United States annually, plus 7,500 foreign flag ships making 51,000 calls on U.S. ports.[8] The DHS transportation security programs and regulations are administered through the Coast Guard (CG), Customs Service (CS), and Transportation Security Administration (TSA).

The Coast Guard patrols the U.S. coastline and internal navigable waterways implementing the various security measures set forth by the DHS. The CG can stop a vessel from entering an U.S. port, board the vessel, and prevent any undesirable freight from being offloaded from a vessel.

The TSA administers the air passenger security-screening processes at U.S. airports. TSA hires and manages the airport screeners and sets forth items that are prohibited from being carried on board commercial passenger aircraft. TSA is testing various security devices and procedures to ensure the safety of passengers as well as reduce delays resulting from the security-screening process.

TSA has conducted a transit and rail inspection program with the goal of implementing rail passenger and luggage screening similar to that in the air passenger sector. In conjunction with Amtrak and the DOT, TSA is implementing phase II of a first-time rail security technology study to evaluate the use of emerging technologies to screen checked and unclaimed baggage as well as temporarily stored personal items and cargo for explosives.

The U.S. Customs & Border Protection agency (CBP) has been focusing on implementing security measures for cargo entering the United States. CBP has established the 24-hour rule that requires shippers to electronically transmit a description of the cargo to CBP 24 hours before loading. CBP can block any prohibited cargo items from being unloaded at any U.S. port or airport. CBP is working in partnership with shippers to streamline the security paperwork in an attempt to reduce the negative consequences on global commerce entering the United States.

Transportation security has been increased to protect the public against future terrorist attacks. As the security measures increase, the impact on the transportation system and transportation users is increased transit times and cost. The transportation security agencies are aware of the commercial impact and are taking steps to reduce the shipping and traveling delays while at the same time maintaining the needed level of security.

Summary

- Imperfections in the marketplace in a free-enterprise economy provide the rationale for government intervention in business operations.
- Potential monopolistic abuses in transportation motivated the federal government to create the Interstate Commerce Commission (ICC) to regulate the transportation industry. The Surface Transportation Board (STB) replaced the ICC.
- The U.S. court system, through decisions under a common law structure, also influences transportation regulation.
- All carriers are subject to safety regulations administered by both federal and state agencies.
- The Department of Transportation (DOT) is the federal organization responsible for developing and implementing the overall transportation policy for the United States.
- Transportation regulation has progressed through four phases: Era of Initiation, Era of Positive Regulation, Era of Intermodal Regulation, and the Era of Deregulation.
- In today's transportation environment, the federal government is a proponent of less regulation, preferring to allow market forces to regulate carrier prices and availability of supply.

Key Terms

air carriers, 66
air traffic control system, 74
Airport and Airway Trust Fund, 75
allocation of resources, 52
Amtrak, 76
Army Corps of Engineers, 77
benefit/cost ratio, 72
cargo preference, 77
Civil Aeronautics Board, 55
Clayton Act, 61
Coast Guard, 77
common carrier, 67
common law, 54
dredging and construction aid, 77
economic deregulation, 80
exempt carriers, 67
existence charge, 79
federal-state conflict, 57
Federal Aviation Administration, 56
Federal Energy Regulatory Commission, 56
Federal Motor Carrier Safety Administration, 56
Federal Highway Trust Fund, 75
Federal Maritime Commission, 55
Federal Railroad Administration, 56
Federal Trade Commission, 61
granger laws, 55
hazardous material, 81
highway development, 75
home-flag airlines, 74
indirect promotion, 77
Interstate Commerce Commission, 55
intrastate commerce, 57
MARAD, 77
minimum safety level, 80
monopoly, 53
National Highway Traffic Safety Administration, 56
National Transportation Safety Board, 57
nationalization, 80
Office of Hazardous Materials Transportation, 57
operation, 52
per se violations, 62
police powers, 57
reasonable rate, 67
Reed-Bulwinkle Act of 1948, 61
relative use, 79
rule of reason violations, 62
Sherman Antitrust Act, 61
Shipping Act of 1984, 78
state regulation, 54
statutory law, 54
Surface Transporation Board, 55
time value of funds, 73
truck intrastate deregulation, 58
unit charge, 79
U.S. Department of Transportation, 55
user charges, 75
vehicle standards, 81

Study Questions

1. Discuss the rationale for economic regulation of transportation.
2. How has common law provided a basis for the government's regulation of transportation in the United States?
3. Discuss the role of antitrust laws in transportation during the regulated era versus the deregulated era.
4. How do the police powers of the Constitution affect transportation?
5. Why does the United States need a national transportation policy? What purpose does it serve?
6. Analyze the major issues addressed by the ICC Termination Act national transportation policy statements.
7. Unlike many industrialized nations, the United States has fostered private ownership of transportation companies. What is the rationale for private ownership?
8. Which governmental entities develop transportation policy? What powers and limitations exist for these agencies?
9. Describe and contrast the types of public promotion that have been provided to the modes. What is the rationale for such public promotion?
10. What are transportation user charges? What is the purpose of such changes?

Notes

1. Dudley F. Pegrum, *Public Regulation of Business*, Homewood, IL: Richard D. Irwin, 1959, pp. 21–24.
2. Ibid.
3. Sherman Antitrust Act of 1890, Sections 1 and 2.
4. U.S. Department of Transportation, *A Statement of National Transportation Policy*, Washington, DC, 1975, p. 1.
5. The material in this section is adapted from: Transportation Policy Associates, *Transportation in America*, 4th ed., Washington, DC: 1986, pp. 28–31.
6. Ibid., p. 31.
7. Paul Stephen Dempsey, "The Empirical Results of Deregulation: A Decade Later, and the Band Played On," *Transportation Law Journal*, Vol. 17, 1988, pp. 69–81.
8. http://www.dhs.gov.

Suggested Readings

Adrange, Bahram, Garland Chow, and Raffiee Kambiz. "Airline Deregulation, Safety, and Profitability in the U.S.," *Transportation Journal*, Vol. 36, No. 4, 1997, pp. 30–43.

Augello, William J. *Transportation, Logistics and the Law*, 2nd ed., Huntington, NY: Transportation Consumer Protection Council, Inc., 2004.

Babcock, Michael W., M. Jarvin Emerson, and Marvin Pratter. "A Model-Procedure for Estimating Economic Impacts of Alternative Types of Highway Improvement," *Transportation Journal*, Vol. 36, No. 4, 1997, pp. 17–29.

Berskin, C. G. "Econometric Estimation of the Effects of Deregulation on Railway Productivity Growth," *Transportation Journal*, Vol. 35, No. 4, 1996, pp. 34–43.

Hazard, John L. *Managing National Transportation Policy*. Wesport, CT: ENO Foundation for Transportation, Inc., 1988.

Lewis, I. and D. B. Vellenga. "The Ocean Shipping Reform Act of 1998," *Transportation Journal*, Vol. 39, No. 4, 2000, pp. 27–34.

Pegrum, Dudley F. *Transportation Economics and Public Policy*, 3rd ed., Homewood, IL: Richard D. Irwin, 1973.

Proper, A. F. "In Defense of Antitrust Immunity for Collective Ratemaking: Life After the ICC Termination Act of 1995," *Transportation Journal*, Vol. 35, No. 4, 1996, pp. 26–33.

Spychalski, John C. "From ICC to STB: Continuing Vestiges of U.S. Surface Transportation Regulation," *Journal of Transport Economics and Policy*, Vol. XXXI, No. 1, 1997, pp. 131–136.

Spychalski, John C. "Social Control of Rail Transport in the United States," *The Institutionalist Approach to Public Utilities Regulation*, Edythe S. Miller and Warren J. Samuels, editors, East Lansing, MI: Michigan State University Press, 2002, pp. 297–339.

Case 2-1

CBN Plastic Wood

CBN Plastic Wood company is a manufacturer of plastic wood products made from recycled plastics. In 1993 James Marr, who was the owner of a lumberyard, saw the potential for plastic lumber in the construction of outside decks and patios, as well as other outdoor buildings, because of plastic's ability to withstand the elements. In addition, there was a growing public concern regarding the preservative materials used to treat wood products that would be exposed to the elements.

James worked with a local polymer consultant who helped him acquire the machinery and the sources for recycled plastic needed to produce the plastic lumber. In September 1993 CBN produced its first line of plastic lumber, 2 × 4 studs. Quickly added to the product mix was 4 × 4 and 4 × 6 lumber, so that by the end of 1993 CBN was capable of providing all the plastic lumber needed to construct an outdoor deck or patio.

Business grew at a slow but steady pace because the price (cost) of plastic lumber was higher than wood. In early 2000 the cost of wood began to escalate, making CBN's plastic wood more affordable. Environmental concerns over the preserving agent used for wood products helped spur sales of plastic wood. By 2005 CBN had 12 plants throughout the United States. It served local lumberyards, national home improvement stores, and contractors primarily working on large construction projects.

A major component of CBN's logistics process is its fleet of 90 tractors and 150 flatbed trailers. The private fleet delivers approximately 60 percent of all CBN loads. (Total loads are estimated to be 50,000 in 2004.) The fleet typically operates within a 200-mile radius of the plant, and loads beyond 200 miles are hauled by contract motor carrier. The CBN drivers and contract carrier drivers assist with the unloading at the local lumberyards and job sites because the flatbed trailers can carry a forklift truck.

In January 2004 James held a meeting with the private fleet manager to discuss the impact of the new hours-of-service regulations for drivers. The new rules would permit the drivers to be on duty a maximum of 14 hours and drive a maximum of 11 hours within the 14 on-duty hours. After 14 hours on duty the driver is required to be off duty for 10 consecutive hours. On the surface, these new rules did not seem to pose much of a problem to the way CBN operated its fleet; in fact, the 11 hours of driving time was an increase of 1 hour over the previous driving time rules.

However, the major change with the new hours-of-service regulations is the calculation of on-duty hours. The new rules count all time on duty from the time the driver reports for work. This means the driver's time spent unloading at a customer's site is counted toward the maximum 14 hours of on-duty time. Previously, the time spent at a customer's site unloading was not counted as on-duty time.

Because all CBN drivers and contract carrier drivers assist with unloading, the new regulations have the potential of reducing the productivity of CBN's transportation process. Of particular concern is the national home improvement store accounts. The home improvement store accounts typically send in orders for all stores in the region served by a plant, and the plant consolidates the orders so that the truck makes multiple stops in a delivery run. Most of the national account distribution centers are notorious for not keeping delivery appointments and making the drivers wait for two to four hours.

On a three-stop load, a 2 hour wait for unloading at each stop means the driver is on duty for six hours waiting for unloading and has only 8 hours (maximum of 14 hours on duty less the 6 hours waiting) available for driving. At an average driving time of 45 miles per hour and a driving range of 400 miles (200 miles one way), a driver of a three-stop load would require 8.9 hours for driving; however, with the 6 hours spent waiting to unload, the driver would exceed the 14 hours of on-duty time and would be required to go off duty for 10 hours before returning to the plant.

The implications of this example are reduced driver and equipment productivity, increased driver lodging costs, increased contract carrier rates, and increased capital requirements for equipment. All of these hours of service implications would require CBN Plastic Wood to increase prices, a strategy that James knew would have a very negative impact on sales.

Case Questions

1. What data would you require to analyze the impact of the new hours-of-service driver regulations on CBN's transportation operations and costs?
2. How would you approach the national accounts regarding the unloading delays at their distribution centers?
3. What actions would you take with the CBN contract carriers?

Case 2-2

The U.S. Airline Industry Public Support

After the September 11 terrorist attack in 2001, the U.S. airline industry was grounded by the federal government for security reasons. During this forced grounding, the air carriers faced ongoing expenses, but no income. After the grounding order was lifted, the airlines began to restore flights, but the flying public was not flying. Planes were virtually empty, so the air carriers reduced the number of flights and placed planes in mothball storage.

The financial plight caused by the grounding and subsequent reduction of demand was tremendous. Congress passed emergency legislation to provide operating funds for the air carriers to assure that U.S. citizens would have a viable air carrier system. These public monies helped sustain the industry while the flying public overcame its fear of flying.

In 2004 a number of major air carriers are either in bankruptcy or facing bankruptcy. There is again a call for a federal bailout of money to help support the vital air carrier industry. There are opponents who claim the air carrier plight is a result of mismanagement, overly aggressive flight scheduling that caused over capacity, and an overall reduction in demand from the business community that is increasingly relying on video conferencing, teleconferencing, and e-mails for communication rather than face-to-face meetings.

Case Questions

1. What are the arguments in favor of the federal government providing financial support to the U.S. airlines?
2. What are the arguments against the federal government providing financial support to the U.S. airlines?
3. If federal financial assistance is provided, should the air carriers and/or flying public be expected to repay the government? If so, what form of repayment would you suggest? Why?

Appendix 2-A

Department of Transportation

The U.S. DOT was established in 1966 to coordinate the administration of government transportation programs and to establish overall transportation policy that enables the provision of fast, safe, efficient, and convenient transportation at the lowest cost. As indicated in Figure 2A.1, the DOT consists of 12 different agencies with the secretary of transportation having the responsibility of coordinating the activities of these agencies as each administers the programs under its respective jurisdiction. The centralization of federal transportation activities under the auspices of one department in the executive branch focuses attention on the critical nature of transportation in the economy.

The operating programs of the individual agencies are basically organized by mode. The secretary and deputy secretary are responsible for overall planning, directing, and controlling the departmental activities but do not exercise direct operating control over the agencies. Rather, the secretary's office is concerned with policy development, resource allocation, program evaluation, agency coordination, and intermodal matters.

The secretary is the principal advisor to the president on matters relating to federal transportation. The responsibility for domestic and international transportation policy development and review is delegated to the assistant secretary for policy and international affairs. On the domestic level, this policy formulation is directed toward assessing the economic impact of government regulations and programs on the industry and the economy. Such policy issues as public trust funds, user charges, energy and environmental concerns, subsidy levels for subsidized carriers, international mail rates, aviation and maritime concerns in multilateral and bilateral negotiations, and coordination of efforts to combat transportation-related terrorists acts and drug smuggling are representative of the wide range of policy responsibilities of the secretary of transportation.

FIGURE 2A.1 Agencies of the U.S. Department of Transportation

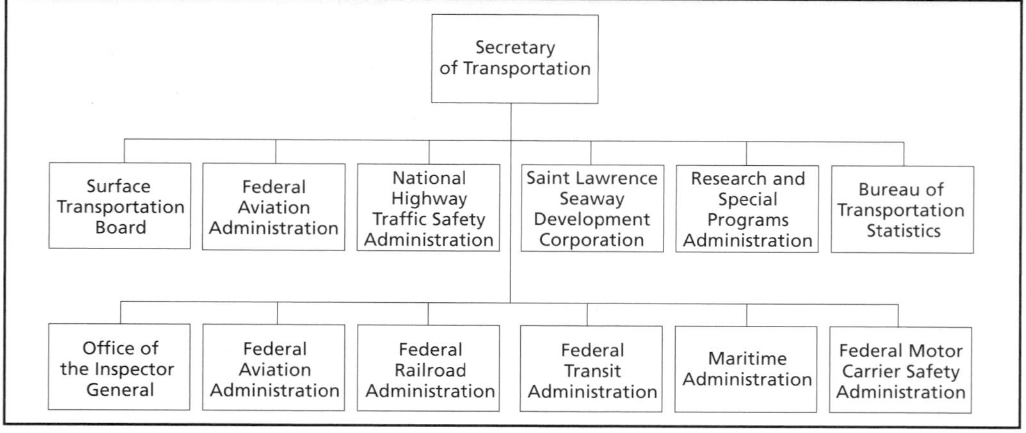

Through its various agencies and departments, the DOT has responsibility and control over transportation safety, promotion, and research. The individual agency programs provide insight into the overall role of government in transportation matters other than economic regulation. A brief description of some of the activities included in the DOT can be found on the following pages.

Federal Aviation Administration

The Federal Aviation Administration (FAA) is responsible for regulating air safety, promoting development of air commerce, and controlling navigable airspace in the interest of safety and efficiency. The FAA is most noted for its air safety regulations governing the manufacture, operation, and maintenance of aircraft, the certification of pilots and navigators, and the operation of air traffic control facilities. It conducts research and development of procedures, systems, and facilities to achieve safe and efficient air navigation and air traffic control. It also enforces the hazardous materials safety regulations.

The FAA administers a grant program for planning and developing public airports and provides technical guidance on airport planning, design, and safety operations. The agency maintains registration and records of aircraft, aircraft engines, propellers, and parts. It promotes international aviation safety by exchanging aeronautical information with foreign authorities, certifying foreign repair facilities and mechanics, and providing technical assistance in aviation safety training.

Federal Highway Administration

The Federal Highway Administration (FHWA) is concerned with the overall operation and environment of the highway systems, including the coordination of research and development activities aimed at improving the quality and durability of highways. In this capacity, the FHWA administers the federal-aid highway program, which provides financial assistance to the states for the construction and improvement of highways and traffic operations. For example, the interstate system is a 42,500-mile network financed on a 90-percent federal/10-percent state basis. Improvements for other federal-aid highways are financed on a 75-percent federal/25-percent state basis. The monies are generated from special highway-use taxes, which are deposited into the Highway Trust Fund. Congress authorizes disbursement of money from the trust fund for payment of the federal government's portion of the highway expenditures.

Federal Railroad Administration

The promulgation and enforcement of railroad safety regulations are major responsibilities of the Federal Railroad Administration (FRA). The safety regulations cover maintenance, inspection, and equipment standards and operating practices. It administers research and development of railroad safety improvements and operates the Transportation Test Center near Pueblo, Colorado, which tests advanced and conventional systems and techniques that improve ground transportation.

The FRA administers the federal assistance program for national, regional, and local rail services. The assistance is designed to support continuation of rail freight and passenger service and state rail planning. In addition, the FRA administers the programs designed to improve rail transportation in the northeast corridor of the United States.

National Highway Traffic Safety Administration

Motor vehicle safety performance is the major jurisdiction of the National Highway Traffic Safety Administration (NHTSA). In this capacity, the NHTSA issues prescribed safety features and safety-related performance standards for vehicles and motor vehicle equipment. The agency reports to Congress and to the public the damage susceptibility, crashworthiness, ease of repair, and theft prevention of motor vehicles. It is charged with the mandate of reducing the number of deaths, injuries, and economic losses resulting from traffic accidents. Finally, the NHTSA establishes fuel economy standards for automobiles and light trucks.

Federal Transit Administration

The Federal Transit Administration (FTA) is charged with improving mass transportation facilities, equipment, techniques, and methods; encouraging the planning and establishment of urban mass transportation systems; and providing financial assistance to state and local governments in operating mass transportation companies. Capital grants or loans of up to 75 percent of the project cost are made available to communities to purchase equipment and facilities. Formula grants are available in amounts of up to 80 percent of the project cost for capital and planning activities and 50 percent for operating subsidies. In addition, FTA makes funding available for research and training programs.

Maritime Administration

The Maritime Administration (MA) oversees programs designed to develop, promote, and operate the U.S. Merchant Marine and to organize and direct emergency merchant ship operations. The MA maintains a national defense reserve fleet of government-owned ships that are to be operated in time of national defense emergency. It also operates the U.S. Merchant Marine Academy, which operates training for future Merchant Marine officers.

The MA administers maritime subsidy programs through the Maritime Subsidy Board. The operating subsidy program provides U.S. flagships with an operating subsidy that represents the difference between the costs of operating a U.S. flagship and a foreign competitive flagship. A construction subsidy program provides funds for the difference between the costs of constructing ships in U.S. shipyards and in foreign shipyards. It also provides financing guarantees for construction of reconditioning of ships.

St. Lawrence Seaway Development Corporation

The St. Lawrence Seaway Development Corporation (SLSDC) is a government-owned operation that is responsible for the development, maintenance, and operation of the U.S. portion of the St. Lawrence Seaway; the SLSDC charges tolls to ship operators who use the seaway. These tolls are negotiated with the St. Lawrence Seaway Authority of Canada. The U.S. and Canadian seaway agencies coordinate activities involving seaway operations, traffic control, navigation aids, safety, and length of shipping season.

Research and Special Programs Administration

The Research and Special Programs Administration (RSPA) is responsible for a number of programs involving safety regulation, emergency preparedness, and research and development. The Office of Hazardous Materials Transportation develops and issues hazardous material transportation safety regulations for all modes. These regulations cover shipper and carrier operations, packaging specifications, and hazardous material definitions. The Office of Pipeline Safety establishes and enforces safety standards for the movement of gas and hazardous liquids by pipeline.

Through the auspices of the Transportation Systems Center in Cambridge, Massachusetts, numerous transportation research and development programs are conducted, including the development and maintenance of important national transportation statistics. The Office of Emergency Transportation administers the transportation civil emergency preparedness programs.

Bureau of Transportation Statistics

The Bureau of Transportation Statistics (BTS) was born as a statistical agency in 1992. The Intermodal Surface Transportation Efficiency Act (ISTEA) of 1991 established BTS for data collection, analysis, and reporting and to ensure the most cost-effective use of transportation-monitoring resources. BTS brings a greater degree of coordination, comparability, and quality standards to transportation data, and it helps to fill important gaps.

Federal Motor Carrier Safety Administration

The Federal Motor Carrier Safety Administration (FMCSA) was established as a separate administration within the U.S. Department of Transportation on January 1, 2000, pursuant to the Motor Carrier Safety Improvement Act of 1999. The primary mission is to reduce crashes, injuries, and fatalities involving large trucks and buses. In carrying out its safety mandate, FMCSA

- develops and enforces data-driven regulations that balance motor carrier (truck and bus companies) safety with industry efficiency;
- harnesses safety information systems to focus on higher-risk carriers in enforcing the safety regulations;
- targets educational messages to carriers, commercial drivers, and the public; and
- partners with stakeholders including federal, state, and local enforcement agencies, the motor carrier industry, safety groups, and organized labor on efforts to reduce bus- and truck-related crashes.

FMCSA develops, maintains, and enforces Federal Motor Carrier Safety Regulations (FMCSRs), Hazardous Materials Regulations (HMRs), and the Commercial Driver's License Program, among others.

Office of the Inspector General

The Office of the Inspector General (OIG) is committed to fulfilling its statutory mission and assisting members of Congress, the secretary, and senior department officials in achieving a safe, efficient, and effective transportation system that meets vital national interests and enhances the quality of life of the American people, today and into the future.

The OIG works within the DOT to promote effectiveness and to stop waste, fraud, and abuse in departmental programs. This is accomplished through audits and investigations. OIG also consults with Congress about programs in progress and proposed new laws and regulations.

Surface Transportation Board

The Surface Transportation Board (STB) was created in the Interstate Commerce Commission Termination Act of 1995 and is the successor agency to the Interstate Commerce Commission. The STB is an economic regulatory agency that Congress charged with the fundamental missions of resolving railroad rate and service disputes and reviewing proposed railroad mergers. The STB is decisionally independent, although it is administratively affiliated with the DOT.

The STB serves as both an adjudicatory and a regulatory body. The agency has jurisdiction over railroad rate and service issues and rail restructuring transactions (mergers, line sales, line construction, and line abandonments); certain trucking company, moving van, and noncontiguous ocean shipping company rate matters; certain intercity passenger bus company structure, financial, and operational matters; and rates and services of certain pipelines not regulated by the Federal Energy Regulatory Commission.

Summary

- The agencies that make up the DOT administer federal programs covering all transportation modes.
- DOT establishes national transportation policy, enforces safety regulations, provides funding for transportation programs, and coordinates transportation research efforts.
- The secretary of transportation is the principal advisor to the president on transportation matters.

Part II

Overview of Transportation Providers

Chapter 3

Motor Carriers

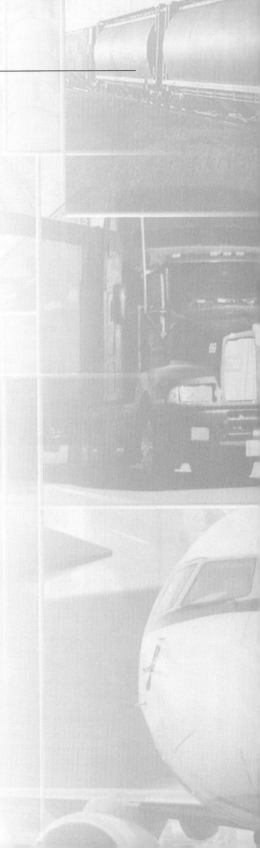

BRIEF HISTORY

The motor carrier industry played an important role in the development of the U.S. economy during the 20th century, and it continues this role in the 21st century. The growth of this industry is noteworthy considering it did not get started until World War I, when converted automobiles were utilized for pickup and delivery in local areas. The railroad industry, which traditionally had difficulty with small shipments that had to be moved short distances, encouraged the early motor carrier entrepreneurs. It was not until after World War II that the railroad industry began to seriously attempt to compete with the motor carrier industry, and by that time it was too late.

The United States has spent more than $120 billion to construct its **interstate highway system** and in the process has become increasingly dependent on this system for the movement of freight. The major portion of this network evolved as the result of a bill signed into law in 1956 by President Dwight D. Eisenhower to establish the National System of Interstate and Defense Highways, which was to be funded 90 percent by the federal government through fuel taxes.

As the interstate system of highways developed from the 1950s to 1980, motor carriers steadily replaced railroads as the mode of choice for transporting finished and unfinished manufactured products. In 1950 the railroad industry moved 1.4 billion tons of freight on an intercity basis, whereas motor carriers moved 800 million tons. In 1980 railroads moved 1.6 billion tons, compared to more than 200 billion tons by motor carriers. By 2001 motor carriers were handling 4.1 billion tons, compared with 2.1 billion tons by rail (see Figures 3.1 and 3.2). On a relative basis, however, the railroads did stabilize their market share.

FIGURE 3.1 Intercity Trucking Ton-Miles

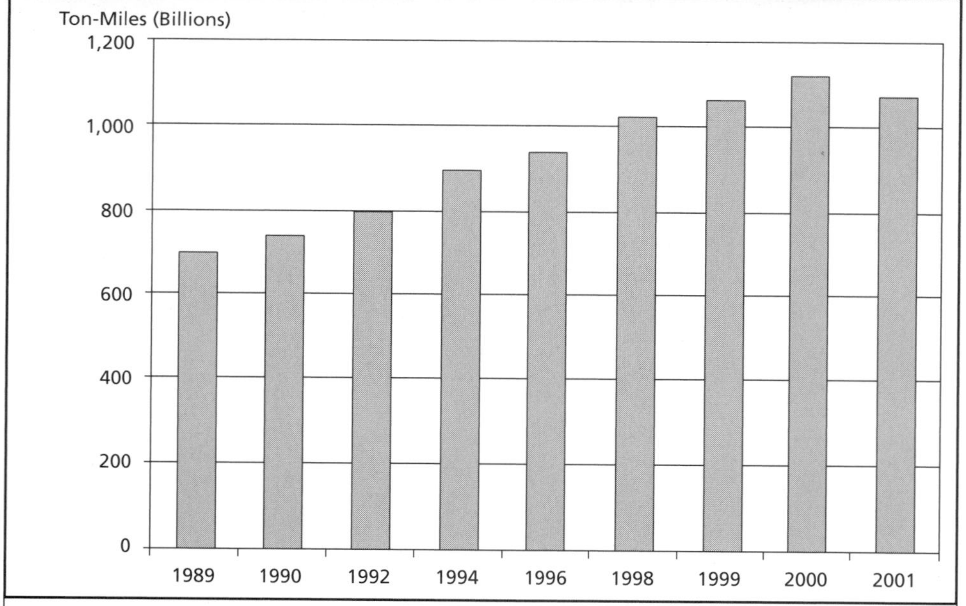

Source: Eno Transportation Foundation, Washington DC, "Transportation in America," 19th ed., 2002.

FIGURE 3.2 Intercity Trucking Tons

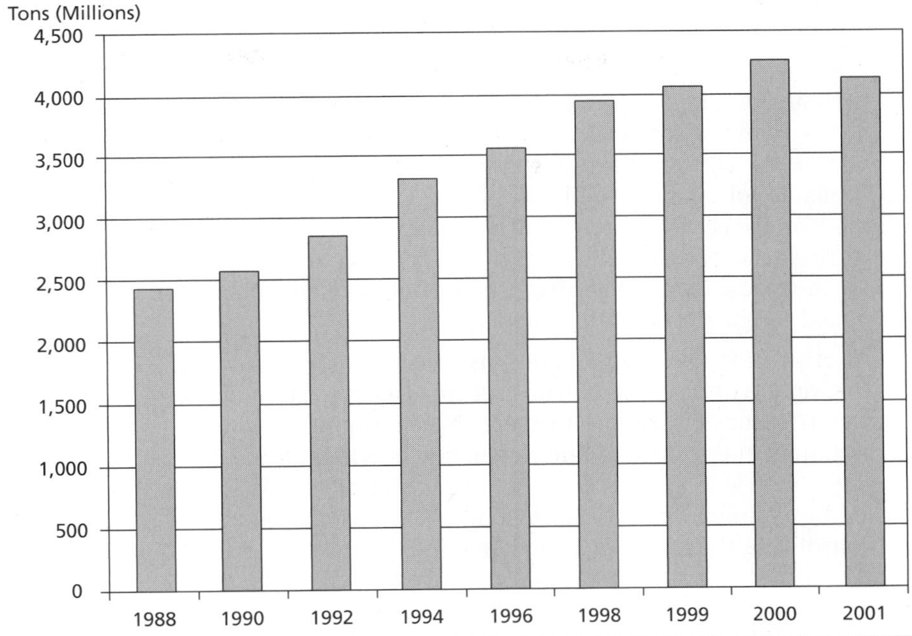

Source: Eno Transportation Foundation, Washington DC, "Transportation in America," 19th ed., 2002.

INDUSTRY OVERVIEW

Significance

In 2002 the United States paid over $585.3 billion for highway transportation, approximately 86.5 percent of the total 2002 Nation's Freight Bill.[1] Motor carriers transported 10.51 billion revenue freight ton-miles in 2001, or 28 percent of the ton-miles transported by all modes.[2] During 2001, approximately 1.8 million people were employed in the motor carrier industry, with an average annual compensation of $40,365.[3] These figures clearly demonstrate the significant role that motor carriers play in our society and the dependence of U.S. companies on motor carrier service. Finally, motor carriers logged 442.1 billion miles used for business purposes in 2002 (excluding the government and farm sectors).[4]

Types of Carriers

The first major division of motor carriers is between for-hire and private carriers. The **for-hire** carrier provides services to the public and charges a fee for the service. The private carrier provides a service to the industry or company that owns or leases the vehicles, and thus does not charge a fee, but obviously the service provider incurs cost. Private carriers might transport commodities for-hire, but when operating in such a capacity, the private carrier is really an exempt for-hire carrier.

For-hire carriers can be either local or intercity operators, or both. The local carriers pick up and deliver freight within the commercial zone of a city. The intercity carriers operate between specifically defined commercial zones to include the corporate limits of a municipality plus adjacent areas beyond the corporate limits determined by the municipal population. Local carriers frequently work in conjunction with intercity carriers to pick up or deliver freight in the commercial zone.

The for-hire carriers may be common and/or contract operators. The common carriers are required to serve the general public upon demand, at reasonable rates, and without discrimination. The contract carriers serve specific shippers with whom the carriers have a continuing contract; thus, the contract carrier is not available for general public use. Contract carriers also typically adapt their equipment and service to meet shipper needs. Shippers must choose to use a commercial carrier or to operate their own private fleet. The decision is based on what is best for their business. Trade-offs exist for both options, but it will ultimately be determined by the needs of the shippers.

Another important distinction is between the truckload (**TL**) and less-than-truckload (**LTL**) carriers. The truckload carriers provide service to shippers who tender sufficient volume to meet the minimum weights required for a truckload shipment and truckload rate or will pay the difference. Less-than-truckload carriers provide service to shippers who tender shipments lower than the minimum truckload quantities, such as 50 to 10,000 pounds. Consequently, the LTL carrier must consolidate the numerous smaller shipments into truckload quantities for the line-haul (intercity) movement and disaggregate the full truckloads at the destination city for delivery in smaller quantities. In contrast, the TL carrier picks up a truckload and delivers the same truckload at the destination.

A hybrid type of carrier that has developed can best be characterized as a "heavy LTL" motor carrier. Shipment sizes carried by this type of carrier are in the upper end of what can be considered LTL shipments (i.e., 12,000 to 25,000 pounds). This carrier utilizes consolidation terminals (like LTL carriers) to fully load trailers but does not utilize break-bulk facilities for deliveries. Rather, it delivers from the trailer, much like a "pool" carrier, charging line-haul rates plus a charge for each stop-off (like TL carriers). This type of carrier specializes in shipment sizes less than the TL carriers haul and more than LTL carriers haul. It has some fixed costs (because of the consolidation terminals) but not as much as in the LTL industry.

Finally, interstate common carriers might be classified by the type of commodity they are authorized to haul. Historically, motor carriers were required to have "operating authority" issued by either federal or state authorities. Since 1996, with the repeal of the Interstate Commerce Act and the elimination of the Interstate Commerce Commission, such authority is no longer required. The ICC Termination Act of 1995 removed virtually all motor carrier regulation and preempted the states from exercising any economic control over the motor carrier industry. Carriers are now only required to register with the Federal Motor Carrier Safety Administration and provide proof of insurance. They can then transport any commodity they wish, with only household goods and related items being subject to any economic oversight.

Number of Carriers

The motor carrier industry consists of a large number of small carriers, particularly in the TL (truckload) segment of the industry. As illustrated in Figure 3.3, as of 2002 a total of 585,677 interstate motor carriers were on file with the Office of Motor Carriers. Of these carriers, 81 percent operate with six or fewer vehicles.[5] This figure supports the small firm composition of the for-hire carrier industry. Keep in mind that many businesses do use their own private fleet.

FIGURE 3.3 U.S. Distribution of Motor Carriers

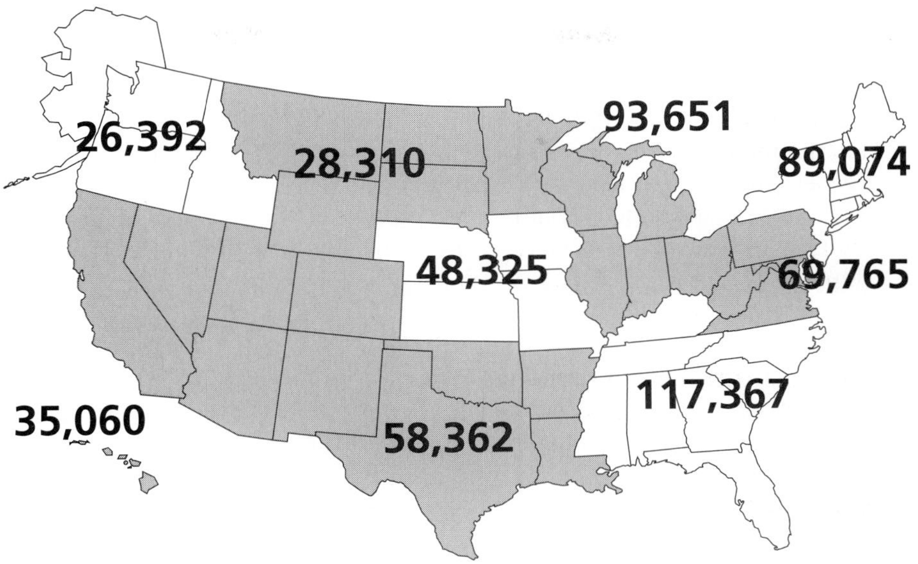

A further explanation of the large number of small carriers is the limited capital needed to enter the TL industry. A motor carrier can be formed with as little as $5,000 to $10,000 equity, and the balance can be financed with the vehicle serving as collateral for the loan. However, LTL carriers have terminals that increase the capital requirements and thus add a constraint to entry.

There is a significant difference between TL and LTL carriers, both in terms of number and start-up costs. The great growth that occurred in the 1980s, when regulated carriers more than doubled, happened primarily in small TL carriers because of the low startup costs indicated above.

The LTL segment of the motor carrier industry requires a network of terminals to consolidate and distribute freight, called a "hub-and-spoke" system. The large LTL carriers moved to expand their geographic coverage after 1980, and many of them eliminated their TL service. Because of this relatively high level of fixed costs, the LTL industry has continued to consolidate. In August 2003 Yellow Corporation announced that it would buy Roadway Corporation for $1.1 billion. After it was approved by the appropriate government agencies, this consolidation created a company that controls approximately 20 percent of the national LTL carrier market.[6]

Perhaps a brief description of an LTL operation would be helpful here. Shippers that have shipping requirements that are small-use LTL carriers (for example, the cubic capacity of a 53-foot trailer is not needed for the shipment). Also, the LTL shipper typically has shipments headed for more than one destination. The LTL carrier collects the shipments at the shipper's dock with a **pickup and delivery (PUD)** vehicle. This vehicle, as its name implies, does the collection and delivery of all shipments. After a PUD vehicle is finished collecting and delivering shipments, it returns to a consolidation or break-bulk facility. Once at the consolidation facility, the packages collected are sorted by their final destination. The next part of the trip is called the **line-haul** segment. For this portion of the trip, the shipments are loaded into 28-foot, 48-foot, or 53-foot trailers. If 28-foot trailers are used, they are hooked together in combinations of twos and threes, depending on the state's trailer configuration permitted over the route of travel. The 28-foot trailer is used in this situation because it is easier to unload two 28-foot trailers at separate bays than to unload one 48-foot or 53-foot trailer at one bay. Another reason for using the 28-foot trailer is because LTL carriers find that it is easier to utilize the capacity of a 28-foot trailer. After the line-haul portion of the trip, the trailers are unloaded at another break-bulk facility and are then sorted and reloaded into a PUD vehicle to be delivered to the receiver.

The TL segment of the industry has been experiencing some limited concentration. Carriers such as J. B. Hunt and Schneider National have become increasingly larger. The ability of the larger TL carriers to compete effectively with small TL companies with their value-added services might change the structure of the TL segment.

With the repeal of the Interstate Commerce Act, combined with changes in distribution patterns, a climate was created in which new TL carriers could easily enter the business (see Figure 3.4). The "trucking recession" of 1994 and 1995, during which capacity greatly exceeded demand, removed many of the weaker firms either through bankruptcy or merger. However, low startup costs in this sector still enabled new entrants to attempt success in this area.

Market Structure

When discussing the motor carrier industry, consideration must be given to the commodities hauled. Motor carrier vehicles, both for-hire and private, primarily

FIGURE 3.4 Overview of the Motor Carrier Industry

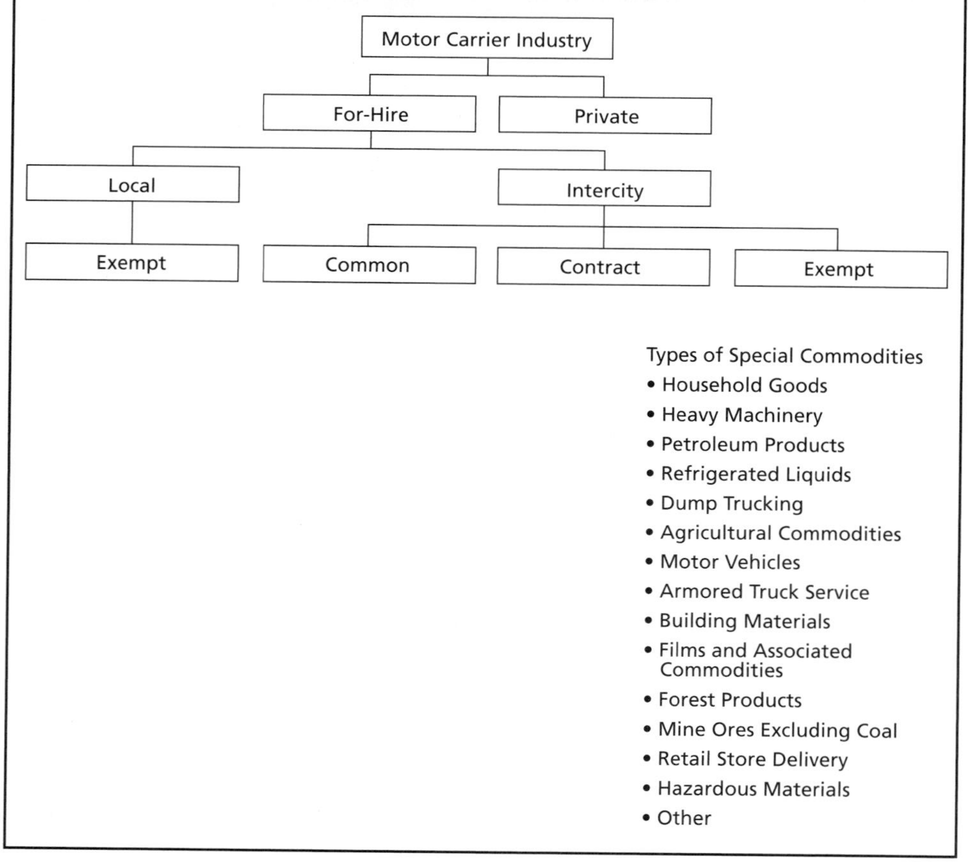

transport manufactured, high-value products. These vehicles carry more than a majority of the various manufactured commodity categories. The commodity list includes food products and manufactured products, consumer goods, and industrial goods. In addition, these vehicles transport almost all of the sheep, lambs, cattle, calves, and hogs moving to stockyards.[7]

Motor carriers transport less of commodities such as grain, primary nonferrous metal products, motor vehicles and equipment, and paper and allied products. Because such commodities generally must move long distances and in large volumes, shipping them by rail and water is usually less expensive.

Competition

Motor carriers compete vigorously with one another for freight. With the large number of for-hire motor carriers, rivalry between firms can be intense. However, the most severe competition for for-hire carriers often comes from the private carrier.

As indicated earlier, the motor carrier industry offers few capital constraints to entry. With a relatively small investment, an individual can start a motor carrier business and compete with an existing carrier. Thus, freedom of entry, discounting, and lack of regulatory constraints appear to dominate the industry and suggest that competition between firms can control the industry. Such a conclusion has been the basis for greater reliance on the marketplace and less reliance on regulation. Even though the LTL segment is more concentrated, there is still intense competition between the top carriers. Other competitors also include United Parcel Service, FedEx, and FedEx Ground.

Certain segments of motor carriers have higher capital requirements than others, as indicated, and therefore have some degree of capital constraint for entry. The major segment that has extensive capital requirements for entry is the LTL carrier. The LTL carrier must invest in terminals and freight-handling equipment that are simply not needed by the TL carrier. Special equipment carriers—carriers of liquefied gases or frozen products—usually have larger investments in equipment and terminals than those involved with general freight. The large TL carriers like J. B. Hunt and Schneider National also have significant capital investment.

On the whole, the motor carrier industry, especially for contract carriers, has been market oriented. Meeting customer requirements has been a common trait of motor carriers. The small size of the majority of for-hire carriers allows them to give individualized attention to customers. As carriers have grown in size, this close carrier–customer relationship has been strained. However, the responsiveness to customer demands for service still dominates all motor carrier organizations, and shippers expect carriers to respond to their needs.

STOP OFF

Yellow and Roadway Get it Together

Surprise merger tightens LTL market a notch; smaller companies may stand to profit.

When the news came down that Yellow Corp. had announced its intention to buy Roadway Corp., the industry didn't just sit up and take notice—it leapt to its feet in surprise. The unexpected announcement hit the industry hard, and its impact was felt from coast to coast.

The deal includes a $966 million payout, translating to $48 per share—a 49-percent premium on Roadway's stock. Yellow also will absorb some $140 million in Roadway's debt, making the total cost of the merger approximately $1.1 billion. The new company, to be called Yellow-Roadway, is expected to pull in roughly $6 billion of revenue annually—twice what Yellow posted last year.

Yellow executives insist they will keep both brands, including existing facilities and drivers, operating separately but acknowledge their intention to consolidate management and "back room" functions such as accounting and information technology.

Separate brands or not, with that kind of market share on the line, some observers naturally have raised the question of whether or not the deal violates antitrust regulations. Indeed, the combined company will command about 20 percent of the national LTL market, but company executives defend the move by noting that Yellow-Roadway's stake in the $600 billion U.S. transportation market will be just 1 percent.

There were none of the typical initial rumblings or harbingers of the transaction, no industry rumors for either side to confirm or deny. But although this particular merger may have come as a surprise, market factors pointed to this sort of deal, says Jon Langenfeld, vice president and senior research analyst with Robert W. Baird & Co. in Milwaukee, Wis. "It wasn't out of the blue," he says. "When you look at the transportation industry in general, there has been a consistent move toward consolidation across all modes. It's taken a pause given what the economy's been doing, but I think that continued consolidation is going to occur, and I think we'll see some more surprises, if you will, down the road."

Which may not be an entirely good thing for shippers. In its July 11 newsletter, the National Industrial Transportation League warned that the merger might trigger a new round of consolidations in the LTL industry that would further reduce the availability of carriers offering competitive rates, transit times, and strong service performance.

Now the question is: What impact will the merger have in the LTL arena?

Despite the insistence of Bill Zollars, chairman, president, and CEO of Yellow-Roadway, that the two companies will operate as separate units, the merger still amounts to the departure of one major player. "In a way they'll work independently, but I'm sure they won't be cutting each others' throats," says industry analyst and *Logistics Management* columnist Ray Bohman. "With CF (Consolidated Freightways) gone and the number one and two companies under the same ownership, I think we'll see some stability in discounting at a level we haven't seen in years."

Some analysts have noted that the combined capacity of the two companies will allow the new entity to more effectively compete with FedEx and United Parcel Service, which have been encroaching on the LTL market for some time. A Bear Stearns analysis, meanwhile, suggests several factors that may have moved Yellow toward the purchase, including current low interest rates, which are very agreeable to large-scale financing.

Still, the "departure" of one LTL giant will create a hole from which smaller carriers should be able to pump more revenue. Many analysts expect that shippers that had been splitting their freight between the original Big Two may not care to do so once they become the Big One. One possible reaction would be to start parceling out business to smaller regional LTLs. If shippers prefer to stick with a national carrier, though, that would put ABF in a strong position.

That is, if ABF remains ABF. Industry buzz suggests that the third-largest unionized LTL carrier could also be a buyout target. One scenario that's often been mentioned since the Yelllow-Roadway announcement has UPS buying ABF to keep pace with its main competitor, FedEx. "There's been speculation since FedEx bought out American Freightways and Viking that UPS will eventually want to offer an LTL service as well," says Bohman. "It wouldn't surprise me at all to see UPS make a move to purchase a major LTL carrier with broad territorial coverage." As one of the last unionized nationwide carriers, ABF would be a likely target, he suggests.

In Langenfeld's view, such a move would make economic sense. "The requirement for scale is a necessity in order to compete," he says. "The leading companies have realized that you have to garner scale—whether it's within a specific vertical or across different verticals—in order to compete over the longer haul."

Now that the shock of the announcement has worn off, other carriers will be watching carefully to see where the pieces from this shake-up fall and looking for a way to scoop those pieces up for themselves. "Whenever you have a merger, you're going to have some attrition of customers," says Langenfeld. "The question is how much. Any attrition off the Roadway and Yellow base, which is obviously very large, should benefit the other players. [Yellow-Roadway's] ability to retain its customer base is going to determine how successful the other companies are going to be at taking advantage of the situation."

Source: "Yellow and Roadway get it together." *Logistics Management*, August 2003. Reprinted with permission of Logistics Management, copyright 2003.

OPERATING AND SERVICE CHARACTERISTICS

General Service Characteristics

The growth and widespread use of motor carrier transportation can be traced to the inherent service characteristics of this method. In particular, the motor carrier possesses a distinct advantage over other modes in the area of accessibility. The motor carrier can provide service to virtually any location, as operating authority of the for-hire carrier no longer places restrictions on the areas served and commodities transported. Motor carrier access is not constrained by waterways, rail tracks, or airport locations. The U.S. system of highways is so pervasive that virtually every shipping and receiving location is accessible via highways. Therefore, motor carriers have potential access to almost every origin and destination.

The accessibility advantage of motor carriers is evident in the pickup or delivery of freight in an urban area. It is very rare to find urban areas not served by a pickup–delivery network. In fact, motor carriers provide the bridge between the pickup and delivery point and the facilities of other modes; that is, the motor carrier is referred to as the universal coordinator.

Another service advantage of the motor carrier is speed. For shipments going under 500 miles, the motor carrier vehicle can usually deliver the goods in less time than other modes. Although the airplane travels at a higher speed, the problem of getting freight to and from the airport via motor carrier adds to the air carrier's total transit time. In fact, the limited, fixed schedules of the air carriers might make motor carriers the faster method, even for longer distances. For example, a delivery to a destination 600 miles away might take 13.3 hours by motor carrier (600 miles at 45 mph). Although the flying time between airports is 1.5 hours, 3 hours might be needed for pickup and 3 hours for delivery, plus time for moving the freight from one vehicle to another. If the airline has scheduled only one flight per day, the shipment could wait up to 24 hours before being dispatched. The motor carrier, however, proceeds directly from the shipper's door to the consignee's door. This service advantage became evident in the wake of September 11, 2001, when U.S. air traffic was shut down. The U.S. Post Office issued a statement alerting customers of delays for any package or letter traveling more than 800 miles because any Post Office shipment moving over 800 miles travels by air and under 800 miles travels by motor carrier.

When compared to the railcar and barge, the smaller cargo-**carrying capacity** of the motor carrier vehicle enables the shipper to use the TL rate, or volume discount, with a lower volume. Many TL minimum weights are established at 20,000 to 30,000 pounds. Rail carload minimum weights are often set at 40,000 to 60,000 pounds, and barge minimums are set in terms of hundreds of tons. The smaller shipping size of the motor carrier provides the buyer and seller with the benefits of lower inventory levels, lower inventory-carrying costs, and more frequent services.

Another positive service characteristic is the smoothness of transport. Given the suspension system and the pneumatic tires used on their vehicles, the motor carrier ride is smoother than rail and water transport and less likely to result in damage to the cargo (although there can still be some cargo damage with motor carrier transportation). This relatively damage-free service reduces the packaging requirements and thus packaging costs.

Lastly, the for-hire segment of the motor carrier industry is customer or market oriented. The small size of most carriers has enabled (forced) the carriers to respond to customer equipment and service needs.

In 2001 interstate truckload motor carriers had an average haul length of 294 miles. LTL carriers averaged 752 miles per trip, railroads averaged 735 miles per trip, and airlines averaged approximately 900 miles per trip.[8] These data suggest that, depending on the commodity being moved and the service level required, there can be a high level of both intramodal and intermodal competition present in the motor carrier industry.

Equipment

Many of the motor carrier service advantages emanate from the technical features of the transportation vehicle. The high degree of flexibility, the relatively smooth ride, and the small carrying capacity of the vehicle are the unique characteristics that result in greater accessibility, capability, frequency of delivery and pickup, cargo safety, and lower transit time.

The motor carrier vehicle can also be loaded quickly. A railroad operation needs to collect a number of freight cars to be pulled by the one power unit; the motor carrier has just one or two. The availability to operate one cargo unit eliminates the time needed to collect several cargo units.

The other dimension of motor carrier equipment flexibility is the lack of highway constraint. Unlike the railroad and water carriers, the motor carrier is not constrained to providing service over a fixed railway or waterway. The motor carrier can travel over the highway, paved or unpaved, servicing virtually every conceivable consignee in the United States.[9] There are, however, gross vehicle weight and axle weight restrictions on vehicles while traveling the highway system.

In most cases, equipment represents the largest operating asset that a carrier maintains. With all of the different types and locations of equipment, positioning becomes critical to successful operations. Seasonal influences such as holidays or harvest times must also be considered, as they can drastically alter demand.

TL and LTL carriers need to make two types of equipment decisions: what type of tractor (power) and what type of trailer. In a TL operation, equipment positioning at terminals is not as important as in an LTL operation. However, power must be specified to be able to handle the size and length of the load, along with the terrain over which it travels. Many different specifications for tractors can be used, including single axle and twin axle, with different engine and drive train combinations. Decisions regarding trailers include length (28 feet, 45 feet, 48 feet, 53 feet, etc.) and trailer type (dry van, refrigerated, ragtop, container, flatbed, etc.). These decisions will be made in light of market demands and the type of carrier operation.

LTL carriers must make the same types of equipment decisions as TL carriers, along with deciding where to deploy this equipment. Similar to an airline equipment decision, LTL carriers need to position certain types of equipment at certain terminals. For example, city delivery vehicles and tractor–trailer combinations (either 28-foot or 40-foot trailers) will be positioned at PUD terminals, whereas line–haul trailers (usually 45, 48, or 53 feet) and line-haul tractors (single or twin axle) will be assigned to break-bulks. Compounding the LTL decision is the inclusion of 28-foot trailers (also called *pups, twins,* or *double bottoms*) in the equipment decision. Having the right mix of power and trailers at a particular terminal location determines the ability to efficiently serve customers.

Types of Vehicles

Motor carrier vehicles are either line-haul or city vehicles. Line-haul vehicles are used to haul freight long distances between cities. City straight trucks are used within a city to provide pickup and delivery service. On occasion, line-haul vehicles also will operate within a city, but the line-haul vehicle is normally not very efficient when operated this way.

LINE-HAUL VEHICLES

The line-haul vehicle is usually a tractor–trailer combination of three or more axles (see Figure 3.5). The cargo-carrying capacity of these vehicles depends on the size (length) and the state maximum weight limits. A tractor–trailer combination with five axles (tandem-axle tractor and trailer) is permitted in most states to haul a maximum of 80,000 pounds gross weight (110,000 pounds in Michigan). For a vehicle to

FIGURE 3.5 Equipment Types

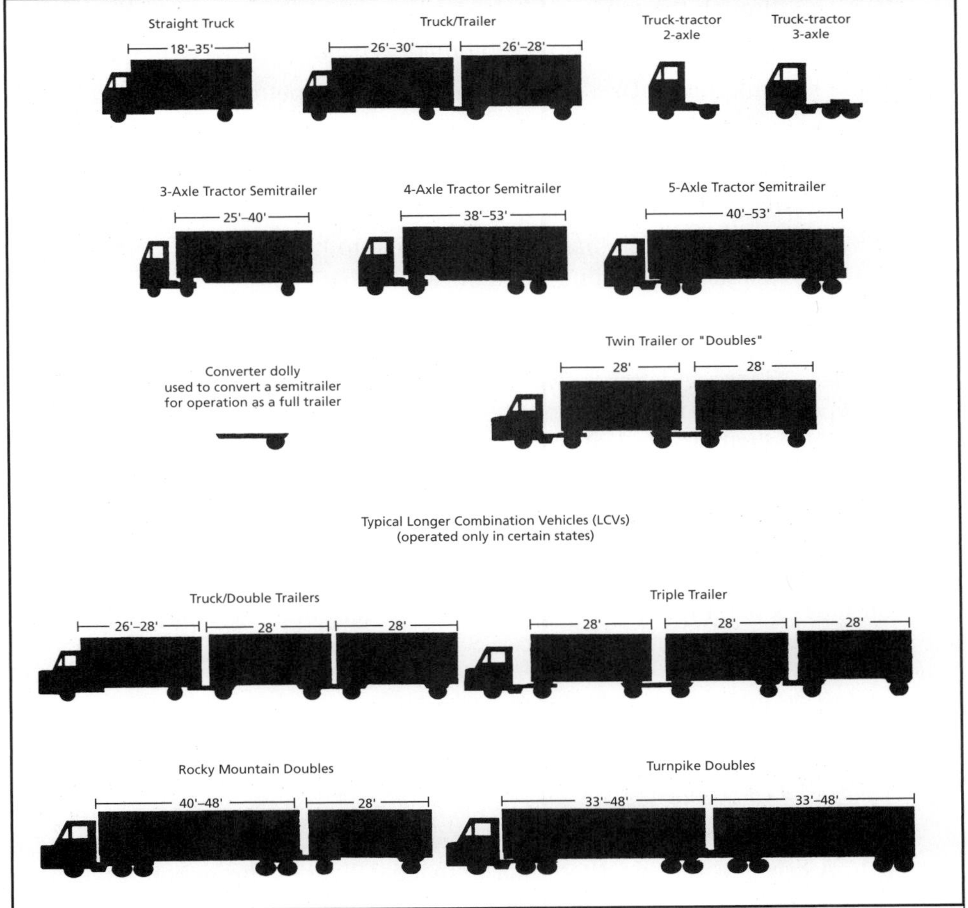

Source: American Trucking Trends 2003, American Trucking Associations (Alexandria, VA: ATA, 2003) p. 60.

run with more than five axles, a permit is required. If the empty vehicle weighs 30,000 pounds, the maximum net payload is 50,000 pounds or 25 tons.

The net carrying capacity of line-haul vehicles is also affected by the density of the freight. A 53 × 8 × 8-foot trailer has 3,392 cubic feet of space. If the commodity has a density of 10 pounds per cubic foot, then the maximum payload for the vehicle is 33,920 (3,392 $ft^3 \times 10\ lb/ft^3$). Shippers of low-density freight (below 16 lb/ft^3) advocate increased payload capacity of motor carrier vehicles.

CITY STRAIGHT TRUCKS

City vehicles, or "straight trucks," are normally smaller than line-haul vehicles and are single units (see Figure 3.5). The city truck has the cargo and power unit combined in one vehicle. The typical city truck is approximately 20 to 25 feet long with a cargo unit 15 to 20 feet long. However, there is growing use of small trailers (28 feet) to pick up and deliver freight in the city. These trailers can also be used for line-haul, which increases efficiency. Shipments can be "loaded to ride," meaning they will not require handling at the origin terminal.

SPECIAL VEHICLES

In addition to the line-haul and city vehicle classifications, the following special vehicles are designed to meet special shipper needs:

- Dry van: Standard trailer or straight truck with all sides enclosed
- Open top: Trailer top is open to permit loading of odd-sized freight through the top
- Flatbed: Trailer has no top or sides; used extensively to haul steel
- Tank trailer: Used to haul liquids such as petroleum products
- Refrigerated vehicles: Cargo unit has controlled temperature
- High cube: Cargo unit has drop-frame design or is higher than normal to increase cubic capacity
- Special: Vehicle has a unique design to haul a special commodity, such as liquefied gas or automobiles

The Department of Transportation's Federal Motor Carrier Safety Administration has established many rules and regulations governing the specifications of motor carrier vehicles. These regulations cover such areas as the number of lights on the vehicle, the type of brakes used, tire specifications, and other operating parts.[10] The overall allowable length and height of the vehicle are prescribed in the various states.[11]

Terminals

Some motor carrier operations, namely TL operations, might not require terminals for the movement of freight. The carrier uses the shipper's plant for loading and the consignee's plant for unloading. Typically, TL terminals normally provide dispatching, fuel, and maintenance services. Some carriers, such as Schneider National, are expanding the services offered by their terminal facilities to include restaurant and hotel offerings to give their drivers alternatives to truck stops. These terminals are designed primarily to accommodate drivers and equipment, but not freight.

Heavy LTL carriers use terminals for loading, or consolidation, only. However, as indicated earlier, LTL freight operations do require terminals. Some of the large LTL carriers, such as Yellow Freight or Roadway Express, have more than 400 terminals each. A driver will leave a terminal to make deliveries throughout the country but will always return to his or her domicile. A driver's domicile is the terminal that the driver originally left. The terminals used by motor carriers can be classified as pickup or delivery, break-bulk, and relay. A discussion of functions performed at each type of terminal follows.

PICKUP AND DELIVERY TERMINALS (PUD)

The terminal is a key facility in the operation of an LTL hub-and-spoke system. This section will present an expanded discussion of the types and roles of the terminal in this system.

The most common type of terminal found in the LTL system is the PUD terminal. These are also called *satellite* or ***end-of-the-line (EOL)*** terminals. The PUD terminal serves a local area and provides direct contact with both shippers and receivers. The basic transportation service provided at this terminal is the pickup and/or delivery of freight on peddle runs. A **peddle run** is a route that is driven daily out of the PUD terminal for the purposes of collecting freight for outbound moves or delivering freight from inbound moves. A PUD terminal will have several peddle runs in its customer operating area. Figure 3.6 gives an example of how a peddle run is designed. The PUD terminal is located in Altoona, Pennsylvania. Attached to it are four peddle runs, one each to Tyrone, State College, Lewistown, and Huntington. Every Monday through Friday morning, a driver will depart the Altoona terminal and deliver freight to customers located on that driver's assigned peddle. During and after the deliveries, freight will be picked up from customers and returned with the driver to the Altoona terminal at the end of the day. When all the drivers return at the end of their shifts, the Altoona terminal will have freight to be consolidated and moved outbound from customers in Tyrone, State College, Lewiston, and Huntington to customers in other areas of the country.

Note that there are two elements of a peddle run, one called **stem time** and the other called peddle time. Stem time is the time that elapses from when the driver leaves the terminal until the driver makes the first pickup or delivery; it is also the time that elapses from when the driver makes the last pickup or delivery until returning to the terminal. This is nonrevenue-producing time because no shipments are handled. A carrier would want to locate PUD terminals in such a way that this

FIGURE 3.6 Terminal Peddle Run

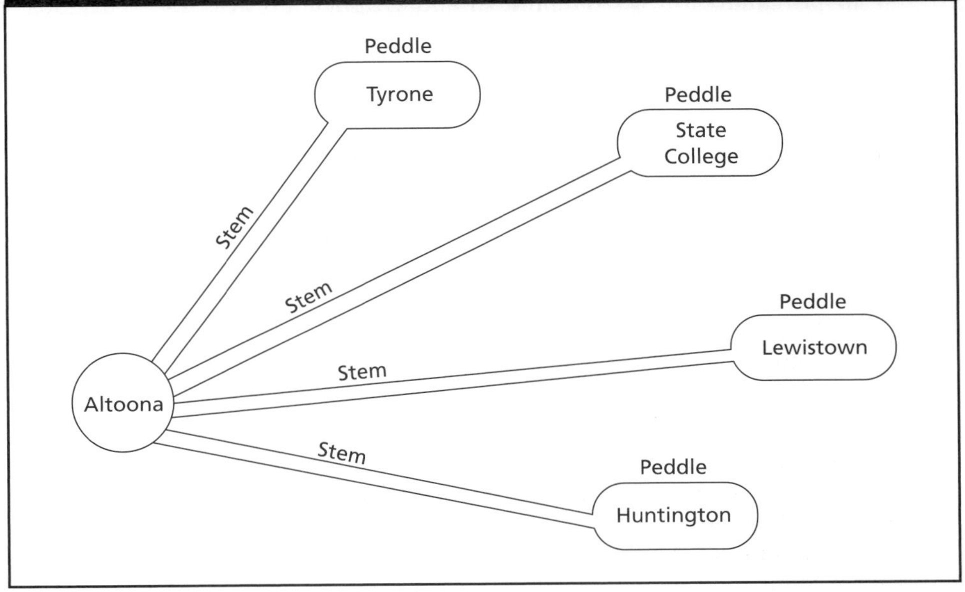

nonrevenue-producing travel time is minimized. (This aspect of LTL service will be discussed later in this chapter.) The other type of time is peddle time. This is the time during which the driver is actively involved in the pickup and delivery of freight. This is revenue-producing time because it occurs when shipments are handled. Obviously, carriers would want to maximize the amount of time a driver spent performing these activities.

The basic terminal services performed at these facilities are consolidation and dispersion. For example, freight moving inbound to Altoona from other terminals (passing through a break-bulk) will be "broken" into individual deliveries by peddle run to be handled by the driver during that particular shift. Freight that is brought back by the peddle drivers for movement inbound from Altoona will be consolidated into line-haul trailers for subsequent movement to the appropriate break-bulk. This is a basic cross-dock type of operation with the direction of freight flow across the dock that changes depending on whether the move is inbound or outbound.

The dispatch operation provided at the PUD terminal is critical to the operating efficiency of the peddle runs. Freight can be picked up on peddle runs in one of two ways. First, a customer on a peddle run might have a standing order for a pickup every day at 10 a.m. The PUD driver is aware of this, so the customer has no need to notify the carrier in advance for the pickup. Second, a customer might call the local PUD terminal to order service for a pickup. This is where the local dispatcher becomes involved. The dispatcher records the nature of the shipment and required time of pickup and assigns that shipment to the driver on the appropriate peddle run. The PUD driver will periodically call in to the dispatcher to determine the order and frequencies of new pickup requests. Obviously, the dispatcher needs to be familiar with the geography of the peddle runs and the capacity of the PUD drivers and trailers to efficiently route freight with the appropriate vehicle.

Other services that are provided at the PUD terminal might include tracing, rating and billing, sales, and claims. However, some carriers are beginning to centralize these functions at break-bulks or other locations by taking advantage of telecommunications technology. For example, some LTL carriers use the Internet for tracing purposes. When the customer accesses the carrier's website, the shipper keys in the pro number or waybill number and the system provides the current status of the shipment.

BREAK-BULK TERMINALS

Another type of terminal found in an LTL hub-and-spoke system is called a **break-bulk**. This facility performs both consolidation and dispersion (or break-bulk) services. Customers will rarely have contact with the operations at the break-bulk facility. The main purpose of this terminal is to provide an intermediate point where freight with common destinations from the PUD terminals is combined in a single trailer for movement to the delivering PUD terminal. This can be seen in Figure 3.7. Break-bulks will have many PUD terminals assigned to them as primary loading points. For example, assume that a shipper in Toledo, Ohio, wanted to send an LTL shipment to a customer in Pottstown, Pennsylvania. The Toledo PUD terminal is attached to the Cleveland, Ohio break-bulk, and the Philadelphia PUD terminal, which handles the Pottstown peddle, is attached to the Lancaster, Pennsylvania, break-bulk. At the completion of the peddle run, the Toledo driver brings the shipment back to the Toledo PUD terminal. There it is sorted and combined with other shipments going to the Lancaster break-bulk service area. (This could include all PUD terminals covering significant portions of Pennsylvania, New

FIGURE 3.7 Break-Bulk Terminal

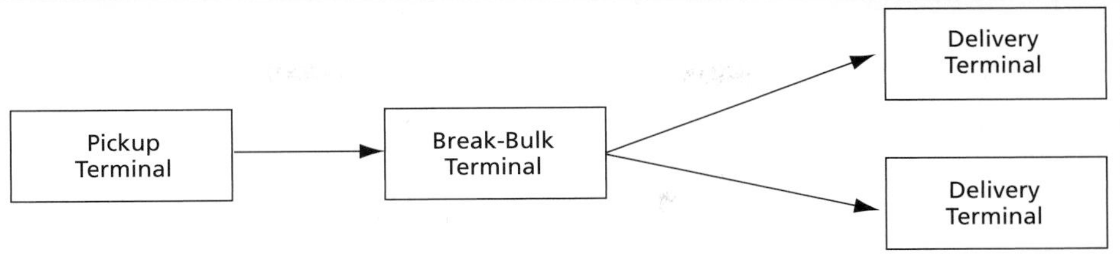

York, New Jersey, and parts of Maryland.) These shipments are consolidated into one trailer that will be dispatched to the Lancaster break-bulk.

Once the trailer arrives in Lancaster, it will be unloaded, and all of the freight destined to Philadelphia and its peddle runs will be loaded into an outbound trailer. This trailer will be dispatched from the break-bulk and arrive at the Philadelphia terminal to be unloaded in the early morning so the freight can be segregated into peddle delivery vehicles for an early morning delivery schedule. So, just as with the airline hub-and-spoke system, the LTL system utilizes the full capacity of its vehicles in the line-haul operation.

Break-bulk facilities also serve as driver domiciles. City drivers located at a PUD terminal will always remain in their local area during their shift and will be able to return home when it is over. Line-haul drivers, however, might or might not be able to return home after a trip, depending on the length of haul they are assigned. For example, a turn means that a line-haul driver is assigned a load to be taken from the break-bulk (domicile) to a PUD terminal that is no more than 5.5 hours away. Because of DOT-mandated driving limits, that line-haul driver can make the trip, drop the trailer, and pick up another shipment destined back to the break-bulk within the hours-of-service driving limit. However, a movement that requires more than 5.5 hours driving time in one direction will require a "layover"; that is, when the driver reaches the destination, a 10-hour rest period is required before that driver will be able to take a return load back to the break-bulk and return to the domicile. Therefore, at the maximum, a driver facing an 11-hour run with an 10-hour layover and an 11-hour return trip will return to the domicile within 32 hours of the original departure. Sometimes, however, a return load is not immediately available, which will delay the driver's return.

RELAY TERMINALS

Relay terminals are different from the PUD and break-bulk terminals in that freight is never touched. The relay terminal is necessitated by the maximum hours-of-service regulation that is imposed on drivers. Under DOT enforcement, drivers were permitted to drive a maximum of 10 hours after 8 consecutive hours off duty. (This was until January 3, 2004. After that, new driving restrictions were enforced. The upcoming section titled "Labor" will discuss these new driving rules.) At the relay terminal, one driver substitutes for another who has accumulated the maximum hours of service. (The term **slip seat** also has been used to describe the relay terminal operation.)

As indicated in Figure 3.8, the location of the relay terminal is a maximum driving time of 11 hours from an origin. If the relay terminal is located 5.5 hours from an origin, the driver can drive to the relay terminal and return within the maximum 11 hours. (This is also called a "turn.")

FIGURE 3.8 Relay Terminal

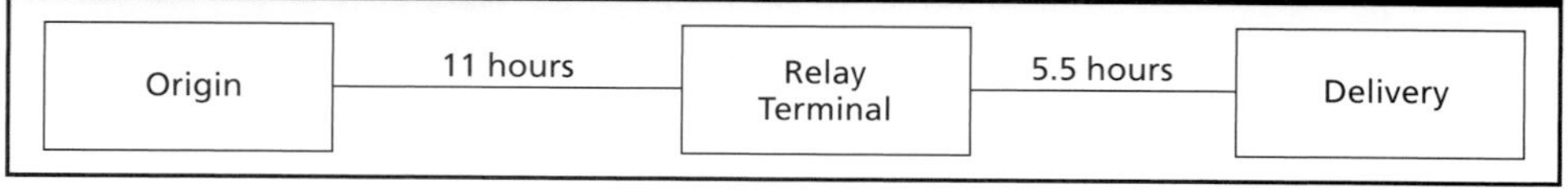

Using the example given in Figure 3.8, assume that the driving time is 15 hours between origin and destination. Without the relay terminal, the transit time is 26 hours. After 11 hours of driving, the driver goes off duty for 10 consecutive hours. Upon resuming duty, the driver drives 5 hours to the destination. The total elapsed time is 26 hours (11 + 10 + 5). The driver drives 11 hours to the relay terminal, and another driver takes over and drives the vehicle to the destination. In this instance, the relay terminal reduces the transit time by 10 hours, the mandated driver off-duty time. Under the new driver hours-of-service rules, relays still play an important role in LTL motor carrier operations. However, some carriers might have to rethink their relay structure because of the new, extended driver hours.

An alternative to the relay terminal is the use of a sleeper team—two drivers. While one driver accumulates the off-duty time in the sleeper berth of the tractor, the other driver is driving. The sleeper team has been most successful for long trips with many destinations.

Terminal Management Decisions

Many types of operating decisions need to be made when utilizing terminals in a carrier's network. Along with making these decisions, carrier management must also consider their strategic implications. This section will address a few of these types of decisions.

NUMBER OF TERMINALS

In many modes, this is a relatively simple decision. For example, passenger airline terminals will be located close to major population centers. This decision, however, usually does not belong to the carrier but to some local government agency. Railroads must also make this decision but are limited by geography and track locations for terminal sites. Railroads will not normally have many terminals in their networks. The mode with probably the most difficult decision in this area is LTL motor carriage, primarily because of the vast numbers of terminals in these systems and the relatively small investment needed to develop a terminal site.

The obvious question for an LTL motor carrier is, "How many terminals should we have?" The obvious answer is, "It depends." First, the degree of market penetration and customer service desired by the carrier will help determine the number of terminals to establish. In theory, the more terminals, the closer to the customer, the better the service. This also has proven to be true in practice. Realistically, at some point additional terminals will result in no incremental increase in service and might even detract from service.

Second, the dilemma of small terminal versus long peddle must be addressed. Figure 3.9 represents this situation. In Example 1, assume that a carrier's market is the state of Pennsylvania, with one terminal located in Harrisburg with peddle runs to Erie, Scranton, Pittsburgh, and Philadelphia. This network utilizes only one terminal but has extremely long and expensive stem times for its peddle runs. The terminal must also be large to accommodate the volume of freight that will come from these four peddles. Example 2 shows a network that utilizes two terminals, each

FIGURE 3.9 Small Terminal Versus Long Peddle

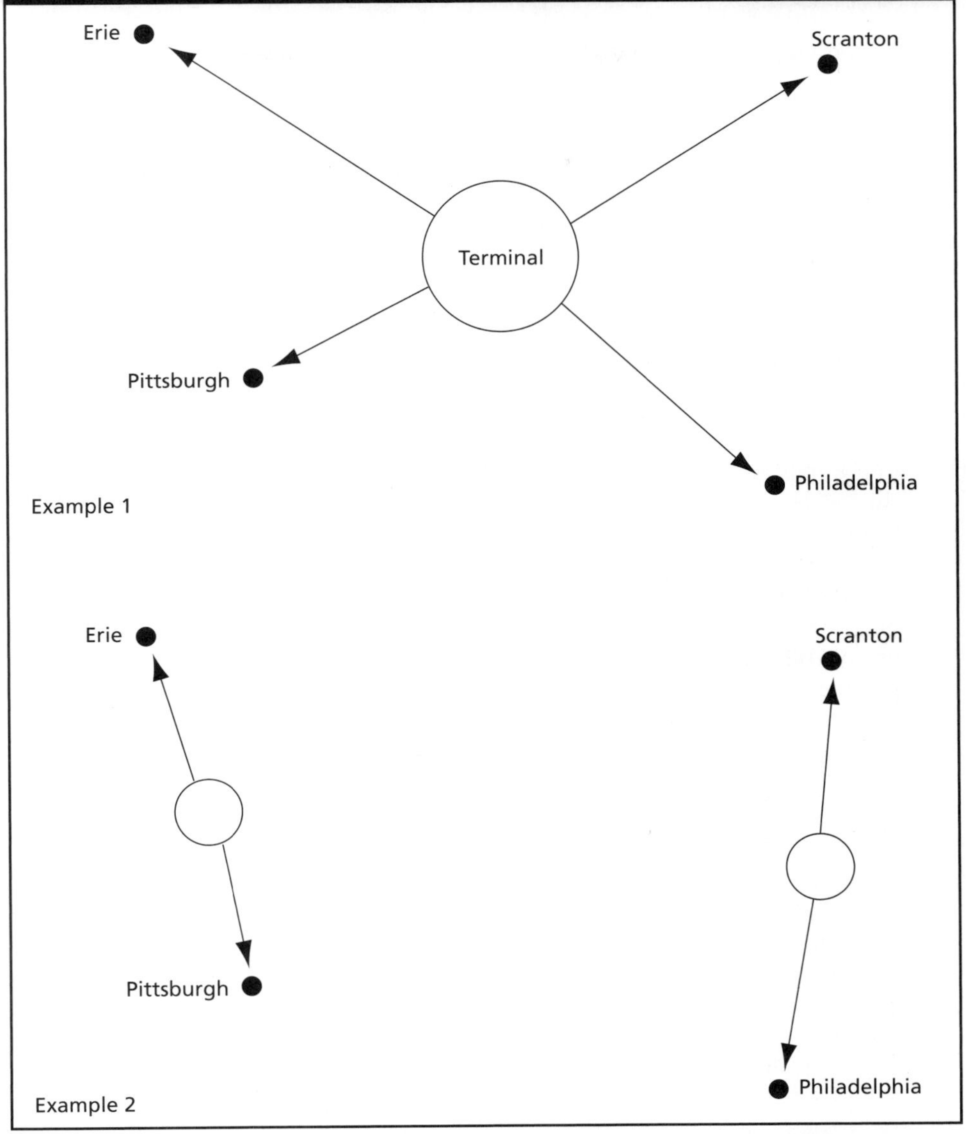

having two peddle runs with significantly shorter stem times. Each terminal in this scenario is smaller than the one terminal in Example 1. Thus, Example 2 has doubled the number of terminals but decreased stem times for customer PUD. The small-terminal-versus-long-peddle decision would be made based on the service implications of establishing terminals closer to customers versus the cost of adding another terminal.

Many times when shippers are making distribution system decisions, they assume that manufacturing facilities are fixed and that warehouse decisions must be made based on this fixed network. This assumption is also part of the terminal decision process for LTL motor carriers, except their "manufacturing facilities" are break-bulk terminals. Whether or not another terminal can be added to a break-bulk's operating region might simply be a question of available capacity at that break-bulk.

Normally, each PUD terminal is assigned at least one door at a break-bulk. To add another PUD terminal means eliminating an existing terminal, physically adding another door to the break-bulk, or improving the productivity at the break-bulk to turn trailers in doors more than once per shift.

LOCATIONS OF TERMINALS

Closely related to the decision of how many terminals to establish is the decision of *where* to establish them. As previously mentioned, for airlines and railroads, this decision can be relatively simple because of geographic, government, and demand variables. LTL carriers, however, must consider some other variables. First, the DOT limits the amount of time a driver can continuously operate a vehicle before a rest period is required. Currently, this limit is 11 hours, so optimally, PUD terminals should be located no more than 11 hours away from a break-bulk. This would allow a driver to complete the run in one trip. Second, PUD terminals should be located to minimize the distance that freight would need to be backhauled to the break-bulk. The assumption here is that freight flows from east to west and north to south in the United States. When a shipment is picked up, the idea is to send that freight in one of these directions as soon as possible. For example, given that a carrier has two break-bulks, one in Lancaster, Pennsylvania, and the other in Columbus, Ohio, where would a PUD terminal based in Pittsburgh send its freight? Based on the assumption made earlier about freight flows, Pittsburgh would send its freight to Columbus; that is, a shipment picked up by a Pittsburgh peddle driver would begin its east–west journey more productively by being sent to Columbus because if it were sent to Lancaster, it would conceptually duplicate this distance when it began its journey from Lancaster to the west (actually passing right by Columbus). Finally, market penetration and potential will help determine terminal location. As mentioned in the decision process for determining the number of terminals, getting closer to the customer can many times improve the level of service given to that customer.

Recent trends in the LTL sector have seen significant reductions in the number of terminals as these carriers strive to provide overnight and second-day delivery to more and more customers. To do this, many interterminal runs have been realigned with the resultant elimination of intermediate handling. This has resulted in increased load factors and reduced transit times. Less handling has also improved the claims experience for the LTL carriers. The long-haul LTL carriers will still favor the hub-and-spoke operation, whereas the regional carriers will still look toward fewer terminals with more direct runs.

COST STRUCTURE

Fixed Versus Variable Cost Components

The cost structure of the motor carrier industry consists of high levels of variable costs and relatively low fixed costs. Approximately 70 to 90 percent of the cost is variable, and 10 to 30 percent is fixed. The public investment in the highway system is a major factor contributing to this low fixed-cost structure because the highway is the motor carrier's "right of way." In addition, the motor carrier is able to increase or decrease the number of vehicles used in short periods of time and in small increments of capacity. Lastly, the carriers as a group (with the exception of the LTL carrier) do not require expensive terminals. The small investment in terminals also contributes to low fixed costs. The bulk of the motor carrier's cost then is associated with daily operating costs—the variable costs of fuel, wages, maintenance, and highway user fees (e.g., fuel tax, vehicle registration).

The discussion of motor carrier cost will begin with the vehicle operating costs of long-distance fleets transporting products in tractor–trailers. These data can be compared only to similar operations; that is, comparisons cannot be made to local motor carrier operations (PUD). Figure 3.10 indicates that in 2001 the total cost to operate a tractor–trailer was 207.1 cents per mile. As indicated, approximately 80 percent of the cost to operate an intercity tractor–trailer is the variable. The remaining 20 percent is associated with the fixed costs of: vehicle interest; depreciation and interest on terminals, garages, and offices; management; and overhead (such as utilities). For carriers handling LTL freight, the fixed cost is higher. That is, additional terminals, management, and overhead expenses are required to handle small-sized shipments.

The two categories with the largest share of the variable costs are labor and fuel. A discussion of each of these two variable costs will follow.

LABOR

The cost of drivers accounts for 19 percent of the total costs per vehicle mile, as shown in Figure 3.10. Labor costs (wages plus fringe benefits) usually absorb about 41 percent of a carrier's revenue dollar. That is, 41 cents out of every dollar in revenue goes to labor. The average annual wage in 2001 was $40,365.[12]

The over-the-road (intercity) driver is typically paid on a mileage basis, such as 32.5 cents per mile; local drivers are paid by the hour. Over-the-road drivers are normally paid an hourly rate for operating delays resulting from loading/unloading, accidents, weather, and the like.

The DOT enforces maximum hours of service regulation. As of January 3, 2004, the DOT's **driving time regulations** permit drivers to drive a maximum of 11 hours

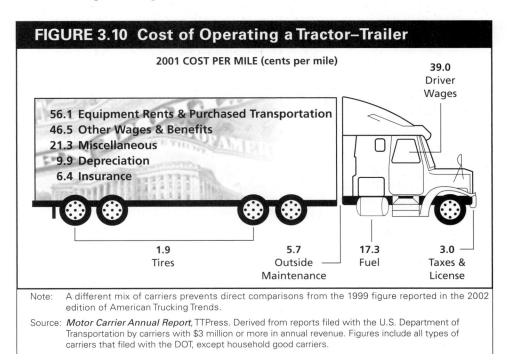

FIGURE 3.10 Cost of Operating a Tractor–Trailer

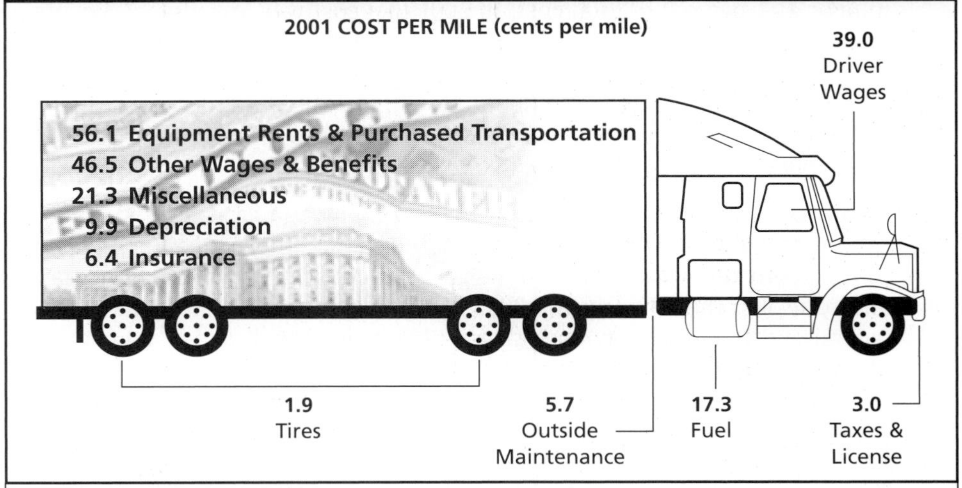

Note: A different mix of carriers prevents direct comparisons from the 1999 figure reported in the 2002 edition of American Trucking Trends.

Source: *Motor Carrier Annual Report*, TTPress. Derived from reports filed with the U.S. Department of Transportation by carriers with $3 million or more in annual revenue. Figures include all types of carriers that filed with the DOT, except household good carriers.

after being off duty for 10 consecutive hours. A driver is permitted to be on duty a maximum of 14 hours after 10 consecutive hours off duty. In addition, no driver can drive after accumulating 60 hours on duty in 7 consecutive days, or 70 hours in 8 consecutive days. Following a federal court decision to overturn the new driving time rules, a law was enacted extending the new driving time rules until September 30, 2005, or until the FMCSA complies with the federal court order.

The most pressing labor issue facing motor carriers, particularly TL carriers, is the shortage of qualified drivers. Part of the problem is that the federal government, as part of an overall safety program, imposed stringent driver licensing requirements. Since April 1992, all operators of vehicles over 26,000 pounds gross vehicle weight must hold a commercial driver's license (CDL). Although CDLs are issued by the driver's home state, the requirements are mandated by the Federal DOT. Along with the new licensing requirements, the DOT also imposed stringent rules dealing with drug and alcohol abuse. Poor driving records and inability to pass the CDL test eliminated many marginal drivers.

The hardships imposed by the very nature of long-haul motor carrier operations have also impacted the availability of drivers. Drivers are frequently away from home for long periods and often have to assist with the loading and unloading of trailers. This life-style is not as attractive as other career choices, so the available pool from which drivers might be drawn has declined. The motor carrier industry has undertaken several initiatives to counteract the problem of driver retention and recruitment. They have raised the per-mile and per-hour pay rates, scheduled drivers home more frequently, and worked with shippers and consignees to make freight more "driver-friendly" (i.e., easier to load/unload, tarp, brace, etc.).

FUEL

Since 1974 the higher price of fuel has resulted in a rise in the relative proportion of fuel cost to total cost. For example, in 1976 fuel cost was 11.6 cents per mile or 19.8 percent of the total cost per mile, but in 1985 fuel cost was 24.6 cents per mile or 21.1 percent of total cost. In 2001 fuel cost was lower at 17.3 cents per mile or about 8 percent of total costs (see Figure 3.10). Carriers have experienced a 181-percent increase in diesel fuel prices from 1976 to 2003—approximately 53 cents per gallon in 1976 to about $1.49 per gallon in 2003. Ever since 1974 fuel prices have changed more frequently over a larger range due to fluctuations in supply.

Included in the price of the diesel fuel is a highway user tax imposed by both the federal and state governments. The fuel tax plus other taxes for highway use are payments made by the carrier to the government for the construction, maintenance, and control of the highways. In 2002 the motor carrier industry paid $30.7 billion in federal and state highway user taxes.[13] The federal fuel tax is 24.4 cents per gallon of diesel fuel plus a state average of 21.9 cents per gallon.[14]

Economies of Scale

There does not appear to be major economies of scale for large-scale motor carrier operations. Economies of scale are realized through more extensive use of large-sized plants or indivisible inputs. However, the extensive use of indivisible inputs is not characteristic of all motor carrier operations. In addition, the large number of small firms, especially in the TL segment, suggests that small-sized operations are competitive. The concentration of the LTL business is indicative of economies of operation in this segment.

In the short run, certain economies exist in the greater use of indivisible inputs such as terminals, management specialists, and information systems. The average cost of such inputs will decrease as output (greater use) increases. Such economies of use justify the rather large-sized firms that operate transcontinentally, especially in the LTL segment. Carriers that operate over wide geographic areas require more terminals, elaborate information systems, and more management specialists than those carriers that operate over narrow geographic areas.

For TL operations, very limited investment is required for terminals, but information systems are becoming increasingly important to efficient operations. Computers in tractors, direct satellite communication to drivers, and bar coding with optical scanners are a few examples of the sophisticated information systems and technology that now exist in the motor carrier industry. Many of the TL carrier inputs (vehicle, labor, fuel) can be increased one vehicle at a time in response to the small increases in demand.

Operational cost trade-offs exist between large and small carriers. A large-scale operation affords savings in purchase economies of equipment and in such inputs as fuel, parts, and interest in loans. (The small carrier might enjoy some of these purchase economies from larger retailers of motor carrier vehicle suppliers, such as truck stops.) On the other hand, large LTL motor carriers might be unionized and thus pay higher labor rates, but the motor carrier industry is less unionized today than it was in 1980.

Overall, long-term economies of scale appear not to be significant in TL motor carrier transportation and are present to some degree in the LTL segment. This degree of scale economies has implications for competition and the market's capability to control such competition.

OPERATING RATIO

A measure of operating efficiency used by motor carriers is the **operating ratio**. The operating ratio measures the percent of operating expenses to operating revenue.

$$\textit{Operating Ratio} = (\textit{Operating expenses/Operating revenue}) \times 100$$

Operating expenses are those expenses directly associated with the transportation of freight, excluding nontransportation expenses and interest costs. Operating revenues are the total revenues generated from freight transportation services; nontransportation services are excluded. Motor carriers might use the operating ratio to support a rate increase request. The closer the operating ratio is to 100, the more indicative of the possible need to raise rates to increase total revenues. In today's market, however, a rate increase might not be a feasible solution. Carriers are more likely to seek supply chain solutions with shippers and receivers to reduce operating expenses, thus increasing operating margin.

An operating ratio of 94 indicates that 94 cents of every operating revenue dollar is consumed by operating expenses, leaving 6 cents of every operating dollar to cover interest costs and a return to the owners. LTL motor carrier operating ratios usually range between 93 and 96, whereas the TL segment could see ratios in the low to mid 80s. The operating ratio is also a benchmark or barometer of financial viability. Obviously, if the operating ratio is equal to or greater than 100, there is no revenue available to cover fixed or overhead costs or to return a profit to owners or stockholders. Increasing revenues and/or reducing costs are viable approaches to resolving the problem of a high operating ratio.

STOP OFF

Discounts Still a Major Factor in LTL Pricing

For well over two decades now, discounting off of less-than-truckload (LTL) motor carrier class rates has been a major factor in pricing in this sector of the trucking industry, and that continues to be the case to this day. In fact, it's unusual to find a shipper these days that isn't receiving some type of discount on their LTL rates.

When discounts first took root in the early 1980s they were pretty modest, with many starting at around 5 percent. But as time went on and competition for shippers' business became stiffer, discounts began to escalate to 10, 20, 30, 40 percent and even higher. Now it's commonplace to see many shippers enjoying discounts in the high 50-percent to low 60-percent range.

To get an idea of the range of discounts that are currently being offered by LTL carriers, all you need to do is look at the annual reports that regional motor carrier rate bureaus are required to file with the Surface Transportation Board (STB). These annual reports list the range of discounts the rate bureaus' collective members have established with their customers.

Here are the ranges for discounts that were just recently filed with the STB by the nation's six major rate bureaus:

- EC-MAC Motor Carriers Association—from 20 percent to 76 percent
- North American Transportation Council—from 5 percent to 85 percent
- Middlewest Motor Freight Bureau—from 25 percent to 85 percent
- Pacific Inland Tariff Bureau—from 30 percent to 76 percent
- Rocky Mountain Tariff Bureau—from 30 percent to 76 percent
- Southern Motor Carriers Rate Conference—from 20 percent to 83 percent

Many readers may be surprised by those high-end numbers. Before you ask your carrier for such deep discounts, however, let me caution you that they are reserved for only the very largest companies. Shippers commanding discounts in the 70- and 80-percent ranges are rare birds indeed.

If you're already enjoying discounts and those discounts haven't changed in some time, there's nothing to stop you from sitting down with your carriers and working out some sort of upward adjustment. Carriers are free to make any revisions to their pricing they may wish, and they don't need to seek prior approval from any rate bureau or governmental agency. All that's necessary is for both sides to come to an agreement. (Of course every shipper should make certain it gets something in writing—what many shippers and carriers refer to as a "pricing agreement"—that sets forth the full terms of the deal and is signed by an officer of the carrier.)

Stay vigilant by watching rate bureaus' annual reports and you'll be sure to keep up with the pack when it comes to discounts.

__Ray Bohman__, a well-known consultant and author, is editor of several highly successful newsletters on transportation and is a consultant to a number of national trade associations. He is president of The Bohman Group, consultants and publishers in the freight-transportation field. His offices are located at 27 Bay Lane, Chatham, MA 02663. Phone: (508) 945-2272.

Source: "Discounts still a major factor in LTL pricing." *Logistics Management*, July 2004, p. 23. Reprinted with permission of *Logistics Management*.

Since the founding of the United States, the federal government has felt that it has the responsibility to provide highways to meet the national defense and commerce needs of the country. At first, the federal government was the sole financier of highways, but over the years, state and local governments have assumed a greater role. Today, the state and local governments assume the responsibility for maintaining the highways, while the federal government provides up to 90 percent of the construction cost of new highways with the designated network. The Federal Highway Administration (FHWA), part of the DOT, oversees the National Highway System (NHS). The NHS was defined in 1995 and consists of the 42,000-mile interstate highway system, 113,7000 miles of existing state and federal noninterstate highways, and

3,000 additional miles devoted to specialized freight transportation needs. Although the NHS includes slightly over 4 percent of the total road mileage, this network sees the transportation of more than 75 percent of intercity freight traffic.

The Intermodal Surface Transportation Efficiency Act (ISTEA) has been replaced by the Transporation Equity Act for the Twenty-first Century (TEA21), which has continued the role of FHWA in this area. Additional funds were added under TEA21, which remained in place until 2003. More than $73 billion was expected to be spent on roads and related projects during this period.

FUNDING

Highway users—motor carrier vehicle and automobile operators—pay for the construction, maintenance, and policing of highways through highway user taxes. The total amount of taxes paid depends on the use of the highway. The motor carrier incurs a cost for the use of the highway that is related to its amount of use. This situation contributes to the high variable cost structure of the motor carrier.

Federal and state governments assess highway user taxes. The federal highway user taxes are paid into the Federal Highway Trust Fund. From the Federal Highway Trust Fund, the federal government pays 90 percent of the construction costs for the interstate system and 50 percent of the construction costs for all other federal-aid roads. Table 3.1 indicates items taxed and the rate assessed by the Federal Highway Trust Fund.

The state also assesses highway user taxes to defray the cost of construction, maintenance, and policing of highways. The state taxes include fuel tax, vehicle registration fees, ton-mile taxes, and special-use permits.

Implied in the highway user tax concept is the philosophy that the highway predominantly confers benefits on specific groups and individuals. Although the general public benefits from increased mobility and the availability of a wide variety of goods and services, the motor vehicle user is presumed to be the major benefactor and therefore is expected to pay a larger share of the costs. An analogy that illustrates this concept is the property owner who pays property taxes that include an assessment for streets (access to the property). Much debate exists as to whether motor carrier vehicles pay a fair share of the total cost of highways. In 2000 all modes paid $89.8 billion in state and federal user taxes and fees, of which motor vehicles paid $36 billion, or 40 percent.[15] The central issue is whether motor carriers should pay for the added construction and maintenance costs caused by their heavier weight.

Table 3.1 Federal Highway Trust Fund Tax Rates

Commodity	Tax
Gasoline	18.4 cents/gallon
Diesel fuel	24.4 cents/gallon
Gasohol	12.3–15.2 cents/gallon
Tires	15 cents/lb. for tires 40–70 lb. $4.50 + 30 cents/lb. for tires 70–90 lb. $10.50 + 50 cents/lb. for tires over 90 lb.
New truck and trailer sales	12% of manufacturer's sales price on trucks weighing more than 33,000 lb. and trailers exceeding 26,000 lb.
Highway vehicle use tax	For trucks weighing 55,000 lb. or more, $100 + $22 for each additional 1,000 lb. up to a maximum of $550

Source: Federal Highway Administration, Highway Trust Fund Primer.

Because each state must pay for the maintenance, policing, and construction of the highways within its boundaries, each state attempts to ensure receipt of taxes for using its highways. For a motor carrier operation over many states, this means buying vehicle registrations in many states and maintaining records of miles driven in a particular state so that the state will receive a fuel tax or ton-mile tax. Such record-keeping adds a cost to the carrier's operation.

CURRENT ISSUES

Safety

Some members of the motor carrier industry have come to realize that improved safety can mean improved profitability. After the regulatory reform that took place in the early 1980s, motor carriers found themselves with more direct control of their economic and operating policies. Deficiencies in safety can translate into decreased profitability because of expensive claims for lost or damaged goods, increased insurance premiums, accidents, fines, and so on. These consequences are not unique to the motor carrier industry; in fact, they apply to the entire transportation industry.

The FMCSA has developed rules under which its inspectors determine whether a carrier is fit from a safety rule compliance perspective. The system includes three categories: Satisfactory, Conditional, and Unsatisfactory. The FMCSA has the right to force a carrier to stop operating after a specific period has passed if the carrier has received an Unsatisfactory rating and improvement is not made. The period varies depending on the type of traffic the carrier is transporting. If the carrier is hauling nonhazardous materials, they must cease operations 60 days after his or her safety rating is found to be Unsatisfactory. If the company hauls hazardous materials, the period is reduced to 40 days. This only applies if the carrier does not correct the problems discovered in the FMCSA safety audit. There is also an appeal process that allows the carrier to correct any concerns as might be necessary.

The carrier might be allowed to continue to operate if there is a "good faith" effort on its part to correct the defects. Government regulations require that the FMCSA review a carrier who is found in violation within 45 days of that company's request. If the carrier transports hazardous materials, the time period for review upon request drops to 30 days.

Many shippers seek safety fitness information as part of their selection process, so there is considerable pressure on carriers to operate safely. Many transportation contracts contain clauses that permit the shipper to cancel the contract if the carrier's safety rating is Unsatisfactory.

A major related concern is that of alcohol and drug abuse. It has been estimated that American industry pays $50 to 100 billion for the effects and results of substance abuse in the workplace every year, either for the cost of accidents or losses in productivity.

In response to this problem, the motor carrier industry has begun to move toward drug screening for its employees. Drug and alcohol testing are required in the following circumstances:

- As a requirement for employment
- As a part of a regular physical exam required of current employees
- For "cause," required after any accident
- On a random selection basis

Drug and alcohol rules require motor carriers to have an anti-drug program, as well as drug testing that includes random and postaccident testing. All fleets, regardless of size, are required to have a complete program, including random and postaccident testing in place. These rules apply to the owner/operator as well. Many states have drug-testing programs of their own as well, with which the carrier must comply.

When proper care is taken to implement a substance abuse program, most drivers support the program because it makes their job safer. Proper care in implementing a substance abuse program involves relating substance abuse to health and problems, while leaving moral judgments to the individual. Such care also includes setting consistent policies that are enforceable and apply to every employee, making policies for violations known, and providing counseling and rehabilitation services for those employees who have substance abuse problems. Support for employees with problems is critical for any substance abuse program to be successful.

Other areas of safety concerns are drivers' hours-of-service and fatigue issues. Before January 3, 2004, the hours-of-service rules dated from before World War II and did not reflect modern realities. Under a complex formula of allowed driving and required rest periods, a driver can be on duty for no more than 60 hours in 7 days or 70 hours in 8 days. As previously discussed, these rules have been altered to address today's changing environment.

Another safety issue receiving attention deals with vehicle size and weight. As shown earlier, there are a number of different sizes of vehicles, and each has its own weight-carrying regulations. Recent studies have analyzed increasing total gross vehicle weight to 94,000 pounds with the addition of a third axle to the trailer. The studies have also addressed increased use of triples. All these issues include safety concerns and will require federal legislation before any changes can be made. In addition to safety, there are significant economic issues for the motor carrier industry because these larger vehicles will improve productivity and lower cost.

Technology

The use of satellite technology has a major impact on the motor carrier industry. Using global positioning technology (GPS), satellites are being used to track vehicles throughout their movement from origin to destination. The use of satellites allows the carriers to pinpoint the location of the vehicle and relay this information to the customer. The interaction between the driver, using an on-board computer, and a home-base computer allows route or arrival adjustment for poor weather or road conditions, and these adjustments can be communicated to the customers.

One area where satellite communication has had a very positive effect is in the movement of hazardous materials. For example, phosphorous pentasulfide (P2S5), a very dangerous chemical if not handled properly, is shipped by Bee Line Trucking for the Monsanto Company, a corporation in the food, medicine, and health industries. The two companies have teamed up to provide safe transportation for this dangerous chemical. The satellites used in the transport allow communication between the driver and a terminal in San Diego, which forwards the information on location and status to both Bee Line and Monsanto. This tracking allows for quick reaction to any accidents or spills, and the computers can give the name of the authority in the area to call in case any emergency action needs to be taken. Satellite communication will continue to play a role in improved safety and customer service for motor carriers into the future.

LTL Rates

Since the early 1980s the LTL segment of the motor carrier industry has used discounts from published tariffs as a means of pricing segments to attract traffic of large shippers. The Interstate Commerce Commission (ICC) was eliminated under the ICC Termination Act of 1995 (ICCTA1995) and with it, most of the last vestiges of motor carrier rate regulation. Although certain portions of rate oversight were transferred to the then newly created Surface Transportation Board, for all practical purposes LTL rates are subject to the free-market environment. In addition, the common carrier obligation to serve was preserved, but absent was an enforcement mechanism, which the marketplace will control as well. As it currently stands, the shipper has more choices for LTL today than existed during the height of regulation.

A limited amount of antitrust immunity was also preserved, but only for classifications, mileage guides rules, and general rate adjustments. Individual carrier rates are subject to antitrust action but cannot be challenged that the rate is unreasonably high. This is a direct reversal of the situation that existed under the old ICC.

There is no longer any requirement to file tariffs, and contracts can be used instead. Although carriers are still required to maintain rates, rules, and classifications, they only need be furnished to the shipper upon request. In a departure from previous regulation, rates need not be in writing to be enforceable. Shippers, however, must exercise due caution because federal oversight and enforcement is greatly diminished.

This law also reduced the time for recovery of disputed freight charges from 3 years to 18 months. If either the carrier or the shipper feels that the charges are incorrect, they must file suit no longer than 18 months from the date of the shipment. The lack of tariffs might make this more difficult unless the shippers have obtained the carrier's prices and rules in writing before tendering the shipment to the carrier.

Financial Stability

Another major concern in the motor carrier industry is financial stability. The operating ratios of many motor carriers have been in excess of 95 percent, and some companies have operating ratios of over 100. The high operating ratios are a clear indicator of the financial plight of many motor carriers and an indication of the low competitive rates.

Immediately after the initial lessening of economic regulation in 1980, a large number of motor carriers failed as the competitive environment became severe. Of the top 100 motor carriers in 1980, fewer than 10 were still in business in 1990. Only one new LTL was formed in this period that survived to the 1990s. The failures after 1990 were fewer but usually involved larger firms that could not continue to compete. In some cases, the unionized carriers were victims of labor unrest or shipper concerns about stability. In other cases, mergers and buyouts reduced the number of Class I carriers. Recent consolidations have also occurred in the TL sector as the larger carriers have taken over smaller firms to achieve market share.

In 2002 a total of 2,345 motor carrier firms failed, mostly with revenues between $5 million and $20 million. However, several larger carriers also succumbed to financial woes, with the two most notable failed carriers being Consolidated Freightways and A-P-A Transport.[16]

Overcapacity has periodically been a severe problem for the motor carrier industry, most recently during 1994 and 1995. Given that there is a finite amount of freight to be transported at any one time and there is little, if anything, that carriers can do to influence this, market share changes generally occur at the expense of one carrier over another. These periods of overcapacity also lead to severe pricing pressure, which can cause weaker carriers to exit the market. Shippers often exploit these factors and the "spot" market can drive prices below costs as carriers seek to move empty equipment.

Shippers have become increasingly cognizant of the failure rate among motor carriers, and many have introduced a financial evaluation of carriers into their overall decision framework for selecting carriers. When a carrier goes out of business, the interruption of service could have serious consequences.

Summary

- Table 3-2 offers a summary of motor carrier industry characteristics.
- Motor carriers have developed rapidly during the 20th century and now represent one of the most important modes of transportation for freight movement in the 21st century. U.S. business and most individuals depend in whole or in part upon motor carriers for the movement of goods.
- The public provision (federal, state, and local government units) of highways has played a major role in the development of the motor carrier because of the ubiquitous level of accessibility provided by the comprehensive U.S. highway system.
- The private carrier is a very important part of the motor carrier industry and a viable option to large and small companies requiring special services, such as grocery or food deliveries. The need of U.S. industry for dependable and controlled service has also contributed to the development.
- For-hire motor carriers can be classified in a number of useful ways, including local versus intercity, common versus contract, regulated versus exempt, general versus specialized, and TL versus LTL.
- One of the manifestations of deregulation has been the tremendous growth in the TL segment of the motor carrier business, especially among the small truckload carriers, which has significantly escalated the degree of intramodal competition.
- The LTL segment of the motor carrier industry has experienced increased concentration; that is, the larger carriers have generated a larger share of the total tonnage, as they have aggressively expanded and marketed their services.

Table 3.2 Summary of Motor Carrier Industry Characteristics

• General Service Characteristics	• Low Investments/Equipment
• Investments/Capital Outlays	• 90% Variable Costs, 10% Fixed
• Cost Structure	• Pure Competition
• Ease of Entry	• Compete on Price/Service
• Market Structure	• High-Valued Products
• How They Compete	• Large Number of Small Carriers (With Few Exceptions)
• Types of Commodities	• Long Distance/Metropolitan Destinations
• Number of Carriers	
• Markets in Which They Compete	
• Accessibility, Speed, Reliability, Frequency, and Lower Loss and Damage Rates	

- The motor carrier industry plays a major role in the movement of manufactured and food products (ie., higher-valued, time-sensitive traffic) because of its generally higher quality of service compared to other modes of transportation.
- The general service characteristics of motor carriers, including accessibility, speed, reliability, frequency, and lower loss and damage rates, have given motor carriers an advantage over other modes.
- Motor carriers offer a variety of equipment for use by shippers that reflect the distance of service and customer requirements.
- The cost structure of motor carriers is dominated by variable costs largely due to the carriers' ability to utilize a publicly provided right-of-way (highways) where payment is based upon user charges such as fuel taxes and licenses.
- Labor costs are an important element of the motor carrier industry, which tends to be much more labor intensive than other modes. Increased equipment size and more nonunion drivers have lessened the impact of wage costs during the 2000s.
- In contrast to railroads, motor carriers are regarded as having limited economies of scale; that is, small-scale operations are viable and competitive. The major exception would be the LTL carriers with their required investment in terminals. There is increasing evidence that there are some economies of scale among large LTL carriers.
- Public funding of highways and the level of user charges paid by motor carriers continue to be arguable issues because it is frequently maintained that motor carriers do not pay their fair share.
- A number of current issues face motor carriers, including safety, substance abuse, technology, undercharge claims, and state regulation.

Key Terms

break-bulk terminal, 108
carrying capacity, 103
driving regulations, 113
end-of-line terminal (EOL), 107
exempt carriers, 97
for-hire, 97
hub and spoke, 99
interstate highway system, 96
line-haul, 99
LTL (less than truckload), 98
operating ratio, 115
peddle run, 107
pickup and delivery (PUD), 99
relay terminal, 109
slip seat operation, 109
stem time, 107
TL (truckload), 98

Study Questions

1. The motor carrier is probably the most visible segment of the transportation system in the United States, but in many ways the motor carrier is also the most significant element of the freight transport industry. What factors account for the motor carrier's visibility and significance?
2. The railroad industry played a significant role in the development and growth of many cities and geographic regions during the 19th century. What role, if any, have motor carriers played during the 20th century in terms of economic development?
3. Private carriage is more important in the motor carrier segment of our transportation industry than any of the other four major modal segments. What factors have contributed to private carriage becoming so prevalent in the motor carrier area?
4. The so-called local carrier is also almost unique to the motor carrier industry. Why?

5. Compare and contrast the TL segment of the motor carrier industry with the LTL segment in terms of infrastructure, cost structure, market structure, and operating characteristics.

6. What is the nature of intramodal and intermodal competition in the motor carrier industry? How have the motor carriers fared in terms of intermodal competition since 1980?

7. Describe the general service characteristics of motor carriers and explain how these service characteristics have contributed to the growth of the motor carrier industry.

8. The cost structure of the motor carrier industry is affected by its infrastructure (such as highways and terminals). Discuss the cost structure of motor carriers and how it is affected by the infrastructure. Should there be changes made in public policy with respect to the motor carriers' use of public highways?

9. Describe the nature of the operation ratio and its usefulness in analyzing a motor carrier's financial viability.

10. What are the major issues facing motor carriers in the 21st century? How should these issues be addressed?

Notes

1. American Trucking Associations, Inc., *American Trucking Trends, 2003,* Washington, DC: American Trucking Associations, 2003.
2. *Transportation in America*, 19th ed., Washington, DC: Eno Transportation Foundation, 2002.
3. Ibid.
4. American Trucking Associations, op. cit.
5. Ibid.
6. "Yellow and Roadway Get it Together," *Logistics Management,* August 2003, p. 19.
7. American Trucking Associations, Inc., *American Trucking Trends, 1977–1978,* Washington, DC: American Trucking Associations, p. 27.
8. *Transportation in America,* op. cit.
9. There are no notable exceptions to this ability to serve. Shippers located on an island are served by water or air transportation. Other unique examples exist where the motor carrier is physically unable to provide the transportation.
10. For a complete listing of federal equipment specifications, see the U.S. Department of Transportation, Federal Highway Administration, Bureau of Motor-Carrier Safety, *Federal Motor Carrier Safety Regulations*, Washington, DC: U.S. Government Printing Office, 2002.
11. Through police powers contained in the U.S. Constitution, each state has the right to establish regulations to protect the health and welfare of its citizens. Vehicle length and height laws are within these police powers, as are vehicle speed and weight laws.
12. *Transportation in America,* op. cit.
13. American Trucking Associations, 2003, op. cit.
14. Ibid.
15. *Transportation in America,* op. cit.
16. "Life After CF," *Logistics Management,* July 2003, p. 35.

Suggested Readings

Kent, John L., R. Stephen Parker, and Robert H. Luke. "An Empirical Examination of Shipper Perceptions of Service-Selection Attributes in Five Truckload Industry Segments," *Transportation Journal*, Vol. 41, No. 1, 2001, pp. 27–36.

Mejza, Michael C., Richard E. Barnard, Thomas M. Corsi, and Thomas Keane. "Driver Management Practices of Motor Carriers with High Compliance and Safety Performance," *Transportation Journal*, Vol. 42, No. 4, 2003, pp. 16–29.

Premeaux, Shane R. "Motor Carrier Selection Criteria: Perceptual Differences Between Shippers and Motor Carriers," *Transportation Journal*, Vol. 42, No. 2, 2002, pp. 28–38.

Saltzman, Gregory M., and Michael H. Belzer. "The Case for Strengthened Motor Carrier Hours of Service Regulations," *Transportation Journal*, Vol. 41, No. 4, 2002, pp. 51–71.

Spiegel, Robert. "Truckload vs. LTL," *Logistics Management*, July 2003, pp. 54–57.

Case 3-1

Hardee Transportation

As we learned in Chapter 1, Jim O'Brien of Hardee Transaportation has his hands full with the requests from his largest customer. However, a new and possibly greater issue has presented itself to Jim: the new hours-of-service rules. Hardee's freight lanes and customer pickup and delivery (PUD) operations are set to reflect the previous 10 hours of maximum drive time for his drivers. The dispatch centers and bobtail patterns to service customer trailer pools are also set up on the previous rules.

Jim's customers don't necessarily agree with his concerns. They argue that drivers will actually have more continuous drive time under the new regulations. They also argue that the reduced on-duty hours for drivers will reduce driver fatigue and result in fewer accidents, lowering Hardee's operating costs. Jim doesn't agree. Even though driving hours are increased, total driving time might actually be reduced. If PUD times are increased at certain customer locations, driving time is reduced to comply with the 14-hour on-duty time.

This is a great concern for Jim because some of his largest customers have the longest PUD times. Plus, some of these customers also require that the driver bobtails to their shipping locations. Jim has approached his sales team with the request that they require their customers to reduce loading and unloading times. If they can't, Hardee has no choice but to either increase detention charges or seriously consider dropping those customers. Obviously, these two options were not well-received by the sales organization. Sales perceived these actions to be against Hardee's service strategy and were fearful that some customers may rebel.

Case Questions

1. Using the information in this chapter, how would you tell Jim to proceed?

Case 3-2

JEI Carrier Corporation

At JEI's annual shareholders meeting, Jean Beierlein of JEI Carrier Corporation is braced for dissent from the JEI union employees. For some time, the company has tried to negotiate for more flexibility in its operations with its union workers. Because of an agreement with the union, JEI has limits on when it can engage in intermodal operations. At present, intermodal transportation can only be used when there are no drivers available at the origin or at key relay points. The problem for the company is that the industry has become increasingly competitive since 1980 with the growth of other alternatives, such as UPS and nonunion carriers.

In many instances, nonunion carriers have taken away market share that the JEI Carrier Corporation once held because the nonunion companies are more flexible with respect to transporting goods. As a result, the nonunion carrier companies continue to grow and increase their share of the market.

The use of intermodal transportation gives carriers the opportunity to use a variety of modes of transportation when moving goods so they can better serve their customers. A frequent intermodal choice within the motor carrier industry is to use rail. In addition, JEI wants to be able to use split shifts with its employees.

With the union not allowing the company to participate in intermodal operations for more than 28 percent of total line-haul, the company does not have much flexibility and is less competitive. The union does not want the company to participate in intermodal operations because it is afraid that some of its members will lose their jobs. Since deregulation, more than 400,000 union jobs have been lost within the motor carrier industry.

The company is in a bad position because it wants to be able to remain competitive. However, with the union restricting the use of intermodal operations, JEI's competitors might be in a good position to capture some of its customers. The motor carrier industry has become very competitive over the years, and many companies are using intermodal operations as a competitive measure to attract and retain customers, as well as to lower cost.

Case Questions

1. What recommendations would you make to JEI for increasing its flexibility while also providing job security for its union employees?
2. What strategies could JEI use to remain competitive if the union still restricts the use of intermodal operations?
3. Do you think that having union employees is an advantage or a disadvantage for JEI? Why or why not?

Case 3-3

Retirement Funds

In the U.S. motor carrier industry there has been a coalition attempting to persuade Congress to place a limit on the amount of payouts of pension funds for workers in the industry. One important concern is that many of the pension funds are not fully funded, yet there continues to be an increase in the number of benefits being offered by these funds. Right now, in one union pension fund, an individual with 30 years of service who is 65 years of age will receive at least $2,500 per month.

Employers want to see an end to the trend of increasing benefits. The unfunded liabilities are growing year by year. In the motor carrier industry, in which many employees belong to a union, there has been a lot of conflict recently concerning this issue. The coalition feels that the only way to stop increasing benefits is to have Congress put a limit on the benefits of pension funds. However, there is union opposition to such a limit.

As a result of not having fully funded pension funds, if a company goes bankrupt and out of business, the government agency that oversees pension funds will be faced with a large number of claims for funds. The position of the union is that it wants to secure the maximum amount of benefits for its members. Employers are worried that by continuing to have increasing benefits, their respective companies will become more and more insolvent. Some employers might have to go out of business, depending on how insolvent they become. The result of going out of business means a loss of jobs and more unemployment. Congress has an important decision to make regarding whether or not to put a limit on the amount of benefits that pension funds will pay. The increasing liabilities of employers can affect the economy in a large way because many employers might pass on the increased liabilities to customers in the form of higher prices.

Case Questions

1. What decision should Congress make regarding the issue of putting a limit on the benefits of pension funds? Justify your answer.
2. Do you think that the unions are being too greedy by not wanting a limit put on the amount of benefits of pension funds? Why or why not?
3. What recommendations do you have for solving the pension fund issue between employers and unions?

Chapter 4

Railroads

NITTANY VALLEY SHORTLINE

Bob Patterson, CEO and president of the Nittany Valley Shortline Railroad (NVSR), called an emergency meeting of the Executive Committee. There had been rumors circulating for 6 months that the Shannon Glass Company was going to close its local plant. The day before, a formal announcement finally was made by Shannon about their plans for the local plant. Bob Patterson received a registered letter from the plant manager informing him that the company was planning to close the plant down in 6 months and would no longer need the transportation services of the Nittany Valley Shortline Railroad.

The letter was especially bad news for Nittany Valley Shortline because Shannon Glass was its largest customer and represented 20 percent of its total revenue. In fact, when Bob developed his initial business plan to start up the railroad and obtain investment capital from local investors and loans from banks, Shannon was the cornerstone of the plan for future financial viability of NVSR.

Company Background

NVSR was established in 1982 to provide rail service to businesses in the Nittany Valley. The company was able to obtain special funding from the state and local governments to buy a branch rail line that recently had been abandoned. The government units felt that rail service was necessary to support established local businesses. The government units were concerned that companies would leave the area, with subsequent loss of jobs and tax erosion if good rail service was not available. They also felt that viable rail service would contribute to continued economic development in the Valley by helping to attract new businesses.

NVSR was able to retain all the customers that were originally served by the branch line, and it developed a good relationship with Conrail and then CSX Transportation to provide through rail service for customers throughout the United States. The key to its long-run financial viability was, obviously, retaining old customers and attracting new customers. The line was originally abandoned because the customer traffic volume was not sufficient to cover the total costs associated with the line. Therefore, NVSR had to develop more traffic from current customers and/or attract new customers. The cost structure of NVSR was comparable to other rails in that it had high fixed costs. Consequently, traffic volume was critical to its financial success. However, NVSR's operating costs were lower because it used nonunionized labor. It also was "closer" to its customers and was able to adapt better to customer requirements.

Current Situation

Bob Patterson's emergency meeting with the Executive Committee was not an anticipated event. The impact of a 20-percent reduction in revenue associated with the Shannon Plant closing had significant implications especially because of the fixed costs of the NVSR. Although it could reduce some of its operating costs (e.g., labor and fuel), the reductions were not significant because the cars that it delivered for Shannon were moved with cars to be delivered for other customers along the line. Therefore, the same basic train crew had to be used and fuel consumption was not reduced significantly. Raising the rates to other customers to make up some or all of the revenue was not feasible because some or all of its customers would probably switch to motor carrier service, which would exacerbate its financial situation. The committee quickly agreed that the only alternative was to find new customers and alternative uses of its facilities.

As you read this chapter, you will gain additional perspective about the special challenge facing NVSR at this stage of its history. More importantly, you should gain some insights that would help you make recommendations to NVSR to remain profitable.

BRIEF HISTORY OF THE RAIL INDUSTRY

Throughout its history, the United States has viewed transportation as being vital to the well-being of commerce, and for well over a century railroads commanded a dominant position in the U.S. transport system. Rail transportation played a significant role in the economic development of the nation from 1850 to 1950. The establishment of a transcontinental railway in 1869 contributed to the population migration to land west of the Mississippi River because expansion was no longer dependent on U.S. inland waterways or slow travel by wagon over poor trails. The population migration, however, was only a part of the significant contribution of the railroads to the economic development of the Western territories. The railroads provided a lifeline for that migration because they provided inbound and outbound movement of products to sustain the people in the area.

The railroads supplanted water transportation, canals in particular, but also river transportation for many products. The railroads were a superior form of transportation compared to water transportation, especially from a service perspective. Their economic advantages led to the development of a comprehensive rail network through out the United States. Many cities and towns were either funded or significantly expanded because they were at important locations along the rail lines.

In some instances, the railroads developed their lines parallel to rivers and canals, which resulted in direct competition for freight movements. The reliance upon private capital to develop and expand the rail system lead to an overexpansion of the network, which lead to financial failures, some scandals, and a need to rationalize the rail system through government intervention at a later date. There is no question that the development of the U.S. rail system in the 19th century was an important part of the foundation for the agricultural and industrial development that ensued.

However, the railroad industry has declined in relative importance during the last half of the 20th century. This decline has been well documented and can be attributed in part to the following events: the alternate transport modes with superior services and/or cost characteristics (primarily motor carriers and pipelines); a resurgence in water transportation; and changing needs of the U.S. economy. In 2001 railroads transported only 41.7 percent of the total intercity ton-miles transported by all modes, which is approximately 33 percent less than 1929 on a relative basis.[1] It is important to note that, on an actual basis, rail ton-miles have continued to increase and railroads are still the largest carrier in terms of intercity ton-miles, but not in terms of tonnage or revenues.

Starting in 1984, the railroad industry adopted a new depreciation accounting system, and **return on investment (ROI)** shot up to 5.7 percent. In 2001 ROI again showed an increase to 7.33 percent.[2] Consequently, some rail stocks have become more attractive investments.

The railroads are still vital to our transportation system and play an important role in our economy. For example, in 2001 rail revenues accounted for approximately 1 percent of the gross domestic product.[3] Railroads in 2001 employed 234,000 people or approximately 0.17 percent of the total civilian labor force.[4] Investment is another indication of importance. In recent years, rail investment in new plant and equipment has accounted for over 1 percent of total private investment. In 1989, for example, rail locomotive and freight car acquisition increased sharply over 1988 (i.e., an increase of more than 7,000 railcars). These indicators have been hailed as further evidence of the success of the Staggers Rail Act of 1980. However, outlays for rail equipment declined sharply in 2001, dropping from 7,108 in 2000 to 4,716 in 2002.[5]

As mentioned earlier, in 2001 the railroads shipped about 41.7 percent of all ton-miles moved by all transport modes in the United States. This percentage of total ton-miles has been declining since its peak of 75 percent in 1929. However, actual ton-miles have, for the most part, been steadily increasing. In 1980 a total of 932 billion ton-miles of domestic intercity freight was moved. The figure dropped to 810 billion ton-miles in 1982 due mostly to the recession of 1982 to 1983. In 2001 the ton-miles moved were 1,558 billion, representing 41.7 percent of transportation's total 3,733 billion.[6]

These figures highlight the fact that, even though railroads continue to move record amounts of goods, they are capturing less of the total transportation market because other modes have been growing even faster. However, there are indications that railroads may experience a resurgence on a relative basis because of more aggressive marketing and growth in intermodal traffic.[7] Intermodal shipments become more attractive as fuel prices escalate and highway congestion increases.

INDUSTRY OVERVIEW

Number of Carriers

Although there were 571 railroads listed in 2001, only 8 were Class 1 companies (see Table 4.1). This meant that they each did more than $266.7 million (2001) annually in revenue, or a total of $33.53 billion. The balance of the railroads is classified as "regional," "local," and "switching" carriers, and they accounted for about $3 billion of revenue. Today there are only 7 Class 1 railroads remaining (http://www.aar.org).

Offsetting the decline in the number of Class 1 lines, significant growth occurred in short-line railroads known as locals and larger lines known as regionals. These new operators took over unwanted trackage of the Class 1 lines and sought to recover lost business. As of 2001, 34 regional railroads existed, of which the Wisconsin Central was the largest. There were also 529 local lines, broken up by line-haul and switching. Some of the roads were as small as two or three miles but still contributed to the overall freight network. There are currently only 33 regional railroads in existence. The largest regional railroad today is the Iowa, Chicago & Eastern Railroad at 1,336 miles.

In addition, a number of holding companies were formed to control a number of short lines scattered around the country. One of the largest is RailAmerica, which operates more than 20 separate railroads in the United States and Canada. The holding companies have economies of scale in purchasing and can share other corporate assets, which reduces the cost of operation.

Table 4.1 Class I Railroads in 2001

Railroad	Number	Miles	Employees	Revenue ($Mil)
Class I	8	97,631	162,155	$33,532.50
Regional	34	17,439	10,302	1,576.30
Local	529	27,563	11,912	1470.00
Total	**571**	**142,633**	**184,369**	**$36,578.80**

Source: Association of American Railroads, *Railroad Facts*, Washington, DC, 2002, p. 3.

Line mileage declined during the same 50-year period (see Table 4.2). Line mileage expanded rapidly during the initial construction period of 1830 to 1910 and reached a peak of 254,251 miles in 1916.[8] By 1929 line mileage was down to 249,433, and in 2001 it had been reduced to about 167,275 track miles.[9] This reduction is traceable largely to the abandonment of duplicate trackage that was built during the "boom" periods of the industry's developmental years that was no longer needed because of technology, market shifts, the rail merger movement, and intermodal competition.

Competition

The competitive position of the railroad industry has changed dramatically during the past 50 years. Railroads were the dominant mode of transportation before World War II; now the industry is faced with intense intermodal competition and selective intramodal competition. Consolidations within the industry have created a situation in which only eight Class I railroads handle over 95 percent of the traffic. In addition, the railways must compete with the other modes of transportation that have either evolved or matured since the 1920s.

The industry's economic structure has developed into a fine example of differentiated oligopoly. In other words, there are a small number of very large railroads, and they serve somewhat different market areas. Their major source of competition is intermodal in nature.

INTRAMODAL

Today, only a few railroads serve a particular geographic region. This situation gives rise to an oligopolistic market structure because there are a small number of interdependent large sellers. Barriers to entry exist because of the large capital outlays and fixed costs required, and, consequently, pricing can be controlled by the existing firms. For this reason, economic regulations implemented by the ICC before 1980 brought the geographic coverage and the rate-making procedures of the railroads under federal scrutiny and control so that intramodal and intermodal competition

Table 4.2 U.S. Railroad Miles and Trackage (Class I)

Year	Miles of Line*	Miles of Track**
1980	164,822	270,623
1985	145,764	242,320
1990	119,758	200,074
1992	113,056	190,591
1993	110,425	186,288
1994	109,332	183,685
1995	108,264	180,419
1996	105,779	176,978
1997	102,128	172,564
1998	100,570	171,098
1999	99,430	168,979
2000	99,250	168,535
2001	97,817	167,275

* This represents the aggregate length of roadway of all line-haul railroads exclusive of yard tracks, sidings, and parallel lines.

** This includes the total miles of railroad track owned by U.S. railroads.

Source: Association of American Railroads, *Railroad Facts*, Washington, DC, 2002, p. 45.

might be promoted. Because of the need to recover many of the high fixed costs while maintaining market share, regulation influenced railroads not only to set prices in a competitive fashion, but also to seek a rate of return adequate to attract investors.

With the merger trend discussed earlier, the intramodal competition has been reduced. Many cities now have only one railroad serving them. Even major rail centers such as Chicago or Kansas City have seen the number of carriers serving those areas significantly reduced. Shippers are concerned that there will not be enough effective intramodal competition to preserve railroad-to-railroad competition. In fact, there has been a growing level of complaint about rail service and the shortage of rail equipment to move freight. Some shippers feel that the service is very unsatisfactory.

INTERMODAL

As noted earlier, the relative market share of railroad intercity ton-miles has been steadily declining because of increased intermodal competition. Inroads into the lucrative commodity markets have been facilitated by governmental expenditures on infrastructure that have benefited competing modes. For example, the government has provided an extensive local and national highway system, especially the interstate network, for motor carrier use. When a railroad company president was asked how his service compares to that offered by trucking firms, he responded:

> Our service is not as fast as truck, but we have discovered that customers will accept a slower transit time in exchange for a lower rate, as long as service is consistent, and we can usually provide a lower freight rate because our costs are less than truck.[10]

Customers look for consistent on-time performance. Railroads need to provide this level of service to stay competitive. Railroad companies usually cannot deliver freight early because the customer then has to find a place to store it.

In addition, through improvements and maintenance of the inland waterway system by the U.S. Army Corps of Engineers, the government has also provided the right-of-way for water carriers. Because of the governmental programs and the response of the railroad industry to change, railways now account for 25.5 percent of total tonnage and 41.7 percent of total ton-miles shipped (see Table 4.3).

Overall, the railroads have been rate-competitive. Government influence, either in the form of economic regulation or expenditure programs aimed at promoting other

Table 4.3 Railroad Intercity Ton-Miles and Tonnage

Year	*Ton-Miles	Percent of Total	**Tonnage	Percent of Total
1950	597	56.1	1421	46.7
1960	579	44.1	1301	36.1
1970	771	39.8	1572	31.1
1980	932	37.5	1589	28.7
1990	1,091	37.7	1738	27.1
1995	1,375	40.4	1911	25.7
2000	1,534	41.0	2139	25.3
2001	1,558	41.7	2121	25.5

* Billions.
** Millions.

Source: Eno Transportation Foundation, Washington DC, "Transportation in America," 19th ed., 2002.

modes, together with intermodal competition, forced the railways into making a determined effort to forestall industry decline by becoming more competitive. The Staggars Rail Act, which removed significant economic regulation, has allowed railroads to be much more price-competitive through contract rates and a more tailored response to customer's service requirements, but overall they are perceived to be lacking in responsiveness to customer needs.

MERGERS

Historically, many mergers have taken place in the railroad industry, and the size of the remaining carriers has correspondingly increased. Early rail mergers grew out of efforts to expand capacity to benefit from large-volume traffic efficiencies and economies. Later, **side-by-side** combinations were made to strengthen the financial positions of many of the railroads and eliminate duplication. More recently though, **end-to-end mergers** were created to provide more effective intermodal and intramodal competition.[11] Customer service and reliability can be improved by these mergers because the many types of operating costs, such as car switching, and clerical costs, such as record keeping, can be reduced; but, such improvements have been slow to develop.

Previously we noted that the number of railroads (refer to Table 4.1) and the number of miles of track (refer to Table 4.2) have declined. One of the major reasons for this decline in both the number of companies and the miles of track has been the significant number of mergers or unifications that have occurred in the railroad industry during the past 30 years. A total of 28 mergers have taken place during the past 30 years, and 50 unifications overall. The latter included not only mergers but also consolidations and outright purchases for control. The decade of the 1970s was very active, but the tempo of rail consolidations in the 1980s was hyperactive.

In 1920 there were 186 Class 1 railroads; by 2001 the number had declined to 8. One reason for this drop was the way in which railroads are classified by revenue, which, as it was adjusted for inflation, fewer roads qualified. The primary reason, however, was the acclerating trend of mergers. After the Staggers Act was passed in 1980, there was a significant increase in mergers and acquisitions so that as of 1999 there were only four major rail lines: Norfolk Southern, CSX Transportation, Union Pacific, and the Burlington Northern Santa Fe.

ABANDONMENTS

Recall that in 1916, at its peak, the railroad industry owned 254,000 miles of track. Today, more than half of that is gone, enough to circle the Earth three times. The early overexpansion left extensive amounts of excess trackage in many areas, and the railroads had to abandon significant portions of rail trackage to remain competitive. Parallel and overlapping routes, therefore, have been eliminated wherever possible.

Many factors led to the abandonment of track around the country. In the late 1950s, the government opened the Interstate Highway System. This allowed trucking service to decrease transit time, which caused shippers to use motor carriers. To effectively compete with trucking companies for time-sensitive traffic, railroads had to focus on efficient routes. In the 1970s and 1980s, bankruptcies forced the shutdown of railroad systems such as Rock Island, Penn Central, and Milwaukee Road. Another critical issue that caused abandonment of railroad tracks occurred in 1980. Deregulation gave companies freedom to buy, sell, or abandon unprofitable track without federal interference. Cities such as Annapolis, Maryland, and Carson City, Nevada, lost all their railroad service. Even tracks that carried the country's most famous passenger trains vanished. Once the railroad companies abandoned the tracks, they sold the rails and ties to scrap dealers. They received as much as $10,000 per mile for this scrap.

The land used for rights-of-way could also be used unless the original deed required the return when the property was no longer being utilized for railroad purposes.

In some cases, all or part of the right-of-way was turned into hiking trails with some bridges left in place. The 13-year-old program, "Rail to Trails Conservancy," has been highly successful in adding over 10,000 miles of trails to the country's recreational facilities. In other cases, the land and sometimes even the track was left in place as part of a program known as "rail-banking." The theory behind this is should the line be needed in the future, it would be much easier to restore it. In one case, a major railroad company reopened a major line after it was closed for over 10 years.

Even though the railroad industry reduced its track mileage by more than half, the lines remaining still carried a major share of the freight. The abandonments were either rural branches or duplicate lines left over from mergers. The ICC, and later the STB, still regulate abandonments, but changes in the law made it much easier for the railroad industry to close unprofitable lines. Not all the lines were scrapped, as discussed above, and regional and short-line operators took over some of this property.

New developments, such as unit trains carrying one commodity like coal or grain from one shipper to one consignee, helped the railroads operate profitably. As more and more traffic was concentrated on fewer and fewer routes, overhead costs were spread over more businesses. Each time a railroad interchanged a car to another line, there was the chance for delay. As mergers reduced the number of railroads, fewer interchanges were needed. For example, until 1993, at least three railroads were needed to go from Chicago to San Francisco, but now one company owns all the track, allowing more efficient service.

With less than half the amount of original track, railroads had to find a way to stay in business profitably. The best solution concentrated on improved service. For one, railroads developed special train units to carry the cargo of only one manufacturer at a time. This provided express service (no stop offs) for the shipper. Railroads also sold track to short lines that provided faster, customized service for smaller shippers who discontinued use of large shippers. Finally, railroads had to eliminate unnecessary delays in service by providing 24-hour service. They also used computer systems to track cargo. In spite of these efforts, railroads are still challenged in attempting to compete against the service offered by motor carriers.

STOP OFF

Rail Shippers Yearn To Be Free

All across the country, captive rail shippers are becoming restless. No longer viewing themselves as individual victims with little or no recourse, they are banding together to change the way they're treated by the railroads that serve them. And whether they do so by applying legislative pressure or by building their own rail lines, captive shippers are determined to gain the right to take advantage of competitive markets—a right shippers using other transportation modes often take for granted.

Although captive rail shippers have protested their treatment in the past, their voices have typically been heard one at a time, echoing through the halls of the Surface Transportation Board (STB) as they trudged through the time- and money-consuming process of filing a rate complaint. Now, however, those voices are being heard in chorus through groups such as Consumers United for Rail Equity (CURE), headed by Platz. Comprising 16 associations from a diverse group of industries, including chemical, agricultural, coal-fueled power, plastics, and paper, CURE may represent the first time that captive rail shippers have addressed their problems en masse.

The issue today, though, is not just that captives pay more; it's that they pay substantially more. Railroads typically charge shippers rates that are roughly 180 percent above the variable costs of the haul—the sum needed to ensure something close to revenue adequacy. (Revenue adequacy, the ability of a railroad to reap a return on investment that's higher than its cost of capital, is a "holy grail" the railroads strive for but have not achieved in some time.) But the 2001 Revenue Shortfall Allocation Methodology study conducted by the STB showed that on average, the largest U.S. railroads—the BNSF, Norfolk Southern, and Union Pacific—charged captives rates averaging 237 percent above their variable costs.

There's one word that crops up in every conversation with captive shippers: *bottleneck*. A bottleneck exists when a shipper's premises are served by a single rail carrier that connects further down the line to another railroad.

Here's why that's a problem: Suppose a shipment must travel 500 miles, but only the first 20 miles are on the sole-serving carrier's line. The shipper would like to pay the first carrier for just the 20-mile segment and negotiate a separate rate with the second railroad for the remaining 480 miles. But because the first carrier owns the one and only connection to the shipper's premises—the bottleneck—the shipper is required to pay that carrier for the entire 500 miles.

What shippers want instead is for the railroads to be forced to quote a bottleneck rate rather than a through rate from point of origin to destination. The railroads, however, say that because they've invested in the entire rail system and not just that small portion of it, it's unfair to ask them to price their services based on that shorter leg.

Neither side, however, appears capable of fixing government policy on its own. Nothing can change until both sides gather at a single table and work out the issues. And when you get down to it, that's what captive shippers would like to see most of all.

Adapted from: *Logistics Management*, November 2003.

OPERATING AND SERVICE CHARACTERISTICS

General Service Characteristics

COMMODITIES HAULED

In the 19th century, when the railroads were the primary source of transportation, they moved almost every available type of product or raw material. Today, the railroad system has evolved into a system that primarily transports large quantities of heavyweight, low-value commodities (or bulk products).[12] Motor carriers concentrate on the handling of small-volume, high-value finished goods, whereas water and pipelines carry the larger volumes of the lowest value types of bulk commodities. The railroads therefore find themselves engaged in intense competition with these other modes for the opportunity to ship many product categories. Although railroads still handle a wide variety of commodities, more than 50 percent of total rail carloadings in 2001 involved the movement of bulk materials. Table 4.4 lists the products with almost 20 million carloadings carried by the railroads in 2001. Of the six commodities shown in the table, only one, motor vehicles and equipment, is not a bulk commodity.

Coal. Railroads are the primary haulers of coal, accounting for 43.8 percent of the total tonnage transported in 2001.[13] In addition, coal constitutes almost one-third of the total tonnage handled by the railways. Its share of carloadings, which make up more than one out of every four rail freight cars loaded in 2001, represents a marked change in transport. Table 4.3 indicates that 7.2 million carloadings moved in 2001, up by more than 300,000 from 2000 levels. Furthermore, rail coal traffic is concentrated among a few railroads, with four firms handling more than 60 percent of the railcar tonnage.[14] Coal is an alternative energy source that will probably continue to be an important commodity shipped by the railroads, and this tonnage may increase if there are political challenges in the Middle East that limit the supply of petroleum and related products.

Table 4.4 Carloads Originated by Commodity

Commodity Group	Carloads (thousands) 2001	2000	Change Cars	Percent
Coal	7,295	6,954	341	4.9
Miscellaneous Mixed Shipments	6,231	6,796	–565	–8.3
Chemicals and Allied Products	1,801	1,844	–43	–2.4
Motor Vehicles and Equipment	1,650	1,860	–210	–11.3
Farm Products	1,461	1,437	24	1.7
Food and Kindred Products	1,446	1,377	68	5.0
Nonmetallic Minerals	1,280	1,309	–29	–2.2

Source: Association of American Railroads, Washington, DC, 2002, p. 25.

Farm products. When considered together, farm and food products constitute the second largest commodity group hauled by railroads. Total movement by rail amounted to about 2.7 million carloads in 2001.[15] The growth in domestic markets and the increase of exports to foreign customers have been steady for many years. For example, the exportation of grain and its related products accounted for more than 50 percent of the total grain market. Because of this growth, distribution patterns might change, but the transportation of farm products will continue to be an important rail commodity movement.

Chemicals. Chemicals and allied products, a great number of which are classified as "hazardous" by the U.S. Department of Transportation (DOT), are transported in specially designed tank cars. Most of this material is carried long distances (more than 500 miles) in 245,137 privately owned tank cars. A total of 151 million tons of this highly rated traffic traveled by rail in 2001.[16] The railroads, in comparison with highway movements, safely transport chemicals, and this safety has been steadily increasing for years. This type of long-haul bulk material is ideally suited for rail movement. Interestingly, motor carriers move more chemicals, and they compete vigorously for this traffic.

Transportation equipment. Transportation equipment carloadings, which are linked to the relative health of the domestic automobile industry, have increased to more than 5 percent of total carloadings, an increase of more than 40 percent since 1982, but decreased by over 200,000 carloads from 2000 to 2001.

Although the commodities shipped by the railroad industry have changed over the years, with the emphasis placed on the movement of low-value, high-volume bulk materials, the railroads are still a possible mode of transport for many different types of goods, including both high-value merchandise and raw materials alike.

TRAFFIC SHIFTS

As indicated previously, the demand for freight transportation is a derived demand; that is, transportation demand is based upon the demand for products and related matters. Consequently, economic conditions have an impact upon the demand for transportation service. This is especially true for railroads because they primarily move basic raw materials and supplies (e.g., coal, chemicals, etc.).

There was almost universal agreement that the U.S. economy was recovering during the last three quarters of 2003. In spite of the economic upturn, standard rail carload shipments during this period did not reflect the economic good news of 2003.

However, intermodal movements by rail increased by 6.9 percent during this period. This trend toward intermodal moves could prove to be very beneficial to the railroad industry and allow them to be more competitive with the motor carriers.

Constraints

Railroads are constrained by fixed rights-of-way and therefore provide differing degrees of service completeness. For example, if both the shipper and receiver possess rail sidings, then door-to-door service can be provided. However, if no sidings are available, the movement of goods must be completed by some other mode. If line-haul mileage continues to decline (as indicated by current industrial trends), the industry will become less service-complete and even more dependent on other modes of transportation for completion of many types of moves.

Unlike motor, air, or water transport, the railroad system provides a truly nationwide network of service. Each railroad serves a specific geographic region, and freight and equipment are exchanged at interchange points. For example, a shipment between Philadelphia, Pennsylvania, and Portland, Oregon, might be handled by two or three railroads, depending on the route chosen. The through service is unique, but multiple handlings can create rate-division problems and delays in delivery.

Although on-time delivery performance and the frequency of service had deteriorated in the past, improvements have been made in recent years. The current position of the industry has been restored to competitive levels on selected movements (particularly over long distances). Railroads dominate the market for hauling 30,000 pounds or more over distances exceeding 300 miles. The industry hopes to expand its service to certain short-haul markets and selected lanes for manufactured products.[17] However, reliability and transit time will have to improve as well as equipment availability.

Strengths

A large carrying capacity enables the railroads to handle large-volume movements of low-value commodities over long distances. Motor carriers, on the other hand, are constrained by volume and weight to the smaller truckload (TL) and less-than-truckload (LTL) markets. Furthermore, although pipelines compete directly with the railroads, they are restricted largely to the movements of liquid and gas (and then only in one direction).

This kind of carload capacity, along with a variety of car types, permits the railroads to handle almost any type of commodity. For the most part, the industry is not constrained to weight and volume restrictions, and customer service is available throughout the United States. In addition, railroads are able to use a variety of car types to provide a flexible service because the rolling stock consists of boxcars, tankers, gondolas, hoppers, covered hoppers, flatcars, and other special types of cars (see Table 4.5).

Another important service is that the **liability** for loss and damage is usually assumed by the railroads. Railroads, however, have had a comparatively high percentage of goods damaged in transit. In 2001 the total pay-out of freight claims for U.S. and Canadian railroads increased to $115 million from $101 million in 2000.[18] Such damage occurs because rail freight often goes through a rough trip due to vibrations and shocks (steel wheel on steel rail). In addition, the incidence of loss is usually higher than on other modes because of the high degree of multiple handlings. Excessive loss and damage claims have tended to erode shipper confidence in the railroad's ability to provide adequate service.

In an attempt to regain traffic lost to other modes and gain new traffic share, the railroads have been placing an increasing amount of attention on equipment and technology. For one, to decrease damage statistics, railroads focus on new technologies.

Table 4.5 Types and Number of Freight Cars in Service in 2001

Type	Total	Class 1 Railroad	Other Railroads	Car Companies and Shippers
Boxcars				
Plain Box	21,367	234	7,597	13,536
Equipped Box	119,209	77,698	38,781	2,730
Covered Hoppers	390,444	122,067	23,348	245,029
Flatcars	149,993	90,261	17,283	42,429
Refrigerator Cars	25,556	19,568	3,890	2,098
Gondolas	201,336	104,289	20,880	76,167
Hoppers	154,206	82,742	12,691	58,773
Tank Cars	246,108	758	33	245,317
Others	5,917	2,223	967	2,727
Total	**1,314,136**	**499,860**	**125,470**	**688,806**

Source: Association of American Railroads, *Railroad Facts*, Washington, DC, 2002, p. 25.

Multilevel suspension systems and end-of-car cushioning devices protect the goods in transit. Also, the Association of American Railroads has developed a quality certification program (M-1003) to ensure freight car quality and technical specifications. Finally, equipping cars with instrumentation packages to measure forces that might cause damage reduces the damage potential. One area that has received much attention has been the intermodal era, namely, trailer-on-flatcar (**TOFC**) and container-on-flatcar (**COFC**) service. The railroads realized the necessity of improving the TOFC and COFC service to compete effectively with motor carriers. The developments include terminal facilities for loading and unloading, as well as changes in the railcars and trailers and containers. However, the changes have not stopped here. The railroads have invested a significant amount of money recently in improving right-of-way and structures to help improve service by preventing delays.

Microprocessors have found their niche in the railroad industry, particularly in communications and signaling. The "chip" is also being used in vital circuits (safety related). Fiber optics are used in this high-tech explosion to improve communications, which will in turn improve service and revenues. The railroad industry hopes that these service-related improvements will increase its traffic. However, the rail industry has to realize that technology alone cannot mitigate their problems. Process change also has to occur.

Equipment

The **carload** is the basic unit of measurement of freight handling used by the railroads. A carload can vary in size and capacity depending on the type of car being used. Historically, the number of carloadings has declined since the turn of the century; there was a total of almost 39 million carloads in 1929. In 2001, the total railroad carloads equaled 27.2 million.[19] This decline has occurred primarily because of the introduction of larger cars and the increase in productivity per car type. Absolute tonnage has increased (see Table 4.3).

The increases in average carrying capacity of railroad freight cars over the past 50 years have been dramatic. In 2001 the average carrying capacity per car stood at almost 93.1

tons, compared to 46.3 tons in 1929.[20] Most of today's new cars have more than twice the capacity of the typical boxcar used 50 years ago. However, the carrying capacity of a new or rebuilt car could easily exceed 100 tons, and the trend of increasing average capacity will continue in the near future. A car with a 100-ton capacity probably represents the most efficient size with the present support facilities.

The railroads own and maintain their own rolling stock. The characteristics of these cars have changed considerably to suit customer requirements; for example, the conventional boxcar has been de-emphasized but has seen resurgence in the past few years. Today's car fleet is highly specialized and is designed to meet the needs of the individual shipper. Following is a list of eight generalized car types:

- Boxcar (plain): Standardized roofed freight car with sliding doors on the side used for general commodities
- Boxcar (equipped): Specially modified boxcar used for specialized merchandise, such as automobile parts
- Hopper car: A freight car with the floor sloping to one or more hinged doors used for discharging bulk materials
- Covered hopper: A hopper car with a roof designed to transport bulk commodities that need protection from the elements
- Flatcar: A freight car with no top or sides used primarily for TOFC service machinery and building materials
- Refrigerator car: A freight car to which refrigeration equipment has been added for controlled temperature
- Gondola: A freight car with no top, a flat bottom, and fixed sides used primarily for hauling bulk commodities
- Tank car: Specialized car used for the transport of liquids and gases

The total number and percentage of freight cars in service in 2001 are shown in Table 4.5 and Figure 4.1. The boxcar has been surpassed by the covered hopper car, which is followed closely in number by the hopper car. In addition, the largest increase in total new cars was in covered hopper cars. The composition of the railroad fleet has shifted from the accommodation of manufactured commodities to the movement of bulk goods. In 2001 more than 50 percent of the total fleet was designed for the transport of bulk and raw materials.

Class I railroads own almost 46 percent of the rolling stock in use, private companies hold title to 37 percent, and other classes of railroads make up the remainder (see Table 4.4).[21] Car companies and shippers are becoming increasingly more important in the ownership of railroad cars. In 1991 they owned almost all of the specially designed tank cars in use, and in the past several years they have purchased a substantial number of covered hopper cars, more than 30,000.

To remain competitive with the other modes of transportation, the railroads have increased their capacity. The average freight train load also has increased; in 2001 more than 3,005 tons per load were carried as compared to barely 800 tons per load in 1929.[22] This increase in capacity will be necessary if more bulk commodities are to be shipped longer distances in the future.

Service Innovations

The railroad cost structure makes it necessary to attract large and regular volumes of traffic to take advantage of scale economies and to operate efficiently. In recent years, rail management has developed or re-emphasized a number of service innovations to increase traffic volume.

FIGURE 4.1 Types of Freight Equipment, 1997

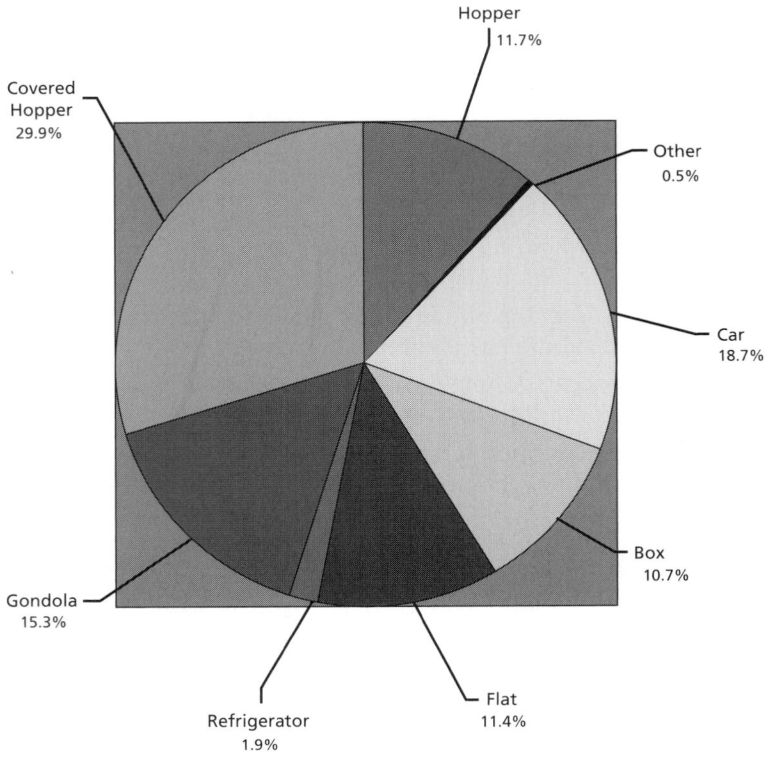

Source: Association of American Railroads, *Railroad Facts*, Washington, DC, 1998, p. 51.

The concept of piggyback service was designed by railroad management to increase service levels to intermodal customers. Piggyback traffic, which includes both TOFC and COFC services, accounted for 15.2 percent of total loadings in 1986, occupying a little less than 3 million cars and ranking second behind coal in total rail carloadings.[23] In 2001 more than 8.9 million trailers and containers were loaded. As can be seen in Table 4.5, intermodal carloadings increased until 2001, when there was a modest decline of 2.7 percent. When discussing piggyback service, consideration must be given to the individual concepts of TOFC and COFC movements.

TOFC service transports highway trailers on railroad flatcars. It combines the line-haul efficiencies of the railroads with the flexibility of local motor pickup and delivery service. On-time deliveries, regularly scheduled departures, and fuel efficiency are the major reasons for the present growth and future potential of TOFC service. For example, a 100-car train (which places two trailers on each flatcar) is more economical to run than 200 trucks over the road. Fuel is saved and railroad economies of scale are realized. Traffic congestion, road damage, and maintenance and repair costs are all reduced because of the reduction of number of trucks out on the highways.

Table 4.6 shows that the intermodal movement of trailers and containers grew rapidly during the 1980s. This growth was stimulated by the advent of double-stack containers used in international trade. Also, the railroads have placed new emphasis on their intermodal business after a number of years of doubting its profitability.

Table 4.6 Intermodal Carloadings

Year	Trailer and Containers
1965	1,664,929
1970	2,363,200
1975	2,238,117
1980	2,059,402
1985	4,590,952
1990	6,206,782
1992	6,627,891
1993	7,156,628
1994	8,128,228
1995	7,936,172
1996	8,143,258
1997	8,698,308
1998	8,772,663
1999	8,907,626
2000	9,176,890
2001	8,935,444

Source: Association of American Railroads, Railroad Facts, Washington, DC, 2002.

In recent years, the railroads have largely segregated their intermodal traffic from regular freight, with most of the intermodal trains operating on a priority schedule.

One result of the new schedules has been more reliable service for shippers, which has led to increased growth in loadings. The railroads have also simplified their billing procedures and made their computers accessible to customers for service innovations.

The growing use of TOFC by motor carrier companies has also contributed to the recent growth. United Parcel Service (UPS) has been a supporter of rail intermodal service for some time and is still their largest single customer. The LTL carriers began using intermodal service during the 1980s to handle their surges of traffic, and as rail service has become more reliable, they are using the rail service on a continuing basis. New union agreements allow truckers to substitute rail for over-the-road for up to 28 percent of the total traffic. The biggest change came recently when two of the largest truckload carriers, Schneider National and J. B. Hunt, purchased equipment to use rail intermodal service on an extensive basis. This commitment by these two large carriers has had a significant influence on the growth of rail intermodal service. Figure 4.2 shows the flows of traffic in the United States.

COFC is the international form of transportation for containers and is equivalent to domestic TOFC movements. A container does not have wheels and must therefore be placed on a flatbed truck for ramp-to-door delivery. The amount of handling is reduced because the container can be loaded and sealed at the origin and shipped directly to the consignee. Economies are realized because putting finished goods in containers means not only lower packaging and warehousing costs but also faster transit times because time and effort are saved in the loading, unloading, and delivery of goods. In addition, the TOFC piggyback plans can apply to COFC shipments with the substitution of the container for the trailer in the movement. Furthermore, land-bridge traffic, which substitutes railroads for ocean vessels for part of the journey, has become more widely used in international commerce because it facilitates the handling

FIGURE 4.2 Intermodal Traffic Flows

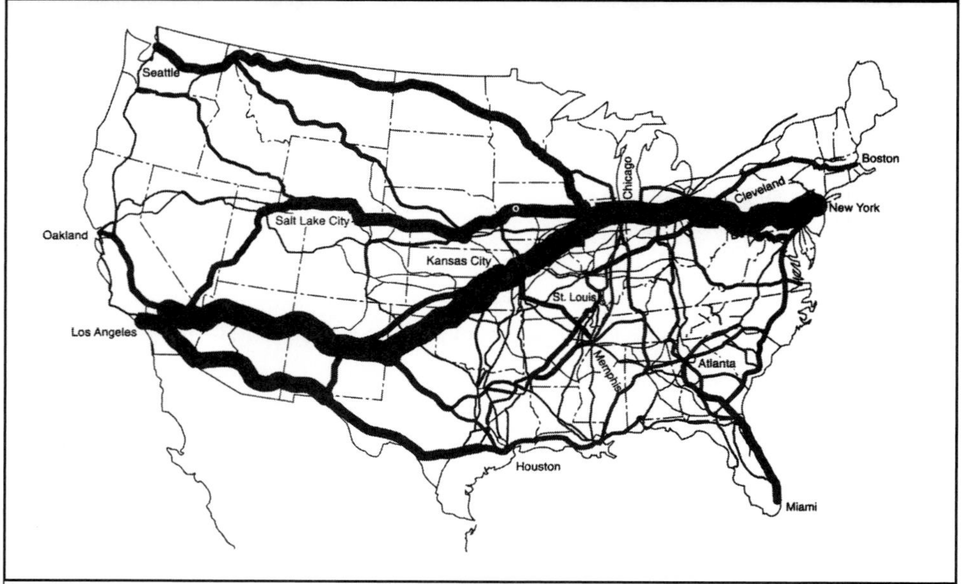

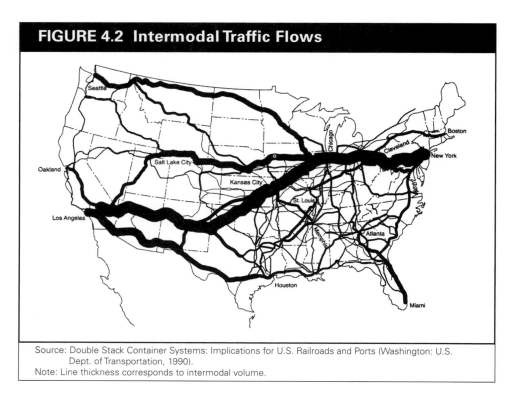

Source: Double Stack Container Systems: Implications for U.S. Railroads and Ports (Washington: U.S. Dept. of Transportation, 1990).
Note: Line thickness corresponds to intermodal volume.

of export–import commodities.[24] The double stacking of the containers on traffic to and from West Coast ports has improved the productivity of the rail COFC service dramatically.

The **unit train**, which evolved from the rent-a-train concept for the movement of goods, specializes in the transport of only one commodity, usually coal or grain, from origin to destination. Many times the shipper owns cars, and the train is, in effect, rented to the shipper for a particular period of time. For example, a typical utility coal unit train move would involve the transportation of 10,000 tons of coal in 100 hopper or gondola cars, each with a 100-ton capacity. The movement would be directly from the mine to an electric power-generating station with no stops in transit, and loading and unloading would be accomplished while the train was moving. Because of the single commodity nature of the concept and the need to maintain regularly scheduled movements, empty backhauls occur. However, this drawback is offset by the high revenue-producing capabilities of the unit train resulting from the improved overall car utilization.

The scale economies of the railroad industry have brought about the division and specialization of labor. Rail management has responded by increasing the use of computers and communications to help improve discipline and maintain control over rail operations. Elaborate information and communication systems have been developed so that a railroad's progress, status, and reliability can be monitored on an online basis. Car ordering and billing is simplified, while cars are traced and located, and orders are expedited at a faster rate. Computers are not a panacea, but they do help bring about increased efficiencies without any loss in service quality.

COST STRUCTURE

Fixed Costs

The railroad industry's cost structure in the short run (a period when both plant and capacity remain constant) consists of a large proportion of indirect fixed costs, rather than variable costs.[25] This situation exists because the railroads, along with the pipelines, are the only modes that own and maintain their own network and terminals.

In addition, railroads, like other modes, operate their own rolling stocks. In the past, it has been estimated by some managers that up to two-thirds of the industry's cost did not vary with volume.[26] Today it is believed that this figure is closer to 30 percent. The investment in long-lived assets has had a major impact on the cost characteristics of the industry. Cost structures will be discussed in more detail in a later chapter.

The major cost element borne by the railroad industry, and not found in the cost structure of other modes (excluding pipelines), is the operation, maintenance, and ownership of rights-of-way. **Rights-of-way** describe what a carrier's equipment uses to provide movement. For example, the railroads use track and ballast, while the motor carriers use highways. Initially, a large capital investment is required and annual maintenance costs become a substantial drain on earnings. Capital expenditures in 2001 alone amounted to $5.4 billion.[27]

Another major component of the railroad industry's high fixed costs is the extensive investment in private terminal facilities. These terminal facilities include freight yards, where trains are sorted and assembled, and terminal areas and sidings, where shippers and connecting railroads are serviced. Because of the large amount of fixed assets, the railroads as a group are not as responsive as other modes to the volume of traffic carried. Motor and water carriers, as well as the airline industry, are able to shift resources faster in response to changes in customer demand because of their use of "free" rights-of-way. Motor carriers, for instance, pay for their costs through user charges, tolls, and various taxes (such as gasoline taxes). These charges are related and vary directly with the volume handled, thereby creating a variable rather than a fixed cost for the user. Circumstances place the railroads at a disadvantage.

The investment for equipment in rail transport, principally for locomotives and various types of rolling stock, has been enormous. In 2001 more than $7.42 billion was spent on plants and equipment.[28] The Class I railroads operated 19,745 locomotives and some 499,860 freight cars in 2001.[29] Other railroads, car companies, and shippers owned or leased about 500,000 cars. The costs associated with equipment are both fixed and variable depending on which costs are used and what time period is being considered.

It is apparent that the railroads have a high proportion of expenses that are fixed and constant in the short run. However, they also have costs that vary substantially with volume.

Semivariable Costs

Semivariable costs, which include maintenance of rights-of-way, structures, and equipment, have accounted for more than 40 percent of railroad outlays in recent years and have amounted to more than $10 billion per year. These figures, however, are deceptive because some railroads that were in poor financial health had allowed their physical plants and equipment to deteriorate at alarming rates. The Federal Railroad Administration estimated that the industry has deferred more than $4 billion in maintenance expenses in some years.[30] Railway management found it necessary to forego maintenance to pay other pressing expenses, such as increased fuel and labor. Recently, maintenance schedules have been implemented on a regular basis so that service would not further deteriorate, and additional business would then be lost.

Variable Costs

Variable costs are one of the immediate concerns of railroad management, accounting for a large proportion of every revenue dollar spent by the railways. Labor cost is the largest single element of variable costs for railroads. Fuel and power costs are the next largest group of variable costs. Together these two categories account for a major portion of variable costs.

LABOR

In 2001 the cost of labor was $11.5 billion for $0.332 cents of every revenue dollar.[31] The average hourly gross earning for all employees was over $20, with an average annual earning of $58,153. Train and engine employees received an annual earning of $59,330, whereas maintenance workers received about $41,700. Together, these groups accounted for 76 percent of all the wages paid by the railroads.[32]

Railroad labor is represented by 14 different unions as opposed to the trucking industry, the vast majority of whose unionized employees are members of one union, the Teamsters. There are three major classifications of labor unions: operating, nonoperating craft, and nonoperating industrial. Each represents a different category of employee. The large number of unions has created difficulties for railroad management because each union guards its rights. Recently, some unions have merged and have shown much more flexibility in allowing innovation.

Railroad management believes that several of the work rules for the operating unions are either out of date or inefficient. The railroad industry has been reducing the size of the standard train crew wherever possible. Many positions, such as that of fireman, a carryover from the steam engine era, are no longer needed. In addition, the dual basis for pay for a full day's work (either 8 hours or 100 miles traveled) is inefficient in today's operating environment. Furthermore, "seniority districts," or the establishment of artificial boundaries beyond which an employee is not authorized to work, is another barrier to operating efficiency. Progress has been made with these issues, but they have not been completely resolved.

The railroad industry has been addressing work rules and staffing requirements in a very aggressive manner in the past several years. Several railroads have negotiated new crew agreements that have reduced the number of personnel required for trains. Conrail started a program in 1981 to buy off unnecessary brakemen and firemen; this program eliminated more than 1,900 positions, yielding a savings of $85 million.[33]

Starting in 1982, rail management took steps to remove cabooses from railroad trains. It has been estimated that the elimination of cabooses saved as much as $400 million per year. The rail brotherhood agreed that railroads could drop cabooses by local agreement, if possible, and by arbitration, if necessary.[34] Two-person crews are now the standard, with both riding on the locomotive.

Railroad managers feel that continuing changes in modifying or eliminating work rules for rail employees must be implemented in the near future if the industry is to survive in its present form. Mutual trust and cooperation should replace impediments between labor and management that restrict productivity gains, labor-savings methods, and technological advances. Progress in other industries has indicated the productivity gains that are possible.

FUEL

Fuel costs make up the second largest percentage of the revenue dollar. Fortunately, railroads have very efficient propulsion units, and productivity and fuel efficiency have increased dramatically since 1929. In the past 50 years, the railroads have more than doubled the revenue of ton-miles while reducing the locomotive units to less than one-half the 1929 level. Thus, the industry has been able to partially offset the increase in fuel costs by making locomotives more efficient. In 2001, only $3.2 billion was spent on fuel, showing a decrease of $0.75 billion from the 1980s level of $3.95 billion. This is a result of using more fuel-efficient engines and other train devices, such as wind-resistance designs.[35] The railroad's efficiency in the use of fuel is an important factor making intermodal movements with the motor carrier more attractive.

Economies of Scale

As previously indicated, railroads have a high level of fixed costs as contrasted with variable costs. Fixed costs, such as property taxes, are incurred regardless of traffic volume. Variable costs, on the other hand, vary or change with the volume of traffic moved; that is, they rise with increases and fall with decreases in traffic levels.

The development of any railroad requires a very large capital investment because of the cost incurred in buying land, laying tracks, building bridges, providing terminals, and providing right-of-way facilities. In addition, equipment investment is significant. Maintenance of right-of-way structures also results in fixed costs because it is usually the weather rather than use that necessitates such expenditures. The same is also true to some extent of equipment maintenance because the equipment spends so much time in freight yards and on sidings.

All costs are generally regarded as being variable in the long run because, as traffic increases, capacity is reached and new investment is needed in plants and equipment. However, because railroads are so large and facilities are durable, the short run can be a long period of time.

Our focus here is primarily on the short run. Consequently, you should make special note of the impact of the high level of fixed costs in the railroad industry. When fixed costs are present, a business will operate under conditions of increasing returns until capacity is reached. In other words, an increase in output (traffic) will not be accompanied by a proportionate increase in total costs because only the variable costs will increase. This will mean a decline in the per-unit costs because the fixed costs will be spread out over an increased number of units with subsequent unit-cost declines.

Let's consider several examples that illustrate the impact of fixed costs and economies of scale. Suppose that C. B. N. Railroad carries 200 million tons of freight at an average charge of $0.035 per ton. It has fixed costs of $3.5 million and variable costs of $2.5 million:

Fixed Costs	$3.5 million
Variable Costs	+ $2.5 million
Total Costs	*$6.0 million*
Revenue	$7.0 million
Profit	$1.0 million
Cost Per Ton	*$0.03*

Let's assume a 20-percent increase in traffic at the same average charge of $.035 per ton and no need to increase plant size:

Fixed Costs	$3.5 million
Variable Costs	$3.0 million
Total Costs	*$6.5 million*
Revenue	$8.4 million
Profit	$1.9 million
Cost Per Ton	*$0.0271*

It is obvious from the above example that, if average revenue stays the same, the economies of scale not only lower costs per unit but also increase profit.

FINANCIAL PLIGHT

As was stated previously, the railroad industry once enjoyed a virtual monopoly on the efficient and dependable transportation of passengers and freight. Railroads played a very important role in achieving various national objectives during the 19th century. Because of this, the government promoted the growth of the industry until a distinct change in public attitudes toward railroads became apparent.

The establishment in 1887 of the Interstate Commerce Commission (ICC), which was created to regulate maximum rates and to prevent discrimination to protect the rail shipper, marked the beginning of this change. In later years, the ICC's objective was to promote competition between modes of transportation while ensuring the financial health of the regulated carriers. However, this objective was never completely accomplished.[36] Competition tended to be restrained under the regulatory environment prior to 1975.

Over the decades, competition from other modes of transportation increased dramatically. By the 1950s, more people selected buses and planes for transportation, rather than rail transportation. The rail industry's share of the intercity freight market also declined to less than 50 percent during this time. Although competition from other modes became progressively more intense, the railroads were subject to strict regulations that frequently treated them as if they were still the dominant form of freight transportation.[37] Government funds were used to provide rail competitors with their rights-of-way without fully charging them the cost of constructing or maintaining them as with the rail industry. Between 1946 and 1975, the federal government spent more than $81 billion on highways, $24 billion on airports and supervision of airways, $10 billion on inland waterways, and only $1.3 billion on railroads.[38]

The financial position of the railroads grew increasingly worse after World War II. During the 1970s, the railroad industry's return on investment remained near 2 percent and never exceeded 3 percent. The railroads were plagued by decreasing market shares, poor future prospects, and high debt ratios. At least 20 percent of the industry was bankrupt by 1970. These poor conditions were evident in delayed or poor maintenance, increasing claims for damages, and accidents that cost the industry many of its much needed customers. The railroads' share of intercity freight revenues had fallen from 72 percent in 1929 to less than 18 percent in the mid-1970s.[39]

It became obvious that the railroad industry could not continue to survive under these conditions and that the main obstacle that needed to be cleared from the railroads' path to survival was probably excessive regulation that restricted their ability to compete. Poor earnings made it difficult for the railroads to earn or borrow sufficient funds to make improvements in track and rail facilities.[40]

Legislation Reform

The Rail Passenger Act of 1970 created the government-sponsored National Railroad Passenger Corporation (**Amtrak**), which relieved the railroads of their requirement to provide necessary passenger operations that were not profitable.[41] While only a few key "corridors" (the Northeast corridor, Boston, New York, and Washington, DC) were profitable enough to fully support regularly scheduled intercity passenger service, Congress still supports this service.

The **Regional Rail Reorganization Act of 1973 (3R Act)** attempted to maintain rail freight service in the Northeast by creating the Consolidated Rail Corporation (Conrail), which was formed from six bankrupt northeastern railroads. The act also created the United States Railroad Association (USRA) as the government agency responsible for planning and financing the restructuring. By 1980, the federal government had granted Conrail more than $3.3 billion in federal subsidies to cover its operating expenses.[42]

Conrail proved to be very successful and was "spun off" to the public with the sale of in 1992. Conrail's management was able to rationalize the excess track while preserving and improving service. After a failed attempt by CSX to take over Conrail, CSX and the Norfolk Southern Railroad agreed to split Conrail between them and paid collectively over $10 billion for the property.

The **Railroad Revitalization and Regulatory Reform Act of 1976 (4R Act)** was the first attempt to deregulate the industry since the railroads came under regulation in 1887. The goals of the 4R Act were to help the railroads obtain funds for capital investment and to allow the railroads more freedom concerning decisions on mergers, abandonments, and rate making.[43] Although the 4R Act was an attempt to deal with regulatory problems, the ICC's interpretation of the act negated much of its positive aspects and in some cases actually increased rail regulation.

The **Staggers Rail Act** did a great deal to enable the railroads to help themselves and avoid further deterioration of the industry, although they still face financial challenges because their return on equity is very low (about 3 percent) compared to many other industries. However, many railroad managers are optimistic that the industry will be able to keep its profitability and financial health if the Staggers Rail Act is not altered to introduce more regulatory control and is allowed to continue working.[44] Many railroads have continuously improved their financial situation during the 1980s.

The **ICC Termination Act of 1995** eliminated the ICC and transferred economic rail regulation to the Surface Transportation Board (STB), which is part of the DOT. The STB has taken a relaxed posture on rail regulation, sometimes to the dismay of the shippers, so the railroads are now subject to market pressures more than economic regulations. It is interesting to observe that the STB faces some of the same challenges faced by the ICC (i.e., rail consolidation, larger shipper bargaining power, capitalization, etc.).

Improved Service to Customers

Since the Staggers Rail Act, the performance of the railroads has been improving in the eyes of some of its customers. Rail freight revenue per ton declined by an inflation-adjusted 27 percent in the period of 1992 to 2001. This decline in freight rates is evident in the two major areas of coal and grain rates. Coal rates dropped by 10 percent and grain rates dropped an inflation-adjusted 40.8 percent during this same period.

As shown in Table 4.6, **intermodal** traffic has expanded by almost 300 percent during the period of 1980 to 2001, while productivity measures also have shown an increase.[45] An important indicator of improved performance is the railroads' continued good safety record. Train accidents declined by over 60 percent from 1980 to 2001. Consequently, injuries and fatalities also have fallen.

A positive effect of the railroads' performance was shown in a survey of rail shippers. The survey showed that 86 percent of the shippers polled approved of government actions for allowing the railroads rate-making freedom.[46] Many signs indicate that deregulation has brought improvement to the railroads (improved financial status) and to their customers. The industry has changed dramatically in many ways, including providing more tailored service and equipment and negotiating contract rates for volume movements. The railroads have worked hard to improve their operating performance times and reliability. Table 4.7 provides a comprehensive summary of railroad characteristics for review.

CURRENT ISSUES

Alcohol and Drug Abuse

Alcohol and drug abuse has affected almost every workplace in the United States. Many industries, including the rail industry, are taking a close look at the problem and at possible methods of dealing with it.

The problem of substance abuse can be brought on by the very nature of railroad work. Long hours, low supervision, and nights away from home can lead to loneliness and boredom, which can then lead to substance abuse. Because of this situation, the railroads have been dealing with the problem of substance abuse for a century. Rule G, which was established in 1897, prohibits the use of narcotics and alcohol on company property. Rail employees violating this rule could be subject to dismissal; however, the severity of this punishment led to the silence of many rail workers who did not want to jeopardize the jobs of their coworkers.

To deal with this problem, the railroad industry has attempted to identify and help employees with substance abuse problems. The industry has established **employee assistance programs** (EAPs) that enable these troubled employees to be rehabilitated.

Employees can voluntarily refer themselves to EAPs before a supervisor detects the problem and disciplinary actions become necessary. However, a Rule G violation—substance abuse while on the job—usually necessitates removal of the employee from the workplace to ensure his or her safety and the safety of coworkers. Employees who

Table 4.7 Summary: Railroad Industry Characteristics

• General service characteristics	• In completion with motor carriers; shippers of bulk products
• Investments/capital outlays	• High investments/equipment, track
• Cost structure	• High fixed costs, low variable costs
• Ease of entry	• Low
• Market structure	• Oligopoly/monopoly
• Ways in which they compete	• Price (intramodal) and service (intermodal)
• Types of commodities	• Low-value, high-volume bulk commodities
• Number of carriers	• Small number of large carriers
• Markets in which they compete	• High-value chemicals, long-haul but large commodities

are removed can still use EAPs for rehabilitation and can apply for reinstatement after they have overcome their problem.

Railroad EAPs have proven to be very effective. A recent Federal Railroad Administration report found that the rate of successful rehabilitation has risen by 70 percent. The success of these programs depends largely on support from rail workers as well as all levels of management.[47]

Energy

The energy shortages of the 1970s made the United States increasingly aware of the need to conserve natural resources. The U.S. government, for example, decided to reduce the quantity of fuels and petroleum products that are imported into the country. Americans want to preserve and, wherever possible, clean up the environment. The railroads today are in a favorable position, especially when compared to motor carriers, because they are efficient energy consumers. For instance, a train locomotive uses less fuel than a tractor–trailer in pulling the same amount of weight. In fact, a study supported by the National Science Foundation indicates that railroads are more energy-efficient per ton-mile than any other freight mode except pipelines, using only 670 BTUs per ton-mile (see Table 4.8).[48]

Another study by the U.S. DOT concluded that railroads are more energy-efficient than motor carriers, even when measured in terms of consumption per ton-mile.[49] In addition to being more energy-efficient, railroads cause less damage to the environment than do trucks. In 1980, railroad emissions (0.9 grams per net ton-mile) were 75 percent less than truck emissions.[50] Railroads, in comparison to trucks—a major competitor—are able to move large amounts of freight with less energy and less harm to the environment.

The railroads economically shipped 8.4 million tons of energy-yielding products in 2001; 95 percent of these loadings were coal movements. Because coal, which can be converted into electricity, is an abundant substitute for oil, electric utility companies can convert their present processes to coal whenever economically possible. Because the railroads already transport approximately three-quarters of all the coal moved, they would be able to increase service to the utilities and capture more of the market by using high-volume-unit coal trains.

Hence, the railroads can be an important factor in the development of the nation's energy policy.

Technology

To become more efficient and consequently more competitive, the railroad industry is becoming a high-tech industry. Computers are playing a large role in every mode of

Table 4.8 Relative Fuel Efficiency of Transportation Modes

Mode	Actual BTU[a] per Ton-Mile	Price (Cents per Ton-Mile)	Haul Length (Miles)	Speed (MPH)
Pipeline	490	0.27	300	5
Railroad	670	1.40	500	20
Waterway	680	0.30	1,000	—
Truck	2,800	7.50	300	40
Airplane	42,000	21.90	1,000	400

a BTU = British thermal units.

Source: Association of American Railroads, *More Miles to the Gallon... The Railroads*, Washington, DC, 1974, p. 4.

transportation, and the railroads are no exception. A line of "smart" locomotives is being equipped with onboard computers that can identify mechanical problems, and the legendary "red caboose" was phased out by a small device weighing 30 pounds that attaches to the last car of the train. This electric device transmits important information to engineers and dispatchers alike, including information about the braking system. Other applications of computer technology are as follows:

- Advanced Train Control Systems (ATCS): A joint venture between the United States and Canada that will use computers to efficiently track the flow of trains through the entire rail system
- Rail yard control: Computer control of freight yards that is used to sort and classify as many as 2,500 railcars a day
- Communications and signaling: Provides quick and efficient communications between dispatchers, yard workers, field workers, and train crews
- Customer service: By calling a toll-free number, customers can receive information on the status of their shipments, correct billing errors, and plan new service schedules
- Radio Frequency Identification (RFID) tags to track equipment and shipments and improve visibility.

The role of high technology and computers will continue to expand and increase the ability of the railroads to provide progressively higher levels of customer service.[51] Please refer to Chapter 11, "Information Management and Technology," for a further explanation of technology.

Future Role of Smaller Railroads

As noted, the deregulation of the railroad industry in 1980 led to a number of important changes. The consolidation among so-called Class I railroads has been duly noted in this chapter. The obvious outcome was a reduction in the number of carriers in this category, but interestingly, it led to an increase in the number of regional and small rail carriers. These small and regional rail carriers typically took over part of the infrastructure abandoned by the large railroads who spun off parts of their system that had low traffic levels and/or were deemed not to be needed for market success.

The small and regional carriers often have to operate at a cost disadvantage compared to the large rail system carriers who have the advantage economies of scale. However, the smaller rail companies have some advantages given that they are more flexible and adaptable in meeting the needs of their customers (shippers). They are usually not unionized, which also helps to make them more flexible. Another possible advantage is local ownership of the rail companies and the related willingness to accept lower returns and/or pay closer attention to customer needs to promote regional economic development.

It should also be noted that local and state governments have assisted in financing the establishment of the new lines that have come into being since 1984. This community support is usually based upon a need to continue the rail service for the economic benefit of existing and potential new businesses. Although truck transportation has often filled the need of smaller communities for transportation service, rail service may be viewed by some communities as a necessary ingredient for the economic viability of the area. Consequently, many communities have had the advantage of continuing rail service that would not have been possible otherwise.

The large Class I railroads have been frequent targets for criticism about the service they provide to their customers. The smaller lines are usually viewed in a more favorable light because of their responsiveness at the local level. However, the small and regional rail carriers are usually more vulnerable if a large shipper along their line decides to close their operations. The future role of some of those carriers is somewhat uncertain because of these factors.

Customer Service

As suggested in this chapter, the large Class I railroads are perceived by some shippers as not being customer focused. This criticism has grown in intercity transport during the 1990s as mergers continued to occur. The new, larger companies appeared insensitive to shipper needs and concerns about equipment and service. Some of the service and equipment issues are attributable to the challenges inherent in combining relatively large organizations with unique systems and procedures, and problems always occur in spite of serious "up-front" planning.

To the extent that those equipment and service problems have persisted during the last several years, is indicative of the legitimacy of shipper complaints. There are differences among the "majors" or Class I railroads in terms of their customer service focus, but unfortunately some shippers are inclined to lump them altogether as being unsatisfactory. Consequently, this is a major issue for railroads, and improvements need to be made to increase rail market shares of freight traffic.

Drayage for Intermodal Service

As indicated previously in this chapter, one of the constraints on rail service is the fixed nature of the rail routes and the high cost to add rail segments to provide direct service. Consequently, the beginning and/or the end of a rail movement may depend upon motor carrier service. This is, obviously, especially true for intermodal service in trailers on containers. The pickup and delivery of trailers and containers in conjunction with a line-haul rail movement is usually referred to as local drayage.

When the railroads are carrying the trailers or containers of a motor carrier as a substitute for the motor carrier providing the line-haul service, local drayage is not an issue because the motor carrier will provide these links. However, when the railroad is the land carrier, it will have to arrange for local drayage for pickup and delivery. Motor carriers that are willing and able to provide this service for the railroads are becoming scarce and charging relatively high rates for the service. In some instances, the pickup and delivery time adds significantly to the total transit time. This is another area that needs attention to improve rail service.

Summary

- The railroads played a significant role in the economic and social development of the United States for about 100 years (1850–1950) and continue to be the leading mode of transportation in terms of intercity ton-miles, but they no longer dominate the freight market.
- The railroad segment of the transportation industry is led by a decreasing number of large Class I carriers, but the number of small (Class III) carriers has been increasing in number since the deregulation of railroads in 1980.
- Intermodal competition for railroads has increased dramatically since World War II, but the level of intramodal competition has decreased as the number of Class I railroads has decreased. The increased intermodal competition has led to more rate competition.

- Mergers have been occurring among railroads for many years, but the pace has accelerated during the past 30 years, leading to rapid decrease in the number of Class I railroads.
- In recent years, the railroads have become more specialized in terms of the traffic they carry, with the emphasis being on low-value, high-density, bulk products; however, there is some evidence of a resurgence of selected manufactured products such as transportation equipment.
- In recent years, railroads have been emphasizing new technologies and specialized equipment to improve their service performance and satisfy customers.
- Intermodal service (TOFC/COFC) has received renewed interest since 1980, and there has been a dramatic growth in the movement of such traffic by railroads.
- Long-distance truckload carriers and other motor-carrier companies such as UPS have also begun to use rail intermodal service.
- The railroads have a high level of proportion of fixed costs because they provide their own right-of-way and terminal facilities. Because the large railroads are multistate operators, the amount of fixed expenditures is significant.
- The cost of labor is the single most important component of variable costs for railroads, but the railroad industry has been striving to reduce labor costs on a relative basis by eliminating work rules that were a carryover from another era.
- The high level of fixed costs helps give rise to economies of scale in the railroad industry, which can have a dramatic impact upon profits when the volume of traffic increases.
- The financial plight of the railroads has improved since deregulation in 1980 as railroads have been able to respond more quickly and aggressively to market pressures from other modes, particularly motor carriers.
- A number of important issues are facing railroads at present, including substance abuse, energy, technology, small railroads and local drayage.

Key Terms

Amtrak, 147
carloads, 138
Container-on-flatcar (COFC), 138
economies of scale, 145
employee assistance program, 148
end-to-end mergers, 133
ICC Termination Act of 1995, 147
intermodal traffic, 148
intramodal competition, 131
liability, 137
local drayage, 151
Railroad Revitalization and Regulatory Reform Act of 1976 (4R Act), 147
Regional Rail Reorganization Act of 1973 (3R Act), 147
return on investment (ROI), 129
right-of-way, 143
side-by-side mergers, 133
Staggers Rail Act, 147
Trailer-on-flatcar (TOFC), 138
types of mergers, 133
unit train, 142

Study Questions

1. Railroads no longer dominate the freight transportation market but they still lead the market in terms of freight ton-miles. What factors contribute to their leadership in this area? Why is their share of the total expenditures for freight movement so small if they lead in freight ton-miles?

2. Since the passage of the Staggers Rail Act of 1980, there has been an increase in the number of small railroads (Class III). Why has this number increased while the number of Class I railroads have decreased?

3. Explain the difference between intramodal and intermodal competition in the railroad industry. Which form of competition is most beneficial to shippers? Why?

4. One of the significant factors in rail development has been the number of mergers that have occurred, but there have been different types of mergers that have occurred over time. Discuss the major types of mergers and explain why they occurred. Will mergers continue to occur in the rail industry? Why or why not?

5. What factors have contributed to the decline in the volume of higher-value freight by the railroads? What changes, if any, could the railroads make to attract back more higher-value freight from motor carriers?

6. Railroads have abandoned a significant number of miles of track (over 260,000 miles) since 1916. Why has this trend developed? Will it continue into the future? Why or why not?

7. The railroad industry has developed a number of new types of equipment to replace the standard boxcar. What is the rationale supporting the diversification of equipment?

8. The railroad industry's cost structure is different than that of the motor carrier industry. What factors contribute to this difference? What impact do these differences have for the railroads in terms of pricing, competiveness, and investment?

9. Discuss the major current issues facing the railroad industry. Select one of these major issues and present appropriate recommendations for resolving the issue.

10. What factors have contributed to the success of intermodal rail service? What barriers exist to future expansion?

Notes

1. *Transportation in America*, 19th ed., Washington DC: Eno Transportation Foundation, 2002, p. 44.

2. Association of American Railroads, *Railroad Facts*, Washington, DC, 2002, p. 5.

3. *Transportation in America*, p. 5.

4. Ibid., p. 61.

5. Ibid., pp. 8–9.

6. Ibid., p. 44.

7. Association of American Railroads, *Railroad Facts*, 2002, p. 3.

8. U.S. Department of Commerce, *Bureau of the Census, Historical Statistics of the United States: Colonial Times to 1975*, Washington, DC: U.S. Government Printing Office, 1960, p. 429.

9. Association of American Railroads, *Railroad Facts*, 2002, p. 44.

10. *Trains*, August 1996, p. 14.

11. The National Commission of Productivity, *Improving Railroad Productivity*, p. 161.

12. The commodity groups included here are metals and metal products; food and kindred products; stone, clay, and glass products; and grainmill products.

13. Association of American Railroads, *Railroad Facts*, 2002, p. 5.

14. Reebie Associates, *The Railroad Situation: A Perspective on the Past, Present, and Future of the Railroad Industry*, Washington, DC: U.S. Department of Transportation, March 1979, p. 687.

15. Association of American Railroads, *Railroad Facts*, Washington, DC, 1997, p. 29.

16. Ibid., p. 29.

17. Donald D. Roth, *An Approach to Measurement of Modal Advantage*, Washington, DC: American Trucking Association, 1977, p. 11.

18. Tom Judge, ed., "Shake, Rattle & Roll," *Progressive Railroading*, Vol. 39, October 1996, pp. 30–32.

19. Association of American Railroads, *Railroad Facts*, 2002, p. 24.

20. Ibid., p. 52.
21. Ibid., p. 51.
22. Ibid., p. 37.
23. Association of American Railroads, *Railroad Facts*, 2002, p. 39.
24. Association of American Railroads, press release, Washington, DC, 1979, p. 342.
25. Fixed costs remain the same over a period of time or a range of output (such as labor costs). Semivariable costs contain some fixed variable elements (such as setup costs on a production line).
26. R. J. Sampson and M. I. Farris, *Domestic Transportation: Practice, Theory, and Policy*, 4th ed., Boston: Houghton Mifflin, 1979, p. 59.
27. Association of American Railroads, *Railroad Facts*, 1997, p. 9.
28. Ibid., p. 15.
29. Ibid., p. 48.
30. U.S. Department of Transportation, *A Prospectus for Change in the Freight Railroad Industry*, Washington, DC: U.S. Government Printing Office, 1978, p. 65.
31. Association of American Railroads, *Railroad Facts*, 2002, p. 11.
32. Ibid., p. 56.
33. Frank Wilner, *Railroads and the Marketplace*, Washington, DC: Association of American Railroads, 1988, p. 7.
34. Ibid., p. 2.
35. Association of American Railroads, *Railroad Facts*, 1997, p. 60.
36. Association of American Railroads, *Railroad Facts*, Washington, DC, 1988, p. 11.
37. Ibid., p. 9.
38. Frank Wilner, *Railroads and the Marketplace*, Washington, DC: Association of American Railroads, 1988, p. 7.
39. Ibid., p. 9.
40. Ibid., pp. 8–12.
41. Ibid., p. 2.
42. Consolidated Rail Corporation, *Summary of Business Plan*, Philadelphia: Consolidated Rail Corporation, 1979, p. 5.
43. Wilner, op cit., p. 15.
44. Ibid.
45. Association of American Railroads, *Railroad Facts*, 2002, p. 26.
46. Association of American Railroads, *Railroad Facts*, Washington, DC, 1992, p. 3.
47. Association of American Railroads, *"What are the Railroads Doing About Drug Abuse?"*, Washington, DC: 1986, pp. 1–4.
48. Consolidated Rail Corporation, *Summary of Business Plan*, p. 5.
49. Wilner, op cit., p. 15.
50. Ibid.
51. American Association of Railroads, *High Technology Rides the Rails*, Washington, DC, 1988, pp. 1–3.

Case 4-1

CBN Railway Company

CEO John Spychalski is concerned about a problem that has existed at CBN railroad for almost 20 years now. The continuous problem has been that the locomotives used by the company are not very reliable. Even with prior decisions to resolve the problem, there still has not been a change in the reliability of these locomotives. Between 1995 and 1997, 155 new locomotives were purchased and one of CBN's repair shops was renovated. The renovated shop has been very inefficient. Spychalski estimated that the shop would complete 300 overhauls on a yearly basis, but instead it has only managed to complete an average of 160 overhauls per year.

The company has also been doing a poor job servicing customers (i.e., providing equipment). CBN has averaged only 87 to 88 percent equipment availability compared to other railroads with availability figures greater than 90 percent. Increased business in the rail industry has been a reason for trying to reduce the time used for repairing the locomotives. CBN's mean time between failure rate is low—45 days—compared to other railroads whose mean time between failure rates is higher than 75 days. This factor, Spychalski feels, has contributed to CBN's poor service record.

CBN is considering a new approach to the equipment problem: Spychalski is examining the possibility of leasing 135 locomotives from several sources. The leases would run between 90 days to 5 years. In addition, the equipment sources would maintain the repairs on 469 locomotives currently in CBN's fleet, but CBN's employees would do the actual labor on the locomotives. The lease arrangements, known as "power-by-the-mile" arrangements, call for the manufacturers doing the repair work to charge only for maintenance on the actual number of miles that a particular unit operates. The company expects the agreements to last an average of 15 years. John Thomchick, the executive vice president, estimates that CBN would save about $5 million annually because the company will not have to pay for certain parts and materials. Problems with the locomotives exist throughout CBN's whole system, and delays to customers have been known to last up to 5 days. Spychalski and Thomchick feel that the leasing arrangement will solve CBN's problems.

Case Questions

1. What are potential advantages and disadvantages of entering into these "power-by-the-mile" arrangements?
2. What should be done if the problem with the locomotives continues even with the agreements?
3. Do you think that the decision to lease the locomotives was the best decision for CBN? Explain your answer.

Case 4-2

Nittany Valley Shortline Railroad

Bob Patterson, CEO of Nittany Valley Shortline Railroad, met recently with Rich Young, president of Central Pennsylvania Distribution and Warehousing Company (CPD&W). Rich and Bob thought that they could help each other. Bob's company was going to lose its largest customer, Shannon Glass, in several months because Shannon was going to close its plant, which was located along its line near Pleasant Gap, Pennsylvania. Rich Young's warehousing company was also located along the rail line closer to Bellefonte, Pennsylvania. Rich Young's company also provided service to Shannon Glass. In fact, Shannon was also 20 percent of CPD&W's business volume.

Patterson and Young believed that they should try to coordinate and expand their services to potential and existing clients. What they envisioned was value-added services that they could offer, including transportation, warehousing, inventory management, and other logistics services.

Case Questions

1. What are the advantages and disadvantages of such a joint-service offering?
2. What special challenges will Young and Patterson face?

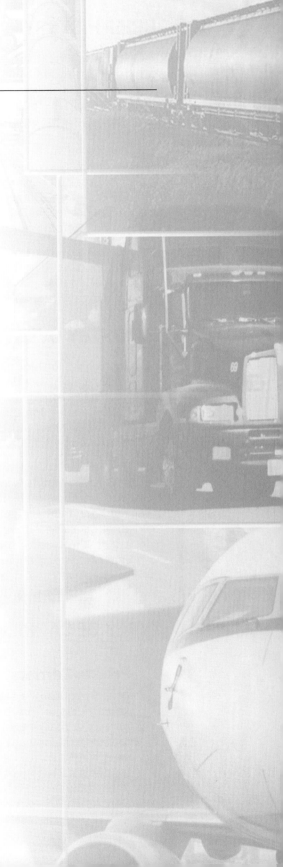

Chapter 5

Air Carriers

BRIEF HISTORY

From the first flight that lasted less than 1 minute to space shuttles orbiting the earth, air transportation has come a long way in a short period of time. Wilbur and Orville Wright made their first flight in 1903 at Kitty Hawk and sold their invention to the federal government. In 1908 the development of air transportation began with the **U.S. Post Office** examining the feasibility of providing air mail service. Although airplanes were used in World War I, the use of airplanes for mail transport can be considered the beginning of the modern airline industry. Passenger transportation services developed as a by-product of the mail business and began to flourish in selected markets. Since that time, airplanes have become faster, bigger, and relatively more fuel-efficient. Although the level and degree of technological improvement have slowed in the airline industry, there is still opportunity for further innovation.

Airline travel is a common form of transportation for long-distance passenger and freight travel and the only reasonable alternative when time is of the essence. The tremendous speed of the airplane, coupled with more competitive pricing, has led to the growth of air transportation, particularly in the movement of passengers.

INDUSTRY OVERVIEW AND SIGNIFICANCE

In 2002 for-hire air carriers had total operating revenues of $106.9 billion, of which $73.3 billion (68.6 percent) came from passenger service.[1] In 2002 air carriers transported 24.5 million revenue ton-miles, or approximately 0.5 percent of total intercity ton-miles.[2] **Employment** in the air carrier industry totaled 601,356 people in 2002, with an average annual compensation of over $74,831 for persons employed by scheduled carriers.[3]

The airline industry is very dependent on **passenger revenues** to maintain its financial viability. However, to characterize airlines simply as movers of people presents too simplistic a view of their role in our transportation system. The airlines are a unique and important group of carriers that meet some particular needs in our society. Although their share of the freight movement on a ton-mile basis is small, the type of traffic that they carry (high-value, perishable, or emergency) makes them an important part of our total transportation system. Emphasis upon total logistics cost in a quick-response lead-time environment will continue to contribute to their growth in freight movements.

TYPES OF CARRIERS

Private Carriers

Air carriers can be segmented into for-hire carriers and private carriers. A private air carrier is a firm that transports company personnel or freight in planes to support its primary business. The preponderance of private air transportation is used to transport company personnel, although emergency freight is sometimes carried on private airplanes as well. Rarely, however, is a private air carrier established to routinely carry freight. The private air carrier is subject to the federal safety regulations administered by the Federal Aviation Administration (FAA) of the U.S. Department of Transportation.

For-Hire Carriers

The for-hire carriers are no longer regulated on an economic basis by the federal government and cannot be easily categorized into specific types because carriers provide many types of services. For our purposes, the for-hire carriers will be discussed according to type of service offered (all-cargo, air taxi, commuter, charter, and international) and annual revenue (majors, nationals, and regionals).

A classification frequently used by U.S. air carriers is one based on annual operating **revenues**. The categories used to classify air carriers in terms of revenue are as follows:

Majors — annual revenues of more than $1 billion

Nationals — annual revenues of $100 million to $1 billion

Regionals — annual revenues of less than $100 million

U.S. major carriers have $1 billion or more in annual revenues and provide service between major population areas within the United States such as New York, Chicago, and Los Angeles. The routes served by these carriers are usually high-density corridors, and the carriers use high-capacity planes. The U.S. **majors** also serve medium-sized population centers such as Harrisburg, Pennsylvania. Examples of major U.S. carriers are American, United, Delta, US Airways, and Southwest.

U.S. **national** carriers have revenues of $100 million to $1 billion and operate between less-populated areas and major population centers. These carriers operate scheduled service over relatively short routes with smaller planes. They "feed" passengers from outlying areas into airports served by the U.S. majors. Today, many of the U.S. national carriers operate over relatively large, regional areas and are stiff competition for the U.S. majors on many routes. Examples of U.S. nationals include JetBlue, Sun Country, and Frontier Airlines.

Regional carriers have annual revenues of less than $100 million and have operations similar to the nationals. The carriers operate within a particular region of the country, such as New England or the Midwest, and connect less-populated areas with larger population centers. Included in the regional category are carriers such as Air Midwest, Allegheny, and PSA. The regional carriers are grouped into two categories: large ($10million–$100 million) and medium (less than $10 million).

The **all-cargo carrier**, as the name implies, primarily transports cargo. The transportation of air cargo was deregulated in 1977, permitting the all-cargo carriers to freely set rates, enter and exit markets, and use any size aircraft dictated by the market. Examples of all-cargo carriers include FedEx and UPS Airlines.

The **commuter** air carrier is technically a regional carrier. The commuter publishes timetables on specific routes that connect less-populated routes with major cities. As certified carriers abandon routes, usually low-density routes, the commuter enters into a working relationship with the certified carrier to continue service to the community. The commuter then connects small communities that have reduced or no air service with larger communities that have better scheduled service. The commuter's schedule is closely aligned with connecting flight schedules at a larger airport. Many commuter firms use turboprop aircraft to feed the major hubs of the major airlines. Today, however, some commuters are adding regional jets that not only continue to feed these hubs but also offer direct service to larger metropolitan areas. Many commuter operators are franchised by the majors, such as US Airways Express.

The **charter carriers**, also known as air taxis, use small to medium size aircraft to transport people or freight. The supplemental carrier has no time schedule or designated route. The carrier charters the entire plane to transport a group of people or cargo between specified origins and destinations. Many travel tour groups use charter carriers. However, a big customer for charters is the Department of Defense; it uses charter carriers to transport personnel and supplies. For example, Operation Iraqi Freedom (OIF) relied upon charters for some of their moves of personnel and supplies. The rates charged and schedules followed are negotiated in the contract.

Many U.S. carriers are also international carriers and operate between the continental United States and foreign countries, and between the United States and its territories (such as Puerto Rico). Because service to other countries has an effect on U.S. international trade and relations, the president of the United States is involved in awarding the international routes. Examples of international carriers include United and American. Many foreign carriers provide services between the United States and their country, such as British Air and Air France.

MARKET STRUCTURE

Number of Carriers

A look at carrier revenues shows a concentration of earnings by a small group of majors, nationals, and regionals. (Table 5.1 provides numbers for these three categories.) Table 5.1 shows that a majority of air movements are made by 141 carriers. The largest increase in number of carriers has occurred with the regionals. In fact, 96 percent of total industry revenue was generated by the top 25 carriers (see Table 5.2).

Private air transportation has been estimated to include approximately 60,000 company-owned planes, with over 500 U.S. corporations operating private air fleets. In addition, thousands of planes are used for personal, recreational, and instructional purposes.

Deregulation in 1978 was expected to result in a larger number of airlines competing for passengers and freight traffic. The number of major airlines did increase initially, but as Table 5.1 indicates, the number of airlines had decreased by 1994. Available seat miles for 2002 declined by 4.1 percent as some carriers traded larger

Table 5.1 Number of Carriers

Carriers	1984	1987	1994	1996	2001	2002
Majors	11	14	11	11	15	14
Nationals	19	20	24	26	39	35
Regionals					46	92
Large	37	32	20	24		
Medium	28	27	20	28		
Total	95	93	85	89	100[a]	141[a]

[a] After 1996, The Air Transport Association stopped categorizing large and medium regionals.

Source: Air Transport Association, 2003 Annual Report.

Table 5.2 Top 25 Airlines by Various Rankings—2002

Passengers (Thousands)			Revenue Passenger Miles (Millions)		
1	**American**	**94,048**	1	**American**	**121,668**
2	**Delta**	**90,799**	2	**United**	**109,395**
3	**Southwest**	**72,448**	3	**Delta**	**93,494**
4	**United**	**68,350**	4	**Northwest**	**72,002**
5	**Northwest**	**51,743**	5	**Continental**	**57,003**
6	**US Airways**	**47,155**	6	**Southwest**	**45,396**
7	**Continental**	**39,486**	7	**US Airways**	**40,024**
8	**America West**	**19,426**	8	**America West**	**19,855**
9	**Alaska**	**14,138**	9	**Alaska**	**13,178**
10	American Eagle	11,835	10	**American Trans Air**	**9,415**
11	AirTran	9,652	11	**JetBlue**	**6,830**
12	Continental Express	9,212	12	AirTran	5,582
13	Comair	8,732	13	**Hawaiian**	**4,450**
14	Atlantic Southeast	8,329	14	Spirit	4,096
15	**American Trans Air**	**7,846**	15	Continental Express	3,951
16	**JetBlue**	**5,672**	16	Comair	3,748
17	Mesaba	5,587	17	American Eagle	3,673
18	**Hawaiian**	**5,183**	18	Frontier	3,363
19	Horizon Air	4,815	19	Atlantic Southeast	3,296
20	**Aloha**	**4,367**	20	National	2,469
21	Frontier	3,722	21	Continental Micronesia	2,394
22	Spirit	3,672	22	**Midwest Express**	**1,966**
23	**Midwest Express**	**2,164**	23	Mesaba	1,607
24	Trans States	2,018	24	**Aloha**	**1,605**
25	National	1,910	25	Horizon Air	1,505

Bolded Airlines = ATA Members.

Freight Ton-Miles (Millions)			Total Operating Revenues ($Millions)		
1	**FedEx**	**9,094**	1	**FedEx**	**15,941**
2	**UPS Airlines**	**4,534**	2	**American**	**15,871**
3	**Atlas Air**	**2,376**	3	**United**	**13,916**
4	**United**	**2,276**	4	**Delta**	**12,410**
5	**Northwest**	**2,224**	5	**Northwest**	**9,152**
6	**American**	**2,014**	6	**Continental**	**7,353**
7	**Delta**	**1,458**	7	**US Airways**	**6,915**
8	**Polar Air Cargo**	**1,349**	8	**Southwest**	**3,522**
9	**Continental**	**859**	9	**UPS Airlines**	**2,852**
10	**Airborne Express**	**685**	10	**American West**	**2,021**
11	Gemini Air Cargo	440	11	**Alaska**	**1,832**
12	**US Airways**	**406**	12	American Eagle	1,199
13	**Evergreen Int'l**	**389**	13	**American Trans Air**	**1,150**
14	Southern Air	249	14	**Airborne Express**	**1,117**
15	Tradewinds	225	15	Atlantic Southeast	752
16	**DHL Airways**	**218**	16	AirTran	733
17	Arrow Air	205	17	**JetBlue**	**635**
18	Air Transport Int'l	199	18	**Hawaiian**	**632**
19	Kalitta	178	19	**Polar Air Cargo**	**527**
20	Express.Net	159	20	Frontier	465
21	World	149	21	Air Wisconsin	445
22	Kitty Hawk Air Cargo	140	22	Horizon Air	415
23	**Southwest**	**128**	23	Spirit	404
24	Florida West Int'l	99	24	World	384
25	Calital Cargo Int'l	86	25	**Evergreen Int'l**	**378**

Source: Air Transport Association, 2003 Annual Report.

aircraft for regional jets.[4] However, the number of flights increased from 8.8 million in 2001 to 9 million in 2002. Part of this was due to the fact that the number of delays decreased from 954 per day in 2001 to 783 per day in 2002.[5]

COMPETITION

Intermodal

Due to their unique service, air carriers face **limited competition** from other modes for both passengers and freight. Air carriers have an advantage in providing time-sensitive, long-distance movement of people or freight. Airlines compete to some extent with motor carriers for the movement of higher-valued manufactured goods; they face competition from automobiles for the movement of passengers and, to a limited extent, from trains and buses. For short distances (under 500 miles), the access time and terminal time offsets the speed of the airline for the line-haul.

Intramodal

Competition in rates and service among the air carriers is very **intense**, even though the number of carriers is small. As noted, passenger air carrier regulation was significantly reduced in 1978, and new carriers entered selected routes (markets), thereby increasing the amount of competition (see Chapter 9 for a discussion of the Theory of Contestable Markets). Also, existing carriers expanded their market coverage, which significantly increased intramodal competition in certain markets. Table 5.2 indicates that the top 25 air carriers accounted for about 96 percent of the total operating revenue. Carriers may also have **excess capacity** (too many flights and seat miles on a route) and attempt to attract passengers by selectively lowering fares to fill the empty seats. Since 1992 airline prices have fallen 8.4 percent (not adjusted for inflation). During this same period, inflation (measured by the Consumer Price Index) has risen 28.2 percent.[6] New entrants to the market, such as Airtran and JetBlue, have taken a very aggressive stance on discounting passenger fares. Recently, JetBlue Airways announced that it was putting 1 million seats on sale for up to half price during the fall of 2004.[7]

New entrants to the airline market initially cause overcapacity to exist on many routes. To counter this and add passengers to their aircraft, carriers reduce prices and fare wars begin. This causes financially weaker carriers to exit the market. This is especially true of carriers with high operating costs (many times due to high-cost union labor contracts), high cost of debt, or high levels of fixed costs. (Many of these maintain high fixed investments in hub-and-spoke terminal operations.) The remaining carriers begin to enjoy economies of density (discussed later in this chapter), and the cost per passenger mile will decrease and margins will increase, even in the existence of relatively low fares. So, even with the discounted prices in today's airline market, many carriers have been able to remain profitable.

Service Competition

Competition in airline service takes many forms, but the primary service competition is the **frequency and timing** of flights on a route. Carriers attempt to provide flights at the time of day when passengers want to fly. Flight departures are most frequent in the early morning (7:00 a.m. to 10:00 p.m.) and late afternoon (4:00 p.m. to 6:00 p.m.).

In addition to the frequency and timing of flights, air carriers attempt to differentiate their service through the **advertising** of passenger amenities. Carriers promote such things as on-time arrival and friendly employees to convince travelers that it has the desired quality of service. Gourmet meals and on-board movies are some of the amenities that a carrier uses to entice passengers to use and reuse its service. JetBlue Airways was the first airline in the world that offered live satellite television free of charge on every seat in its fleet.[8] Frequent flyer programs and special services for high-mileage customers are popular examples of other services to attract loyal customers.

A postderegulation development in service competition was **no-frills service**. The no-frills air carrier (for example, Southwest Airlines) charges fares that are lower than that of a full-service air carrier. However, passengers receive limited snacks and drinks (coffee, tea, or soft drinks). Southwest offers passengers an opportunity to purchase a boxed meal at the gate before they enter the aircraft. Another hallmark of such carriers is that they only provide one class of service. Also, the passengers provide their own magazines or other reading materials. Overall, there are fewer airline employees involved in no-frills services operations, which contribute to lower costs. The "no-frills" carriers have had a significant impact on fares where their service is available.

Cargo Competition

For cargo service, competition has become intense. As a result of the complete deregulation of air cargo in 1977, air carriers have published competitive **rates**, but these rates are still higher than those available via surface carriers. Freight schedules have been published that emphasize low transit times between given points. To overcome accessibility problems, some carriers provide door-to-door service through contacts with motor carriers. Major airline freight companies (e.g., FedEx, UPS Airlines, and DHL) have their own fleets of surface delivery vehicles to perform the ground portion of this door-to-door service.

Although the number of major and national carriers is small (approximately 26), the competition among carriers is great. An interesting development has been the number of surface carriers that have added air cargo service, such as UPS. Competition for nonpassenger business will become even greater as more carriers attempt to eliminate excess capacity resulting from currently reduced passenger travel patterns. Another interesting dimension has been the growth in volume of express carrier traffic, which is an important reason for the attraction of surface carriers into this segment of the business.

STOP OFF

FedEx Buys Kinko's to Increase Retail Presence

Although FedEx long ago achieved its goal of becoming a household name, the integrated carrier is aggressively moving deeper into the retail market, which serves individuals and small business customers.

FedEx recently announced that it had purchased long-time partner Kinko's, the nationwide provider of copying, printing, and other business services. For the past 15 years, FedEx has staffed separately run booths or drop boxes in roughly 100 of Kinko's 1,100 outlets.

Company executives expect that increasing the number of staffed booths will significantly increase shipment volumes. "Our market analysis shows that locations that are staffed by a FedEx employee typically have up to 10 times as many packages shipped there than in an area with just a drop box." says Jess Bunn, manager of media relations for FedEx. With staffed locations, the company also can offer ground service to Kinko's customers, he says. At present, the company only offers FedEx Express service at those locations.

The acquisition of Kinko's is designed to bring the FedEx brand closer to small businesses and what Bunn refers to as "mobile professionals." "It's like their office away from home," he says. "They can avail themselves of the services at Kinko's, and shipping is one of those services. We see it being particularly attractive to small and medium-size businesses."

Because Kinko's operates around the clock, some have wondered whether FedEx would also offer 24-hour service at store locations. Bunn says that's under consideration. "I wouldn't rule it in or out right now. Certainly if it turned out that we thought there was some value there, we'd be likely to do it."

Some industry experts believe that the Kinko's purchase is also designed to keep pace with rival UPS and its Mailboxes Etc. outlets, which last year were rebranded as "The UPS Store." "One can't overlook that they are obviously very mindful of what UPS is doing with Mailboxes Etc.," says Satish Jindel of SJ Consulting in Pittsburgh, Pa. But this latest move will also help FedEx compete against its other rivals, Jindel adds. "This is a recognition of the changes in the industry. It's not just what UPS is doing, but also with Airborne now becoming part of DHL and going after those small customers Airborne didn't serve before. This is a recognition that [FedEx needs] to get a lock on the market with their strong brand name for those small customers before the other [companies] gain a huge leverage."

Source: *Logistics Management*, February 2004, p. 18. Reprinted with permission.

OPERATING AND SERVICE CHARACTERISTICS

General

As indicated above, the major revenue source for air carriers is passenger transportation. In 2002 approximately 68.6 percent of total operating revenues were derived from passenger transportation. This **revenue** was generated from about 611.7 million passenger enplanements in 2002.[9] Air transportation dominates the for-hire, long-distance passenger transportation market.

In 2002 approximately 12.5 percent of the total operating revenues were generated from **freight** transportation.[10] The majority of freight using air service is high-value and/or emergency shipments. The high cost of air transportation is usually prohibitive for shipping low-value routine commodities unless there is an emergency.

For **emergency shipments**, the cost of air transportation is often inconsequential compared to the cost of delaying the goods. For example, an urgently needed part of an assembly line might have a $20 value, but if the air-freighted part arrives on time to prevent the assembly line from stopping, the "opportunity" value of the part might become hundreds of thousands of dollars. Thus, the $20 part might have an emergency value of $200,000, and the air freight cost is a small portion of this emergency value.

Examples of **commodities** that move via air carriers include mail, clothing, communication products and parts, photography equipment, mushrooms, fresh flowers, industrial machines, high-priced livestock, racehorses, expensive automobiles, and jewelry. Normally basic raw materials such as coal, lumber, iron ore, or steel are not moved by air carriage. The high value of these products provides a cost-savings trade-off, usually but not always from inventory, that offsets the higher cost of air service. The old adage "Time is money" is quite appropriate here.

Speed of Service

Undoubtedly, the **major** service **advantage** of air transportation is speed. The terminal-to-terminal time for a given trip is lower via air transportation than via any of the other modes. Commercial jets are capable of routinely flying at speeds of 500 to 600 miles per hour, thus making a New York to California trip, approximately 3,000 miles, a mere 6-hour journey.

This advantage of high terminal-to-terminal **speed** has been dampened somewhat by reduced frequency of flights and congestion at airports. As a result of deregulation, the air traffic controllers strike of 1981, and lower carrier demand, the number of flights offered to and from low-density communities has been reduced to increase the utilization of a given plane. As previously noted, commuter airlines have been substituted on some routes where major and national lines find the traffic volume to be too low to justify using large planes. The use of commuters requires transfer and rehandling of freight or passengers because the commuter service does not cover long distances.

Air carriers have been concentrating their service on the **high-density** routes like New York to Chicago, for example. In addition, most carriers have adopted the hub-and-spoke terminal approach, in which most flights go through a hub terminal; Atlanta (Delta) and Chicago (United) are examples. These two factors have aggravated the air traffic congestion and ground congestion at major airports and have increased total transit time while decreasing its reliability. Also, some carriers have been unable to expand because of limited "slots" at major airports. At hub airports, these slots are controlled by the dominant carrier, making it difficult for new carriers to offer service at that hub.

The shippers who use air carriers to transport freight are primarily interested in the speed and reliability of the service and the resultant benefits, such as reduced inventory levels and inventory carrying costs. Acceptable or improved service levels can be achieved by using air carriers to deliver orders in short time periods. Stock-outs can be controlled, reduced, or eliminated by responding to shortages via air carriers.

Length of Haul and Capacity

For passenger travel, air carriers dominate the long-distance moves. In 2002 the average length of haul for passenger travel was 852 miles for air carriers.[11] The capacity of airplanes is dependent on its type. A wide-body, four-engine jet has a seating **capacity** of about 370 people and an all-cargo carrying capacity of 16.6 tons. Table 5.3 provides capacity and operating statistics for some of the more commonly used aircraft in both domestic and international markets.

Normally, small shipments that are time-sensitive are moved by air carriers. Rates have been established for weights as low as 10 pounds, and rate discounts are available for shipments weighing a few hundred pounds. Adding freight to the baggage compartment on passenger flights necessitates rather small-size shipments and thus supports rate-making practices for these shipments.

In addition to small shipment sizes, the packaging required for freight shipped by air transportation is usually less than other modes. It is not uncommon in air

Table 5.3 Aircraft Operating Characteristics—2002

Model	Seats	Cargo Payload (Tons)	Speed Airborne (mph)	Flight Length (miles)	Fuel (Gallons per Hour)	Operating Cost $ per Hour	Operating Cost $0.01 per Seat Mile
B747-200/300*	370	16.60	520	3,148	3,625	9,153	5.11
B747-400	367	8.06	534	3,960	3,411	8,443	4.6
B747-100*	–	46.34	503	2,022	1,762	3,852	–
B747-F*	–	72.58	506	2,512	3,593	7,138	–
L-1011	325	0.00	494	2,023	1,981	8,042	5067
DC-10*	286	24.87	497	1,637	2,405	7,374	5.11
B767-400	265	6.26	495	1,682	1,711	3,124	2.71
B-777	263	9.43	525	3,515	2,165	5,105	3.98
A330	261	11.12	509	3,559	1,407	3,076	2.51
MD-11*	261	45.07	515	2,485	2,473	7,695	4.75
A300-600*	235	19.12	460	947	1,638	6,518	5.93
B757-300	235	0.30	472	1,309	985	2,345	2.44
B767-300ER*	207	7.89	497	2,122	1,579	4,217	4.38
B757-200*	181	1.41	464	1,175	1,045	3,312	4.47
B767-300ER	175	3.72	487	1,987	1,404	3,873	5.08
A321	169	0.44	454	1,094	673	1,347	2.05
B737-800/900	151	0.37	454	1,035	770	2,248	3.88
MD-90	150	0.25	446	886	825	2,716	4.93
B727-200*	148	6.46	430	644	1,289	4,075	6.61
B727-100*	–	11.12	417	468	989	13,667	–
A320	146	0.31	454	1,065	767	2,359	4.14
B737-400	141	0.25	409	646	703	2,595	5.48
MD-80	134	0.19	432	791	953	2,718	5.72
B737-700LR	132	0.28	441	879	740	1,692	3.28
B737-300/700	132	0.22	403	542	723	2,388	5.49
A319	122	0.27	442	904	666	1,913	4.22
A310-200*	–	25.05	455	847	1,561	8,066	–
DC-8*	–	22.22	437	686	1,712	8,065	–
B737-100/200	119	0.11	396	465	824	2,377	6.08
B717-200	112	0.22	339	175	573	3,355	12.89
B737-500	110	0.19	407	576	756	2,347	6.49
DC-9	101	0.15	387	496	826	2,071	6.86
F-100	87	0.05	398	587	662	2,303	8.46
B737-200C	55	2.75	387	313	924	3,421	19.89
ERJ-145	50	0.00	360	343	280	1,142	8.63
CRJ-145	49	0.01	397	486	369	1,433	9.45
ERJ-135	37	0.00	357	382	267	969	9.83
SD 340B	33	0.00	230	202	84	644	11.6

*Data includes cargo operations.

Source: Air Transport Association: 2003 Annual Report.

transportation to find a palletized shipment that is shrink-wrapped instead of banded. The relatively smooth ride through the air and the automated ground-handling systems contribute to lower damage and thus reduce packaging needs.

Accessibility and Dependability

Except in adverse conditions such as fog or snow, air carriers are capable of providing **reliable** service. The carriers might not always be on time to the exact minute, but the variations in transit time are small. Sophisticated navigational instrumentation permits operation during most weather conditions. On-time departures and arrivals are within 15 minutes of scheduled times. Departure time is defined as the time the aircraft door is closed and, in the case of passenger aircraft, the vehicle is pushed away from the gate. Arrival time is defined as the time when the aircraft wheels touch down on the runway.

Poor **accessibility** is one disadvantage of air carriers. Passengers and freight must be transported to an airport for air service to be rendered. This accessibility problem is reduced when smaller planes and helicopters are used to transport freight to and from airports, and most passengers use automobiles. Limited accessibility adds time and cost to the air service provided. Even with the accessibility problem, air transportation remains a fast method of movement and the only logical mode when distance is great and time is restricted. The cost of this fast freight service is high, about three times greater than motor carrier and 10 times greater than rail. Nevertheless, the high speed and cost make air carriage a premium mode of transportation.

EQUIPMENT

Types of Vehicles

As previously mentioned, there are several different sizes of airplanes in use, from small commuter planes to huge, wide-body, four-engine planes used by the nationals. These various-sized planes all have different costs associated with using them; these costs will be addressed later in the section titled "Cost Structure." Table 5.3 compares some of the major aircraft types in terms of seats, cargo payload, speed, fuel consumption, and operating cost per hour. Airlines have many options to select from when purchasing equipment.

Terminals

The air carriers' **terminals** (airports) are financed by a government entity. The carriers pay for the use of the airport through landing fees, rent and lease payments for space, taxes on fuel, and aircraft registration taxes. In addition, users pay a tax on airline tickets and air freight charges. Terminal charges are becoming increasingly more commonplace for passenger traffic. Table 5.4 summarizes the various types of taxes paid by carriers, shippers, and passengers in the airline industry.

The growth and development of air transportation is dependent upon adequate airport facilities. Therefore, to ensure the viability of air transportation, the federal government has the responsibility of financially assisting the states in the construction of airport facilities. The various state and local governments assume the responsibility for operating and maintaining the airports.

At the airport, the carriers perform passenger, cargo, and aircraft servicing. Passengers are ticketed, loaded, and unloaded, and their luggage is collected and dispersed. Cargo is routed to specific planes for shipment to the destination airport or to delivery vehicles. Aircraft servicing includes refueling; loading of passengers, cargo, luggage, and supplies (food); and maintenance. Major aircraft maintenance is done at specific airports.

As carrier operations become more complex, certain airports in the carriers' scope of operation become hubs. Flights from outlying, less-populated areas are fed into the hub airport, where connecting flights are available to other areas of the region or country.

Table 5.4 Federally Approved Taxes and Fees: 1972-2003

Fee	1972	1992	2003	Round Trip[3]	Unit of Taxation
Passenger Ticket Tax[1]	8.0%	10.0%	7.5%	nmf	Domestic Airfare
Passenger Flight Segment Tax[1]	–	–	$3.00	$12.00	Domestic Enplanement
Passenger Security Surcharge	–	–	$2.50	$10.00	Enplanement at U.S. Airport
Passenger Facility Charge	–	$3.00[2]	$4.50[2]	$18.00	Enplanement at Eligible U.S. Airport
International Departure Tax	$3.00	$6.00	$13.40	nmf	International Passenger Departure
International Arrival Tax	–	–	$13.40	nmf	International Passenger Arrival
INS User Fee	–	$5.00	$7.00	nmf	International Passenger Arrival
Customs User Fee	–	$5.00	$5.00	nmf	International Passenger Arrival
APHIS Passenger Fee	–	$2.00	$3.10	nmf	International Passenger Arrival
Cargo Waybill Tax[1]	5.00%	6.25%	6.25%	nmf	Waybill for Domestic Freight
Frequent Flyer Tax	–	–	7.5%	nmf	Sale of Frequent Flyer Miles
APHIS Aircraft Fee	–	$76.75	$65.25	nmf	International Aircraft Arrival
Jet Fuel Tax[1]	–	–	4.3¢/gal	nmf	Domestic Gallon
LUST Fuel Tax[1]	–	0.1¢/gal	0.1¢/gal	nmf	Domestic Gallon
Air Carrier Security Fee	–	–	Carrier-Specific	nmf	CY2000 Screening Costs

[1] Tax applies only to domestic transportation; prorated on flights between mainland U.S. and Alaska/Hawaii.
[2] Legislative maximum.
[3] Single-connection round trip with maximum passenger facility charge (PFC).

NOTES:
Nmf = not meaningful
INS = Immigration and Naturalization Service
APHIS = Animal and Plant Health Inspection Service
LUST = Leaking Underground Storage Tank
Source: Air Transport Association, 2003 Annual Report.

For example, Chicago, Denver, and Washington-Dulles are major **hub** airports for United Airlines. Flights from cities such as Toledo and Kansas City go to Chicago, where connecting flights are available to New York, Los Angeles, and Dallas. Delta Airlines uses the Atlanta and Cincinnati airports in the same way. By using the hub airport approach, the carriers are able to assign aircraft to feed passengers into the hub over low-density routes and to assign larger planes to the higher-density routes between the hub and an airport serving a major metropolitan area. In essence, the hub airport is similar to the motor carrier's break-bulk terminal.

Airport terminals also provide services to passengers, such as restaurants, banking centers, souvenir and gift shops, and snack bars. The new Denver airport also includes some major general purpose attractions similar to a shopping mall. The success of the Pittsburgh airport has resulted in other airports expanding restaurants to include many popular chains (McDonald's, TGI Friday's, Pizza Hut, etc.) and popular shops for clothing, accessories, books, and other items.

COST STRUCTURE

Fixed Versus Variable Cost Components

Like the motor carriers, the air carriers' cost structure consists of high variable and low fixed costs. Approximately 80 percent of total operating costs are variable and 20 percent are fixed. The relatively low fixed cost structure is attributable to government (state and local) investment and operations of airports and airways. The carriers pay for the use of these facilities through landing fees, which are variable in nature.

As indicated in Table 5.5, 30.4 percent of airline operating costs in 2002 was incurred for flying operations and amounted to $35.13 billion; maintenance costs equaled 12.3 percent of total operating costs. Both of these expenses are variable costs. The next major category of expense is aircraft and traffic servicing, which totaled $19.48 billion in 2002 and about 17 percent of total operating costs. In 2002 depreciation accounted for about 6.0 percent of total operating expenses.

Table 5.5 provides a comparison of operating costs for 1991, 2000, 2001, and 2002. The cost of flying operations increased from 1991 to 2002, as did total operating expenses. Total costs decreased in 2002 from 2001 because of the decrease in maintenance costs, flying operations, and promotion and sales. From 1991 to 2002, every cost item increased by more than a factor of two except for promotion and sales.

The increased price competition in the airline industry has caused airlines to try to operate more efficiently by cutting costs where possible. There has been much effort put forth to decrease labor costs because the airline industry tends to be labor-intensive compared to other modes, such as railroads and pipelines. The airlines have negotiated significant labor cost reductions with many of the unions represented in the industry.

Fuel

Escalating **fuel costs** have caused problems in the past for the airlines. The average price per gallon of fuel for domestic operations was about 89 cents in 1983 compared

Table 5.5 U.S. Scheduled Airlines Operating Costs

Expense	1991	2000	2001	2002
	($Billions)			
Flying Operations	16.8	38.19	37.54	35.13
Maintenance	6.7	15.23	15.34	14.21
Passenger Service	5.1	10.57	10.47	10.19
Aircraft and Traffic Servicing	9.1	19.39	19.94	19.48
Promotion and Sales	8.8	13.37	11.76	8.97
General and Administrative	2.9	7.18	9.43	8.83
Depreciation and Amortization	3.2	6.91	8.42	6.93
Transport Related	4.1	13.01	12.58	11.72
Total Operating Costs	56.7	123.85	125.49	115.45

Source: Air Transport Association, 2003 Annual Report.

to 57 cents in 1979 and 30 cents in 1978. It dropped to under 60 cents in 1986 but rose again in 1990 to above the 1983 level. It decreased again by 1998 to about 55 cents per gallon. By December 2002 the price per gallon of aviations fuel was $0.77 per gallon.[12]

The impact that such fuel increases have had can be shown by analyzing fuel consumption for certain aircraft that are commonly used today. The Air Transportation Association's annual report shows that the number of gallons of fuel consumed per hour for the following planes is as follows (see Table 5.3):

367-seat 747	3,411 gallons/hour
286-seat DC-10	2,405 gallons/hour
148-seat 727	1,289 gallons/hour
101-seat DC-9	826 gallons/hour

Using a cost of $0.77 per gallon, the fuel cost per hour is $2,626.47 for a 747, $1,851.85 for a DC-10, $992.53 for a 727, and $636.02 for DC-9. Consequently, rapidly escalating fuel costs in recent years have caused airlines to suffer financially in an already depressed pricing market.

When fuel costs rise, carriers scrutinize planes in the fleet as well as routes served. More **fuel-efficient** planes have been developed and added to carrier fleets. In the short run, carriers are substituting smaller planes on low-density (low demand) routes and eliminating service completely on other routes. Commuter lines have provided substitute service on the routes abandoned by major and national carriers. Even though the average cost per gallon of fuel increased from $0.62 to $0.77 from January 2002 to December 2002, fuel consumption declined by 1.2 billion gallons (6.5-percent reduction) from 2001 to 2002, resulting in a fuel savings of over $2 billion.[13]

Labor

Labor costs represented over 65 percent of total operating expenses in 2002. In 2002 carriers employed about 601,000 people at an average annual compensation of $74,831.[14] Average compensation includes wages and fringe benefits.

Airlines employ people with a variety of different **skills**. To operate the planes, the carrier must employ pilots, copilots, and flight engineers. The plane crew also includes the flight attendants, who serve the passengers. Communications personnel are required to tie together the different geographic locations. Mechanics and ground crews for aircraft and traffic service provide the necessary maintenance and servicing of the planes. The final component of airline employment consists of the office personnel and management. Overall employment has decreased as airlines have moved aggressively to reduce costs to improve their competitiveness and lower prices in selected markets.

Strict **safety** regulations are administered by the FAA. Acceptable flight operations, as well as hours of service, are specified for pilots. Both mechanics and pilots are subject to examinations on safety regulations and prescribed operations. FAA regulations also dictate appropriate procedures for flight attendants to follow during takeoff and landing.

The **wages** paid to a pilot usually vary according to the pilot's equipment rating. A pilot who is technically capable (has passed a flight examination for a given type of aircraft) of flying a jumbo jet will receive a higher compensation than one who flies a single-engine, six-passenger plane. Table 5.6 shows the average pilot compensation for the major airlines in the United States. Delta averages the highest pilot wages, whereas Airtran has the lowest. Pilot wages as a percent of total airline revenue has increased from 7.8 percent in 1999 to 13.4 percent in 2003.[15]

Table 5.6 Average Annual U.S. Airline Pilot Salaries—2003

	5-Year Copilot	10-Year Copilot of Smallest Jet	Senior Captain of Biggest Jet
Delta	$125,640	$195,828	$275,256
Northwest	104,676	158,532	229,908
Continental	98,436	152,988	200,532
United	84,024	137,400	194,736
US Airways	102,312	144,228	188,220
Southwest	93,444	152,256	155,628
American	72,432	112,800	156,624
AirTran*	53,702		138,000

*AirTran figures supplied by the airline. Copilot figures are for 2nd year; captain figures are for 5th year or higher.

Source: *The Atlanta Journal-Constitution*, Atlanta, GA, June 6, 2004, p. F.1.

Wages can also vary according to whether a person works for a **union** airline or not. In 2003 the average salary for a captain of the biggest jet who belonged to a union was well over $275,000, whereas an employee with the same credentials and a position at a nonunion airline received about $138,000.[16]

Equipment

As mentioned earlier, the cost of operating airplanes varies. Larger planes are more costly to operate per hour than smaller planes, but the cost per seat-mile is lower for larger planes. That is, the larger plane has the capacity to carry more passengers; thus, the higher cost is spread out over a large number of output units.

Table 5.3 shows the hourly operating costs for four aircraft used by major carriers in 2002. The cost per *block hour* was $8,443 for the 367-seat 747 and $2,071 for the 101-seat DC-9. However, the cost per seat-mile was $0.0046 for the 747 and $0.00686 for the DC-9. This reduced operating cost per seat-mile for the larger planes indicates that economies of scale exist in aircraft.

Economies of Scale/Economies of Density

Large-scale air carrier operations do have some **economies of scale**, which result from more extensive use of large-size planes or indivisible units. Of the small number of major and national carriers, approximately 25 transport over 90 percent of the passengers, indicating that large-scale operations exist.

The information contained in Table 5.3 suggests the existence of economies of scale with large-size planes. Market conditions (sufficient demand) must exist to permit the efficient utilization of larger planes (i.e., if the planes are flown near capacity, the seat-mile costs will obviously decrease). Contributing to the existence of economies of scale for an aircraft is the inability to inventory an unused seat. For example, a 367-seat 747 is about to close its doors with 10 seats empty. If the plane takes off with the empty seats, the seats are "lost" for that flight because the airline cannot inventory the excess capacity for another flight that might be overbooked. On the other hand, the marginal cost of filling those 10 empty seats right before the doors on the aircraft are closed are negligible. This is the same concept of economies of scale as found in the railroad industry. The marginal cost of adding one more rail car to a train right before departure is negligible.

Another factor indicating large-scale operations for air carriers is the integrated **communication** network required for activities such as operating controls and passenger reservations. Small local or regional carriers find the investment required for such a communication system rather staggering, but without the communication system, the emerging carrier cannot effectively operate (provide connecting service with other carriers and ticketing to passengers). Such carriers have purchased passenger reservation systems from large carriers to be competitive.

The air carrier industry overall has a cost structure that closely resembles that of motor carriers. Long-run economies of scale, as compared to short-run economies of plane size and utilization, are not significant in the air carrier industry. Industries characterized by high variable cost ratios (airlines and motor carriers) can relatively easily add equipment to a given market. As such, the ability to decrease fully allocated cost per mile by adding aircraft does not exist. On the other hand, when high fixed-cost industries (pipe and rail) add fixed capacity, they can decrease fully allocated cost per mile by adding volume to the fixed capacity. In high fixed-cost industries, however, capacity is not easily added in small increments.

Economies of density exist when a carrier has significant volume between an origin–destination pair to fully utilize capacity on forward-haul movements as well as utilize significant capacity on back-haul movements. This concept can exist across all modes of transportation. Southwest Airlines uses this concept aggressively when deciding which markets to enter, choosing those city pairs that offer high volumes of potential passengers to fill outbound aircraft. Table 5.7 shows the top 25 passenger markets in the United States. Of these, 14 have New York City as the originating point. JetBlue, based out of JFK Airport in New York, currently serves Fort Lauderdale, Orlando, San Juan, Tampa, and West Palm Beach. Economies of density, then, are important for all airlines to achieve to fully utilize capacity in a given market. History has shown that this has been a successful strategy for new entrants to the airline passenger market.

Over the years the federal government has provided direct operating **subsidies** (i.e., public service revenues) to air carriers. The subsidies have been provided to ensure air carrier service over particular routes where operating expenses exceed operating incomes. The subsidies enable regional carriers to provide service to less-populated areas that otherwise would probably not have air service.

RATES

Pricing

Airline pricing for passenger service is characterized by the **discounts** from full fare. Seats on the same plane can have substantially different prices depending on restrictions attached to the purchase, such as having to stay over a weekend or having to purchase the ticket in advance. Business people generally pay more for their airline travel due to the more rigid schedules they are on and the fact that they usually depart and return during the high-demand times. JetBlue, Southwest, and AirTran have aggressively discounted prices in major passenger markets. JetBlue announced in July 2004 that it will reduce fares by up to 50 percent for travel in the fall of 2004. This would reduce the one-way fare from New York to Florida to $49. Bestfares.com estimated that passengers can fly between 351 city-pairs for under $99 roundtrip.[17] The price of seats on different flights and the price of the same seat on a particular flight can vary due to competition with other airlines, the time and day of departure and return, the level of service (first class versus coach or

Table 5.7 Top 25 Domestic Airline Markets—2002[1]

Passengers (Thousands)[2]

1	New York	Fort Lauderdale	3,158
2	New York	Chicago	2,707
3	New York	Orlando	2,646
4	New York	Los Angeles	2,401
5	New York	Atlanta	2,215
6	Honolulu	Kahului, Maui	2,019
7	New York	Boston	1,637
8	New York	Washington, DC	1,627
9	Chicago	Los Angeles	1,521
10	Dallas/Fort Worth	Houston	1,520
11	New York	San Francisco	1,500
12	New York	Las Vegas	1,472
13	Honolulu	Lihue, Kauai	1,430
14	Chicago	Las Vegas	1,421
15	New York	West Palm Beach	1,410
16	New York	San Juan	1,393
17	New York	Miami	1,345
18	Los Angeles	Las Vegas	1,330
19	New York	Tampa	1,272
20	Honolulu	Kona, Hawaii	1,263
21	Los Angeles	Oakland	1,241
22	Chicago	Orlando	1,210
23	New York	Dallas/Fort Worth	1,209
24	Chicago	Phoenix	1,124
25	Honolulu	Hilo, Hawaii	1,103

[1] Includes all commercial airports in a metropolitan area.
[2] Outbound plus inbound; does not include connecting passengers.

Source: Air Transport Association, 2003 Annual Report.

no-frills service), and advance ticket purchase. Discount pricing has continued throughout the 2000s as airlines have attempted to increase their "payload." Industry load factors in 2002 are 71.6 percent, up from 70 percent in 2001.[18] This is a result of aggressive pricing as well as more systematic allocation of capacity to markets.

Cargo pricing is dependent mainly on **weight** and/or cubic dimensions. Some shipments that have a very low density can be assessed an over-dimensional charge, usually based on 8 pounds per cubic foot. This over-dimensional charge is used to gain more appropriate revenue from shipments that take up a lot of space but do not weigh much. An exaggerated example of a shipment to which this rule would apply is a shipment of inflated beach balls. Other factors affecting the price paid to ship freight via air transportation include completeness of service and special services, such as providing armed guards.

Operating Efficiency

An important measure of operating efficiency used by air carriers is the **operating ratio**. The operating ratio measures the portion of operating income that goes to operating expenses:

$$\text{Operating Ratio} = (\text{Operating Expense}/\text{Operating Income}) \times 100$$

Only income and expenses generated from passenger and freight transportation are considered. Like the motor carrier industry, the air carrier industry's operating ratio was in the low to mid-90s, between 1994 and 2000, ranging from 96.9 in 1994 to 94.7 in 2000. However, the operating ratio for the industry in 2002 was 108.8.[19] The overall profit margin is small, and a loss is incurred when the operating ratio exceeds 100.

Another widely used measure of operating efficiency is the load factor (previously discussed). The load factor measures the percentage of a plane's capacity that is utilized.

$$\text{Load Factor} = (\text{Number of Passengers/Total Number of Seats}) \times 100$$

Airlines have raised plane load factors to the 65- to 70-percent range. The particular route and type of plane (capacity) directly affect the load factor, as does price, service level, and competition.

Again, referring to Table 5.3, the relationship among load factor, cost, plane size, and profitability can be seen. Assume that a route requires 1 hour to traverse and has a load factor of 65 percent; the average operating cost per passenger for a 747 is $35.39 ($8,443 per hour/(367 [capacity] × 0.65 [load factor]). If the demand drops to 80 passengers on the route, the load factor for the 747 would be 21.8 percent (80/367), and the hourly operating cost per passenger would be $105.54 ($8,443/80). At this level of demand, the carrier would substitute a smaller capacity plane, a 727 or DC-9. With 80 passengers, the load factor for the DC-9 would be 79.2 percent (80/101) and the average operating cost would be $25.89 ($2,071/80). The small aircraft would be more economical to operate over this lower-density (demand) route, and the carrier would substitute this more efficient plane (DC-9) on this hypothetical route.

Equipment substitution, however, might not be possible, and substitution might result in excess capacity. The jumbo planes have large carrying capacities that might not be utilized in low-demand routes. Thus, large-capacity planes are used on high-demand routes such as New York–Chicago and New York–Los Angeles, and smaller capacity planes are used on low-demand routes such as Toledo–Chicago and Pittsburgh–Memphis.

CURRENT ISSUES

Safety

The issue of airline safety is of great importance to the airline industry. Any incident involving airplanes receives a great deal of publicity from the media because of the large number of people affected at one time. (Accidents involving motor vehicles affect only a few people in each incident but affect a greater number of people than do airline accidents in the long run.)

Several factors affect airline safety. First, airport security has come under close scrutiny over the past several years. On September 11, 2001, four aircraft were hijacked and two were flown into the Twin Towers in New York City, killing and injuring thousands of people. As a result, airport security has reached an all-time high, causing more delays at airport terminals. The U.S. Government created the Office of Homeland Security to be the agency that monitors and manages the security of the U.S. borders.

Air travel is more popular than ever, as indicated previously, but there is still great concern about safety. The 1990s had some major air disasters among major carriers, such as TWA, American, US Airways, SwissAir, and the ValuJet crash in the Florida Everglades. In addition, the frequent reportings of near collisions, minor accidents, and airplane recalls have heightened public awareness of the air safety

Table 5.8 U.S. Air Carriers Operating Under 14 CFR 121—Scheduled Service

Year	Departures (Millions)	Total Accidents	Fatal Accidents	Fatal Accident Rates[1]	Fatalities
1992	7.5	16	4	0.053	33
1993	7.7	22	1	0.013	1
1994	7.8	19	4	0.051	239
1995	8.1	34	2	0.025	166
1996	7.9	32	3	0.038	342
1997	9.9	44	3	0.030	3
1998	10.5	43	1	0.009	1
1999	10.9	46	2	0.018	12
2000	11.0	50	3	0.027	92
2001	9.8	41	6	0.020	531
2002	10.1	34	0	0.000	0

[1] Fatal accidents per 100,000 departures; excludes incidents resulting from illegal acts.

Source: National Transportation Safety Board.
Air Transport Association, 2003 Annual Report.

problem. However, air travel is still the safest way to travel. Table 5.8 shows the trend of aircraft accidents from 1992 through 2002. The spike in 2001 was caused by the incident in New York City on September 11. Table 5.9 shows that even though there is a significant loss of life in an airline tragedy, air travel is still the safest mode for passenger travel, with automobiles being the most dangerous.

Finally, as with other transportation modes, the issue of substance abuse concerning pilots and ground crews has become important. Strict drug-testing policies and

Table 5.9 U.S. Passenger Fatalities Per 100 Million Passenger Miles

Year	Autos[1]	Buses[2]	Railroads[3]	Airlines[4]
1991	0.91	0.04	0.06	0.03
1992	0.83	0.04	0.02	0.01
1993	0.86	0.02	0.45	0.01
1994	0.91	0.03	0.04	0.06
1995	0.97	0.03	0.00	0.04
1996	0.96	0.02	0.09	0.08
1997	0.92	0.01	0.05	0.01
1998	0.86	0.05	0.03	0.00
1999	0.83	0.07	0.10	0.003
2000	0.80	0.01	0.03	0.02
10-Yr. Avg.	**0.88**	**0.03**	**0.08**	**0.02**

[1] Passenger cars/taxis; drivers considered passengers; data from the National Safety Council Fatality Analysis Reporting System.
[2] Does not include school buses; data from the National Safety Council Fatality Analysis Reporting System.
[3] Data from the Federal Railroad Administration.
[4] Large and commuter scheduled airlines, excluding cargo; from the National Transportation Safety Board.

Source: Air Transport Association, 2003 Annual Report.

alcohol consumption guidelines are in effect for pilots and other aircraft personnel. In spite of these concerns, airline travel is still a very safe form of transportation; however, these issues are currently being addressed by the airlines to ensure that airline transportation remains safe.

Technology

Because the airline industry must offer quick and efficient service to attract business, it constantly needs more sophisticated equipment. With other modes such as railroads and water carriers, travel times are measured in days; however, air carriers measure travel time in hours.

For this reason, the airline industry has developed automated information-processing programs like the Air Cargo Fast Flow Program, which was designed by the Port Authority of New York/New Jersey. The Fast Flow Program is a paperless system that speeds the processing of air freight cargo through customs processing, which was found to take 106 out of 126 hours of processing time for international shipments. The system allows the air freight community to tie into customs-clearing systems and thus reduce paperwork and time requirements dramatically. The system also will provide better tracking of shipments and better communication between connecting carriers. These improvements will allow customers to receive their inbound shipments faster than ever before.

Summary

- The airline industry began its development in the early part of the 20th century, and its growth was influenced to a great extent initially by government interest and policy.
- The airline industry is dominated by revenue from passenger service, but air freight revenue is growing in importance.
- Both private and for-hire carriers operate as part of the airline industry, but private carrier service is predominantly passenger movement.
- For-hire carriers can be classified based on service offered (all-cargo, air taxi, charter, etc.) or annual operating revenue (majors, nationals, or regionals).
- All-cargo carriers and commuter operators have grown in importance in recent years and play a more important role in the total airline industry.
- A relatively large number of airline companies exist, but a small number (25) account for more than 90 percent of the total earnings.
- Deregulation of airlines was rationalized to some extent with the argument that an increase in the number of carriers would increase competition. Initially, there was an increase followed by a decrease; today the number is higher.
- Airlines are unique in that they face limited intermodal competition, but intramodal competition is very keen in terms of pricing and service and has been exacerbated by unused capacity.
- Airline service competition is usually in terms of frequency and timing of flights, but special passenger services and programs are important.
- The express portion of air freight has grown dramatically. A growing number of commodities use air freight service, and increased growth is expected.

- Speed is the major advantage of airlines for both passengers and freight, but the airlines' speed of service has been offset recently by congestion and fewer flights.
- The higher cost of airline service can be a trade-off against lower inventory and warehousing costs, as well as other logistics-related savings.
- Airline carriers are essentially long-haul service providers for passengers and freight because the cost of takeoffs and landings makes short hauls relatively uneconomical.
- Airlines usually provide service for small shipments where value is high and/or the product may be perishable.
- Airlines offer a generally reliable/consistent service, but their accessibility is limited.
- Airlines use different types of equipment that limits their carrying capacity, but their overall equipment variety is also limited.
- Airlines use publicly provided airways and terminals, but pay user charges on both, which helps make their cost structure highly variable.
- Major and national airlines use a hub approach to their service, which contributes to operating efficiency but often adds travel time.
- Fuel and labor costs are important expense categories for airlines and have received much managerial attention. The low fuel cost of the late 1990s helped the airlines improve their profitability; today, however, rising fuel prices are having a negative impact on industry profits.
- Economies of scale and economies of density exist in the airline industry, making larger-scale carriers usually more efficient, based on equipment, markets, and communications.
- In the era of deregulation, discount pricing has become very popular, and it has made the rate schedules of airlines for passenger services complex.
- Airline safety is a very important issue, but overall airlines have a very good record.
- Traditionally, airlines have capitalized on new equipment technology to improve their operating efficiency and to expand capacity. In recent years, technology improvements have come in a variety of other areas.

Key Terms

accessibility, 167
advertising, 163
all-cargo carriers, 159
capacity, 165
changing fuel costs, 168
charter carriers, 160
commodity examples, 164
communication, 172
commuter carriers, 159
discount pricing, 172
economies of density, 172
economies of scale, 171
emergency shipments, 164
employee skill variety, 170
employment, 158
equipment size, 171
equipment substitution, 174
excess capacity, 162
freight revenue, 164
frequency and timing, 162
fuel costs, 169
fuel efficiency, 170
high-density routes, 165
hub, 168
limited competition, 162
major advantage, 165
major carriers, 159
national carriers, 159
no-frills service, 163
operating ratio, 174
passenger revenues, 158
pilot wages, 170
private carriers, 160
public terminals, 167
rates and service, 163
regional carriers, 159
reliability, 166
revenue classes, 164
safety, 170
skills, 170
subsidies, 172
terminals, 167
time factor, 165
U.S. Post Office, 158
union wages, 170, 171
weight, 173

Study Questions

1. What are the types of carriers as defined by revenue class? Who are some of the members of each class? Do you think the members of each class would compete against or work together with members of the other classes? What about members of their own class? Use examples obtained from advertising or websites.
2. Discuss the ways in which air carriers compete with each other. How have regulatory changes affected this competition?
3. What is the major advantage of air carriers? How does this advantage impact the inventory levels of those firms using air transportation? Explain how this advantage relates to the choice of modes when choosing between air carriage and other modes of freight and passengers transport.
4. Discuss the length of haul and carrying capacity of the air carriers. Explain how they both favor and hinder air carriers from a competitive standpoint.
5. What is the role of government in air transportation? Include both economic and safety regulations in your answer.
6. How does fuel cost and efficiency affect both air carrier costs and pricing?
7. What is the current situation of labor within the air industry? Are unions a major factor? How does skill level vary within the industry? Do you think this situation is similar to other modes? If so, which one(s) and explain why.
8. Do air carriers have economies of scale at any level? Economies of density? Discuss and support your answer with examples.
9. How do air carriers price their services? Is the weight or density of the shipment a factor? Explain this factor as part of your answer. How does air carrier pricing relate to the value of the goods being transported?
10. What are the current issues facing the air industry? Discuss how each impacts the industry, its customers and employees?
11. What is the cost structure of the air industry? How does it compare with other modes? How does this affect pricing, particularly for passengers? Be sure your answer includes examples from either advertising or the Internet.

Notes

1. Air Transportation Association, *2003 Economic Report*, Washington, DC: 2003, p. 6.
2. Ibid., p. 7.
3. Ibid., p. 15.
4. Ibid., p. 9.
5. Ibid., p. 9.
6. Ibid., p. 12.
7. David Koenig, "Airlines Cut Fares to Fill Seats," *Center Daily Times*, July 14, 2004, p. B7.
8. Hoover's Online, June 7, 2004, http://www.jetblue.com/learnmore/factsheet.html.
9. Air Transport Association, op.cit., p. 6.
10. Ibid., p. 6.
11. Ibid., p. 8.
12. Ibid., p. 13.

13. Ibid., p. 13.

14. Ibid., p. 15.

15. Russell Grantham, "Overweight Overhead Putting Brakes on Pilot Pay Only a Start for Strapped Airline," *The Atlanta Journal-Constitution,* June 6, 2004.

16. Ibid.

17. Monica Roman, "Bargains in the Sky," *BusinessWeek,* July 26, 2004, p. 47.

18. Air Transport Association, op.cit., p. 10.

19. Ibid., p. 7.

Suggested Readings

Baldwin, Gordon, and Michael W. Pustay. "Trade and Transportation: The Impact of the 1995 Transborder Air Services Accord," *Transportation Journal*, Vol. 43, No. 2, 2004, pp. 5–15.

Brady, Stephen P., and William A. Cunningham. "Exploring Predatory Pricing in the Airline Industry," *Transportation Journal,* Fall 2001, pp. 5–15.

Breskin, Ira. "Higher Security Hurdles Confront Forwarders," *Logistics Management,* October 2003, pp. 39–42.

Carey, Susan, Henry Sender, and Amy Schatz. "UAL Again Fails to Get Loan Aid, Hurting Airline's Chapter 11 Plan," *The Wall Street Journal,* Tuesday, June 29, 2004, p. A3.

Cooke, James A. "East Beats West: Why Fujitsu Supplies the U.S. from Japan," *Logistics Management,* June 2003, pp. 24–26.

Costa, Peter R., Doug S. Harned, and Jerrod T. Lundquist. "Rethinking the Aviation Industry," *The McKinsey Quarterly*, No. 2, 2002.

Curry, Andrew. "Taking Flight," *U.S. News & World Report*, July 21, 2003, pp. 40–46.

Doig, Stephen J., Adam Howard, and Ronald C. Ritter. "The Hidden Value in Airline Operations," *The McKinsey Quarterly*, No. 4 (2003).

Forster, Paul W. and Amelia C. Regan. "Electronic Integration in the Air Cargo Industry: An Information Processing Model of On-Time Performance," *Transportation Journal,* Summer 2001, pp. 46–61.

Gecker, Rachel. "The New Frontier of Border Security," *Inbound Logistics,* March 2004, pp. 54–61.

Golicic, Susan L., Teresa M. McCarthy, and John T. Mentzer. "Conducting a Market Opportunity Analysis for Air Cargo Operations," *Transportation Journal,* Summer 2003, pp. 5–15.

Gooley, Toby B. "Airfreight Packaging: Don't Take it Lightly," *Logistics Management,* April 2004, pp. 49–54.

Grow, Brian. "Can Delta Carry Song's Tune?," *BusinessWeek,* August 2, 2004, pp. 80–81.

Helyar, John. "A Tale of Two Bankruptcies," *Fortune,* February 17, 2003, pp. 68–70.

Johnson, Keith, and Daniel Michaels, "Big Worry for No-Frills Ryanair: Has it Gone as Low as it Can Go?," *The Wall Street Journal,* Thursday, July 1, 2004.

Lin, Jiun-Sheng Chris, Martin Dresner, and Robert Windle. "Determinants of Price Reactions to Entry in the U.S. Airline Industry," *Transportation Journal,* Winter/Spring, 2001–2002, pp. 5–22.

McCartney, Scott. "Hit Hard by Low-Cost Airlines, AMR Tries Behaving Like One," *The Wall Street Journal,* Monday, June 7, 2004.

Putzger, Ian. "Airlines and Forwarders: Redefining Partnerships," *AirCargo World,* June 2003, pp. 22–25.

Quinn, Francis J. "Security Matters," *Supply Chain Management Review,* July/August 2003, pp. 38–45.

Suzuki, Yoshinori. "The Effect of Airfares on Airport Leakage in Single-Airport Regions," *Transportation Journal*, Vol. 42, No. 5, 2003, pp. 31–41.

Suzuki, Yoshinori. "The Impact of Airline Service Failures on Travelers' Choice: A Case Study of Central Iowa," *Transportation Journal*, Vol. 43, No. 2, 2004, pp. 26–36.

Toh, Rex S., and Peter Raven. "Perishable Asset Revenue Management: Integrated Internet Marketing Strategies for the Airlines," *Transportation Journal*, Vol. 42, No. 4, Summer 2003, pp. 30–43.

Trottman, Melanie. "At Southwest, New CEO Sits in a Hot Seat," *The Wall Street Journal,* Monday, July 19, 2004.

Walter, Clyde Kenneth, and Yoshinori Suzuki. "Perceived High Air Fares: Effects on Location and Business Travel Decisions," *Transportation Journal*, Vol. 42, No. 1, 2002, pp. 42–50.

Case 5-1

Hardee Transportation

Jim O'Brien has become well aware that the demand for freight has blurred among the modes. Customers no longer are concerned about which mode is used for a transportation move and instead focus more on service standards. Jim's customers are asking for faster, more time-specific deliveries of heavy LTL freight (10,000 pounds or more) on longer shipping lanes. Jim's TL operation is straining to fulfill these requests.

Jim has become interested in the air freight market to cover these new moves. He has seen successful freight companies such as UPS get into this market by owning their own aircraft. He has also seen, however, other firms complementing their ground operations by becoming air freight forwarders. He also knows that both passenger and freight airlines compete in this market.

Jim needs to prepare an analysis to determine the feasibility of entering the air freight market for heavy LTL shipments. He sees it as a necessary step to meet the increasing demands of his customers.

Case Questions

1. Using the information in this chapter, how would you suggest Jim approach this analysis?
2. Is this a market Hardee should enter?
3. If you agree that this is a good opportunity, how should Hardee implement this new service? Owned aircraft? Freight forwarder?
4. What are the risks and opportunities for a ground freight company in entering the air freight market?

Case 5-2

US Airways

The U.S. airline industry has faced growing intramodal competition, as well increased fuel and labor costs over the past several years. New carriers such as Airtran, JetBlue, and Southwest have collectively changed the financial operating results for many of the traditional airlines. Companies such as American, Delta, United, and US Airways have seen these rising costs and increased competition as a threat to their survival. As of this writing, both United and US Airways have declared reorganization under bankruptcy, and Delta could be facing a similar fate.

However, none have struggled as has US Airways. Their relatively short-haul, Northeast-dominated routes have made US Airways extremely susceptible to low-cost competition. This case is based on facts found in the popular press and is intended to present the current state of US Airways and its competitors. It will present a synopsis of the operating strategies and characteristics of US Airways and its three new competitors: AirTran, JetBlue, and Southwest. A summary of 2002 operating characteristics for these four airlines can be found in Table 5.10.

Table 5.10 2002 Annual Operating Characteristics

	AirTran[1]	JetBlue	Southwest	US Airways
1. Aircraft	84	37	375	280
2. Employees	5,500	2,924	33,056	33,321
3. Departures	182,500	44,149	948,169	538,279
4. Revenue Passengers (000)	9,654	5,672	72,448	47,155
5. Revenue Passenger Miles (millions)	5,582	6,830	45,396	40,024
6. Available Seat Miles (millions)	N/A	8,240	68,907	56,338
7. Passenger Revenue ($millions)	890	615	5,237	5,224
8. Cargo Revenue ($millions)	0.7	2	85	138
9. Operating Revenue ($millions)	918	635	5,522	6,915
10. Operating Profit (Loss) ($millions)	N/A	106	418	(919)
11. Net Profit (Loss) ($millions)	100.5	55	241	(1,659)
12. Aircraft				
• A320	3	37	–	24
• A319	–	–	–	66
• A321	–	–	–	28
• A330	–	–	–	9
• B737	–	–	375	110
• B757	–	–	–	32
• B767	–	–	–	11
• B717-200	71	–	–	–
• CRJ (Regional Jet)	10	–	–	–
13. Cost per Available Seat-mile	6.42¢	6.08¢	7.82¢	11.68¢
14. Hubs	Atlanta	JFK/NYC	Chicago, Los Angeles, Dallas	Pittsburgh, Philadelphia, Charlotte, NC
15. Rank 2002				
• Passengers	11	16	3	6
• Revenue Passenger Miles	12	11	6	7
• Revenue	9	10	6	7

[1] Items 1 through 14 are for 2003; comparable 2002 data not available from ATA 2003 annual report. Item 15 is 2002 data.

AirTran

Based in Atlanta, AirTran Airways makes nearly 500 departures daily to 45 cities (mostly eastern and Midwestern destinations). Its top competitors are Delta, Southwest, and US Airways. AirTran's strategy is to focus on both business and leisure travelers using low fares. Its labor costs are among the lowest in the industry. The nonunion environment allows AirTran to have flexible labor scheduling. It is the world's largest operator of Boeing 717 and will begin taking deliveries of the new Boeing 737-700 on 2004. AirTran, unlike Southwest, operates a hub-and-spoke network out of its Atlanta hub. Revenues have increased from $624 million in 2000 to $918 million in 2003, with net income increasing from $47.4 million to $100.5 million during the same period. AirTran is facing significant competition in Atlanta from Delta and from American in Dallas. It will begin entering markets served by Southwest. It is in direct competition with US Airways at Baltimore, Philadelphia, Pittsburgh, and Orlando.

JetBlue

Based in John F. Kennedy International Airport in New York City, JetBlue is one of the fastest growing airlines in the United States. Revenues grew from $104.6 million in

2000 to $998 million in 2003, with net income increasing from a loss of $21.3 million to a gain of $103.9 million during the same period. It currently operates 37 Airbus 320 aircraft to 24 cities. JetBlue's strategy is to offer low fares in one class of service on its aircraft. It is one of the only airlines to offer 24 channels of live satellite television free at every seat. JetBlue was the first U.S. airline to introduce "paperless cockpit" flight technology and the only U.S. airline to be 100-percent ticketless. Its routes are point-to-point and rely mostly on nonstop, long-distance flights. Right now, its main competitors are American, Southwest, and United. However, its Florida market is in direct competition with US Airways.

Southwest

Located in Dallas, Texas, Southwest has enjoyed 31 profitable years. Southwest was the first of the new low-cost, no-frills airlines. Passengers sit wherever they want and free meals are not served on-board. Meals may be bought at the gate and brought on-board. Southwest locates its operations in major cities but not at major airports. For example, in Chicago Southwest has avoided the congestion and high cost of using O'Hare and has opted for using Midway Airport. Southwest's growth was well planned. It entered specific market pairs where economies of density were present. Its low-cost structure (nonunion labor) allowed it to attract both business and leisure travelers from existing carriers by offering much lower fares. It only utilizes Boeing 737's in its fleet. Its major rivals are American (at Dallas), Delta, and JetBlue. A new entrant called Song, a low-cost subsidiary of Delta, will begin to provide some significant competition to Southwest in its major markets. However, Southwest made a significant strategic move into the main markets serviced by US Airways. Its first move was into Baltimore (a Piedmont hub operated by US Airways), making US Airways downplay its significance in its hub-and-spoke network servicing the Southeast. Recently Southwest made a major move into Philadelphia, the new major hub in the US Airways network.

US Airways

US Airways, originally known as Allegheny Airlines, is one of the original major hub-and-spoke airlines in the U.S. Based in Arlington, Virginia, US Airways has major hubs in Pittsburgh, Philadelphia, and Charlotte, North Carolina. Rising labor and fuel costs, coupled with its relatively short-haul network in the Northeast, forced US Airways into bankruptcy reorganization (it successfully emerged from the restructuring in 2003). US Airways currently has the highest operating cost per mile of any major U.S. airline. The unions have made many wage and operating concessions to help bring US Airways out of bankruptcy. However, continued pressure from nonunion, low-cost airlines has presented major challenges for US Airways to grow back to profitability.

US Airways predominantly utilizes feeder, or commuter, airlines (i.e., US Airways Express) to bring passengers from small metropolitan areas to its major hubs where it consolidates passengers into larger aircraft traveling to more distant locations. Its major hub was in Pittsburgh. However, rising costs at the Pittsburgh International Airport has forced the airline to cut flights significantly from this hub and focus its efforts on the Philadelphia International Airport. Basing its major operations in the Northeast also brings with it delays and cancellations because of weather.

US Airways has begun to introduce regional jets into some of its medium markets, hoping to reduce its operating cost per mile and to compete with the low-cost airlines. Traditionally, the main competitors for US Airways were United, American, and Delta (all union, hub-and-spoke carriers). However, its new competitors are AirTran, JetBlue, and Southwest.

Case Questions

1. If you were the CEO of US Airways, what would you do to confront the competition from its new low-cost competitors?
2. Can US Airways survive by remaining the same carrier it is today?
3. If you were AirTran, JetBlue, or Southwest, how would you continue to take market share away from US Airways?
4. Do American, Delta, and United still pose competitive threats to US Airways?

Case 5-3

Southwest Airlines

Southwest Airlines started its passenger service as an intrastate carrier in Texas.

Initially, it offered service between Dallas, Houston, and San Antonio. The original founders of Southwest were probably considered eccentric or even crazy during the early years of the company's development. After all, their strategies were contrary to the conventional wisdom of the 1970s and 1980s.

Most airline executives felt that interstate service offered the most potential for profit and that an important ingredient of efficiency was to use the hub concept for service. These same executives also felt that in-flight service of beverages, snacks, and/or food should be included in the fare and that guaranteed seating and baggage checking were necessary ingredients for success. Perhaps even more important was their vision that air service was a premium transportation alternative and should be priced accordingly.

The Southwest Approach

Dissatisfied with the then-current airline service, the founders of Southwest Airlines felt that there was a great opportunity for an intrastate carrier to serve the growing metropolitan areas of Dallas, Houston, and San Antonio. Southwest also, after a while, switched its service to the old airports in Dallas and Houston that had been almost abandoned by the larger carriers.

Southwest used a no-frills, low-price service approach in their marketing strategy. After deregulation of the airline industry in 1978, there was greater opportunity to offer "rock bottom" fares, point-to-point, in selected market areas.

Another important ingredient of the Southwest strategy was its approach with employees. Southwest is run like a democracy, with all of its employees given the opportunity to participate in running the company and having an ownership stake through stock investment. Employees are viewed as the most important asset of the company and its number one priority. Underlying this philosophy is the belief that happy employees will help make the company efficient and will provide better overall customer service. This approach has worked for Southwest—their profitability, customer service, and employee morale are the stuff that legends are made of.

The key points of their continuing success have been:

- Dominance of the short-haul, high-density markets using secondary airports
- Discount fares
- Aggressive advertising

- High level of service
- Employees' attitude and buy-in
- Fiscally sound and conservative

Current Situation

Southwest has recently seen its operating costs rise and its labor relations become more challenging. Its strategy of low-cost, no-frills service is no longer unique to the airline industry. New carriers, such as AirTran, JetBlue, and Song (a Delta subsidiary) have been able to successfully copy this strategy on many of Southwest's major routes. Recent union wage increases (31-percent increase for flight attendants over a 6-year contract) have eroded profits and weakened Southwest's stock price.

Southwest can combat the current financial situation in two ways: increase fares and/or decrease costs. Price increases will certainly result in lost market share to competitors. Price decreases at major cities have been met aggressively by American and by US Airways in Philadelphia. Further cost reductions will provide a challenge. Major cost-reduction opportunities have already taken place at Southwest. In fact, its cost per seat-mile increased to $0.0809 in the 2nd quarter of 2004 from $0.0788 cents the same period in 2003. Further cost reductions might not have the substantial impact as some of the initial initiatives.

Finally, CEO James Parker suddenly retired in July 2004. He has been replaced by Southwest CFO Gary Kelly. Although Mr. Kelly has a thorough knowledge of the costs and budgets involved with Southwest, he brings little operating experience into the top job.

Case Questions

1. What is your evaluation of Southwest Airlines as it stands today?
2. What changes, if any, would you recommend to help keep it competitive and profitable?
3. What difficulties would a new entrant to this low-cost market likely face? If you wanted to start an airline and compete with Southwest, how would you do it?

Chapter 6

Water Carriers and Pipelines

MON VALLEY COAL AND AGGREGATES COMPANY

Joe Hulich and his son-in-law, Andy Kersnick, were having a "heated" discussion about the future of their family business, Mon Valley Coal and Aggregates Company of Monessen, Pennsylvania, which was located in the so-called Mon Valley along the Monoghela River in the southwestern part of the state. Joe, who was CEO, and Andy, who was COO, were involved in a strategic planning session trying to chart the future of their company. Both Joe and Andy recognized the need to transform their organization, but they had different visions about the future strategic direction of Mon Valley Coal and Aggregates Company.

The company was founded in the early 1900s when Monessen was a bustling steel town along the river south of Pittsburgh. The town benefited from good rail service and access to the Ohio River via the Monoghela. The company got its start distributing coal from the rich reserves in Pennsylvania and West Virginia to the numerous steel plants along the river. Other raw materials were added over time as opportunities developed, especially the road system where aggregates were needed for construction and related purposes.

The company was at a crossroads now because the local steel mill had closed, as well as mills located in other towns along the river. Business volume and profits had declined, and drastic action was needed if they wanted to continue operating the business.

Joe's father had established the business, and he was now over 65 years old with a strong desire to retire. Andy was the heir apparent to succeed Joe in the near future. Joe wanted to assure the future viability of the company before his retirement. Andy and Joe did not see eye to eye on the appropriate strategies for the company.

A key to the success of Mon Valley Coal and Aggregates Company was an efficient and effective transportation strategy. Historically, the company accepted large shipments of materials by barge or by rail hopper car. Its location on the river made either approach a viable alternative. Deliveries to customers were usually made by truck. In fact, Mon Valley had its own fleet of trucks for deliveries but were considering other options, namely, for-hire carriers.

The closing of the Monessen Steel Mill changed the economics of the company because it could no longer justify the large-volume deliveries required by rail and barge. Delivery to its location by truck was possible, but it was a more expensive alternative. Joe's strategic vision was a slow change from coal as the primary product to aggregates and home-heating oil. Andy felt that coal should continue to be a major product that they sell and distribute. His view was based upon extending their market boundary and using barge transportation for delivery to customers in the Midwest via the Ohio River and/or rail shipments to the Port of Toledo and then barge on the Great Lakes to appropriate locations.

Andy also wanted to eliminate having all shipments stop in Monessen for eventual delivery to customers, which obviously contributed to the cost of doing business. Andy's analysis convinced him that they could price their product competitively for the Midwest market area by changing their transportation/distribution strategy. He also felt that the increase in oil prices would increase the opportunity for coal sales to public utility companies and other businesses, especially coal retailers who sold for home use. He was also counting on a revival of interest in barge service and government investment in port facilities in the Monessen area. Joe was of the opinion that they should change to all-truck transportation and minimize their inventory levels. As you read this chapter, analyze these two strategies.

INTRODUCTION

Water carriers and pipelines are frequently overlooked by the general public. The public is well aware of trucks, trains, and planes, but has limited appreciation of the role and contribution of water and pipeline transportation to businesses and our economy. These two modes of transportation are an important part of our transportation infrastructure, particularly for certain types of goods. In this chapter, we will explore the role and importance of water carriers and pipelines to a modern transportation system to gain an understanding and appreciation of their significance.

BRIEF HISTORY OF WATER TRANSPORTATION

The inland or domestic waterways (rivers, lakes, and oceans) have provided an important link for freight and people movement for centuries. Waterways are a natural highway, and even some motive power (currents and wind) can be provided by nature. Water transportation has, of course, been improved by modern technology and federal investment to enhance motive power, vessel carrying capacity, and even the waterways by building dams and canals, and dredging to increase the potential of water transportation for economic development.

Water transportation played an important role in the early development of the United States, providing the settlers with a link to markets in England and Europe. In addition, many of our major cities developed along the coasts and still thrive in those locations. As the internal sections of the country developed, water transportation along the rivers and the Great Lakes linked the settlements in the wilderness with the coastal cities and also gave rise to interior cities such as Pittsburgh, Cincinnati, and Memphis. The natural highway, or waterway, was the only viable form of economical transportation available until the railroads were developed and was a prime determinant of population centers, as well as industrial and commercial concentration at port cities along the rivers or Great Lakes. Early private and public sector construction projects in transportation were the Erie, C&O, and other canals to provide inexpensive water transportation.

This chapter focuses on the basic economic and operating characteristics of domestic water and pipeline transportation. An overview is given first, followed by a consideration of types of carriers, market structure, operating and service characteristics, equipment cost structure, and current issues.

WATER TRANSPORT INDUSTRY OVERVIEW

Significance of Water Transport

Water transportation remains a viable mode of transportation for the movement of products and especially basic raw materials. Domestic water carriers compete with railroads for the movement of bulk commodities (such as grains, coal, ores, and chemicals) and with pipelines for the movement of bulk petroleum, petroleum products, and chemicals.

As indicated previously, over $259 billion was spent for freight transportation in 2001 in the United States, which was less than a 1-percent increase over 2000. However, since 1991 freight transportation expenditures have risen by 63 percent, which represents an increase of about $224 billion. Intercity ton-miles rose 29 percent during that same period. Expenditures for truck transportation dominated the market, whereas water transportation market share declined from 5.7 to 4.8 percent of freight expenditures in 2001 even though international freight revenue rose more than 73 percent.[1]

The distribution of domestic intercity freight as measured in ton-miles has changed dramatically since the advent of transportation deregulation. Motor carriers have been the biggest beneficiary, as noted previously, but water carriers have not fared as well. Barge (river) traffic declined by 2 percent and Great Lakes traffic declined by 3 percent from 2000 to 2001. In total, water transportation's ton-miles declined from 16.4 percent in 1980 to 13.2 percent in 2001.[2]

Coastwise domestic shipping has historically not been included in the data for domestic water transportation's share of intercity ton-miles because of the long distances involved (e.g, from the Atlantic Coast to the Pacific Coast through the Panama Canal). Such movements generate high ton-mile figures for a relatively small tonnage figure. For example, if coastwise shipping had been included in 1980, the water carrier share would have been 33.3 percent instead of 16.4 percent. However, the 2001 figures still would have declined to 15.6 percent (as opposed to 13.2 percent noted above).[3]

If the measurement was based solely on tonnage and not ton-miles, water carriers collectively (rivers, Great Lakes, and coastal) had a decrease in tonnage of 6 percent in 2001 compared to 2000 because tonnage shipped declined from 998 million to 939 million tons. Their market share of freight tonnage (as opposed to ton-miles) declined from 15.5 percent in 1991 to 11.3 percent in 2001.[4]

Strong competitive pressures have pushed average freight rate levels down for some modes during the 1990s. However, prices for producers or manufacturers have increased 16 percent during the last decade, but average freight rates for barge shipments have decreased by 8 percent. Rail rates also declined during this period, reflecting the competitiveness of the marketplace, especially intermodal competition.

It is obvious that the water carriers' importance in the U.S. transportation system declined over the past decade. However, many manufacturers and suppliers would experience serious problems in maintaining their competitive position without the availability of low-cost water transportation. The decline in water transportation is attributable in part to the transformation of the U.S. economy from basic manufacturing to service industries and technology. The focus on logistics and supply chain management has also impacted water transportation because companies have switched to carriers offering better service (e.g., motor carriers to offset other costs such as carrying cost for inventory, warehousing cost, packaging cost, etc.).

Types of Carriers

Like motor carriers, the first major classification of the domestic water carrier industry is between for-hire and private carriers. A **private carrier** cannot be hired and only transports freight for the company that owns or leases the vessel. Private water carriers are permitted to transport, for a fee, exempt commodities; when they are hauling such exempt goods, they are technically exempt for-hire carriers. Bona fide private water carriers (transporting company-owned freight and exempt commodities) are excluded from federal economic regulation, as are water carrier shipments of three or fewer commodities within the same barge unit.

The **for-hire** water **carriers** consist of regulated and exempt carriers that charge a fee for their services. Exempt carriers, as indicated above, are excluded from the federal economic regulations administered by the **Surface Transportation Board** (STB). When authority was transferred to the STB under the **ICC Termination Act of 1995**, the STB's authority was expanded over domestic water traffic. In addition to inland river traffic, the STB has jurisdiction over port-to-port traffic when both ports are in the United

States as well as transportation between the United States and its territories. Water carriers are exempt from economic regulation when transporting bulk commodities, both dry and liquid. Because the majority of freight transported by domestic water carriers consists of bulk commodities, exempt carriers dominate the for-hire segment of the industry.

Regulated water **carriers** are classified as either common or contract carriers. Economic regulation, similar to that controlling motor carriers (e.g., operating certificates, rates, etc.), is administered by the STB. Although the majority of water traffic is exempt from regulation, a small number of regulated common and contract carriers do exist.

The domestic water carrier industry is most commonly classified by the waterway used. Carriers that operate over the inland navigable waterways are classified as **internal** water **carriers**. Internal water carriers use barges and towboats and operate over the principal U.S. rivers—Mississippi, Ohio, Tennessee, Columbia, and Hudson—plus smaller arteries. Internal water carriers dominate the north–south traffic through the central portion of the United States via the Mississippi, Missouri, and Ohio rivers.

The Great Lakes carriers operate along the northeastern portion of the United States and provide service between ports on the five Great Lakes that border the states of New York, Pennsylvania, Ohio, Michigan, Indiana, Illinois, Wisconsin, and Minnesota. The lake ships normally remain on the lakes, but access to the Atlantic and Gulf ports is possible via the Saint Lawrence Seaway. This Great Lakes-to-Atlantic traffic is classified as a coastal operation.

Coastal carriers operate along the coasts serving ports on the Atlantic or Pacific oceans or the Gulf of Mexico. Intercoastal carriers transport freight between East Coast and West Coast ports via the Panama Canal. Coastal and intercoastal carriers use ocean-going vessels, but some operators use ocean-going barges (18,000-ton capacity). Currently, large quantities of petroleum, crude and refined, are moved between points on the Atlantic and Gulf of Mexico. Likewise, oil from Alaska moves via coastal carriers to refineries along the Pacific coast.

Number and Categories of Carriers

The domestic for-hire water carrier industry consists of a limited number of relatively small firms. The latest numbers available from the Bureau of Transport Statistics is for 1996, when it was reported that there were 554 vessel operators in service, and that number was relatively constant over a 3-year period. The number of employees for 2000 was 193,900, which was an increase of 8,400 over 1999. There are 25,777 miles of navigable waterways in the United States. This number has remained constant since 1983.[5]

Based upon operating revenues for hauling domestic freight, the inland waterways (rivers and canals) were the most important, followed by the coastal waterways and then the Great Lakes carriers. Operating revenues on the inland waterway has remained relatively constant over the last decade, whereas revenue on the Great Lakes has increased about 23 percent because of an increase in higher-valued freight movements. Freight revenue on the coastal waterways declined about 40 percent during the 1990s as explained below. Water carriers have experienced increased competitive pressure, but the intensity has varied from segment to segment, with carriers operating along the coastal waterways experiencing the greatest impact of the competition especially from railroads and pipeline carriers.[6]

Competition

Water carriers vigorously compete for traffic with other modes and, to a limited degree, with other water carriers. The relatively small number of water carriers results in a limited degree of competition. Because the number of carriers on a given waterway is limited, there is little incentive for the water carriers to compete with one another by lowering rates because they realize that the rate decrease will most likely be matched.

The major water carrier competition is with two other modes, namely rail and pipelines. Water carriers compete with railroads for the movement of dry bulk commodities such as grain, coal, and ores. For example, the movement of grains from the Midwest to New Orleans (export traffic) is possible by rail as well as by water carrier. The water carriers can use the Mississippi and Missouri River systems to connect the plain states with New Orleans. Both modes move sizable amounts of grain along this traffic corridor.

Rail and water carriers compete heavily to move coal out of the coal-producing states of Pennsylvania, West Virginia, and Kentucky. The water carriers are capable of transporting coal via the Ohio and Mississippi rivers to southern domestic consuming points (utilities), as well as to export markets.

On the Great Lakes, water carriers compete with railroads for the movement of coal, ores, and grain. Iron ore and grain originating in Minnesota, Michigan, and Wisconsin are moved across the Great Lakes to other Great Lakes ports, or out of the Great Lakes region via the Saint Lawrence Seaway to Atlantic and Gulf ports or to export markets.

The Port of Toledo has become an interchange point between rail and water carriers for the transport of coal. Railroads haul coal out of the coal-producing states to Toledo, where the coal is loaded onto laker ships for movement to northern Great Lakes ports. In essence, the railroads have helped to overcome the water carrier accessibility problem by moving coal from the mines to Toledo, which suggests that the modes are partners rather than competitors. Because the cost of the water–rail combination is lower than the all-rail route, shippers continue to request the combined water–rail service.

Water carriers and pipelines are vigorous competitors for the movement of bulk liquids (petroleum and petroleum products). Bulk liquids (petroleum, petroleum products, and chemicals) account for about one-third of the total tonnage transported by domestic water carriers. Bulk liquids are important commodities to both modes, and vigorous competition exists for moving bulk liquids along the Gulf, Atlantic, and Pacific coasts, as well as the Mississippi River system.

To a very limited degree, water carriers compete with trucks. However, trucks are usually used to overcome the accessibility constraints of water carriers because trucks tie inland areas to the waterways for pickup and/or delivery. Shipment quantities argue against an all-motor carrier movement for long hauls because one barge can transport the equivalent of 58 tractor–trailers.

Operating and Service Characteristics

COMMODITIES HAULED AND RELATED CHARACTERISTICS

In 2000, water carriers hauled 91 billion ton-miles of crude oil, which represents 24.2 percent of the total ton-miles hauled that year. Water carriers were second to pipelines but only transported about one-third of the ton-miles hauled by pipelines. The water carrier share of the refined petroleum movements was higher in 2000 when they moved almost 31 percent of the total ton-miles compared to 59 percent by pipelines. Chemicals accounted for about 9 percent of the water carrier total. Dry bulk commodities transported by water carriers are typically raw materials such as coal and coke and represent about 28 percent of the total freight moved by water carriers. Agricultural products account for about 15 percent of the total. Other products include iron and steel, scrap, pulp, and so on.[7] It is obvious that water carriers are important for low-value, bulk movements of liquid and dry materials. The low rates of water carriers are attractive to the shippers of such commodities.

Water carriers are considered to be medium-to-long-haul carriers. Their carrying capacity is relatively large, which makes short hauls with frequent stops uneconomical. However, the length of haul varies by segment from about 400 miles (inland water carriers) to over 1,500 miles for coastal carriers. As noted, the carrying capacity is large. Barges are capable of carrying 1,500 to 3,000 tons, and lake carrier vessels can carry about 20,000 tons. A 1,500-ton load represents the typical carrying capacity of 15 railcars or about 50 trucks. The long hauls and the large carrying capacity combined with fuel efficiency allow water carriers to offer low-cost service—about 72 cents per ton-mile on average.[8]

The low cost of the water carrier comes with some service disadvantages that need to be considered by shippers. Water carriers are relatively slow, with average speeds on inland rivers, for example, of 5.5 to 9 miles per hour. The limited accessibility of the water carrier usually necessitates pickup or delivery by another mode of transportation to bridge the accessibility gap. The transfer between modes will obviously add to the total cost.

Service can also be disrupted by weather. Rivers and lakes freeze during the winter months in the northern states, which can interrupt service for several months. Drought conditions can lower water levels and restrict traffic flow. Conversely, heavy rains can cause flooding, which is also disruptive to service. The waterways are a natural highway, but "Mother Nature" can also constrain the flow of traffic.

Overall, water carriers are an attractive alternative for low-value traffic, where transportation rates are a significant part of the total delivered cost and price of the good. However, the poor service characteristics may add cost for the user, which has to be traded off against the low rate to calculate the true total cost.

Equipment

TYPES OF VEHICLES

Because most domestic water carriers transport bulk materials, they use ships with very large **hold** openings to facilitate easy loading and unloading. Watertight walls dividing the holds allow a ship to carry more than one commodity at a time. However, most carriers will carry a limited variety of products at one time.

The largest ship in the domestic water carriage industry is the tanker. A **tanker** can carry anywhere from 18,000 to 500,000 tons of liquid, generally petroleum or petroleum products. Due to oil spill problems, the use of double-hulled tankers has become preferable to the use of the more conventional single-hulled tankers. However, the building of these ships has diminished greatly since 1991.

Another type of vessel is the **barge**, a powerless vessel towed by a tugboat. Barges are most commonly used by internal waterway carriers. Additional barges can be added to a tow at very little additional cost. Consequently, barge transportation offers a capacity flexibility comparable to railroads plus lower rates.

TERMINALS

Water carrier terminals are often provided by the public. Most ports are operated by local government agencies, and many ports have publicly operated storage facilities.

It has been recognized for a long time that water transportation is a catalyst to economic activity in the community, and it is this belief that has spurred public investment in the operation of ports.

Some volume users of transportation invest in and operate port facilities or **shipper run terminals**. Individual firms that handle such commodities as grain, coal, and oil commonly build docks, terminals, and commodity-handling facilities to meet their unique needs. The water carriers have the opportunity to use these private facilities owned by shippers.

Over the past few decades, major port improvements have centered on the mechanization of materials-handling systems, especially for internal waterway ports. Efficient handling of larger volumes of bulk commodities has been a prerequisite for ports that desire to remain economically competitive with other ports along the waterway and for water carriers that seek to be competitive with other modes.

The port facilitates ship loading and unloading, which means that the port must be equipped with cranes, forklifts, and other handling equipment. Certain commodities like oil, grain, and coal require more technically advanced loading equipment, such as pneumatic loaders and railcar dumping equipment. Such materials-handling equipment reduces unproductive port delays and enables water carriers and ports to remain economically viable.

The port also facilitates the transfer of freight from one mode to another. The port is usually served by railroads and motor carriers. Terminals at the port will have railroad sidings to handle inbound and outbound rail freight as well as parking lots for motor carrier equipment. Ports play a key role in promoting the efficiency of intermodal transportation.

Because barges and ships carry larger loads than rail or motor carrier vehicles, storage facilities are necessary at the port. The storage areas receive cargo from many trucks and railcars. This freight is held until sufficient volume is obtained to be handled effectively by barge or ship. Conversely, when a loaded vessel arrives at port, the freight is unloaded, stored, and then dispatched in hundreds of railcars or trucks at some later date.

Cost Structure

FIXED VERSUS VARIABLE COST COMPONENTS

The basic cost structure of water carriers consists of relatively high variable costs and low fixed costs. Like motor carriers and air carriers, water carriers do not provide their own highways (rights-of-way). The waterways are provided by nature (except canals) and are maintained, improved, and controlled by the government. The carriers pay **user charges**—lock fees, dock fees, fuel taxes—for the use of government-provided facilities. These user charges are directly related to the volume of business, and therefore, are considered variable costs.

The **operating costs** for water carriers are approximately 85 percent variable and 15 percent fixed. Fixed costs include depreciation and amortization, and general expenses. The major variable expenses are line-operating costs, operating rents, and maintenance. Line-operating costs are those expenses associated with renting operating equipment and facilities.

INFRASTRUCTURE

As indicated above, the domestic water carrier's low fixed costs can be attributed in part to **public aid** in the area of infrastructure. For water carriers, the major public aid is the construction and maintenance of waterways. The construction of canals with public fund opens new markets and sources of revenue for water carriers. The construction of locks and dams on rivers makes the waterways navigable for domestic water carriers. The dredging of the Mississippi River, for example, is performed by the **Army Corps of Engineers** to maintain channel depth and width. Port facilities are maintained by federal and local monies.

An example of a major public aid for domestic water carriers is the **Tennessee Tombigbee** (Tenn-Tom) **project**. Opened in 1985, the project connects the Tennessee River and the Warrior River via the Tombigbee River. Another example of public aid was when, in 1986, the federal government built two 1,200-foot locks and a new dam at Lock and Dam Number 26 on the Mississippi River systems.

Critics of waterway projects like Tenn-Tom often refer to them as "**pork barrel projects**," suggesting that they are funded by government funds for the benefit of only a small number of the legislator's constituents. Critics question their value to society and maintain that these projects probably would not have been constructed if the actual users or local taxpayers had to assume the full burden of the costs. The U.S. Army Corps of Engineers has been responsible for conducting benefit/cost analysis to determine if such projects deserve to be funded by federal dollars, but critics question whether the Corps' analysis are realistic and whether the projects' expected benefits will ever be realized.

LABOR

Water transportation is not labor-intensive. In 1997, 2.72 million ton-miles of freight were transported for each water carrier employee. This compares to 4.74 million ton-miles for each rail employee, 0.4 million ton-miles for each motor carrier employee, and 39.3 million ton-miles for each pipeline employee.[9]

Labor is required at the terminal to load and unload general commodities. The freight is moved from the dock onto the ship and into the appropriate hold for the voyage (and vice versa for unloading). In addition, labor is required to handle the loading of freight from connecting modes, such as truck and rail, and to store the freight waiting to be loaded onto the ship or connection carriers.

Domestic water carriers ususally do not require much labor at the terminal, because the carriers primarily transport bulk commodities that can be loaded mechanically. Great Lakes carrier companies have developed ships that are equipped with automatic unloading devices that reduce the amount of labor required to unload the ships.

CURRENT ISSUES

DRUG AND ALCOHOL ABUSE

The grounding of the Exxon tanker ***Valdez*** off the shores of Alaska in March 1989 exemplifies the need for strong measure against drug and alcohol abuse in the water transportation industry. The captain of the *Valdez* was found to be intoxicated at the time the ship ran aground and spilled 10 million gallons of oil off Alaska's shores. The full impact of this disaster will not be known for many years to come; however, it is known that the environmental damage resulted in the deaths of hundreds of animals, including some endangered species, and the loss of income and jobs for many of Alaska's citizens (such as fishermen, for example).

In recognition of the problem of substance abuse, the U.S. Coast Guard now tests American seamen for drug abuse before they are issued a seamen's license and before they can be employed. Seamen are also tested randomly during their employment.

PORT DEVELOPMENT

Because of today's environmental concerns, ports are having trouble keeping pace with the accelerated developments in global trade. Ports are now having to balance competitive economic concerns with the concerns of the public, which, rightly or wrongly, often view ports as a main source of air, water, and noise pollution.

An example of the struggle would be the problems the port of Oakland, California, faced in trying to get permission to dredge its harbors to a lower depth in order to berth new, larger vessels. Without the dredging, Oakland's competitiveness would decrease. But proposals for dumping the spoil from the dredging were denied at every turn. Soon another problem developed. The city's mayor decided to siphon port revenues into the city's coffers to alleviate budget problems. After local and international business people united in support of the port's autonomy, the mayor backed down. Months later, thanks to the concerted efforts of two U.S. representatives and California's governor, the port got approval to dredge and dump the spoil in a cost-effective spot in the bay. Although that issue was resolved, now California is considering a bill that would allow the state to take revenue from the ports to replenish the state's depleted treasury.

Also, a current issue facing North American ports is the growth of multicarrier alliances, leading to the expansion of the already gargantuan ships. An increase from 6,000 20-foot equivalent units (TEU) to 8,000 TEU's has many ports worried for the future. The larger the ships are, the deeper they go, meaning that many of the smaller ports will need to begin the dredging process as soon as possible to be able to compete in the future. The dredging process would allow ports to make their waterways deeper and wider in order to accommodate these new, larger ships and allow them to stay competitive. However, as indicated above, the approval process for the dredging is problematic.

BRIEF HISTORY OF PIPELINES

Pipelines have played an important role in the transportation industry in the post-World War II era. Originally, pipelines were used to feed other modes of transportation, such as railroads or water carriers. The Pennsylvania Railroad initiated the development of pipelines in the oil fields of Pennsylvania in the 19th century and then sold out to the Standard Oil Company, establishing the precedent of pipelines being owned by the oil companies. Early in the 20th century, the oil companies operated the pipelines as integrated subsidiaries and often used them to control the oil industry by not providing needed transportation service to new producers. Consequently, after World War II, in a decision rendered by the U.S. Supreme Court known as the **Champlin Oil Case**, pipelines were required to operate as common carriers if there was a demand by shippers for oil for their services. This decision was coupled with the growth in demand for gasoline after World War II and the need to move oil and oil products from the oil fields in Texas and Oklahoma to the markets in the Northeastern states.

Pipelines Industry Overview

The pipeline industry is unique in a number of important aspects, including the type of commodity hauled, ownership, and visibility. The industry is relatively unknown to the general public, which has little appreciation of the role and importance of pipelines. Pipelines are limited in the markets they serve and very limited in the commodities they can haul. Furthermore, pipelines are the only mode with

Table 6.1 Pipeline Share of Intercity Traffic

Year	Ton-miles Shipped (Billions)	Total Transportation Intercity Ton-miles (%)
1975	507	24.5
1980	588	23.6
1985	564	22.9
1990	584	20.2
1995	601	17.6
2000	617	16.5
2001	616	16.5

Source: Eno Transportation Foundation, Washington DC, "Transportation in America," 19th ed., 2002.

no **backhaul**; that is, they are unidirectional with products that only move in one direction through the line.

Significance of Pipelines

As seen in Table 6.1, pipelines accounted for 16.5 percent of the total intercity ton-miles shipped in the United States in 2001. This figure is comparable to the share of water carriers, and pipelines' relative position, on a strict tonnage basis, is comparable to that of all water carriers. Few people in the United States would guess that pipelines compare to motor carriers and rail companies in terms of traffic relevance. Pipelines are virtually unknown to the general public but represent a key component in our transportation system.

As shown in Table 6.2, the pipeline network grew steadily until the early 1980s, allowing pipelines to move an increased amount of tonnage. However, Table 6.2 does not adequately reflect the increase in total capacity because it does not show the diameter of pipelines. As we will discuss later, pipeline diameters have increased in recent years, and the larger diameters have increased capacity significantly because of the increased volume that can move through the pipeline. The larger diameter has also allowed the total network shown in Table 6.2 to decrease since the early 1980s to about 177,000 miles in 2000.

Table 6.2 Pipeline Network

Oil (000)

Year	Miles
1960	191
1970	219
1980	218
1985	214
1990	209
1995	201
2000	177

Source: Eno Transportation Foundation, Washington DC, "Transportation in America," 19th ed., 2002.

The tonnage comparison shown in Table 6.1 is a sharp contrast to the revenue picture indicated in Table 6.3. Here the low rates of the pipeline, which are discussed later in this chapter, are reflected in the very low percentage of the total intercity revenue paid to all pipeline carriers. The pipelines account for approximately 4 percent of the total transportation revenues, compared to motor carriers, for example, which account for more than 75 percent of the total revenue.

Types of Carriers

As noted earlier, due to the decision rendered by the U.S. Supreme Court in the Champlin Oil Case, many pipelines operate as **common** carriers. Hence, although some private carriers exist today, the for-hire carriers dominate the industry. Common carriers account for approximately 90 percent of all pipeline carriers.

Ownership

With some exceptions, oil companies have been the owners of the oil pipelines. Beginning with Standard Oil Company buying out the Pennsylvania Railroad and developing pipelines more extensively in order to control the industry and enhance its market dominance, oil companies have been the principal owners of pipelines. The federal government entered the pipeline business briefly during World War II when it developed two pipelines to bring crude oil and oil products from the oil fields of the Southwest to the Northeast to ensure an uninterrupted flow of oil. These two pipelines, known as the Big Inch and the Little Inch, were sold to private companies after the war.

Some pipelines are joint ventures among two or more pipeline companies because of the high capital investment necessary for large-diameter pipelines. Individual, vertically integrated oil companies control the largest share of the pipeline revenues followed by jointly owned pipeline companies. Railroads, independent oil companies, and other industrial companies control the remaining percentage.

Number of Carriers

Like the railroad industry, the pipeline industry has a small number of very large carriers that dominate the industry. In 2001 approximately 239 carriers of oil and oil products offered for-hire service, accounting for approximately 85 percent of the ton-miles carried. The remaining 15 percent were carried by private carrier operations.

Table 6.3 Revenue Position of Pipelines

Oil (Millions)

Year	Revenue
1960	895
1970	1,376
1980	7,548
1985	8,910
1990	8,506
1995	9,077
2000	8,958
2001	9,066

Source: Eno Transportation Foundation, Washington DC, "Transportation in America," 19th ed., 2002.

The oligopolistic nature of the industry is demonstrated by the fact that 20 major integrated oil companies control about two-thirds of the crude oil pipeline mileage.[10]

There are a number of reasons for the limited number of pipeline companies. First, startup costs (capital costs) are high. Second, like railroads and public utilities, the economies of scale are such that duplication or parallel competing lines would be uneconomic. Large-size operations are more economical because capacity rises more than proportionately with increases in the diameter of the pipeline and investment per mile decreases, as do operating cost per barrel. For example, a 12-inch pipeline operating at capacity can transport three times as much oil as an 8-inch pipeline.

The procedural requirements for entry and the associated legal costs also contribute to the limited number of companies. An additional factor is the industry itself, which has been dominated by the large oil companies that joined together in the post-World War II era to develop pipelines from major fields and entry ports.

OIL CARRIERS

The pipeline industry experienced rapid growth after World War II, but the rate of growth has since decreased dramatically. Intercity ton-miles increase to 623 billion in 2001. The reported operating revenue decreased slight from 1995 to 2001. There were corresponding changes in other data, including the number of employees, which also decreased. Overall, however, oil pipelines play a major role in our transportation network because, as previously mentioned, they transport about 16.5 percent of the total intercity ton-miles.[11]

NATURAL GAS CARRIERS

Another part of the pipeline industry is involved with the transportation of natural gas, which, like oil, is an important source of energy. The movement data for natural gas are recorded in cubic feet, rather than ton-miles. The industry is comparable in size to the oil pipeline industry in terms of the number of companies and, as in the oil pipeline industry, there has been a growth in the number of companies since 1975. It should be noted that there has been a reclassification of some companies since 1975, so the growth numbers are not exactly comparable. Finally, operating revenues have increased by about 25 percent between 1995 and 2001.[12]

STOP OFF

This Politics of Global Pipelines

Like other forms of transportation, pipelines can provide the links for bringing nations together because they can establish alliances based upon convenience and/or necessity. In today's world, they may be viewed as the trade routes of the 21st century. Pipelines can be a vital delivery system for water, oil and natural gas. They help sustain the economic and, perhaps, social well being of some countries.

For countries that produce oil but do not have ports, pipelines carry material resources for hundreds, or even thousands, of miles. The pipelines, therefore, allow foreign revenue to flow into the producing country to support the local citizenry and they can provide social capital to support economical improvements.

On one hand, pipelines can enable wealth, development, power, economic stability, global leverage, etc., but they also can lead to political tensions. It has been estimated by several sources that there are over a million miles of oil and natural gas pipelines crisscrossing the globe among independent nations. They are the arteries of modern commerce in some parts of the world.

Pipelines crossing national boundaries create an environment of interdependence, which sometimes give rise to not only national issues but also international issues. Pipelines can drive political strategy and foreign policy. The United States, for example, consumes more oil than it produces and for political and security reasons purchases oil from a variety of sources. Some of those sources are landlocked which necessitates pipeline transportation usually to a port in another country where the oil can be transshipped to a tanker ship for movement to a designated refinery.

When new oil sources are discovered in a landlocked country, it usually necessitates the development of a pipeline to unlock the newly discovered resource. Russia is a good example of such a situation; Russia is the second largest exporter of oil after Saudi Arabia. The former Soviet Republics around the Caspian Sea also figure into this equation. Consequently, the United States is supporting the development of new pipelines (BTC) designed to transport crude oil from the Caspian Port Baku, Azerbaijan through Tbilisi, Georgia to Ceyhan (port) in Turkey. The pipeline should generate about $65 million in transit fees for Georgia when it is functioning at capacity. This is only one example and there are others.

Pipelines that have been described as an almost invisible part of the U.S. transportation infrastructure are much more visible in global situations as described above. They do connect nations and give rise to alliances, which, in turn, may promote stability in the geographic area of the pipeline. The economic interdependence can go a long way to helping to stabilize alliances, as long as there are not any outside influences, which disrupt or impose the flow of oil through the pipelines.

Adapted from: "Pipeline Diplomacy" by Steve Goldstein, *The Philadelphia Inquirer*, October 26, 2003, pp. C1 and C3.

Operating and Service Characteristics

COMMODITIES HAULED

Pipelines are a very specialized carrier in that they transport a very limited variety of products. The four main commodities hauled by pipeline are oil and oil products, natural gas, coal, and chemicals.

OIL AND OIL PRODUCTS

The bulk of pipeline movements are crude oil and oil products. In 2001 crude oil and oil products accounted for about 60 percent of total pipeline use. Pipelines move about 66 percent of the total ton-miles of crude oil and petroleum products.

The total volume of petroleum transported domestically in the United States has declined slightly during the 1990s. However, the split by modes between pipeline and water carrier has changed for several reasons. A pipeline was built across Panama during the 1800s, virtually eliminating long movements of Alaskan crude oil tankers around South America. The Alaskan crude oil is now transshipped via the pipeline to Atlanta tankers for Gulf and Atlantic Coast deliveries to refineries. Also, another large crude oil pipeline has been built, providing service from the West Coast to Midwest refineries and reducing the need for tanker movements even further.

The length of haul in the oil pipeline industry is medium in length compared to other modes. Crude oil movements average about 800 miles per shipment, and product lines average about 400 miles per movement. The average shipment size for these movements is very large. (This will be discussed later in the section titled "Equipment.")

NATURAL GAS

Natural gas pipelines are an important part of our total pipeline network. They account for the second largest number of miles of intercity pipelines. The natural gas pipeline companies produce about 10 percent of the gas they transport. Independent gas companies produce the remaining 90 percent and transport it via the pipelines.

COAL

Coal pipelines are frequently called **slurry lines** because the coal is moved in a pulverized form in water (one-to-one ratio by weight). Once the coal has reached its destination, the water is removed and the coal is ready for use. Coal pipelines are primarily used for transporting coal to utility companies for generating electricity. The large slurry pipeline that operates between Arizona and Nevada covers 273 miles and moves 5 million tons of coal per year. Coal pipelines use enormous quantities of water, which causes concern in several western states where their installation has been proposed, because there is a scarcity of water and the water is not reusable (no backhaul).

CHEMICALS

Chemical lines are another type of product line, although only a limited number of different types of chemicals are carried by pipelines. The three major chemicals are anhydrous ammonia, which is used in fertilizer; propylene, which is used for manufacturing detergents; and ethylene, which is used for making antifreeze.

Relative Advantages

A major advantage offered by the pipeline industry is low rates. Pipeline transportation can be extremely efficient, with large-diameter pipelines operating near capacity. Average revenues for pipeline companies are below one-half of a cent per ton-mile, which is indicative of their low-cost service.

Two additional user cost advantages complement the low rates. First, pipelines have a very good **loss and damage record** (L and D). This record is attributed in part to the types of products transported, but it is also related to the nature of the pipeline service, which provides underground and completely encased movement.

The second important cost advantage is that pipelines can provide a warehousing function because their service is slow. In other words, if the product is not needed immediately, the slow pipeline service can be regarded as a form of free warehousing storage. (Products move through pipelines at an average of 3 to 5 miles per hour.)

Another positive service advantage of pipelines is their dependability. They are virtually unaffected by weather conditions, and they very rarely have mechanical failures. Although the service time is slow, scheduled deliveries can be forecasted very accurately, diminishing the need for safety stock. The risk of terrorism is reduced when the pipelines are buried in the ground.

Relative Disadvantages

Although the pipeline's slow speed can be considered an advantage due to its use as a free form of warehousing, in some instances the pipeline's slow speed can be considered a disadvantage. For example, if a company's demand is uncertain or erratic, it will have to hold higher levels of inventory to compensate for possible shortages because the pipeline will not be able to deliver an extra amount of the product in a short period of time.

Pipelines are also at a disadvantage when it comes to completeness of service because they offer a fixed route of service that cannot be easily extended to complete door-to-door service. That is, they have limited geographic flexibility or accessibility. However, because the source of the pipelines and the location of the refineries are known and are fixed for a long period of time, the fixed-route service factor may not be a critical problem. Frequently, pipelines depend on railroads and motor carriers to complete delivery, which adds to user costs.

The use of pipelines is limited to a rather select number of products: crude oil, oil products, natural gas, coal, and a limited number of chemicals. There is interest in using pipelines for other products because of their cost advantage, but the technology for such use has not yet been fully developed. Capsule and pneumatic pipelines can carry and extend the low-cost, high-volume, reliable service to other bulk products. Frequency of service (the number of times a mode can pick up and deliver during a particular period) is a characteristic of interest to some users. On one hand, the large tenders (shipment size requirements) and slow speed of pipelines reduces the frequency. On the other hand, service is offered 24 hours a day, 7 days a week.

Pipelines are generally regarded as somewhat inflexible because they serve limited geographic areas and limited points within that area. Also, they carry limited types of commodities and only offer one-way service. Finally, the operations technology precludes small shipment sizes.

In summary, pipelines offer a good set of services for particular types of products, but they have some serious limitations for many other products.

Competition

INTRAMODAL

Intramodal competition in the pipeline industry is limited by a number of factors. First, there are a small number of companies—slightly more than 100. The industry, as noted previously, is oligopolistic in market structure, which generally leads to limited price competition. Second, the economies of scale and high fixed costs have led to joint ownership of large-diameter pipelines because the construction of smaller parallel lines is not very efficient. Finally, the high capital costs preclude duplication of facilities to a large extent.

INTERMODAL

The serious threats to the pipeline industry are in terms of traffic diversion to other modes of transportation. Technically, pipelines compete with railroads, water carriers, and motor carriers for traffic. However, even with these forms of transportation, the level of competition is limited. The most serious competition is water, or tanker operations, because their rates are competitive with pipelines. However, the limited coverage of water carrier service also limits its effective competitiveness. Trucks have increased the number of products they carry that can also be carried by pipelines. However, truck service complements rather than competes with the pipeline because trucks often perform a distribution function for pipelines (i.e., delivery).

Once a pipeline has been constructed between two points, it is difficult for other modes to compete. Pipeline costs are extremely low, dependability is quite high, and there is limited risk of damage to the product being transported. The major exception is probably coal slurry pipelines because the need to move the pulverized coal in water can make the costs comparable to rail movements. Water carriers come closest to matching pipeline costs and rates as indicated.

Equipment

The U.S. Department of Transportation estimates that the total pipeline investment is in excess of $21 billion, based on historical costs. Also, the department estimates it would cost about $70 billion to replace the system at today's costs.[13] This great investment in the equipment is necessary to finance the complex operation of getting oil from the well to the market.

Pipelines can be grouped into other categories in addition to for-hire or private carriers. For instance, they are frequently classified as gathering lines or trunk lines, particularly in reference to the movement of oil. The trunk lines are further classified or subdivided into two types: crude and product lines. The gathering lines are used to bring the oil from the fields to storage areas before the oil is processed into refined products or transmitted as crude oil over the trunk lines to distant refineries. Trunk lines are used for long-distance movement of crude oil or other products, such as jet fuel, kerosene, chemicals, or coal.

Early in the history of the oil industry, the refineries were located primarily in the eastern part of the United States, and thus the long-distance movement of oil was basically the movement of crude oil. The state of technology in the industry also made it much easier to control leakage with crude oil than with refined oil products such as gasoline or kerosene. After World War II, however, refineries were developed at other locations, especially in the Southwest, when better technology (limited seams and welding techniques) made the long-distance movement of oil products easy to accomplish.

When comparing **gathering lines** and trunk lines, there are several important differences to note. First, gathering lines are smaller in diameter, usually not exceeding 8 inches, whereas trunk lines are usually 30-50 inches in diameter. Gathering lines are frequently laid on the surface of the ground to ensure ease of relocation when a well or field runs dry. Trunk lines, on the other hand, are usually seen as permanent and are laid underground.

The term **trunk line** is often used in conjunction with oil movements and can refer to crude oil trunk lines or oil product lines. Oil trunk lines move oil to tank farms or refineries in distant locations, whereas oil product lines move the gasoline, jet fuel, and home heating oil from refineries to market areas. Technically, however, any long-distance movement via a large-diameter, permanent pipeline implies a trunk-line movement. Therefore, when coal, natural gas, or chemicals move via pipelines, such movement is usually classified as trunk-line movement.

Commodity Movement

Gathering lines bring oil from the fields to a gathering station, where the oil is stored in sufficient quantity to ship by trunk line to a refinery. After the oil is refined, the various products are stored at a tank farm before they are shipped via product line to another tank farm with a market-oriented location. A motor carrier most frequently makes the last segment of the trip, from the market-oriented tank farm to the distributor or ultimate customer.

Trunk lines, as indicated previously, are usually more than 30 inches in diameter and are the major component of the pipeline system. Stations that provide the power to push the commodities through the pipeline are interspersed along the trunk line. For oil movements, pumps are located at the stations, which vary in distance from 20 to 100 miles, depending on the viscosity of the oil and the terrain. Figures 6.1 and 6.2 illustrate the major interstate and intrastate pipelines in the United States.

The pumping stations for large-diameter pipelines can provide 3,000 to 6,000 horsepower. Compressors are used for the movement of natural gas, and pumps are used for the liquid items that move through the pipelines.

Computers at the pumping stations continually monitor the flow and pressure of the oil system. Any change indicating a leak is easily detected. Routine visual checks and searches by airplane are sometimes used to locate leaks. Great care is rendered, not only because of the potential losses but also because of the lawsuits that could ensue as a result of damage to property and the environment.

FIGURE 6.1 Major Interstate and Intrastate Crude Oil Pipelines

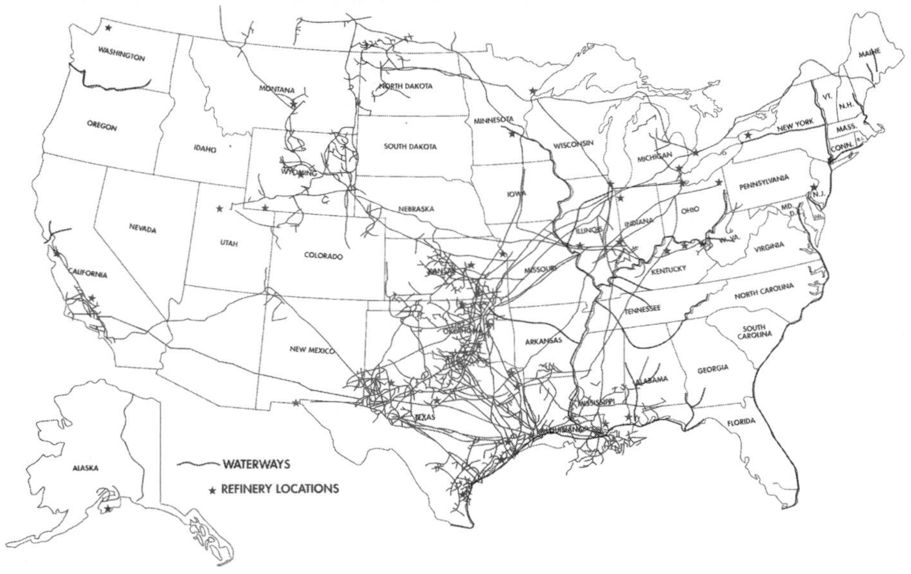

Source: Association of Oil Pipelines

FIGURE 6.2 Major Interstate and Intrastate Products Pipelines

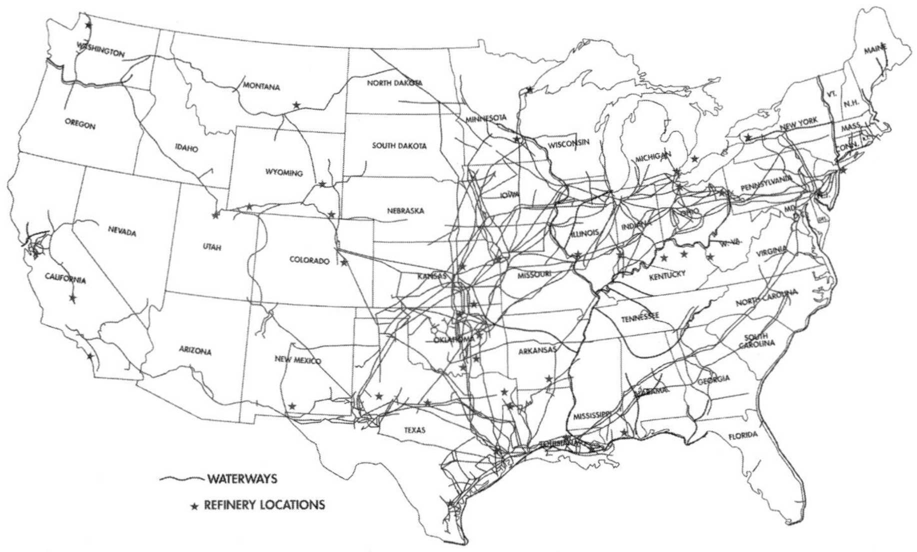

Source: Association of Oil Pipelines

In the oil segment of the pipeline industry, sophisticated operating and monitoring techniques are used because of the different petroleum products moving through the product lines and the different grades of crude oil moving through the crude oil lines. There are 15 grades of crude oil and a range of products including jet fuel, kerosene, and aviation fuel. When two or more grades of crude oil or two or more products move through a system at one time, the "batches" may need to be separated by a rubber ball called a **batching** pig. However, this is not always necessary because the different specific grades of the products helps to keep them separated. Any mixing (shop) that does occur is only of minor lower-grade items with which they are mixed. Usually, products are scheduled 1 month in advance with kerosene moving first, then high-grade gasoline, then medium-grade gasoline, then various other products, with home heating oil last. Before the cycle starts again, the pipeline is usually scoured to prevent mixing problems.

Cost Structure

FIXED- VERSUS VARIABLE-COST COMPONENTS

Like the railroad industry, the pipeline industry has a high proportion of fixed costs with low capital turnover. The pipeline owners have to provide their own right-of-way by purchasing or leasing land and constructing the pipeline and pumping stations along the right-or-way. The property taxes, amortizations of depreciation, the return to investors, and preventative maintenance all contribute to the high ratio of fixed to variable expenses.

In addition to the right-of-way costs, the terminal facilities of pipelines contribute to the high level of fixed costs. The same types of expenses associated with the right-of-way, such as depreciation and property taxes, are incurred by the pipeline terminals.

As stated previously, the pipeline industry has significant economies of scale. The high fixed costs and the economies of scale help to explain the joint ownership and investment in large-diameter pipelines. Pipelines do not operate vehicles like other modes of transportation because the carrying capacity is the pipe itself, which is best regarded as part of the right-of-way. This unique element of the pipeline operation helps to explain the low variable costs because vehicles are frequently a major source of variable expense.

Labor costs are very low in the pipeline industry because of the high level of automation. One example is the Trans-Alaska Pipeline System, built at a cost of $9.2 billion and operated by 450 employees. Another variable cost is the cost of fuel for the power system. The pipelines employ about 8,000 people compared to about 10 million in the motor carrier industry for comparable ton-miles on an intercity basis.

RATES

Pricing in the pipeline industry is unique compared to its major modal competitors. First of all, pipelines do not use the freight classification system that underlies the class rates of railroads and motor carriers. The limited number and specialization of commodities make such a practice unnecessary. A crude oil pipeline or natural gas pipeline has little need for an elaborate classification system.

Even though pipelines have high fixed costs, the differential pricing practices common in the railroad industry are virtually nonexistent among pipelines. The nature of operation (one-way movement, limited geographic coverage of points, limited products, etc.) provides little opportunity to provide differential pricing practices. Pipelines quote rates on a per-barrel basis (one barrel equals 42 gallons). Quotes for rates are typically point-to-point or zone-to-zone. Also, minimum shipment sizes, usually called tenders, are required; these range from 500 barrels to 10,000 barrels.

Pipeline rates are very low, which is reflected in the fact that they carry more than 15 percent of the total intercity ton-miles and receive only about 2 percent of the total revenues.

Summary

- Water carriers played a key role in the development of many U.S. cities and regions.
- The water carrier system is still a viable part of the total transportation system and competes with the railroad system and pipelines for the movement of bulk, low-value commodities.
- The domestic water carrier system can be classified in terms of inland carriers (rivers, canals, and Great Lakes) and costal/intercoastal carriers, all three of which are vital to water transportation.
- Intramodal competition among water carriers is not as important as intermodal competition, especially railroads and pipelines.
- Water carriers offer low-cost services, but their transit time is slow and can be interrupted by weather conditions. Accessibility and potential product damage are also service disadvantages.
- Water carriers have relatively low fixed costs because they use a right-of-way provided by the government for which they pay user charges like motor carriers and airlines.
- Water carriers are not labor-intensive for their movement operations but may require more labor in terminal areas for certain types of freight.
- The development of pipelines began in the 19th century in Pennsylvania by the Pennsylvania Railroad, but subsequently the ownership and development were taken on by the oil companies, who operated them as integrated subsidiaries.
- Ownership by oil companies has continued to the present, but some oil pipelines are owned by non-oil companies. Also, joint ownership by several companies has become common because of the large investment of capital necessary.
- The pipeline industry is a large component of our transportation industry (more than 20 percent of intercity ton-miles), but it is largely invisible to many people.
- Because of market-control tactics used by some oil companies, an important U.S. Supreme Court ruling after World War II required pipelines to operate as common carriers, even if owned by an oil company.
- Pipelines are very specialized in terms of the commodities that they carry. Most of the traffic are oil and oil products, but they also carry natural gas, chemicals, and coal.
- Only a small number of pipeline companies exist (about 100), and they only have limited intermodal competition.
- Pipelines are low-cost carriers when operated at capacity, but they have high levels of fixed cost because of the heavy investment necessary in infrastructure.
- Pipeline service is slow and has limited accessibility, but it is also very reliable with little or no loss and damage.
- Intercity pipeline service is provided by large-diameter (30-50 inches) pipelines called trunk lines. Small-diameter pipelines, called gathering lines, are used to

bring the oil from the producing area to the terminals for storage before processing and/or transporting.

- Pipelines are a highly automated, efficient form of transportation. Oil moves in one direction in large volumes at a steady, slow speed.
- Although there is always some concern about safety and the environment, pipelines have been a relatively safe mode of transportation.

Key Terms

Army Corps of Engineers, 193
backhaul, 195
barge, 191
batching, 203
Champlin Oil Case, 194
classification, 188
coastal carriers, 189
common carriers, 196
fixed costs, 192
for-hire carriers, 188
gathering lines, 201
holds, 191
ICC Termination Act of 1995, 188
intermodal competition, 188
internal carriers, 189
intramodal competition, 200
loss and damage record (L and D), 199
natural highway, 187
operating costs, 192
pork barrel, 193
private carriers, 188
public aid, 192
regulated carriers, 189
shipper terminals, 192
slurry lines, 199
Surface Transportation Board (STB), 188
tank farms, 201
tanker, 191
tenders, 200
Tennessee Tombigbee Project, 193
transit time, 207
trunk lines, 201
user charges, 192
Valdez, 193

Study Questions

1. The integrated ownership of pipelines was initially used by some oil companies to gain control of oil-producing area. What other reasons can be offered for integrated ownership? Are these reasons valid in today's business environment?

2. The pipeline industry has approximately 100 companies, as compared to the motor carrier industry with more than 50,000. How do you account for this difference, given the fact that they both carry approximately the same volume of intercity ton-miles?

3. The typical pipeline company has high fixed costs. What economic factors account for this situation? What special problems does this present?

4. Pipelines account for more than 20 percent of the intercity ton-miles but less than 5 percent of the revenue paid by shippers to transportation companies. What factors account for this contrast? Is this situation likely to change? Why or why not?

5. The economic and market position of the pipelines has been described as mature and stable with little likelihood of significant growth in the near future. Do you agree? Why or why not?

6. Water carriers played a dominant role in the transportation system of the United States in the 18th and 19th centuries. Why has their relative position declined during the 20th century?

7. What would be the impact of higher fuel charges on the water carrier industry? Provide a rationale for your position.

8. Technology often offers the potential of improving efficiency and effectiveness. How could improved technology help the water carrier industry to improve its competitive position?

9. "Pipeline companies face limited competition." Do you agree with this statement? Why or why not? What market competition do pipelines actually face?

10. Why are pipelines unknown to many individuals? Do you think the pipelines should advertise to change this?

Notes

1. *Transportation in America*, 19th ed., Washington, DC: Eno Foundation, 2002, pp. 7–12.
2. Ibid.
3. Ibid.
4. Ibid.
5. Ibid., pp. 22–23.
6. Ibid., pp. 9–12.
7. National Transportation Statistics, 2002 edition, Washington, DC: U.S. Department of Transportation, 2002, pp. 187–191.
8. Ibid.
9. Ibid.
10. Ibid., pp. 192–196.
11. Op.Cit., *Transportation in America*, pp. 14–15.
12. Ibid.
13. Op.Cit., *National Transportation Statistics*, pp. 193–95.

Suggested Readings

Anonymous, "Internet Freight Exchanges Court Ocean Carriers," *Logistics Management and Distribution Report*, Radnor: June 2000, Vol. 30 pp. 75–78.

I.N. Lagoudis, C.S. Lalwani, M.M. Naim, "A Generic Systems Model for Ocean Shipping Companies in the Bulk Sector," *Transportation Journal*, Lockhaven: Winter 2004 Vol. 43 pp. 55–76.

R.G. Emonson, "Beyond the Water's Edge," *Journal of Commerce*, New York: June 9, 2003 p. 1.

Anonymous, "Breathing New Life into older Hulls," *Marine Log*, New York: June 2004, pp. 59–60.

R.J. Black, L.L. Freeman, J.A. Calderone, "Pioneering Deepwater Gulf Pipeline System," *Oil and Gas Journal*: Tulsa, May 12, 2003, Vol. 101, Issue 19, pp. 58–59.

M. Mikulis, "Project Intelligence for Gas Pipelines and Large Capital Projects," *Oil and Gas Journal*: Dallas, Vol. 231, Issue 4, pp. 34–40.

Mike Coppoch, "Oil From the Land of the Midnight Sun," *American History*, Dallas, Vol. 39, Issue 4, pp. 40–42.

D. Thomlinson, O. O'Sullivan, J. Adams, "Building a Bridge to the Gas Future," *Pipeline and Gas Journal*, Dallas: July 2004, pp. 30–32.

N.J. Watson, "Controversial Pipeline Takes a Step Forward," *Petroleum Economist*: London, December 2003, p. 1.

S.W. Crispin, "Pipe of Prosperity," *Far Eastern Economic Review*: Hong Kong, Feb. 2004 Vol. 167, pp. 12–16.

Case 6-1

Great Lakes Bulk Carriers

During the summer of 2004 Meghan Rondner, president and chief operating officer of Great Lakes Bulk Carriers (GLBC), and Gracie Klauser, vice president of marketing, visited with the port directors of every major port on the Great Lakes. Their objective was to seek additional business for GLBC's bulk cargo transportation division with a sub-objective of examining potential demand for a container ship operation on the Great Lakes.

GLBC was founded in 1940 by Meghan's grandfather with one ship hauling coal and iron ore from the mines along the Great Lanes to the steel mills in Cleveland and surrounding areas of Youngstown and Pittsburgh. Today the company has a fleet of seven bulk ore vessels that haul primarily iron ore from Duluth to Cleveland and Toledo as well as grain from the upper Great Lakes area to Chicago and Buffalo. The demand for the movement of both commodities has decreased during the past five years; iron ore movements decreased because of increased foreign competition for steel and railroads increased their share of the grain movement.

Gracie had suggested to Meghan that there is a void of container ship service on the Great Lakes and this might be a golden marketing opportunity for GLBC. Container traffic between the United States and the EU moves via railroad to the port of Montreal where it is trans-loaded to an ocean-going container ship. Substantial NAFTA container traffic (USA-Canada) moves via either railroad or truck to major cities adjacent to the Great Lakes. Lastly, the area surrounding the Great Lakes is a major manufacturing region with huge volumes of traffic moving among the major port cities.

Meghan and Gracie discussed the type of vessel that would be needed to move containers and concluded a current GLBC could not be retrofitted for container operations. Furthermore, the new ship would have a maximum carrying capacity of 1,000 containers because of the size limitations imposed by the locks on the Saint Lawrence Seaway. The typical ocean-going container ship has a minimum carrying capacity of 2,500 containers.

The proposed operation would consist of weekly sailing schedules beginning in Duluth and stopping at Chicago, Detroit, Toledo, Cleveland, Buffalo and Montreal. Containers would be picked up and delivered at each port along the route. The transit time from Duluth to Montreal is estimated to be 7 days, which compares to 4 days by rail and 2 days by truck. For intermediate origin-destinations, such as Chicago to Cleveland, the transit time is estimated to be 3 days and compares very favorably with railroad service, while the truck transit time is 1 day. The rate for the container service is estimated to be 30 percent of the current truck rate and 65 percent of the current rail rate.

The meetings with the port directors confirmed the volume of grain and iron ore being handled by Great Lakes carriers was on the decline and the predictions for the next 5 to 10 years was for the decline to continue. The lack of container ship service on the Great Lakes was also confirmed and the port directors, in general, were quite excited about the possibility of GLBC initiating such service.

As the 2004 Great Lakes shipping season came to a close, Meghan and Gracie began the planning and analysis of container ship business with a goal of having a decision made by the start of the next shipping season.

Case Questions

1. What marketing data would you want to have available to make the decision?
2. What cost data would you need to make a rational decision?
3. What are some of the logistics supply chain issues that GLBC should consider?
4. Based on what you know what recommendation would you make to the GLBC Board of Directors regarding a container ship operation?

Case 6-2

CBN Pipeline Company

At the weekly brown-bag brainstorming sessions, Robert Norwalk, president of CBN Pipeline Company (CBNPC), suggested CBNPC build a new pipeline from Elizabeth, New Jersey, to Chicago to move refined petroleum product, gasoline and diesel fuel. Following some discussion, he asked the strategic planning department to consider the idea before the next brown-bag session.

Ed Brown, vice president for Strategic Planning, thought Robert had gone off the deep end with this scheme. How could CBNPC obtain land to build the pipeline, let alone obtain the necessary capital to finance the project? Then, there is the question of the existing refineries located in Ohio, Indiana, and Illinois. Ed knew refined petroleum products were being transported from the Gulf of Mexico refineries via barge and pipeline to the Chicago market areas.

Ed turned over the project to John Coines, chief strategy analysts, to develop some preliminary thoughts as to the viability of building a new New Jersey-Illinois pipeline. In a span of 6 days John found the following strategic issues for the project:

- At least three mid-west refineries were being planned for closure within the next 10 years because of environmental and cost considerations.
- A number of major refineries were considering the building of new refineries offshore, closer to the sources of foreign oil. Both cost and environmental considerations favored this consideration.
- The New Jersey-Illinois corridor is one of the highest developed land regions in the United States with the highest land values.
- The demand for refined petroleum products is expected to increase by 5 percent each year through 2015.
- The project will require approximately 10 years to complete, including the time to obtain land via the eminent domain process.
- The capital requirements for the project are estimated at $600 billion.
- The expected average annual rate of return on investment is 10 percent given the expected construction and land acquisition cost, rate per barrel and demand over the next 20 years.

Case Questions

1. Do you feel the project has any merit for further investigation? Why?
2. What additional information is needed beyond that provided by John Coines to make a better decision?
3. Discuss the political assessment of building a pipeline that traverses five states.

Chapter 7

Intermodal and Special Carriers

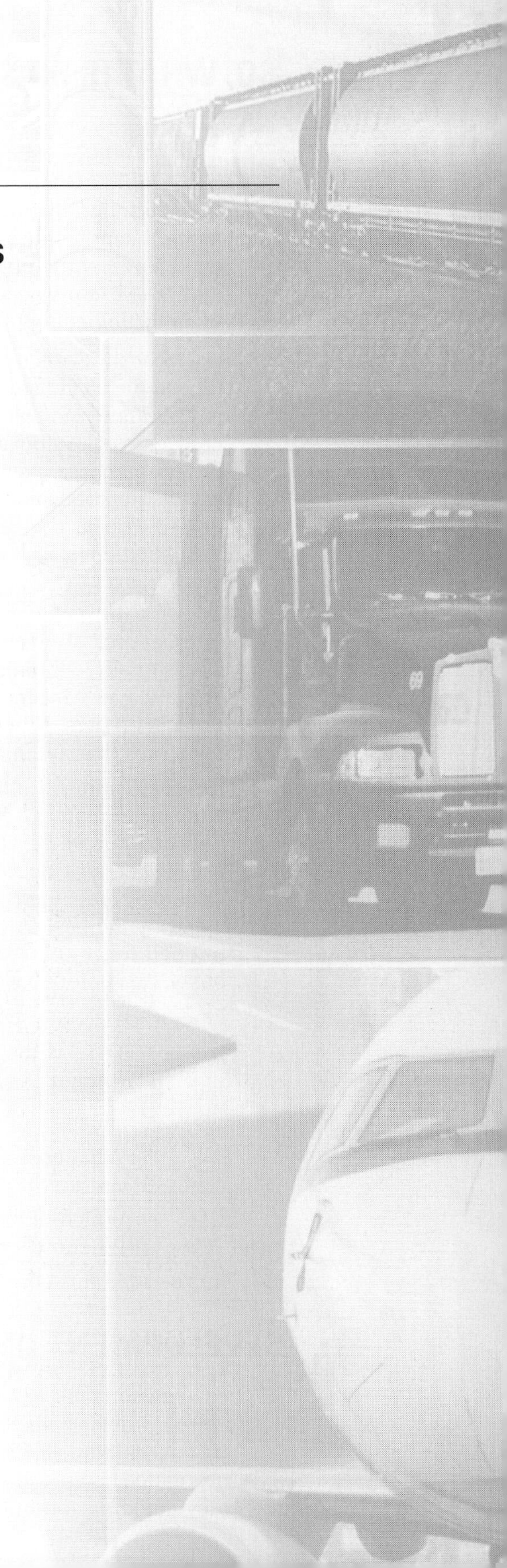

SO, WHAT IS SO SPECIAL ABOUT A SPECIAL CARRIER?

The newly appointed supply chain manager of OverStock, USA, Lauren Rondow, just returned from the Council of Supply Chain Management Professionals (CSCMP) annual meeting where she attended a number of transportation management sessions and picked up ideas about transportation cost containment techniques involving the use of special carriers. Lauren has extensive experience with procurement, inventory management, warehouse management, and SCM software, but her exposure to transportation is limited to the loading/unloading processes at the receiving and distribution warehouses.

OverStock, USA is a retailer of overstocked, out-of-season, overproduction, and distressed merchandise. OverStock has 65 retail outlets throughout the United States and is well known for offering very favorable prices for high-quality products. The company employs 50 buyers located throughout the United States, Europe, and Asia. The buyers purchase overstock, overproduction, and distressed merchandise from retailers, distributors, and manufacturers. The purchased merchandise is shipped to one of three distribution warehouses in the United States (Elizabeth, NJ; Atlanta; and Tacoma, WA) and then shipped to the individual stores from the distribution centers (DCs).

The typical transportation process involves receiving inbound products at the DCs by truck in truckload or containerload quantities. Ocean conference carriers move international shipments in containers to U.S. ports and then to the DCs by truck. Occasionally, inbound shipments of small, high-value items, such as jewelry, will arrive via air carriers. Outbound shipments from the DCs to the retail outlets move via LTL carriers. When an item is in high demand, express carriers are used to supply stores that are in a stockout situation.

After attending a number of the CSCMP transportation sessions, Lauren was amazed to learn of the many special carriers that were available to reduce cost and/or improve service over that provided by a basic modal carrier (truck, rail, ocean, and air). Some of these special carriers could be classified as air carriers or trucking companies; however, they provided some value-added services not provided by the basic modal carrier. These value-added services benefited the shipper through freight cost savings or service improvements that lowered the shipper's or buyer's inventory cost.

Lauren's basic questions regarding special carriers are as follows:

- What is the basic mode utilized by the special carrier?
- What are the benefits of using special carriers?
- What are the disadvantages of using special carriers?
- What are the cost and service characteristics of the different special carriers?
- Which of the special carriers offers potential benefit for OverStock? Where would each be used in the supply chain? Why?

As you read this chapter, try to answer these questions.

DEVELOPMENT OF SPECIAL CARRIERS

Historically, transportation service was purchased directly from basic modal providers such as railroads, motor carriers, or airlines. Shippers dealt directly with the carrier and, to the extent possible under the old regulatory scheme, negotiated rates and service requirements. After World War I the railroads found they could not profitably handle less-than-carload (LCL) traffic. Freight forwarders (nonrailroad firms) were developed to assist LCL shippers by collecting several small shipments, loading them together into boxcars, and sending them to the destination city, where the process was reversed. Shipper cooperatives began in the 1930s to provide this railroad consolidation service to their members on a not-for-profit basis. When intermodal rail-truck (piggyback) service started growing during the 1950s, railroads were concerned that shippers would shift freight from boxcars to trailers. They created a number of rules designed to prevent this from happening, and, in so doing, they created yet another agency: the consolidator or intermodal marketing company. The consolidator collected shipper freight, loaded it into motor carrier trailers, and transported the trailers to the railroad terminal; the railroads moved the trailers on flatcars to the destination city, where the process was reversed. Today, consolidators are wholesalers of intermodal rail service and the major intermodal customers of the railroads. In the trucking industry, firms known as freight brokers were developed to serve as intermediaries between truckers and farmers. These brokers would bring together farmers with commodities to be hauled to market and truckers who had empty trucks going toward the market. Brokers also were involved in household goods movement by truck.

With the removal of economic regulation starting in 1980, these various agencies grew and prospered. With the easing of entry for brokers, the number of these firms grew to more than 6,000 by the mid-1980s. Freight forwarders also benefited from the ease in regulation, and the growth was equally explosive.

During this period, a new entity came on the scene, that being third-party providers. These firms were either linked to motor carriers or were started specially to manage the transportation sector of a shipper's business. These firms have since expanded into supplying related services such as warehousing, inventory control, and other value-added services.

INTERMODAL TRANSPORTATION

Intermodal transportation involves the use of two or more modes of transportation in moving a shipment from origin to destination, primarily through the use of the "container." The development of the container allowed the growth of intermodealism to be possible. In the mid-1950s Malcolm McLean, a successful truck line owner, developed the concept of using a trailer to move freight by both highway and water. McLean's operation grew into sea–land services, one of the largest water carriers. Although this was a logical outgrowth of the use of the highway trailers for railroad piggyback service, the development of a standard container that could be interchanged among all modes made modern intermodalism possible. Standarization of dimensions, hold-down devices, and related items allowed the service providers to design ships, railcars, and highway chassis, knowing the container or "box" would fit.

The intermodal service combines the advantages (and disadvantages) of each mode used. For example, air–truck intermodal transportation combines the advantages of the motor carrier's accessibility and lower cost with the speed of the air carrier. At the same time, the combined service includes the air carrier's high cost and the motor carrier's slow speed. Air–truck intermodal rates are lower than all-air rates but higher than all-truck rates, and the transit times are shorter than by all-truck but longer than by all-air.

The **growth** of intermodal transportation has been aided by the deregulation of U.S. transportation, growth in global business, and changes in the business environment. The economic deregulation of rail piggyback transportation and air cargo reduced the regulatory barriers to modes working together to provide through service. Substantial growth in global business, particularly in the off-shore sourcing of goods in the Pacific Rim countries by the United States, led to the increased use of water–rail–truck intermodal service. Lastly, the economic reality of higher operating costs and driver shortages caused numerous motor carriers to divert long-haul traffic from all-truck to piggyback in order to save costs and remain competitive.

Overstock currently uses intermodal for inbound international shipments (ocean and truck) and for small, high-value shipments (air and truck).

The motor carrier industry experienced a severe driver shortage, starting in 1986 with the commencement of stringent licensing of truck drivers. This, combined with the promise of lower costs, induced the motor carriers to make greater efforts to utilize piggyback. Recent teamster union agreements also permitted the diversion of up to 28 percent of line-haul LTL movement to intermodal, which made this sector one of the railroad industry's largest customers.

A mode common to most forms of intermodal transportation is the motor carrier. The motor carrier's high degree of **accessibility** enables it to serve points that other modes are physically incapable of serving. Trucks can go to the shipper's door, pick up the freight, deliver it to the airport, and at the destination airport deliver the freight from the airport to the consignee. The air carrier is incapable of providing service to points beyond the airport. Similar conditions exist for rail, water, and pipeline transportation.

Piggyback

Piggyback transportation includes the movement of motor-carrier trailers on flatcars **(TOFC)** plus containers in flatcars **(COFC).** In 2001 railroads moved approximately 10.2 million containers and trailers, a 1.0-percent reduction from the volume in 2000. This high volume is due in part to economic deregulation of piggyback and technological advancements such as the double-stack train. With a double-stack train, two containers are loaded onto one flatcar, increasing the operating efficiency of the railroad and lowering the cost per container, thereby making possible a lower rate per container (See Figure 7.1).

FIGURE 7.1 Examples of a Piggyback and Double-Stack Train Car

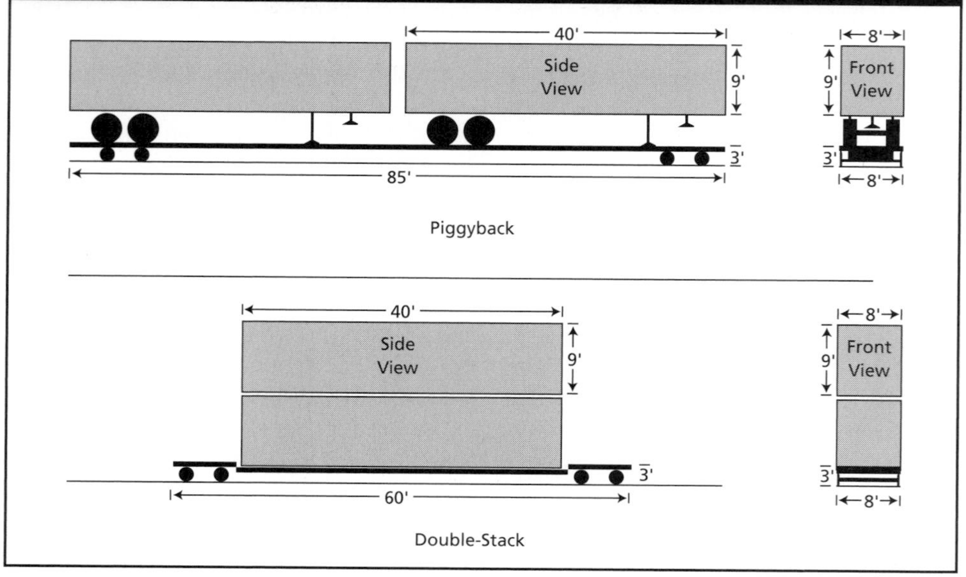

Piggyback also permitted the railroads to follow their industrial customers to the suburbs. As manufacturers moved from the cities to build new and more efficient plants, many of these new sites did not have railcarload access. Without the ability to provide intermodal, the railroads would have lost this business to truck. Their success is illustrated by the fact that 8.7 million trailers and containers were transported during 1997.

In principal rail corridors such as Los Angeles or Chicago, transit time is motor carrier-competitive as well as cost-effective. In recent years, the rail industry has concentrated on major point pair lanes, focusing resources on providing truck-competitive offerings. Many small, older ramps were closed, with service either being withdrawn or truck-substituted service being provided. By doing this, the railroad industry has acknowledged that motor carriers are their primary competitors. Recent railroad mergers have created new options for intermodal service. The acquisition of Conrail by CSX and Norfolk Southern created several new corridors for intermodal. The longer hauls within the merged railroads mean fewer interchanges. This has speeded intermodal service while reducing the number of times the trailer must be handled between origin and destination.

A new innovation is the RoadRailer®, which provides a railroad with the ability to haul trailers on special wheel sets and avoid the use of flatcars. RoadRailers® do not require special mechanical equipment for loading or unloading because the train can be made up on a paved area with a spur track. The cost structure of RoadRailer® operation is such that railroads are now competitive within a 500- to 800-mile range. Historically, intermodal shipments had to travel more than 1,000 miles before the railroad could compete effectively. RoadRailers® are available in 48- and 53-foot lengths, and refrigeration units have been introduced. Amtrak added RoadRailer® to their fleet, allowing them to compete for truckload shipments and to transport mail as the postal sorting facilities, similar to their industrial counterparts, have also moved to the suburbs. (Amtrak no longer offers RoadRailer® service.) One disadvantage is that the higher empty weight of the RoadRailer® reduces the shipment weight that can be legally hauled on the highway.

Increased use is being made of piggyback (COFC) for the domestic portion of product movements between the United States and foreign countries. In such moves, the container is commonly used because of its easy transferability from one mode to another and minimal additions to handling costs and total transit times. For example, Japanese automobile plants located in the United States are supplied with some parts produced in Japan. These parts are loaded into containers at the Japan supply sources, moved by ship to the West Coast (Long Beach or Seattle) and hauled into the Midwest plant locations via double-stack railroad service. If the rail terminus is not within the plant, a motor carrier is used to deliver the containers from the rail siding. The items in the container are handled only two times: once at loading in Japan and once at unloading in the Midwest.

Piggyback is a potential intermodal service for OverStock's container loads. A lower freight cost is possible with piggyback vs. truck from the ports to the DCs, but transit times may increase.

Under the old regulations of the Interstate Commerce Commission, a number of "plans" prescribed the type of intermodal service that could be offered. For example, Plan I, for trucking companies, required that the trucker supply the trailer. Under Plan II, the railroad supplied the trailer, flatcar, and all related services. Each plan was detailed, and this limited customer choice.

With the end of most economic regulation in 1996, these plans were scrapped and the free market took over. Service providers, whether they are motor carriers, intermodal service companies, or railroads, can offer any type of service combination that the customer desires. Current offerings range from intermodal service offered through motor carriers to transporting shipper-owned trailers with the customer providing the highway portion of the service.

Containerization

As noted above, the container, which is nothing more than a big box into which the freight is loaded, improves the efficiency of interchange among modes. The container also reduces the potential for damage and theft because the actual freight is not rehandled after it is loaded at the shipper's facility. Cargo interchange efficiency increases with the container, and both overall transit time and the transit time consistency of containerized intermodal shipments improve.

The motor carrier trailer is essentially a container on wheels. The trailer comes in various sizes, ranging in length from 28 to 53 feet. The railroad flatcar is capable of handling various sizes of trailers, but longer trailers preclude loading two trailers on one flatcar, thereby increasing the cost per freight unit hauled. The trailer is loaded onto the flatcar by a variety of methods including driving, hoisting with a crane, or lifting by means of a forklift-type device.

The use of trailers as containers for movement by ship presents technical problems. Therefore, the containers used for water transportation are boxes without wheels or a chassis. The water container comes in two standard lengths: 20 feet (TEU or 20 feet equivalent unit) or 40 feet (FEU or 40 feet equivalent unit). Container rates are quoted by water carriers on a TEU or FEU basis.

In an effort to address the varying sizes of containers, both marine and highway, the railroads developed a method whereby containers can be "double stacked" on specially designed railcars (see Figure 7.1). These cars can accommodate a wide variety of sizes, and by placing the smaller containers in the "well" of the cars, larger containers can be stacked on top. This has also increased the efficiency of the railroads. Under the old method of placing two trailers on a flatcar, as many as three or four containers can be shipped on a double-stack car. The elimination of chassis from the rail portion of the move has also reduced the gross weight, allowing more units to hauled by the same number of engines.

Containers are unloaded from the ship by crane and are transferred to either railroad or motor carriers. As noted above, containers can be placed two high on double-stack cars or one high on regular flatcars. For movement by motor carriers, the containers are either placed on a flatbed trailer or on a chassis (frame with wheels). The transfer of the container from water to either railroad or truck takes less than 1 day and usually is accomplished in a matter of hours.

The most recent trend in rail–ocean transfer has been to load or unload the containers from the railcars directly at shipside. The "on-dock" transfer saves both time and money by eliminating the drayage between the pier and the rail yard.

The container used in intermodal air shipments is not the standard rectangular, 40-foot-long shape. Rather, the air container is smaller (usually under 20 feet), narrower than the standard 8-foot ocean container, and typically rounded at the top to fit the contours of the aircraft. Many air carriers utilize hydraulic handling equipment to quickly and easily move the container into and out of the aircraft.

THIRD-PARTY TRANSPORTATION

In 2001 the use of outside firms to provide logistics support amounted to about $60 billion. This third-party activity grew out of many companies' desire to concentrate their resources on what they do and leave other, nonincome-producing tasks to these specialists. The trend toward focusing on "core competencies" has also benefited from management's desire to streamline operations and move such nonproductive facilities as warehouses off the firm's balance sheet by transferring that activity to a third party. Many of these third-party firms enjoy economies of scale that allow them to provide a manufacturer with logistics services at lower costs than the firms, could do themselves.

Table 7.1 shows the different **types** of third-party transportation providers in operation today. These include either management of information-based providers or asset- and operation-based providers. The management-based firms tend to be either shipper or consultant spin offs, whereas the asset-based firms are outgrowths of either carriers or leasing firms. Each has its own unique benefits and must be considered in light of the tasks to be performed for the customer. The information-based third-party providers generally, but not exclusively, provide transportation management, freight bill payment, auditing, reporting, and consulting services.

The asset-based companies provide many of these services plus basic transportation. Table 7.2 contains examples of third-party provider services.

In all of these third-party arrangements, information **links** exist between the shipper and/or receiver, and the third-party "carrier" is part of an integral link. Many of them have over-the-road trucking equipment with computer-transponder links to satellites that can give the exact location of the truck at all times and information regarding specific package pickups and deliveries to company headquarters at the exact moment the transfers are taking place.

The people typically initiating these new forms of **services** have been innovative and entrepreneurial transportation experts who see valuable opportunities in the efficient linking of shippers and receivers. The benefits to shippers and receivers are more efficient processes, lower labor rates, and/or improved services.

OverStock may want to explore using a third party to manage outbound shipments from the DCs to the stores to achieve lower freight costs through consolidation. Also, the third party could break down container loads at the port and ship items directly to the stores.

Another recent development has been for third-party firms to place their own personnel at the manufacturer's plant or the consignee's warehouse to handle the details of outsourced services. This frees the client's staff to devote their attention to those areas that are beyond the day-to-day details.

Table 7.1 Types of Third-Party Transportation Providers

Type/Example Company	Website
Asset Based	
CRST Logistics, Inc.	http://www.crstlogistics.com
DHL Worldwide Express	http://www.dhl.com
England Logistics, Inc.	http://www.englandlogistics.com
FedEx Supply Chain Services	http://www.fedex.com
Schneider Dedicated Operations	http://www.schneider.com
Non-Asset Based	
Cass Information Systems	http://www.cassinfo.com
Caterpillar Logistics Services, Inc.	http://www.catlogistics.com
C.H. Robinson	http://www.chrobinson.com
Hub Group, Inc.	http://www.hubgroup.com
Pittsburgh Logistics Systems, Inc.	http://www.pghlogistics.com

Table 7.2 Examples of Third-Party Provider Services
Consulting
Freight Bill Auditing
Freight Bill Payment
Freight Brokering
Inventory Management
JIT
Kitting
Order Fulfillment
Transportation Management
Transportation Network Optimization
Warehouse Management Systems

The following are examples of outsourcing services:

- Menlo Worldwide Logistics is managing the actual assembly of build-to-order golf clubs at the Nike Golf facility in Tigard, Oregon, as well as providing distribution services such as component inventory management and finished goods exportation for clubs.
- Wheeling-Pittsburgh Steel outsourced its traffic function to Pittsburgh Logistics, who is responsible for contracting and scheduling carriers and tracking delivery for Wheeling-Pittsburgh Steel's customer deliveries.
- England Logistics offers a state-of-the-art pallet tracking system that tracks, records, and reports the pallet activity for each England Logistics' customer and each of its customer locations.
- Emery Forwarding is providing seamless, door-to-door global transportation management services to Cabela, an outfitter of fishing, hunting, and outdoor gear, for its worldwide air shipments.

In each of the above examples, the third party is providing more than basic transportation services. One key service provided is information technology that enables the shipper to exercise greater control over shipments throughout the supply, whether it is tracking on-time deliveries or pallets in a pallet exchange program. In the Menlo example, the third-party provider is going beyond traditional transportation and logistics services and is managing the assembly function for the shipper. The possibilities for third-party services are numerous and are constantly expanding to meet the needs of shippers.

STOP OFF

CP Expands Expressway Service

When Canadian Pacific launched its Expressway trailer on flat car service in 1996, some industry observers were puzzled. Hadn't CP been the chief proponent of domestic containers as trailer replacements as early as 1979?

CP was actually seizing an opportunity. Expressway came out of the realization there were three million non-reinforced trucker- and shipper-owned trailers on North American highways. They couldn't be toplifted conventionally and their owners weren't going to replace them with containers. In short, adapt or reject a huge market opportunity.

Beginning with Iron Highway equipment leased from CSX Intermodal, Expressway was inaugurated on the 332-mile Toronto-Montreal corridor.

This is where CP intermodal service began on Dec. 1, 1952, with overnight piggyback trains. Rail peaked with 48% of this market, but nose-dived as government poured billions into highways. CP eventually pulled out altogether. Too short a haul and too much price competition, was the conventional view.

"We've changed that view," says Expressway Vice President Paul Gilmore. "The key is not just equipment and fast terminal turnaround, but the approach to the market. Formerly, we were competing head-to-head with motor carriers in traditional intermodal. We partner with the motor carriers on Expressway."

The service has grown to two trains in each direction, six days per week, with up to 90 platforms, linking Montreal, Toronto, and Detroit. The test equipment, which split into two segments for loading, has been replaced by 310 CP-designed five-platform sets that separate into multiple cuts for faster circus loading with portable ramps and shunt tractors. Loading time is less than one hour for a typical consist. The fleet now includes 240 new-builds from National Steel Car and 70 former piggyback flats, redesigned with premium trucks and slackless drawbars by CP General Manager-Mechanical Support Dave Meyler.

Five terminals-prominently advertised on public roads as "Expressway On Ramps"-have replaced two temporary facilities shoehorned into existing yards. They serve Detroit, Windsor, Montreal, and Toronto (one each for the east and west sides of that city). Electronic check-in and Internet pre-booking have sliced trucker turnaround to 15 minutes. With this investment of more than $50 million, traffic has more than tripled, from 25,000 trailers in 2000 to 85,000 in 2002.

Gilmore emphasizes partnership as the reason for Expressway's success attracting three types of customers: "We have pure motor carriers, who use us to replace their highway haul. We have fleet owners, such as retailers Hudson's Bay Company and Frito-Lay, which now use their tractors and drivers for drayage only. And we have truckers who support the automotive industry's just-in-time parts needs. This takes advantage of our fast transit times and provides balanced loads in both directions between parts and assembly plants on both sides of the border."

CP doesn't market directly to DaimlerChrysler, GM, and Ford, but points out that Expressway's reliability and rates should be of interest to their motor carriers. When the car companies solicit trucking bids, they now request them with and without Expressway. Part of this success is a border issue. No Expressway train has ever been significantly delayed for customs inspection. In the wake of 9/11, an emergency Expressway train shuttled trailers between the two cities to bypass the clogged highway crossings, preventing production line shutdowns.

Says Gilmore, "This product needs a heavy truck lane to succeed, and when you look around North America, there aren't many with as heavy a concentration as Montreal-Chicago-Minneapolis. Customers are calling for more frequencies, especially between Toronto and Montreal, but this corridor is pushing its capacity limit now." CP has proposed a $2 billion public/private partnership with the Canadian and Ontario governments to double-track the entire Montreal-Detroit corridor and replace CP's former New York Central Detroit River Tunnel. Expressway features prominently.

"We're succeeding in a market that was conceded to trucks years ago," says Gilmore. "We're answering the problems motor carriers are having with driver shortages, fuel prices, and equipment costs."

Source: "CP Expands Expressway Service," *Railway Age*; Bristol; Jan 2003, 20. Reprinted with permission of *Copyright Simmons-Boardman Publishing Corporation Jan 2003.*

SPECIAL CARRIER FORMS

Several special types of carrier services represent a significant segment of the transportation services purchased by shippers. These forms of transportation often use the long-haul services of the five basic transportation modes.

Surface Forwarders

Surface freight forwarders hold a unique place among carriers. A forwarder is both a carrier and shipper in as much as they are recognized as a "carrier" by their customer, while being treated as a "shipper" by the company who actually provides the transportation service. Once regulated as another form of common carriage, forwarders are now exempt from economic oversight. Forwarders must still register with the Department of Transportation and maintain cargo insurance in the amount prescribed.

A forwarder's role is still defined under current regulations as found at 49 United States Code, Section 13102, Part 8. A forwarder is a "person" holding oneself out to the general public (other than as a pipeline, rail, motor, or water carrier) to provide transportation or property for compensation in the ordinary course of its business. The definition goes on to state that the forwarder (a) assembles and consolidates shipments and performs break-bulk and distribution operations for shipments; (b) assumes responsibility for the transportation from the place of receipt to the place of destination; and (c) uses the services of another mode, such as a motor or rail carrier. Air freight forwarders are specifically exempted from this definition.

OPERATIONS

Historically, forwarders consolidated small shipments into truckloads or carloads. (See Figure 7.2) In most cases, the forwarder provided local pickup and delivery but used boxcars to provide line-haul service. Since the 1960s, motor carriers, and to some extent intermodal, have become the primary means of transport used by the forwarder.

The forwarding industry nearly had died out by the mid-1980s because of severe competition from LTL motor carriers. The LTL carriers were able to provide better service and, in many cases, lower prices, including generous discounts from their base rates. Passage of the Freight Forwarder Act of 1986 removed nearly all regulatory oversight from this industry. The industry rebounded quickly and has become a significant factor as a transportation service provider. It is estimated that several thousand surface freight forwarding companies are in business today.

With the elimination of economic regulation, forwarders have evolved into a role similar to truckers. They have moved away from the traditional LTL market and have concentrated on volume shipments. Some forwarders still provide the classic consolidation or small shipment service, but most have expanded into the intermodal and truckload areas.

A forwarder must "issue" a bill of lading to the shipper, the same as a railroad or motor carrier. In so doing, the forwarder accepts responsibility for the shipment. Because of this, a forwarder must maintain cargo insurance and accept liability for loss and/or damage to a shipment that it accepts. A copy of the insurance policy must be filed with the Surface Transportation Board for the protection of the forwarder's customers.

A surface freight forwarder may help OverStock lower freight cost by consolidating outbound loads from the DCs to stores. The freight forwarder also provides cargo damage risk protection because it is liable for damage.

As with other carriers, for the most part, forwarders are no longer required to file their prices with the federal government. The exception relates to those forwarders

FIGURE 7.2 Surface Forwarder Operation

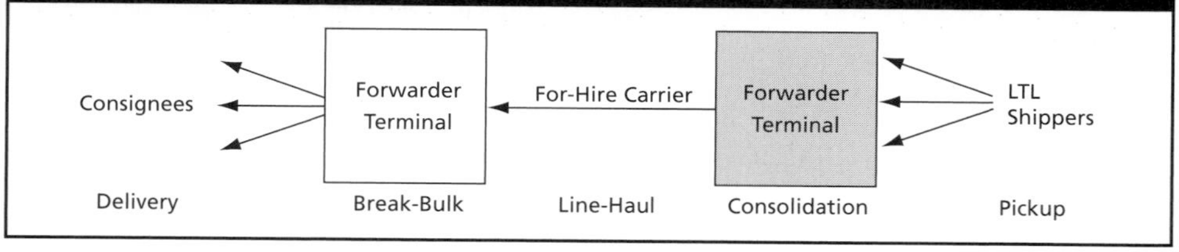

who handle household goods. This allows forwarders the freedom to negotiate prices on a shipment-by-shipment basis with their customers, giving them the same flexibility as motor or oil carriers. Because they are required to "issue" bills of lading, they are subject to the same terms and conditions as other carriers.

Air Freight Forwarders

Air freight forwarders act in much the same way as surface forwarders by consolidating small shipments for long-haul and eventual distribution. They primarily use the services of major passenger and freight airlines for long-haul service. The air freight forwarder serves the shipping public with similar pickup service, a single bill of lading and freight bill, one-firm tracing, and delivery service, as does the surface forwarder. The air freight forwarder, though, is generally used by shippers of goods having high-product-dollar value or time-sensitivity value, or both.

CHARACTERISTICS

Use of air freight **forwarders** has grown over the past two decades. As the air industry grew, so did acceptance of this generally high-cost form of transportation for emergency and high-time-value moves. A reason also often stated for air forwarder growth has been that these firms have concentrated upon offering door-to-door service from shipper to consignee. This service relieves a significant traffic arrangement burden from shippers and consignees. It also fills a void because airlines tend to emphasize terminal-to-terminal services and have been involved only to a limited degree in surface pickup and delivery services.

Many air freight forwarders have expanded into aircraft operations as the airline industry consolidated because of mergers and bankruptcies. Emery and Airborne are examples of two such firms that started as pure forwarders but now operate a large fleet of aircraft. This trend was accelerated by increased passenger loads brought about by deregulation of air fares. As the passenger aircraft became more crowded, there was little room for freight after the baggage and mail was loaded. Changes in passenger schedules eliminated many flights that forwarders relied on for overnight service. This, along with basic changes in air service patterns as the airlines moved toward hub-and-spoke operations, forced many forwarders to acquire their own freight airplanes.

SERVICE BENEFITS

The air freight forwarder industry presents some major transportation service benefits to the shipping community. For one, speed of service is vital for many movements such as spare parts, emergency replenishment goods, medical components, and business documents. Further, this industry represents a single-carrier, full door-to-door service. Its main disadvantage lies in its high rates, but these are usually considered by shippers in light of the service benefit received relative to the product's value and time sensitivity. New "deferred" rate plans provide for second- or third-day shipment at significant savings. In some areas, these new plans are truck competitive.

The air freight forwarder may offer OverStock an opportunity to lower freight cost on the small, high-value shipments via air carriers.

AIR FORWARDER FUTURE

The future of air freight forwarding is mixed. On the positive side, the pickup and delivery movements of air freight are unrestricted. Air freight movements became unregulated in 1977, and the pickup and delivery portions of the moves were unregulated in 1980. Thus, new origin and destination points far from terminal cities presented expanded opportunities for these firms. However, deregulation of air freight has brought about price and service competition and innovation. Mergers and acquisitions have strengthened the industry so that most firms are well positioned for the new century.

In the international arena, air freight forwarders provide the shipping public with transportation movement and the handling and processing of many international documents. Thus, in this sector, the air forwarders provide a value-added service in addition to simple movement.

Freight Brokers

Brokers function as "middlemen" between the shipper and the carrier much the same as a real estate broker does in the sale of property. The definition of a broker is still found in the United States Code under Title 49, section 13102, subpart (2). This regulation defines as broker as a "person" other than a motor carrier, an agent, or an employee that, as a principal or agent, sells, offers for sale, negotiates for, or holds itself out by solicitation, advertisement, or otherwise as selling, providing, or arranging for transportation by motor carrier for compensation.

Most truckload motor carriers cannot afford to maintain a nationwide sales force, but their trucks operate throughout the United States. The broker normally represents the carrier and seeks freight on their behalf to avoid moving empty equipment. They may also represent the shipper and will provide trucks for loading. Brokers can provide intermodal services as well as other logistics offerings, such as warehousing and cross docking.

Historically, brokers were confined to the agricultural area, but after the partial repeal of economic regulation in 1980, combined with the elimination of the Interstate Commerce Act in 1996, the brokerage industry saw explosive growth. The restrictions to entry into the brokerage business were removed, with the only requirement being retained that the broker post a $10,000 surety bond. This bond is for the protection of the carrier because many brokers bill the shipper and pay the trucker. In the event the broker fails to do so, the bond would be available to make good on the lost revenue.

Brokers do not have to file any price schedules with the federal government. A broker does not issue a bill of lading and they are not required to maintain cargo liability insurance because they are not considered to be a carrier. These two factors are the primary difference between a broker and a freight forwarder. Many brokers provide cargo insurance at their expense for the protection of their customers to relieve the shipper of that concern.

Brokers and surface freight forwarders are represented by a trade association, Transportation Intermediaries Association (TIA), located in Alexandria, Virginia. TIA conducts educational programs and holds annual meetings, as well as represents these carriers before Congress and federal agencies.

ROLES

Brokers assume some of the functions of shippers and truckers. They also relieve shippers of a major traffic function burden. Client truckers use brokers to relieve them of a major fixed-cost burden and communicating expense. These are both traffic management and carrier sales and pricing roles.

Surveys indicate that individual brokers service anywhere from a few to several thousand shippers. Basic shipper services include the arrangement of service, the verification of the trucker's insurance and safety rating, verification of equipment condition, and the negotiation of a freight transportation price. Brokers also are involved in LTL and warehouse consolidation for shippers, as well as insurance acquisition for truckers.

Although brokers traditionally dealt with owner-operators, today they also deal with regular for-hire carriers, acting in a sales role for these firms. The broker typically charges the shipper for the freight movement, deducts a brokerage fee between 8 and 10 percent, and then remits the net amount to the trucker.

The value-added services offered by brokers may be useful for OverStock's outbound moves from DCs to stores. Of particular interest is the freight consolidation services that may offer freight cost reductions.

The future is quite bright for brokers, and one of the largest transportation firms, C.H. Robinson, does more than $3 billion in revenue, much of it from brokerage.

The computer and communications networks available today provide access to information about current and upcoming shipments and the availability of equipment. The broker industry will no doubt grow as it seeks ways to expand solicitation, movement availability, and third-party service opportunities.

Shippers' Associations

These transportation entities are **nonprofit** cooperative consolidators or distributors of shipments owned or shipped by member firms. Their prime purpose is to group together members' shipments for line-haul in much the same way as for-hire, for-profit freight forwarders. In the past, these organizations consolidated many local shippers' small shipments into line-haul piggyback shipments. In this role, they were a form of nonprofit surface freight forwarder.

SERVICES

Shippers' associations benefit members through better service and lower total transportation costs. These include broker-like services for line-haul truckload movements, piggyback consolidations services for smaller shipments, the arrangement of over-the-road truckload services, and tailored third-party services for special transportation needs. The breadth of services and buying power enables the shippers' association to provide traffic management services to small and medium shippers.

The **future** for shippers' associations is bright. In an unregulated environment with changing transportation supply and price settings, the shippers' association provides small- to medium-size shippers with a high level of expertise and buying power.

Intermodal Marketing Companies

Intermodal marketing companies (IMCs) are intermediaries between shippers and railroads and are also known as consolidators or agents. They are facilitators or arrangers of transportation only. They assume little or no legal liability; the legal shipping arrangement is between the shipper and long-haul carrier and not with the agent. Freight charge payment usually is made to the agent who, in turn, pays the long-haul carrier.

Piggyback shipments were exempted from regulation by the ICC in 1981. This expanded the market opportunities available to IMCs. The deregulation meant that specific service features and rates could be established through negotiation and contracting.

CHARACTERISTICS

IMCs maintain simple management structures. They are either locally or nationally based and rely upon personal solicitation and advertising. Examples of IMCs include Alliance Shippers, Hub Group, Inc., and C. H. Robinson Co.

The trend of this shipping sector is generally positive. IMCs play a cost-savings role for both the shipper and the railroad. Little specific industry-wide knowledge exists as to the number, size, and particular services they perform because they are not subject to regulation. Most IMCs have volume, wholesale contracts with the railroads. They can offer lower prices than most shippers could obtain on their own.

Rail equipment use is enhanced as trailers are matched and shipped by the IMC. Many IMCs actively assist in managing rail equipment for better turnaround. These agents solicit freight for the carriers, sparing the railroad this expense.

A disadvantage associated with IMCs is in the area of liability. The shipper usually pays the IMC, who, in turn, pays the rail carrier. Ultimate freight payment liability, however, still rests with the shipper. There is the possibility, and it has occurred occasionally, that the IMC will retain the freight charges and cease operations, leaving the shippers with, in effect, a second freight bill. Therefore, before hiring any IMC, the shipper should investigate the agent's reputation and stature.

Shippers often find that these firms can save transportation costs for them even after their fee is paid. This segment of the industry is represented by the Intermodal Association of North America (IANA), based in Greenbelt, Maryland. IANA, who has about 600 intermodal freight members including IMCs, railroads, motor carriers, port authorities, and ocean carriers.

The future is also relatively bright for IMCs, especially in light of the increased use of intermodal transportation by long-haul motor carriers and international container shippers. IMCs represent the pooled buying power of shippers. Opportunities exist for these firms to negotiate low rail contract rates and better service.

The IMC offers OverStock potential cost and service advantages on international shipments from the ports to the DCs.

Owner-Operators

The term *owner-operator* was traditionally applied to a person who owned or leased a truck, and often a trailer, and made his or her equipment and driving service available to for-hire carriers. Owner-operators were confined to serving regular for-hire carrier firms that needed the service on an overflow basis when carrier equipment and labor were not available. They also commonly worked for special-commodity carriers that did not have the equipment but booked freight and used owner-operators to carry it from origin to destination. The owner-operator rented his or her services and equipment to the carrier that possessed the operating rights to move the goods. Owner-operators are often paid a percentage of the amount received in exchange for the carrier's retention of the operating rights.

Owner-operators are playing a key role for some newly evolving for-hire carriers. Some new carriers do not have employee drivers or company-owned equipment. That is, long-haul movement as well as regular pickup and delivery operations are often performed under an arrangement between the carrier and the terminals and owner-operators. These relationships are often contractual, but they give the carrier flexibility in operations and reduced financial risk. Many of these carriers offer incentive plans and pay scales that allow them to be very competitive against the unionized, traditional for-hire carriers.

OverStock may consider using owner-operators on moves from the DCs to the stores. The owner-operator freight cost may be lower than that of the larger LTL carriers.

Express Services and Expedited Services

The growth in express and expedited services is related to today's business focus on supply chain speed, or cycle-time reduction. The higher value of today's products places greater emphasis on reducing inventory, which is achieved, in part, through lower transit times. In addition, manufacturers are utilizing new processes such as Lean Manufacturing and JIT that have as one of their goals the reduction of inventory. Lastly, the advent of e-business, with ordering just a click away, gives the buyer an expectation of faster shipment time. The combined impact of these changes is frequent, smaller shipments and the need for low transit times to reduce inventory levels.

Express and expedited carriers are typically motor and air carriers who specialize in the movement of small shipments, generally under 250 pounds. These carriers specialize in moving small packages with published transit times, Internet-based tracking and tracing capabilities, and, for some services, a delivery guarantee. Their transit times are usually lower than the basic shipment time provided by an LTL carrier or nonexpress air carrier. Thus, the express and expedited carrier target market is the shipper of high-value, low-weight, and time-sensitive products.

The most widely known express and expedited service carriers are FDX, Inc., UPS, Airborne Express, DHL, and BAX Global. These carriers can best be described as integrated express carriers because they utilize both ground and air transportation equipment. With an integrated carrier, a shipper has the choice of shipping by air or ground at varying prices and transit times. For example, a shipper of a 20-pound package from Atlanta to Dallas has the choice of air services ranging from same-day delivery to second-day delivery, plus a ground service with third-day delivery. The rate for same-day delivery is 12 times greater than that for third-day ground service.

Although these carriers were limited as to the size of the shipments they would handle, firms such as UPS and FDX, Inc. have moved aggressively into the LTL market. These firms are now competing directly against companies such as Roadway Express, Yellow Freight System, and ABF Freight System. Although they started as package carriers, most firms in this category offer a full range of services; the distinction between a package and express carrier and an LTL company is becoming much less clear. Many of the express companies have expanded into the international market as well.

Express firms operate with large networks of terminals, pickup and delivery vehicles, and line-haul service. UPS is most notable in this regard. It began as a retail store delivery system and has since grown to a worldwide firm with revenues of $31.2 billion in 2002. UPS has operations in over 200 countries and territories worldwide. UPS transports an average of 13.5 million packages per day.

FDX, Inc, a major competitor of UPS, earned revenues of about $20 billion in 2002 and averaged approximately 4.8 million shipments per day.

The United States Postal Service (USPS) provides package service and in 2001 handled 1.1 billion packages, generating revenues of $1.993 billion. Other package and express services include those provided by national and local bus companies such as Greyhound, air couriers such as AirNet Systems, Inc., and many local, regional, and national motor carriers.

As mentioned above, some express carriers offer time-definite service; that is, the delivery time is guaranteed. Shippers who require time-definite service typically opt for air service because of its speed, although motor carriers do offer time-definite transit times that are less than those offered by air carriers between locations with limited air carrier service. The cost of time-definite service is quite high when compared with normal delivery, as noted above with the same-day delivery being 12 times greater than the "normal" ground service of 3 days transit time.

To reduce the high cost associated with all-air, time-definite service, some shippers have contracted with motor and air carriers to provide time-definite service over two or more links to make up a total move. The shipper-developed time-definite services offer lower total costs but higher transit times than all-air transit. In some situations, such as in remote areas, the overall transit time with the blended truck and air service may be equal to or better than that of all-air service.

For OverStock, the express and expedited services are viable options for hot-selling items that are in a stockout situation at a retail site. Before using a time-definite service, OverStock must compare savings from reduced lost profit to the cost of the speedier service.

Drayage Carriers

A drayage carrier is a motor carrier that provides pickup and delivery service in the local metropolitan area, piggyback ramp area, and/or container area. The drayage firm will load product from a local warehouse and deliver it to the consignee in the metropolitan area. Likewise, the drayage firm will pick up freight from shippers and bring the shipments to a warehouse, carrier terminal, or container yard for consolidation and long-haul shipment preparation.

The drayage carrier plays an important role in intermodal container shipments. The drayage firm provides the truck to haul the container from the container or piggyback yard to the consignees location, and vice versa. Many of the drayage carriers that haul containers to and from ports and piggyback yards are independent owner-operators and are typically contracted by the railroad or ocean carrier to provide the service.

OverStock utilizes the services of drayage carriers for its international container shipments. The company might explore the possibility of contracting with a drayage carrier instead of having this service be included in a through-ocean rate.

HOUSEHOLD GOODS INDUSTRY

This industry sector consists of a group of motor carriers that are specifically organized to move the household goods of people and businesses. These firms, often called van lines, are geared to serve the market with specialized vehicles, local agencies with warehouses for storage, and pickup and delivery equipment, as well as central dispatching operations. In all areas, however, the overall corporate name, or franchise, will appear on vehicles, local agencies, and in national advertising.

The top 4 household goods carriers generated 2001 revenues of $1.68 billion. This compares with $7.17 billion of the top 4 truckload carriers for the same period.

The specific segments of this industry fall into four groups. The first is the **central franchise firms** whose corporate name and operating certificate are used by the agencies and over-the-road vehicles. The franchise firms also provide a central dispatch to coordinate the most efficient flow of vehicles possible between all points.

The second group is the **local agencies,** which consists of a terminal and storage warehouse. The terminal is the local contact point for customer contact and shipment initiation. It generally supplies the packing and the pickup vehicle loading labor, as well as delivery and unpacking manpower. In the event the household goods owners wish to move goods when vehicles are not available, or they wish to store goods temporarily, local agencies provide storage facilities.

The third segment of this industry is the **over-the-road vehicle** owned by the local agency. Many local agents own their own tractor and trailer and hire employees who will perform outbound and inbound moves dispatched by the central firm.

A fourth entity in this industry is the **owner-operator**, who displays the corporate identity on the vehicle and loads, hauls, and unloads shipments that are dispatched by the central franchise firm and are coordinated by local agents.

This four-party system is not apparent to individual shippers who typically think that they are dealing with one corporate entity that has direct supervisory control over drivers and vehicles as well as all agencies. Instead, the household goods industry is a loose alliance of entities that share a single franchised **identity** and a communication system.

Shipment Process

The household goods shipment process reveals the makeup of the functional relationships in this transport sector. Initially, the individual agent joins the franchise by paying an entry fee and adhering to certain centrally established standards. An individual owner-operator who generally performs long-haul services acquires a vehicle and moving firm identity in much the same way.

The actual shipment process is as follows. First, a home or apartment dweller contacts the local agent, who generally visits the pickup point, estimates the shipment weight, and evaluates the need for any special move tasks. The agent, in turn, estimates a total move cost for the shipper. The shipper–carrier relationship is initiated when the shipper signs an **"order for service"** document that is transmitted to the central firm dispatch office for over-the-road vehicle assignment and scheduling. Generally, if an individual shipment is 7,500 pounds or more, a new run will be created based on that shipment. Smaller shipments are tacked onto existing runs and the home owner is then informed of the estimated arrival date. If packing is to be part of the hired service, local agency personnel perform this task a few days prior to pickup.

The over-the-road vehicle then arrives, after the driver has determined the total vehicle weight prior to loading. The driver will inspect the possessions, label them, and log them onto an inventory tally sheet along with notations about the condition of each item. The goods are then loaded, and the shipper is given a receipt (bill of lading). The pickup goods are usually loaded into a vehicle with other shipments that are often dropped off to other homes along the route (and where others might be picked up) prior to the specific shipment delivery. The vehicle is then reweighed to determine the total shipment weight.

The actual **charges** are based on that weight, as well as special charges that might be added for such things as weekend work; movement of large, heavy, special, or fragile items; or the need to climb stairs or use an elevator. Agency packing, too, is included in these charges, all of which can boost the total shipment cost by 30 to 50 percent.

The shipment then moves to the delivery point. The driver can, and usually does, demand payment of freight charges in cash or by certified check unless certain credit arrangements are made in advance. Then the shipment is unloaded. The new local agency then unpacks the boxes, if packing and unpacking are part of the hired service. Any loss and damage claims are then filed through the new local agency.

Revenue distribution is usually made on the following basis: 10 percent to the corporate franchise, 50 percent to the vehicle owner (agency or owner-operator), 25 percent to the pickup agency, and 15 percent to the destination agency. Packing service charges are distributed in various ways between the two local agencies.

Problems

Many problems exist in this industry. First, people's possessions are being handled and moved—a major event for the shipper and family. Second, moving causes the shipper and his or her family a significant degree of stress, and problems in the actual move may aggravate the entire process. Third, the industry is made up of three or four separate parties (franchise, pickup, vehicle, and destination agencies). Fourth, unless the shipper is being transferred by the military or a major national firm, the individual has little influence over the movers. Traditionally, none of these agencies has had any direct control over the others. Further, long-distance communications are necessary between all of them.

Trends in this industry are mixed. The market basically consists of about 17 percent military moves; the remainder is divided equally between individual shipper moves and moves booked under supervision of employers. It is a very seasonal business. Typically 70 percent of all moves take place in the 5-month period between May to September (representing only 42 percent of the year). This peak situation creates a great demand during a short period, and manpower and equipment use is low for the remaining part of the year.

Some household goods moving firms have withdrawn completely from the field, while a few have discontinued shipping household goods in favor of moving fragile electronic items, such as computers and copying equipment. This traffic requires the special equipment and handling expertise of the moving firms, but it is less seasonal in nature. Other firms divested from the household goods operations altogether in the 1970s when the military and corporations began what appears to be a long-term trend toward reducing the number of employee transfers.

Summary

- The transportation user is not confined to firms and services of the basic modes. Carriers that appear as hybrids of these modes, as well as special forms within each, are also available forms of transportation service.
- Regulatory changes governing air, motor, rail, and household goods transportation aided the development of the special carriers.
- Intermodal transportation involves the joint efforts of two or more modes to complete the through movement. The most common forms of intermodal include piggyback (rail–truck), water–rail (container on flatcar), and truck–air. The container improves the freight interchange efficiency between the modes and enhances the value of intermodal service.
- Third-party transportation providers offer a total package of logistics services in which transportation is one component. Third-party transportation involves outsourcing transportation services ranging from simple freight bill payment to carrier selection and routing of shipments to storage, partial assembly of parts, and transportation.
- Today's transportation system is supported by a number of intermediaries who provide shipment consolidation, marketing, information, and premium services to both carriers and shippers. Forwarders, shippers' associations, brokers, intermodal marketing companies, owner-operators, and express and expedited companies are the primary providers of these intermediary services.

- The household goods moving industry consists of specialized motor carriers who move the household goods of people and businesses. The industry faces peak demand during the summer months and utilizes a system of local agents and owner-operators to provide service.

Key Terms

air forwarder trends, 218
central franchise firm, 224
charges, 225
COFC, 212
common identity, 225
drayage carrier, 224
expedited service, 223
express service, 223
future, 221
growth, 211
intermodal marketing companies, 221
key links, 215
local agency, 224
nonprofit forwarders, 221
ordering service, 225
over-the-road vehicle, 224
owner-operator, 225
package service, 223
revenue distribution, 225
services, 215
time-definite service, 223
TOFC, 212
truck accessibility, 212
two or more modes, 211
types, 215

Study Questions

1. Intermodal rail transportation in the form of TOFC and COFC has been growing since the 1980s. What factors have contributed to this growth?
2. Discuss the role the container has played in intermodal transportation.
3. Third-party transportation is a growing sector of the transportation industry. What are the advantages and disadvantages of using a third-party provider for transportation and other logistics services?
4. Describe the similarities and differences between a surface freight forwarder and an air freight forwarder. How do these special carriers differ from the freight broker?
5. Intermodal marketing companies and similar organizations control about 75 percent of all intermodal rail traffic. Explain why this is true and its implications for the railroad industry.
6. Discuss the role of shippers' associations in today's transportation market. What type of shipper benefits from using a shippers' associations? Why?
7. What is the value-added service provided by express and expedited carriers? What types of shipping situations justify use of these services? Why?
8. Why have there been problems with service reliability in the household goods industry?
9. Currently, there are federal economic regulations imposed on the household goods carriers but not on other sectors of the trucking industry. Why?
10. Define, compare, and contrast the following special carriers: owner-operator, drayage carriers, and consolidators.

Suggested Readings

Bardi, Edward J., and Michael Tracey. "Transportation Outsourcing: A Survey of U.S. Practices," *International Journal of Physical Distribution and Logistics Management*, Vol. 21, No. 3, 1991, pp. 15–21.

Bienstock, C.C., and J. T. Mentzer. "An Experimental Investigation of the Outsourcing Decision for Motor Carrier Transportation, *Transportation Journal*, Vol. 39, No. 1, pp. 42–59.

Bradley, Peter. "Railroads, The Big Get Bigger," *Logistics Management*, July 1998.

Burns, Gregory. *Freight Forwarding/Logistics*, New York: Gerard, Klauer Mattison & Co., 1997.

Evers, P. T., and C. J. Johnson. "Performance Perceptions, Satisfaction and Intention: The Intermodal Shipper's Perspective, *Transportation Journal*, Vol. 40, No. 2, pp. 27–39.

Foster, Thomas A. "Sweet on Intermodal," *Logistics Management*, March 2003.

Gooley, Toby B. "Express: The Competition Heats Up," *Logistics Management*, July 1998.

Jedd, Marcia. "Big Battle for Small Packages," *Logistics Management*, February 1999.

Hoffman, Kurt C., "Tight Supply Chains Respond to Guaranteed Truck Service," *Global Logistics & Supply Chain Strategies*, February 2000.

Robert Motley. "Logistics Consultant Roger Urban Reflects on Outsourcing, Collaboration, and How Many Numbers Can Go Before 'PL'," *American Shipper*, August 2002.

Krause, Kristin S. "Taking Off the Gloves—FedEx Expands Freight Business," *Traffic World*, March 1, 1999.

Sheffi, Yosef. "Third Party Logistics: Present and Future Prospects," *Journal of Business Logistics*, Vol. 11, No. 2, 1990, pp. 27–40.

Thomas, Jim. "Transportation Intermediaries—How David Lives with Goliath," *Logistics Management*, December 1998.

Newbourne, Malcolm J. *Intermodal Transport by Land in the United States: A Guide to Intermodal Trucking*, Marco Island, FL: Cargo Transport Corporation, 2002.

Case 7-1

Specialty Gift Foods

Mr. Bob Gatshell, president of Specialty Gift Foods, Inc., (SGF) was pondering the implications of a transportation management article he read in a business journal. The article concluded that leading-edge companies are limiting the number of carriers used to about 50 or fewer, placing the carriers under contract, consolidating shipments, and utilizing piggyback for long-haul shipment. Bob felt SGF was a leader in the specialty foods industry, having won numerous awards for its innovative products and business model. However, Bob realized that SGF's transportation process was completely opposite of that described for leading-edge companies.

SGF began in 1940 as a catering company, providing hot meals to factory workers in Chicago. Bob's mother would prepare sandwiches in her kitchen, and Bob's father would drive a van loaded with the sandwiches to the factory entrance and sell them to the workers at lunchtime. The business grew quickly with the addition of new menu items, including breakfast and hot lunches. After World War II, SGF continued the hot meal delivery business but expanded into selling gift boxes of food for holidays, particularly Christmas. From its beginning in Chicago, the SGF operation now consists of 250 stores (including kiosks in shopping malls), 20 production facilities (specialty meats and cheeses), and three packaging/distribution centers. At the package centers the various SGF products are assembled into gift boxes for distribution to the sales outlets. In 1999 SGF began selling via the Internet, with all Internet sales fulfilled from its packaging/distribution centers.

In response to Bob's questions about why SGF was not using the leading-edge transportation practices sited in the article, Fred Cane, transportation manager, collected the following data for 2003 transportation activities:

- SGF shipped 3.5 million gift boxes.
- 90 percent of the annual sales occurred in December.
- Production facilities operate 5 months (August to December).

- SGF's carrier base consisted of 485 carriers:

  310 motor carriers

  100 freight brokers

  20 air carriers

  55 express/local cartage carriers
- Motor carriers are used for shipments from the production facilities to the packaging centers and from the packaging centers to the sales outlets.
- Freight brokers arrange for motor carriers service during the peak shipping periods of October to December.
- The air carriers and express companies handle the Internet shipments.
- SGF has contracts with only a few of the motor carriers and relies on the standard shipping documents for all other carriers.
- Piggyback is not utilized and consolidation occurs only for loads going to the packaging centers.

Fred also noted the severe service requirement imposed on a short selling timeframe, October to December. Approximately 3.2 million gift boxes were moved in 3 months. If the products were not at the sales outlets for the Christmas buying season, SGF would lose the sale.

Case Questions

1. Why does SGF use so many carriers? Can it operate with a smaller number of carriers?
2. What role does the freight broker play in SGF's transportation strategy?
3. Do you see opportunities for freight consolidation and piggyback?
4. What value would contracting with the carriers have for SGF?
5. Can SGF implement the leading-edge transportation strategies suggested in the article Bob read?

Case 7-2

Rare Book Sellers

Rare Book Sellers (RBS) is a retailer of rare, hard-to-find books. RBS was started by Grace Renay in 1970 while she was working on her Ph.D. in literature. Grace was a collector of old books and would spend most of her free time scouring book stores, attending estate auctions, and perusing library out-of-date book sales in search of those rare books. She developed quite a network of book suppliers and rare book collectors. Upon graduation, Grace continued her RBS business as a hobby while she taught literature at a major university.

In 1998 Grace took an early retirement from the university and turned her attention full time to RBS. Her original store was filled with books, and RBS was known in the industry as the source for obtaining that almost-impossible-to-find book. In 1999 RBS began selling books on the Internet. The RBS website increased the number of suppliers available to RBS because individuals and companies would electronically contact RBS with books for sale. What started as a hobby in 1970 turned out to be a $200 million business in 2003.

As the business grew, Grace turned her attention to the numerous management issues confronting a growing concern. In a recent staff meeting the director of marketing raised a pricing question regarding the handling of shipping costs in light of the rising rare books cost and falling prices for rare books. For a number of years RBS included free shipping in the price of the book. In 2003 shipping costs amounted to approximately 10 percent of sales or $20 million. This amount had been increasing during the past 3 years because of rising transportation rates and greater use of express delivery service.

The typical book order is for one book that weighs about 3 pounds (including packaging) and has a value of $50. RBS uses three transportation carriers to deliver books to its customers: FedEx, UPS, and United States Postal Service (USPS). Each carrier has different rates and different delivery service levels. For example, FedEx and UPS have same-day service, next day by 8:00 a.m., next day by 10:00 a.m., next day by 4:00 p.m, second day, plus ground service of 2 or more days. USPS also has next-day delivery, second-day delivery, etc. There are different rates for each delivery service, with higher rates for quicker delivery.

Generally, the customer wants the book as quickly as possible and is not concerned about the cost as long as it is built into the selling price. But the pricing strategy proposed by the marketing director would add the shipping cost to the selling price of the book. Grace's initial questions dealt with the types of services available from these three carriers, the relative costs of each service level, and the relative costs among the three carriers. Before Grace agrees to the pricing strategy change she wants to determine if the current shipping costs can be lowered by changing the delivery service level.

Case Questions

1. Using the Internet, determine the types of services offered by FedEx (http://www.fedex.com), UPS (http://www.ups.com), and USPS (http://www.usps.com).

2. For a typical shipment of 3 pounds with a value of $50 from New York City (zip code: 10001) to Atlanta (zip code: 30310), determine the relative cost for same-day, next-day and second- or third-day service levels.

3. Given your cost analysis, what service level will result in a shipping cost that is less than 10 percent of the selling price of $50?

Chapter 8

Global Transportation

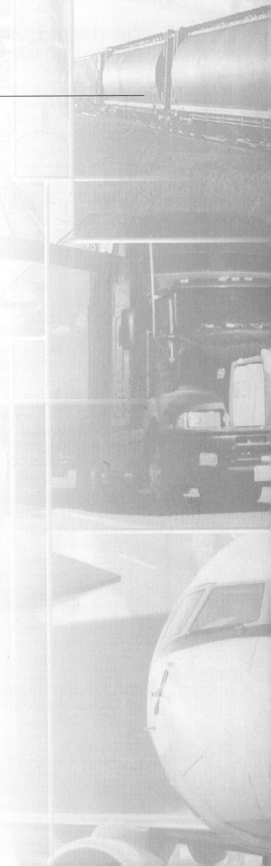

THE BALANCING ACT: SECURITY VERSUS GLOBAL COMMERCE

Global commerce with the United States came to a halt on September 11, 2001, when terrorists attacked the United States. Air transportation into and within the United States was suspended for days, and ocean shipments stopped at the ports. Global transportation as we knew it changed dramatically after 9/11 because of the new security procedures implemented to prevent a reoccurrence of that tragic event.

Prior to 9/11, shipments could clear U.S. ports, gateways, and airports in a matter of hours. Today's security measures require more cargo inspection, more paperwork, and longer time to clear the U.S. borders. Ships may be stopped and inspected by security personnel and cargo containers opened and the contents checked. Cargoes that might be used by terrorists, as well as shipments originating from suspected terrorist areas in the world, are given close scrutiny.

A delicate balance exists between security and global commerce. That is, if security is too tight it could stop or seriously impede global commerce. Ports, gateways, and airports could become so congested with inspections that shipments could take months to clear customs. For example, border crossings between the United States and Canada were accomplished in less than 1 hour prior to 9/11 but increased to days immediately following. This long customs clearance time caused considerable economic upheaval at plants in the United States that are dependant on Canadian supplies, and vice versa for Canadian companies awaiting supplies from U.S. vendors.

The security measures have been amended to improve the flow of product through border crossings, while at the same time increasing security over that existing before 9/11. As an example, workers at some ports are required to have a criminal background check, be fingerprinted, and obtain a special port identification. Adding more inspectors enables more cargo inspections while easing the inspection delays.

Electronic filing of cargo information has improved the border clearance times. The Trade Act of 2002 requires exporters to electronically submit shipping documents to U.S. Customs 24 hours after delivery to the port and at least 24 hours before the vessel's departure. The Act also makes illegal the tendering of improperly documented shipments to carriers. For imports to the United States, the U.S. Custom's 24-Hour Manifest Rule requires ocean carriers and consolidators to electronically file cargo manifest data with customs at least 24 hours before U.S.-bound cargo is loaded on the vessel at a foreign port.

Canada is a major trading partner of the United States, with a total trade volume between the two countries of approximately $370 billion. Prolonged trade flow blockages at the borders could mean serious consequences for the economies of both countries. Recognizing this unique trade relationship, U.S. Customs developed the Free and Secure Trade (FAST) program, which enables participants to receive unique identifiers making them eligible for expedited processing at U.S.–Canadian border crossings. The trucking company and driver must be preapproved to receive the expedited processing.

The U.S. Maritime Transportation Security Act of 2002 authorizes the U.S. Coast Guard to assess U.S. ports' vulnerability. The agency has the authority to assess foreign ports' vulnerability and to deny entry to ships from countries that do not meet security standards. The Act also requires development of standards for container seals and locks, cargo tracking, identification, and a screening system for ocean containers.

As you can see from this overview of recent security measures for global trade, officials are recognizing the impact of tighter security on global trade. Electronic transmission of global shipment data plus increased focus on the personnel and processes at the borders are the cornerstones of the improved security measures. Global shippers realize the tightened security measures are here to stay, and they are adjusting their shipping processes and inventories to allow for the added transit times.

Global transportation is an integral part of the study of transportation. Foreign trade is growing in tonnage and value for the United States and for most other nations of the world. Further, it is a purchase or sales activity engaged in by more and more firms, even medium and small firms and carriers. Although the primary economics and techniques of carrier management efficiencies are similar in a global setting to those in domestic settings, the supply of transportation and the public policy require separate treatment.

This chapter examines foreign trade and presents the basic forms of transportation found in this realm. Rate-making systems are examined for both air and ocean trades. Several major areas of policy concern are covered that bear on the carriers, the United States, and relations with foreign nations. Finally, often overlooked in many texts but a crucial part of global transportation, is the role of port planning.

EXTENT AND MAGNITUDE OF TRADE

The United States is a large trading partner in the world. Although foreign trade is not as significant to the United States as it is to the gross national product of some other nations, the magnitude and value of U.S. tonnage imported and exported makes U.S. global trade an important area of study. The United States trades with nearly all nations of the world, with the exception of a few nations that are excluded due to political reasons.

The U.S. trading partners are indicated in Table 8.1. The largest U.S. trading partner is Canada, with a 2002 trade value of $371.39 billion. Mexico is the second largest, with an annual trade value of $232.26 billion. Japan, China, and Federal Republic of Germany are the next largest trading partners, with annual trade values of $172.93 billion, $147.22 billion, and $89.11 billion, respectively. The 10 countries in Table 8.1 account for 70 percent of U.S. imports and 65 percent of U.S. exports of goods.

As noted in the opening vignette, there is a delicate balancing act between security and global trade. Excessive security restrictions can strangle global trade and cause serious economic problems for countries. The top 10 U.S. trading partners generated $1,277 billion in trade in 2002. This translates into hundreds of thousands of jobs and a quality of life citizens are accustomed to living. Excessive security restrictions that stop trade among the 10 countries could spell economic turmoil for these countries as well as other countries around the world.

The United States has taken steps to increase security at the borders to protect its citizens while at the same time attempting to mitigate the negative impact on global trade. Many of the steps involve improving the quality and timeliness of cargo information, thereby permitting security review before the shipment reaches the border. (See the opening vignette, "The Balancing Act: Security versus Global Commerce.")

Table 8.1 U.S. Trading Partners

Country	2002 Trade Value ($ in billions)
Canada	371.39
Mexico	232.26
Japan	172.93
China	147.22
Federal Republic of Germany	89.11
United Kingdom	74.12
Korea, Republic of	58.17
Taiwan	50.59
France	47.43
Italy	34.38

Source: U.S. Census Bureau, "Top Ten Countries with which the U.S. Trades," December 2002.

Trading with Canada and Mexico is a relatively simple procedure because truck and rail transportation can be used in a manner similar to that used for domestic moves. Documentation and custom processes still exist, but this form of international transportation does not require differentiation from that of domestic U.S. transportation. Both countries are adjacent to the United States, and both serve as markets for U.S. goods as well as sources of raw materials and production and assembly operations. The United States, Mexico, and Canada have signed the **North American Free Trade Agreement (NAFTA)**, easing import duties and encouraging trade among the three countries.

Overview of the North American Free Trade Agreement

The North American Free Trade Agreement (NAFTA) was signed by leaders of Canada, the United States, and Mexico in 1993 and was ratified by Congress in early 1994. NAFTA establishes free trade between these three countries and provides the way the Agreement is to be interpreted. The Treaty states the objectives of the three countries is based on the principles of an unimpeded flow of goods, most-favored-nation (MFN) status, and a commitment to enhance the cross-border movement of goods and services. MFN status provides the lowest duties or customs fees, if any, and simplifies the paperwork required to move goods between the partner countries.

Canada and the United States have agreed to suspend the operation of the Canada–U.S. Free Trade Agreement (FTA) to allow NAFTA to prevail. Any sections of the FTA that are not covered by NAFTA remain in place.

From a transportation standpoint, by 2000 motor carriers of each country were to have been able to operate freely in all three countries. There have been meetings between trucking executives and government officials the United States, Canada, and Mexico, but no overall agreement has been put in place. Although cross-border operations between the United States and Mexico were to have started in 1995, a number of problems remain to be resolved and such operations are still prohibited. The original agreement allowed U.S. or Mexican carriers to pick up or deliver, but not both, in each country's border states with their own equipment and employees. A number of concerns including safety and environmental issues remain to be addressed.

A problem has been the allowable trailers that could operate into Mexico. While American carriers have standardized on the 53-foot van, many Mexican carriers do not operate this type of trailer. The Mexican government announced new size regulations in early 1997 that would seem to permit 53-foot trailers in Mexico. These regulations limit overall combination tractor and trailer length to just over 68 feet. This requires an extremely short wheel base tractor, which very few Mexican or American carriers operate. This issue is the subject of ongoing negotiations between the United States and Mexico.

Since June 1996, Mexican regulations will not allow U.S.-owned vehicles to operate more than 12.5 miles from the border without obtaining a permit from the Mexican government for each vehicle. (Mexican-owned trucks are restricted to a 20-mile border zone in the United States.) The Department of Commerce and Industrial Development issues the permit, and the U.S. trucking company is required to post a bond. The permit is good for 30 days and will allow only one entrance and one exit for that trailer during the life of the permit. The other alternative is to transfer the freight to a trailer owned and operated by a Mexican-based trucking company. A bond is required for each separate trailer and the bond fee is not refundable.

Much work still has to be done in connection with NAFTA implementation as it relates to the United States and Mexico. However, there has been significant change related to Canadian motor carriers' operation in the United States.

Canadian motor carriers now have the same rights in the United States as U.S. truckers have in Canada. Historically a "foreign" carrier was not allowed to pick up and deliver shipments within the United States. Current regulations permit Canadian and U.S. carriers to enjoy the same privileges while operating in the other's country.

Canadian carriers are now allowed to transport domestic U.S. traffic when such transportation is incidental to a return trip to Canada. For example, a Canadian trucker could deliver a load in Chicago, pick up a shipment for Detroit and upon arrival in Detroit, pick up a shipment destined to Canada. However, the truck must be driven by a citizen of the country in which the truck is operated.

An example of the trading arrangement between the United States and Mexico is a unique international operation known as a **Maquiladora**. A Maquiladora is a U.S. manufacturing or assembly operation located along the U.S.–Mexico border, or other locations specified by the Mexican government. U.S. raw materials and component parts are sent to the Maquiladora, where the semi-finished or finished product is manufactured or assembled. All or part of the Maquiladora output is subsequently returned to the United States without any Mexican import duties being paid. The U.S. companies with Maquiladora operations are taking advantage of the lower labor rates in Mexico.

A unique situation exists for truck movements to and from Mexico. Mexican trucks are permitted to operate in the United States within a 20-mile border zone. U.S. trucks are likewise restricted to border zone operations in Mexico. These restrictions add additional delay and shipment hand-offs for U.S–Mexico trade. As Figure 8.1 depicts, southbound traffic moves from the U.S. shipper by a U.S. trucking company to a freight forwarder/Mexican Customs broker for inspection and document filing. The forwarder contacts a Mexican drayage carrier to haul the load across the border to the Mexico Customs for inspection and approval. The load is then transferred to a Mexican carrier, who hauls it to the Mexican consignee.

For northbound moves, the Mexican carrier moves the load to the border where a Mexican customs broker files the appropriate documentation for U.S. entry and

FIGURE 8.1 U.S.–Mexico Border-Crossing Process

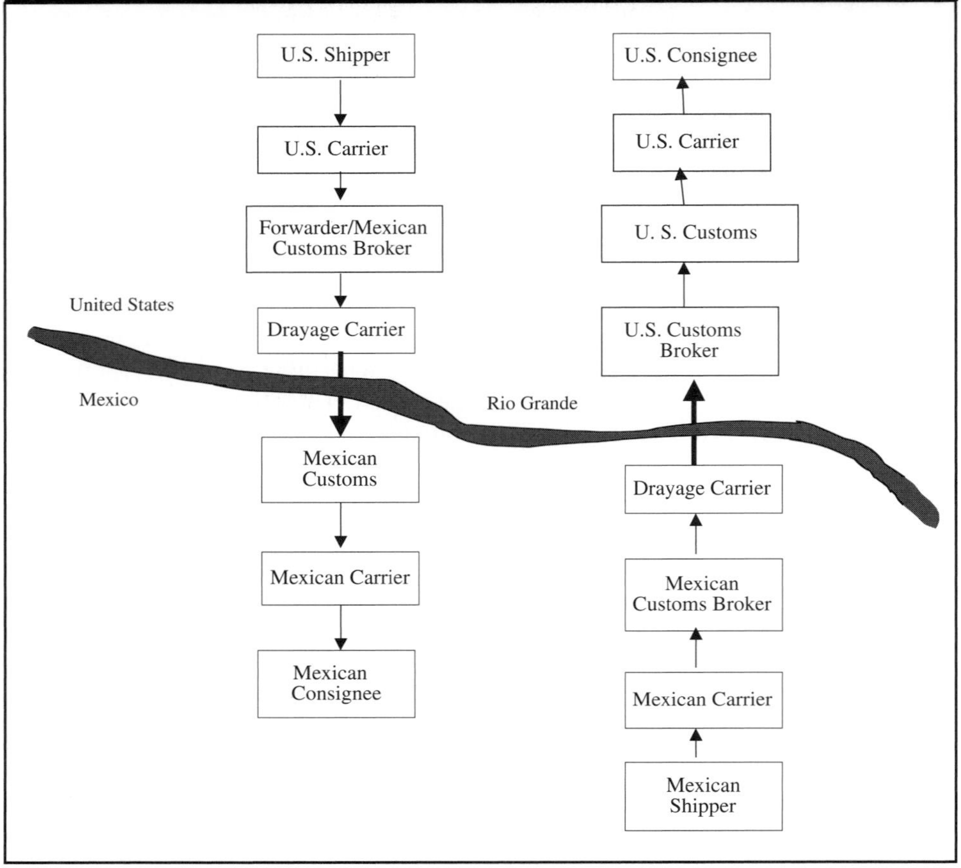

arranges for a drayage carrier for the cross-border move. A U.S. Customs broker files the appropriate documentation with U.S. Customs for inspection and approval. A U.S. carrier then transports the load to the U.S. consignee.

In 2001 (prior to 9/11) the Federal Highway Administration conducted a truck travel time and delay study at three U.S.–Mexico port-of-entry sites. The study measured the travel time for trucks from initial queuing in the export country up to and through the first inspection point in the importing country. The average inbound times (from Mexico) were 31, 37, and 35 minutes, respectively, for Laredo, El Paso, and Otay Mesa. The time required for 95 percent of the truck to traverse the study distance was 55, 77, and 65 minutes for the three respective ports of entry. Average outbound (to Mexico) times were lower: 17, 13, and 19 minutes, respectively, for the three ports of entry.[1]

Since 9/11, the travel time through the ports of entry have increased because of security reasons as noted in the introductory case to this chapter. The NAFTA agreement does not override the security concerns of the country. Today, the travel times required to cross the U.S.–Mexican border require hours, not minutes. (See "Stop Off: Could You Do What Denso Did?" for a description of what one company did to improve the transit time for U.S.–Mexico shipments.)

STOP OFF

Could You Do What Denso Did?

The numbers are alluring: Denso Manufacturing Tennessee, an automotive components manufacturer, cut transit times to Mexico by 70 percent, slashed safety stocks by three to four days, and found significant cost savings not just for itself and its service providers.

Who wouldn't jump at the chance to make improvements like that? Many shippers undoubtedly could realize similar benefits by mapping transportation processes, identifying problems and bottlenecks, and developing solutions that maximize speed and efficiency, just as Denso did. But it doesn't come easily. It achieved those rewards only after months of planning, site visits, and countless meetings with service providers. Along the way, Denso and its providers learned some lessons that helped them reach their goals. Here's their advice on how you can do the same:

- **Go see for yourself.** "This is not a business you can do from your desk. You really have to go and physically see and experience what's happening to get the full picture," says Paige Rose, assistant director of transportation at Denso Manufacturing Tennessee.
- **Find out who's really calling the shots.** Rose and colleagues discovered that the choice of local drayage and Mexican longhaul carriers, whose performance was questionable, was made by Denso's Mexican customs broker and its sister company in Laredo. "Once we identified who had that responsibility and held them accountable, service improved," she said.
- **Make your expectations clear.** Denso failed to communicate expectations or set deadlines for service providers, so there was no impetus for those providers to cut transit times. "You have to be specific, even if you have to say hour-by-hour how long it should take to go through the process," says Daniel B. Hastings, Jr., president of customs broker at Daniel B. Hastings, Inc.
- **Measure performance against established standards.** Hastings recommends tracking the date and hour that a shipment completes each step in the process, then measuring the time elapsed against predetermined parameters for each transaction. Analyzing that information by lane, service provider, and customer should bring bottlenecks and their causes to light.
- **Set realistic timelines.** Denso built 12 extra hours into its schedule to allow for customs inspections at the border. Even if customs authorities should decide to conduct an intensive inspection, there will still be enough time to meet the delivery deadline, according to Denso's truckload carrier, Contract Freighters, Inc.
- **Use Mexican customs laws to your advantage.** Some little-known provisions of Mexican customs laws allow more flexibility than Mexican brokers would have you believe, says Hastings. One example is *revision en origen* (verification of origin), under which a Mexican importer guarantees to Mexican customs authorities that the U.S. exporter's shipments and data are always accurate. If *revision en origen* is granted, then no verification of the shipment contents by the Mexican broker is required. If the information is not 100 percent accurate all the time, the shipper and Mexican customer will be in serious trouble.
- **Ask for feedback and be willing to change.** When Denso asked what it could do to help its service providers meet its stringent new requirements, it learned that some of Denso's own practices were partly to blame for delays. By listening to providers' concerns and implementing their suggestions, Denso not only enabled its supply chain partners to improve their on-time performance but also communicated its commitment to their success.
- **Negotiate in person.** Mexican business culture places greater emphasis on personal relationships than does its U.S. counterpart. "I can't stress enough the importance of face-to-face meetings," says Rose. "Even when you're not happy with service, the way you communicate is important."

Source: Toby B. Gooley, "Could You Do What Denso Did?" *Logistics Management*, March 2003, p. 52. Reprinted with permission.

GLOBAL TRANSPORTATION PROVIDERS

International transportation is provided by all modes of transportation, including pipelines in North America. However, the majority of non-North American shipments are made via air and water transportation. Because the shipments from and to Canada and Mexico are quite similar to the domestic moves, this section will emphasize ocean and air transportation. In addition, attention is given to the transportation intermediaries who are critical components in most global shipments.

Ocean Transportation

The specific types of carriers that transport U.S. ocean-borne trade are liners, tramps, and private vessels. Each type provides specific service features to the international transportation user as discussed below. Table 8.2 contains some major ocean carriers.

LINERS

Liners are ships that ply fixed routes on published schedules. They typically charge according to published tariffs that are either unique to the ship line or are made by several lines in a particular trade route. Liner services are either container or break-bulk types.

Freight must be moved to the liner company's terminal at the port after the shipper has arranged for the freight booking or reservation. This freight is loaded by machine if bulk, or crane if containerized, and stowed in accordance with ship weight and balance requirements. The frequency of various liner departures from New York, Los Angeles, and Long Beach has caused these ports to be highly preferred by many shippers.

Container movement is gaining over the traditional **break-bulk** method of ocean carriage. When goods have to be heavily crated and packaged for break-bulk movement, a container often provides much of that needed protection. Further, whereas a break-bulk ship might require many days to unload and load its cargo by small crane and manpower, an entire container ship can enter, unload, load, and clear a port in less than 12 hours. Such speed has brought about labor savings to both the shipper and the liner company, as well as increased ship (and capital) utilization. Because a ship is only earning revenue at sea, it is easy to see why containers have become a dominant form of packaged-goods shipping.

Table 8.2 Major Ocean Carriers

Ocean Carrier	Website
APL (American President Lines)	*http://www.apl.com*
COSCO (China Ocean Shipping Company)	*http://www.cosco-usa.com*
CrowleyMarine	*http://www.crowley.com*
Evergreen Group	*http://www.evergreen-marine.com*
Lykes Lines	*http://www.lykeslines.com*
MaerskSealand	*http://www.maersksealand.com*
Matson Navigation Company	*http://www.matson.com*
Hapag-Lloyd AG	*http://www.hapag-lloyd.com*
NYK Lines	*http://www.nykline.com*
P&O Nedllod B.V.	*http://www.ponl.com*

Container service, although saving port and ship time, has brought about different operating and management concerns for the ship company. For one, this service requires a large investment in containers because, while some are at sea, many others are being delivered inland or are being loaded there for movement to port. Although a ship might carry 1,000 containers, an investment of 1,500 to 2,500 containers is necessary to support that ship. Another concern is control over the containers. Previous shipping line managements were port-to-port-oriented. With inland movement of containers, control over this land movement becomes a necessity. The container itself is a large investment and is attractive to thieves in areas of warehouse or housing shortages.

The **lighter-aboard ship (LASH)** is a liner that carries barges that were loaded at an inland river point and moved to the ocean port via water tow. A specially designed ocean ship carries the payload and barge intact to a foreign port to be dropped off in the harbor. This system avoids port handling and enables fast ship turnaround and high utilization.

The economics of the LASH ship are similar to that of the container ship in that the ocean ship is high in capital cost, and the presence of barges or containers decreases high stowage density. These two factors are generally traded off against the fast port turnaround provided by these systems.

Another type of ship found in liner services is a **roll-on/roll-off ship,** often referred to as a **RORO** ship. These ships carry trucks, trailers, and construction equipment much like a multilevel ferryboat. When in service with trailers, a RORO ship is like a container ship except that it has the wheel chassis attached to the trailer body en route. RORO ships are especially useful in carrying heavy construction equipment because they are unable to maintain an even keel while the equipment is being loaded and unloaded. This stability allows loading and unloading without the use of dockside cranes that may not even be available.

TRAMPS

The **tramp ship** is one that is hired like a taxi or leased auto. That is, it is a bulk or tank ship that is hired on a voyage or time basis. On a voyage basis, a U.S. exporter of grain will seek a tramp ship that will become empty at a desired U.S. port. It will then be hired for one-way movement to a foreign port. Port fees, a daily operating rate and demurrage, will be part of the charter contract. Time charters are usually longer-term charters in which the shipper will make or arrange for more than a one-way move. Such charters are made with or without crews being provided by the shipowner.

PRIVATE VESSELS

Private ships are owned or leased on a long-term basis by the firm moving the goods. Many oil ships fit this category, as do automotive and lumber vessels. The economics of this form of ship movement are similar to those of private motor trucks.

Another element of interest in ocean shipping is that of ship registry. Although a ship might be U.S.-owned and ply a route between the United States and the Persian Gulf, it might be registered in and fly the flag of Liberia or Panama. These nations represent what are called **flags of convenience.** That is, the owners derive certain benefits of taxes, manning, and some relaxed safety requirements by being registered in those countries, rather than in the United States, Canada, or wherever. The top flags of convenience nations include Panama, Liberia, the Bahamas, Greece, and Malta.

Air Carriers

Just as with domestic moves, air transportation offers the global transportation user speed. The fastest method of movement for the non-North American international shipment is air carriage. Four types of air carriers are available for international shippers: air parcel post, express or expedited service, passenger, and cargo.

AIR PARCEL POST

Air parcel post service is provided by the postal service of a country and is designed to handle small packages. The postal service contracts with an air carrier to pick up and deliver the item from one country to another. There are restrictions as to the size and weight of the shipment handled by air parcel post, and these restrictions vary by country. In the United States, the maximum size permitted is 108 inches of length and girth and no more than 70 pounds of weight.

EXPRESS OR EXPEDITED SERVICE

Express or courier service is provided by air carriers and is generally restricted to small shipments weighing less than 70 pounds. Speed is the essential characteristic of this service, with next-day or second-day delivery a standard service level. Examples of major carriers providing this service include Federal Express, United Parcel Service (UPS), and DHL.

PASSENGER CARRIERS

Regularly scheduled international passenger flights haul freight in the "belly" of the plane. These carriers focus on the movement of passengers, but the excess capacity in the nonpassenger compartment permits the transporting of cargo along with passengers. Cargo capacity and cargo size are limited by the size of each plane, but the regular schedules afford the use of numerous flights between origin and destination. Examples of U.S. international passenger carriers that transport cargo are American, Delta, Northwest, and United.

ALL-CARGO CARRIERS

All-cargo carriers specialize in the movement of freight, not passengers. The airplanes are outfitted with larger hatch openings, cargo compartments, and floor-bearing ratings. Many air cargo planes have mechanized materials-handling devices on board to permit the movement of heavier cargo inside the plane. Some of the larger planes are capable of transporting a 40-foot container, trucks, and other motor vehicles. Generally, these carriers haul heavier shipments weighing more than 70 pounds. BAX Global, Federal Express, and UPS Air are examples of U.S. all-cargo carriers.

Ancillary Services

Other service firms exist in addition to the basic modes that are available to the international transportation user. These ancillary service companies provide a variety of functions that offer the user lower costs, improved service, and/or technical expertise.

AIR FREIGHT FORWARDERS

International air freight forwarding firms operate in a manner similar to domestic air freight forwarders. The air freight forwarder books space on an air carrier's plane and solicits freight from numerous shippers to fill the booked space. The air freight forwarder offers the shipper of small shipments a rate savings resulting from the advanced purchase of space. In addition, the air freight forwarder offers convenience to the shipper, especially when more than one airline must be used in an interline setting, or when ground transportation is necessary at one or both ends of the air move.

INTERNATIONAL FREIGHT FORWARDERS

These firms arrange movement for the shipper. They do not necessarily act as consolidators or earn their revenues in the manner like domestic forwarders. International freight forwarders act as agents for shippers by applying familiarity and expertise with ocean shipping to facilitate through movement. They represent the shipper in arranging such activities as inland transportation, packaging, documentation, booking, and legal fees. They charge a percent of the costs incurred for arranging these services. They play an invaluable role for shippers who are not familiar with the intricacies of shipping or those who do not have the scale or volume to warrant having in-house expertise in this area.

NONVESSEL OPERATING COMMON CARRIERS (NVOCC)

Nonvessel operating carriers assemble and disperse less-than-container shipments and move them as full-container shipments. They serve much the same role as the domestic freight forwarders. A shipper moving a small item would otherwise have to move it via break-bulk ocean carrier or air freight. The NVOCC consolidates this shipment with many others and gains the economies of container movement. Some NVOCCs operate from inland cities, where they unload inbound containers and distribute the goods to consignees. They in turn solicit outbound freight, **consolidate** shipments into the containers, and move them back to a seaport for outbound movement. The steamship line gains opportunities from broadened territorial traffic, and it gains services and control over containers from the NVOCC solicitations. Shippers and receivers gain from the shipping expertise and processes of the NVOCC, as well as from expanded and simplified import and export opportunities.

SHIP BROKERS

These firms act as middlemen between the tramp shipowner and a chartering shipper or receiver. The brokers' extensive exposure, contacts, and knowledge of the overall ship market make them valuable parties in these arrangements. They are compensated on the basis of a percentage of the chartering fees.

SHIP AGENTS

Ship agents act on behalf of a liner company or tramp ship operator (either owner or charter company) to represent their interests in facilitating ship arrival, clearance, loading, unloading, and fee payment while at a specific port. Liner firms will use agents when the frequency of sailings are so sparse that it is not economical for them to invest in their own terminals or to have management personnel on site.

LAND, MINI-, AND MICRO-BRIDGES

These three services have become significant parts of global shipping over the past decade. Their development is largely due to the carrier efficiencies they provide that also benefit the shippers.

The **land bridge** system consists of containers moving between Japan and Europe by rail and ship. That is, originally, containers were moved entirely by ship between Asia and Europe across the Pacific and Atlantic Oceans and through the Panama Canal. Ship fuel and capital costs, as well as trouble in Panama, created economies in moving the containers by water to a U.S. Pacific Coast port, then by entire trainload across the United States to another ship for transatlantic crossing to Europe. This system reduces transit time and liner company ship investment.

A **mini-bridge** is a similar system that is used for movements between, say, Japan and New York, Philadelphia, Baltimore, Charleston, New Orleans, or Houston. Rather than move all-water routes from Asia to these cities through the Panama Canal, a mini-bridge consists of transpacific water movement to Seattle, Oakland, or Long Beach, then by rail to the destination East Coast or Gulf Coast city. Mini-bridge services likewise operate from Europe to West Coast cities and New Orleans and Houston, with water–rail transfer taking place at New York or Charleston.

Examples of two mini-bridges are shown in Figure 8.2. The all-water route from Japan to New York requires about 21 to 24 days. This route is 9,700 miles and it involves transit through the Panama Canal, which requires a toll. The alternative is to unload the freight in Seattle and use rail to move it across the country. This route is only 7,400 miles long and takes about 16 days. The savings to the shipper is in the transit time. The second route is Europe to Houston. The all-water route is 4,600 miles, whereas unloading at Charleston and using rail to Houston is 4,500 miles. The mileage is not significant, but the savings here is in faster transit time. The steamship company can turn the ship around and return it to Europe faster than before. In fact, this option enables the steamship company to offer weekly service between Europe and Houston using one fewer ship than is used in the all-water

FIGURE 8.2 Mini-Bridge System

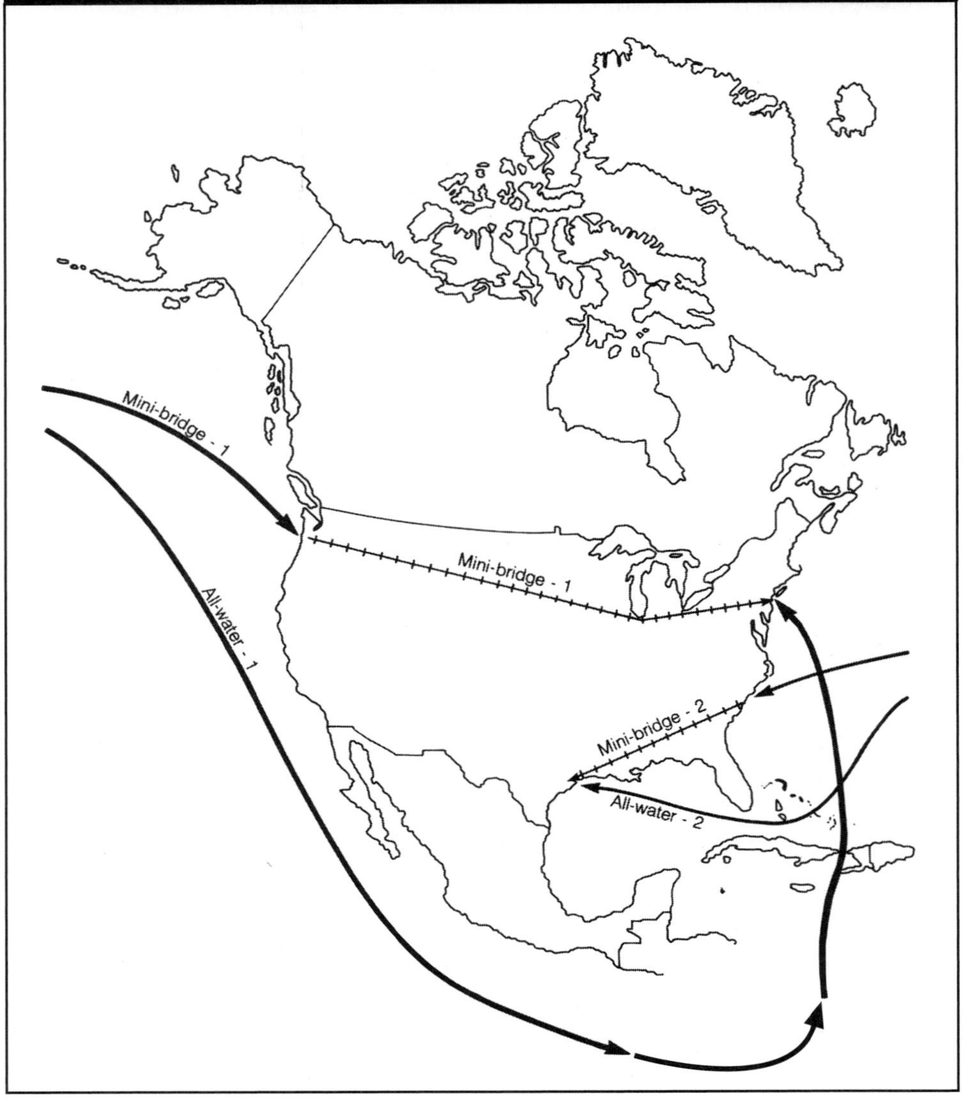

route. That ship can be redeployed onto another route altogether. The mini-bridge gives the steamship company effective freight-hauling capacity while saving the investment in one ship.

A mini-bridge saves transit time and ship line separating costs and investment, but previously another benefit accrued to the shipper/receiver in loading and unloading cost savings was avoiding what was called a "50-mile rule." When containers replaced break-bulk shipping, many stevedores lost work and income. As part of a labor settlement, it was arranged that any consolidated container had to be loaded or unloaded by stevedores if it was stuffed or unstuffed within 50 miles of the container point of embarkation or debarkation. This system often required handling at times that were inconvenient for the shipper/receiver or were at a cost much higher than what would be incurred by the shipper's own labor. An all-water movement from a San Jose, California, shipper to a consignee in Europe through ship loading at Oakland required such stevedore container packing. However, in a mini-bridge move by container train from California for containership movement from New York to Europe, San Jose was beyond the 50-mile radius of the New York containership loading point. Thus, the San Jose shipper avoided stevedore loading and enjoyed faster transit time to Europe.

In early 1989, the 50-mile rule was struck down in a court decision. This did not have a major impact upon traffic patterns. Mini-bridges are firmly entrenched because it provides faster transit time and avoids Panama Canal tolls and congestion.

Micro-bridge is an adaptation of mini-bridge, only it applies to interior nonport cities such as St. Louis. The origin or destination of the shipment is a U.S. interior, nonport city. Micro-bridges operate similarly to the NVOCC system. Here, too, a container is loaded at the interior point for transference to the ship at the port. This avoids truck movement to the port for actual loading of the container at the port terminal.

RATE MAKING IN GLOBAL TRANSPORTATION

Rate making is presented from the standpoint of three major transportation supply sources available to shippers: air, liners, and chartered tramp ships.

Shipping Conferences

A steamship conference is a voluntary organization of vessel-operating carriers whose main function is to set acceptable rates for steamships and shippers. The goal of the conference is to maintain a stable market and fair competition among carriers. Another important element of the steamship conference is to administer operating rules that guarantee the shipper a consistent level of service from participating lines.

For many years it was believed that the members of steamship conferences were "the cream of the crop"—providing the best service coupled with the highest cost. On the other hand, a shipper could get a cheaper price than what was offered by choosing a nonconference carrier but at the cost of a lower service level. Several factors have begun to erase this line between conference and nonconference carriers. First, the demand for highly sophisticated services has forced all carriers, conference and nonconference alike, to upgrade their service level to remain in business. Second, the development of containerization has enabled even the smallest carrier to compete in the door-to-door markets. Third, the Shipping Act of 1984 and the Ocean Shipping Reform Act of 1998 provided greater pricing freedom to the carriers and limited conference restrictions on independent actions of conference members.

As a result of these factors, the conferences are losing their significance in ocean transportation. As the Stop Off shows, the Trans-Atlantic Conference, a once powerful conference that exercised market control over even the largest Europe–U.S. shippers, is losing its influence.

Global Air

The economies of global air freight carriage are largely similar to those of domestic movement. The differences lie primarily in institutional factors relating to national agreements and the International Air Transport Association (IATA). This is an international air carrier rate bureau for both passenger and freight movement. IATA has long served as a collective rate-making body composed of the U.S. overseas airlines in various trade routes. Prices for both passenger and freight traditionally tend to be set at sufficient levels so as to cover most costs of the higher-cost or lower-load factor carriers. This system enhances a supply of service and brings a stability to the rate structure. U.S. government policy shifts in the late 1970s tended to encourage rate flexibility and greater route expansion; these factors were initially seen as decreasing the effectiveness of IATA-made prices. This situation is discussed further in this chapter along with other policies.

AIR CARGO RATE

Air cargo rates are based on the value of service or the cost of service. **The value of service,** as discussed in Chapter 2, "Transportation Regulation and Public Policy," is demand based and considers the sensitivity of the cargo being shipped to freight rates. The less sensitive cargo is to rates, the higher the rate will be. On traffic lanes where demand is strong and plane capacity is limited, the air rates will be high, and vice versa for traffic lanes where supply exceeds demand. Also, products with high prices or emergency conditions surrounding the move will be charged high rates because the freight rate is a small portion (less than 1 percent) of the landed selling price.

Cost factors enter into air carrier pricing of cargo. Given the limited cargo-carrying capacity of a plane, space is a premium. The utilization of this space is related to the **density** of the cargo, with low-density cargo requiring more space per weight unit than high-density cargo. Rates are based on a product density of 10.4 pounds per cubic foot. For shipments with lower densities, the air carrier calculates the weight based on the shipment's number of cubic feet times the standard density of 10.4 pounds per cubic foot. For shipments with densities greater then 10.4 pounds per cubic foot, the actual weight is used.

For example, an international shipment weighing 480 pounds and measuring 6 feet × 3 feet × 5 feet, or 90 cubic feet, has a density of 5.33 pounds per cubic foot (480 pounds/90 cubic feet). The international air carrier will charge the shipper a calculated weight of 936 pounds (90 cubic feet × 10.4 pounds per cubic foot) for moving the shipment.

Three types of international air carrier rates are based on the commodity shipped: general cargo, class, and specific commodity rates. The **general cargo rate** is a standard rate that applies to commodities for which there is no other applicable rate (class or specific). The general cargo rate is available for any commodity, can vary with distance and direction, and/or is applicable between specific origin–destination pairs. Discounts are available for larger shipment sizes and may or may not include ground transportation to and from the airport

The **class rate** is applicable to cargo grouped into classes. There is no classification system in international air transportation as is found in domestic surface transportation.

The rate for a particular class expressed as a percentage of the general cargo rate is usually lower than the general cargo rate and can be door-to-door or airport-to-airport.

The specific **commodity rate** is applicable to a specific commodity between a specific origin–destination pair. The specific commodity rate is generally lower than the general cargo rate. A high minimum weight is usually required for each shipment. Because the air carrier utilizes the specific commodity rate to attract freight and to enable shippers to penetrate certain market areas, it may have a time limit. As with the other commodity-based rates, the specific commodity rate can be either door-to-door or airport-to-airport.

Container rates are also available for cargo shipped in a container. The rate is cost based, rather than value of service or commodity based. The rate applies to a minimum weight in the container. Some carriers offer a container rate discount per container shipped over any route of the individual carrier. The discount is deducted from the tariff rate applicable to the commodity being moved in noncontainerized form and a charge is assessed for returning the empty container.

Liner Rate Making

COSTS

Liner operation, as with most ship operation, is largely fixed and common in nature. Approximately 80 to 90 percent of total cost is fixed and 10 to 20 percent is variable. Liner companies tend to have large overhead costs in the form of managements that are necessary for solicitation purposes.

The liner ship is often specifically constructed for a particular trade route. That is, such things as ship size and type, dimension, hatches, cargo space configuration, and engine type are designed around the ports to be visited, cargoes to be moved, and even the wave patterns experienced in a particular trade. These factors cause a ship that is designed for, say, Asian traffic to be less economical for United States-to-European trades.

A majority of the total costs of operating a ship are fixed. Because cargo loading, unloading, and fuel are the only primary variable costs, the ship's operation cost is roughly the same regardless of the commodity hauled. The problem of determining a cost per pound entails a difficult fixed-cost allocation process, which can be arbitrary at best. Ship operators will often determine unit costs in terms of cost per cubic foot of ship space so as to better evaluate and price for the range of commodities handled.

Because the cost of owning and operating the ship manifests itself as a relatively fixed cost per day regardless of the commodity hauled, ship operators attempt to solicit and charge rates that will maximize the total revenue of the entire ship. This condition brings about the tendency to price according to the principles of value of service. That is, a floor of variable costs must be covered as a minimum; then the blend of high- and low-value-per-pound commodities, as well as the host of traffic elasticities, leads to pricing according to what the traffic will bear to maximize revenue.

THE CONFERENCE OF RATE MAKING

Liner firms have long banded together into collective rate-making bodies called **steamship conferences**. These serve a similar purpose as those provided by domestic rail and motor rate bureaus. Conferences date back to the last century, when several liner firms banded together in the United Kingdom to calculate Calcutta trade. Since then they have developed into their current state in which several characteristics can be noted.

Conferences comprise member liner firms only. The organization is international in scope because liner firms of many nations will belong to one. They are also territorial in scope. For example, the Pacific Westbound Conference includes the United States and foreign carriers originating freight at Pacific Coast ports between California, Alaska, and Canada for destinations in Japan, Korea, Taiwan, and Hong Kong. Another conference made up of some of the same countries as well as others will cover eastbound traffic between the same points. A range of firms belongs to conferences. Some operate on sparse schedules, whereas others might offer weekly service. American carriers with new ships costing up to $15,000 per day to operate will be in the trade, along with foreign carriers, some of whose ships might cost only $6,000 to $7,000 per day to operate.

The actual rate system in conferences reflects the ship and liner firm economics previously discussed. Because ship operators experience a relatively fixed cost per day, and weight is not necessarily a variable cost expense, rates are constructed to also accommodate the density of freight. Many rates are assessed on a weight basis, either on a 2,000-pound short ton or a 2,240-pound long ton. Products that might occupy more of a proportionate share of space relative to their weight are often charged on a "weight or measure" (W/M) basis. That is, the carrier would charge a dollar rate per ton based upon shipment weight or "measurement ton," which is computed as 40 cubic feet equals one measurement ton. A shipment assessed at $60 W/M that weighs 5 weight tons but occupies 280 cubic feet would be charged $420 (7 cubic tons at $60). This system somewhat enables the carrier to recoup a minimum cost per cubic foot of space of ship capacity.

Another feature of conference rate making deals with contract rates and noncontract rates. Noncontract rates are the base rates, whereas contract rates are charged to shippers who have signed "exclusive patronage agreements" with the conference. This means that the shipper is charged rates approximately 10 to 15 percent lower than noncontract rates in exchange for using only member liner firms of the conference. The exclusive patronage agreement evolved from a deferred rebate system, but that was replaced by the agreement in U.S. trade as a result of American regulatory policy. The two rates are the reason this system is referred to as a dual-rate system. A shipper not having signed an agreement must pay the noncontract rate. Contract shippers unable to book space on a conference ship can use a nonconference liner without jeopardizing the discount. Further, a contract shipper can use tramp ships for bulk cargoes without conflicting with the agreement. Competitive pressures and regulatory changes caused many steamship lines to eliminate the contract/noncontract system and replace it with a single-rate system.

Time/volume rates are a rate feature new to ocean shipping to and from the United States. These rates are much like the service contracts found in motor carriage transport. They often provide for a rate reduction in exchange for a guaranteed amount of tonnage or containers over a certain time period. The carrier or conference receives the benefit of a larger or guaranteed amount of tonnage.

One problem facing conferences and shippers in recent times is fluctuating international currency levels. That is, a Japanese steamship firm receiving revenues in dollars might find that rate and revenue to be unprofitable due to an upward relationship of the yen against the dollar. This does not necessarily harm the American flag carrier that pays the ship mortgage and wages in dollars, but the Japanese ship is hurt because its obligations must be paid in yen. The conferences consequently developed a currency adjustment factor (CAF), which is a surcharge on the rates used to recover any such related losses. These surcharges also fluctuate with currency relationship shifts. Problems have occurred with different conferences charging different CAFs, as well as land portions of mini-bridges also being subject to the charge. In essence, the CAFs tend to harm U.S. exports. Carriers charge extra fees for moving U.S. exports; thus, a low dollar that makes exports cheaper to foreigners is actually charged at a proportionally higher rate. This is a continuing subject of debate and policy consideration by the Federal Maritime Commission.

Another problem relating to ocean export and import movements is the competitiveness, location, and rail network relationship of various U.S. ports. Some ports are in direct lines between producing and consuming areas of the nation and major ocean routes, but others require longer land moves or experience less frequent ship sailings. As a result, railroads traditionally serving the less-competitive ports often charge a rate for inland moves on export and import shipments that cause a through-move to be the same rate as that over a direct port route. This traditionally was encouraged by the Interstate Commerce Commission (ICC) in an effort to equalize port relationships. Since the ICC has been eliminated, the STB is not following the same course of action.

The conference system has withstood a great amount of pressure and criticism over the years. The criticism has focused mainly on two situations. One is over tonnage of shipping capacity. That is, the amount of ship-carrying space plying the oceans is greater than the freight being moved. This situation leads to price cutting in any cartel-like relationship, and in the late 1970s ship conferences experienced the pressure when some carriers withdrew from the conference.

Another problem area has been with price cuttings by ship firms owned and operated by the Soviet Union in United States-to-Japan and United States-to-European markets. The Atlantic and Pacific Ocean arms of the Russian steamship organizations entered into these markets in the 1970s with significant rate cutting that severely affected the traditional firms. In many instances, this practice was seen by many as unfair because the Russian firms appeared to be operating at below variable cost. However, labor and capital costs of these ships were paid in Russian currency, and profit was not necessarily the motive. Market entry and obtaining hard Western currencies was no doubt the objective; that is, the motive for operating was different than the other liners' long-run profit objective. The situation came to a head in 1980 when U.S. stevedores refused to service these ships as a result of the Russian invasion of Afghanistan.

The conference system has often been criticized from several vantage points. These criticisms are similar to those against domestic rate bureaus because rates are higher than they would be under free-market competition. Inefficient liner firms are protected, and rate innovations are not encouraged. Further, the practice of restricted conference membership by liner firms might leave poor-quality service to some areas.

For example, in the 1980s, 10 conferences existed between Western Europe and the East Coast of the United States. One superconference, Trans-Atlantic Conference Agreement (TACA), was available to shippers on this trade route. In 1992, TACA, then the Trans-Atlantic Agreement (TAA), reduced the available supply of ship space, increased rates by approximately 20 percent, and eliminated the door-to-door rate. That is, the shippers faced an ocean rate 20 percent greater than the previous door-to-door rate, plus they had to incur additional inland transportation charges. Also, certain ports, such as Philadelphia, were eliminated from the regular TAA schedule, thereby reducing the shippers' flexibility and negotiating abilities for inland transportation. This trend toward superconferences was evident on other major trade routes such as U.S.–Asia (Transpacific Westbound Rate Agreement).

Rate conferences do provide some benefits that contribute to their long-term existence. They provide a somewhat stable rate structure that fosters uniformity of rates and procedures. Further, individual shipper discrimination is reduced because any economic discrimination that is taking place is done uniformly.

The changes made by the Ocean Shipping Reform Act of 1998 may spell the end of the conference system. The new flexibility granted to ship lines and their customers may result in much rate-making activity done outside the conference environment. The new freedom to enter into contracts will also impact the conferences. (See "Stop Off: Hard Times for TACA.")

Tramp Ship Cost Rate Factors

COSTS

Tramp ships are generally not controlled by a specific route with a single commodity. Large oil tankers that are built for time charters for specific origin–destination markets are the exception. The basic tramp vessel might haul coal, grain, fertilizers, and lumber in the same year. Adaptability is necessary to minimize lost revenue possibilities that will arise. These vessels might not always be of low-cost, optimal design for any of the movements, but that is a basic trade-off to being flexible.

The economies of ship construction are critical to the tramp vessel, especially the tanker. The nontanker vessel is generally built to hold between 5,000 and 8,000 tons of cargo. This is a good range for a majority of cargo lot sizes shipped by firms. The tanker, on the other hand, is usually designed for crude oil movements, and here the large tankers can competitively move oil at costs much lower than small vessels. This is due to economies of scale in both construction and operation. In fact, many 200,000-deadweight-ton (DWT) tankers have the same number of crew members as those carrying only 40,000 DWT. Labor economies exist on new ships through the technological advances in navigation and operating systems. Whereas boiler rooms previously required a large number of personnel, many now function through computerized and automated control direct from the bridge. Navigational safety and optimum route planning are even enhanced with direct satellite links that can pinpoint ships' locations within a few hundred yards.

A major consideration of tramp owners is the nation in which the ship is registered. The nation of registry requires the shipowner to comply with specific manning, safety, and tax provisions. Panama, Liberia, Bahamas, Greece, and Malta are the leading ship registery nations.

TRAMP SHIP RATE MAKING

A tramp shipowner experiences costs, like those of the liner, that are largely fixed in nature. Ownership costs present themselves in depreciation and interest costs. Fuel is not as greatly variable with the commodity weight load, as is ship speed or at-sea versus port time. The key is that the shipowner minimizes empty nonrevenue miles and days.

Three primary forms of ship rental or chartering systems are in use. These are the voyage, time, and bareboat or demise charter. Each one is distinct. The **voyage charter** is one in which the shipowner mans, operates, and charters the vessel, similar to a taxicab for a specific voyage. Shippers seek voyage charters for primarily one-way and sometimes two-way trips. The owner is constantly seeking charters subsequent to present charters to minimize empty moves to the next charter.

The **time charter** is one in which the shipowner rents the vessel and crew to a shipper for use over a period of time that often includes use for several shipments. The owner has his or her ship productively tied up for a longer period of time than in the voyage charter, and the shipper might judiciously arrange the moves, making the time charter more economical than several voyage charters.

The **bareboat** or demise **charter** is one in which the owner usually rents the vessel for a long period of time while the chartering party supplies the crew and performs the physical operation of the vessel. In this setting, the owner is seeking to recoup capital and interest costs and to be assured that the ship will be safely operated. Ship brokers in New York and London handle most ship chartering in this area.

The market for ship chartering is a fluid supply-and-demand situation. At any one time, the charter rate situation can be one of feast or famine for shipowners. This market can fluctuate over both the short and long term. In the short run, the demand for a ship and charter rates at a single port area will depend on shipper movement needs and available ship supply within a time span as short as a month. In another way, the market can be considered glutted or tight, depending on the number of ships or types of ships that are available in the world during a span of a year.

Long-run conditions have affected the work charter market in several ways. In one context, the growth in world oil consumption dropped after the 1973 energy crisis. Much ship tonnage was still being constructed at the time that was expected to be profitably used throughout the 1970s. So the growth rate of new ship capacity coming online continued to exceed the growth rate of oil demand. Another market-depressing factor was the reopening of the Suez Canal in the mid-1970s. For several years, ships carrying oil from the Persian Gulf to Europe and North America had to travel around Africa. Once the Suez Canal reopened, a medium-sized ship could make a round trip in much less time. With the same number of ships in the market suddenly capable of making more trips per year, the world capacity of ship carriage effectively increased, which caused supply to exceed demand. A major U.S. grain sale to Russia or China had the effect of boosting charter markets in both existing grain-carrying ships and tankers that can be converted for such cargoes. This market was not very continuous during the 1970s, and, in fact, the 1980 U.S. grain embargo to Russia harmed this market until other nation sales took up some of the supply. All of these factors point to the high capital commitment and risk situation in this area of shipowners.

STOP OFF

Hard Times For TACA

The Trans-Atlantic Conference Agreement may get the rate increases it is seeking this year, but it is facing hard times on other fronts and its influence appears to be waning.

While tariff rates set by TACA influence how non-conference carriers set rates, around 80 percent of cargo in the transatlantic trade moves under confidential contracts between shippers and individual carriers. Membership in TACA has declined from 12 lines in 1997 to only seven today, and the conference, which had to remake itself in 1998 under pressure from European regulators to comply with reforms set out in the U.S. Ocean Shipping Reform Act (ORSA), is facing increased scrutiny from the European Commission.

Last November the EC, after a protracted battle, found that TACA was in compliance with European Union competition rules but at the same time opened the door for a reappraisal of its antitrust exemptions. Nicolette van der Jagt, secretary general of the European Shippers Council, said that a review of the block exemptions from competition rules could provide the impetus for new rules to prevent conferences from being used as a vehicle by which carriers collectively discuss and set rates.

The EC likely will take action on antitrust immunity soon, van der Jagt said. The Belgium-based Court of First Instance, which last year upheld a ban on price fixing in inland transport as well as European Union rulings on carrier capacity management and price-fixing practices, also will hear TACA's appeal of the nearly $275 million in fines that were levied against it in 1996 for violating competition rules.

Total removal of antitrust immunity has long been a European Shippers Council priority. "We don't think it provides any benefits to shippers or that it provides the stability it claims to provide," said van der Jagt.

In the United States, after OSRA, most conferences were replaced by discussion agreements, which permit rate guidelines to be issued by carriers. Discussion agreements are illegal in the European Union but are common among lines operating in U.S. trade lanes.

Many U.S. shippers also are hoping to see the end of conferences as rate-setting entities. "Pressures will continue from a shipper community that is always looking at ways to eliminate antitrust immunity," said Paul Bingham of Global Insights, Inc. "The EU is signaling that it will be consistent across industries and there is no reason why the maritime industry should be any different."

Bingham sees TACA as an organization in decline. "The future is not too bright for the rebuilt TACA," he said. "Whether or not they will wither quickly or sustain market share at plateau levels is not yet clear to us."

While transatlantic rates are currently favorable for shippers, other trends are less shipper-friendly. Even with private service contracts shippers are not always getting the contract lengths they prefer, and they must contend with surcharges that make up an increasingly higher percentage of freight costs. Bunker, currency, security, fuel, and war-risk surcharges are non-negotiable, making cost certainty difficult.

"We would like the surcharges to be agreed upon between carriers and shippers," said van der Jagt. "They are now addressed in conferences, which is not as transparent as we would like."

Source: David Biederman, "Hard Times for TACA," *Traffic World*, April 28, 2003, p. 20. Reprinted with permission.

GLOBAL TRANSPORTATION PROBLEMS, ISSUES, AND POLICIES

Two major policy areas are of concern in global transportation. One relates to the Federal Maritime Commission (FMC) in regulation of international waterborne rates and practices to and from the United States. The other revolves around international air transportation.

Federal Maritime Commission Regulation of U.S. Ocean Rates

OCEAN SHIPPING REFORM ACT

President Clinton signed the Ocean Shipping Reform Act into law October 14, 1998, and it became effective May 1, 1999. There are a number of significant provisions of the Ocean Shipping Reform Act. Some of them are listed below.

Rate Regulation. As with the domestic surface carriers, the new law eliminated the requirement that ocean carriers file rates and tariffs with the Federal Maritime Commission. Carriers are now required to maintain and post pricing information on the Internet or other such methods. Tariff rates must be applied without discrimination or rebates. Ocean carriers may negotiate with nonocean carriers for inland rates and services (door-to-door service). Carriers are not required to publish tariffs for exempt commodities, including assembled motor vehicles, bulk cargo, forest products, recycled metal scrap, waste paper, and paper waste.

Service Contracts. Ocean carriers now have the authority to enter confidential contracts with shippers. This also parallels the deregulation of domestic carriers. Only certain details must be released to the public. Carriers are no longer required to match service contract provisions for similarly situated shippers, the so-called "Crazy Eddie" clause.

Conference Antitrust Immunity. Antitrust immunity for ocean carrier conferences is continued, but some new restrictions have been added. A primary one is the degree to which such agreements can restrict independent rate actions by individual ocean carriers. Conferences cannot prohibit individual conference carriers from negotiating and signing service contracts.

Ocean Transportation Intermediaries. Freight forwarders and nonvessel operating common carriers (NVOCCs) will now be referred to as "ocean transportation intermediaries." They will be licensed and bonded, and it will remain unlawful for carriers to provide service to a NVOCC that is not in compliance with the FMC's regulation. An ocean transportation intermediary may not enter into service contracts as a carrier for a shipper, but it can enter into a service contract as a shipper with an ocean carrier.

The new Act has changed the traditional common carrier, tariff-based pricing to contracts, as has occurred with domestic surface carriers. Now that carriers or groups of carriers can legally enter into confidential contracts with shippers or groups of shippers, it is expected that contracting will eventually replace the old tariff-based system.

Freight forwarders and NVOCCs are becoming more significant in international distribution. These companies are moving into the role of "retailers" of ocean freight, similar to domestic intermodal service providers. However, they can be both an asset to and a competitor with ocean carriers. This new law increases regulatory control over these firms more than it does over companies who actually operate ships. Under the Act, an NVOCC shipping 10,000 TEUs (20 foot equivalent) per year must be bonded and licensed. A major exclusion deals with an "ocean carrier," which does not own or operate ships but charters space aboard another company's ships, does not have to comply with the bonding and licensing requirements, can offer confidential contracts, and has immunities from the antitrust laws.

Global Air Regulation

Matters of concern in global air carriage relate to air safety and economic regulation. No single international regulatory body covers rate and route matters in the international air area. Instead, the pattern of route and rate establishment has evolved from national policy, use of the bilateral system of operating rights as negotiated after World War II by many nations of the world, the new U.S. policy of open competition, and policies of the **International Air Transport Association (IATA)**, a long-standing international rate bureau.

SAFETY

International air safety issues are addressed by the International Civil Aviation Organization (ICAO), which is part of the United Nations. ICAO, headquartered in Montreal, is concerned with the technical and safety issues of aircraft operation. The organization has developed operating standards such as navigating practices, rules of the air, navigation charts, and communications. In addition, it is concerned with maintenance personnel and practices, meteorology, search and rescue, air accident investigation, and air traffic control. The focus of ICAO is international flying safety and is similar to the U.S. Federal Aviation Administration.

U.S. OPEN POLICY

The deregulatory shift in the U.S. rail and motor modes has spilled over into a more liberal U.S. international air policy. Many U.S. cities, other than New York, Miami, Los Angeles, and San Francisco, are originating or developing sufficient traffic volumes to warrant direct overseas air service. The Civil Aeronautics Board (CAB), and White House policy during the late 1970s and early 1980s encouraged the opening up of more U.S. cities to direct service. This coincides with a shifted national policy of seeking more competition between the airlines. As a result, the United States has awarded international routes to both U.S. and foreign carriers at cities such as Atlanta, Boston, Dallas, Denver, Minneapolis, and St. Louis. The open policy has brought direct service, which is a convenience over having to change airlines at gateway cities such as New York. Many foreign nations are slow to accept the new open policy because the policy is expected to open up other major foreign cities in exchange for gaining access to other U.S. cities.

The availability of international air carrier service is determined by bilateral agreements negotiated between nations. The bilateral agreements are based on the concept of airline freedoms or rights to provide certain types of services. The freedoms are as follows:

1. The right to fly over a foreign territory with approval.
2. The right to stop in a foreign country for fuel and repairs.
3. The right to carry passengers and cargo from an airline's home country to a foreign country.
4. The right to carry passengers and cargo from a foreign country to an airline's home country.
5. The right to carry passengers and cargo from one foreign nation to another foreign nation.
6. The right to utilize the third and fourth freedoms to carry cargo between foreign nations (the cargo is trans-shipped through the airline's home country).

These first and second freedoms are automatically granted to countries that are part of international airline conventions. The remaining freedoms are negotiated before being included in bilateral agreements. Freedom 5 is the most controversial because it allows a carrier to carry cargo or passengers from country A to country B and then from country B beyond to a third or fourth country.[2]

IATA

The IATA is a collective rate-making body of international air carriers that is based in Montreal and has traditionally functioned in ways similar to a domestic rate bureau.

Collective fare and rate making in international air carriage under the IATA has fostered a relatively stable pricing system over the past few decades. New York to London fares have usually been the same regardless of the carrier. "Competition" under this type of system is generally limited to schedule positionings and in-flight amenities. This system also protects the higher-cost carrier while providing possibly higher than normal economic profits to the low-cost carrier.

The IATA has been the subject of official government criticism under the recent deregulatory thrusts in the United States. The more liberal route award actions by the CAB in the late 1970s and early 1980s along with the White House administration tended to weaken the strength of the IATA, because these awards are often predicted upon the applicant airliners' promotional fare plans.

The future picture of international air policy is unclear. On one hand, nearly every nation of the world has a home airline operating on routes emanating from it as well as leading to prime third-flag routes. The opportunity for monopoly profits and strong one-nation influence upon a route (something more common in the past) is perhaps a diminishing phenomenon. The influence of the United States and major Western European nations in international air markets is not as great as it once was because modern equipment can be acquired by almost any airline in the world. Finally, many major nation governments are reluctant to subsidize the home nation airline deficits. These lines will then be seeking strategies for profit or positive cash flow opportunities in ways heretofore not used in their management approaches. This trend might cause the foreign governments to protect the home carrier, thereby enabling it to earn a profit. Such moves might include, but are not limited to, a strengthening of an IATA-like fare setting, and schedule and flight limitations by competing flag carriers.

Port and airport development represents large capital outlays and planning activities that are often beyond the normal capabilities of individual carriers. For these reasons, nations, states, and cities throughout the world are deeply involved in port and airport development. The vitality of a region's economic activity is closely linked with that of the capacity and efficiency of the airports and ports it uses to interface with other regions and nations.

ROLE OF PORT AUTHORITIES IN GLOBAL TRANSPORTATION

The term **port authority** applies to a state or local government that owns, operates, or otherwise provides wharf, dock, and other terminal investments at ports. In many instances, these include the major city airport as well. The primary reasons for the existence of these organizations are to allow for comprehensive planning, to provide the large physical investment base, and to provide for certain political needs within the area.

Port authorities are organized along various lines. One is local to the port or terminal. This body seeks to maximize benefits to one particular port site. An example is Oakland, California, which actively competes against and, in fact, has diverted significant amounts of traffic away from the Port of San Francisco, which is in the same bay area. Another authority organization is statewide. Maryland, Virginia, Georgia, and Louisiana are examples. Here, one agency oversees all the ports within the state. The general taxing authority of the state backs up the financing efforts of these bodies. The third major authority organizational structure is concerned with a port area across state lines. The Port Authority of New York and New Jersey covers the water area and airports in New York City, and the Delaware River Ports Authority spans Philadelphia and Camden, New Jersey.

Port authorities serve various roles. Some own all waterfront rights and rent waterside access rights to shipping companies and terminal firms. This is the case under Louisiana law, which evolved from French legal precedent in which the state controls access to the water. Some others actually develop waterways and pier terminal facilities and rent them to users (on short- and long-term bases) who do not have the scale of operations to support or perhaps do not wish to actually own such assets. This capital financing role is perhaps the major benefit provided by these port authorities. In the container boom of the 1960s and 1970s, ports acquired container-loading facilities to develop such traffic through them. These assets, in many cases, would not exist, nor would the traffic be found there today, were it not for these public investments. Port authorities also promote overall trade through their port areas. This includes industrial development efforts, the offering of favorable financing, representation before regulatory bodies, and the encouragement of adequate transportation facilities on land.

FUTURE OF GLOBAL TRANSPORTATION

Global transportation will grow in importance as more manufacturing and merchandising firms become involved in overseas sourcing and marketing. Long-standing domestic firms in many industries face competition against foreign-based manufacturers that can produce and load goods at customer docks as cheaply as the goods can be produced locally. This phenomenon is fostered by reduced trade barriers, relative currency fluctuations, and the competitiveness of ocean carriers. This exporting and importing used to be confined to the large firm; it is now a basic activity in many medium and small U.S. firms.

The cloud on the global trade horizon is nationalism. This ranges from tariff protection to political constraints and home flag carrier protection. Such nationalism tends to appear whenever a home industry is threatened by foreign competition or forces. The Jones Act in the United States, which requires domestic movements only by U.S. flag ships and domestic airlines, is one such example, though not a significant one on the world scene.[3] Be that as it may, pressures in supply-short or economically sluggish nations can tend to cause constraints that hinder international trade and transportation.

A final point on this topic relates to individual traffic and distribution managers. Most firms are becoming involved in international purchasing and marketing. The process requires different procedures than those for domestic trade. It is a discipline that is different in many ways from related domestic activities. The supply of transportation, rate making, and public policy concerns are somewhat different than counterpart domestic areas.

Summary

- Global transportation is governed by the same set of underlying economic principles as domestic forms of carriage, but its ownership patterns, processes, procedures, and government policies are different. Today companies view markets as global, rather than domestic, and the international transportation system is being called upon to move ever-increasing quantities of goods between the countries of the world.
- The United States trades with nearly all countries of the world; Canada, Japan, Mexico, the United Kingdom, and Germany are the largest U.S. trading partners.
- All modes of transportation are available for shipments from the United States to Mexico and Canada, but air and water are the dominant forms of shipments to other countries.
- Ocean carriers consist of liners, tramps, and private carriers. Liner or conference carriers offer scheduled services over fixed routes at a published rate. Tramp carriers follow the trade with no fixed schedules or rates. Private carriers are ships operated by the firm moving the goods, which are usually basic raw materials moving in large quantities.
- Air carriers offer low transit times and high rates. Four types of air carriers exist: air parcel post, express or courier service, passenger, and all cargo.
- Ancillary service companies provide numerous functions to assist the international shipper. These companies provide technical expertise, freight consolidation, vehicle booking, and other services that offer users lower cost and improved service.
- Global carrier rates are established on the basis of cost and service. Air carrier rates tend to be based on value of service, whereas ocean rates are based on cost. Line carriers publish rates via conferences; the International Air Transport Association acts as a domestic rate bureau. Both published and contract rates are available from both modes, and ship/plane chartering is available.

- The Federal Maritime Commission regulates ocean carrier rates. No federal agency regulates international air rates. Major changes in regulation have taken place under the Ocean Shipping Reform Act of 1998.
- Port authorities are state or local government agencies that own, operate, finance, or provide services at local ports and/or airports.

Key Terms

all-cargo carriers, 240
bareboat charter, 249
break-bulk, 238
class rate, 244
commodity rate, 245
consolidate, 241
container rate, 245
containers, 239
density, 244
flags of convenience, 239
general cargo rate, 244
International Air Transport Association (IATA), 251
land bridge, 241
lighter-aboard ship (LASH), 239
liners, 238
Maquiladora, 235
micro-bridge, 243
mini-bridge, 241
North American Free Trade Agreement (NAFTA), 234
nonvessel owning carriers, 241
port authority, 253
private ships, 239
RORO ship, 239
steamship conferences, 245
time charter, 248
tramp ships, 239
value of service, 244
voyage charter, 248

Study Questions

1. Describe the economic factors that indicate international transportation will become increasingly important in the future.
2. Why would a shipper select a liner ocean carrier? What are the disadvantages of using a liner carrier?
3. How has the Ocean Shipping Reform Act of 1998 impacted ocean conferences?
4. Discuss the business conditions necessary for air transportation to be an economical international carrier choice. Compare this to domestic air modal choice.
5. Discuss the advantages and disadvantages of using an international freight forwarder.
6. The use of the land, mini-, and micro-bridges has improved international water transportation. Describe these "bridges" and discuss their economic advantage.
7. Discuss the advantages and disadvantages of conference rate making.
8. Both air and water carriers establish container rates. What are the similarities and differences between air and water container rates?
9. What forms of economic regulation are imposed upon international air and water carriers by the United States?
10. Describe the role of port authorities in international transportation.

Notes

1. "Measurement of Commercial Motor Vehicle Travel Time and Delay at U.S. International Border Stations," U.S. Federal Highway Administration, 2002.
2. Toby B. Gooley, "When Air Freight and Politics Collide....," *Logistics Management*, May 1997, pp. 74–75.
3. The Jones Act, 46 U.S.C. A.

Suggested Readings

Brooks, M. R., and J. J. Button. "The Determinants of Shipping Rates: A North Atlantic Case Study," *Transport Logistics*, Vol. 2, No. 1, 1996, pp. 21–30.

Clarke, Richard L. "An Analysis of the International Ocean Conference System," *Transportation Journal*, Vol. 36, No. 4, 1997, pp. 17–29.

Clott, C. B. "Ocean Freight Intermediaries: An Analysis of Non-Vessel Operating Common Carriers (NVOCC's) and Maritime Reform," *Transportation Journal*, Vol. 40, No. 2, 2001, pp. 17–26.

Gooley, Toby B. "Will Security Tie Us In Knots?" *Logistics Management*, January 2003, pp. 26–30.

Harley, Stephen. "Transportation: The Cornerstone of Global Supply Chain Management," *Council of Logistics Management Annual Conference Proceedings*, 1996, pp. 635–641.

Maltz, Arnold B., James R. Giermanski, and David Molina. "The U.S.-Mexico Cross-border Freight Market: Prospects for Mexican Truckers," *Transportation Journal*, Vol. 36, No. 1, 1996, pp. 5–19.

Lewis, I., and David B. Vellenga. "The Ocean Shipping Reform Act of 1998," *Transportation Journal*, Vol. 39, No. 4, 2000, pp. 27–34.

Morash, Edward A., and Steven R. Clinton. "The Role of Transportation Capabilities in International Supply Chain Management," *Transportation Journal*, Vol.36, No. 3, 1997, pp. 5–17.

Oster, C. V., Jr., and J. S. Strong. "Transport Restructuring and Reform in an International Context," *Transportation Journal*, Vol. 39, No. 3, 2000, pp. 18–32.

Wood, Donald F., Anthony Barone, Paul Murphy, and Daniel L. Wardlow. *International Logistics*, New York: Chapman & Hall, 1995.

Case 8-1

Natural Footwear Company

Natural Footwear Company, located in Detroit, Michigan, is a manufacturer of specialty shoes. The company was started in 1990 by Mary Crawled, who is an avid mountain climber and hiker. In early 1985, following a fruitless search for a comfortable pair of hiking boots, Crawled designed and produced a model hiking boot that was comfortable and durable. The design was patented, and she began limited production and marketing of the Natural Hiker in 1987.

In 2000 Crawled attended an international footwear trade show in Paris. She received many positive inquiries from shoe distributors throughout Europe, and in July of 2000 she selected Barrett Brothers of Liverpool, England, to be the exclusive distributor of the Natural Hiker and other Natural Footwear products. The demand for the Natural Hiker in Europe exceeded Crawled's wildest expectations. As of January 2004 Crawled committed to producing and shipping 100 40-foot containers (FEU) per year to Barrett Brothers. The delivery requirement specified the receipt of one container on Monday and Thursday of each week, except the first 2 weeks of July.

John Vangen, traffic manager for Natural Footwear, was not experienced in international shipping. During the initial start-up period with Barrett Brothers, Vangen merely called the local international freight forwarder, described the shipment specifics, and let the freight forwarder make all the arrangements. Vangen felt that he had learned a considerable amount from the freight forwarder and decided to manage the international shipping for the new Barrett Brothers contract for 100 FEUs.

After contacting a number of liner and nonliner ocean carriers, Vangen discovered the FEU rate from Baltimore to Liverpool was $2,850 by the liner carriers and $2,668 by the nonliner carriers. The liner carriers published a biweekly departure schedule from Baltimore and a five-day sailing schedule to Liverpool. The nonline carriers promised a biweekly departure schedule but would not give Vangen a commitment as to this sailing schedule or the sailing time. The cost to transport a container to Baltimore by truck is $905 and requires 1 day.

A sales representative from Canadian Maritime learned of Vangen's shipping needs and presented a proposal to move containers from Detroit via railroad to Montreal and from Montreal to Liverpool via ship. The Canadian Maritime quoted Vangen a total cost from Detroit to Liverpool of $3,600 per container. The total transit time, including the rail move from Detroit to Montreal, is 6 days and the published departure schedule is four sailings per week.

Case Questions

1. What additional information would you require before making a decision?
2. What ocean route would you recommend John Vangen use?

Case 8-2

Ohio Plastics

Ohio Plastics (OP) is an extruder of plastic sheets of varying color and size that are sold to engraving and business promotional firms who make signs, name tags and award trophies from the plastic sheets. OP is well known in the industry for making a high-quality product and for providing quick response times for orders. In 2003 OP had 75 percent of the U.S. market for plastic engraving sheets.

During the last half of 2003 OP sales declined. Discussions with OP's major distributors and engravers revealed a softening of demand for engraved items, and the outlook for 2004 was a further reduction in sales.

To counter the U.S. market decline, OP began to sell its products in Mexico in August 2003. OP signed agreements with distributors in Mexico City, Monterrey, and Guadalajara. During the first 6 months distributors in these Mexican cities had double-digit monthly sales increases. However, during the first quarter of 2004, monthly sales increased at a slower rate.

Discussions with the Mexican distributors indicated the lead time for shipments had increased to 7 days from the 4-day norm during 2003, and the consistency of the transit time had dropped to 70 percent. This longer, less consistent lead time for shipments resulted in frequent stockouts and lost sales. Because OP did not have brand recognition in Mexico, the Mexican engravers would buy other brands from the distributors. Thus, OP incurred the lost sales while the distributors substituted other brands to meet their engraver demands.

OP initiated a study of the transportation process to Mexico, and the results are presented below.

- The sheets are picked up by CBN Trucking at OP's Ohio plant and transported to its terminal in Laredo, Texas.
- When the shipment arrives at CBN's terminal, CBN calls BCJ Forwarding and Brokerage and notifies it that a shipment has arrived.

- BCJ Forwarding will not arrange for pickup until after the shipment arrives at CBN's terminal. BCJ will not prepare the Mexican import documentation until it inspects the shipment, assures the payment of the correct Mexican import duties, and prepares the correct Mexican documentation. Mexican law places the burden for any errors in customs duties owed to the Mexican government on the broker, not the shipper or consignee.
- After being notified of the shipment arrival at CBN's terminal, BCJ prepares the Mexican import document, the *pedimento*, and files the export declaration with U.S. Customs.
- BCJ then contacts a local drayage company to pick up the trailer at CBN's terminal and transport it to the Mexican customs area. The drayage company has the required documentation for Customs clearance.
- After the shipment clears Mexican Customs, the trailer is delivered to CBN-Mexico, a subsidiary of CBN Trucking. Because the trailer contains OP orders for all three Mexican distributors, CBN-Mexico operates a drop-ship operation, stopping at each of the three distributor locations.
- CBN does not use its tractors to haul the trailer across the bridge into the Mexican Customs area because of the long time required (a tractor can make one trip per day) and the lower Mexican driver wage.

Case Questions

1. Outline the steps in OP's Mexican transportation process.
2. What changes to would you recommend to reduce overall transit time?
3. What recommendations would you make to improve the shipment transit time consistency?

Part III

Transportation Management

Chapter 9

Costing and Pricing in Transportation

The regulation of business on a comprehensive basis by federal statute was initiated in the United States in 1887 when Congress passed the original Act to Regulate Commerce. This legislation established a framework of control over interstate rail transportation.

The federal government continued intensive regulation of the modes until 1978, when air carriers were deregulated. This was followed by significant changes in motor carriers (the Motor Carrier Act of 1980) and railroads (the Staggers Act of 1980). In the 1980s, further regulatory reduction efforts continued, with buses being deregulated in 1982 and surface, domestic freight forwarders being given similar treatment in 1986. The deregulation efforts that have swept through various segments of the transportation industry in recent years have focused on issues associated with rate control.

Problems created by the partial deregulation under the preceding laws created the need for more attention from Congress. The ICC Termination Act took effect in 1996. This legislation removed virtually all motor carrier economic regulation and significantly reduced the remaining oversight of the railroad industry. The ICC was terminated, and some of its functions were referred to the newly created Surface Transportation Board (STB), part of the Department of Transportation (DOT).

With the removal of economic regulation, the marketplace prevails as to pricing. Due to the monopolistic nature of the railroad industry, some rate regulation has been retained by the STB.

The motor carrier industry is totally free to operate wherever it wants geographically and charge any rates it desires. Certain functions within the less-than-truckload (LTL) sector remain, including the classification that assigns products to a "category" based on transportation characteristics and the use of rate bureaus that publish "class rates." However, all aspects of transportation pricing are negotiable.

The use of contracts has ensured that both the carrier and the shipper have a clear understanding of each other's requirements. The material discussed in this chapter is no less relevant than in the past. If anything, it is even more important, because no federal agency is available to assist should a shipper fail to negotiate wisely.

Individuals studying transportation should understand the theoretical underpinnings of the rates and prices of transportation agencies. A key point to master at the outset is the idea that a difference exists between the terms *rate* and *price.*

In the recent past when transport regulation was at its peak, it was more appropriate to use the term *rate* than *price.* A rate is an amount that can be found in a rate tariff book, as payment to a carrier for performing a given transport service. This rate is the *lawful* charge that a carrier can impose on a given commodity movement; therefore, a rate has the full force of the law behind it for its timely payment. A rate is determined primarily by considering a carrier's costs only and not by assessing the overall market situation at that moment in time and how these market forces influence supply and demand. A discussion of cost concepts can be found in Appendix 9-A.

A price, however, is a much clearer notion of how postderegulation transportation firms determine and impose charges for their services. A price implies a value or level that is determined based on prevailing market forces. Clearly, the notion of price implies a dynamic economic environment, one that is receptive to changes in customer demand and carrier supply.

Although the transportation industry is not completely unique compared to other industries, there are enough differences to justify a thorough discussion of transportation pricing. The first part of this chapter on transport prices will explore the market structure of the transportation industry. The section on market structure will be followed by an analysis of cost-of-service pricing. This analysis will provide the basis for a discussion on value-of-service pricing. The final part of the chapter will address rate systems and pricing in transportation.

MARKET CONSIDERATIONS

Before discussing the characteristics of the transportation market, a brief review of basic market structure models is appropriate. Such a discussion will provide some insights into the unique nature of the transportation market situations.

Market Structure Models

The necessary conditions for **pure competition** are generally stated as follows:

- There are a large number of sellers.
- All sellers and buyers are of such a small size that no one can influence prices or supply.
- There is a homogeneous product or service.
- There is unrestricted entry.

The demand curve facing the individual firm is one of perfect elasticity, which means the producer can sell all output at the one market price, but none above that price. Although pure competition is not a predominant market structure, it is frequently used as a standard to judge optimal allocation of resources.

If pure competition is one type of market structure, the other extreme is a perfectly monopolistic market with only one seller of a product or service for which there is no close competitor or substitute. In such a situation, the single seller is able to set the price for the service offered and should adjust the price to its advantage, given the demand curve. To remain in this situation, the single seller must be able to restrict entry. The single seller maximizes profits by equating marginal cost and marginal revenue and might make excess profit.

A third type of market structure is **oligopoly**. Oligopoly can be defined as competition between a "few" large sellers of a relatively homogeneous product that has enough cross-elasticity of demand (substitutability) so that each seller must, in pricing decisions, take into account competitors' reactions. In other words, it is characterized by mutual interdependence among the various sellers. The individual seller is aware that in changing price, output, sales promotion activities, or the quality of the product, the reactions of competitors must be taken into account. All modes encounter some form of oligopolistic competition.

The fourth type of market structure is **monopolistic competition**. In this type of market structure there are many small sellers, but there is some differentiation of products. The number of sellers is great enough and the largest seller small enough that no one controls a significant portion of the market. No recognized interdependence of the related sellers' prices or price policies is usually present. Therefore, any seller can lower price to increase sales volume without necessarily eliciting a retaliatory reaction from competitors.

This brief description of the four basic market models is by no means complete. The interested student can obtain additional perspectives from any standard microeconomics text. For our purposes, the above discussion provides enough background to focus more closely on transportation markets.

Theory of Contestable Markets[1]

The relevant market structure faced by each mode of transportation provided the basis for arguments made by proponents of deregulation. This was especially the case with airline deregulation. For deregulation to work for a mode, its market structure must closely resemble pure competition. On the surface, it appeared that the passenger airline industry was oligopolistic and therefore would prevent the free entry of competitors. However, there was some consensus that the airline industry could perform in a competitive manner. This rationale resulted in what can be called *the theory of contestable markets,* which substitutes potential competition for the active participation of many sellers.[2]

For this theory to work, several conditions had to be met. First, barriers to entry could not exist. Such barriers could include physical barriers, informational barriers, and capital barriers.[3] Second, economies of scale could not be present. In the airline industry, this meant that operating many aircraft could not have a cost advantage over operating a single aircraft. Third, consumers had to be willing and able to switch quickly among carriers.[4] Finally, existing carriers had to be prevented from responding to new entrants' lower prices, assuming that the entrant possessed a lower cost structure than the incumbent.[5]

Although the theory of contestable markets proved to be correct in the early days of deregulation, incumbent airlines have been able to remove the potential threat of new entrants in today's operating environment, thus weakening the theory's application.[6] This conclusion points to the importance of understanding the market structures of the modes and how they will behave in a deregulated environment. It also leads to the conclusion that the passenger airline industry is indeed an oligopoly, and thus is subject to the potential abuses of this type of market.

Relevant Market Areas

A general statement classifying the market structure of the entire transportation industry cannot be made because it is necessary to view structures in particular market areas. In the railroad industry, for example, there exists a variety of different services, involving the transportation of thousands of different commodities between tens of thousands of different stations or geographic points, via a multiplicity of different routes and under various conditions of carriage.[7] The market structure in transportation must describe the situation at any one point, and even then the situation will differ between commodities. Therefore, to determine pricing in transportation, we must describe the situation between two points, for one commodity, in one shipment size, moving in one direction.[8]

For example, a particular railroad that provides service between Pittsburgh and Cincinnati might find that the movement of ordinary steel approximates what we have described as monopolistic competition. There is likely to be a large number of other carriers, especially common and contract motor carriers, that provide essentially the same service.

However, for the movement of a very large, sophisticated generator, the railroad might face an oligopolistic market on the move between Pittsburgh and Cincinnati because none of the motor carriers might be able to haul such a large piece of equipment and the railroad might be competing with only a few water carriers. It is possible that we could find some commodity where the railroad would be operating in a monopolistic position because of restrictions on operating authorities. Finally, there might even be a product for which the situation approaches pure competition. In fact, this might be true for certain steel products, given the availability of rail, motor, water, and private carrier. In summary, the relevant market situation for transportation consists of one commodity, moving between two points, in one shipment size, in one direction.

We could describe, of course, the market structure for a particular mode of transportation in one market in more detail. This is especially true with respect to the railroad industry, the water carrier industry, and the pipeline industry. We could describe a typical situation in *each* of these industries and make it fit one of the economic models described. For example, we could say that between two particular cities the water carriers are faced with oligopolistic conditions. From this, we could discuss the general pricing behavior of the industry.[9] However, there is intermodal competition present in transportation, and it is necessary to take this fact into consideration to adequately describe the market situations. Also, as we have stated, the situation varies by commodity.

The complexity of the situation does not eliminate the validity of the economic models described above. It only means that in order to make use of these models we must have knowledge of the situation that exists in the particular market. Although this might seem to be too much to expect at first, it can be accomplished. The elaborate classification system for rates (discussed later in this chapter) distorts the situation somewhat, but in our economy commodity rates are the most important in terms of total intercity ton-miles. Commodity rates are competitive on commodities between specific points. In setting prices, a carrier must have knowledge of the relevant market area. With this knowledge, it is possible to use one of the economic models described. Although there will be instances when carriers might find it expedient to generalize in adjusting prices, a much narrower focus is customary in the day-to-day negotiation and analysis of these prices.

The deregulation that has occurred in transportation in the last 26 years has made these conclusions even more appropriate. Although it is true that there has been a general increase in competition, the competition has been uneven among market areas, commodities, and shipment sizes. The new competitive environment has made carriers and shippers more sensitive to the importance of the relevant market area concept. More prices are being negotiated by shippers and carriers and are taking into account the particular demand and supply situations for the movements affected.

The important point about our analysis is that, although transportation competition has indeed become more intense in the last three or four decades, the intensity is uneven. Therefore, all four types of markets can be found in transportation markets. This makes pricing very challenging. In addition, the derived nature of transportation demand further complicates the pricing situation.

COST-OF-SERVICE PRICING[10]

There are two separate concepts in **cost-of-service pricing**: basing prices upon average cost or basing prices upon marginal cost. To give adequate treatment to both sides, let us make some simplifying assumptions and make use of diagrams. The assumptions are that the product or service is homogeneous, only one group of customers is involved, and this group of customers is responsible for all costs.

If the firm desires to maximize its profits (see Figure 9.1), it will produce quantity Q_m and charge price P_m. The firm would be making excess profits in the economic sense because the price is above average cost and the firm is not producing at a point for optimal allocation of resources. This is a monopoly situation.

FIGURE 9.1 Cost-of-Service Pricing

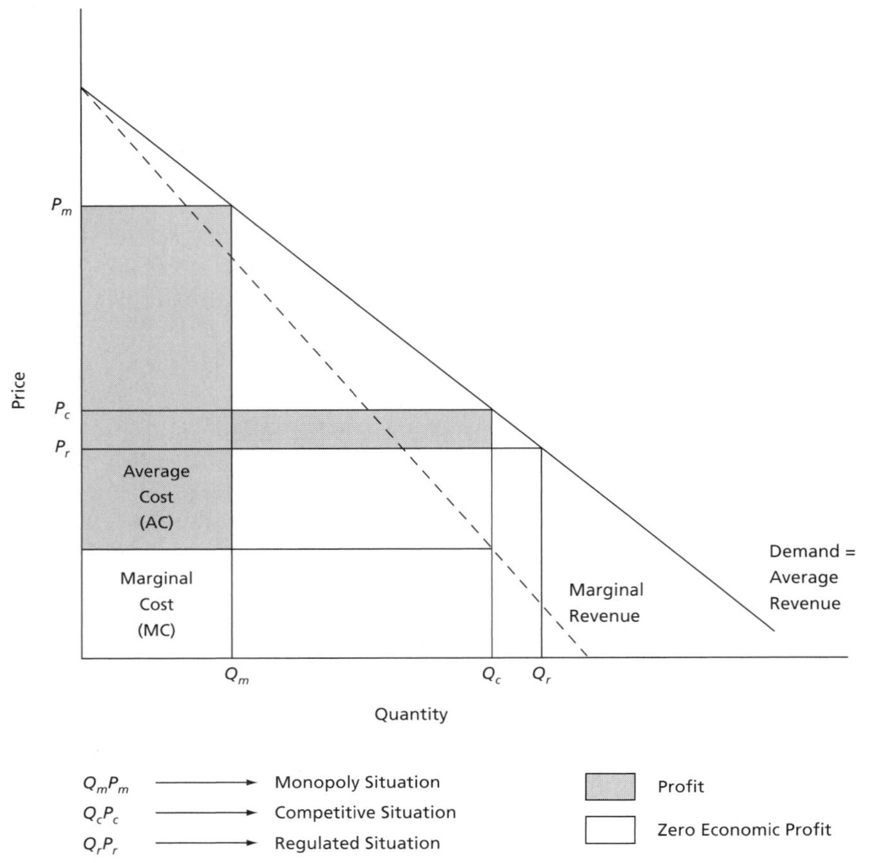

P = Profit, Q = Quantity, Q_mP_m Monopoly situation, Q_cP_c Competitive situation, Q_rP_r Regulatory situation.

Based on what might appear to be undesirable features, we might decide to impose regulation upon this firm. Now, if the "regulators" want to set a single price that would cover the firm's cost of production and at the same time sell all the output, then the price should be P_r and the output Q_r. In this instance, we would be basing the price on **average cost**. There would not be any excess profit in the economic sense, and consumers would be receiving more output at a lower price. This is the regulated situation.

It appears that the average-cost approach is more socially desirable than the unregulated, profit-maximizing approach. What are the attributes of the marginal-cost approach? If price is set at **marginal cost** equal to marginal revenue, we have a higher price (P_c) and less output (Q_c) than the average-cost approach yields. The advocates of an absolute marginal-cost approach argue that the output between Q_c and Q_r is such that the marginal cost of producing these additional units of output is greater than what buyers are willing to pay for the extra units supplied because the marginal-cost curve is above the demand curve over this range of output.[11] This is the competitive situation.

In Adam Smith's terminology, we are saying that the value in use is not as great as the cost of producing the additional output. Therefore, there are alternate uses in which the resources used to produce this additional output are valued more highly by consumers. When stated in this manner, the argument is based upon logic usually advanced under a label of "welfare economics."[12] Under the marginal-cost solution presented in Figure 9.1, there would be excess profits because price is above the average cost. However, this need not be a problem because the excess profits can be used to pay taxes.

One of the arguments frequently raised against a strict marginal-cost approach to pricing is that, under decreasing cost conditions, if the firm equates marginal cost with demand, then it will necessitate the firm's operating at a loss (see Figure 9.2). However, the advocates of a strict marginal-cost approach would still present the argument that individuals are willing to pay the marginal cost of the additional output between Q_m and Q_r and therefore it should be produced. There is one obvious solution and that is to allow the government to make up the deficit through a subsidy.[13] These subsidies could be offset by the taxes collected in the previous example. These are also additional ways to offset governmental subsidies.

Thus far in our discussion, no attempt has been made to substantiate one approach or the other. We have merely presented the arguments advanced by advocates of each approach. Before any critique can be presented of these alternate approaches, we should examine the assumptions that were made at the outset.

In regard to the assumption that only one group of customers is served, this is not the typical situation, except in very special cases among transportation companies. Likewise, costs are not usually separable according to the classes of customers, but rather, common costs are quite typical, particularly with respect to railroads. We have already mentioned that output is not homogeneous in many instances; rather, what we have are heterogeneous or multiple services. Transportation firms are not peculiar in this respect because so many firms have common costs.

FIGURE 9.2 Decreasing Cost Situation

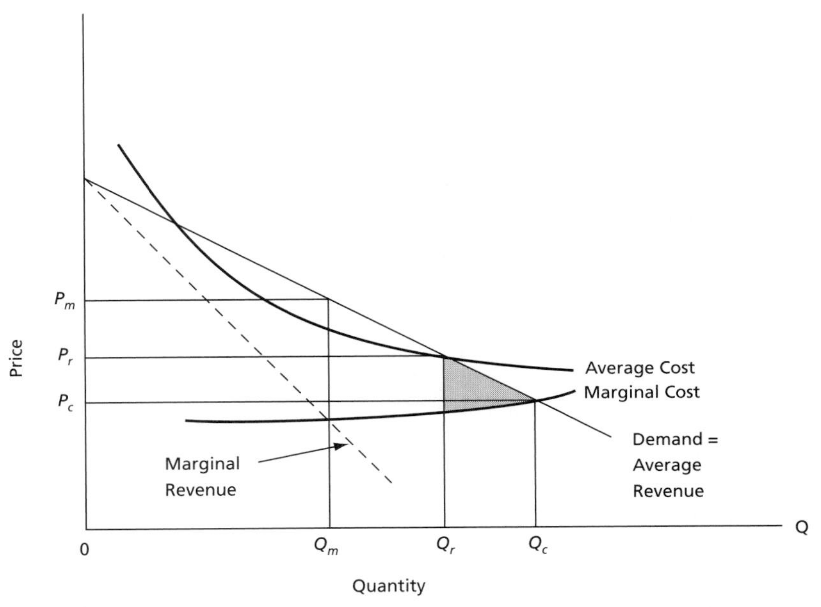

The presence of **common costs** raises some problems for cost-of-service pricing, particularly the average-cost approach. If we are to base rates upon average or fully allocated costs, it becomes necessary to apportion these costs by some arbitrary means. Average cost pricing with fixed or common costs, or both, makes these costs price-determining when they should be price-determined. In other words, fixed costs per unit depend on the volume of traffic, and the volume of traffic depends on the rate charged. To some extent then, cost is a function of the prices; the prices are not a function of the cost.[14] In fact, it could be argued that not only do costs determine prices, but that prices determine cost; in other words, the situation is analogous to the chicken and the egg argument.

The presence of common costs does not raise the same theoretical problem for marginal-cost pricing because no arbitrary allocation of these costs is technically necessary. However, we might encounter problems because marginal cost can only be determined with large blocks of output as a trainload or even a truckload. The output unit we want to price can be smaller with LTL shipments. There are some additional problems of a more practical nature, however, with respect to strict marginal-cost pricing. For example, in transportation, marginal costs could fluctuate widely, depending on the volume of traffic offered. The requirement of published rates would necessitate the averaging of these marginal costs to stabilize them, which would make them unequal with theoretical marginal costs.

We have raised some theoretical and practical problems with cost-of-service pricing. An obvious question is whether cost-of-service pricing has any relevance for establishing prices. Prices charged by transportation companies are actually one of the criteria that guide intelligent shippers in selecting the mode of transportation or carrier that is most appropriate for their shipment. When the modal choice or carrier decision is made properly, the shipper will balance the carrier's price against the carrier's service characteristics such as transit time, reliability, and loss and damage record.

For the transportation decision to be properly made, the price charged should reflect the cost of providing the service to ensure carrier and economic system efficiency. The price(s) of carriers should be related to cost, but not to some arbitrary allocation of cost.

Railroads and pipelines require large, indivisible capital inputs because of their rights-of-way, terminals, and so on. The associated high fixed costs that are common costs to most of the traffic, if averaged over the units of traffic, will have to be allocated on an arbitrary basis, which will in turn lead to unwise and uneconomical pricing decisions. Adherence to an average cost or fully allocated cost approach does not make any sense in such situations.

Cost-oriented prices should be related to what we have defined as marginal cost or variable cost. Such costs, measured as precisely as possible, should serve as the conceptual floor for individual prices. Some traffic will move if prices are above marginal or variable cost, whereas other traffic will move at prices close to marginal cost, particularly under competitive circumstances. In other words, differential pricing seems to make sense in most instances, but our rationale needs further explanation.

In the presentation of cost-of-service pricing, mention was made of **decreasing cost industries**. Some transportation firms fall into this category. If prices are based on strict marginal cost, the firm experiences a loss. A subsidy could be paid, but this is not likely to be done. Therefore, the firm has to recover its fixed costs. To accomplish this on the basis of an average-cost approach is not acceptable. However, it can be accomplished by using marginal cost as a floor for prices and using the value of service, or demand, to establish how far above this minimum the rate or price should be set.

Value-of-service pricing is sometimes defined as **charging what the traffic will bear**. In actuality, this phrase can assume two meanings. First, it can be used to mean that prices are set so that on each unit the maximum revenue is obtained regardless of the particular costs involved. That is, no service should be charged a lower price when it could bear a higher price. The second meaning, which can be more conveniently expressed in a negative form and which is germane to our discussion, is that no service should be charged a price that it will not bear when, at a lower price, the service could be purchased. This lower price will always cover the marginal cost incurred by the company in providing the service.

The differences in the elasticities of demand for the different services will determine the actual level of the prices. The presence of indivisibilities in the cost structure necessitates the dissimilar pricing. Therefore, the greater the amount of the indivisibilities in the cost structure, the greater the need for dissimilar pricing and its consequent practice of segregating services according to demand elasticity.

One final point should be treated, and that is the desirability of dissimilar pricing. Dissimilar pricing allows common and fixed costs to be spread out over large volumes of traffic. In other words, dissimilar pricing might render economical benefits because prices might be lower than they otherwise would be. It is not unusual to hear statements in the railroad industry that the prices on captive traffic subsidize competitive traffic; coal, for example, will not move unless the rates are relatively low. It could be argued that, as long as the coal rates cover more than the marginal cost of the movement, they allow the railroad to charge lower rates on other traffic.

As previously mentioned, the variable, or marginal, cost of providing the service should serve as the floor for carriers when setting prices. This is going to rely entirely on how marginal, or variable, cost is defined, as we will see in this discussion. With this mentality, a carrier will be able to recover, at least in the short run, related costs of providing a service. This relationship can be seen in Figure 9.3. In this example, a carrier's variable cost for a particular move is $90, its average cost (also called *fully allocated cost*) is $100, and its potential price is $110 (which could result in a $10 profit). This example assumes that (1) the carrier knows its costs and (2) it is able to charge a price that will result in a profit. This second assumption can be called *value-of-service pricing*, which will be discussed in the next section.

FIGURE 9.3 Cost of Service as Price Floor—Generic Example

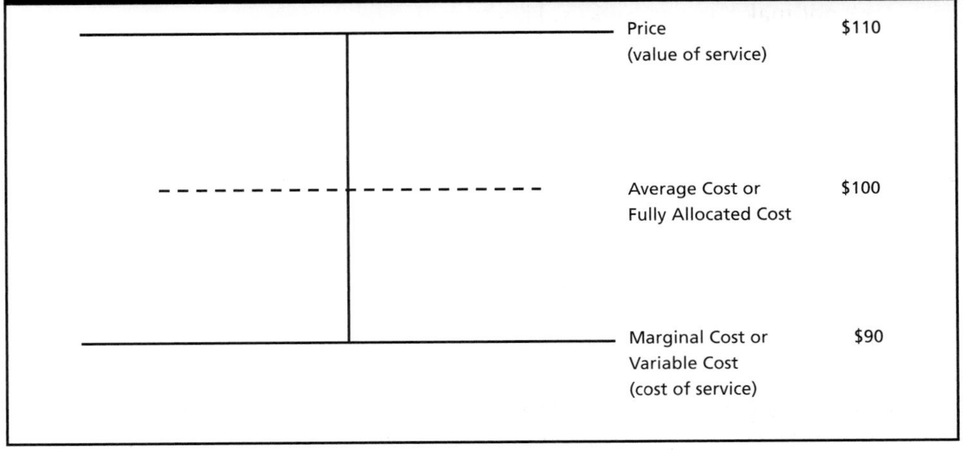

It can be said that dissimilar pricing is the logical approach for pricing in regulated industries. Cost indivisibilities necessitate the practice of discriminatory pricing, but this was approached within what might be called a cost framework. Marginal cost sets the minimum basis for prices, whereas fixed or common costs are, in effect, allocated on the basis of demand elasticity.

STOP OFF

LTL Rate Increases on Par with Last Year's GRIs

Every summer, most major national and regional less-than-truckload carriers implement a round of general rate increases (GRIs), and this year certainly is no exception.

Starting in late April and continuing through June and July, with a handful holding out until August, most LTLs are raising rates for their non-contract customers.

Most LTL carriers have raised their rates by the same amounts as they did last year—an average of 5.9 percent. A handful came in at 5.95 percent, and two carriers, Saia and Jevic Transportation, topped the list at 6.2 percent. To date, only ABF Freight System has announced an increase below 5.9 percent, coming in with 5.85 percent.

Most regional motor carrier rate bureaus also are taking action to raise their LTL class rates. The first bureau to do so was the Pacific Inland Tariff Bureau. On July 1, it boosted its rates by an average 5.98 percent. California intrastate rates, however, were hit with increases averaging 6.5 percent. The Middlewest Freight Bureau has set July 28 for an average 5.95 percent GRI. That will be followed by an average hike of 6.1 percent from SMC3 (Southern Motor Carriers), which is slated to be effective August 1.

In keeping with the trend of the past three to four years, some carriers have advanced the effective dates of their GRI's by anywhere from a few days to nearly two months.

[Below] is a partial list of LTL carriers that boosted their class rates in June, together with a comparison of this year's effective dates with last year's.

Other LTL carriers have set effective dates for July or August. Roadway Express, for example, will implement a GRI averaging 5.9 percent on July 13.

Bear in mind that the published GRIs are *average* increases. These percentages, therefore, do not apply to all rates and lanes across the board. This is the time of year when LTL carriers "tweak" their base rates, and rates on some lanes will be increasing by percentages that are higher than the average—sometimes substantially higher. To avoid surprises, you may want to check out the new rates for the major lanes you use.

Ray Bohman, a well-known consultant and author, is editor of several highly successful newsletters on transportation and is a consultant to a number of national trade associations. He is president of The Bohman Group, consultants and publishers in the freight-transportation field. His offices are located at 27 Bay Lane, Chatham, MA 02633. Phone: (508) 945-2272.

Source: *Logistics Management*, July 2003. Reprinted with permission.

Carrier	Average % Increase	2003 Effective Date	2002 Effective Date
USF Bestway	5.9%	June 2	June 24
USF Dugan	5.9%	June 2	June 24
USF Holland	5.9%	June 2	June 24
USF Reddaway	5.9%	June 2	June 24
USF Red Star	5.9%	June 2	June 24
Central Freight Lines	5.95%	June 2	June 10
Jevic Transportation	6.2%	June 2	July 29
Saia	6.2%	June 9	July 29
Overnite Transportation	5.95%	June 23	July 1
Motor Cargo Industries	5.9%	June 30	June 30
FedEx Freight	5.9%	June 30	July 22

VALUE-OF-SERVICE PRICING

Value-of-service pricing is a frequently mentioned and often criticized approach to pricing that has generally been associated with the railroad industry. Part of the problem associated with value-of-service pricing is that a number of different definitions of it are offered by various sources. Therefore, we will first develop a workable definition of the term.

One rather common definition of value-of-service pricing in transportation is pricing according to the value of the product; for example, high-valued products are assessed high prices for their movement, and low-valued commodities are assessed low prices. Evidence can be found to substantiate this definition by examining the class-rate structure of railroads.

Several points are in order here. First, even if a cost-based approach is taken to setting prices, high-valued commodities would usually be charged higher prices because they are typically more expensive to transport. There is generally more risk involved in moving high-valued commodities, and more expensive equipment is necessary. Second, the value of the commodity is a legitimate indicator of elasticity of demand; for example, high-valued commodities can usually bear higher prices because transportation cost is such a small percentage of the final selling price.

This concept can be seen in Figure 9.4. The demand curves of two different types of commodities for transportation services are shown. The high-value item has a steeply sloping demand curve implying price inelasticity. On the other hand, the low-value item has a gradual slope, implying price elasticity. To see how these elasticities relate to how a transportation firm can set prices based on product value, consider a price increase from price *P*1 to price *P*2. When the price of the transport service increases for the high-value product, a small quantity-demanded decrease is observed from quantity *Q*1 to quantity *Q*2. For the same price increase, the low-value product cannot absorb the increased price. This inability to support the added price of the service is seen as a drop in the quantity demanded from *Q*1

FIGURE 9.4 Influence of Value and Demand Elasticity on Price

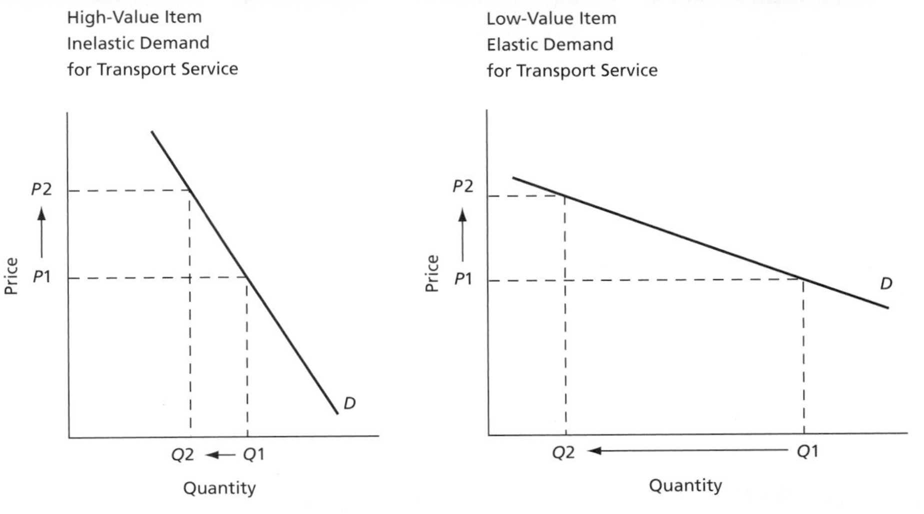

to *Q*2. Clearly the decrease in quantity demanded for the low-value product is of a larger magnitude than the decrease for the higher-value product for the same price increase.

In a situation where a carrier has a complete monopoly, to consider value-of-service pricing only in terms of the commodity's value would not lead to serious traffic losses. It would be analogous to the idea behind progressive income taxes, that is, setting prices upon the ability or willingness to pay.[15] But where alternatives are present at a lower price, shippers are not willing to pay higher prices based upon the value of the product alone. This is one of the reasons why the motor carriers were able to make serious inroads in rail traffic during their early development. They undercut the prices on high-valued commodities when the railroads were the most susceptible to competition. In essence, the value of the commodity gives some indication of demand or the ability to bear a charge, but competition also will affect the demand for the service, that is, the height and slope of the demand curve.

Value-of-service pricing also has been defined as **third-degree price discrimination** or a situation in which a seller sets two or more different market prices for two or more separate groups of buyers of essentially the same commodity or service.[16] Three necessary conditions must exist before a seller can practice third-degree price discrimination. First, the seller must be able to separate buyers into groups or submarkets according to their different elasticities of demand; this separation enables the seller to charge different prices in the various markets. The second condition is that the seller must be able to prevent the transfer of sales between the submarkets. That is, the buyer must not buy in the lower-priced market and sell in the higher-priced markets. Third, the seller must possess some degree of monopoly power.

Another name given to value-of-service pricing is **differential** pricing. Differential pricing can be done based on several methods of segregating the buyers into distinct groups. It can be done by commodity (such as coal versus computers), by time (seasonal discounts/premium rates), by place (as Figure 9.5 demonstrates), or by individual person. It should be noted, however, that discrimination based on an

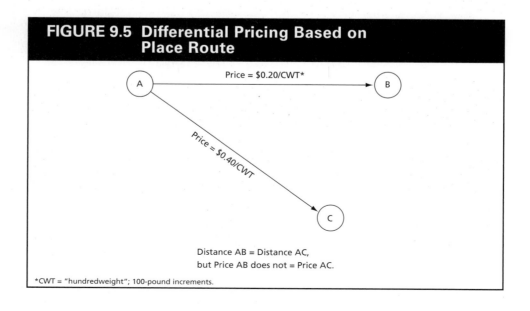

FIGURE 9.5 Differential Pricing Based on Place Route

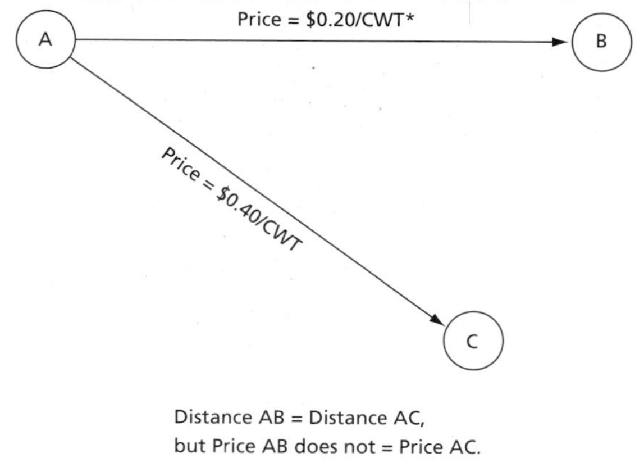

*CWT = "hundredweight"; 100-pound increments.

individual person is illegal per se on traffic that remains economically regulated by the STB.[17]

These conditions for third-degree price discrimination can be fulfilled in the transportation industry, as well as in other regulated industries such as the telephone industry. For example, in transportation shippers are separated according to commodities transported and between points of movement. The previous discussion of the relevant market area in transportation implied that there were different or separable customer-related markets—for example, one commodity between each pair of shipping points, each with a separate elasticity.

Another point that is relevant is the nature of "essentially the same commodity or service."[18] Actually, we need only recognize that many transportation companies sell multiple or heterogeneous services that are technically similar. For example, rail movements of television sets or glassware are very different in terms of time, equipment, terminal facilities, and so on.

Value-of-service, or differential pricing, makes sense from the perspective of the railroads, considering their high level of fixed costs and need to attract traffic. Remember that railroads will experience declining average costs with increases in volume. If shipments are priced properly, this could mean increased revenues from higher volumes with more profit.

The key to success lies in being able to determine the appropriate costs and to estimate demand elasticity in the various markets. This essentially means determining what the shipper is willing to pay for the service, given the competition in the market from other carriers, the demand for the product itself, and any other factors affecting demand.

Assume that a particular railroad is establishing prices on three different commodities.[19] One of the commodities is large computer systems, which has a very high value and for which there is limited substitutability. The second commodity is color television sets, which are of medium value and have some substitutes. The third commodity is coal, which is low in value and has substitutes.

Assume further that the value of a particular computer system is $200,000 and that it weighs 1 ton. If the rate charged for movement was $1,000 per ton, it would still only be one-half percent (0.005) of the value of the product. The color television might have a value of $10,000 per ton. Therefore, a rate of $1,000 between the same points would represent 10 percent of the value. Finally, the coal might be worth $50 per ton. A rate of $1,000 would represent 2,000 percent of its value. Therefore, charging a common price would discourage some shippers, particularly of low-value products.

This example is obviously simplified. However, it does point out some of the underlying logic behind value-of-service or differential pricing. In all three instances, each particular commodity is paying more than its variable cost and making a contribution to average cost, which also might be a concept of fully allocated cost.

One might argue that the coal shippers are not paying their full share and the computer shippers are paying too much. However, another argument that is frequently advanced in such instances is that, if the coal did not move (remember it is paying more than the associated variable cost), then the other traffic (computers and televisions) would have to pay an even higher price to help cover the costs of running the railroad. The same analogy applies to the supersaver fares charged by the airlines. Full-fare passengers complain sometimes that they are subsidizing discount-fare passengers. Actually, full fares might be higher if the special fares were not offered.

The essential ingredient in the value-of-service analysis is the notion that each commodity movement has its own unique demand characteristics. If the railroad placed the same price on all commodities shipped, it would discourage some shippers from moving their goods at that price. Consider what would happen if the meat counter at the local supermarket priced all the various cuts and types of meats at the same level. Obviously, it would sell the T-bone steaks quickly and have only chopped steak left.

Several points about this example need to be emphasized. First, the example is simplified. The determination of cost is a difficult task. Second, most railroads and many other carriers would be considering more than three commodities between two points. Third, the example applies to the railroad because it is more attractive in situations with high fixed costs, yet other carriers, even motor carriers, might find differential pricing attractive. Fourth, some difference would exist in rates among commodities because of cost differences; for instance, televisions cost more to handle than coal. Finally, the elasticity of demand for a particular commodity might change with competition, or because of some other factors. Therefore, high rates on higher-valued commodities have to be continually evaluated.

The three commodity examples presented here are extensions of the example presented for cost-of-service pricing, as shown in Figure 9.3. Conceptually, if cost-of-service pricing serves as the floor for carrier pricing, then value-of-service pricing can serve as the ceiling. This can be especially seen in the color television and computer examples. However, if we accept the notion that value-of-service pricing is pricing based on "what the traffic will bear," then an argument can be made that value-of-service pricing is also the floor for carrier prices, rather than the marginal cost of providing the service. This will depend on how marginal cost is defined in the context of the move.

An example might best represent this hypothesis. Assume that a truckload carrier moves a shipment from point A to point B with a variable cost of $90, an average cost of $100, and a price of $110. This relationship can be seen in Figure 9.6. This is called the carrier's **headhaul** because it is this move that initiated the original movement of the carrier's equipment and the shipper's goods. As such, the carrier might be able to use value-of-service pricing, charging $110 (profit maximization) because of commodity and competitive circumstances. With the carrier's equipment at point B, it is necessary to bring the equipment and driver back to point A. This is called a *backhaul* because it is the result of the original move (headhaul). The carrier now faces a totally different market in this backhaul lane. Assume that marginal cost in this backhaul lane is defined as the variable cost of fuel and driver wages, or $90. If the carrier decides to price based on its marginal cost of $90 (cost-of-service pricing), it is very possible that the market from point B to point A will not "bear" this price and the carrier will be forced to return empty. This will result in a loss to the carrier of $90. Now suppose that the carrier prices this backhaul in accordance with market demands at a level of $80. Although this results in a price below marginal cost, the carrier has minimized its losses by losing only $10 on the move instead of $90. Pricing in this manner can be called *loss minimization.* So it can be argued that value-of-service pricing can be used as the price ceiling (profit

FIGURE 9.6 Value of Service as Price Floor and Price Ceiling

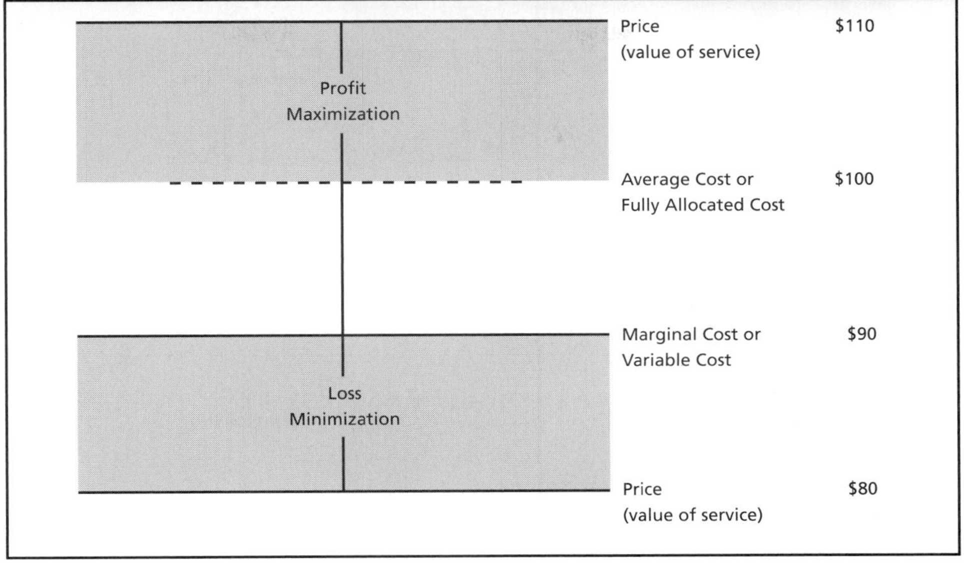

maximization) and as the price floor (loss minimization). Both situations can be seen in Figure 9.6, and both assume that the carrier knows its costs and the market environment.

Now assume that the marginal cost in this backhaul lane is defined as those costs that would be avoided if the carrier, in fact, returned empty; that is, because the vehicle and driver are going to return anyway, the $90 for fuel and wages now becomes the fixed cost, which will now be included in the average cost figure. Marginal cost now becomes the added cost of loading the shipment and the reduced fuel efficiency, which will be assumed to be $20. Figure 9.7 shows these relationships. On the headhaul, the price of $110 covers both the average cost of $100 and the marginal cost of $90. On the backhaul, the $90 is allocated as a fixed cost over the units of output to result in an average cost of $50. Now the $80 price charged covers both the average cost and marginal cost and results in a profit, just as the price produced a profit in the headhaul example. In this example, value of service provided the price ceiling and cost of service provided the price floor, as shown in Figure 9.3. The point of showing how different price floors can be justified is that prices will be set depending on how costs are defined. In Figure 9.6, backhaul variable costs were defined from an accounting perspective, that is, those costs directly related to the return move. In Figure 9.7, backhaul variable costs were defined from an economic perspective, that is, those costs that would be avoided if the carrier, in fact, returned empty. These two definitions result in two distinct perspectives on the profitability of the move for the carrier and would probably affect pricing and operations decisions of the carrier. Thus, when using costs as a base for price, care must be taken to identify the proper role and definition of those costs in the pricing decision.

FIGURE 9.7 Cost of Service as Price, Floor, and Value of Service as Price Ceiling—Headhaul/Backhaul Example

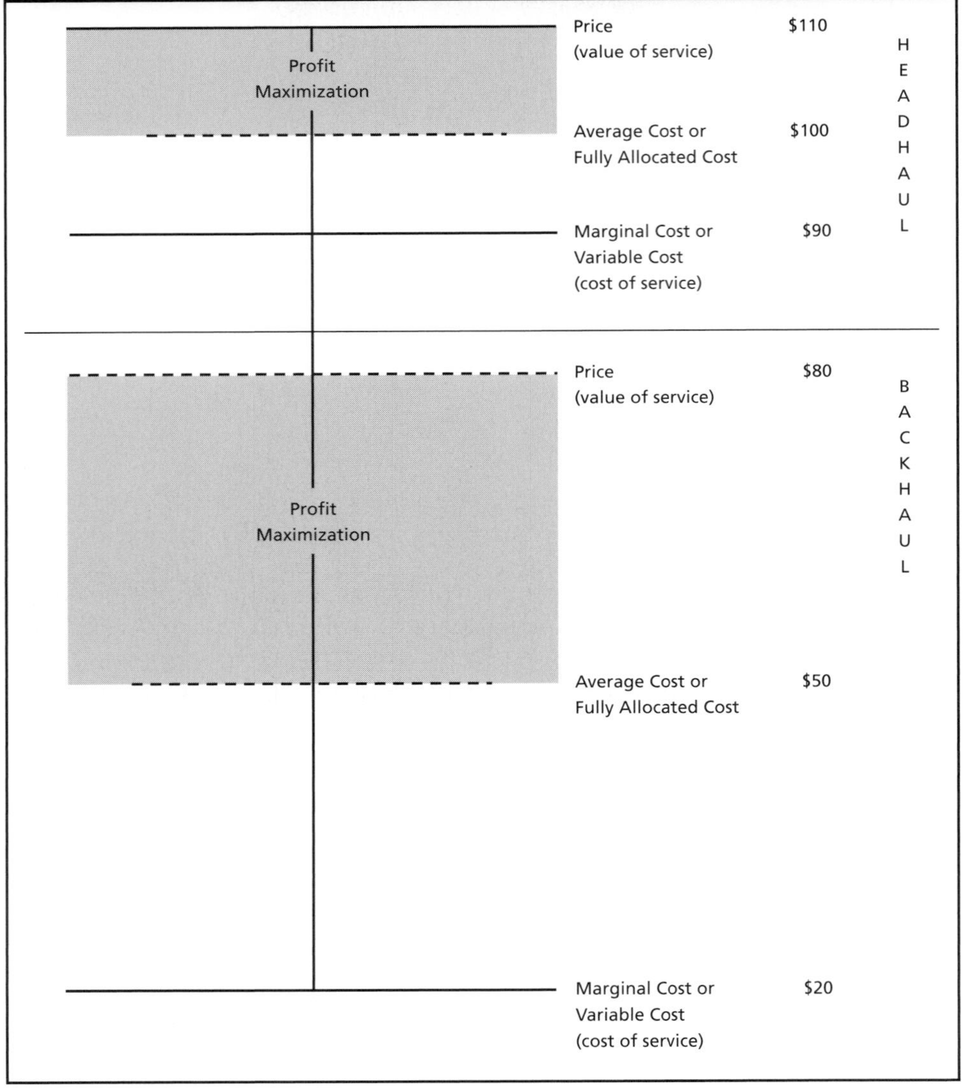

RATE MAKING IN PRACTICE

A complete understanding of carrier cost economics and behavior is a necessary prerequisite to effective management of carrier pricing. This section presents an overview of the general forms of pricing that are employed by carriers of all types. The form of each rate is discussed and analyzed, along with the primary inducements for the carrier and its users.

The overall carrier pricing function revolves around costing, rates, and tariffs. Carriers employ costing personnel who are responsible for determining the overall cost and productivity of the carrier operations as well as the specific routes, customer services, or equipment needs. The work of cost analysts should serve as a pricing input to rate personnel who are responsible for establishing specific rates and general rate levels for the carrier. Tariffs are the actual publications in which most rates are printed. Some firms print their own tariffs, which are often referred to as *individual tariffs,* or they use a rate bureau that is common to many carriers to establish and publish rates. These tariffs are referred to as *bureau tariffs.*

General Rates

These are the class, exception, and commodity rate structures in the United States. The **class rate** system provides a rate for any commodity between any two points. It is constructed from uniform distance and product systems. **Exception rates** are designed so that carriers in particular regions can depart from the product scale system for any one of many possible reasons, which will be discussed later. **Commodity rates**, on the other hand, are employed for specific origin–destination shipping patterns of specific commodities. Each one of these three systems has a particular purpose.

It would be simple if all transportation services were sold on the basis of ton-miles; that is, we would have to pay x dollars to move 1 ton, 1 mile. But, in fact, transportation services are not sold in ton-miles; they are sold for moving a specific commodity in a specific shipment size between two specific points—for example, moving 10,000 pounds of glass from Toledo to New York City. This fact gives some insight into the enormous magnitude of the transportation pricing problem. There are more than 33,000 important shipping and receiving points in the United States. Theoretically, the number of different possible routes would be all the permutations of the 33,000 points. The result is in the trillions of trillions of possible rates. In addition, it is necessary to consider the thousands and thousands of different commodities and products that might be shipped over any of these routes. There are also the different modes to consider and different companies within each mode. It also might be necessary to consider the specific supply–demand situation for each commodity over each route.

CLASS RATES

Because it is obviously impossible to quote trillions and trillions of rates, the transportation industry has taken three major steps toward simplification. Figure 9.8 summarizes this class rate simplification.

FIGURE 9.8 Class Rate Simplification

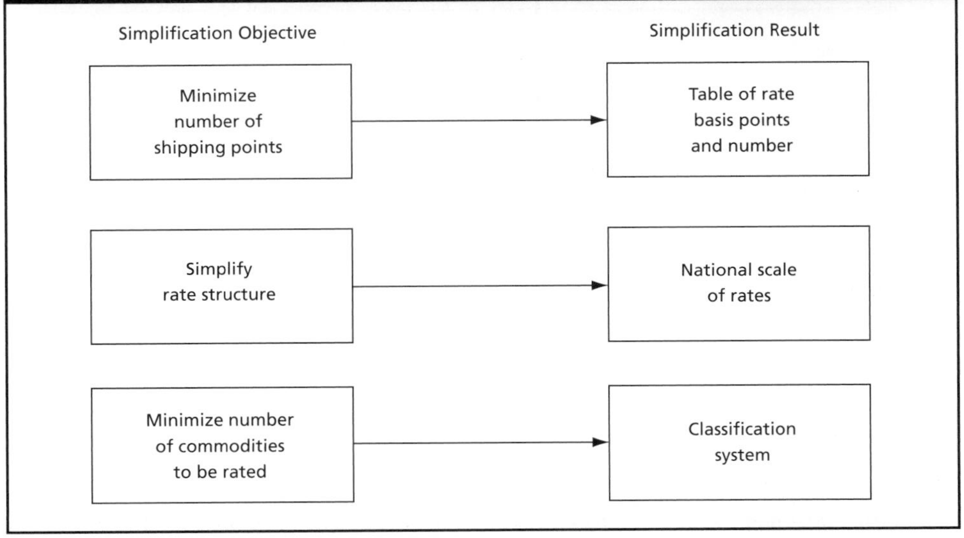

The first step consolidated the 33,000 shipping points into groups by dividing the nation into geographic squares. The most important shipping point for all other shipping points (based on tonnage) in each square serves as the **rate base point** for all other shipping points in the square. These grouped points are found in a groupings tariff. This reduces the potential number of distance variations for rate-making purposes. The distance from each base point to each other base point was determined by the railroads and placed on file with the Interstate Commerce Commission (ICC, now the STB) and published in the National Rate Basis Tariff. The distance between any two base points is referred to as the **rate basis number**. The first simplifying step reduced the number of possible origins and destinations for pricing purposes. (See Tables 9.1 and 9.2 for examples of grouping and rate basis number tariffs.)

The second step deals with the thousands and thousands of different items that might be shipped between any two base points. The railroads have established a national scale of rates that has been placed on file with the ICC (now the STB) and gives a rate in dollars per hundredweight (cwt), which is dollars per cwt for each rate basis number. (The motor carriers established a similar rate structure.) The actual rate to move a commodity considered the commodity's transportation characteristic by means of the classification, the third simplification step.

The third step simply groups together products with similar transportation characteristics so that one rating can be applied to the whole group. Now one rate is quoted for the group into which a number of different commodities have been placed, thereby reducing the number of rates quoted by the carriers. Items that are placed into class 125 will be charged 125 percent of the first-class rate found in the uniform scales of rates. This percentage number is called a *class rating,* and it is the group into which the commodity is placed for rate-making purposes. Table 9.3 is a classification example from the National Motor Freight Classification.

CLASSIFICATION FACTORS

The factors that are used to determine the rating of a specific commodity are the product characteristics that impact the carrier's costs. In particular, the ICC has ruled and the STB has maintained that four factors are to be considered: product density, storability, handling, and liability. Although no specific formulas are

Table 9.1 Groupings Tariff Example[a]

State	Point	Apply Rates From or To
Michigan	Climax	Battle Creek
	Coleman	Clare
	Comstock	Kalamazoo
	Columbiaville	Flint
	Crossvillage	Cheyboygan
Ohio	Clay Center	Toledo
	Clifford	Chillicothe
	Clement	Dayton
	Cleves	Cincinnati
	Climax	Marion

[a]Alphabetical listing of points by states from and to which rates apply.

Source: Tariff ICC CMB 575-C.

Table 9.2 Rate Basis Numbers Tariff Example

And Points Taking the Following Basing Points	Between Points Taking the Following Basing Points: Chilicothe OH	Cincinnati OH	Columbus OH	Dayton OH
	Rate Basis Numbers			
Cheboygan, MI	550	570	490	510
Clare, MI	400	420	360	380
Flint, MI	275	300	227	214

Source: Tariff ICC CMB 575-C.

Table 9.3 National Motor Freight Classification

Item	**Articles**	**Classes** LTL	TL	MW
	PLASTIC MATERIALS, OTHER THAN EXPANDED, GROUP: subject to item 156100			
156300	Sheet or Plate, NOI. Self-supporting (rigid), see Note, item 156302, other than in rolls or coils, in boxes, crates or Packages 248, 384, 930, 1029, 2187, 2207 or 2310			
Sub 1	Exceeding 9 feet, 6 inches in two dimensions or 20 feet in one dimension	85	45	30
Sub 2	Not exceeding 9 feet, 6 inches in more than one dimension nor 20 feet in one dimension	60	35	30
156500	PLASTIC OR RUBBER ARTICLES, OTHER THAN EXPANDED, GROUP: Articles consist of Plastic or Rubber Articles, other than foam, cellular, expanded or sponge articles, see Item 110, Sec. 15 and Note, item 156502, as described in items subject to this grouping.			
156600	Articles, NOI, in barrels, boxes or crates, see Note, item 156602, also in Packages 870, 1078, 1170, 1241, 1273, 1409, 1456, 2195, 2212, 2213 or 2230:			
Sub 1	LTL, having a density of, subject to Item 170:			
Sub 2	Less than one pound per cubic foot, see Note, item 156608	400		
Sub 3	One pound per cubic foot, but less than two pounds, see Note, item 156608	300		
Sub 4	Two pounds per cubic foot, but less than four pounds, see Note, item 156608	250		
Sub 5	Four pounds per cubic foot, but less than five pounds, see Note, item 156608	150		
Sub 6	Six pounds per cubic foot, but less than 12 pounds, see Note, item 156608	100		
Sub 7	12 pounds per cubic foot, but less than 15 pounds, see Note, item 156608	85		
Sub 8	15 pounds or greater per cubic foot	70		
Sub 9	TL		100	10
			70	16
			60	21
			45	30
155000	Personal effects, other than household effects or furnishings, of commissioned or enlisted personnel of the U.S. Army, Air Force, Navy, or Marine Corps, or deceased veterans, moving on government bills of lading, see Note, item 155024, in bags, traveling bags, boxes, or in army trunk lockers or navy cruise boxes or foot lockers securely locked or sealed:			
Sub 1	Each article in value in accordance with the following, see Note, item 155022:			
Sub 2	Released value not exceeding 10 cents per pounds	100	70	16
Sub 3	Released to value exceeding 10 cents per pounds, but not exceeding 20 cents per pounds	125	77½	16
Sub 4	Released to value exceeding 20 cents per pounds, but not exceeding 50 cents per pound	150	85	16
Sub 5	Released to value exceeding 50 cents per pounds, but not exceeding $2.00 per pound	200	110	16
Sub 6	Released to value exceeding $2.00 per pound, but not exceeding $5.00 per pound	300	150	16

Source: National Motor Freight Classification 100-H.

used to assign a commodity to a particular class, the four factors are considered in conjunction by a carrier classification committee. An individual carrier can establish a commodity classification that differs from the national classification; this individual carrier classification is termed an exception and takes precedence over the national classification.

Product density directly impacts the use of the carrier's vehicle and the cost per hundredweight. The higher the product density, the greater the amount of weight that can be hauled and the lower the cost per hundredweight. Conversely, the lower the product density, the lower the amount of weight that can be hauled and the higher the cost per hundredweight hauled.

As shown in Table 9.4, only 6,000 pounds of a product that has a density of 2 pounds per cubic foot can be loaded into the trailer, which means the cost per hundredweight shipped is $6.67. However, 48,000 pounds of a product with a density of 16 pounds per cubic foot can be hauled at a cost of $0.83 per hundredweight. Therefore, the higher the product density, the lower the carrier's cost per weight unit and the lower the classification rating assigned to the product.

Stowability and handling reflect the cost the carrier will incur in securing and handling the product in the vehicle. Product characteristics such as excessive weight, length, and height result in higher stowage costs for the carrier and a corresponding higher classification rating. Likewise, products that require manual handling or special handling equipment increase the carrier's costs and are given a higher rating.

The final classification factor, **liability**, considers the value of the product. When a product is damaged in transit, the common carrier is liable for the value of the product. Because higher-valued products pose a greater liability risk (potential cost), higher-valued products are classified higher than lower-valued products. In addition, products that are more susceptible to damage or are likely to damage other freight increase the potential liability cost and are placed into a higher classification rating.

In Table 9.3, the stowability and handling factors are evidenced in the classification of Item 156300. Plastic sheets or plates that exceed 9 feet, 6 inches (Sub 1) have a higher rating than the same product that does not exceed 9 feet, 6 inches (Sub 2). The density factor is embodied in the classification item 156600, Subs 1 through 8; the higher the density, the lower the rating. Finally, product liability is a primary factor in the classification of Item 155000, personal effects of military personnel; the higher the declared value of the shipment, the higher the rating.

Table 9.4 Product Density and Carrier Cost Per Hundredweight (cwt) Hauled

	Product Density		
	16 lb/ft^3	**10 lb/ft^3**	**2 lb/ft^3**
Shipment Weight (lb)[1]	48,000	30,000	6,000
Carrier Cost[2]	$400.00	$400.00	$400.00
Cost/cwt[3]	$0.83	$1.33	$6.67

[1] Shipment weight = product density × 3,000 ft^3 assumed capacity of 48-ft. trailer.
[2] Carrier cost assumed for a given distance to be the same for each shipment weight.
[3] Carrier cost/shipment weight/100.

DETERMINING A CLASS RATE

The procedure for determining a class rate for moving a specific commodity between two points is outlined in Figure 9.9. The first step is to determine the rate base points for the specific origin and destination from the groupings tariff. Next, from the rate basis number tariff, determine the rate basis number for the relevant rate basis points. The class rating for the particular commodity being shipped is found in the classification. Finally, the rate is found in the class rate tariff for the appropriate rate basis number and class rating. The shipping charge for moving a product between a specific origin and destination is determined by multiplying the class rate, which is in cents per hundredweight, by the total shipment weight in hundredweight.

As an example, we will determine the total shipping charges for moving 11,000 pounds of plastic sheets, exceeding 9 feet, 6 inches, from Crossvillage, Michigan, to Clifford, Ohio. From the groupings tariff (Table 9.1), we find that the rate basis point for Crossvillage is Cheboygan, Michigan, and that for Clifford it is Chillicothe, Ohio. Next, the rate basis numbers tariff (Table 9.2) indicates that the rate basis number for rate basis points Cheboygan and Chillicothe is 550. From the classification (Table 9.3), we find the class rating for plastic sheets (Item 156300, Sub 1) is 85. Consulting the class tariff (Table 9.5) for a rate basis number of 550 and a class rating of 85, we find the class rate is 846 cents per hundredweight for the weight group M10M (minimum of 10,000 pounds).

The computation of total shipping charges is as follows:

Shipment weight in cwt = 11,000/100 cwt
Shipping charges at class rate = \$8.46/cwt × 110 cwt = \$9.30 930.60

The term *tariff* is commonly used to mean almost any publication put out by a carrier or publishing agency that concerns itself with the pricing of services performed by the carrier. All the information needed to determine the cost of a move is in one or more tariffs.

FIGURE 9.9 Procedure for Determining a Class Rate

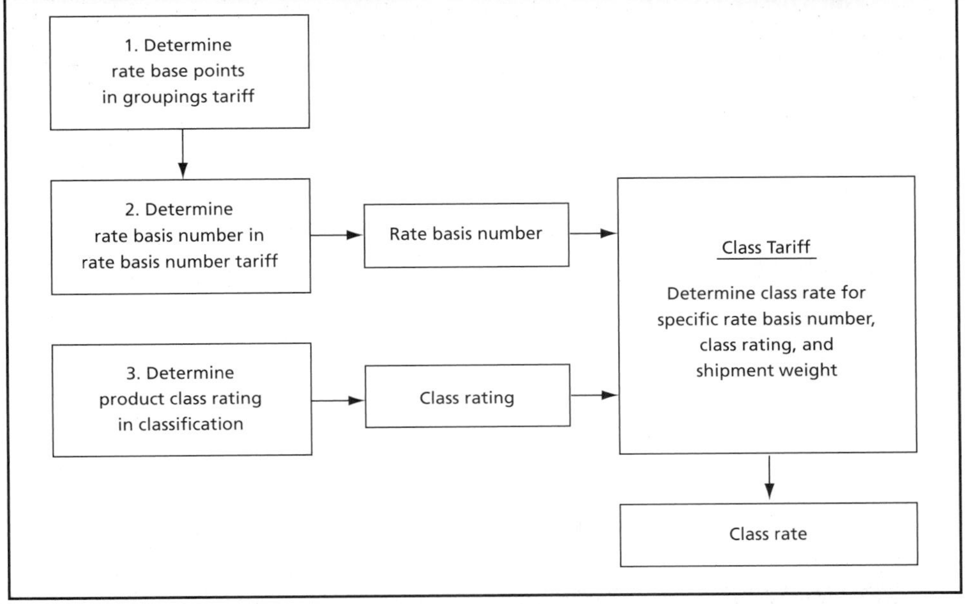

Table 9.5 Sample Class Rate Tariff

Rate Basis Number	Minimum Charge	Weight Group	Classes (cents/100 lb) 200	100	85
201 to 250		L5C	3,850	1,860	1,650
	4,500	M5C	3,105	1,500	1,325
		M1M	2,231	1,078	957
		M2M	1,825	882	781
		M5M	1,370	662	582
		M10M	1,264	611	540
		M20M	813	393	319
		M30M	650	314	255
		M40M	586	283	229
501 to 550		L5C	4,556	2,201	1,957
		M5C	3,775	1,824	1,633
	4,500	M1M	2,900	1,401	1,264
		M2M	2,488	1,202	1,092
		M5M	2,035	983	888
		M10M	1,933	934	846
		M20M	1,459	705	640
		M30M	1,292	624	572
		M40M	1,223	591	547

EXCEPTION RATES

An exception rate is a modification (change in rating, minimum weight, density groups, etc.) to the national classification instituted by an individual carrier. Exception ratings are published when the transportation characteristics of an item in a particular area differ from those of the same article in other areas. For example, large-volume movements or intensive competition in one area might require the publication of a lower exception rating; in this case the exception rating applies, rather than the classification rating. The same procedures described above apply to determining the exception rate, except now the exception rating (class) is used instead of the classification rating. There does not have to be an exception rate for every class rate.

COMMODITY RATES

A commodity rate can be constructed on a variety of bases, but the most common is a specific rate published on a specific commodity or group of related commodities between specific points and generally via specific routes in specific directions. Commodity rates are complete in themselves and are not part of the classification system. If the commodity being shipped is not specifically stated, or if the origin–destination is not specifically spelled out in the commodity rate, then the commodity rate for the particular movement is not applicable.

When the commodity rate is published, it takes precedence over the class rate or exception rate on the same article between the specific points. A sample is shown in Table 9.6. The commodity rate in the table applies only to reclaimed, dispersed, liquid, or paste rubber. In addition, the commodity is directional-specific and applies from Akron, Barberton, Ravenna, and Cleveland, Ohio, to Warren, Michigan. This commodity rate is not applicable from Warren to Akron, for example.

This type of rate is offered for those commodities that are moved regularly in large quantities. Such a pricing system, however, completely undermines the attempts to simplify transportation pricing through the class-rate structure. It has caused transportation pricing to revert to the publication of a multiplicity of rates and adds to the complexity of the pricing system.

Table 9.6 Example of Commodity Rate

Item	Commodity	From	To	Rate (cents per 100 lb.)	Minimum Weight (lb)
2315	Rubber (reclaimed, dispersed, liquid, or paste)	Akron, OH Barberton, OH Ravenna, OH Cleveland, OH	Warren, MI	726 518 496	2,000 5,000 10,000

Rate Systems Under Deregulation

General rate structures were the basis of tariffs published by rate bureaus. These rate-making bodies consisted of carriers that collectively met, established rates, published them in tariff form, and sold them on a subscription basis. Deregulation changes in both rail and motor modes have prohibited rate bureaus from discussing or voting on rates that involve only a single carrier. Similarly, joint rate making is limited to only those carriers involved in a movement and not all carriers in the bureau.

The diminished role of the rate bureau in carrier rate making has resulted in a plethora of individual carrier tariffs. In addition, the greater reliance upon the marketplace to control carrier rates has enabled the shippers to greatly increase *negotiations,* resulting in rate reductions, discounts, and contract rates. Although deregulation has somewhat diminished the use and application of the class, exception, and commodity tariff systems, various features of these tariff systems are widely used today for the pricing of small LTL freight.

The product classification feature of the former class rate system will no doubt survive for some time to come. This system of describing and classifying products simplifies the entire product description processes for all carriers. Carriers that are not even a part of the classification process often refer to these groupings to simplify their rate-making processes.

The class rate system also serves as a benchmark against which specific carrier rates and contract rates are created. Discount plans for specific shippers often are published as a percentage from the published class or exceptions-based rate.

Commodity rates published by individual carriers are similar in form to those published by the former rate bureaus. Most individual carriers publish commodity rates in a form similar to the one shown in Table 9.6.

Many innovative carriers have simplified their own class and commodity rate structures further. One way of accomplishing this is by providing shippers with small tariffs for moves from one or a few shipper points to any points within three-digit zip codes throughout the country. Thus, instead of describing more than 30,000 points in the United States, as in the rate base-point system, a maximum of 1,000 groupings is used. For a five-state region, one carrier has 85 three-digit groupings.

Many large motor carriers have computerized and/or web-based zip code tariffs. The shipper enters into the computer the three-digit zip code for the origin, destination, and class rating of the commodity being shipped. The computer program searches for the appropriate rate and determines the freight charges with any applicable discounts. These computerized zip code tariffs are simply a variation of the class rate structure, relying on the classification rating and zip codes to delineate the product being shipped and the origin and destination (rate basis points) of the shipment.

Another variation on the commodity tariff system is the **mileage rate.** The mileage rate is quoted in cents per mile and not in cents per hundredweight. For example, the shipper pays $1.25 per mile times the number of miles the shipment moves, regardless of the shipment weight, which is limited by the physical or legal operating constraints.

In summary, the innovative rate structures being used in today's deregulated environment are variations of the class and commodity rate structures. The next section discusses the special rates used by carriers.

STOP OFF

STB Will Enforce "Truth in Rates" Rules for Motor Carrier Rate Bureaus

Shippers will be the primary beneficiaries this fall when motor carriers that participate in rate bureaus will have to comply with two new requirements mandated by the Surface Transportation Board (STB).

These requirements have been a long time coming. Back in 1997, the STB began a proceeding titled "EC-MAC Motor Carriers Service Association Inc., et. al." in response to provisions of the Interstate Commerce Commission Termination Act of 1995. The purpose of that proceeding was to consider whether and under which conditions the board should continue to approve existing rate bureau agreements.

Since then, the STB has focused much of its efforts on ensuring that the rate bureaus' collective rate-setting process does not skew pricing or mislead shippers as to the rates prevailing in the market. One of the board's primary concerns about the way motor carrier rate bureaus set "class" rates is that those rates are being set at artificially high levels in order to serve as the basis for rate discounting.

To address that concern, the STB on March 21, 2003, issued two new requirements that the 11 motor carrier rate bureaus will have to include in their Section 5a antitrust immunity agreements.

The first requirement is that rate bureau members publish a "truth in rates" notice that is designed to ensure that "occasional or uninitiated shippers" are not misled into thinking that class rates are the going rates for most motor carrier traffic.

Under that rule, a bureau member that publishes or quotes—either in writing or orally—a rate that is based on or references bureau-set class rates must give the potential shipper a "truth in rates" notice that prominently discloses the range of discounts provided to shippers by bureau members.

The second requirement set conditions for member carriers' loss-of-discount provisions. The STB now will prohibit motor carriers from applying a loss-of-discount penalty for late payments that references or is linked in any way to a class rate that was collectively set by a rate bureau. The STB, furthermore, has set this requirement as a condition of rate bureau membership.

In its decision, the board said that although credit regulations adopted by the Interstate Commerce Commission and now administered by the Federal Motor Carrier Safety Administration (FMCSA) permit carriers to employ reasonable procedures to recover collection costs incurred in connection with overdue charges, they are not entitled to use those procedures for "unjust enrichment." "Bureau members are not precluded from imposing other permissible, reasonable late-payment charges under the FMCSA regulations," the new rule says. "They simply will not be allowed to peg such charges to the class rates that are the product of the collective ratemaking process."

It's still too early to tell if these new rules, particularly the "truth in rates" notice requirement, will be so distasteful as to prompt some rate bureau members to withdraw altogether from collectively setting rates.

Ray Bohman, a well-known consultant and author, is editor of several highly successful newsletters on transportation and is a consultant to a number of national trade associations. He is president of The Bohman Group, consultants and publishers in the freight-transportation field. His offices are located at 27 Bay Lane, Chatham, MA 02633. Phone: (508) 945-2272.

Source: *Logistics Management*, June 2003. Reprinted with permission.

SPECIAL RATES

A myriad of special rate forms have evolved over the years either as a result of special cost factors or to induce certain shipment patterns. In their basic form, these special rates appear as class, exception, or commodity rates.

Character-of-Shipment Rates

One set of special rates relates to the size or character of the shipment. Carriers generally have certain fixed costs for each shipment. Many rate forms have been developed that take advantage of the fact that additional units or weight in each shipment do not incur additional amounts of these fixed costs.

LTL/TL RATES

Less-than-truckload (LTL) shipments require several handlings. Each one of these handlings requires dock personnel, materials-handling equipment, terminal investment, and additional communications and tracking effort. A truckload (TL) shipment, on the other hand, is generally loaded by the shipper and moved intact to the destination, where the consignee unloads it. No intermediate handlings are required, nor does it have to be loaded or unloaded by carrier personnel. The direct movement also avoids intermediate terminals. As a result of these factors, larger TL shipments have lower rates than LTL shipments.

MULTIPLE-CAR RATES

Railroads offer volume discounts for moves of more than one carload that are shipped as a single string of cars from one point to another. The cost of moving several cars in a single shipment is proportionally less than the cost of each car moved singly. For example, the multiple-car movement of 10 cars can be handled by the same effort (empty car drop-off, pickup, intermediate and delivery efforts, and documentation) as a single-car shipment. The only basic difference is the additional weight moved in the larger string of cars. Because of this economy of movement, railroads offer such rates in coal, grain, fertilizer, chemical, and many other basic commodity moves.

INCENTIVE RATES

The term **incentive rates** generally applies to a rate designed to induce the shipper to load existing movements and equipment more fully. These special rates usually apply only to weight or units loaded over and above the normally shipped quantities. For example, suppose an appliance manufacturer typically ships in carload quantities that only fill a car to 80 percent of its actual capacity. That is, the carload rate minimum is 40,000 pounds and the car is typically loaded to 48,000 pounds, but 60,000 pounds of appliances can be physically loaded into it. The carrier would prefer to have this car more fully loaded. In an incentive rate situation, the carrier would offer a rate lower than the carload rate that would only apply to the weight above the 48,000-pound norm in this example. It is more economical for the carrier to handle more weight in existing moves than to handle additional moves. By inducing the shipper to load each car more fully, fewer cars and moves would be required over the course of a year, and the same actual volume would be shipped.

UNIT-TRAIN RATES

Unit trains are integrated movements between an origin and destination. These trains usually avoid terminals and do not require intermediate switching or handling of individual cars. In many situations, the shipper or consignee provides the car investment. The railroad experiences economies through high car utilization and reduced costs of movement because the rates are low in comparison to individual moves. Again, it is more economical to handle larger single movements than many individual moves. Rail carriers many times use this type of rate for TOFC or COFC movements.

PER-CAR AND PER-TRUCKLOAD RATES

Per-car or per-truckload rates are single-charge rates for specific origin–destination moves regardless of shipment commodity or weight. These rates also apply to container movements where the carriers' costs of movement are dominated by moving the equipment and not specifically by the weight of the shipment.

ANY-QUANTITY RATES

Any-quantity (AQ) rates provide no discount or rate break for larger movements. That is, there exists an LTL rate but no TL rate for large shipments. The AQ rates apply to any weight in a shipment. They are usually found with large, bulky commodities such as boats, suitcases, and cages where no economies are realized by the carrier for larger shipments.

DENSITY RATES

Some rates are published according to density and shipment weight, rather than by commodity or weight alone. These rates are common in air container shipments. For example, a density rate is published as, say, $10 per hundredweight for shipments up to 10 pounds per cubic foot, $9 per hundredweight for 11 to 20 pounds per cubic foot, and $8 per hundredweight for 21 pounds per cubic foot and up. These are applied when the carrier assesses rates on the basis of weight but does not experience lower costs for lighter-weight containers. Here, in fact, the carrier would experience a loss of revenue (due to a low weight) when moving a given amount of cubic footage.

A motor-carrier variation on the density rate is the linear foot rule. The generalized linear foot rule applies on shipments that weigh more than 2,000 pounds and occupy more than one linear foot of space for every 350 pounds. If the shipment meets these criteria, the carrier reconstructs the weight of the shipment based on 350 pounds times the number of linear feet of space occupied and eliminates any discounts the shipper has negotiated. Air carriers use a similar approach to handling low-density articles. All rates except household goods are exempt.

Area, Location, or Route Rates

A number of rates relate to area, location, or route. These special rates deserve consideration and discussion.

LOCAL RATES

Local rates apply to any rate between two points served by the same carrier. These rates include full-cost factors for pickup, documentation, rating, billing, and delivery.

JOINT RATES

Joint rates are single rates published from a point on one carrier's route to another carrier's destination. They are usually lower in total charges than the combination of the local rates because of through-movement economy.

PROPORTIONAL RATES

Many carriers experience a competitive disadvantage when their line is part of a through line that competes with another, more direct line. If a combination of local rates were charged, the through-movement cost might still be higher than the charges over the direct route. In this situation, the carrier might publish a proportional rate (lower than the regular local rate) that applies only to through moves to certain destination points beyond its line.

DIFFERENTIAL RATES

The term *differential rates* generally applies to a rate published by a carrier that faces a service time disadvantage compared to a faster carrier or mode. For example, water carriers often publish differential rates that are below those of railroads. In this way, the lower rate somewhat overcomes the longer transit time disadvantage inherent to the water carriers. The term *differential* is also found in situations where an extra charge is assessed for high-cost services such as branch lines. With all the recent mergers, this type of rate making has fallen from widespread use.

PER-MILE RATES

Some rail, motor, and air carriers provide rates that are based purely upon the mileage involved. This is a common practice in bulk chemical truck moves and air charter movements. Railroads also use these rates in special train movements (high, wide, and heavy). Similarly, special moves, such as the movement of circus trains and some postal moves, are based on these rates.

TERMINAL-TO-TERMINAL RATES

Terminal-to-terminal rates, often referred to as *ramp-to-ramp rates,* apply between terminal points on the carrier's lines. These rates require the shipper and consignee to perform the traditional pickup and delivery functions. Many air freight rates and some piggyback rates are found in this form.

BLANKET OR GROUP RATES

These rates apply to or from whole regions, rather than points. For example, all shippers of lumber from an area in Oregon and Washington are generally treated as having the same origin. Destinations eastward are grouped into zones in which all receivers in an entire state pay the same rates regardless of the special origin point in the Pacific Northwest. Blanket systems are found in food shipments from California and Florida. These rates equalize shippers and consignees because plant location is not a factor in determining the rate charged.

Time/Service Rate Structures

The Staggers Rail Act of 1980 specifically sanctioned rail contract rates, many of which can be classified as time/service rate structures. These rates are generally dependent on the transit time performance of the railroad in a particular service. One such contract provides for a standard rate for a transit time service norm. The shipper pays a higher rate for faster service and a lower rate for slower service. Another contract calls for additional shipper payments to the carrier for the fast return of empty backhaul shipper-leased cars. These rate forms either place incentives or penalties in areas where they tend to create desired results, or they reduce undesirable performance.

CONTRACT RATES

Contract services are commonplace in motor carriage and rail moves, as well as in water and some air moves. These services are governed by contracts negotiated between the shipper and carrier, not by generally published tariffs. Some specific contract service features that are typically found are described here.

One basic contract service feature calls for a reduced rate in exchange for a guarantee of a certain minimum tonnage to be shipped over a specified period. Another contract service feature calls for a reduced rate in exchange for the shipper tendering a certain percentage of all tonnage over to the contracting carrier. In both these instances, a penalty clause requires the shipper to pay up to the regular rate if the minimum tonnage is not shipped.

Another type of rail contract service feature calls for the rate to be higher or lower depending on the specific type of car supplied for loading and shipment, called a **car-supply charge.** The higher rates apply on cars whose contents have not been braced or blocked by the shipper; the higher charge is used to compensate the carrier for a potentially higher level of damage to the contents and ultimately to the higher liability level of the carrier. These are also the same cars that represent higher capital investment or daily per diem expense for the railroads.

A few contract service features require the shipper to pay a monthly charge to the railroad that supplies certain special equipment for the shipper's exclusive use. This charge tends to increase the shipper's use of the cars; the shipper no longer views them as free capital goods that can be used for temporary storage or loosely routed and controlled. Here the shipper firm has the incentive to use these cars in a way that benefits the firm and the carrier.

Many different rate and service configurations are found in motor carriage. These contract rates call for such services as scheduled service, special equipment movements, storage service in addition to movement, services beyond the vehicle (such as retail store shelf stocking by the driver), small package pickup and movement, bulk commodity movement, or hauling a shipper-owned trailer.

A great degree of flexibility surrounds the contracts of both rail and motor carriage. Carriers and shippers are relatively free to specifically tailor contract services to particular movements, equipment, and time-related services. The key in any contract service is to identify the service and cost factors important to each party and to construct inducements and penalties for each.

DEFERRED DELIVERY

The deferred delivery rate is common in air transportation. In general, the carrier charges a lower rate in return for the privilege of deferring the arrival time of the shipment. For example, air express companies offer a discount of 25 percent or more for second- or third-day delivery, as opposed to the standard next-day delivery. The deferred delivery rate gives the carrier operating flexibility to achieve greater vehicle utilization and lower costs.

Other Rate Structures

Several other rate forms serve particular cost or service purposes.

CORPORATE VOLUME RATES

A rate form called the corporate volume rate came into existence in 1981. It is a discounted rate for each LTL shipment that is related to the total volume of LTL shipments that a firm ships via a specific carrier from all shipping points. Generally, the more volume a shipper tenders to a particular carrier, the greater the discount.

The corporate volume rate is not widely used today, but the principle of gaining lower rates for shipping larger volumes via a carrier is the basis of many negotiated rates. The corporate volume concept brings the full market power of the shipper (total dollars spent on moving all inbound and outbound company freight) to bear on negotiations. Also, the practice of placing blocks of freight up for bid, such as all the freight moving into and out of the southeastern United States, uses the corporate volume approach to gain special rates from the accepted bidder.

DISCOUNTS

In the motor carrier industry, a discount is a common pricing practice for LTL shipments moving under class rates. The typical discount ranges from 25 to 50 percent, with some discounts as high as 60 to 65 percent, off the published class rate. The discounts might apply to specific classes of LTL traffic moving between given origins and destinations, or all LTL commodities moving between any origin and destination. For the smaller shipper that does not have the corporate volume to effectively negotiate lower rates, the discount is a viable alternative to achieving reduced rates.

LOADING ALLOWANCES

A loading (unloading) allowance is a reduced rate or discount granted to the shipper that loads LTL shipments into the carrier's vehicle. Motor carriers are required to load and unload LTL shipments and their LTL rate structures include this loading and unloading cost. The shipper/receiver that performs this function is incurring a cost that would have been incurred by the carrier. Thus, the carrier agrees to reimburse the shipper for this expense in the form of a lower rate.

AGGREGATE TENDER RATES

A reduced rate or discount is given to the shipper that tenders two or more class-rated shipments to the carrier at one time. Usually, the aggregate shipment weight must equal 5,000 pounds or some other minimum established by the carrier. By tendering two or more shipments to the carrier at one time, the shipper reduces the carrier's pickup costs by reducing the number of times the carrier goes to the shipper's facility to pick up freight. With the aggregate tender rate, the shipper reaps part of the cost-reduction benefit that the carrier realizes from the multiple shipment pickup.

FAK RATES

FAK rates, also known as *all-commodity rates or freight-all-kinds rates,* are rates expressed in cents per hundredweight or total cost per shipment. The specific commodity being shipped is not important, which means the carrier is basing the rate on the cost of service, not the value of service. The FAK rate is most valuable to shippers that ship mixed commodity shipments to a single destination, such as a grocery distributor shipping a wide variety of canned goods, paper products, and so on, to a local warehouse.

RELEASED RATES

Released rates are lower than the regular full-value rates that provide for up-to-total-value carrier compensation in the event of loss or damage. Instead, released rates only provide for carrier obligation up to certain limited dollar amounts per pound shipped. They traditionally are found in air freight, household goods, and a small number of motor- and rail-hauled commodities. The 1980 and 1995 regulatory changes allowed flexible use of this rate form in most types of service and commodities.

EMPTY-HAUL RATES

An empty-haul rate is a charge for moving empty rail or motor equipment that is owned or leased by, or assigned to, a particular shipper. The existence of this type of rate tends to induce the shipper to fully load all miles of the equipment movements.

TWO-WAY OR THREE-WAY RATES

The terms *two-way rates* and *three-way rates* apply to rates that are constructed and charged when backhaul or triangular moves can be made. The intent here is to tie a fronthaul move with what would have been another firm's backhaul move. In this way, neither firm incurs the penalty for empty backhauls. Some bulk chemical motor carriers offer these rates. They reduce total transportation charges for the shippers, and the carrier's equipment is more fully utilized than it would be otherwise.

SPOT-MARKET RATES

"Spot-market" rates can be used to facilitate the movement of the equipment or product. For example, if an excess supply of empty trailers begins to accumulate in a geographic region, spot-market rates can be quoted to allow the trailers to begin moving full back to their origin. These are similar to those types of prices used in the buying and selling of commodities on the "spot market." This is also common in air freight.

MENU PRICING

Carriers are beginning to provide more and more value-added services for shippers, such as loading/unloading, packaging, merge-in-transit, and sorting, along with traditional transportation services. Menu pricing allows the shipper to pick and choose those services the carrier should perform, and the shipper is charged accordingly. This concept is the same used in "a la carte" menus in restaurants. This type of pricing also requires the carrier to understand and know its costs of providing these services.

The regulatory standards legislated in 1980 and 1995, as well as altered administrative STB policies, have created a realm of flexibility and creativity in rate forms. Carriers are relatively free to develop rate systems to benefit them and shippers in ways that were neither common in the past, nor even existent. Any pricing system, however, should induce the buyer to buy in ways beneficial to the seller, be simple to understand and apply, and maximize the financial resources of the seller.

Many carriers have published their rate forms and structure in computerized form or on websites. Computerization of the former rate structures in the 1960s and 1970s was frustrated by the multitude of product classifications, locations, and footnote items that applied to specific movements. Tariffs of today are often greatly simplified, and computers are capable of greater memories and computational processes.

PRICING IN TRANSPORTATION MANAGEMENT

For many years, carriers relied on tariffs as their "price" lists for their services. Under traditional economic regulation, little incentive was present for carriers to differentiate themselves through either service enhancements or pricing strategies. Today, however, both of these differentiating tactics are critical to carriers in all modes, regardless of market structure. Unfortunately, however, many carriers still rely on the "tariff" mentality when setting prices as a competitive weapon. This way of thinking normally uses cost as a base and pays little or no attention to price as a part of the marketing mix. Many carriers will admit that they know their costs but do not know how to price.

This section will present a basic discussion on pricing for transportation management. Its intent is to introduce some common pricing strategies and techniques that are commonly used in such industries as retailing. Further in-depth discussions on these topics can be found in any basic marketing textbook.[20]

Factors Affecting Pricing Decisions

Many carrier pricing decisions are based on some reaction to a stimulus from the business environment. In transportation, the environment comprises many constituencies, four of which include customers (market), government, other channel members, and competition.

The discussion presented on value-of-service pricing in this chapter focused on the role of the market to determine prices. Obviously, a profit-maximizing–oriented carrier will not set a price in the long run that prohibits the movement of freight or passengers. The carrier's price will be set at the level that maximizes its return. This, however, is dependent on what the market perceives to be a reasonable price and/or what the market is forced to pay (in monopolistic situations). The concept of price elasticity also plays an important role in the market's impact on carrier prices. For example, business travelers might be willing to absorb increases in air fares in exchange for the convenience of short-notice reservations, whereas leisure travelers might not. Customers then have a formidable impact on carrier prices.

Transportation had been economically regulated by the federal government for well over 100 years because of potentially monopolistic abuses. Part of this regulation dealt with carrier prices in the forms of how they are constructed and how they are quoted. Most of the economic transportation regulation falls under the responsibility of the STB. After the deregulatory efforts of the late 1970s through the 1990s, however, the Justice Department also entered the carrier pricing arena to monitor for antitrust violations. In some respects, these government agencies help mitigate the imperfections in the marketplace to control carrier pricing. As such, governmental controls affect how carriers price their services. (Government impact on carrier pricing is discussed at length in Chapter 2, "Transportation Regulation and Public Policy.")

In the case of carriers, other **channel members** can include other carriers in the same mode and in different modes. For example, interline movements between different carriers that involve revenue splits will certainly impact how each carrier prices its services. If one carrier decides to raise its price, the other carrier either has to reduce its price or risk losing business, given that the market has a high price elasticity. This can be especially true in airline movements using two different trunkline carriers or using trunkline/commuter combinations. Another case involves interline agreements between railroads for track usage. Because there is no single transcontinental railroad, it is quite likely that a shipment will have to use the tracks of more than one railroad. If costs increase, rail carriers might have to increase their prices to customers, reduce their operating margins, or risk losing tonnage on that move.

Finally, competitors will impact carrier-pricing strategies. History has shown that even in transportation oligopolies (such as airlines and LTL motor carriers), price leaders that offer discounts to customers will find that competitors will match those discounts, even at the risk of reducing industry profits. This could be a symptom of the continual pressure on carrier customers to reduce transportation costs in their firms. Across-the-board price increases are also usually matched by all the major competitors in a particular mode. However, occasions do occur when competitors do not follow price leader actions. An attempt by one airline to simplify its pricing structure by reducing the number of special fares was not matched by its competitors. Because of this, that airline was forced to abandon its original simplification strategy and return to normal airline pricing tactics.

Carriers then must respond to changes and directions from their operating environment. Sometimes these changes might not favor the carriers, such as when government regulations force carriers to make a change that reduces efficiency. However, these environmental forces do exert pressure on carrier-pricing strategies and price levels.

Major Pricing Decisions

Every firm involved in delivering either a product or service faces major pricing decisions. These decisions can range from the very simple to the extremely complex. However, pricing decisions can be grouped into three categories. First, a carrier faces a decision when setting prices on a new service. For example, Federal Express had no precedent when setting prices on its first overnight delivery service. Such a decision could be difficult because it is based on little knowledge concerning the elasticity of the market to prices and the actual cost of providing the service. Also, if the price is set high enough to generate substantial profits, competitors will be enticed to enter the market at perhaps a lower price. On the other hand, if the price is set too low, although significant traffic might be generated, the carrier will not be maximizing its profits.

Second, a carrier must make decisions to modify prices over time. Market changes, operating changes, and service changes will require prices to be changed.

An important aspect of this decision is how and when to announce the changes to the market. For example, a major price increase by a carrier after announcing record company profits might get negative reactions in the market. In a manufacturing or retailing environment, price increases are sometimes announced in advance so customers can increase purchases to help offset the higher price. However, in transportation, services cannot be inventoried, so prior notification of a price increase does not accomplish the same objective, yet prior notification does allow for customers to seek alternative sources of supply.

Finally, carriers will make decisions initiating and responding to price changes. The concept of a "price leader" within an industry is not new. If you are the price leader, then you initiate the change; if not, then you respond to the change. In transportation, where many of the markets are oligopolistic, downward price changes can be dangerous because of their potential to decrease industry revenues. Upward price changes can make a carrier the sole high-price service provider if competition does not follow the change, so how this decision is made can have a substantial impact on market share and profits.

Although there might be other types of price decisions, these represent the major ones that carriers will make. These can be considered strategic decisions because of the importance they have on carrier market position within the industry. For example, People's Express once offered a low-price, no-frills airline service and did not expect other carriers to match the low fares. However, some of the major trunk lines actually offered fares below People's, even though it meant a loss. With a high debt and stiff competition, People's eventually went out of business. Pricing then is a major marketing decision for every carrier.

Establishing the Pricing Objective

Pricing objectives for a carrier should reflect overall company objectives and reflect, in many ways, how the carrier will compete in its markets. Pricing objectives might also change for a particular service offering as it progresses through its product life cycle. Carriers with multiple markets might also establish various pricing objectives for these markets. For example, passenger airlines have separate pricing objectives for first-class and coach markets as well as for business and leisure travelers. This section will present several different pricing objectives that can be utilized in the transportation industry.

Especially in the case of ailing passenger airlines, survival-based pricing is aimed at increasing cash flow through the use of low prices. With this price level, the carrier attempts to increase volume and also encourage the higher utilization of equipment. Because an empty airline seat cannot be inventoried and is lost at takeoff, the marginal cost of filling that seat is small. Survival pricing then tries to take advantage of the marginal cost concept. Closely related is a **unit volume pricing** objective. This attempts to utilize a carrier's existing capacity to the fullest, so the price is set to encourage the market to fill that capacity. Multiple pickup allowances in the LTL industry, space-available prices in the freight airline industry, and multiple-car prices in the railroad industry are examples of this type of pricing objective.

Another price objective is called *profit maximization,* which can occur in the short run or in the long run. Carriers using this type of pricing usually are concerned with measures such as return on investment. This type of objective also can utilize what is called a **skimming price.** A skimming price is a high price intended to attract a market that is more concerned with quality, uniqueness, or status and is insensitive to price.[21] For example, although a high-cost move, pricing for the maiden flight of the Concorde was certainly aimed at those who would be willing to pay a high price because of the limited number of seats. This strategy works if competition can be kept out of a market through high investment costs or firm loyalty.

Many times a skimming price strategy is followed by a **penetration price** strategy. This can lead to a sales-based pricing objective, which can be an effective strategy because (1) a high price can be charged until competition starts to enter; (2) a higher price can help offset initial outlays for advertising and development; (3) a high price portrays a high-quality service; (4) if price changes need to be made, it is more favorable to reduce a price than to raise it; and (5) after market saturation is achieved, a lower price can appeal to a mass market with the objective of increasing sales.[22] A sales-based pricing objective also follows the life cycle approach of using skimming during the introduction and growth stages and penetration during the maturation stage. The recent reintroduction of luxury passenger railroad service might be a good example of this type of strategy. In transportation, this strategy would more likely be successful with passenger movements because of the reliance it places on the price–value relationship.

A market share pricing objective can be used in an industry whose revenues are stagnant or declining. This objective tries to take market share from competitors through the use of lower prices. This strategy is used frequently in passenger airlines and the LTL motor carrier industries. In some cases, this strategy assumes that competitors' offerings are substitutes and that competitors are not in a position to match the lower prices; if the services were not substitutes, a lower price would not provide a competitive advantage. For example, an airline that lowers its fares for business travelers to gain more of this market but does not offer the same number of departures and arrivals as a competitor might not succeed at gaining any market share.

Finally, a social responsibility pricing objective forgoes sales and profits and puts the welfare of society and customers first.[23] For example, after the tragic incident in New York City on September 11, 2001, many carriers offered to carry such items as food, clothing, building supplies, and medical supplies into the devastated area at greatly reduced prices or for free.

Because carriers in the various transportation industries service multiple markets, it is quite possible for them to employ several pricing objectives at one time. A carrier must be careful when setting an overall company pricing strategy that these multiple pricing objectives are complementary, not conflicting.

Estimating Demand

Probably one of the most difficult tasks associated with pricing is estimating demand. In a perfectly competitive market, unit demand will decrease as price increases. This is reflected in the traditional demand-and-supply curve offered in basic economic theory. However, transportation carriers do not function in perfectly competitive markets. Demand estimation can become very tedious and difficult. However, certain concepts and procedures can be used in this process. One of these is the concept of price elasticity. Price elasticity refers to the change in demand because of a change in price. In an established market for a carrier, this relationship should be well developed to the point where demand implications from a price change should be easy to estimate. We can again use the example of business versus leisure travelers in the airline industry. Business travelers are relatively price inelastic because demand for business travel by air does not fluctuate widely with increases in price. However, leisure travelers are very price elastic and might tend to delay travel or seek travel by an alternative mode if there is an increase in air fares. In a new market, estimations of price elasticity can be made by comparing the new market with a similar existing market.

A direct attitude survey might also be used in determining demand under a new pricing structure. For example, asking customers and/or potential customers how much business they would provide at certain price levels might produce some feel of how sensitive demand is to price. Caution has to be used in this method in how this question is asked because customers will usually tend to favor the lowest price.

Finally, a market test is a possible way to determine potential demand when market testing is feasible. This might involve a carrier introducing a new service at a high price in one area and at a higher price in another area to see how sensitive demand is to price. Important in this method is choosing test market areas that resemble the entire market for which the service is applicable.

Although not a science, demand estimation is a critical part of pricing strategy. Demand estimation results in potential revenue estimation. (Some of the theory behind demand estimation was presented earlier in this chapter under the topic, "Value-of-Service Pricing.") With revenue estimated, costs should next be established.

Estimating Costs

A significant portion of this chapter is devoted to the concepts of costs and cost-of-service pricing, so a detailed explanation of either is not necessary here. However, a decision must be made as to which costs should be included in the total cost analysis. In the example given under value-of-service pricing, the fuel expense and driver wages generated on a backhaul can be considered a fixed cost and, as such, need not be included in the backhaul pricing decision.

Another cost relationship that must be examined is how costs behave at different levels of output or capacity. The existence or nonexistence of scale economies in transportation, for example, will affect how costs behave at different capacity levels. This information can be used to determine such concepts as break-even points. Regardless of the methods used, the cost of providing a service must be calculated to determine the attractiveness of a market for a carrier.

Price Levels and Price Adjustments

With demand and cost estimates generated, it is possible to set the actual price. Many methods for doing this exist, including demand-based methods, cost-based methods, profit-based methods, and competition-based methods. Lengthy discussions of these can be found in any basic marketing-text chapter on pricing.[24] However, a discussion of price adjustments might be warranted because of the federal government regulations over such concepts as rebates.

Discounts are a reduction from a published price that rewards a buyer for doing something that is beneficial for the supplier.[25] In transportation, LTL versus TL prices reflect carrier savings from larger shipments, a portion of which is passed on to the customer in the form of a lower price. This could be called a quantity discount. Airlines use a form of seasonal discounts to encourage vacation passengers to travel during carrier off-peak periods. Cash discounts, relatively new to the transportation industry, reward customers who pay their bills within a stated period of time. A common form of a cash discount is "2/10, net 30," which means that the customer can take a 2-percent discount if the bill is paid within 10 days, or else pay the full amount within 30 days. This helps speed the cash flow for carriers, which is important for their financial stability.

Geographic adjustments are common in the transportation industry. Although not directly used by carriers, geographic adjustments are used by shippers and receivers to compensate for transportation costs in the final price to the customer. One common type of geographic price is FOB origin or FOB destination pricing. In FOB origin pricing, the buyer is responsible for transportation costs; in destination pricing, the shipper is responsible (see Figure 9.10).

Uniform-delivered pricing, a form of FOB destination pricing, offers a final price to customers for a product that includes all transportation costs. Related to this is **zone pricing**, in which every customer within a certain zone pays exactly the same price for a product based on average transportation costs within the zone.

When using discounts and allowances in the transportation industry, an important rule to remember is that a discount or allowance passed on to a customer must be the result of a reduction in carrier costs because of an action by the customer. Also, the discount or allowance given to the customer may not exceed the cost savings to the carrier. Violating either of these rules of thumb exposes the carrier to the jurisdiction of the STB (rebates) and the Justice Department (antitrust and rebates).

Most Common Mistakes in Pricing

As previously mentioned, carriers have not had many years of experience in setting and managing prices on a strategic level. However, just like firms in any other industry, they are prone to certain mistakes. The first common mistake is to make pricing too reliant on costs. Although it is important to know the costs of providing a service, many other factors play a role in setting the appropriate price for a market. Competitive factors, customer preferences and values, and government regulations will affect the level at which the price will be most beneficial to the carrier.

The second common mistake is that prices are not revised frequently enough to capitalize on market changes. Under the previous regulatory environment, it was difficult for carriers to change prices because of the requirement of public notice and the burden of proof on the carrier. However, today's environment has allowed tremendous freedom and the flexibility for carriers to change prices. Unfortunately, for some carriers, the traditional mentality remains and can prevent a carrier from entering a market or, in some cases, creating a new market.

Setting the price independently of the marketing mix is a third common mistake. The **marketing mix**, also known as the "4Ps," consists of product, price, promotion, and place. A carrier's product or output is transportation; its promotion is how it creates demand or advertises itself to customers; price is what it charges for its

FIGURE 9.10 The Variety of FOB Pricing Arrangements

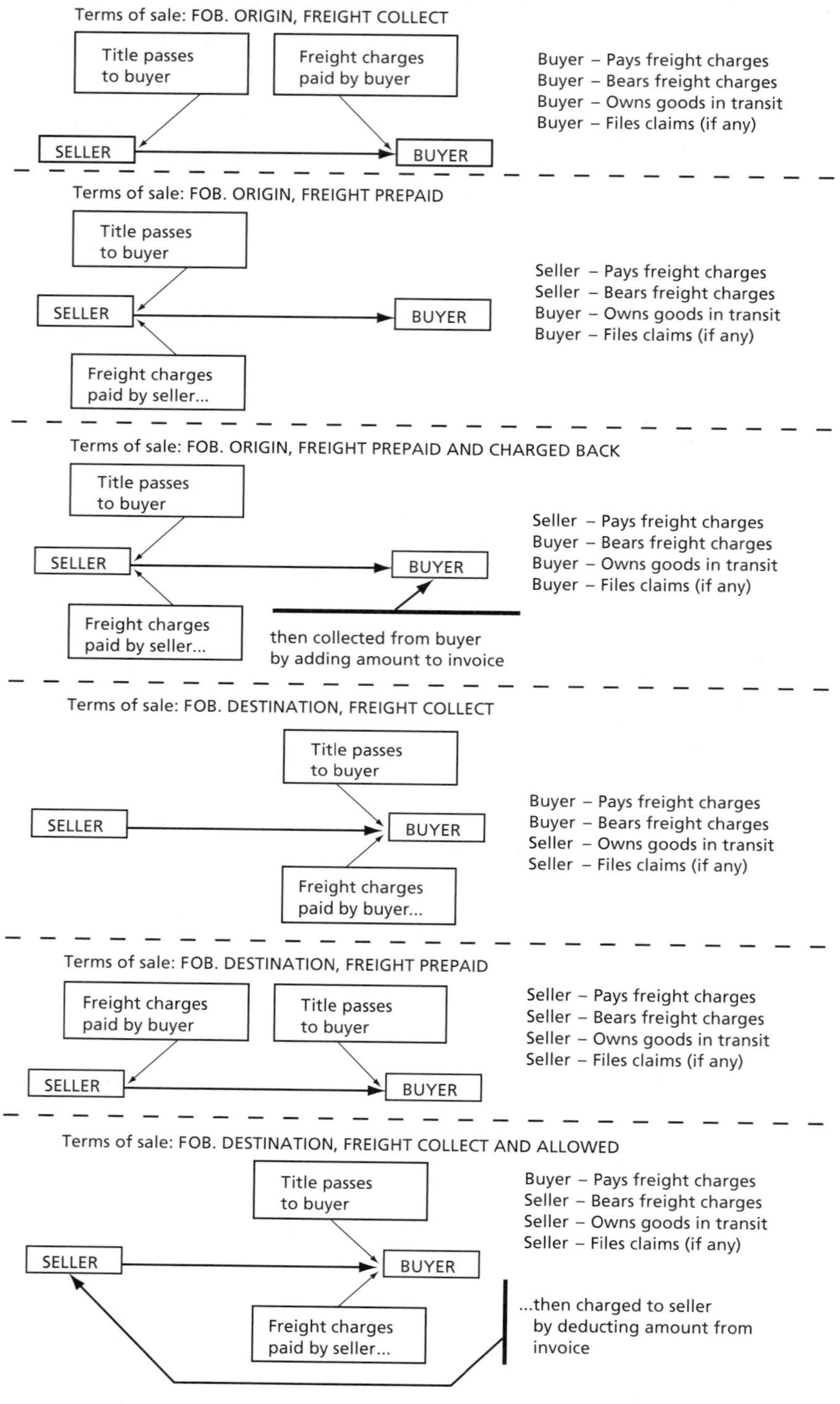

Source: Bruce J. Riggs, "The Traffic Manager in Physical Distribution Management," *Transportation & Distribution Management*, June 1968, p. 45. Penton Media Inc.

product or output; place is how it delivers its service to customers. All of these interact within a carrier's organization to provide access to and, it is hoped, success in current and potential markets. Managing one of these areas independently of the others will result in a suboptimization of the carrier's resources and its profits.

Finally, price is sometimes not varied enough for different service offerings and market segments. A "one price for all" mentality does not work in the transportation industry. As previously stated, carriers service multiple markets with differing service/price requirements. Airlines use a concept called "yield management" pricing, a form of value-of-service pricing, which relates price to the availability of capacity and the willingness of passengers to pay, or to address this situation.[26] Charging one price for all services is not going to maximize the profits for the carrier.

Pricing is a complex and challenging process that applies to all business entities. Pricing is also critical to a business's competitive advantage, position within its markets, and overall profitability. It must, however, be managed within the context of the carrier's overall strategic plan, not independently of it.

Summary

- The market structure for a carrier will be related to its cost structure; having a knowledge of this cost structure is necessary for the development of carrier prices.
- Cost-of-service pricing relies on the marginal cost of providing a service.
- Value-of-service pricing relies on the average cost of providing the service or on "what the market will bear."
- Because of the high number of possible freight rates for commodities, tariffs were constructed to simplify them into class, exception, or commodity rates.
- Various types of special rates exist that allow carriers and shippers the flexibility to tailor rate structures to meet market needs.
- Pricing in transportation can be a strategic advantage if managed within the context of corporate strategy.
- Setting and managing prices in transportation are affected by actions of government, customers, competition, and other channel members.

Key Terms

average cost, 266
car-supply charge, 288
channel members, 291
class rate, 277
commodity rate, 277
cost-of-service pricing, 265
decreasing cost industries, 268
differential, 272
charging what the traffic will bear, 269
common costs, 268
exception rate, 277
liability, 280
rate base point, 278
rate basis number, 278
stowability and handling, 280
freight-all-kinds (FAK) rates, 289
headhaul, 274
incentive rates, 285
marginal cost, 266
marketing mix, 295
mileage rate, 284
monopolistic competition, 263
oligopoly, 263
penetration price, 293
pure competition, 263
skimming price, 293
third-degree price discrimination, 272
unit-volume pricing, 293
value-of-service pricing, 269
zone pricing, 295

Study Questions

1. Compare and contrast pure competition with monopoly from a pricing perspective. If you were a shipper, which would you prefer? Which would a carrier prefer?
2. Describe an oligopolistic market structure. What alternatives to price competition exist in such markets? Why would these alternatives be important to shippers?
3. What is value-of-service pricing? Is this approach to pricing valid today?
4. What is cost-of-service pricing? What is the relationship between value-of-service pricing and cost-of-service pricing?
5. What is a released value rate and how does its use affect a shipper's transportation costs?
6. What are the major forces that affect carrier pricing strategies?
7. How might pricing strategies differ among carriers in competitive markets, oligopolistic markets, and monopolistic markets?
8. What are the various factors used in classifying commodities for tariff purposes?
9. What are the differences among class, exception, and commodity rates?
10. Why were tariffs created? Are they still useful in today's transportation environment?

Notes

1. For a more thorough discussion of contestable market theory, see W. J. Baumol, J. C. Panzar, and R. D. Willig, *Contestable Markets and the Theory of Industry Structure,* New York: Harcourt, Brace, Jovanovich, 1982.
2. Stanley E. Fawcett and Martin T. Farris, "Contestable Markets and Airline Adaptability Under Deregulation," *Transportation Journal,* Vol. 29, No. 1, 1989, pp. 12–24.
3. Ibid., p. 17.
4. Ibid., p. 14.
5. Ibid.
6. For a more detailed discussion of this conclusion, see Fawcett and Farris, op. cit.
7. Winthrop M. Daniels, *The Price of Transportation Service,* New York: Harper and Brothers, 1942, p. 1.
8. John R. Meyer, et al., *The Economics of Competition in the Transportation Industries,* Cambridge, MA: Harvard University Press, 1959, p. 205.
9. For an excellent analysis of industry pricing behavior, see Meyer, *The Economics of Competition,* pp. 203–211.
10. This section is based on the discussion in J. J. Coyle, "Cost-of-Service Pricing in Transportation," *Quarterly Review of Economics and Business,* Vol. 57, 1964, pp. 69–74.
11. Ibid., p. 27.
12. Harold Hotelling, "The General Welfare in Relation to Problems of Taxation and of Railway and Utility Rates," *Econometrics,* Vol. 6, No. 3, 1938, p. 242.
13. R. W. Harbeson, "The Cost Concept and Economic Control," *Harvard Business Review,* Vol. 17, 1939, pp. 257–263.
14. Ibid.
15. George W. Wilson, "Freight Rates and Transportation Costs," *The Business Quarterly,* Summer 1960, pp. 161–162.
16. John J. Coyle, "A Reconsideration of Value of Service Pricing," *Land Economics,* Winter 1964, pp. 193–199.
17. George W. Wilson, *Theory of Transportation Pricing,* Bloomington, IN: Indiana University, 1985, p. 160.
18. For an extended discussion, see Coyle, "A Reconsideration of Value of Service Pricing," pp. 195–198.

19. This example is adapted from Wilson and Smerk, "Rate Theory," pp. 7–10.
20. See, for example, Eric N. Berkowitz, Roger A. Kerin, Steven W. Hartley, and William Rudelius, *Marketing*, 3rd ed., Homewood, IL: Richard D. Irwin, 1992.
21. Joel R. Evans and Barry Berman, *Marketing*, New York: Macmillan, 1982, p. 532.
22. Ibid.
23. Berkowitz, et. al., op. cit., p. 321.
24. Berkowitz, et. al., op. cit., pp. 339–352.
25. Ibid., p. 354.
26. For a discussion of yield management pricing, see Sheryl Kimes, "The Basics of Yield Management," *The Cornell H.R.A. Quarterly*, November 1989, pp. 14–19; Walter J. Relihan III, "The Yield Management Approach to Hotel Room Pricing," *The Cornell H.R.A. Quarterly*, May 1989, pp. 40–45; Peter P. Belobaba, "Application of a Probabilistic Decision Model to Airline Seat Inventory Control," *Operations Research*, Vol. 37, No. 2, 1989.

Suggested Readings

Bohman, Ray. "Check Carrier's Tariffs for Extra P&D Charges," *Logistics Management*, August 2003, p. 33.

Cooper, Robin, and Robert S. Kaplan. "Profit Priorities from Activity-Based Costing," *Harvard Business Review*, May–June 1992, pp. 130–135.

Coyle, John J., Edward J. Bardi, and C. John Langley. *The Management of Business Logistics*, 7th ed., Cincinnati, OH: Southwestern, 2003.

Harmatuck, Donald J. "Motor Cost Function Comparisons," *Transportation Journal*, Vol. 31, No. 4, 1992, pp. 31–46.

Kahn, Alfred E. *The Economics of Regulation: Principles and Institutions*, Vol. 1, New York: John Wiley and Sons, 1970, Part 3.

Kortge, G. Dean, and Patrick A. Okonkwo. "Perceived Value Approach to Pricing," *Industrial Marketing Management*, Vol. 22, 1993, pp. 133–140.

Locklin, D. Philip. *Economics of Transportation*, 7th ed., Homewood, IL: Richard D. Irwin, 1972, Chapters 3, 7, and 8.

Malone, Robert. "Cutting Costs on Urgent Shipments," *Inbound Logistics*, August 2003, pp. 18–20.

Nelson, James R., ed. *Criteria for Transport Pricing*, Cambridge, MD: Cornell Maritime Press, 1973.

Pegrum, Dudley F. *Transportation: Economics and Public Policy*, Homewood, IL: Richard D. Irwin, 1973, Chapters 7–10.

Schultz, John D. "Yield Management Rate Strategies May Boost Truckers' Ailing Fortunes," *Traffic World*, October 7, 1991, pp. 33–34.

Shanahan, John. "Demystifying LTL Pricing," *Logistics Management*, October 2003, pp. 31–36.

Simon, Hermann. "Pricing Opportunities—and How to Exploit Them," *Sloan Management Review*, Winter 1992, pp. 55–65.

Taylor, Mark A. "12 Ideas to Lower Shipping Costs," *Parcel Shipping and Distribution*, July-August, 2003, pp. 38–39.

Case 9-1

Hardee Transportation

Jim O'Brien has realized for quite some time that some of his customers are more profitable than others. This is also quite true for certain freight lanes. However, Hardee has traditionally structured its prices around discounts on their published tariff rates. Most of the discount has been based on freight volume only. Jim knows that his drivers and dock people do more for certain customers than move volume; they count freight during loading, sort and segregate freight on the dock, weigh shipments, and do some labeling.

Jim foresees some of the new service demands from his customers being very difficult to cost and price because they won't necessarily be based on freight volume. Some of these new demands will include merge-in-transit, event management, continuous shipment tracking, RFID capability, and dedicated customer service personnel. Traditionally, Hardee has used average cost pricing for its major customers. Some of his pricing supervisors have strongly urged Jim to consider marginal cost pricing. However, Jim has developed a keen interest in value-of-service pricing methods versus the traditional cost-of-service pricing.

The problem with both approaches for Hardee is that they have no form of activity-based costing or any other methodology that will allow them to really get a handle on where there costs are hidden. Jim knows what Hardee pays its drivers, knows the costs of equipment and fuel, and knows the overall costs of dispatch and dock operations. Hardee's average length of haul is 950 miles and its loaded mile metric is 67 percent.

Case Questions

1. Using the information in this chapter, how would you advise Jim to proceed on his costing journey?
2. What strategies would you suggest he use in pricing existing and evolving service operations?

Case 9-2

Hardee Transportation

One of Jim O'Brien's customers presented him with an opportunity for a significant amount of freight moving into a new market for Hardee. Hardee is a truckload carrier primarily moving freight in the East/West market in the United States. Although it has some movements in and out of Canada and Mexico, Hardee has focused on moving freight between the two U.S. coasts. Hardee has dispatch centers located throughout the United States that have some dock capacity.

The new move would be one between Pittsburgh and Miami. Hardee has avoided this market because of the lack of backhaul opportunities that exist outbound from Florida. However, this new move offered a significant increase in volume for Hardee. A complicating factor in this move is the request that Hardee perform sorting and segregation at its dispatch centers. Each shipment will consist of straight pallet-loads of various types of consumer goods freight destined for a retailer's distribution center in Miami. Sorting and segregation at Hardee's locations would consist of breaking the pallets and sorting the freight by the retailer's store locations, then repalletizing into rainbow pallets for each store.

Hardee has never experienced this type of request before. Jim knew that he needed to put some type of costs to this move to make sure that the moves are profitable. Because of the large volume involved, not covering Hardee's costs in its pricing could result in large losses for Hardee.

The relevant information for costing this move is as follows:

Equipment Cost Data

Equipment Purchase Price

1. Line-haul tractors = $40,000
2. Line-haul trailers = $20,000

Depreciation

1. Tractors = 5-year straight line
2. Trailers = 10-year straight line

Interest

1. Tractors = 10% APR for 5 years
2. Trailers = 10% for 10 years

Fuel

1. $1.50 per gallon for diesel
2. Line-haul tractors = 6 miles per gallon

Labor

1. Line-haul drivers = $0.40 per mile
2. Pickup and delivery (PUD) operation drivers = $30 (fully loaded) per hour
3. Dock workers = $25 (fully loaded) per hour

Miscellaneous

1. Insurance cost = $0.05 per mile
2. Maintenance cost = $0.15 per mile
3. Billing cost = $5.00 per freight bill
4. Tractors and trailers are available for use 20 hours per day (80% uptime), 365 days per year
5. Administrative/overhead cost = 8% of total cost of move
6. Dock facility cost = $15.00 per hour
7. Line-haul vehicles average 45 mph between origin and destination

Route and Time of Move

The shipment (40,000 lb) originates at a customer location in Pittsburgh, located 20 miles from Hardee's dispatch center. A PUD operations driver is dispatched from the Hardee location at 8:30 a.m. on Monday, January 12, 2004, and arrives at destination at 9:00 a.m. The shipment is loaded from 9:00 a.m. to 12:00 p.m. The PUD operations driver departs the customer location at 12:00 p.m. and arrives back at the Hardee dispatch center at 12:30 p.m.

The sort process starts at 12:30 p.m. and ends at 8:30 p.m. It requires unloading the trailer, sorting, and repalletizing the load. This operation requires two dock workers, each working 4 hours on the load, for a total of 8 hours in the dispatch center.

The line-haul portion begins with the vehicle being dispatched from the Pittsburgh location at 8:30 p.m. on Monday and traveling to Charlotte, North Carolina, a distance of 481 miles, and arriving at Charlotte at 7:12 a.m. on Tuesday, January 13. The driver rests from 7:12 a.m. until 5:12 p.m. The trip continues with the vehicle departing Charlotte at 5:12 p.m. on Tuesday and traveling to Jacksonville, Florida, a distance of 399 miles, and arriving at Jacksonville at 2:06 a.m. on Wednesday, January 14. The driver rests from 2:06 a.m. until 12:06 p.m. The line-haul portion concludes with the vehicle departing Jacksonville at 12:06 a.m. and traveling to the customer's location in Miami, a distance of 369 miles, and arriving at the DC at 8:18 p.m. on Wednesday.

The line-haul drivers stays with the vehicle while it is being unloaded (2 hours unload time). The driver then deadheads at 10:18 p.m. from the customer's DC and arrives at a Hardee dispatch center located in Miami at 10:48 p.m., a distance of 15 miles from the DC.

Case Questions

1. What are the pickup, sort, line-haul, and delivery costs to Hardee for this move?
2. What is the total cost of this move? Cost per cwt? Cost per revenue mile?
3. What if Hardee put two drivers in the vehicle for the trip? What would happen to total costs?
4. How would you account for the empty backhaul costs associated with this move? Would you include those in this move? How would impact your pricing strategy?

Case 9-3

Startruck, Inc.

Startruck, Inc., is a small parcel trucking firm specializing in overnight deliveries of small parcels and documents. The evolution of the Internet has significantly impacted the volume of overnight document business that Startruck handles. Because of this shrinking market, Startruck decided to focus its efforts on building its small parcel business. However, Startruck's president, John T. Work, knew that to leapfrog the competition in the industry would require a significant technological breakthrough. His chief scientist, Mr. Shock, was able to provide that breakthrough in the form of a transporter device that could instantly transport freight and small parcels by disassembling their molecules, transporting them through space, and reassembling them at destination. This technology would eliminate the need for transportation vehicles and could provide immediate transportation for freight and small parcels. It was, in effect, an Internet technology for packages. In fact, shippers and receivers would only require an investment in what could be called a "transporter bay" to use this technology.

The key to this technology was imbedded in a special computer chip that was invented by Mr. Shock. Both he and Mr. Work realized that it would not be long before competitors were able to copy this chip and expand on it. In fact, a major competitor, Hang-On Shipping, was working on technology that could also transport people through space. Work and Shock realized that they, too, would soon have that technology but felt it important to quickly boost market share in small packages before getting into a new line of business.

Scotty, Startruck's chief of marketing, was asked by Mr. Work to devise a marketing plan to introduce this new service and technology. Because of the reduced investment in transportation equipment needed by Startruck and the significant improvement in speed of transportation, Scotty felt that the pricing strategy used by Startruck for this new service would be critical to its success in the marketplace.

Case Questions

1. What should Startruck's pricing objective be for this new service?
2. How will Startruck estimate demand for this service? Where will the market(s) be?
3. Which costs will be incurred by Startruck in offering this service?
4. Should any type of price adjustments be included in Startruck's pricing strategy for this service?

Appendix 9-A

Cost Concepts

Accounting Cost

The simplest concept or measure of cost is what has sometimes been labeled accounting cost, or even more simply as money cost. These are the so-called bookkeeping costs of a company and include all cash outlays of the firm. This particular concept of cost is not difficult to grasp. The most difficult problem with accounting costs is their allocation among the various products or services of a company.

If the owner of a motor carrier, for example, were interested in determining the cost associated with moving a particular truckload of traffic, we could quickly arrive at all the cost of fuel, oil, and the driver's wages associated with the movement. It might also be possible to determine how much wear and tear would occur on the vehicle during the trip. However, we must also consider how much of the president's salary, the terminal expenses, and the advertising expense should be included in the price. These costs should be included in part, but how much should be included is frequently a perplexing question. Our computation becomes even more complex when a small shipment is combined with other small shipments in one truckload.

Some allocation would then be necessary for the fuel expense and the driver's wages.

Economic Cost

A second concept of cost is economic cost, which is different from accounting cost. The economic definition of cost is associated with the alternative cost doctrine or the opportunity cost doctrine. Costs of production, as defined by economists, are futuristic and are the values of the alternative products that could have been produced with the resources used in production.

Therefore, the costs of resources are their values in their best alternative uses. To secure the service or use of resources, such as labor or capital, a company must pay an amount at least equal to what the resource could obtain in its best alternative use. Implicit in this definition of cost is the principle that if a resource has no alternative use, then its cost in economic terms is zero.

The futuristic aspect of economic costs has special relevance in transportation because, once investment has been made, one should not be concerned with recovering what is sometimes referred to as **sunk costs**.[1] Resources in some industries are so durable that they can be regarded as virtually everlasting. Therefore, if no replacement is anticipated, and there is no alternative use, then the use of the resource is costless in an economic sense. This is of special importance in the railroad industry.

Railroads have long been regarded as having durable and therefore costless resources. That is, some of the resources of railroads, such as concrete ties, some signaling equipment, and even some rolling stock, are so durable and so highly specialized that they have no alternative production or use potential. So the use of such resources, apart from maintenance, is costless in an economic sense. Consequently, in a competitive pricing situation, such resources could be excluded from the calculation of fixed costs. Also, such specialized resources can be eliminated in comparing cost structures.[2]

Although the economic logic of the above argument on the use of durable, specialized resources is impeccable, it is frequently disregarded by pricing analysts and regulators. In a sense, the elimination of such costs from pricing calculations defies common sense. From the money or accounting cost perspective, these costs usually should be included.

The conclusion that must be drawn is that economic costs differ from money or accounting costs. Money costs are by their very nature a measure of past costs. This does not mean that money costs do not have any relevance in the economic sense. Past costs do perform a very important function because they provide a guide to future cost estimates. However, complete reliance should not be put upon historical costs for pricing in the transportation industry.

Social Cost

A third category of costs—social cost—might also be considered. Some businesses might not concern themselves with social costs unless required to do so by law. These costs take into consideration the cost to society of some particular operation and, in fact, might outweigh money cost. For example, what is the cost to society when a company releases its waste materials into a stream? Today many regulations and controls are administered by various regulatory agencies to protect society from such costs. These agencies make the business organizations responsible for social costs. (For example, strip-mining operators are customarily required to backfill and plant.) In spite of such controls, however, there are still instances when chemicals or other hazardous materials are discharged or leak out and society has to bear the cost of the cleanup operations as well as the health hazards.

We are not trying to castigate business organizations or suggest that all investment decisions result in negative social costs because, in fact, there can be social benefits from business investments. However, to ensure that our discussion is complete, social costs must be considered.

Analysis of Cost Structures

There are two general approaches to an analysis of a particular cost structure. Under one approach, costs can be classified as those that are directly assignable to particular segments of the business (such as products or services) and those that are incurred for the business as a whole. These two types of cost are generally designated as separable and common costs, respectively. Usually, common costs are further classified as joint common costs or conjoint common costs. **Separable costs** refer to a situation in which products are necessarily produced in fixed proportions. The classic example is that of hides and beef. Stated simply, the production or generation of one product or service necessarily entails the production or generation of another product. In terms of transportation, joint costs occur when two or more services are *necessarily* produced together in fixed proportions. One of these services is said to be a by-product of the other. The most obvious illustration is that of the backhaul situation; the return capacity is the by-product of the loaded trip to the destination.[3]

It is a generally accepted fact that large transportation companies, especially railroads, have a significant element of common costs because they have roadbed, terminals, freight yards, and so on, the cost of which is common to all traffic. However, the only evidence of true jointness appears to be the backhaul.[4] Nonjoint common costs are those that do not require the production of fixed proportions of products or services. Nonjoint common costs are more customary in transportation. For example, on a typical train journey on which hundreds of items are carried, the expenses of the crew and fuel are common costs incurred for all the items hauled (see Figure 9A.1).

A technique for allocating costs directly to activity centers has been implemented in

FIGURE 9A.1 Directly Assignable Cost Approach

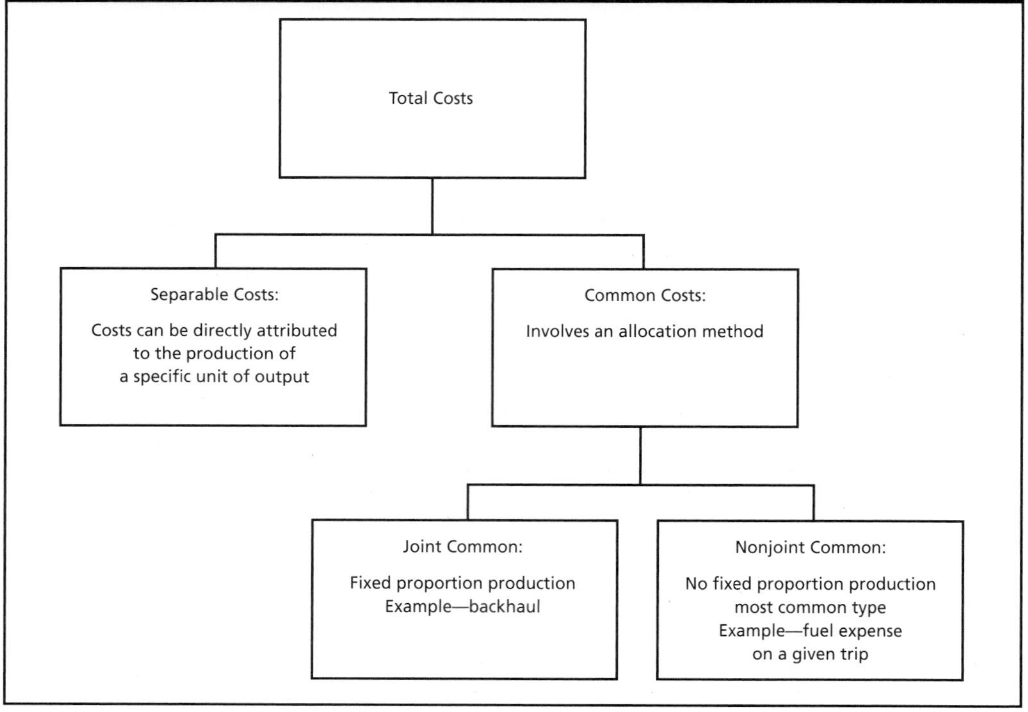

both the carrier and shipper communities. **Activity-based costing (ABC)** identifies costs specifically generated by performing a service or producing a product. ABC does not allocate direct and indirect costs based on volume alone; it determines which activities are responsible for these costs and burdens these activities with their respective portion of overhead costs.

One application for ABC today by both carriers and shippers is the calculation of customer profitability.[5]

Under the other basic approach to analyzing a particular cost structure, costs are divided into those that do not fluctuate with the volume of business in the short term and those that do. The time period here is assumed to be that in which the plant or physical capacity of the business remains unchanged, or the "short run." The two types of costs described are usually referred to as fixed and variable costs, respectively.

In the first approach, the distinction between common and separable costs is made with the idea that costs can be traced to specific accounts or products of the business. In the second approach, the distinction between fixed and variable is made to study variations in business as a whole over a period of time and the effect of these variations upon expenses. In other words, with fixed and variable costs we are interested in the fact that some costs increase and decrease with expansion and contraction of business volume, whereas other costs do not vary as business levels change.

Because of the two different approaches to studying costs, it is possible that a certain cost might be classified as common on one hand and variable on the other, or common under one approach and fixed under the other, and so on, for all the possible combinations. Therefore, the only costs directly traceable or separable are the variable costs, which are also separable. For example, fuel expense is generally regarded as a variable cost, but it would be a common cost with a vehicle loaded with LTL traffic.

The second approach of cost analysis—namely, fixed and variable costs—is important and should be discussed further. As indicated previously, **fixed costs** are constant regardless of the enterprise's volume of business. These fixed costs can include maintenance expenses on equipment or right-of-way (track) caused by time and weather (not use), property taxes, certain management salaries, interest on bonds, and payments on long-term leases.

A business has a commitment to its fixed costs even with a zero level of output. Fixed costs might, in certain instances, be delayed, or to use the more common term, deferred. The railroads frequently delay or defer costs. For example, maintenance of railroad rights-of-way should probably be done each spring or summer, particularly in the northern states. Freezing and thawing, along with spring rains, wash away gravel and stone (ballast) and may do other damage. Although this maintenance can be postponed, just as, for example, house painting might be postponed for a year or two, sooner or later it has to be done if the business wants to continue to operate. There is a fixed commitment or necessity that requires the corrective action and associated expense.[6] The important point is that the fixed expenses occur independently of the volume of business experienced by the organization.

Variable costs, on the other hand, are closely related to the volume of business. In other words, firms do not experience any variable costs unless they are operating. The fuel expense for trains or tractor-trailers is an excellent example of a variable cost. If a locomotive or vehicle does not make a run or trip, there is no fuel cost. Additional examples of variable costs include the wear and tear on tractor-trailers and the cost for tires and engine parts.

Another related point is that railroads and pipelines, like many public utility companies, are frequently labeled as decreasing cost industries. The relevance of this phenomenon to pricing was discussed earlier in this chapter, but it also deserves some additional explanation now. (Economies of scale were discussed in Chapter 3, "Motor Carriers.") Railroads and pipelines have a high proportion of fixed costs in their cost structures. There is some debate about the percentage, but the estimates range from 20 to 50 percent. Contrast this with motor carriers whose average is 10 percent. As railroads produce more units, the proportion of fixed costs on each item will be lower. More importantly, this decline will occur over a long range of output because of the large-scale capacity of most railroads.

An example of the above situation is useful here. Let us assume that a particular railroad incurs $5 million of fixed costs on an annual basis. In addition, let us assume that the railroad is analyzing costs for pricing purposes between Bellefonte, Pennsylvania, and Chicago. In its examination of cost, the railroad determines that the variable cost on a carload is $250 between Bellefonte and Chicago.

Although it might be unrealistic, let us assume that the railroad only moves 10 cars per year. The cost would be as follows:

Fixed cost $5,000,000
Variable cost $2,500 (10 cars × $250)
Total cost $5,002,500
Average cost $500,250 per car

If it moves 1,000 cars, the cost would be:

Fixed cost $5,000,000
Variable cost $250,000 (1,000 cars × $250)
Total cost $5,250,000
Average cost $5,250 per car

If it moves 100,000 cars, the cost would be:

Fixed cost $5,000,000
Variable cost $25,000,000 (100,000 × $250)
Total cost $30,000,000
Average cost $300 per car

The relationship is easy to see. If we continued adding cars to our example, the average cost would continue to decline. Theoretically, average cost would have to level out and eventually increase due to decreasing returns, but the important point is that the high proportion of fixed costs and the large capacity cause the average cost to decline over a great range of output (see Figure 9A.2). There would be a point,

FIGURE 9A.2 Average Cost and Output

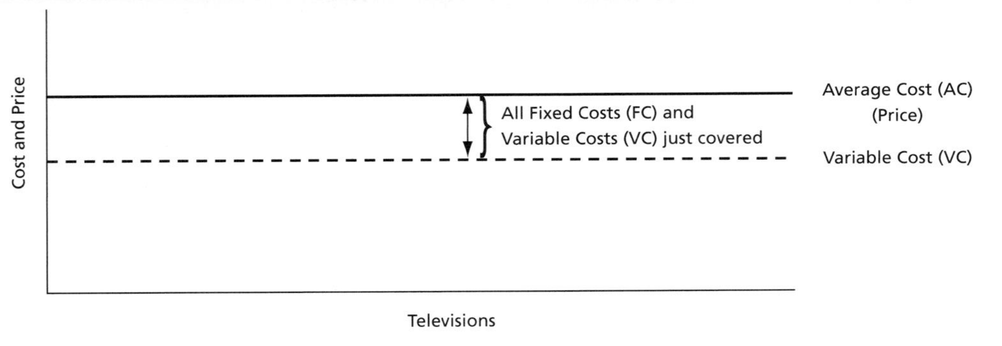

however, at which additional cars would require another investment in fixed cost, thus shifting the average cost curve.

The significance of the declining cost phenomenon to a railroad is that volume is a very important determinant of cost and efficiency. Furthermore, pricing the service to attract traffic is a critical factor in determining profitability, particularly where there is competition from alternate modes of transportation.

Another cost concept that is of major importance in our analysis is marginal cost because of its key role in understanding pricing decisions. Marginal cost can be defined as the change in total cost resulting from a one-unit change in output, or as additions to aggregate cost for given additions to output. This latter definition probably makes more sense in transportation because of the difficulties of defining the output unit. Marginal cost also can be defined as the change in total variable cost resulting from a one-unit change in output because a change in output changes total variable cost and total cost by exactly the same amounts. Marginal cost is sometimes referred to as *incremental cost,* especially in the transportation industry.

There is one other type of cost that should be mentioned because of its importance in price decision—**out-of-pocket costs**. Out-of-pocket costs are usually defined as those costs that are directly assignable to a particular unit of traffic and that would not have been incurred if the service or movement had not been performed. Within the framework of this definition, out-of-pocket costs could also be either separable costs or variable costs. Although the above definition states that out-of-pocket costs are specifically assignable to a certain movement, which implies separable costs, they can definitely be considered as variable costs because they would not have occurred if a particular shipment had not been moved. The definition also encompasses marginal cost because marginal cost can be associated with a unit increase in cost.

The vagueness of the out-of-pocket costs definition has left the door open to the types of cost included as a part of their calculation. The difficulty lies in the fact that from a narrow viewpoint, out-of-pocket costs could be classified as only those expenses incurred because a particular unit was moved. For example, the loading and unloading expense attributable to moving a particular shipment, plus the extra fuel and wear and tear on equipment (relatively low for railroads) could be classified as out-of-pocket costs. On the other hand, a broad approach might be used in defining out-of-pocket costs in regard to a particular shipment, thereby including a share of all of the common variable expenses attributable to a particular movement between two points.

The confusion surrounding the concept of out-of-pocket costs would seem to justify elimination of its use. However, the continued use of the term would be acceptable if its definition was made synonymous with the definition of one of the particular economic costs that its definition implies—marginal costs—because this term is important in price and output decisions and evaluations of pricing economics. Typically, out-of-pocket costs are most important to the firm's accounting system because they are payments that must be made almost immediately as an operating expense. The out-of-pocket cost concept is useful in that it is used as a way to estimate the amount of liquid funds that a transportation firm must keep on hand for daily operations.[7]

Figure 9A.3 gives a good breakdown of the methods of cost analysis. It illustrates the close relationship between the three cost concepts of variable, marginal, and out-of-pocket costs.

Although attention is devoted to cost structure in the separate chapters dealing with each of the modes of transportation, some consideration will be given in this section to an analysis of modal cost structures. Such discussion is useful and necessary background to the analysis of the approaches to pricing.

Rail Cost Structure

One of the characteristics of railroads, as previously noted, is the level of fixed costs present in their cost structures. It is a commonly accepted fact that a relatively large proportion of railway costs are fixed in the short run. At one time it was believed that more than half of rail costs were fixed, and some individuals estimated that these costs ran as high as 70 percent of total cost. The exact proportion of fixed expenses is subject to some debate; however, it is generally accepted that fixed expenses constitute a significant portion of railroad total costs, ranging from 20 to 50 percent. The high proportion of fixed costs can be explained by railroad investment (in such things as track, terminals, and freight yards), which is much larger than the investment of motor carriers, for example. For this reason, railroads are generally regarded as having increasing returns, or decreasing costs per unit of output.[8]

As has been indicated, a significant amount of railroad costs also include common expenses because replacement costs of a stretch of track are shared by all traffic moving over it. This is also true with respect to other items of cost, including officers'

FIGURE 9A.3 Short-Run Cost/Volume Output Approach

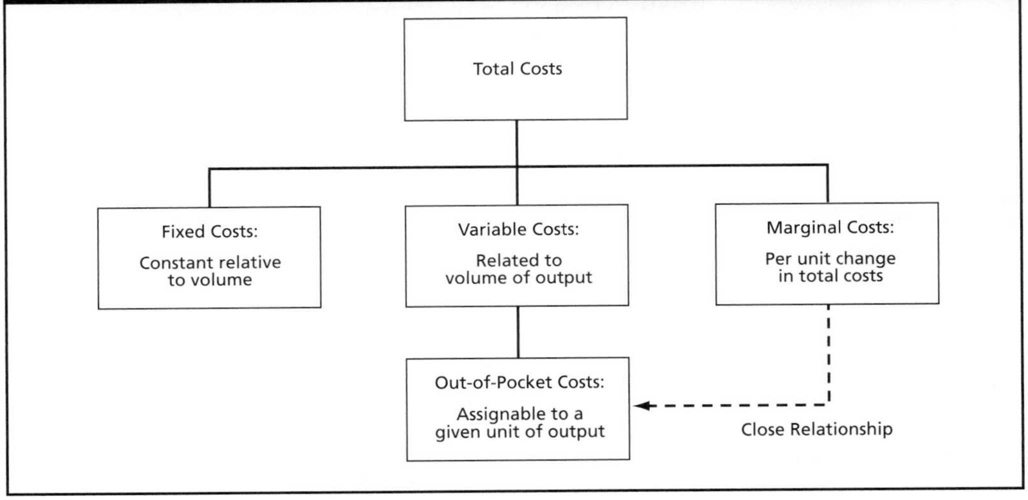

salaries. Some of these common costs are also fixed costs, while others are variable costs (refer to Chapter 4, "Railroads").

Motor Carrier Cost Structure

The motor carrier industry is exemplified by a high proportion of variable costs. It has been estimated that variable costs in the motor carrier industry are 90 percent or more of total costs.[9] This high degree of variability is explained to a large extent by the fact that motor carriers do not have to provide their own right-of-way because roads are publicly provided. It is true that motor carriers do pay fuel taxes and other taxes to defray the cost of providing the highways, but these expenses are variable because they depend on the use made of the highway.

The economic concept of the "long run" is a shorter period in the motor carrier industry than in the railroad industry. The operating unit, the motor carrier vehicle, has a shorter life span than the rail operating unit. It is smaller and therefore more adaptable to fluctuating business conditions. The capital investment required is smaller too, and fleets can be expanded and contracted easier.

The motor carrier situation varies greatly with respect to common costs. Companies that specialize in LTL traffic will have a significant proportion of common cost, whereas contract carriers with only two or three customers who move only TL traffic will have a high proportion of separable costs. Other companies that carry a mixture of TL and LTL traffic will be in the middle of the two extremes (refer to Chapter 3).

Other Carriers' Cost Structures

Information on water carrier cost structure is less prevalent because many companies are privately owned or exempt from economic regulation. The cost structure is probably very similar to that of motor carriers because their right-of-way is also publicly provided. There are some differences, however, because the investment per unit of output is greater, and a large volume of traffic is necessary to realize mass movement potentialities.[10] (See Chapter 6, "Water Carriers and Pipelines.")

The pipeline companies have a cost structure similar to that of railroads. The fact that they have to provide their own right-of-way and the fact that their terminal facilities are very specialized mean that they have a large element of fixed and usually sunk costs. They also usually have significant common costs because they move a variety of oil products through the pipeline (see Chapter 6, "Water Carriers and Pipelines").

The airline companies have a cost structure similar to that of water carriers and motor carriers because of the public provision of their right-of-way. Also, terminal facilities are publicly provided to a large extent, and the airlines pay landing fees based upon use. Airlines tend to have a significant element of common cost because of small freight shipments and the individual nature of passenger movements; for example, airlines very seldom sell a planeload to one customer (see Chapter 5, "Air Carriers").

The differences in the cost structures of the modes of transportation and their differing service characteristics make pricing of their services very important. If motor-carrier service is better than rail service, motor-carrier prices can exceed rail prices. The cost structure of the motor carrier may dictate that their prices can exceed rail prices. The cost structure of the motor carrier may dictate that their prices have to be higher than the rail prices. The critical question is what is the relationship between demand and cost (supply) in such cases.

APPENDIX 9-A TERMS

Notes

1. William J. Baumol, et al., "The Role of Cost in the Minimum Pricing of Railroad Services," *Journal of Business,* Vol. 35, October 1962, pp. 5–6. This article succinctly presents the essence of sunk versus prospective costs.

2. A. M. Milne, *The Economics of Inland Transport,* London: Pitman and Sons, 1955, p. 146.

3. Robert C. Lieb, *Transportation, the Domestic System,* 2nd ed., Reston, VA: Reston Publishing, p. 138.

4. This problem was argued in the economic journals at an early date by two notable economists. See F. W. Taussig, "Railway Rates and Joint Cost Once More," *Quarterly Journal of Economics,* Vol. 27, May 1913, p. 378; F. W. Taussig and A. C. Pigou, "Railway Rates and Joint Costs," *Quarterly Journal of Economics,* Vol. 27, August 1913, pp. 535 and 687; A. C. Pigou, *The Economics of Welfare,* 4th ed., London: Macmillan, 1950, Chapters 17 and 18. An excellent discussion of this debate is contained in D. P. Locklin, "A Review of the Literature on Railway Rate Theory," *Quarterly Journal of Economics,* Vol. 47, 1933, p. 174.

5. For a more thorough discussion of this topic, see Terrance L. Pohlen and Bernard J. LaLonde, "Implementing Activity-Based Costing (ABC) in Logistics," *Journal of Business Logistics,* Vol. 15, No. 2, 1994, pp. 1–23.

6. For an excellent discussion, see George W. Wilson and George W. Smerk, "Rate theory" in *Physical Distribution Management,* Bloomington, IN: Indiana University, 1963, pp. 2–4.

7. Wayne K. Talley, *Introduction to Transportation,* 1st ed., Cincinnati, OH: Southwestern, 1983, p. 27.

8. George W. Wilson, *Essays on Some Unsettled Questions in the Economics of Transportation* (Bloomington, IN: Foundation for Economic and Business Studies, 1962), pp. 32–33.

9. Interstate Commerce Commission, Bureau of Accounts and Cost Finding, *Explanation of Rail Cost Finding Principles and Procedures,* Washington, DC: Government Printing Office, 1948, p. 88.

10. John R. Meyer, et al., *The Economics of Competition in the Transportation Industries,* Cambridge, MA: Harvard University Press, pp. 112–113.

Appendix 9-B

LTL and TL Costing Models

As mentioned in this chapter, understanding costs for costing purposes is critical to a carrier's ability to price in order to maximize profits. Costing and pricing can be extremely complex exercises, depending on the amount and complexity of inputs. However, if we look at LTL and TL operations, we might find that defining their activities for costing purposes can be relatively simple. The purpose of this appendix is to offer basic and simplistic costing models for LTL and TL that can be used to get a feel for the costs associated with a particular move. Obviously, these are not complex models and would need to be adjusted for actual costing purposes. The authors would like to give special thanks to the late Dr. Pete Patton, Professor of Transportation and Logistics at the University of Tennessee, for his pioneering efforts on these costing models.

Operational Activities

If we look at LTL and TL operations, we might think that they are significantly different in how they operate. Actually, they are very similar. The major difference between the two is in the dock rehandling that is associated with the LTL operations, not the TL. However, to move a shipment, both operations provide a pickup service, a line-haul service, and a delivery service. We can use these three activities, along with dock rehandling for LTL, to begin to break out the appropriate costs associated with a move.

Cost/Service Elements

Within each operational activity, we need to identify those cost/service elements that will actually be responsible for shipment costs. These cost/service elements can be defined as time, distance, and support. The time it takes a carrier to pick up, cross-dock, line-haul, and deliver a shipment will impact its fixed costs, such as depreciation and interest, because these costs are allocated and determined by units of time. The distance a carrier has to move a shipment during these operational activities will affect its variable costs, such as fuel and wages. Support costs, such as equipment insurance and maintenance, are considered semi-fixed and semi-variable because they will exist if no activity takes place but will increase as activity increases. Finally, shipment billing can be considered a fixed cost because normally the cost to generate a freight bill is not related to shipment size or distance.

Having identified four operational activities (pickup, cross-dock, line-haul, and delivery) and three cost/service elements (time, distance, and support), it is possible to develop a costing methodology that will allow us to approximate the costs a carrier could incur for moving a shipment.

TL Costing

This section will present a simplified TL costing model that can be used to approximate the costs of moving a shipment between two points. This model can be used for calculating headhaul costs but does not include an adjustment for a possible empty return trip. However, as will be seen, headhaul costs could be adjusted to compensate for variable costs of an empty backhaul.

The following scenario is used.

Shipment and Equipment Characteristics

The shipment consists of 400 cartons at 90 pounds each with each carton measuring 3 cubic feet. Carriers' trailers have a weight capacity of 40,000 pounds and 2,880 cubic feet. The shipment weighs 36,000 pounds (90 percent of weight capacity) and occupies 1,200 cubic feet (almost 50 percent of trailer cubic capacity).

Equipment Cost Data

Equipment Purchase Price

1. Line-haul tractors = $32,000
2. Trailers = $13,000

Depreciation

1. Tractors = 5-year straight line
2. Trailers = 8-year straight line

Interest

1. Tractors = 10% APR for 5 years
2. Trailers = 10% APR for 8 years

Fuel

1. $1.00 per gallon for diesel
2. Line-haul tractors = 4.5 miles per gallon

Labor Cost

1. Line-haul drivers = $0.30 per mile
2. PUD operation drivers = $22.00 per hour

Miscellaneous

1. Insurance cost = $0.03 per mile
2. Maintenance cost = $0.15 per mile
3. Billing cost = $1.95 per freight bill
4. Tractors and trailers are available for use 365 days, 24 hours per day
5. Administrative/overhead cost = 10% of total cost of move

Route and Time of Move

The shipment originates on June 1, 2003, from Pennsylvania State University (located 35 miles from the carrier's dispatch/maintenance facility). A line-haul tractor and trailer are dispatched from the terminal at 7:30 a.m. (all times are Eastern Standard Time) and arrive at the shipper's dock at 8:30 a.m. The shipment is loaded from 8:30 a.m. to 12:00 p.m. Driver and tractor remain at Penn State during loading to visit the famous Nittany Lion statue. Driver and vehicle return to the carrier's terminal at 1:00 p.m. to pick up paperwork.

Total time for pickup = 5.5 hours
Total distance for pickup = 70 miles

The vehicle and the driver depart from the terminal at 1:00 p.m. on the same day for Dallas, Texas. The driver operates from 1:00 p.m. to 11:00 p.m. and travels 450 miles. The driver rests from 11:00 p.m. to 7:00 a.m. (on June 2) in Knoxville, Tennessee, and then operates another 8 hours (7:00 a.m. to 3:00 p.m.) and 375 miles. The driver rests again from 3:00 p.m. to 11:00 p.m. in Memphis, Tennessee. The driver concludes the trip by traveling 450 miles from 11:00 p.m. to 9:00 a.m. (June 3) to the consignee in Dallas, George Bush's summer home.

Total time for line-haul = 44 hours or 1.83 days
Total distance for line-haul = 1,275 miles

The trailer is unloaded from 9:00 a.m. to 12:00 p.m. with the driver and tractor remaining at the home to tour the museum dedicated to George Bush's college baseball days. The driver and vehicle then go to the carrier's Dallas terminal, located 45 miles from Bush's home, arriving at 1:00 p.m. to wait for further dispatch instructions.

Total time for delivery = 4 hours
Total distance for delivery = 45 miles

Cost Analysis

Using the equipment cost data and the distance traveled and time elapsed for the shipment, we can calculate an approximate cost for this move. This analysis can be seen in Table 9B.1. In a real costing situation, certain changes might need to be made to the cost data included in this

Table 9B.1 TL Costing Example

I.	**Pickup**				
	1. Depreciation:	tractor	5.5 hr @ $0.73/hr =	$4.02	
		trailer	5.5 hr @ $0.186/hr =	$1.02	
	2. Interest:	tractor	5.5 hr @ $1.18/hr =	$6.49	
		trailer	5.5 hr @ $0.40/hr =	$2.20	
	3. Fuel		70 miles @ $0.22/mile =	$15.40	
	4. Labor		5.5 hr @ $22/mile =	$121.00	
	5. Maintenance		70 miles @ $0.15/mile =	$10.50	
	6. Insurance		70 miles @ $0.03/mile =	$2.10	
	7. Billing			$1.95	
			TOTAL PICKUP COST		**$164.68**
II.	**Line-haul**				
	1. Depreciation:	tractor	44 hr @ $0.73/hr =	$32.12	
		trailer	44 hr @ $0.186/hr =	$8.18	
	2. Interest:	tractor	44 hr @ $1.18/hr =	$51.92	
		trailer	44 hr @ $0.40/hr =	$17.60	
	3. Fuel		1,275 miles @ $0.22/mile =	$280.50	
	4. Labor		1,275 miles @ $0.30/mile =	$382.50	
	5. Maintenance		1,275 miles @ $0.15/mile =	$191.25	
	6. Insurance		1,275 miles @ $0.03/mile =	$38.25	
			TOTAL LINE-HAUL COST		**$1002.32**
III.	**Delivery**				
	1. Depreciation:	tractor	4 hr @ $0.73/hr =	$2.92	
		trailer	4 hr @ $0.186/hr =	$0.74	
	2. Interest:	tractor	4 hr @ $1.18/hr =	$4.72	
		trailer	4 hr @ $0.40/hr =	$1.60	
	3. Fuel		45 miles @ $0.22/mile =	$9.90	
	4. Labor		4 hr @ $22/hr =	$88.00	
	5. Maintenance		45 miles @ $0.15/mile =	$6.75	
	6. Insurance		45 miles @ $.03/mile =	$1.35	
			TOTAL DELIVERY COST		**$115.98**
IV.	**Total Cost**				
	1. Pickup, line-haul, delivery			$1282.98	
	2. Administrative/overhead (10%)			$128.29	
			TOTAL TL COST		**$1411.27**
V.	**Revenue Needs**				
	1. Per cwt ($1411.27/360) = **$3.92**				
	2. Per revenue mile ($1411.27/1310 miles) = **$1.08**				

example. Tractor fuel economy, for example, might need to be increased or maintenance cost per mile might need to be decreased. The cost analyst would need to determine the appropriate levels for each cost element, depending on the type of equipment and nature of the move.

Pickup

As can be seen in Table 9B.1, the pickup operation generated seven types of costs. *Depreciation expense* per hour is calculated by

equipment cost/years depreciation/365/24.

This formula gives the hourly cost for depreciation for both the tractor and the trailer. *Interest expense (includes both principal plus interest)* per hour can be calculated using the appropriate compound factor (CF) for each piece of equipment. The CF can be found in tables in any introductory finance text. This formula is

interest = amount borrowed x CF for the length of the loan, annual percentage rate; interest per hour = interest for the life of the loan/length of loan in years/365/24.

In this example, the CF for 5 years at 10 percent APR is 1.611 and for 8 years at 10 percent APR it is 2.144. Fuel cost per gallon and tractor fuel economy determine *fuel cost per mile.* This formula is

fuel cost per gallon/miles per gallon

Labor, maintenance, insurance, and billing costs are given and are relatively easy to calculate. *Total pickup costs for this move are $164.68.*

Line-haul

Notice that the line-haul costs categories for this move are the same as for the pickup operation, except for the billing expense. This is simply because only one freight bill needs to be generated for this move. This will also be seen by the absence of a billing cost in the delivery section.

Also, during the pickup operation, the driver was paid by the hour because waiting time was involved. In the line-haul section, the driver was paid by the mile. Obviously, pay scales for drivers will be determined by company or union policies. *Costs in the line-haul section are calculated in the same manner as they were in the pickup section.* Obviously, however, the time and distance generated by the line-haul activity are used. *Total line-haul costs for this move are $1,002.32.*

Delivery

The delivery activity generates the same type of costs as did the pickup activity, except for billing. Again, the time and distance associated with delivery need to be used in calculating costs. *Costs for delivery are calculated in the same manner as they were in the pickup section. Total costs for delivery for this move are $115.98.*

Total Cost

Adding the costs associated with pickup, line-haul, and delivery generates the total cost for this move of $1,282.98. Remember, however, that a 10-percent additional cost is added to make a contribution to the carrier's administration and overhead, so the *total cost for this move is $1411.27.*

Revenue Needs

Carriers quote prices in many forms. Two of the more common methods are price per hundredweight (cwt) and price per revenue, or loaded, mile. In this example, although profit has not yet been added, to recover the fully allocated or average cost for this move, the carrier would quote a *price per cwt of $3.92 ($1411.27/360.00 cwt)* or a *price per revenue mile of $1.08 ($1411.27/ 1310 miles).*

Once again, this model is a simplified version of those used by carriers. Certain adjustments and additions would need to be made to this model to make it more reflective of an actual move. However, it does give the analyst some idea of the approximate costs associated with a shipment.

LTL Costing

This section will present a simplified version of an LTL costing model. LTL costing is more difficult than TL costing because it requires arbitrary allocations of common and fixed costs to individual shipments. Although this does not make costing an LTL shipment impossible, it does require that the individual using the costs understand that averages and allocations were used. Thus, the resulting costs might not be as accurate as would be desired. However, this model will produce "ballpark" estimates for the cost of moving an individual shipment. *All* of the formulas for calculating depreciation costs, interest costs, and fuel costs are the same as those used in the TL costing example.

Shipment and Equipment Characteristics

The shipment to be costed consists of 15 cartons, each weighing 40 pounds and measuring 16 cubic feet. The carrier's trailers have a weight capacity of 40,000 pounds and 2,880 cubic feet. This shipment then occupies 1.5 percent of the trailer's weight capacity and 8.3 percent of its cubic capacity. Because the cubic feet requirement is greater, it will be used to allocate costs in the line-haul move.

Equipment Cost Data

Equipment Purchase Price

1. PUD tractor = $23,600
2. LH tractor = $32,000
3. PUD trailer = $10,000
4. LH trailer = $13,000

Depreciation

1. Tractors = 5-year straight line
2. Trailers = 8-year straight line

Interest

1. Tractors = 10% APR for 5 years
2. Trailers = 10% APR for 8 years

Fuel

1. $1.00 per gallon for diesel
2. PUD tractors = 5 miles per gallon
3. LH tractors = 4.5 miles per gallon

Labor Cost

1. PUD drivers = $22.00 per hour
2. Dock handlers = $20.00 per hour
3. LH drivers = $22.00 per hour

Miscellaneous

1. Terminal variable cost per shipment at both origin and destination = $1.00
2. Terminal fixed cost per shipment at both origin and destination = $1.50
3. PUD equipment maintenance cost = $0.15 per mile
4. LH equipment maintenance cost = $0.15 per mile
5. PUD equipment insurance cost = $0.03 per mile
6. LH equipment insurance cost = $0.03 per mile
7. Billing cost = $1.95 per bill
8. Equipment is available 365 days, 24 hours per day
9. Administrative/overhead cost = 10% of total cost of move

Route and Time of Movement

The shipment is picked up by the carrier's driver in a PUD city tractor/trailer unit on June 1, 2003, as one of 23 stops made by the driver that day from 7:30 a.m. to 6:30 p.m. The stops covered a total of 60 miles within the Altoona, Pennsylvania, satellite terminal service area. The shipment was one of four handled by the carrier at this particular shipper's location. Once the pickup vehicle returns to the Altoona terminal, it takes 15 minutes to move the shipment from the city unit across the dock to the line-haul trailer.

Total time for pickup = 11 hours
Total distance for pickup = 60 miles
Total dock time = 15 minutes

The line-haul tractor/trailer departs from the Altoona terminal at 11:00 p.m. on June 1 and arrives at the Cleveland break-bulk terminal, which is approximately 200 miles from the Altoona satellite, at 4:00 a.m. on June 2. The shipment moves from the line-haul trailer across the dock to a PUD city tractor/trailer unit in 15 minutes.

Total time of line-haul = 5 hours
Total distance for line-haul = 200 miles
Total dock time = 15 minutes

The shipment is delivered to the Cleveland consignee by the PUD driver in a PUD city tractor/ trailer unit on June 2 as one of 16 stops made by the driver over the period 7:30 a.m. to 6:00 p.m. The stops covered a total of 45 miles in the Cleveland area. This shipment is one of three delivered to this particular consignee by the driver.

Total time for delivery = 10.5 hours
Total distance for delivery = 45 miles

Cost Analysis

With the equipment cost data and route and time of movement, an individual LTL

Table 9B.2 LTL Costing Example

I. Pickup					
A. Route Costs					
1. Depreciation:	PUD tractor	1 day @ $12.93/day =	$12.93		
	PUD trailer	1 day @ $3.42/day =	$3.42		
2. Interest:	tractor	1 day @ $20.83/day =	$20.83		
	trailer	1 day @ $7.34/mile =	$7.34		
3. Fuel		60 miles @ $0.20/mile =	$12.00		
4. Labor		11 hr @ $22/hr =	$242.00		
5. Maintenance		60 miles @ $0.15/mile =	$9.00		
6. Insurance		60 miles @ $0.03/mile =	$1.80		
	SUBTOTAL		**$309.32**		
	# Stops		23		
	COST PER STOP		**$13.45**		
	# Shipments at stop		4		
	ROUTE COST PER SHIPMENT		**$3.36**		
B. Shipment Costs					
1. Billing			$1.95		
2. Terminal variable cost			$1.00		
3. Terminal fixed cost			$1.50		
4. Dock		0.25 hr @ $20/hr =	$5.00		
	INDIVIDUAL SHIPMENT COST		**$9.45**		
C. Total Pickup Cost Per Shipment				**$12.81**	
II. Line-haul					
1. Depreciation:	PUD tractor	5 hr @ $0.73/hr =	$3.65		
	PUD trailer	5 hr @ $0.186/hr =	$0.93		
2. Interest:	PUD tractor	5 hr @ $1.18/h. =	$5.90		
	PUD trailer	5 hr @ $0.40/hr =	$2.00		
3. Fuel		200 miles @ $0.22/mile =	$44.00		
4. Labor		5 hr @ $22/hr =	$110.00		
5. Maintenance		200 miles @ $0.15/mile =	$30.00		
6. Insurance		200 miles @ $0.03/mile =	$6.00		
	TOTAL LINE-HAUL FULL TRAILER		**$202.48**		
	% capacity occupied by shipment		8.3%		
	SHIPMENT LINE-HAUL COST			**$16.81**	
III. Delivery					
A. Route Costs					
1. Depreciation:	PUD tractor	1 day @ $12.93/day =	$12.93		
	PUD trailer	1 day @ $3.42/day =	$3.42		
2. Interest:	PUD tractor	1 day @ $20.83/day =	$20.83		
	PUD trailer	1 day @ $7.34/mile =	$7.34		
3. Fuel		45 miles @ $0.20/mile =	$9.00		
4. Labor		10.5 hr @ $22/hr =	$231.00		
5. Maintenance		45 miles @ $0.15/mile =	$6.75		
6. Insurance		45 miles @ $0.03/mile =	$1.35		
	SUBTOTAL		**$292.62**		
	# Stops		16		
	COST PER STOP **$18.29**				
	# Shipments at stop		3		
	ROUTE COST PER SHIPMENT		**$6.10**		

Continued

Table 9B.2 LTL Costing Example (Cont.)

B. Shipment Costs				
	1. Terminal variable cost		$1.00	
	2. Terminal fixed cost		$1.50	
	3. Dock	0.25 hr @ $20/hr =	$5.00	
		INDIVIDUAL SHIPMENT COST	**$7.50**	
C. Total Delivery Cost Per Shipment				**$13.60**
IV. Total Cost Per Shipment				
	1. Pickup, dock, line-haul, delivery		$43.22	
	2. Administrative/overhead (10 percent)		$4.32	
		TOTAL COST PER SHIPMENT		**$47.54**
V. Revenue Needs				
	1. Per cwt ($47.54/6)		$7.92	

shipment can be costed. This analysis can be seen in Table 9B.2. Once again, *the calculations for depreciation, interest, and fuel costs are the same as they were in the TL example.*

Pickup

In this example, a PUD tractor and trailer were used in the pickup operation. This is specialized equipment that really has no alternative uses in the line-haul operation. As such, when this equipment is done with the PUD operation during the day, it will normally sit idle at the satellite terminal. This explains why a full day's depreciation and interest are charged to both the PUD tractor and PUD trailer, even though they were only utilized for 11 hours during this particular day. Some arguments might exist that this places an excessive cost burden on these shipments through fixed-cost allocation. This might be true. However, the cost analyst must make the decision as to where fixed costs will be recovered. If not through this allocation, then fixed costs must be covered by some other method so debt can be serviced and plans for equipment replacement can be implemented.

The fuel, labor, maintenance, and insurance cost calculations are relatively straightforward. *Total route costs for this move are $309.32.* Remember, however, that this cost is for all shipments picked up and delivered by the driver during the day. We want to calculate the cost of only one shipment. To do this, we must first divide the total route cost by the number of stops made by the driver. *This results in a route cost per stop of $13.45.* Second, we must divide the per stop cost by the number of shipments at the shipper's location that had our individual shipment. *This results in a route cost per shipment of $3.36.* Both the stop cost and the shipment cost are averages that assume that each stop is basically the same and each shipment is the same. Adjustments could be made to these figures to more accurately reflect the time and distance actually used for our individual shipment. Remember, however, the per-shipment-route costs used in this example are averages.

Shipment costs are those assigned to each individual shipment that are not generated by the PUD operation. Billing, terminal variable cost, and terminal fixed cost are not dependent on shipment size but are allocated to each shipment. Our shipment took 15 minutes for its cross-dock operation resulting in the dock charge of $5.00. *Total shipment cost for this move is $9.45. Combining the route cost per shipment and the shipment cost results in a total pickup cost per shipment of $12.81.*

Line-haul

Depreciation and interest for the line-haul equipment is charged only for the actual time our shipment is on this equipment. This is the same as in the TL example. Unlike the PUD equipment, this assumes that the line-haul equipment has alternative uses and is 100-percent utilized. Again, actual utilization rates can be used to adjust the allocation of depreciation and interest charges.

As previously mentioned, our shipment occupied 8.3 percent of the cubic capacity of the line-haul trailer. This is the basis used for allocating line-haul costs in a *line-haul cost per shipment of $16.81*. This allocation method assumes that all shipments in the line-haul trailer have approximately the same pounds per cubic foot requirement and that the trailer would probably be cubed out. The analyst might want to make adjustments for this based on the known average weight and cube per shipment in the carrier's system.

Delivery

The calculations for delivery cost are the same as those used for pickup costs. For route shipment cost, 16 stops and 3 stops per shipment are used to determine the *average route cost per shipment of $6.10*. Shipment costs are also the same, except that billing cost is not included, resulting in a *shipment cost of $7.50 and a total delivery cost per shipment of $13.60*.

Total Shipment Cost

Combining the pickup cost of $12.81, the line-haul cost of $16.81, and the delivery cost of $13.60 results in a total cost per shipment of $43.22. Remember, like the TL example, a 10-percent cost is added to cover administrative and other overhead expenses, resulting in a *total cost for our shipment of $47.54*.

Revenue Needs

Although prices are quoted in many different forms in the LTL industry, one popular form is in price per cwt. Taking our total shipment charge of $47.54 and dividing it by 6 cwt results in a *price per cwt of $7.92*. Remember this price does not yet include an allowance for profit for the carrier.

Conclusion

Determining the cost for a particular shipment can be a very complex and time-consuming task.

Detailed data requirements and knowledge of a carrier's operations are necessary inputs to developing accurate costs. However, a simplified approach can be taken to shipment costing that does not need these complex requirements and results in approximate shipment costs. Thus, the advantage of these costing models is their simplicity and ease of calculation. Their disadvantage is that they use general data, allocations, and averages to determine shipment costs. The analyst must trade off these characteristics to determine the level of complexity needed for costing and whether these models will provide a sufficient level of cost detail.

Chapter 10

Carrier Strategies

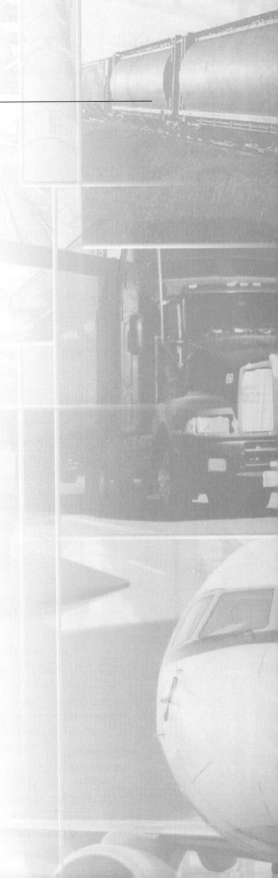

CBN TRUCKING

CBN Trucking is a regional less-than-truckload (LTL) carrier with operations in all states east of the Mississippi River. It has a network of 55 terminals, employs 3,500 persons, and has a fleet of 350 tractors and 750 trailers. Over the years CBN has developed a reputation for providing quick delivery of small shipments (less than a full truck) to points within its operating scope. The business model has worked well for CBN until the early 2000s.

In 2000 CBN experienced its first financial loss. Revenues were up but profit was down. In 2001 the loss was greater due in part to the events of September 11, 2001, which led to the halting of service in the Boston, New York, and Washington, DC, corridor. The financial performance for 2002 and 2003 was slightly better as a result of increased prices and the exiting of a major LTL competitor.

Bill Scaner, CEO and third-generation Scaner to lead CBN, recently held a planning retreat for CBN executives. The goal of the planning retreat was to elicit the strategic challenges facing CBN in the next 5 years and to develop a strategic plan that will bring CBN back to its traditional level of profitability.

The following excerpts from the retreat describe the challenges facing CBN.

- Revenues continue to grow every year.
- Major customers have been retained and new ones are continually added.
- Profit margin from operations has slipped to 0.7 percent from the traditional 3.5 percent.
- Overnight and second-day service, the primary focus of CBN, is being provided for shipments moving less than 600 miles compared to 800 miles in the late 1990s.
- Express ground and air carriers have cut into the traditional, less than 500-pound shipment market, and CBN's revenue from this market has dropped by 70 percent.
- CBN's current information system is late 1990s vintage and is not capable of providing the customer information its competitors provide.
- Costs have escalated for the major resources such as fuel and insurance.
- Labor productivity in terms of pounds handled per dockworker has remained constant over the past 5 years.
- Long-haul driving times have increased along the East Coast, and local pickups and deliveries in major urban areas require more time.
- CBN has equipment replacement and maintenance programs that keep the fleet relatively new (average age of the power units is 2 years) and in good operating condition.

Bill knows that CBN is a financially solid, well-respected carrier with good customer loyalty. He is focusing his strategic planning efforts on the internal operations to improve profitability. As you read this chapter, consider recommendations you would make to Bill so he can achieve his goal.

Transportation firms experience the same laws of economics that production entities experience, but in transportation these guiding principles often manifest themselves in different ways. The transportation industry faces and manages its particular set of economic rules in its own way.

Transportation is a service, not a production activity. Except for pure pleasure cruise travel and some auto travel, transportation faces a derived demand and not a primary demand for its services. Further, transportation is a service that cannot be stored; it is unlike a physical product that can be produced according to certain manufacturing efficiencies and then held until the market demands it. Transportation managers must seek efficient management approaches through various efficiency techniques and through responsive management structures.

This chapter presents many of the transportation efficiency strategies that are inherent to sound economic principles and that have been used by successful carrier managements. It also covers the role of the terminal, which is a basic element of a transportation network. A review of the operating conditions that influence the carrier's business environment is presented initially.

CARRIER OPERATING CONDITIONS

Carrier operating conditions create the business environment within which carrier management establishes strategies and tactics to achieve corporate goals. The discussion in this section will provide an overview of the operating parameters faced by carrier management and a background of the strategies adopted by carriers. Attention is given to the network, operations, labor, and performance measurement.

Operating Network

The carrier's operating network is spread over a vast geographic territory. In the case of a local drayage firm, the geographic territory is the metropolitan area. For a major railroad or motor carrier the territory is the entire United States, whereas the world is the operating territory for many ocean and air carriers. The greater the operating territory, the greater the difficulty of managing the carrier's assets, personnel, and operations.

With assets spread over vast geographic territories, managers face difficult management control issues. First, assets and equipment must be deployed to the shippers' location, which requires continuous monitoring of equipment location and customer demand. Carriers are constantly faced with the dilemma of "deadheading" equipment—operating the vehicle empty—to a shipper's location, incurring operating cost without revenue.

Second, a high proportion of operating tasks is performed beyond the scope of supervisors. Truck drivers, pilots, engineers, and the like perform their duties in the absence of immediate supervision. The supervisors of equipment operators are typically hundreds or thousands of miles away. Technology is the link that enables the supervision of geographically separated operators.

Third, the vast geographic operating network is interrelated and interdependent. That is, the origin terminal, pickup vehicles, consolidation terminals, and so on, all must work together to accomplish the delivery of the shipper's freight. This interdependence among the network operations asserts the need for information technology to connect the many participants in the production of the delivery service.

Fourth, the carrier's operations and equipment are continually exposed to weather conditions and other hazards beyond the control of management. Across the United States weather conditions can vary extremely, and management must keep abreast of the changing weather conditions that may impair the equipment operator's ability to complete the delivery on time or cause damage to the cargo. Management cannot control the weather, but it can respond to changing weather conditions to ensure customer satisfaction.

Other hazards beyond management control include traffic congestion and calamities. Increased highway traffic and the resultant increased traffic congestion have caused increased driving times and cost for motor carriers. The congestion in large metropolitan areas has reduced motor carrier pickup and delivery productivity and increased transit times. Likewise, traffic congestion at airports and water ports has caused added costs and delays to the carriers. Calamities usually result in the stoppage of a carrier's operation in the impacted area. For example, the events of September 11, 2001, halted air transportation for days and disrupted or halted other forms of transportation in the northeastern United States. Riots, strikes, and civil disturbances can have the same impact on transportation operations.

Lastly, the operating equipment is located throughout a widespread area, making it difficult for carriers to protect equipment against vandalism, pilferage, and sabotage. On any given day a major motor carrier may have equipment located in thousands of different locales. Many of these vehicles are stopped at shipper properties, truck stops, or rest areas, and these locations are not under the control of carrier management. Carriers have attempted to implement procedures, such as parking vehicles in lighted areas and locking the vehicle when unattended, that lessen the chance of vehicle sabotage or cargo theft.

Operations

Transportation operations come into direct contact with the general public, making safety a critical factor. Trucks share the highways with automobiles, airplanes fly over populated areas, trains intersect highways and operate in metropolitan areas, and ships operate on internal waterways as well as at port areas adjacent to populated areas. Because of these interactions with the general public, transportation accidents have the potential for doing great harm to many people.

The need for safety, coupled with the high proportion of tasks performed without immediate supervision, necessitates extensive operating rules. Management attempts to prescribe the proper procedures to operate transportation equipment throughout the network. These rules interject a certain degree of rigidity into the operations and stifles personnel creativity. However, the consequences of accidents resulting from unsafe operations are so excessive that the cost of rigidity is miniscule in comparison.

Government has recognized the need for safe operations in transportation and has promulgated numerous safety regulations aimed at protecting the public. The air carriers face the most rigorous safety regulations because an airplane accident has the potential of taking hundreds of passenger lives as well as lives on the ground. Air safety regulations cover most air carrier operations including maintenance, plane operations, plane manufacturing, and passenger support. Trucking safety regulations focus on equipment, equipment operation, and driving times. Similar safety regulations exist for rail and water transportation.

An area of great safety concern is the transportation of hazardous materials. Unsafe transportation of hazardous materials has the potential of causing considerable harm to the public as well as the environment. A chemical spill has the potential for taking lives of those in the immediate area, contaminating water and air supplies that could further impact humans miles away, and causing harm to animals and vegetation in the area. For hazardous materials transportation the government has taken a cradle-to-grave approach, in essence regulating every phase of a hazardous material from its manufacture to its final disposition.

Finally, carriers are concerned with the safe delivery of the cargo. That is, the carriers desire delivery of cargo and passengers without damage or undue delay. Safe delivery of passengers has been addressed above as a humanitarian concern. Generally, cargo safety does not impact human life, but it does impact the operating cost of the shipper and/or receiver. Cargo that is delivered damaged or is lost or delayed causes the receiver to incur lost sales (profits) costs because the product is not available for use or sale. In addition, the receiver may increase inventory levels and incur higher inventory carrying costs to guard against damaged cargo and stockouts (lost sales).

Labor

As noted in the modal chapters, the importance of labor varies among the modes. Pipelines require little labor to operate, whereas motor carriers and air carriers require considerably more for the same amount of freight moved. In addition, a driver is required for each truck, a pilot for each airplane, and a captain for each ship. Railroads, on the other hand, require one engineer for up to 100 railcars.

Transportation has a high degree of unionization. The unions tend to be craft-based (i.e., maintenance, operating, clerical, etc.). This multiplicity of unions creates difficulty for continued operations if all but one union representing a carrier's personnel agree to a contract. For example, air carriers must deal with unions representing mechanics, pilots, and flight attendants. If the air carrier cannot reach a negotiated agreement with one of the three, the one union may halt the carrier's operation.

As noted above, transportation is a service, and one of the characteristics of a service is that it cannot be inventoried. If a labor strike occurs in a transportation company the operation is stopped and no service is provided. The carrier cannot produce the service in anticipation of the strike, inventory the service, and then sell it during the strike. This inability to provide service during a strike causes considerable disruption to society in the form of canceled travel, plant closings, and product shortages.

Government has a propensity for influencing labor unionization in transportation. The most notable government influence is in the trucking industry union, the Teamsters. At one point the government actually headed up the Teamsters. The other government influence is in regulations requiring unions to return to work during a strike. This influence has been seen in air carrier and rail work stoppages. The cost to society of disruptions in the services provided by these modes was viewed as being so high that a number of U.S. presidents signed orders requiring airline and railroad workers to go back to work and continue negotiations.

Performance Measures

The interdependent nature of a carrier's network requires management to measure the performance of the overall company as well as the individual components of the network. In this section we will address the service and financial performance measures of the overall company.

The service performance measurements include time, consistency, and damage. Time encompasses transit time from pickup to delivery, the time element important to shippers. Carriers also monitor the transit time components of pickup, terminal, and delivery times, as well as the terminal-to-terminal time. Consistently producing a desired transit time, free of damage, is a value to a carrier because it provides a value to the shipper in the form of reduced inventory and stockout costs. Lastly, damage to cargo negatively impacts the shipper and/or receiver by rendering the delivered item useless, thereby setting the stage for the shipper and/or receiver to incur stockout costs.

Financial performance measures are critical to the long-term survival of a carrier, and carrier management tends to focus on these performance measurements. By monitoring financial performance, carrier management attempts to efficiently use resources (capital and human) employed in the business. The following financial performance measurements consider the short- and long-term financial performance of a carrier and the efficient use of resources.

Some modes are more capital-intensive than others; for example, railroads are more capital-intensive than motor carriers. Within the modes, some carriers are more capital-intensive than others; for example, truckload (TL) carriers are less capital-intensive than LTL carriers. For more capital-intensive modes and carriers, fixed and common costs are higher and the pricing strategy used to cover variable costs and contribute to overhead is critical. This high capital cost issue is more common to the railroads and air carriers.

Carrier management uses a number of financial performance measurements. Table 10.1 contains 2002 financial data for four different carriers—UPS (a ground and air express carrier), Yellow Freight (an LTL carrier), J.B. Hunt (a TL carrier), and Norfolk Southern (a railroad). Air carriers were not included in the analysis because of the negative financial performance on the industry caused by the events of September 11, 2001.

Table 10.1 contains selected 2002 income statement and balance sheet data for each carrier. Operating revenues range from a low of $2.248 billion to a high of $31.272 billion and net income from a $3.182 billion profit to a $94 million loss.

The financial performance measurements considered in this section include profitability, liquidity, and solvency. Profitability performance measures consider the relative profit generated from operations and assets and the return provided to owners. Common financial ratios used to measure profitability include the profit margin, operating ratio, return on assets, and return on equity.

The liquidity measures examine the company's ability to meet current financial obligations—those due within 1 year. The current ratio, acid test ratio, working capital, and cash flow are widely used measures of liquidity. Finally, the solvency measurement considers the carriers ability to repay principal and interest on long-term debt. The debt ratio and debt-to-equity ratio are the solvency financial measurements.

Referring to Table 10.1 we can see that the profit margin (net income/operating revenue) is 10.18 percent for UPS, 7.34 percent for Norfolk Southern, 2.31 percent for J.B. Hunt, and –3.58 percent for Yellow Freight. UPS, which offers expedited ground and air services, earned the highest profit margin, whereas the Yellow Freight, a LTL carrier, generated a loss. Examination of the operating ratio (operating expenses/operating revenue) reveals a similar profitability picture; that is, Yellow Freight had the highest operating ratio and incurred a loss, whereas UPS had the lowest operating ratio and highest profit margin.

The return on assets considers profit generated by the assets employed in the business. UPS, with the highest profit margin, generated the highest return on assets (net income/total assets). Conversely, Yellow Freight had a –9.01-percent return on assets. Another interesting financial measure of asset utilization is the amount of revenue generated by the assets deployed. Norfolk Southern generated $0.31 of revenue per asset dollar ($6,270/$19,956); UPS, $1.18 ($31,272/$26,357); J.B. Hunt, $1.70 ($2,248/$1,319); and Yellow Freight, $2.52 ($2,624/$1,043). One conclusion is Norfolk Southern and UPS are more capital-intensive than the motor carriers.

The final profitability measure is the return on equity. UPS provided owners with the highest return of the four carriers (Table 10.1) and Yellow Freight provided the lowest. Carrier management must monitor the return on equity because this determines the carrier's ability to attract future investment capital.

Table 10.1 Carrier Financial Performance Measurements

2002 Annual Data	UPS	Yellow Freight	J.B. Hunt	Norfolk Southern
INCOME STATEMENT (millions)				
Operating Revenue	$31,272	$2,624	$2,248	$6,270
Depreciation	$1,464	$79	$146	$529
Operating Expenses	$27,176	$2,577	$2,147	$5,112
Income from Operations	$4,096	$47	$101	$1,158
Net Income	$3,182	($94)	$52	$460
BALANCE SHEET (millions)				
Inventories		$11	$10	$97
Current Assets	$8,738	$425	$433	$1,299
Total Assets	$26,357	$1,043	$1,319	$19,956
Current Liabilities	$5,555	$450	$325	$1,853
Total Liabilities	$13,902	$683	$728	$13,456
Total Equities	$12,455	$360	$591	$6,500
Deferred Taxes	$162	$1	$12	$184
FINANCIAL RATIOS				
Profit Margin (Net Inc/Op Rev)	10.18%	–3.58%	2.31%	7.34%
Operating Ratio (Op Exp/Op Inc)	86.90%	98.21%	95.51%	81.53%
Return on Assets (Net Inc/Tot Assts)	12.07%	–9.01%	3.94%	2.31%
Return on Equity (Net Inc/Tot Equity)	25.55%	–26.11%	8.80%	7.08%
Current Ratio (Cur Assts/ Cur Liab)	1.57	0.94	1.33	0.70
Acid Test Ratio (Cur Assts-Invt/ Cur Liab)	1.57	0.92	1.30	0.65
Debt Ratio (Tot Liab/ Tot Assts)	0.53	0.65	0.55	0.67
Debt/Equity Ratio (Tot Liab/Tot Equity)	1.12	1.90	1.23	2.07
Working Capital (Cur Assts-Cur Liab) (millions)	$3,183	($25)	$108	($554)
Cash Flow (Net Inc + Depr + Def Tx) (millions)	$4,808	($14)	$210	$1,173

Source: All data from individual carrier 2002 annual reports.

The current ratio (current assets/current liabilities) and the acid test ratio (current assets less inventories/current liabilities) measure a carrier's liquidity or ability to meet current (within 1 year) obligations. For all carriers in Table 10.1 the current ratios and acid test ratios are essentially the same because the carriers generally carry very limited inventory. A ratio above 1 means the carrier has sufficient current assets (cash and assets that can be converted to cash within 1 year) to meet current liabilities (debts due within 1 year).

Working capital (current assets less current liabilities) provides a measure of the excess current assets over current liabilities. Yellow Freight and Norfolk Southern had negative working capital, meaning the current liabilities exceeded current assets. Finally, cash flow (net income plus depreciation and deferred taxes) measures the amount of cash available to meet short-term obligations. All carriers shown in Table 10.1, except Yellow Freight, had a positive cash flow.

The solvency measure considers the carrier's ability to repay principal and interest on long-term debt. The debt ratio (total liabilities/total assets) examines the amount of assets available to repay all debt. All carriers in Table 10.1 had debt ratios less than 1, meaning total assets exceed total debt. Finally, the debt-to-equity ratio (total liabilities/total equity) considers the relative amount of debt to ownership. High debt-to-equity ratios mean the creditors have a greater claim on the company than the owners do, and a high debt-to-equity ratio could imply the debtors could control the company. Yellow Freight and Norfolk Southern have higher debt-to-equity ratios than UPS and J.B. Hunt.

In the next section attention is given to the operating strategies employed by carriers.

OPERATING STRATEGIES

The **rule of efficiency** states that it is most efficient to move in a continuous, straight line whenever possible. This rule describes the most efficient movement for goods and people. It calls for little or no circuitry and minimized stopping and restarting. Sporadic movement means energy loss, chances for delay and damage, and an overall increase in costs.

This general rule can be observed in practice in many areas. Unit trains such as coal or grain avoid intermediate classification yards between the shipper and receiver. Truck firms attempt to consolidate long-haul loads so that a single through run, with no intermediate handling, is made and the goods can be sorted for final local delivery at the ultimate destination. The airline industry strives to maximize long-haul nonstop flights because major fuel and engine-wear costs are incurred in takeoffs. Further, the costs of maintaining a transportation vehicle in constant motion are small in relation to the energy and effort expended to get a vehicle from rest to a constant cruise speed.

Intermediate handlings should be minimized. This rule of thumb bears special attention when different transportation firms meet as part of a through move. Railroads often use run-through trains with the engines and cars remaining intact in interline moves to minimize interchange time loss. Preblocked cars are another example of this technique in which interlined cars are handled in groups rather than singly. Truck firms interline trailer loads. Freight is moved from interior points in the United States to Europe inside containers via rail, truck, and ship without the individual goods being handled.

STOP OFF

Workin' on the Railroad

Bottlenecks in the railroad systems usually are a matter of capacity, according to David Dealey, vice president of transportation with Burlington Northern/Santa Fe Railroad, speaking at the national Industrial Transportation League 1999 annual conference. "Creating capacity and managing it are two different matters," he claims. "We've built the capacity."

Dealey links bottlenecks to recent mergers, pointing out most occur at major interchange points and gateways or at joint trackage and facilities. "The traditional remedy here, too, is to throw money at it. We'll do capacity improvement by buying moving stock," he adds. "Mergers have added capacity and freed up routes. We need to coordinate operations and interchange partnerships, and look at service design. We're building run-through trains between eastern and western railroads. A new overpass allows continuous operation of north/south and east/west trains in Kansas City."

"The easy part is throwing money at the problem. The next frontier is to manage congestion in industrial zones caused by peaks and valleys. Making service more reliable will allow us to remove excess equipment."

"Reliability and dependability are what the shipper wants, not penalties. For example, they want communication when the railroad knows of a delay, not when the shipment is already late."

Source: Helen L. Richardson, "Tame Supply Chain Bottlenecks," *Transportation & Distribution*, March 2000, p. 26. Reprinted with permission from *Transportation & Distribution*, March 2000, published by Penton Media, Inc.

The full capacity of the transportation vehicle should be maximized on each run. Transportation costs of trucks, trains, ships, and planes are similar in that the costs of personnel, depreciation, licenses, and taxes are relatively fixed costs that are incurred for each run. The variable amount of goods or people in the run will affect fuel costs, some servicing costs, and loading and unloading costs. On the whole, the firm experiences less per-unit costs as more passengers or freight are added to a run. Therefore, most transportation managers seek to fill the capacity of the vehicle before dispatching it. In the railroad and trucking industries, managers often will delay runs so that more freight can be accumulated for the long haul. The driver or engine crew is paid the same regardless of the weight in the truck or the cars on the train. Airline marketing and pricing managers use low-cost excursion fares to entice vacationers to fill what normally would be empty seats.

As an example, Table 10.2 illustrates the cost per passenger of different passenger loadings on a plane with a capacity of 50 passengers. With an assumed fixed cost per flight of $8,000 (equipment, crew, fuel, and overhead) and a variable cost of $1 per passenger (beverage service), the cost per passenger ranges from $401 with 20 passengers to $161 with 50 passengers. At full plane capacity utilization, the cost per passenger is approximately 40 percent of that at a capacity utilization of 20 passengers (40-percent utilization [20/50]). This capacity utilization example provides the rationale for airlines lowering the ticket price to entice more passengers on the flight and/or canceling a flight and placing the passengers on the next flight that has excess capacity.

Consolidation and break-bulk activities should be used to achieve full capacity for long-haul moves. One means of attaining full equipment use is to use a pickup and delivery network to accumulate freight for the line-haul efficiency. Trucking firms do this with city vehicles that bring different shipments to a terminal for sorting, accumulation, and shipping in bulk to the destination city terminal. This system avoids the prohibitive use of many small trucks and shipments by using large, efficient single units on 400- to 500-mile runs. Railroads perform this task in much the same way. Many airlines have adopted hub-and-spoke route strategies around such cities as Atlanta, Denver, St. Louis, Pittsburgh, and Chicago. Here smaller planes bring passengers from less populated, outlying cities to the hub where the larger, more efficient planes can be used for the long haul. At the destination, the process is reversed: Goods or people are distributed outwardly from the large destination terminal.

Empty mileage should be minimized. The cost of moving an empty vehicle is almost that of moving a loaded one without the offset of revenue. Energy is a major cost in transportation systems. In very few instances can a firm afford one-way loaded movements with empty return hauls. Each mile traveled requires the use of energy, and often the payload in freight or passengers represents only a small part of the total energy consumed in the move. That is, the movement of the vehicle itself can

Table 10.2 Airplane Capacity Utilization and Cost per Passenger

	Passenger Loading			
	20	**30**	**40**	**50**
Fixed Cost per Flight	$8,000	$8,000	$8,000	$8,000
Variable Cost	$20	$30	$40	$50
Total Cost per Flight	$8,020	$8,030	$8,040	$8,050
Cost per Passenger	$401	$267	$201	$161

often be responsible for a large part of the fuel consumed. For this reason, transportation route strategies, carrier marketing and pricing personnel, and dispatchers strive to arrange two-way or three-way moves with almost all miles bearing revenue payloads. Empty miles represent wasted fuel, labor, capital costs, and lost revenue. Motor carriers strive to maintain empty miles at 10 percent or less of total miles.

Movements should be scheduled and dispatched so as to fully use labor and equipment in line with the market. Transportation service cannot be stored. Because the service must be in place for the market, this rule calls for the optimal equipment levels to be in place with the required personnel. Neither the equipment nor the required labor should delay the move. In some rail and trucking firms, power units accumulate at one end of the system while there is a need for them elsewhere, but no crews are available to move them back. Likewise, a waste occurs when crews arrive for work and there is no equipment available for the trip or little freight to be handled that day. Some motor carriers avoid this problem through the use of online shipment record systems that indicate to terminal managers how much freight will be arriving inbound during future shift periods. Thus, crews of optimal size can then be called for particular shifts of work.

TECHNOLOGY AND EQUIPMENT

The more expensive the long-haul vehicle, the greater the required investment in fast load/unload and other support equipment. Transportation vehicles represent capital investments. The economies of high capital investment call for high utilization of the equipment throughout the day, week, month, or year. Because these expensive investments are only earning revenue when they are running, firms strive to operate with a minimum of down time or loading and unloading time. This principle can be seen at airports where aircraft costing $110 million each arrive and depart within as little as 1 hour. Instead of being hand-loaded onto planes, food, luggage, and freight are loaded by mechanized equipment with food placed into expensive containers that are later unloaded by crew members while the plane is enroute. The basic financial principle here is that the cost of ground support equipment is less than the lost revenue that would result from not having the large vehicle itself in operation.

Generally, the larger the vehicle, or the more freight or passengers that can be moved in it, the less each unit will cost to move. Economies of scale suggest that railroad operating managers generally prefer to operate one long train per day than two shorter trains every 12 hours. This can be counterproductive in terms of service, so the trade-offs must be examined. With most transportation vehicles, the larger they are, the lower the ton-mile or seat-mile cost will be—for several reasons. One reason is that the manufacturing cost of most forms of propulsion engines makes larger horsepower or thrust engines cost less per horsepower than smaller units.

A second reason is that larger planes, trains, trucks, and so on can carry more payload without a proportionate increase in crew requirements. Simply illustrated, both a 10-passenger van and a 60-passenger bus are operated by one driver. Tankers capable of carrying 100,000 deadweight tons of oil require a 42- to 45-member crew. In addition, there are a multitude of other efficiencies in having fewer but larger vehicles in the fleet (in maintenance, training, and spare parts inventories). Overall, this principle of the larger the vehicle, the less each unit will cost to move is reflected in the trucking industry's efforts to get larger highway vehicle length and weight limits as well as barge industry efforts to get larger locks and dams for larger tows.

Carriers may dedicate vehicles to particular routes based on power, speed, and maneuverability. For example, in mountainous terrain motor carriers use high horsepower tractors with lower gear ratios to enable efficient traversing of the mountains. For open highway operations (e.g., interstates and turnpikes) the carriers utilize tractors that have higher gear ratios to permit operations at higher sustainable speeds. Conversely, tractors with lower horsepower are used in local delivery operations in which the speed requirements are less and the vehicle load is typically small.

In addition, the size of vehicle used on a particular route is determined in part by the demand on the route. Carriers attempt to match the vehicle carrying capacity with the demand on the route so as to eliminate excess capacity (vehicle too large for demand), minimize stockouts (vehicle too small for demand), and maximize service (vehicle of proportionate size to demand to permit desirable frequency of service). For example, an air carrier would not utilize a Boeing 747 with a carrying capacity of 450 passengers on a route that has a demand of 100 passengers per day. A smaller plane, probably one with a capacity of 125 passengers, would be utilized. But when consideration is given to frequency of service, the carrier might opt to use a regional jet with a carrying capacity of 50 passengers and offer two flights per day.

As indicated in Table 10.3, the carrier's load factor (passengers carried/seats available) is 100 percent with the 50-passenger plane, 80 percent with the 125-passenger plane, and 22 percent with the 450-seat plane. With the 50-seat plane, two flights per day are needed to meet daily demand, whereas only one flight per day is needed with the 125-passenger plane. Using a 450-passenger plane, a flight schedule of one flight every third or fourth day would be needed to increase the load factor to an acceptable level (above 60 percent). Clearly, the use of the 50- or 125-seat planes is desirable from a service perspective.

The fastest possible speed is not always the most efficient for economical operations. The cost of fuel consumption in relation to speed for most transportation vehicles is shown in Figure 10.1. As shown, the cost of fast speeds is very high. In the water carrier industry, this is often expressed as follows: As the speed of a vehicle doubles, the fuel consumption and horsepower requirements are squared. On the other hand, even with very low speeds, fuel consumption can be costly. For every form of vehicle (including planes and ships), a rough *J* curve represents fuel consumption in which the most fuel-efficient speeds are somewhat less than the vehicle's maximum possible speed.

Vehicle weight (tare weight) should be minimized in relation to **gross weight**. Transportation propulsion equipment as well as wings, hulls, rails, and highway pavements and bridges are designed for certain fixed gross weights (weight of the vehicle and the payload in freight or passengers). Therefore, the less the vehicle itself weighs, the more it can carry in the form of freight or passengers. Similarly, when a BTU of energy is burned, it is better for it to be spent on revenue-producing

Table 10.3 Equipment Size and Market Demand

	Plane Carrying Capacity (Passengers)		
	50	125	450
Route Demand/Day	100	100	100
Passengers/Flight	50	100	100
Plane Load Factor	100%	80%	22%
Service (Flights/Day)	2	1	1

FIGURE 10.1 Fuel Consumption in Relation to Speed

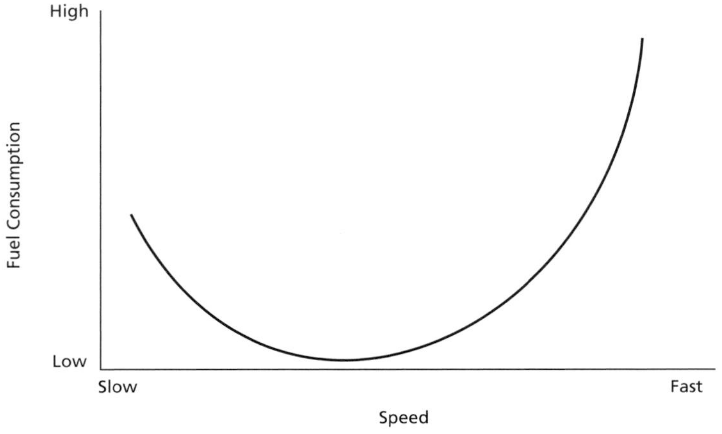

weight than on moving the vehicle itself. This is the reason why lighter metals and plastics are designed for use in motor carrier tractors and in aircraft. Several airlines are changing their aircraft color schemes to show bare metal on the main body fuselage. Paint represents several hundred pounds of weight that can be more effectively used for more freight or passenger carriage. Many motor carriers buy tractors that utilize fiberglass and plastic in the body of the vehicle.

Carriers attempt to maximize the length, width, and height of vehicles so as to increase cubic carrying capacity and loadability. However, vehicle dimensions are restricted by regulations and infrastructure constraints. For example, motor carrier trailers are limited to 53 to 57 feet in length, 102 inches in width, and 13 to 13.5 feet in height. Airplanes dimensions are constrained by airport runway size and ship by waterway structures such as locks and dams, harbor space, and bridges.

Larger vehicle dimension strategy is particularly important to carriers moving low-density freight. As Table 10.4 indicates, a larger vehicle permits the shipper to increase the shipment size that in turn lowers the cost per unit shipped. The longer the trailer, the greater the cubic capacity, the higher the shipment weight, and the lower the cost per pound transported. Cubic capacity increases by 26.7 percent between 45- and 57-foot trailers, and the cost per pound decreases by 21 percent. Shippers of low-density freight desire carriers to have high cubic capacity vehicles permitting larger loads and lower freight costs.

Table 10.4 Vehicle Size, Product Density and Cost per Unit

	Trailer Length (8 feet high × 8 feet wide)		
	45 Feet	**53 Feet**	**57 Feet**
Carrier Cost for 200-Mile Move	\$200	\$200	\$200
Trailer Cubic Capacity (ft^3)	2,880	3,392	3,648
Maximum Shipment Weight[a] (lb)	5,760	6,784	7,296
Cost per Pound	3.47¢	2.95¢	2.74¢

[a] Assumes product density of 2 lb/ft^3.

Equipment should be standardized as much as possible. Standardized equipment simplifies planning, purchasing, crew training, maintenance, and spare parts inventories. When equipment is standardized among firms, efficient equipment interchange can take place. Standardization came early to the railroad industry in the form of the standard track width of 4 feet, 8.5 inches. This allowed cars from most railroads to move over other lines and to avoid rehandling of freight. Truck trailer-hitch systems now are made so that almost total interchange can take place between any two power units and trailers. Even the airline industry's computerized reservation systems are designed so that other airlines can key in and make joint reservation and ticketing arrangements.

Equipment should be adapted to special market and commodity requirements. Many shipping firms require specialized equipment for the economical movement of particular commodities. During the 1960s, grain shippers desired the larger, more economical covered hopper cars in place of the traditional small boxcar. Airlines use the smaller DC-9 to serve shorter-distance routes and smaller cities; B-727s are used in longer-range markets; and jumbo planes are used in transcontinental long hauls. Each plane is designed for economical operation on certain routes. Transportation managers, however, must take care in adapting equipment. On one hand, there is the need to adapt equipment to special markets, and on the other hand, there is the need to recognize the advantages of standardization. Given the high capital cost and long life of transportation equipment, only long-range market planning and sound engineering and financial analysis can provide an optimum balance in this area.

The transportation industry is also characterized by extremely sophisticated communications technology. The railroads, for example, have utilized microwave communications for many years in the operation of trains. In fact, the communication network developed by the Southern Pacific Railroad was later sold and became what is known today as SPRINT. Nearly all truckload carriers such as Schneider National and J.B. Hunt have installed satellite technology and computers on their tractors to be able to communicate in real time with drivers. Aircraft, of course, employ sophisticated avionics in the cockpit to not only keep in touch with air traffic control but also to help maneuver the aircraft. Communications technology continues to be an important asset to carriers in their attempt to maximize the efficiency of their operations.

THE HUB-AND-SPOKE ROUTE SYSTEM

Many motor carriers in the 1970s, as well as airlines in the 1970s and 1980s, realigned route structures to the **hub-and-spoke system**. Figure 10.2 illustrates how this is applied. In the former point-to-point system, carriers attempted to use routes with stops that would maximize passenger or freight revenue. For example, a run might have been set up for A-G-C-F, another for E-B-A, and still another for E-C-G-D. Because too many stops resulted in loss of business to and from far points, demand was limited to nonstop and one-stop routes. Many times the carrier served two points between which passengers seldom traveled. Some routes were densely traveled, whereas others were sparse.

The hub-and-spoke system concentrates the flow of passengers and freight along a fewer number of routes with a main mixing point (hub) at a center. All flights or runs meet at this hub where passengers or freight can be switched to runs to any other point in the system. Thus, passengers from point A can quickly reach B, C, D, E, F, and G all within a few hours. It expands the number of points the carrier can offer travelers with good schedules, and it concentrates more business into a fewer number of runs. The motor carrier industry employs this structure using break-bulk terminals that consolidate freight to faraway points with a minimum of intermediate handling.

FIGURE 10.2 Point-to-Point System Versus Hub-and-Spoke System

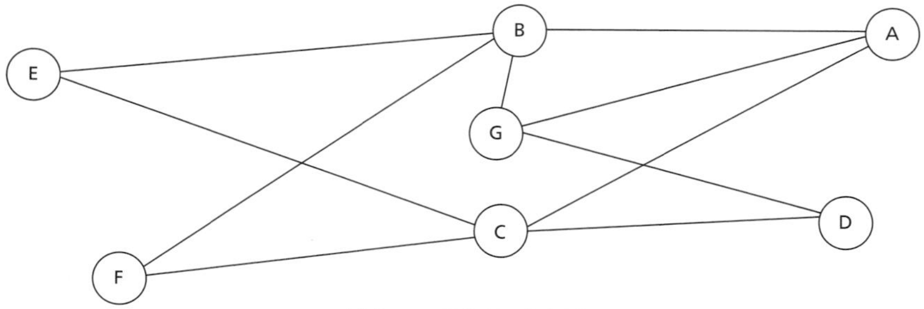

(a) Former Point-to-Point System

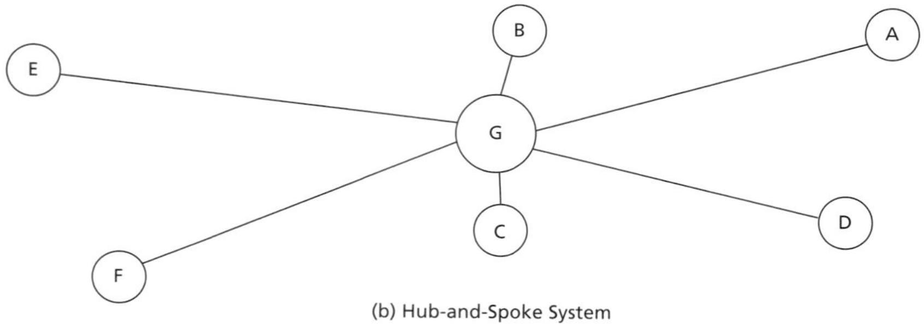

(b) Hub-and-Spoke System

A type of intermediate terminal is more common in the air industry. Called **hub terminals**, they serve as connection points for passengers departing from feeder, short-, and intermediate-haul flights from smaller cities and catching outbound spoke flights on long-haul jumbo planes. Northwest employs this concept at Detroit, American at Dallas-Fort Worth, United at Chicago, and Delta at Atlanta. At these cities, a major proportion of enplaning passengers is not originating from the hub city itself. This concept allows economical use of commuter lines and allows company DC-9s and B-727s to feed longer-haul B-757 and B-747 jumbos.

MARKETING

In a manufacturing firm, customer services complement the tangible output. In a service firm, customer service *is* the output. The intangibility of a service makes it more difficult to both sell and purchase. Transportation firms are faced with the challenge of developing and marketing something that cannot be felt, inventoried, or tested. This makes the marketing of carrier services extremely important to the profitability of the firm, and a knowledge of marketing concepts is critical to this success.

Service marketing is different from product marketing because of the differences between products and services. First, services are intangible. The inability to see, feel, and try a service before it is produced makes it more difficult to sell and more difficult for buyers to make purchase decisions. Second, there is a focus on the service provider. For example, the satisfaction an airline traveler feels toward a flight can be greatly influenced by the service provided by cabin attendants and ticket agents. Likewise, truck drivers who make customer deliveries can reinforce the positive image of a carrier or change a customer's perception of that image. Third, service providers are usually highly labor-intensive. This can make service quality subject to more variability. Although carriers have high investments in equipment, people actually provide the service. In fact, for most modes, labor is the largest cost category. Fourth, there is a simultaneous production and consumption of services; that is, there is no inventory. Transportation services cannot be produced before demand occurs to take advantage of production economies. Equipment, in the form of capacity, can be put into place in anticipation of demand, but production of transportation service occurs at the same time as demand. Finally, services are perishable. A move by rail has no shelf life. Likewise, empty seats on an airplane are lost forever immediately after takeoff.

These characteristics of services make the application of marketing concepts challenging, but not impossible. In fact, some transportation firms, such as Federal Express, are quite adept at marketing their offerings to the public. This was not always the case. Before the deregulation of the transportation industry, most carriers had an operational focus, rather than a marketing focus. This occurred because regulation, it has been argued, removed the incentive and opportunity for carriers to differentiate themselves in their markets. Pricing was controlled so service became the competitive factor.

Today, however, many carriers have adopted a marketing focus because of the freedoms given them by deregulation. Carriers that stress operations are more likely to optimize their existing system at the expense of customer satisfaction. These carriers see themselves as separate entities, rather than as a part of a buyer or receiver's logistics system. They tend to be inflexible and are very inwardly focused. On the contrary, marketing-oriented carriers stress customer satisfaction by tailoring their system and services to meet customer needs. These carriers are outwardly focused, are very flexible, and perceive themselves to be supportive of a buyer or receiver's logistics and business needs. More and more carriers are making the transition to a marketing orientation because of the demands of the market for this way of conducting business. In some cases, carriers have expanded to include tasks once performed by the shipper or consignee. An example is a carrier that hauls garments on hangers, adding labels and price tags prior to delivery.

The logical extension of this marketing orientation is the establishment of carrier-outsourcing, third-party operations. Most of the major trucking companies and air cargo carriers have outsourcing subsidiaries that offer a wide variety of value-added services to their customers. These outsourcing subsidiaries enable the carrier to differentiate its services from its competitors and gain customer business. Some carrier outsourcing subsidiaries offer very sophisticated computer software that enables the customer to have shipment visibility throughout the transportation process.

The magnitude of value-added services being offered by carrier outsourcing subsidiaries is immense. Carrier outsourcing subsidiaries offer a full range of services from basic storage to product enhancement to e-logistics. The carriers view these value-added services as critical service differentiation components in their overall marketing strategy. Generally, the carriers' value-added services lower the shipper's overall logistics costs and assures the carrier freight volume that will increase the utilization of its equipment. For example, at its Memphis hub, FedEx receives orders for electronic parts, picks up the orders from inventory held in Memphis, prepares the order for shipment, and moves the shipment to the destination in its planes and trucks.

COORDINATION

Marketing and operations should be coordinated. Many transportation firms operate with a loose coordination between marketing and operations. While sales personnel strive to attract more business and revenue, operating personnel strive to reduce total costs, which means minimized runs, trains, and so on. The two departments often come into conflict over daily decisions and long-term planning. A hallmark of successful carrier firms is that a close coordination exists between the two departments. A close link ensures that marketing efforts are conducted with operational costs in mind and that an operating department does not allow marketing efforts to be wasted on poor service.

Accountability for profit should begin in the lowest-level divisions of the firm. It is often difficult for every person in the firm to relate each of his or her actions to overall profitability. When no accountability system exists, it is difficult to measure good performance. Good accountability systems attempt to measure and present profitability by shipment, traffic lane, terminal, or another responsibility area. A good accountability system should also measure operating performance against selected standards so that minimizing total cost through slow or unreliable service is not always the operating department rule. The accountability system should relate company profit to operating and marketing performance within the realm of the company's market opportunities and needs.

Consistent, reliable service is often more desirable than the fastest possible service. Many surveys of traffic managers and travelers indicate that a later but reliable arrival time is generally preferred to a faster time that is less reliable. Many successful carriers set transit time standards that are attainable 95 percent of the time. This system is often preferred by shippers over promises of faster delivery that are only attainable 50 percent of the time. Because both early and late arrivals usually incur cost penalties, shippers often will select carriers that might take a day longer but that are more reliable in deliveries. Discounting the occasional need for fast, emergency shipment service, the cost of reliable but longer service time often is perceived as less than that of shorter but unreliable service time. Airlines recognize the marketing advantage of reliable arrival times and adapt to normal delays by padding schedules.

These efficiency approaches have evolved over time and are cited by firms as part of the reason for their success. The list is by no means exhaustive; more guidelines exist in the pricing area. Changes in the business environment, markets, and transportation technology might cause these rules to change as we move through the 21st century. The key is that planners and managers should always observe the economies of the firms they operate within and should steer their companies to the above-mentioned long-standing approaches or implement new or altered approaches as the conditions change.

CHALLENGES AFFECTING CARRIER MANAGEMENT

Transportation companies face some conditions that are not always present in manufacturing firms. These conditions, combined with the available ways in which carriers attempt to work around and with them, mean that there is no *one* ideal form of carrier management.

Transportation firms are geographically dispersed. By their very nature, carrier operations take place over vast distances. Unlike some manufacturing firms where all operations and management are often under one roof, transportation firms typically operate across oceans, through difficult mountain terrain, and in different countries. This causes carriers to rely upon tight controls, often with decentralized structures and close communications. The dispersion problem is compounded by the fact that the firm's product availability is constantly in motion.

The carrier employee who came in contact with the customer traditionally had been given relatively low status and training within the carrier organization. Today's carriers, however, have realized the importance these customer-contact personnel play in shaping customer perceptions concerning service quality. Examples of such personnel would include truck drivers, ticket agents, cabin attendants, and city dispatchers. More and more firms are investing in training for these individuals in an attempt to elevate their status within the organization and to prepare them to deal with the many problems that can occur in a service delivery operation. The driver shortage in the trucking industry and attempts to deal with this problem are an example of the trend. It is also important, however, that these trained individuals have access to upper or middle management to express ideas or to make suggestions concerning service improvements. In some cases, carrier organizations have used the concept of "empowerment" to allow customer contact personnel to solve problems and make decisions concerning dissatisfied customers immediately. Problems can result if the employee is not trained on how to use empowerment or does not "buy into" the concept.

Transportation operating employees are often minimally supervised. Operating personnel in trucks, trains, barges, and so on are often out of reach of minute-by-minute management supervision. Unlike production crews that are under close supervision, carrier crews often come into contact with their supervisors for only minutes per day and often only by phone or radio. Motor carrier managers know that one of the key productivity problem areas is in local pickup and delivery operations. Without supervision, a driver has the potential opportunity for low performance and little accountability to the terminal managers. This has caused many carriers to implement strong communication and performance measurement systems.

The wireless telephone and commercialization of satellite communication enable carrier management to keep in very close communication with operating employees. As wireless telephone providers have increased the geographic service coverage, wireless telephone service permits management to have virtually constant vocal contact with domestic operating personnel. The development of wireless airport Internet devices and satellite communication enables management and operating personnel to transmit data, such as routing instructions, weather conditions, traffic problems, and so on, that will improve operating efficiency.

Satellite communication technology also permits carrier management to track the progress of operating equipment and personnel. Many trucking companies use satellite communications with computers in the truck to monitor the progress of the vehicle, change delivery schedules, and arrange for unscheduled pickups without having the driver call the dispatcher, or conversely, the dispatcher call the driver. The satellite tracking systems can provide management with valuable performance data such as speed, time at each delivery, or time spent not operating. Ocean, air, and rail carriers utilize satellite communication in the same way.

The task of efficiently operating the transportation technology of the firm can create "monolithic" management structures. Every mode of transportation operates with vehicles and equipment requiring large investments and numbers of people. Coupled with the problem of geographic dispersion, carrier managements traditionally have attempted to organize along lines of skill specialization. This phenomenon is largely solidified by union labor contract job classifications in this industry. As a result, many carrier structures have evolved into very strong vertical hierarchies consisting of operations, finance, marketing, and many other disciplines. Modern systems management theory shows that a vertical management organization is inflexible, resistant to

STOP OFF

Keeping Freight Safe South of the Border

When a Mexican truck hauling 96 containers of cyanide was hijacked last May in Mexico, authorities on both sides of the border were concerned that a terrorist plot was about to unfold when they feared the truck had crossed the border into the United States. Though all containers were found in Mexico, this story could have easily had a more disastrous ending.

To combat theft, hijackings, and potential terrorist activity, Pinkerton Consulting and Investigations has teamed up with Safe Freight Technology to provide transportation companies operating in Mexico a solution that offers 20/20 supply chain visibility and security.

Safefreight offers real-time theft deterrence and 24/7/365 tracking through satellite, cellular, and radio frequency technologies to safeguard transportation and cargo assets. As the digital "eyes and ears" inside the trailer, this security system protects the freight trailer and its contents and immediately notifies predetermined key contacts should a security breach occur.

Pinkerton will use its security agents to provide continuous monitoring, and if necessary, respond to alarm-triggering events identified by the onboard security system. The company's expertise in Mexico and in supply chain security will provide transportation operators in Mexico and authorities on both sides of the border with reassurance that reasonable steps have been taken to safeguard cargo and public safety.

Source: "Keeping Freight Safe South of the Border," *Inbound Logistics*, July 2003, p. 34. Reprinted with permission of Inbound Logistics, http://www.inboundlogistics.com/articles.

change, a hindrance to cross-communications at low and middle management levels, and often inconsistent with overall corporate goals and missions. This specialization phenomenon often is cited as the reason that larger, mature firms sometimes tend to be unresponsive to the market and business environment, whereas smaller growing firms in the same mode display growth and vitality. The rise of the low-fare, regional airlines in the late 1990s and early 2000s is partial evidence of this phenomenon.

Single accountability for the transportation service "product" is often minimal. Because of the geographic dispersion factor, carriers often divide the operating department into distinct districts, regions, or divisions. A shipment often will pass through the responsibility sphere of several top operating managers. In interline movements, this situation is further complicated because the transportation "production function" is carried out by several carriers between the shipper and consignee. Without specific service performance systems measuring their tasks, individual operating personnel can lose sight of the need to maintain the company service standard or the assurances made to the customer by the salesperson. In manufacturing settings, the production manager can easily be held responsible for the quality of factory output. Although transportation service standards can be established, without effective discipline and accountability, reliable service is difficult to maintain.

It is often very difficult to determine the exact cost of transportation. Transportation is an activity in which the total cost consists of large amounts of fixed, overhead, and joint costs. These costs, presented in Chapter 9, "Costing and Pricing in Transportation," complicate the task of determining the cost of moving a passenger or package of freight. Specific production costs can easily be determined in most manufacturing activities, but in transportation costs can be affected by season, direction of traffic, volume of other goods in the same movement, the equipment being used, and the relative amounts of business in other parts of the firm.

All of these factors represent management challenges and conditions under which transportation managers function. Some of the factors appear to make transportation different from manufacturing, but the same principles of economics are at play here as in any other business entity. The difference lies in the extent of the challenges and how transportation firms handle them.

THE TERMINAL: THE BASIC TRANSPORTATION SYSTEM COMPONENT

The physical flows of carrier equipment and personnel are linked to the location and activities of terminal networks. Terminals are the nodes in a carrier system and perform various duties to facilitate the movement of their passengers or freight. All modes of transportation use terminals in one context or another. This discussion will address the terminals of all modes, but additional discussions will be presented on LTL carrier hub-and-spoke networks.

General Nature of Terminals

A terminal is any point in a carrier's network where the movement of freight or passengers is stopped so some type of value-adding activity can be performed. Important here is the concept of "value-adding." One of the basic tenets of logistics is to keep an item moving at a constant speed through the system. Once this item is stopped, costs are incurred, so a delay at a terminal must add more value than it incurs costs.

An overview of the terminal's role in the transportation process is given in Figure 10.3. Carrier A picks up the shipment at the origin and moves it to the consolidation terminal. At the consolidation terminal the small-size shipments are consolidated to increase the line-haul vehicle loading and achieve operating efficiency. Carrier A hauls the shipment to the transfer terminal where the shipment is transferred to Carrier B. Carrier B transports the shipment to the break-bulk terminal where it is separated from the consolidated load, loaded onto a delivery vehicle, and delivered to the consignee. The terminals in this example are providing various value-adding functions that are described below.

Terminals provide various **value-adding** activities in their role in a carrier's network. One of the more common activities is called concentration or **consolidation**. This activity takes small shipments or groups of passengers and combines them to make larger units. For example, the airlines use commuter operators from small communities to feed their major hubs where larger aircraft are dispatched to the next larger hub. Consolidation can offer the benefit of operating efficiencies for carriers because vehicle capacity is more fully utilized. However, consolidation can also affect service

FIGURE 10.3 Overview of Terminals in Carrier Network

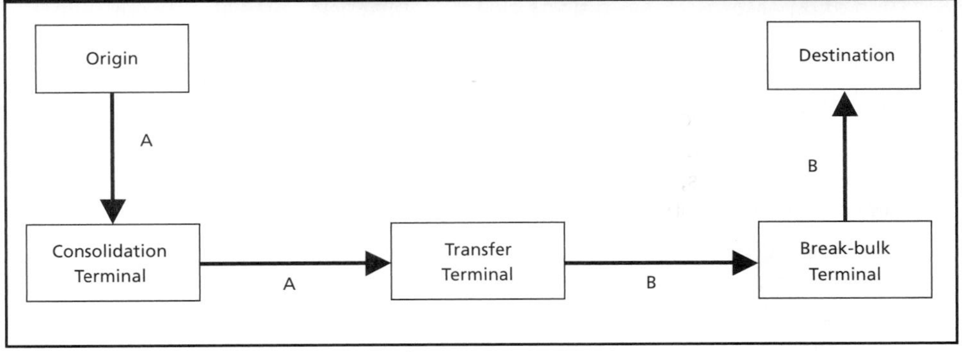

because shipments or passengers might be delayed until a vehicle is full. On the other hand, a fully consolidated vehicle (with similar destinations) in an LTL network might enjoy better service because its freight will not need to be handled at each intermediate terminal on the way to its final destination.

A second terminal value-adding activity is called *dispersion* or **break-bulk**. The opposite of consolidation, this activity involves separating larger units of freight or passengers into smaller units, normally for delivery to final destination. Consolidation and dispersion are usually performed simultaneously at most types of terminals.

Shipment services are also performed at terminals. These involve the storage of freight or accommodating passengers in transit, the protection of freight or passengers from the elements, and routing and billing (or ticketing). Passengers waiting in an airline terminal for the next flight are actually being warehoused. They are moved, segregated at their proper gate, and stored in the waiting area until their flight is ready to depart.

Many types of terminals are used to provide vehicle services, which could include equipment maintenance and the storage of equipment until it is needed. In LTL networks, break-bulks serve as major maintenance facilities for line-haul equipment and also temporarily store equipment that is not needed during periods of slow business.

Finally, terminals can provide shipment process services such as weighing services, customs inspections, claims processing, and interchange operations. All of these terminal activities are performed in an attempt to add value to either freight or passengers. These represent part of the carrier's "service package" offering to the customer and are critical to the successful delivery of the shipment or passenger.

Terminal Ownership

Terminals can represent a high level of fixed investment within a carrier's network. As discussed in Chapter 9, these costs will have a definite impact on a carrier's pricing structures and competitive stance within its markets, so how these costs are allocated to a carrier is important to its cost structure.

If the terminal is owned by the carrier, it will incur fixed costs, such as interest, depreciation, and taxes that will not vary in total with the volume of freight. As volume increases through these terminals, however, the fixed-cost allocation per unit will decrease, which can be an indicator of economies of increased utilization. Railroads, motor carriers, and pipelines almost exclusively own their terminals. Air freight and some port terminals also fall under private ownership.

The other method of terminal financing is through government ownership. In this case, the government (state, local, or federal) owns the terminal facility and charges carriers a user fee based on their activity level at the facility. This still results in the burden of high fixed costs. However, the government bears this burden and passes it along to users as a variable cost. This variable cost can affect the carrier's cost structure and, ultimately, its pricing structure. For example, passenger airlines pay a landing fee at airports and pay rent for ticketing and other space within the facility. Many port facilities are also provided by the government, with charges assessed for loading and unloading ships at these facilities.

Types of Terminals

Carriers utilize different types of terminals within their networks. This section will briefly describe these different types and specifically discuss the types of terminals used in an LTL motor carrier network.

RAIL

The most common form of rail terminal is called a **hump** or marshalling **yard**. Freight cars go through these yards and are then reclassified into new trains according to their destination or are sent to their final destination via a switching operation. Trains enter the receiving yard, where the road locomotives are removed and a yard engine is attached to the rear car. From here, the cars are moved to an inspection area where running gear is inspected for defects. The cars are then moved to the hump, which is an artificial hill that uses gravity to direct the car to a new train on another track. The speed of the cars going down the hump is controlled by retarders; these retarders also control car speed on the tracks so the humped car does not bang into the other cars. These new trains are held on classification tracks, also called *bowls*. From here, the trains move to the departure and forwarding yard where they receive road motive power, where appropriate.

The railroad industry also uses what can be called **transloading terminals**, where TOFC and COFC units are moved by road tractors to and from rail flatcars. These intermodal terminals operate in a similar manner to LTL terminals, consolidating and dispersing trailer and container units. In some cases, this is how interchange between railroads is handled.

WATER

Water terminals consist of a harbor and a port. The harbor provides the water portion for the staging, loading, and unloading activities of ships, whereas the port is the land area that provides space for freight and the loading and unloading of equipment. Harbors are either natural (such as bays) or constructed (such as a seacoast).

The port area of a water terminal includes pilotage and towage facilities for ships not able to use their own power to enter the port. Also included here are the mechanical aids used in the loading and unloading of the ships, such as overhead cranes, conveyors, and fork trucks. The port area also provides warehouse space, both open and closed, for the storage of goods and the holding of freight until it is cleared by customs. Several types of ancillary services are also performed at the port area. These would include ship repairs, bunkering or refueling, victualling (supplying the ship with food, drink, and other provisions), customs, security services, and medical services.

AIR

Freight and passenger terminals perform the same activities but do them in a somewhat different manner. Freight terminals include an area for staging the aircraft during the loading and unloading process and for staging before departure and after landing. Another area in the terminal itself is used for the consolidation and dispersion activities and the readying of air freight containers for the next portion of their journey. Also in the terminal area is storage space used for intermodal containers and oversize freight.

Passenger terminals also perform the consolidation and dispersion activities. However, because these are done using people, the terminal is designed to meet their needs. Gate areas are staging areas for individuals before departure. The walkways in the terminal allow for the movement of people to their proper destination, facilitating the consolidation and dispersion processes. Baggage-handling facilities allow passengers to match up with their luggage after arrival and prepare luggage for departing flights.

Because individuals are the units being handled in a passenger airport, various ancillary services are offered in the terminal. The more common types are restaurant, medical, and small shopping areas for people to utilize before departure. Various types of land transportation are also offered at these terminals. Pittsburgh's new airport has expanded on these ideas by developing a "mall" atmosphere within the terminal that includes numerous shops and eating establishments. So, passenger terminals are unlike freight terminals in ambiance but like them in their operations.

PIPELINE

Pipeline terminals consist of storage facilities, gathering lines, trunk lines, and pumping stations. These facilities provide temporary storage for a commodity (such as oil), provide movement of the commodity from gathering lines to trunk lines, and allow movement of the commodity to customers. Much of the operation at a pipeline terminal is automated, requiring very little intervention by personnel. These terminals provide consolidation and dispersion activities, much like terminals in other modes.

MOTOR CARRIER (TRUCKLOAD)

Truckload movements consist of one shipment between one consignor and one or more consignees. As such, these movements do not require intermediate handlings, nor do they require consolidation and dispersion activities. Truckload terminals, thus, do not generally offer freight-handling services. Rather, these facilities normally provide dispatching, maintenance, and fuel and maintenance services. Some carriers, such as Schneider National, are expanding the services offered by their terminal facilities. These carriers are adding restaurant and hotel services to give their drivers an alternative to truck stops. These terminals are designed primarily to accommodate drivers and equipment, but not freight, and provide the nucleus for the operation of the truckload network.

MOTOR CARRIER (LTL)

The terminal is a key facility in the operation of an LTL hub-and-spoke system. This section will present an expanded discussion of the types and roles of the terminal in this system.

The most common type of terminal found in the LTL system is the pickup and delivery (PUD) terminal, also called a *satellite* or *end-of-the-line (EOL)* terminal. The PUD terminal serves a local area and provides direct contact with both shippers and receivers. The basic transportation service provided at this terminal is the pickup and/or delivery of freight on peddle runs. A **peddle run** is a route that is driven daily out of the PUD terminal for the purposes of collecting freight for outbound moves or delivering freight from inbound moves. A PUD terminal will have several peddle runs in its customer operating area. During and after the deliveries, freight will be picked up from customers and returned with the driver to the terminal at the end of the day. When all the drivers return at the end of their shifts, the terminal will have freight to be consolidated and moved outbound to customers in other areas of the country.

The basic terminal services performed at these facilities are consolidation and dispersion. For example, freight moving inbound from other terminals (passing through a break-bulk) will be "broken" into individual deliveries by peddle run to be handled by the driver during that particular shift. Freight that is brought back by the peddle drivers for movement inbound will be consolidated into line-haul trailers for subsequent movement to the appropriate break-bulk. This is a basic cross-dock type of operation with the direction of freight flow across the dock that changes depending on whether the move is inbound or outbound.

Other services that are provided at the PUD terminal may include tracing, rating and billing, sales, and claims. However, some carriers are beginning to centralize these functions at break-bulks or other locations by taking advantage of telecommunications technology. For example, most LTL carriers use the Internet for tracing purposes. When the customer accesses the carrier's website, the shipper keys in the pro number or waybill number and the system provides the current status of the shipment.

Another type of terminal found in an LTL hub-and-spoke system is called a break-bulk. This facility performs both consolidation and dispersion (or break-bulk) services. Customers will rarely have contact with the operations at the break-bulk facility. The main purpose of this terminal is to provide an intermediate point where freight with common destinations from the PUD terminals is combined in a single trailer for movement to the delivering PUD terminal. Break-bulks will have many PUD terminals assigned to them as primary loading points.

Break-bulk facilities also serve as driver domiciles. City drivers located at a PUD terminal will always remain in their local area during their shift and will be able to return home when it is over. Line-haul drivers, however, might or might not be able to return home after a trip, depending on the length of haul they are assigned. For example, a turn means that a line-haul driver is assigned a load to be taken from the break-bulk (domicile) to a PUD terminal that is no more than 5.5 hours away. Because of DOT-mandated driving limits of 11 hours, that line-haul driver can make the trip, drop the trailer, and pick up another shipment destined back to the break-bulk within the 11-hour limit. However, a movement that requires more than 5.5 hours driving time in one direction will require a "layover"; that is, when the driver reaches the destination, a 10-hour rest period is required before that driver will be able to take a return load back to the break-bulk and return to the domicile.

LTL networks utilize what is called a **relay terminal**. A relay provides a layover point between break-bulks that are more than 11 hours apart. Relays do not handle freight; they are service facilities for drivers and equipment. For example, a line-haul run between Kansas City and Seattle might require a layover somewhere in Wyoming. If a break-bulk is not located in Wyoming, a relay is established. A shipment from Kansas City to Seattle will be dispatched in a vehicle with a Kansas City-domiciled driver. That driver will run to the relay in Wyoming, where the driver must go off duty. It is hoped that when that driver reaches the relay, there will be a Seattle-domiciled driver finishing the rest period who can get into the vehicle, continue it on its journey to Seattle, and return to the Seattle domicile.

LTL hub-and-spoke networks are sophisticated operations requiring hundreds of different types of terminals and thousands of pieces of equipment. Even within types of terminals, there are different sizes and terminals that are more "inbound" or "outbound" than others. This makes the management of such a system very complex and requires that certain management decisions be made to make it operate efficiently and effectively. These decisions are the focus of the next section.

Terminal Management Decisions

Many types of operating decisions need to be made when utilizing terminals in a carrier's network. Along with making these decisions, carrier management must also consider their strategic implications. This section will address a few of these types of decisions.

NUMBER OF TERMINALS

In many modes, this is a relatively simple decision. For example, passenger airline terminals will be located close to major population centers. This decision, however, usually does not belong to the carrier but to some local government agency. Railroads must also make this decision but are limited by geography and track locations for terminal sites. Railroads will not normally have many terminals in their networks. The mode with probably the most difficult decision in this area is LTL motor carriage, primarily because of the vast numbers of terminals in these systems and the relatively small investment needed to develop a terminal site.

The obvious question for an LTL motor carrier is "How many terminals should we have?" The obvious answer is "It depends." First, the degree of market penetration and customer service desired by the carrier will help determine the number of terminals to establish. In theory, the more terminals, the closer to the customer, the better the service. This also has proven to be true in practice. Realistically, at some point additional terminals will result in no incremental increase in service and might even detract from service.

The decision as to the number of terminals in a carrier's network is ultimately based on total cost. The carrier will examine the fixed and variable costs of operating different numbers of terminals in a system and select the number that minimizes total costs. Included in the total cost equation is the cost of different levels of service and the resultant effect on sales. The fewer the terminals in a system the longer the delivery times will be and consequently the lower the service level provided to shippers. The carrier will assess the probable cost of lost sales attributable to the lower service level and build this into the total cost equation. In the late 1990s most major LTL carriers made a strategic decision to reduce the total number of terminals in the network, in some cases a reduction of about 50 percent.

Many times in distribution system decisions for shippers, an assumption is made that manufacturing facilities are fixed and warehouse decisions must be made based on this fixed network. This assumption is also part of the terminal decision process for LTL motor carriers, except their "manufacturing facilities" are break-bulk terminals. Whether or not another terminal can be added to a break-bulk's operating region might simply be a question of available capacity at that break-bulk. Normally, each PUD terminal is assigned at least one door at a break-bulk. To add another PUD terminal means eliminating an existing terminal, physically adding another door to the break-bulk, or improving the productivity at the break-bulk to turn trailers in doors more than once per shift.

LOCATIONS OF TERMINALS

Closely related to the decision of how many terminals to establish is the decision of *where* to establish them. As previously mentioned, for airlines and railroads, this decision can be relatively simple because of geographic, government, and demand variables. LTL carriers, however, must consider some other variables. First, the Department of Transportation (DOT) limits the amount of time a driver can continuously operate a vehicle before a rest period is required. Currently, this limit is 11 hours, so optimally, PUD terminals should be located no more than 11 hours away from a break-bulk. This would allow a driver to complete the run without having to go off duty or use team drivers. Second, PUD terminals should be located to minimize the distance freight would need to be backhauled to the break-bulk. The assumption here is that freight flows from east to west and north to south in the United States. When a shipment is picked up, the idea is to send in that freight in one of these directions as soon as possible. For example, given that a carrier has two break-bulks, one in Lancaster, Pennsylvania, and the other in Columbus, Ohio, where would a PUD terminal based in Pittsburgh send its freight? Based on the assumption made earlier about freight flows, Pittsburgh would send its freight to Columbus; that is, a shipment picked up by a Pittsburgh peddle driver would begin its east–west journey more productively by being sent to Columbus because if it were sent to Lancaster, it would conceptually duplicate this distance when it began its journey from Lancaster to the west (actually passing right by Columbus). Finally, market penetration and potential will help determine terminal location. As mentioned in the decision process for determining the number of terminals, getting closer to the customer can many times improve the level of service given to that customer.

Recent trends in the LTL sector have seen significant reductions in the number of terminals as these carriers strive to provide overnight and second-day delivery to more and more customers. To do this, many interterminal runs have been realigned with the resultant elimination of intermediate handling. This has resulted in increased load factors and reduced transit times. Less handling has also improved the claims experience for the LTL carriers. The long-haul LTL carriers will still favor the hub-and-spoke operation, while the regional carriers will still look toward fewer terminals with more direct runs.

Yellow Freight reduced its number of terminals to 350 from 650, while Roadway Express has shrunk from more than 600 facilities to fewer than 435. This trend will continue as the competition in the 500- to 1,200-mile lanes increases. The regional LTL carriers are challenging the national carriers in these lanes so that each must find more efficient handling methods to stay competitive from both a cost and service standpoint.[1]

EQUIPMENT SELECTION AND DEVELOPMENT

In most cases, equipment represents the largest operating asset that a carrier maintains. With all of the different types and locations of equipment, positioning becomes critical to successful operations. Seasonal influences such as holidays or harvest times must also be considered, as this can drastically alter demand. Airlines must decide which type of aircraft to dedicate to a specific flight, depending on length of flight and passenger demand. The longer the flight, the more efficient a larger aircraft will be.

Truckload and LTL carriers need to make two types of decisions: what type of tractor (power) and what type of trailer. In a TL operation, equipment positioning at terminals is not as important as it is in an LTL operation. However, power must be specified to be able to handle the size and length of the load along with the terrain over which it travels. Many different specifications for tractors can be used, including single axle and twin axle with different engine and drive train combinations. Decisions regarding trailers include length (45 feet, 48 feet, 57 feet) and trailer type (dry van, refrigerated, ragtop, container, flatbed). These decisions will be made in light of market demands and the type of carrier operation.

LTL carriers must make the same types of equipment decisions as a TL carrier, along with deciding where to deploy this equipment. Similar to an airline equipment decision, LTL carriers need to position certain types of equipment at certain terminals. For example, city delivery vehicles and tractor–trailer combinations (either 28-foot or 40-foot trailers) will be positioned at PUD terminals, while line-haul trailers (usually 45 or 48 feet) and line-haul tractors (single or twin axle) will be assigned to breakbulks. Compounding the LTL decision is the inclusion of 28-foot trailers (also called *pups*, *twins*, or *double bottoms*) in the equipment decision. Having the right mix of power and trailers at a particular terminal location determines its ability to efficiently serve its customers.

Rail equipment decisions can become increasingly difficult because of the numerous types of cars utilized in a rail operation. Different types of cars can be assigned to specific customers depending on the type of commodity moved. This means that the empties have to be repositioned to the customer's location at the proper time for loading. Railroad operations include hopper cars, gondola cars, boxcars, dry bulk cars, and tank cars. Also, decisions concerning motive power must be made. The length and weight of trains along with the type of terrain will determine the proper mix of motive power. For example, engines that operate in some western states are equipped with snow plows on the front to help clear a snowy track. In other operations, unmanned helpers (engines without human operators controlled by radio from the front engine) are used over hilly terrain.

Water carriers normally have fixed types of ships; for example, they will operate a container ship or a tanker. Of concern here, especially for container ships and general cargo ships, is having the right mix and type of containers or other freight-storage devices in the correct position. Many shipping lines have their own containers and also participate in common container pools with other ship lines. Because ocean containers normally come in two lengths—20 feet and 40 feet—it is important to have the right container in place to be loaded with freight. Because containers need chassis for road transportation, this must also be factored in the equipment mix. Also, ships are often configured for a certain mix of container lengths (although they can be changed to accommodate a different mix). Finally, pipelines must also make equipment decisions. Although one might not think that pipelines operate "equipment," their pipes represent their rolling stock. Decisions concerning pipe diameter (affected by distance, type of commodity, and speed), pipe length, and type of pipe are made when pipelines are constructed. Unlike the other modes, pipeline decisions are usually made only once because of the large fixed investment involved.

Equipment decisions are important to all modes of transportation. Equipment represents the rolling stock of the carrier and provides the actual movement of freight between modes. Carriers have significant investments made in their equipment and utilize sophisticated maintenance programs to keep their investment roadworthy. These decisions, then, are critical to successful terminal management.

Summary

- The carrier operating network and assets are spread over a vast geographic territory and are interrelated and interdependent.
- A high proportion of operating tasks is performed beyond the scope of supervisors.
- Carrier operations come into direct contact with the general public, making safety a critical factor.
- Transportation has a high degree of craft-based unionization.
- Time, consistency, and damage are service performance measures used by carriers. Profitability, liquidity, and solvency are financial performance measures used.
- The basic transportation efficiency techniques include moving in a straight line, minimizing handling, utilizing full vehicle capacity, minimizing empty miles, and effective scheduling.
- The hub-and-spoke carrier network allows for the efficient use of carrier capacity through hub and PUD-type terminals.
- The marketing of transportation services is different than that for products because of the intangibility of the service.
- The terminal is the basic component of carrier operating networks. Various types of terminals exist, and each has its own role in successful carrier operations.
- Carrier management terminal decisions include the number of terminals, the location of terminals, and equipment selection and deployment.

Key Terms

break-bulk, 340
consolidation, 339
gross weight, 331
hub terminals, 334
hub-and-spoke system, 333
hump yard, 341
peddle run, 342
relay terminal, 343
rule of efficiency, 328
transloading terminal, 341
value adding, 339

Study Questions

1. Discuss the characteristics of the transportation operating network.
2. Describe the financial ratios used by carriers to measure profitability, liquidity, and solvency.
3. Explain the strategic implication of transportation producing a service.
4. Discuss the rationale for government safety regulations of transportation.
5. During the early 2000s the demand for air passenger transportation declined but the load factors for the major air carriers increased. Please explain.
6. Cite the techniques of efficiency and the underlying economic principle(s) in the following transportation practices:
    a. Lower airline passenger rate for a Saturday stayover
    b. Replacing 48-foot trailers with 57-foot trailers
    c. Railroad and motor carrier contract rates
7. Explain the economic rationale for having an efficient communication system in today's transportation company.
8. Describe the value-added role of the carrier's terminal.
9. Discuss the economic strategy for the different types of terminals used in an LTL carrier operation.
10. Describe the hub-and-spoke system. What purpose does it serve in carrier operations?

Notes

1. Peter Bradley, "In It For the Long Haul," *Logistics Management,* January 1997, pp. 47–50.

Suggested Readings

Bond, David. "Mixed Bag for Airlines," *Aviation Week & Space Technology*, April 7, 2003, p. 56.

Bowman, Robert J. "Are Bigger Ocean Carriers Better? Shippers and Lines Don't See Eye to Eye," *Global Logistics & Supply Chain Strategies*, March 2000.

"DC Air Outlines Low Cost Strategy," *Commuter/Regional Airline News*, June 12, 2000, p. 1.

Hannon, David. "Carriers Fight Hard for Your LTL Business," *Purchasing*, March 7, 2002, p. 37.

Menachof, D., and O. Wasenberg. "The Application of Benchmarking Techniques by Road Transport Companies in the United Kingdom and the Netherlands," *Transportation Journal*, Vol. 40, No. 2, 2001, pp. 40–56.

Min, Hokey and Thomas Lambert. "Truck Driver Shortage Revisited," *Transportation Journal*, Vol. 42, No. 2, 2002, p. 5–17.

Saltzman, G. M., and Michael H. Belzer. "The Case for Strengthened Motor Carrier Hours of Service Regulations," *Transportation Journal*, Vol. 41, No. 4, 2002, pp. 51–71.

Suzuki, Y. "The Effect of Airline Positioning on Profit," *Transportation Journal*, Vol. 39, No. 3, 2000, pp. 44–54.

Thomas, Jim. "LTL Carriers: Can They Survive an Economic Downturn?" *Logistics Management*, July 2001, p. 55.

Case 10-1

Shiner International Transportation Company (A)

Shiner has been a TL carrier for the past 20 years and is currently the largest carrier of its type in North America. It has been able to establish its leadership in its industry through aggressive marketing, intermodal agreements, and leading-edge communications technology. However, Shiner sees its growth as being limited in its current markets and continuously faces new competitors in the truckload business.

Top management at Shiner has agreed that growth could come with entry into a relatively oligopolistic industry—LTL trucking. Because Shiner is a TL operation, it has a relatively low debt load and could absorb an initial high investment in terminal facilities. Shiner also sees that entry into this market could offer its already stable customer base a larger service package over a wider range of shipment sizes. Shiner feels that its experience in the TL transportation business will position it favorably for entry into the LTL business.

Shiner is also aware that this entry into a free market-based segment of the transportation industry will not go unchallenged. Current carriers in the LTL industry have established terminal networks, have gained economies of scale and of scope, and have very loyal customer bases. These existing carriers could certainly start a price war or develop special services that would make survival difficult for Shiner in the LTL market. However, Shiner's management feels that the time is right for new competition in this segment of the market and have prepared a public stock offering to get equity capital for terminal facility investments. Success for Shiner rests with its ability to generate customer interest and demand and not only meet existing competitor service levels but exceed them on new and innovative services.

Case Questions

1. Perform an environmental analysis of the LTL industry and of Shiner to determine its strengths, weaknesses, opportunities, and threats.
2. Develop a marketing plan to help guide Shiner in its entrance into the LTL industry.

Case 10-2

Shiner International Transportation Company (B)

Following the environmental analysis of the LTL market segment, Shiner management concluded that the market potential was quite high. At the executive management team meeting the discussion centered on the business model that Shiner should implement as it moves into the LTL business sector.

Two different business models were developed in the meeting. The first model is a Shiner asset-based and operated model, whereas the second is a hybrid-outsourcing model. In the first model, Shiner would invest in the terminals, materials-handling equipment, pickup and delivery vehicles, and information system. The labor force at the terminals plus the drivers would be full-time Shiner employees. The financial risk plus the operations risk of not having terminal operation experience is high for the asset-based model, but the control and profitability is higher than the outsourcing model.

The modified outsourcing model would utilize a third-party logistics-outsourcing firm to provide the terminal operations and pickup and delivery services. Shiner would utilize its TL fleet to haul the consolidated LTL shipments among the terminals. The outsourcing model requires a lower investment and has a lower financial risk if the venture is not successful. However, the customer-critical services of pickup and delivery operations are under the control of the third party, not Shiner. Some members of the executive management team feel the outsourcing model will not produce the desired service levels LTL customers desire. These executives believe that direct control over all LTL operations is the only model that will assure success.

Case Questions

1. Examine the benefits of the asset-based and outsourcing business models for Shiners new LTL venture.
2. Are there other business models that Shiner could employ to enter the LTL market?
3. Which business model would you recommend? Why?

Chapter 11

Information Management and Technology

The use of technology to collect and convey information is not new to the transportation industry. Railroads use microwave technology to manage and track train movement, airlines use sophisticated avionics to manage the flight of their aircraft, ocean vessels use onboard computers to navigate domestic and international waterways, motor carriers use onboard computers and satellite systems to efficiently manage their asset base, and pipelines use computer technology to manage pumping stations to ensure the smooth flow of their products. What is new is the integration of this technology among carriers, shippers, receivers, and third parties to efficiently and effectively manage the supply chain.

The adoption of information technology (IT) in the supply chain exploded during the 1990s, and its use continues to grow in the 21st century. What has caused this exponential growth in the use of information technology? Many companies have found that using information technology has allowed them to significantly reduce assets (inventories or equipment) and better manage information, product, and cash flows among all supply chain partners. The cost of information technology has also decreased significantly over the past 10 years.

A related driver of the growth in IT over the past several years was the "Y2K" problem. Rather than fix existing legacy information systems to accommodate the year 2000, many firms opted to totally reengineer their information systems with new systems and technology. This chapter will examine information systems and technology from a supply chain perspective; it will look at both topics from the perspectives of the shipper, carrier, and receiver. This focus is important because of the need for carriers and their customers to be able to integrate the flow of information. To accomplish this goal, this chapter is divided into four major sections: 1) Information Systems, 2) Information Sources, 3) Information Technology, and, 4) Types of Information Technology. The authors would like to acknowledge the contributions to this chapter from Dr. William L. "Skip" Grenoble, executive director of the Center for Supply Chain Research at the Pennsylvania State University.

INFORMATION SYSTEMS

Before a discussion on technology can begin, the concept of information systems must be addressed. Logistics and transportation operations are sometimes overwhelmed with the vast amount of data available to them. Information systems are designed to use the available data to portray meaningful information to decision makers. Decisions are made at various organizational levels within carrier firms and their customers' firms. These decisions can be made at the transactional levels as well as at the strategic level. For example, a transactional carrier decision might be how to best dispatch a driver and vehicle to minimize empty miles and maximize revenue. A strategic carrier decision might address fleet sizing based on forecasted freight flows over the next 5 years. The transactional decision is influenced by the strategic decision and vice versa. Similar types of decisions are made by shippers and receivers. The point is that some type of information system integration is necessary to link all of the players in the supply chain. The diagram in Figure 11.1 can be used as a mechanism to help link the different types of information systems in a shipper or receiver organization.[1] The importance of this diagram is its ability to link database files with transactional decisions and strategic decisions. This diagram also identifies the types of data necessary to make these decisions. Decisions regarding inventories, warehousing, manufacturing, and transportation are linked to a common database. This is the basis for enterprise resource planning (ERP) systems. The sources of data necessary to manage the transportation process will also be discussed in more detail later in this chapter.

Certain types of information are necessary to facilitate the transportation process between a shipper and a receiver. All of the elements in Figure 11.1 provide inputs to and receive outputs from transportation. More specifically, information required to make the transportation process work can be classified into pretransaction, transaction, and posttransaction information.[2] Pretransaction information includes all information necessary to plan the carrier movement, transaction information includes all information necessary while the shipment is in motion with the carrier, and posttransaction information includes all information necessary after the shipment has been delivered.

Table 11.1 shows the requirements for all three types of information for the shipper, carrier, and receiver. Although it is not comprehensive, the table does show that information flows must be linked among all three parties to make the shipment arrive as promised. In the pretransaction phase, the shipper needs purchase order information and possibly forecast and point-of-sale (POS) data to help plan carrier capacity and selection decisions. The shipper also needs information from the carrier as to equipment availability and scheduled pickup time. Strategically, the carrier needs volume forecast data from the shipper to plan capacity appropriately. Transactionally, the carrier also needs bill of lading (BOL) information as well as desired pickup and delivery times from the shipper. The receiver requires an advance shipment notice (ASN) from the shipper as well as a scheduled delivery time from the carrier (or from the shipper in the ASN).

FIGURE 11.1 Integration of Logistics Information Systems on a Hierarchical and Make-to-Stock Basis

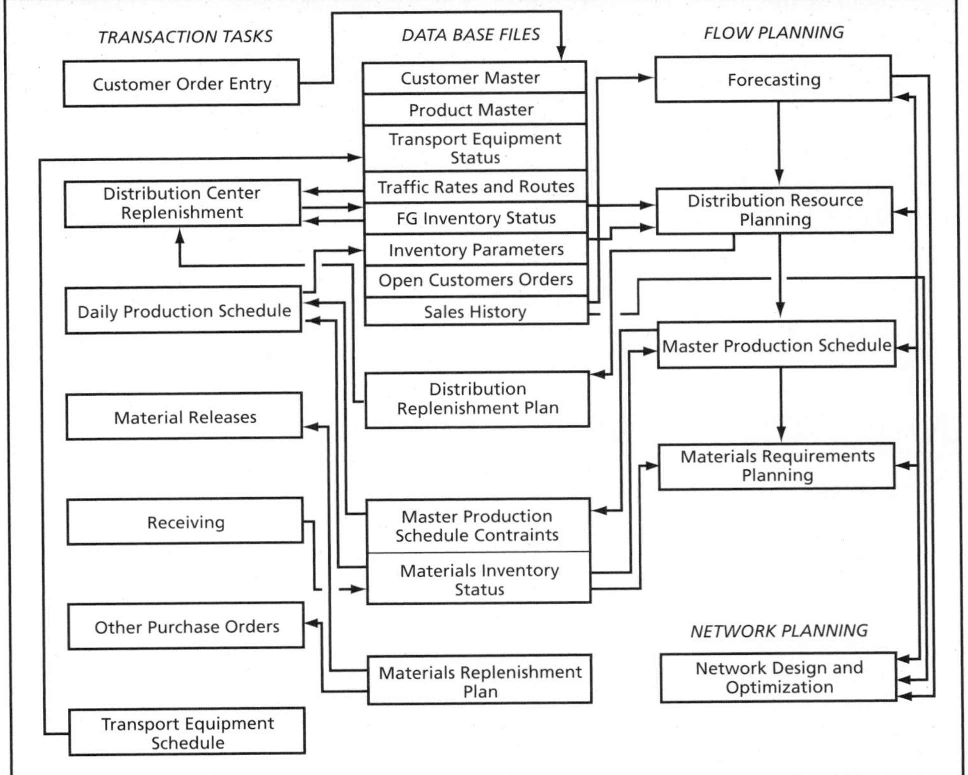

Source: Alan J. Stenger, Steven C. Dunn, and Richard R. Young, "Commercially Available Software for Integrated Logistics Management," *The International Journal of Logistics Management*, Vol. 4, No. 2, 1993, p. 63. http://www.ijlm.org

Table 11.1 Information Needed to Manage the Transportation Process

Transportation Activity	Information User		
	Shipper	**Carrier**	**Receiver**
Pretransaction	P.O. Information Forecasts Equipment Availability	BOL Information Forecasts Pickup/Delivery Time	Advance Ship Notice Delivery time
Transaction	Shipment Status	Shipment Status	Shipment Status
Posttransaction	Freight Bill Carrier Performance Proof of Delivery Claim Information	Payment Claim Information	Carrier Performance Proof of Delivery Claim Information

The transaction phase requires that all three parties receive information regarding shipment status (such as, will it arrive as planned?). Many carriers manage shipment status through technologies such as satellite tracking, onboard computers, and bar coding. Normally, it is the carrier that generates shipment status information. Often this is handled on an exception basis where the shipper and/or receiver are notified of shipment status only if changes occur in delivery times or other shipment requirements.

Finally, the posttransaction phase requires a freight bill from the carrier if the shipment is free onboard (FOB) destination, as well as a proof of delivery (POD) and other verification of carrier performance, such as damage or claims information. The carrier requires payment information (when and how much) from the shipper as well as claims information, if necessary, from the receiver. The receiver might require carrier performance information (on-time, damage-free) from the carrier as well as POD from the shipper or carrier to initiate the payment process to the shipper for the product. These various types of information and their flows are captured in Figure 11.2.[3]

Again, a critical component of the transportation process is that all the information flows among the various parties are integrated, just as they are for the logistics process shown in Figure 11.1.

INFORMATION SOURCES

The previous section identified the various types of information needed to manage the transportation process. This section will identify the sources of this information. Traditionally, transportation information has come from what can be called "documentation." This implied paperwork was generated by the shipper and carrier to initiate, transport, and terminate a shipment. The paperwork required to perform this service included bills of lading, waybills, manifests, and freight bills. In many cases, this paper trail was produced manually and caused many problems for the successful delivery of a shipment. Bills of lading and freight bills were required to be generated by the carrier with their requirements defined by the Surface Transportation Board (STB).

FIGURE 11.2 Examples of Information Flows

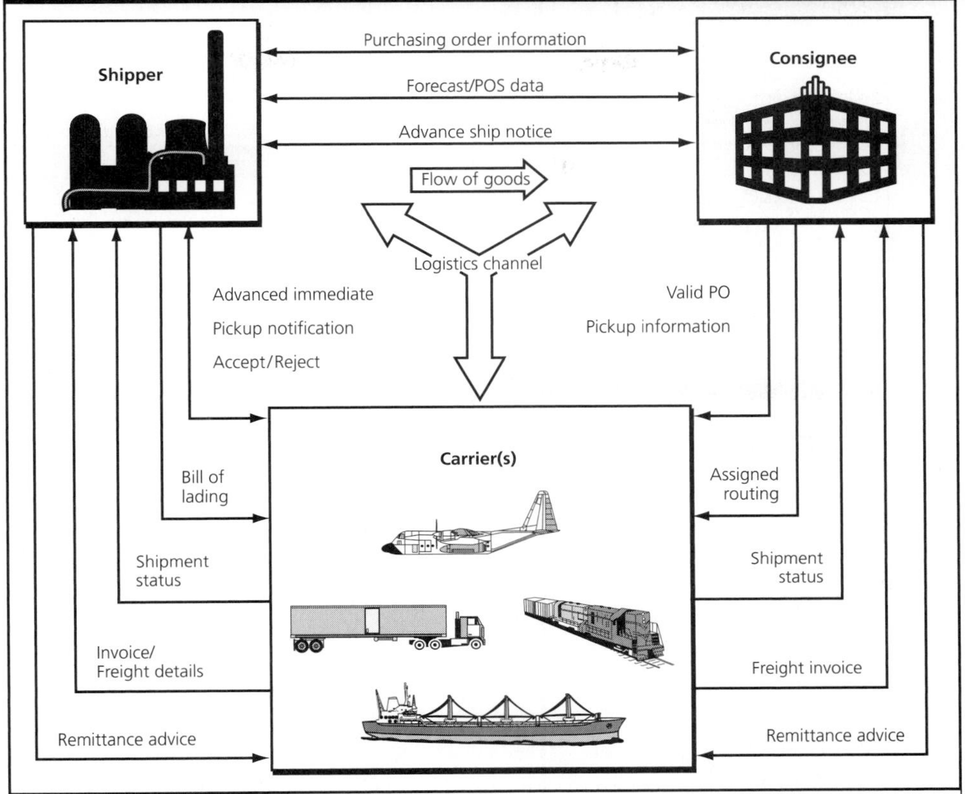

Source: From *The Management of Business Logistics*, 7th edition by Coyle/Bardi/Langley.© 2003. Reprinted with permission of South-Western, a division of Thomson Learning: http:// www.thomsonrights.com. Fax (800) 730-2215.

Today many of these transactions have become "paperless" through the use of electronic data interchange (EDI) or Intranets among carriers, shippers, and receivers. This has eliminated many of the problems associated with manually generated documents and has improved transportation service for shippers and receivers as well as cash flow for carriers. This discussion will not focus on the legal requirements of the various sources of transportation information but will pay attention to the role of these various "documents" and the information they convey.

Bill of Lading

The **Bill of Lading** (BOL) is the document used to initiate the request for a transportation movement. This is probably the most important transportation document because it provides information necessary for the carrier to plan for and perform the transportation service. Although the federal government requires common carriers to generate a BOL for every shipment, most BOLs are customized and generated by the shipper. Figure 11.3 is an example of a BOL.

The BOL serves five legal purposes: 1) It is a receipt for the goods; 2) it contains a description of the shipment; 3) it can be evidence of title; 4) it is an operating document; and 5) it defines the terms of the contract between a shipper and a carrier.

FIGURE 11.3 Bill of Lading Example

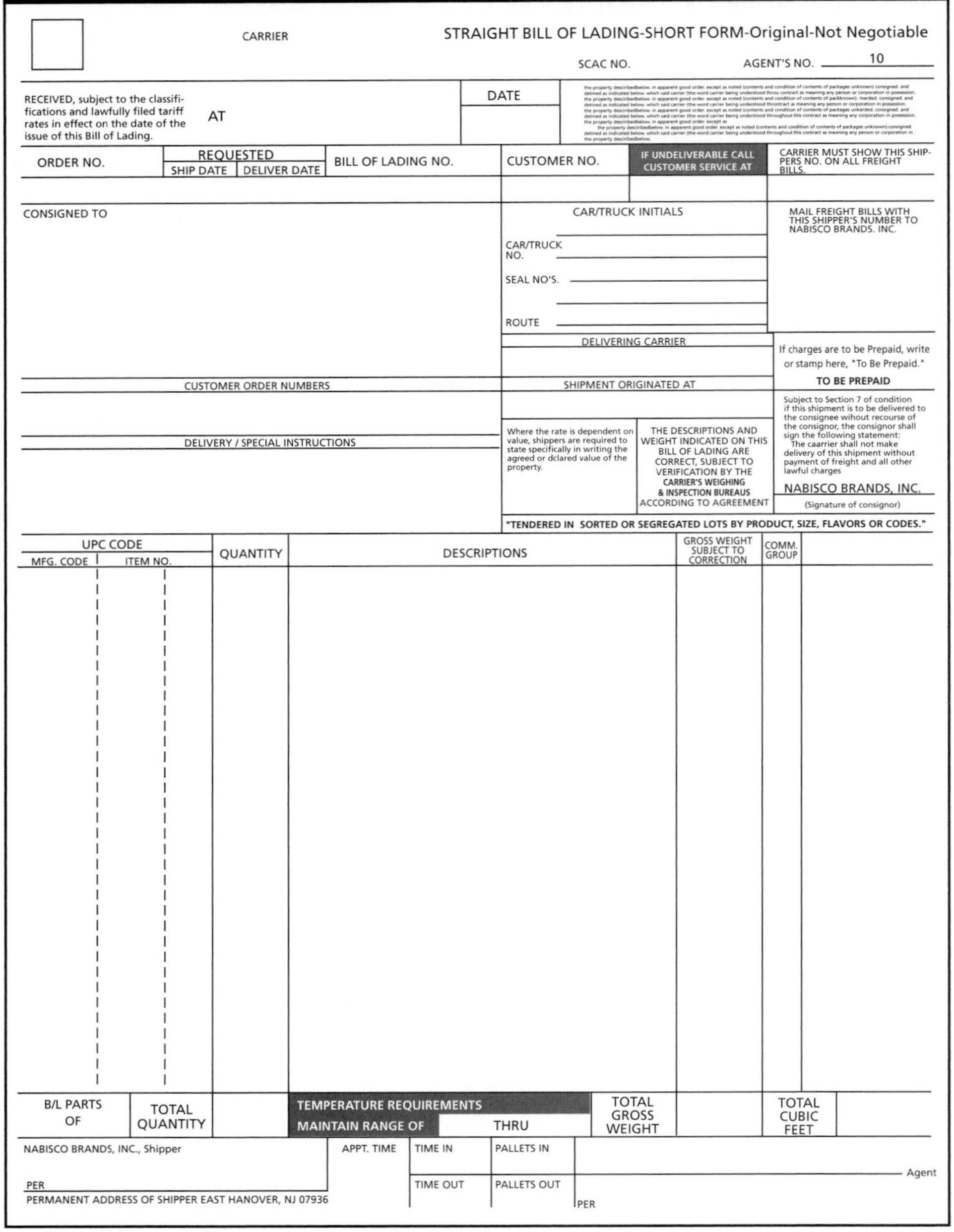
CARRIER
STRAIGHT BILL OF LADING-SHORT FORM-Original-Not Negotiable
SCAC NO. AGENT'S NO. 10

RECEIVED, subject to the classifications and lawfully filed tariff rates in effect on the date of the issue of this Bill of Lading. AT
DATE

ORDER NO.	REQUESTED SHIP DATE	REQUESTED DELIVER DATE	BILL OF LADING NO.	CUSTOMER NO.	IF UNDELIVERABLE CALL CUSTOMER SERVICE AT	CARRIER MUST SHOW THIS SHIPPERS NO. ON ALL FREIGHT BILLS.

CONSIGNED TO
CAR/TRUCK INITIALS
CAR/TRUCK NO.
SEAL NO'S.
ROUTE
DELIVERING CARRIER
SHIPMENT ORIGINATED AT
MAIL FREIGHT BILLS WITH THIS SHIPPER'S NUMBER TO NABISCO BRANDS, INC.
If charges are to be Prepaid, write or stamp here, "To Be Prepaid."
TO BE PREPAID
CUSTOMER ORDER NUMBERS
DELIVERY / SPECIAL INSTRUCTIONS
Where the rate is dependent on value, shippers are required to state specifically in writing the agreed or dclared value of the property.
THE DESCRIPTIONS AND WEIGHT INDICATED ON THIS BILL OF LADING ARE CORRECT, SUBJECT TO VERIFICATION BY THE CARRIER'S WEIGHING & INSPECTION BUREAUS ACCORDING TO AGREEMENT
Subject to Section 7 of condition if this shipment is to be delivered to the consignee wihout recourse of the consignor, the consignor shall sign the following statement: The caarrier shall not make delivery of this shipment without payment of freight and all other lawful charges
NABISCO BRANDS, INC.
(Signature of consignor)
"TENDERED IN SORTED OR SEGREGATED LOTS BY PRODUCT, SIZE, FLAVORS OR CODES."

UPC CODE MFG. CODE	UPC CODE ITEM NO.	QUANTITY	DESCRIPTIONS	GROSS WEIGHT SUBJECT TO CORRECTION	COMM. GROUP	

B/L PARTS OF | TOTAL QUANTITY | TEMPERATURE REQUIREMENTS MAINTAIN RANGE OF THRU | TOTAL GROSS WEIGHT | TOTAL CUBIC FEET

NABISCO BRANDS, INC., Shipper
PER
PERMANENT ADDRESS OF SHIPPER EAST HANOVER, NJ 07936
APPT. TIME | TIME IN | PALLETS IN | TIME OUT | PALLETS OUT
Agent
PER

Although BOLs are usually customized to fit a shipper's needs, certain basic types of information are included at a minimum on all BOLs. Table 11.1 specifies the information contained in the BOL as necessary in the pretransaction phase of the transportation process. The following represents the minimum requirements for BOL information:

1. *Origin/destination of the shipment*. This information is used by the carrier to identify the freight lane that will be used for the shipment. It also allows the carrier to identify the availability of equipment and personnel to provide the transportation, or to begin to position capacity to move

the shipment. This might not be the same as the billing location. This can also be used by the carrier to determine pickup and delivery times.

2. *Carrier designation.* Shippers will generally integrate their BOL-generation process with their carrier-routing process. This allows the shipping location to comply with its contracts and/or routing guides and helps identify the initial contact with the pickup carrier.
3. *Special operating instructions.* This information allows the carrier to perform the transportation service in compliance with the needs of the shipper. Special instructions might include temperature control, loading/unloading requirements, blocking/bracing, pickup or delivery requirements, and so on. The point of this information is to make the carrier fully aware of the nature of the shipment and what might be necessary, above and beyond normal transportation service, to deliver the shipment in compliance with the demands of the shipper.
4. *Shipment description.* This information includes not only a description of the commodity but also the quantity and weight of the commodity or commodities.

   The carrier will use this for equipment selection, pickup, and rating/billing decisions.

   This section can also alert the carrier of any hazardous materials that might be in the shipment.
5. *Billing instructions.* If not the same as the origin identified above, this provides the carrier the information concerning the identity of the party responsible for paying for the transportation service.

Two types of BOL exist: 1) straight, or non-negotiable; and 2) order, or negotiable. The title to the shipment cannot be transferred to another party using a straight BOL. An order BOL can be used to transfer the title to the goods. A sample order BOL can be seen in Figure 11.4. The order BOL actually becomes evidence of the title to a shipment and is very indicative of the product, cash, and information flows present in a supply chain. Figure 11.5 represents a schematic of how the order BOL works.

The order BOL is signed by the carrier and is sent by the shipper to a bank, indicating the shipment is in progress. The bank notifies the consignee that it has received the order BOL and requests payment of the invoice. If the consignee forwards payment to the bank, the bank releases the order BOL to the consignee as evidence of the title. Before the carrier can deliver the shipment to the consignee, the consignee must present the order BOL to the carrier. Most cash and information flows using the order BOL are done electronically in today's environment.

Waybill

What a BOL does for a shipment, a **waybill** does for a railcar. It is the operating document that governs the movement of the car as well as the descriptive document of the car's contents. The waybill assigns a car to a train, designates switching points, identifies routes, specifies trailer numbers for TOFC/COFC shipments, and contains billing information. Every railcar will be identified by a waybill. Today most railroads generate and transmit waybills electronically.

Manifest

A **manifest** is used as the operating and descriptive document for motor-carrier trailers.

FIGURE 11.4 A Sample Order Bill of Lading

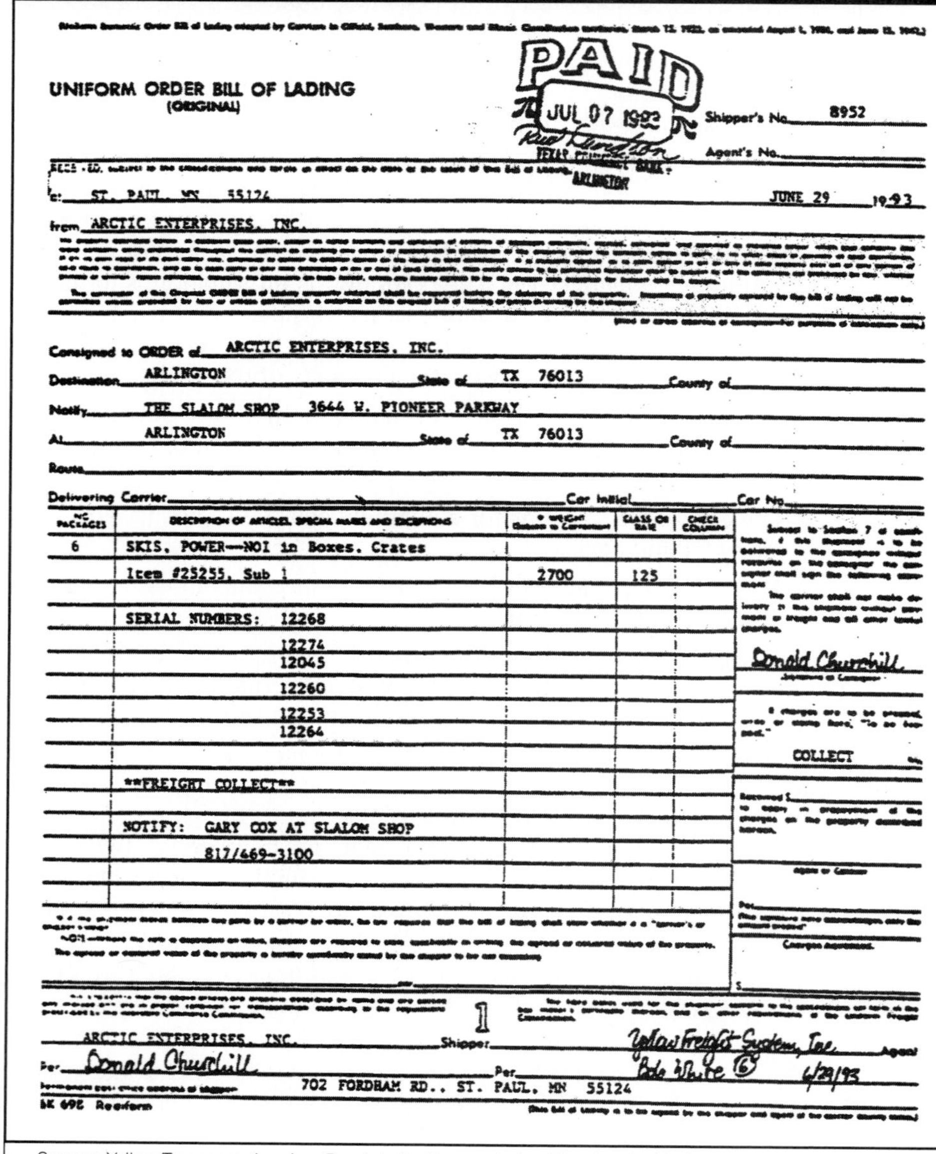
UNIFORM ORDER BILL OF LADING
(ORIGINAL)

PAID JUL 07 1993

Shipper's No. 8952
Agent's No.

At: ST. PAUL, MN 55124 JUNE 29 1993
From: ARCTIC ENTERPRISES, INC.

Consigned to ORDER of: ARCTIC ENTERPRISES, INC.
Destination: ARLINGTON State of: TX 76013 County of:
Notify: THE SLALOM SHOP 3644 W. PIONEER PARKWAY
At: ARLINGTON State of: TX 76013 County of:
Route:
Delivering Carrier: Car Initial: Car No.

No. Packages	Description of Articles, Special Marks and Exceptions	Weight	Class or Rate	Check Column
6	SKIS, POWER—NOI in Boxes, Crates			
	Item #25255, Sub 1	2700	125	
	SERIAL NUMBERS: 12268			
	12274			
	12045			
	12260			
	12253			
	12264			
	FREIGHT COLLECT			
	NOTIFY: GARY COX AT SLALOM SHOP			
	817/469-3100			

Donald Churchill
COLLECT

ARCTIC ENTERPRISES, INC. Shipper
Per Donald Churchill
Yellow Freight System, Inc. Agent
Per Bob White 6/29/93
702 FORDHAM RD., ST. PAUL, MN 55124

Source: Yellow Transportation, Inc. Reprinted with permission. The data in this figure is fictitious.

It has basically the same function as a waybill. A sample manifest can be seen in Figure 11.6. One specific difference is that the manifest documents the weight loaded in each quartile of the trailer. This is done specifically to address axle weight restrictions on the highway system.

Freight Bill

A **freight bill** is the carrier's invoice for transportation and related charges. A sample freight bill can be seen in Figure 11.7. The freight bill has some of the same information as the BOL, such as origin/destination and commodity description. The freight bill also serves the purpose of notifying the buyer of the charges and how they were assessed.

FIGURE 11.5 The Process of Using an Order Bill of Lading

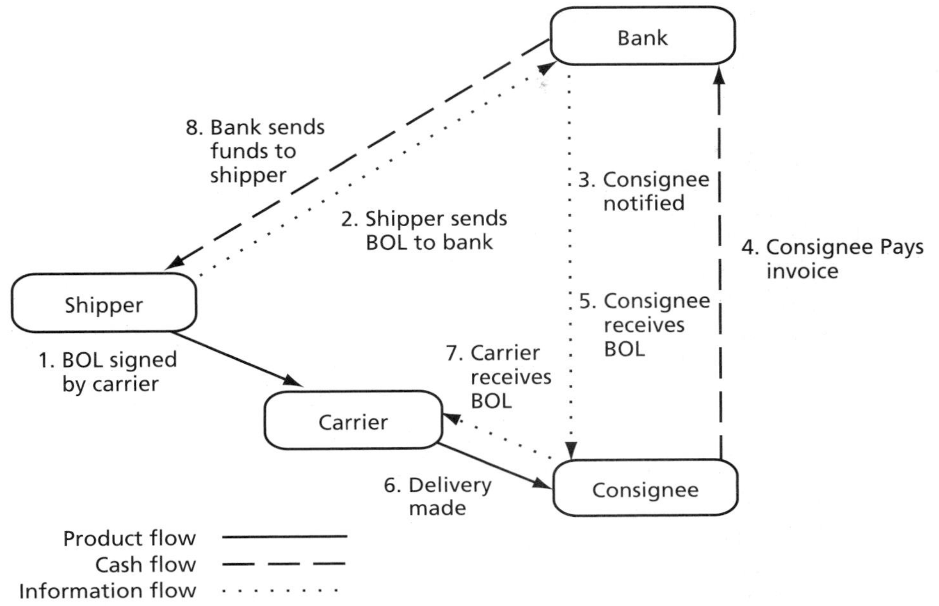

Source: John F. Tyworth, Joseph L. Cavinato, and C. John Langley, Jr., *Traffic Management*, Addison Wesley, Reading, MA, 1987.

It also can serve as proof of delivery. These two pieces of information are identified as important to the transportation process, as shown in Table 11.1.

Many buyers will not begin the payment process until a proof of delivery (signed freight bill) is matched with a BOL, a packing list for the shipment, and possibly an ASN. Some carriers, like FedEx, use electronic signatures on their delivery receipts. When a shipment is delivered to a customer, the carrier will capture the receiver's signature electronically on a hand-held computer. This receiving information, along with time and date, is then stored in the carrier's database and linked with the BOL. Proof of delivery can then be supplied electronically by the carrier. The generation of a hard copy proof of delivery using traditional methods can be a lengthy process and negatively impact the carrier's cash flow. However, electronic signature capture has reduced the time necessary to prove delivery by the carrier and has improved the carrier's ability to collect freight charges quickly.

The evaluated receipts process, used in the automobile industry with its suppliers, has also drastically reengineered the payment process between carriers and their customers. The charges for the transportation are agreed upon between the carrier and the customer; many times these charges are stated in contracts. When the shipment arrives, the ASN is checked against the packing slip and/or the BOL. If they match, the documents are sent to accounts payable and a check is sent to the carrier or an electronic funds transfer is made to the carrier's bank. The carrier does not produce a freight bill and a separate proof of delivery document is used. This process, although not yet common in the transportation industry, has reduced the cost of the payment process for both the carrier and its customers as well as improved the carrier's cash flow.

FIGURE 11.6 A Freight Manifest

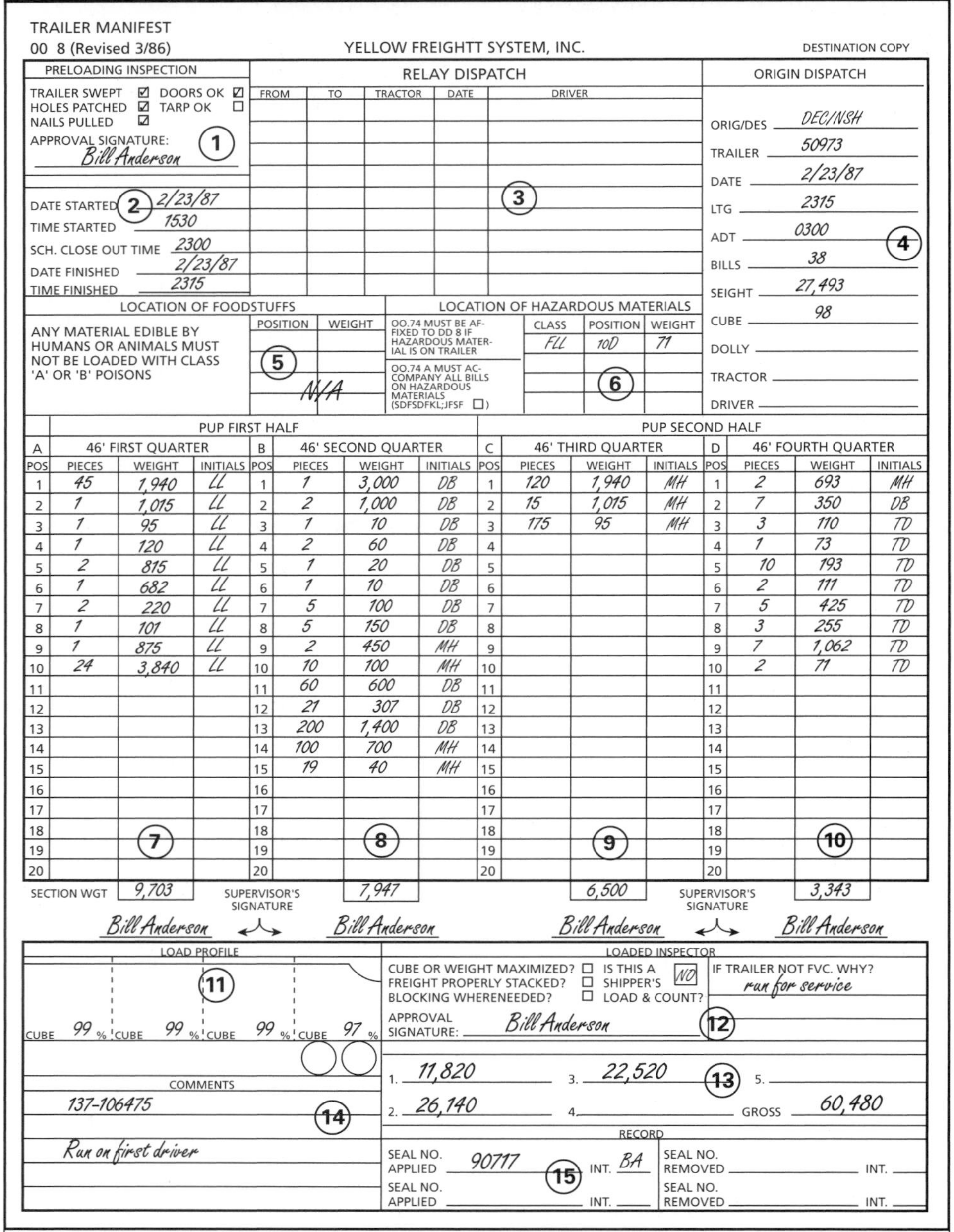

TRAILER MANIFEST
00 8 (Revised 3/86)
YELLOW FREIGHTT SYSTEM, INC.
DESTINATION COPY

PRELOADING INSPECTION
TRAILER SWEPT ☑ DOORS OK ☑
HOLES PATCHED ☑ TARP OK ☐
NAILS PULLED ☑
APPROVAL SIGNATURE: (1) Bill Anderson

DATE STARTED (2) 2/23/87
TIME STARTED 1530
SCH. CLOSE OUT TIME 2300
DATE FINISHED 2/23/87
TIME FINISHED 2315

RELAY DISPATCH (3)

FROM	TO	TRACTOR	DATE	DRIVER

ORIGIN DISPATCH (4)
ORIG/DES DEC/NSH
TRAILER 50973
DATE 2/23/87
LTG 2315
ADT 0300
BILLS 38
SEIGHT 27,493
CUBE 98
DOLLY
TRACTOR
DRIVER

LOCATION OF FOODSTUFFS
ANY MATERIAL EDIBLE BY HUMANS OR ANIMALS MUST NOT BE LOADED WITH CLASS 'A' OR 'B' POISONS

POSITION	WEIGHT
(5) N/A	

LOCATION OF HAZARDOUS MATERIALS
00.74 MUST BE AFFIXED TO DD 8 IF HAZARDOUS MATERIAL IS ON TRAILER
00.74 A MUST ACCOMPANY ALL BILLS ON HAZARDOUS MATERIALS (SDFSDFKL;JFSF ☐)

CLASS	POSITION	WEIGHT
FLL	10D	71
	(6)	

PUP FIRST HALF / PUP SECOND HALF

A POS	46' FIRST QUARTER PIECES	WEIGHT	INITIALS	B POS	46' SECOND QUARTER PIECES	WEIGHT	INITIALS	C POS	46' THIRD QUARTER PIECES	WEIGHT	INITIALS	D POS	46' FOURTH QUARTER PIECES	WEIGHT	INITIALS
1	45	1,940	LL	1	1	3,000	DB	1	120	1,940	MH	1	2	693	MH
2	1	1,015	LL	2	2	1,000	DB	2	15	1,015	MH	2	7	350	DB
3	1	95	LL	3	1	10	DB	3	175	95	MH	3	3	110	TD
4	1	120	LL	4	2	60	DB	4				4	1	73	TD
5	2	815	LL	5	1	20	DB	5				5	10	193	TD
6	1	682	LL	6	1	10	DB	6				6	2	111	TD
7	2	220	LL	7	5	100	DB	7				7	5	425	TD
8	1	101	LL	8	5	150	DB	8				8	3	255	TD
9	1	875	LL	9	2	450	MH	9				9	7	1,062	TD
10	24	3,840	LL	10	10	100	MH	10				10	2	71	TD
11				11	60	600	DB	11				11			
12				12	21	307	DB	12				12			
13				13	200	1,400	DB	13				13			
14				14	100	700	MH	14				14			
15				15	19	40	MH	15				15			
16				16				16				16			
17				17				17				17			
18				18				18				18			
19		(7)		19		(8)		19		(9)		19		(10)	
20				20				20				20			
SECTION WGT		9,703				7,947				6,500				3,343	

SUPERVISOR'S SIGNATURE: Bill Anderson, Bill Anderson, Bill Anderson, Bill Anderson

LOAD PROFILE (11)
CUBE 99 % CUBE 99 % CUBE 99 % CUBE 97 %

LOADED INSPECTOR
CUBE OR WEIGHT MAXIMIZED? ☐ IS THIS A SHIPPER'S LOAD & COUNT? NO
FREIGHT PROPERLY STACKED? ☐
BLOCKING WHERENEEDED? ☐
IF TRAILER NOT FVC. WHY? run for service
APPROVAL SIGNATURE: Bill Anderson (12)

1. 11,820 3. 22,520 (13) 5.
2. 26,140 4. GROSS 60,480

COMMENTS
137-106475 (14)
Run on first driver

RECORD
SEAL NO. APPLIED 90717 (15) INT. BA SEAL NO. REMOVED INT.
SEAL NO. APPLIED INT. SEAL NO. REMOVED INT.

Source: Yellow Transportation, Inc. Reprinted with permission. The data in this figure is fictitious.

Many other documents might be needed for a shipment, depending upon the information needed to manage the transportation process. This is especially true for international shipments. This discussion was by no means meant to be exhaustive. The intent was to identify the types of information needed to manage transportation and identify where the information is to be found. Traditionally, this information was generated and transmitted manually, complicating product, information,

FIGURE 11.7 A Sample Freight Bill

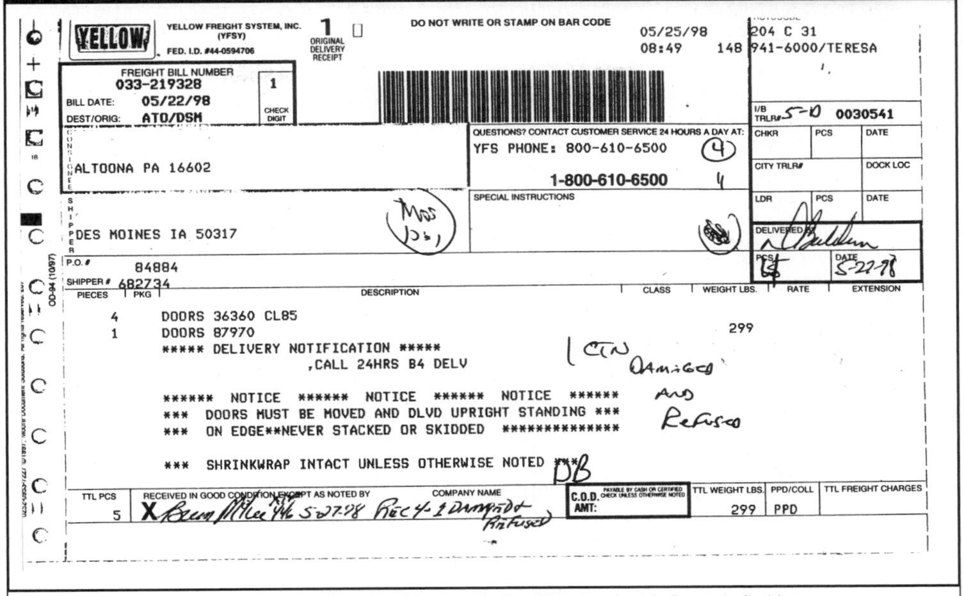
YELLOW
YELLOW FREIGHT SYSTEM, INC. (YFSY)
FED. I.D. #44-0594706
1 ORIGINAL DELIVERY RECEIPT
DO NOT WRITE OR STAMP ON BAR CODE
05/25/98
08:49 148
204 C 31
941-6000/TERESA
FREIGHT BILL NUMBER 033-219328 1
BILL DATE: 05/22/98
DEST/ORIG: ATO/DSM
CHECK DIGIT
I/B TRLR# 0030541
CHKR | PCS | DATE
QUESTIONS? CONTACT CUSTOMER SERVICE 24 HOURS A DAY AT:
YFS PHONE: 800-610-6500
1-800-610-6500
CONSIGNEE ALTOONA PA 16602
CITY TRLR# | DOCK LOC
SPECIAL INSTRUCTIONS
LDR | PCS | DATE
SHIPPER DES MOINES IA 50317
DELIVERED BY
PCS | DATE
P.O.# 84884
SHIPPER# 682734
PIECES | PKG | DESCRIPTION | CLASS | WEIGHT LBS. | RATE | EXTENSION
4 DOORS 36360 CL85
1 DOORS 87970 299
***** DELIVERY NOTIFICATION *****
,CALL 24HRS B4 DELV
****** NOTICE ****** NOTICE ****** NOTICE ******
*** DOORS MUST BE MOVED AND DLVD UPRIGHT STANDING ***
*** ON EDGE**NEVER STACKED OR SKIDDED **************
*** SHRINKWRAP INTACT UNLESS OTHERWISE NOTED ***
TTL PCS 5 | RECEIVED IN GOOD CONDITION EXCEPT AS NOTED BY X | COMPANY NAME | C.O.D. AMT: PAYABLE BY CASH OR CERTIFIED CHECK UNLESS OTHERWISE NOTED | TTL WEIGHT LBS. 299 | PPD/COLL PPD | TTL FREIGHT CHARGES

Source: Yellow Transportation, Inc. Reprinted by permission. The data in this figure is fictitious.

and cash flows between carriers and their customers. Today information technology has totally changed this practice. This will be the topic of the next section.

INFORMATION TECHNOLOGY

The adoption of IT is a leading concern of logistics and transportation managers today. The push to be more competitive from a cost and service perspective has driven firms to take a hard look at how they traditionally provided logistics and transportation services. A recent survey conducted by the United States Chamber of Commerce shows that IT is an important issue for logistics managers, especially in large firms. These results can be seen in Table 11.2.[4] An argument could be made that many issues on this list have an IT application. Two issues arise when deciding to implement IT in a transportation or logistics setting: 1) where to start, and 2) how to integrate the different systems. The purpose of this discussion is not to answer these two questions. The main purpose is to introduce the concept of IT and the various aspects of its implementation for carriers and their customers.

Areas of Application

In a recent study, information system executives were asked which areas of their firms' significant investments will be made in IT. The results of this study are shown in Table 11.3. Obviously, connecting to customers, suppliers, and partners is a critical business decision for all carriers. In fact, all of the top 10 issues in this table are related to the supply chain and its members.

Four reasons push this investment in the supply chain. First, information can be a substitute for supply chain assets, costs, and even services. Making inventory visible through information allows firms in the supply chain to reduce or, in some cases,

Table 11.2 Top 10 Logistics Issues by Revenue

Less than $10M (161 companies)	$10M to $499M (100 companies)	$500M or more (69 companies)
1. Customer service	1. Customer service	1. E-commerce
2. Access to capital	2. Productivity and quality issues	2. Customer service
3. Carrier selection and rate negotiation	3. Workforce recruiting and development	3. Supply-chain technology and software
4. Carrier-shipper contracts	4. Inventory management	4. Productivity and quality issues
5. EPA environmental rules	5. EPA environmental rules	5. Carrier selection and rate negotiation
6. Workforce recruiting and development	6. OSHA/ergonomics issues	6. Inventory management
7. OSHA/ergonomic issues	7. Carrier selection and rate negotiation	7. Carrier-shipper contracts
8. Using brokers and freight forwarders	8. Customs procedures and requirements	8. Workforce recruiting and development
9. Productivity and quality issues	9. Supply-chain technology and software	9. EPA environmental issues
10. Risk management	10. Risk management	10. Customs procedures and requirements

Source: Managing the Supply-Chain: A Survey of Logistics Leaders, prepared and published by the U.S. Chamber of Commerce. Reprinted with permission.

eliminate safety stock inventories. This ultimately takes costs out of the supply chain, rather than pushing costs back to suppliers or carriers. For example, **satellite technology** for carriers has allowed them to know exactly where a shipment is and whether it will meet its scheduled delivery time. If a delay is expected, the receiver is notified so proper actions can be taken. This allows firms to reduce the uncertainty of late deliveries and the necessity of extra inventories. Second, the cost of information continues to fall. This trend has been accelerated by the decreasing cost of technology. For example, desktop personal computers today can be purchased for less than $1,000; the same system cost five times that much 10 years ago. So as processing and storage technology declines in price, so will the cost of information.

Table 11.3 Top Information Systems Issues for 2000 (Global Responses)

Rank	Issue	Percentage of Respondents
1	Connecting to customers, suppliers, and/or partners	65.9
2	Optimizing organizational effectiveness	62.8
3	Optimizing enterprise-wide information systems services	59.9
4	Developing an e-business strategy	59.3
5	Organizing and utilizing data	57.7
6	Aligning information systems and corporate goals	52.7
7	Integrating systems with the Internet	52.1
8	Using IT for competitive breakthroughs	51.6
9	Using obsolete systems	51.3
10	Instituting cross-functional information systems	46.1

Source: Computer Sciences Corporation, *13th Annual Critical Issues of Information Systems Management Survey*, Cambridge, MA: Computer Sciences Corporation, 2001. Available at http://www.csc.com.

Third, demands for information from supply chain partners are increasing. The availability and effectiveness of information regarding supply chain operations are causing firms to need more information to manage their processes. Initiatives such as collaborative planning, forecasting, and replenishment (CPFR) in the retail industry are requiring not only more information but also the sharing of that information with all relevant supply chain partners. Sharing demand forecasts with carriers allows them to better manage and position capacity. An important point to be made here is that the information shared must be relevant to the supply chain partner. Firms are beginning to develop logistics data warehouses with storage capacities measured in terabytes. Sharing all information with all partners will result in data overload and be counterproductive.

Finally, in supply chain management, managing information flows is as important as managing product and cash flows. Chapter 1, "Transportation, the Supply Chain, and the Economy," included all three flows in its description of the supply chain. These three flows are inseparable; one cannot work without the other two. An argument might even be made that managing information might be the most important because it can be used to manage product and cash flows. The point, however, is that information flows are critical in managing the relationships that exist among all members of a supply chain.

Types of Information Technology

The number and types of technology that exist to facilitate transportation and logistics operations continue to grow at a rapid pace. However, certain types of technology are critical to these processes. Table 11.4 is a listing of what can be considered the basic, emerging, and future technologies to be applied to logistics and transportation. This section will present discussions on the most relevant of these technologies.

THE BASICS—COMPREHENSIVE, QUALITY ELECTRONIC DATA INTERCHANGE

Electronic data interchange (EDI) is probably one of the oldest forms of technology used in logistics and transportation. It can be defined as the application-to-application

Table 11.4	Information Technology for Transportation
	➤ **The Basics**
	✓ Comprehensive, Quality EDI ✓ Automatic ID: Bar Coding ✓ Track and Trace
	➤ **Emerging**
	✓ EPC Tags ✓ Internet ✓ Transportation Planning
	➤ **The Future**
	✓ Internet-Intelligent Applications ✓ Transparent EDI ✓ Data Warehousing

Source: W.L. Grenoble, Center for Supply Chain Research, Penn State University, 2003.

exchange of standard format business transactions. Once thought to be a luxury, EDI today is becoming a requirement for doing business.

Many reasons exist for carriers and their customers to electronically transmit transactional data. First, EDI eliminates human intervention, which can help to reduce or eliminate human errors in transcription and interpretation. Second, EDI reduces the cost of the transaction because it eliminates much of the labor cost associated with filling out a BOL, freight bill, manifest, waybill, or purchase order. Third, EDI improves customer service by automatically alerting customers of exceptions to their shipments, allowing them to reduce the cost of the exception. Fourth, EDI is used in many cases because customers demand it. Large customers, like manufacturers, demand that all suppliers use EDI to transmit operational as well as billing information.[5] This can cause significant investments on the part of the suppliers. However, this cost can be recouped through an increase in the number of transactions with that customer. Plus, once a supplier (such as a carrier) is "up" on EDI, adding other customers to the system adds only marginal costs. This last reason is actually the one most cited by carriers for adopting EDI. However, other reasons do exist, and carriers and their customers have found the use of EDI to be extremely beneficial to managing supply chain relationships.

EDI transmissions between trading partners are based on standards. These might be universal standards developed through organizations like ANSI or they might be standards developed for use in a particular industry, such as the Automotive Industry Action Group (AIAG). A standard specifies the data to be transmitted, the order of the data, and the length of the field containing the data. Using standards, any two trading partners will know that an 856 transmission (advance shipment notice) will always be the same. This allows multiple trading partners to communicate electronically using only one translation protocol, rather than having proprietary translations for every trading partner. This discussion will not attempt to define what every standard is because there are too many. Table 11.5 shows a listing of the more common types of EDI transmissions utilized in the transportation process and their corresponding ANSI number. Figure 11.8 is an example of what some of these transmissions and their standard numbers might look like when they are used between members of an automobile supply chain.

The most popular use of EDI transactions is normally for receiving customer orders and for sending orders to suppliers. Figure 11.9 is a summary of the current uses of EDI and the predicted use in 3 years. This also shows that advance shipment notices are very popular. There is also a growing use of invoicing and electronic funds transfer (EFT) transmissions between firms in the supply chain. Historically, firms were reluctant to apply EDI to the flow of cash between trading partners for fear of losing control over float and/or payment terms. However, EFT has proven to improve the control of float and significantly reduce the cost of invoicing and payment.

Implementing EDI, however, has its barriers within many firms.[6] These barriers include hardware/software compatibility, consistent formats, security, investment, senior management support, and ownership (MIS department versus operational units). Many, if not all, of these barriers exist for the initial implementation of an EDI system. Like any technology installation, the first attempt requires a large investment and causes all of the challenges. However, the learning curve with EDI is very positive; each succeeding application should become easier. Economies of scale also exist with subsequent applications. Some firms decide to reduce implementation and operational costs as well as improve security by using third-party providers called value-added networks (VANs). These firms receive EDI transmissions from multiple firms that might have proprietary standards and translate them

Table 11.5 Commonly Used ANSI ASC X12 Standards for Transportation EDI Transmissions

Standard	Description
104 SA	Air Shipment Information
110 IA	Air Freight Details and Invoice
125 MR	Multilevel Railcar Load Details
204 SM	Motor Carrier Shipment Information
210 IM	Motor Carrier Freight Details and Invoice
213 MI	Motor Carrier Shipment Status Inquiry
214 QM	Transportation Carrier Shipment Status
217 FG	Motor Carrier Loading and Route Guide
218 FH	Motor Carrier Tariff Information
250 PV	Purchase Order Shipment Management Document
300 RO	Reservation (Booking Request)(Ocean)
301 RO	Confirmation (Ocean)
303 RO	Booking Cancellation (Ocean)
304 SO	Shipping Instructions (Ocean)
309 SO	U.S. Customs Manifest
310 IO	Freight Receipt and Invoice (Ocean)
312 IO	Arrival Notice (Ocean)
313 QO	Shipment Status Inquiry (Ocean)
315 QO	Status Details (Ocean)
317 SO	Delivery/Pickup Order
319 SO	Terminal Information
322 SO	Terminal Operations Activity (Ocean)
323 SO	Vessel Schedule and Itinerary (Ocean)
324 SO	Vessel Stow Plan (Ocean)
325 SO	Consolidation of Goods in Container
350 SO	U.S. Customs Release Information
352 SO	U.S. Customs Carrier General Order Status
353 SO	U.S. Customs Master In-Bond Arrival
361 SO	Carrier Interchange Agreement (Ocean)
404 SR	Rail Carrier Shipment Information
410 IR	Rail Carrier Freight Details and Invoice
414 CR	Rail Car Hire Settlements
417 WB	Rail Carrier Waybill Interchange
418 IC	Rail Advance Interchange Consist
419 SR	Advance Car Disposition
420 CH	Car-Handling Information
421 IS	Estimated Time of Arrival and Car Schedule
422 DM	Shipper's Car Order
423 RL	Rail Industrial Switch List
425 WT	Rail Waybill Request
426 SR	Rail Revenue Waybill
435 SF	Standard Transportation Commodity Code Master
440 WR	Shipment Weights
451 EV	Rail Event Report
452 PL	Rail Problem Log Inquiry or Advice
453 ST	Rail Service Commitment Advice
456 EI	Rail Equipment Inquiry or Advice
466 TP	Rate Request
468 TP	Rate Docket Journal Log
475 RF	Rail Route File Maintenance
485 TP	Rate-Making Action

Table 11.5 Commonly Used ANSI ASC X12 Standards for Transportation EDI Transmissions (Cont.)

490 TP	Rate Group Definition
492 TP	Miscellaneous Rates
494 TP	Scale Rate Table
601 SE	Shipper's Export Declaration
602 TS	Transportation Services Tender
622 IP	Intermodal Ramp Activity
810 IN	Invoice
820 RA	Payment Order/Remittance Advice
830 PS	Planning Schedule with Release Capability
853 RI	Routing and Carrier Instruction
854 DD	Shipment Delivery Discrepancy Information
856 SH	Ship Notice/Manifest
857 BS	Shipment and Billing Notice
858 SI	Shipment Information
859 FB	Freight Invoice
862 SS	Shipping Schedule
869 RS	Order Status Inquiry
870 RS	Order Status Report
920 GC	Loss/Damage Claim — General Commerce
925 GC	Claim Tracer
926 GC	Claim Status Report and Tracer Reply
940 OW	Warehouse Shipping Order
945 SW	Warehouse Shipping Advice
990 GF	Response to a Load Tender

Source: Penske Logistics

into standard formats, which are then transmitted to their trading partners. This process allows a transmitting firm to develop a single transmission network, rather than a dedicated transmission network for each customer. Many carriers use VANs for their EDI transmissions. For example, a motor carrier that uses satellite technology to monitor shipment status for all of its customers will transmit shipment status data to a VAN. The carrier's customers can then access the VAN, using a customer ID, to download status information on their shipments alone. If all of that customer's carriers also use the same VAN, the customer can also reduce its number of dedicated EDI connections. A VAN for EDI transactions can be compared to a wholesaler for product transactions.

What does the future hold for EDI? Speculation has grown concerning the use of the Internet to replace dedicated EDI networks. Internet sites currently exist that can be used to transmit EDI documents. Both the sender and receiver have to subscribe to the service to receive an account number. The sender specifies the type of document to be transmitted, and the screen automatically formats to the desired data requirements. Some feel that the Internet system will work for small firms that do not have many transmissions and cannot justify the investment. Some feel that because the Internet is "free," the investment in any type of dedicated network is not worth it, regardless of the number of transactions. However, an issue with the Internet is capacity. If EDI transactions continue to grow on the Internet, no guarantee could be given to the trading partners that capacity would be added to avoid delays in transmission. However, the Internet could provide an option to some firms for their EDI transactions.

FIGURE 11.8 MCS Corporation Logistics Information Flows ("Big 3" Model)

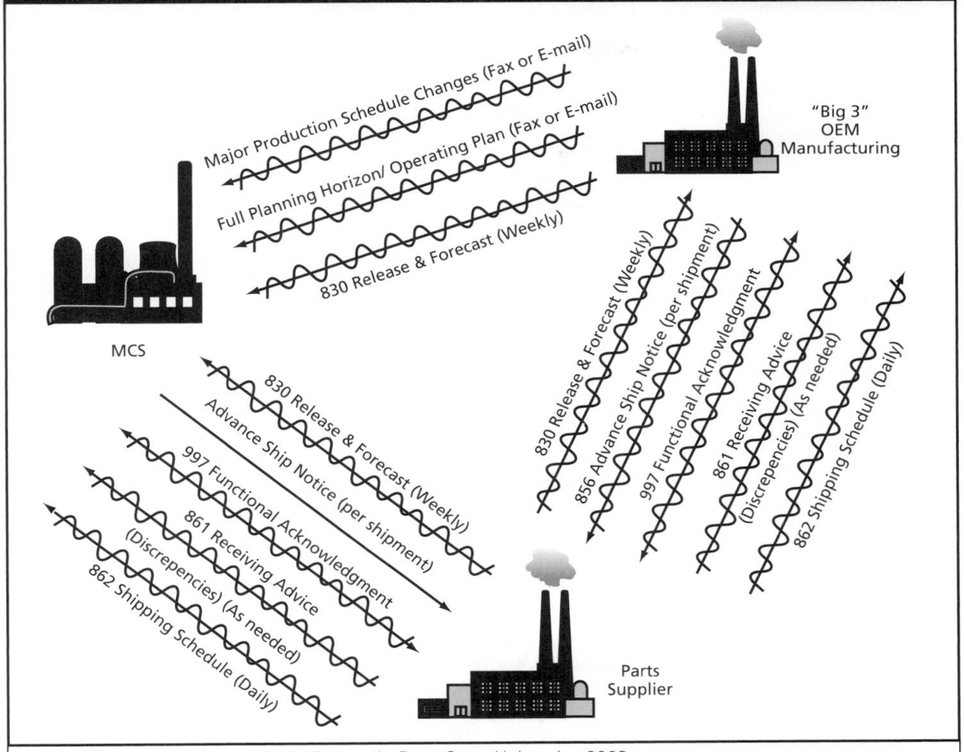

Source: Center for Supply Chain Research, Penn State University, 2003.

The introduction of **XML** (extensible mark-up language) formatting to EDI messages has minimized the need for standards when transmitting data between business partners. XML uses text language to identify the different fields on a document. For example, traditional standards for transmitting "ship to" information on a BOL might require that the 14th to 28th digits in a transmission always identify the "ship to" point. In XML, the "ship to" destination is preceded by the term "ship to" in the message. So, standard formats are not required in XML messaging. This could open up a wide range of data-exchange possibilities in the supply chain.

THE BASICS—AUTOMATIC ID: BAR CODING

Bar coding is another technology that has been in use for quite a while. Bar codes can be seen in grocery stores, retail stores, warehouses, manufacturing plants, and carrier terminals. Coupled with EDI, bar codes provide a powerful tool for providing information about product movement throughout the supply chain.

Bar codes are rather simple in their design, consisting of spaces and bars arranged in a pattern. When a scanning device is passed over the bar code, light waves are reflected off of the code and read by the scanner. These waves are converted to a frequency and assigned a "0" or a "1" (this is called a binary code) based on whether light is reflected or absorbed by the code. A dark bar would absorb light; a light space would reflect light. The relative width of bars and spaces is important in basic bar codes, not the absolute width. The method used to assign the 0 or 1 to the reflections is called the primary algorithm. This algorithm describes the combinations of bars and spaces that result in a 0 or 1. For example, a wide bar and a narrow space in combination might be

FIGURE 11.9 EDI Company Utilization

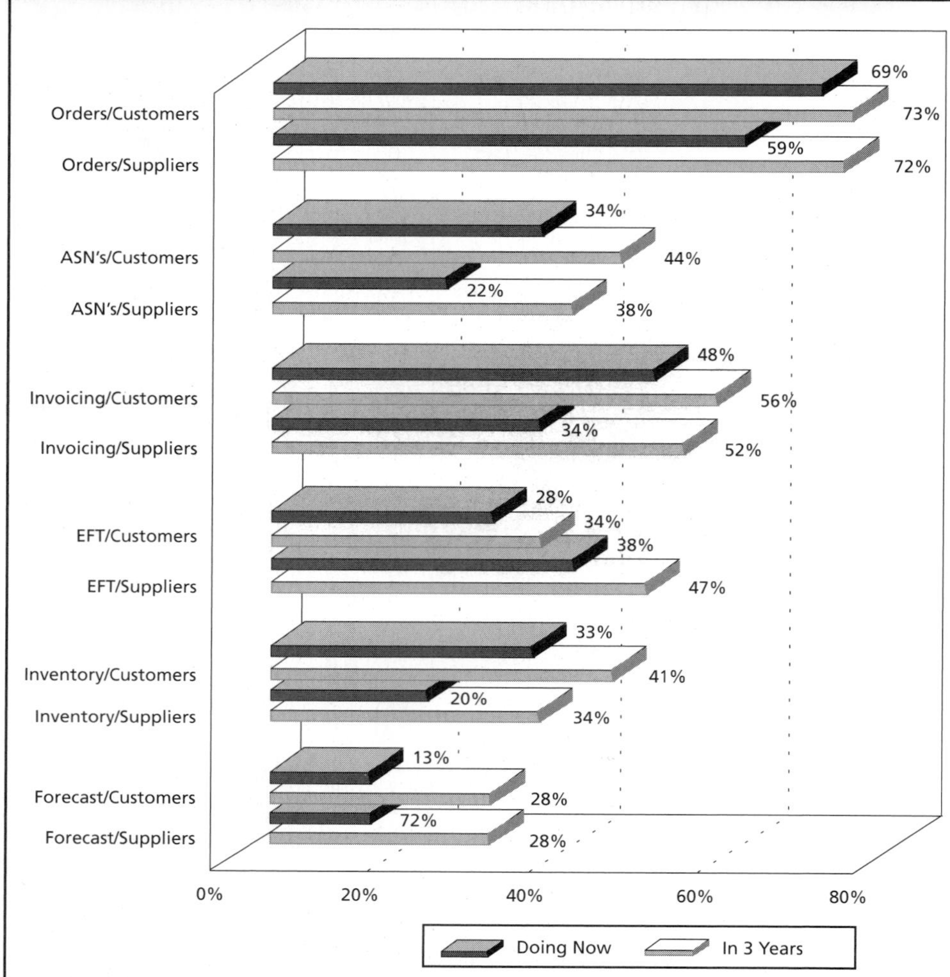

Source: Center for Supply Chain Research, Penn State University, 1998.

encoded as a 0. Once a series of 0s and 1s are created from a bar code, a secondary algorithm is used to translate it to meaningful data. These data might be used to access a product file in a grocery store so the price can be used to check out a customer.

Three variations can be used to encode data in a bar code. A "2 of 5" bar code measures bar-to-bar relationships; a "2 of 5 interleaved" is used to measure bar-to-bar and space-to-space relationships; and "MSI" measures bar-to-space relationships. The most common bar code in use today is called Code 39.[7] Figure 11.10 shows an example of a **Code 39** bar code, which uses five bars and four spaces. In the figure, two bars and one space are wide (three wide) and the remaining six spaces and bars are narrow. The three wide elements out of the nine total is where the name Code 39 comes from.

Another common format for bar codes is Code 128. An example can be seen in Figure 11.11. This code consists of 11 total modules per character with each encoded character containing three bars and three spaces. This code can cover the full 128 ASCII character set, which gives this code its name.[8]

FIGURE 11.10 Code 39 Bar Code

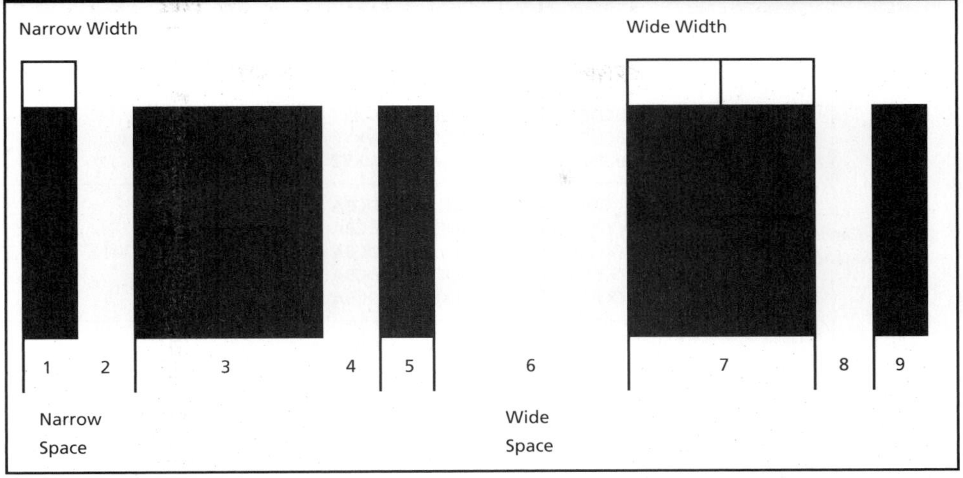

A relatively new development in bar codes is called 2-D, or two-dimensional. Several variations of the 2-D code exist. The first type is called a stacked bar code. Figure 11.12 shows an example of this code. An example of a stacked bar code is Code 49. Code 49 contains two to eight rows of fixed-width bar codes stacked on top of one another. Each row has 49 possible values, giving this code its name.[9] An advantage of this 2-D code is its adaptability to conventional bar code scanners. Figure 11.13 is an example of Code 49.

The second type is called a **PDF 417 bar code**. An example of this can be seen in Figure 11.14. This **2-D bar code** can hold up to 1.1 kilobytes of data, text, graphics, biometrics, or voice records.[10] Both the Department of Defense and General Motors have adopted this technology to manage inventories in their supply chains.

FIGURE 11.11 Code 128 Bar Code

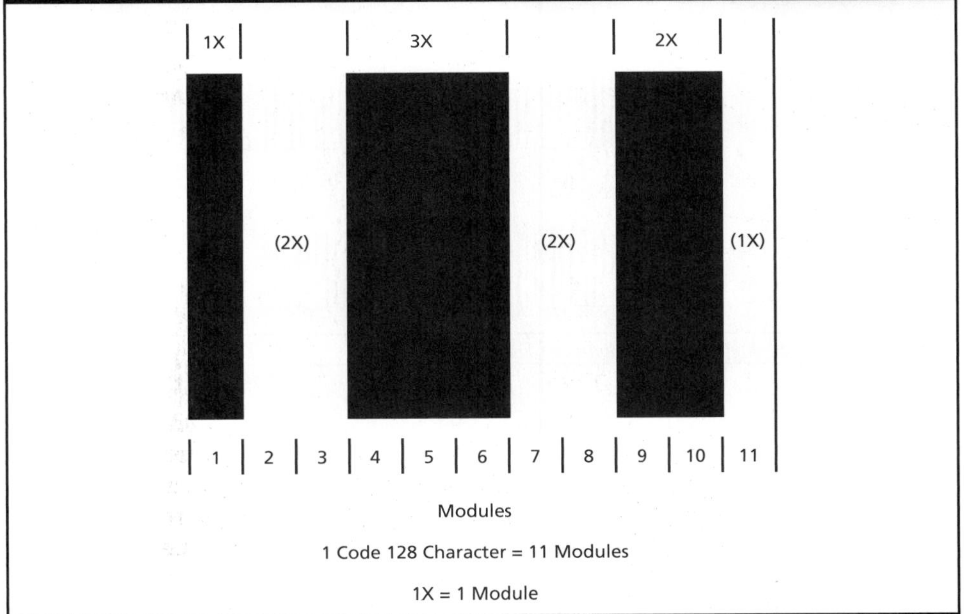

Source: Penton Media Inc.

FIGURE 11.12 Stacked Bar Code

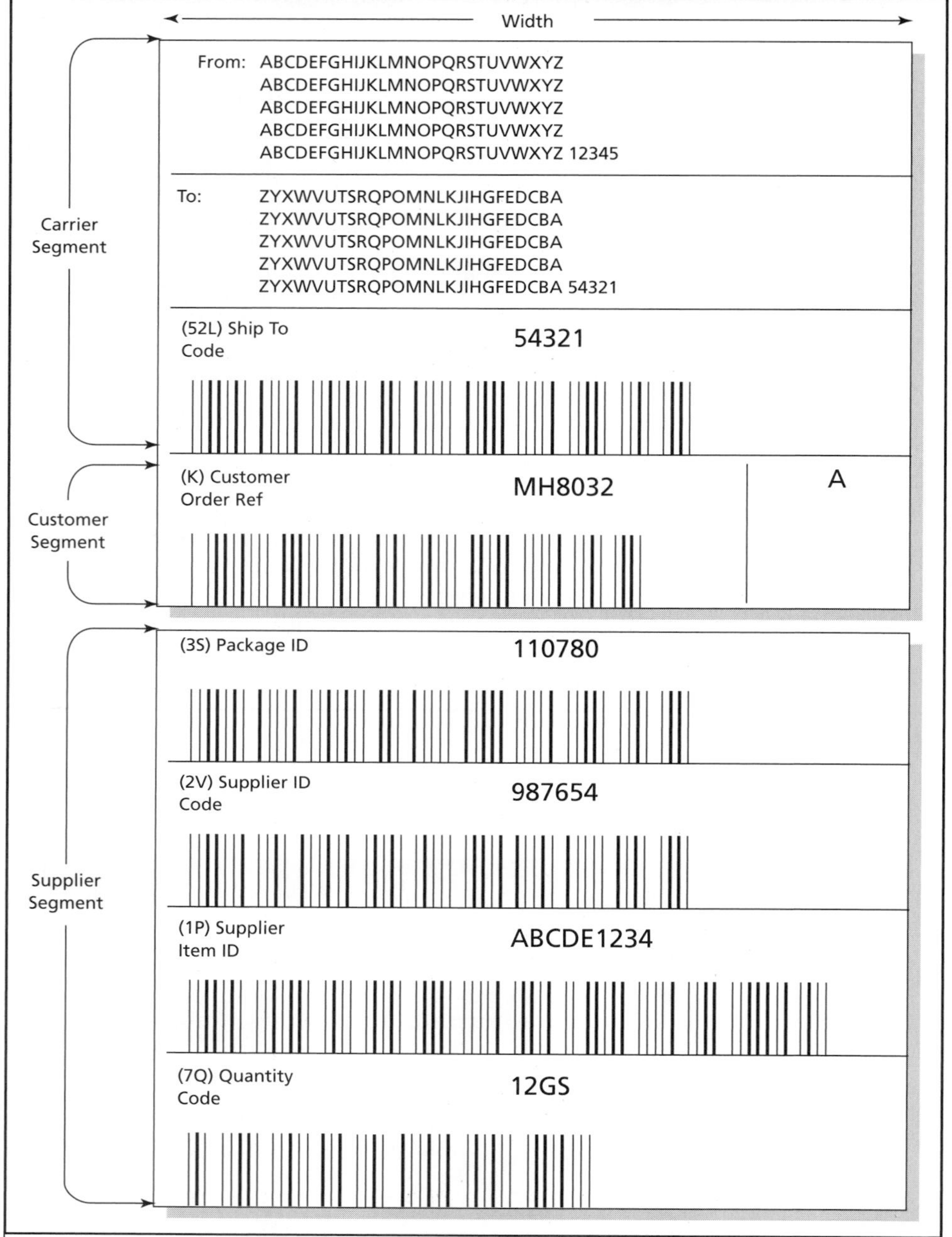

Source: *Transportation and Distribution*, October 1991, p.26

Finally, several types of **matrix bar codes** have been developed that have significantly increased the amount of data portrayed by the bar code. The matrix bar code resembles a checker board with the absence or presence of a black or white dot in a cell portraying the data. One of the earliest successful matrix bar codes was developed by the United Parcel Service (UPS). It resembles a checkerboard pattern with a bull's eye in the middle. Figure 11.15 shows the UPS matrix code. This code is now in the public domain. Another application of this is called Data Matrix symbols. This can be seen in

FIGURE 11.13 Code 49 Bar Code

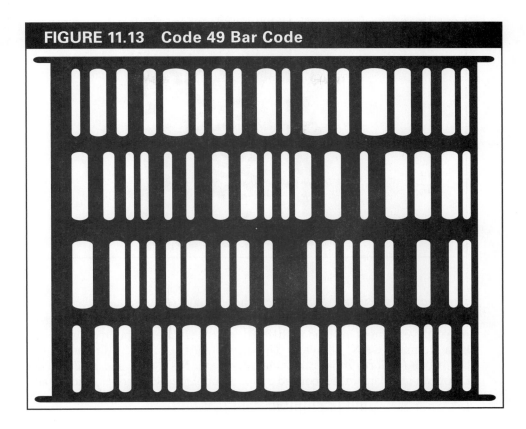

Figure 11.16. A 2-D image-capture device, like a CCD camera, is necessary to scan this matrix code.[11] Both the pharmaceutical and consumer electronics industries have adopted this technology for its ability to capture lot information and product authenticity codes.

Another advancement in the development of bar codes is called the "**license plate**." This bar code, called SSCC-18, is used to identify and manage pallets, rather than traditional consumer or industrial packages.[12] When a pallet is created by the manufacturer, an SSCC-18 is applied and identifies the product, quantity, production lot, date of manufacture, hold status, and storage location.[13] Because these codes use Code 128 formats and are globally unique and context neutral, they can be used anywhere in the

FIGURE 11.14 PDF417 Bar Code

PDF 417 bar codes, like those on the back of driver's licenses in many states, can carry data, text and even some graphics. GM uses a PDF 417 label to track shipping histories.

Source: Reprinted from *Modern Materials Handling*, Copyright 2003 *Modern Materials Handling*, Reed Business Information, a division of Reed Elsevier.

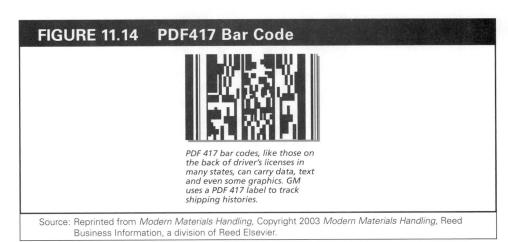

FIGURE 11.15 Matrix Bar Code

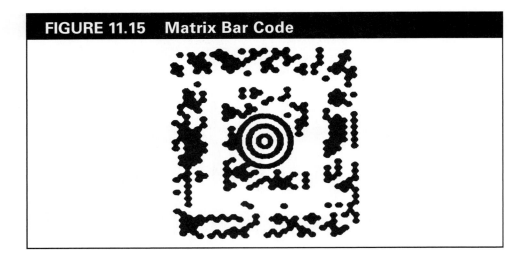

supply chain.[14] This allows shippers, carriers, and receivers alike to share common information about the movement of a pallet through their respective networks.

A new development in standard bar codes has been the adoption of the Global Trade Item Number (GTIN) standard. This new standard can read and store the 8-digit UPC Code (a North American standard), the EAN's 8-digit and 13-digit codes (the European standard), the Reduced Space Symbology (RSS) codes, and an additional digit that identifies how products are packed. This would bring the number of digits in a typical bar code to 14.[15]

A key to the effective use of bar code technology is linking it to other types of technology to allow for inventory visibility. One of these technologies is called track and trace, which is the focus of the next section.

THE BASICS: TRACK AND TRACE

Full visibility of a shipment in the supply chain requires the ability to know where it is in a warehouse or terminal as well as knowing where it is in transit. Bar codes provide an important source of information to be able to provide both types of visibility.

FIGURE 11.16 Data Matrix Symbols

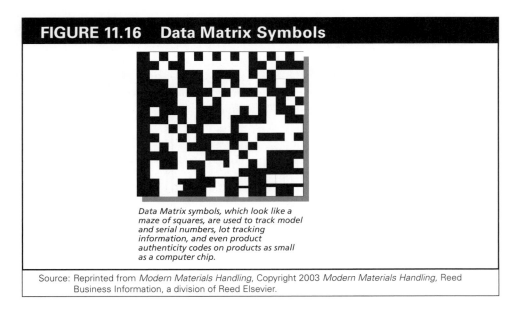

Data Matrix symbols, which look like a maze of squares, are used to track model and serial numbers, lot tracking information, and even product authenticity codes on products as small as a computer chip.

Source: Reprinted from *Modern Materials Handling*, Copyright 2003 *Modern Materials Handling*, Reed Business Information, a division of Reed Elsevier.

In a warehouse or carrier's terminal, bar codes can track a shipment from when it arrives until it leaves, providing status updates along the way. Normal bar code readers store data on product movements and then periodically download this data to a host computer. A technology called **radio frequency** (RF) can provide real-time data. When the bar code is scanned using an RF reader, the data are transmitted immediately using RFs to the host computer. The smart tag is another application where RF technology can be used.

Until recently, tracking a shipment inside a facility was relatively easy when compared to tracking it in transit. However, developments in tracking technology have allowed carriers to communicate with their vehicles in transit as well as determine their location. The major breakthrough in making this visibility a reality is the use of satellite technology. Motor carriers, such as Penske, Schneider, Jevic, and Prime, have installed satellite transponders in the roofs of their tractors to interface with various satellite systems. Coupled with onboard computers, this satellite communication has allowed carriers to not only know the position of their vehicles and their freight but also better manage their asset base. This two-way communication between driver/vehicle and dispatcher has actually allowed carriers to reduce their fleet size while improving utilization. One of the more popular satellite systems is provided by a company called Qualcomm. The Qualcomm system can update the position of a vehicle in transit as often as the user requires, as well as provide a two-way communication between a driver and the dispatcher. The Global Positioning System (**GPS**), initially developed by the U.S. government to detect incoming missiles, is another system used to track vehicles in transit. Composed of multiple satellites in various orbits above the Earth, the GPS can not only track vehicles but also provide directions to a destination for a vehicle. Although used in freight transportation, GPS is also used on passenger cars for navigation and emergency purposes. These updates, along with RF data from warehouses and terminals, can help provide total supply chain visibility for freight.

Some satellite technology applications are used for one-way communications. These passive "transponders" can be applied to trailers or railcars and are used to either transmit data or help determine vehicle position. A disadvantage of the satellite technology on motor-carrier tractors is the inability to track the freight in the trailer when the trailer is unhooked. For example, TOFC trailers can become "lost" in the rail system because their capability to transmit location data resides with the tractor. However, putting a transponder on the trailer allows the trailer to be "live" on the rail.

Another application for this technology is being tried in the refrigerated motor carrier industry. Putting refrigerated trailers on a railcar has presented problems in the past with being able to monitor and control the temperature inside the trailer. However, some carriers are experimenting with these transponders to periodically transmit temperature data back to a central dispatch location. Although they cannot yet control the temperature, this technology allows the motor carrier dispatcher to alert the railroad if a temperature problem occurs.

Tracking and tracing have come a long way in the past 10 years. Shippers have demanded better ways to determine where their shipments are and if they will arrive on time. Carriers have also needed a better way to manage fleet utilization. However, not every firm has taken advantage of technology to provide full inventory visibility. Shippers will normally fall into one of three categories of tracking and tracing capability: lagging edge, mainstream, or leading edge. Table 11.6 summarizes the characteristics of each category. Lagging edge firms can be described as reactive and using little or no technology to track and trace. They are very slow to respond to requests from customers on shipment location, and the track and trace process is completely manual. Mainstream firms are reactive but use some technology, possibly the carrier's, to

Table 11.6 Tracking and Tracing Capability

Attribute	Degrees of Performance Lagging Edge	Mainstream	Leading Edge
Responsiveness	Reactive, Phone based	Reactive, Systemized	Proactive, Systemized
Database	None	Uses carrier capability	Has own capability, SKU-entry
Connectivity	Phone	Terminal inquiry	EDI
Operations Mode	Batch Daily	Batch 3-4 times daily	Online Real time
Shipment Location Specificity	Which carrier/ company	Company and general location. ETA	Geographic-specific satellite/radio links
Use of Info	React to customer request	React and maintain performance data	Automatic pass on to customers

Source: William L. Grenoble, Center for Supply Chain Research, Penn State University, 2003.

track and trace. Because the process is systematic, these firms are able to respond rather quickly to customer requests. Because the track-and-trace process of these firms uses terminal inquiry, some manual activities have been replaced with technology. Finally, leading-edge firms are proactive in their approach to track and trace. They utilize technologies such as EDI and satellite/RF to capture and transmit data automatically. These firms supply real-time shipment status information to their customers, eliminating the need for the customer to request a status update. These firms will sometimes proactively alert a customer if a shipment will be late. Very little, if any, manual interaction is necessary for track and trace for these firms because of the extensive use of technology.

There have been dramatic advances in this area in the past 5 years even though the original technology dates from the late 1980s. First, the current systems were enhanced to add features that allow a dispatcher to monitor the tractor's engine condition, the speed of travel, and other related areas. Features were added to control refrigerator units remotely including monitoring the temperature and starting the refrigeration unit if required. The enhanced systems have more accurate location placement information and have incorporated geographic data to assist with vehicle placement. GPS uses road net and mapping information to graphically depict where the vehicle is located on a specific highway.

The newest systems have overcome the problem of monitoring trailers when not hooked up to a tractor. Past systems relied on power from the tractor and once the trailer was dropped, that portion of the tracking no longer functioned.

The development of long-lasting power supplies and additional technology now allows the trailer's location to be monitored regardless of whether it is attached to a tractor. One system not only maintains the trailer location, it can determine whether the trailer is loaded or empty. This is accomplished by a sensor in the nose of the trailer that scans for light or the absence of light to determine if there is cargo on the trailer.

This technology will spread beyond the motor carrier industry as other modes adopt this control system. Railcars and containers are the next logical choice, and shipper demand will no doubt push carriers to implement tracking technology as a competitive advantage.

Satellite and RF technologies have certainly helped both carriers and shippers achieve efficiency and profitability goals. Some track-and-trace systems are proprietary between a carrier and a shipper. Other carrier track-and-trace systems are in the public domain and are available from the Internet. UPS and Federal Express are two examples. The use of smart tags and the Internet in transportation will be the focus of the next section.

EPC TAGS

Bar codes were developed to allow for quick data capture as packages move through the supply chain. They require some type of reader and contain static information. A new technology developed by Texas Instruments, called the "tag-it," is a revolutionary way to identify packages and manage inventory.[16] Called a "smart tag," this new technology takes the place of a bar code and uses radio frequency to make it work. An advantage of the smart tag is the capability to update its information anywhere along the supply chain. The smart tag can be manufactured into shipping labels or other types of documentation following a shipment. This technology will allow shippers and carriers to manage inventories through distribution centers as well as break-bulk terminals.

These electronic product code (**EPC**) **tags** work in conjunction with RFID to transmit information to computers. Companies like Gillette are experimenting with putting these tags onto individual consumer packages. Wal*Mart is requiring its top suppliers to have these tags on individual pallets by January 1, 2005, and on individual cases by January 1, 2005.[17] These tags carry significantly more data than even the new 14-digit bar codes and transmit their information via radio waves. They can provide real-time data on inventory visibility in the supply chain, from source to shelf. However, three issues must be resolved before their acceptance is universal. First is the issue of cost. Because volumes are not large right now, the cost per tag is about 50 cents. To be realistic for universal use, their cost needs to come down to a fraction of a penny. Second is the issue of standards. Global standards for EPC tags do not currently exist. The UCC and the EAN have joined forces with MIT's Auto-ID Center to develop EPC standards. Finally is the issue of compatibility with existing software. These tags need to be compatible with ERP systems as well as with inventory, transportation, and warehousing software.[18]

STOP OFF

RFID Costs Aren't Likely to Impede Adoption

The buzz surrounding radio frequency identification (RFID) died down somewhat when the consulting firm A. T. Kearney released a study that for the first time quantified the full cost of implementing that technology. The consulting firm estimated compliance costs for individual companies will exceed half a million dollars. Even so, companies under pressure to implement RFID aren't likely to drop their plans to incorporate it into their operations.

The Kearney study based its predictions on Wal-Mart's dictum that its top 100 suppliers be RFID-ready by the end of 2004, with the lion's share of suppliers in line by 2005. The consultants estimated that the cost for those suppliers to acquire and implement electronic product code (EPC) and RFID capabilities that meet the retail giant's expectations will reach $400,000 per distribution center and an additional $100,000 per store. Additional costs for integrating the systems could range from $35 million to $40 million dollars. On the upside, the study notes, much of those expenditures will be fixed costs.

Larger companies might not flinch at dropping that much money to comply with the demands of a single—albeit huge—retail customer, but a small company might balk at such an outlay. At some point, small businesses will have to ask: Is it worth it?

The answer, it seems, is yes—and not just for those laboring in the shadow of Wal-Mart, but also for the industry in general. With RFID widely accepted as a coming necessity, the cost will be largely unavoidable. But the impact can be lessened, says Harry Forbes, senior analyst with Automation Research Corp. (ARC) in Dedham, Mass. "We're telling people not to budget for deployment, but to budget for a pilot program," he says. "We see 2004 as a time of rapid learning for this because it's the manufacturers that have most of the learning to do. What they need to know is what their cost is to implement the Wal-Mart compliance.

Forbes says that ARC will soon be coming out with its own figures on the cost of RFID—figures that are higher than those in the Kearney report. Even so, he says, adoption of the technology will continue, but cautiously. "I think you'll [initially] see a wholesale rollout of pilot projects, not a rollout of deployment projects," he says.

The Kearney report suggests several ways suppliers could lessen the financial blow when it comes to outlays for RFID. For example, RFID-tagging pallets but using EPC barcodes on individual cases could reduce the number of tags 60-fold compared to putting RFID tags on every case. Delaying implementation could also save companies money as the price of tags is expected to drop as the technology becomes more prevalent. Although these and other recommendations in the report may not fully apply to companies that must follow Wal-Mart's guidelines, they may be effective for others should the technology become more widely implemented.

Source: *Logistics Management*, January 2004, pp. 18–19. Reprinted with permission of *Logistics Management*.

THE INTERNET EMERGES

The **Internet** actually began in the 1960s as a network of networks linking government and university computers. Mostly used for research, this linkage allowed for participating institutions to share information. Because its members were volunteers, no formal ownership of the Internet ever existed. This is still true today. A major advantage of the Internet during the 1960s as well as today is that its use is free.

The three major uses of the Internet are for information resources, communications, and transactions. Companies developed Internet sites to provide potential customers with product and price information. Many carriers have developed Internet sites to allow customers to track their shipments. Once on a carrier's site, the customer enters a customer code and shipment identifier to find the status of a shipment. Federal Express can even provide a copy of the receiver's signature on the delivery receipt. Appendix A contains a short compilation of some carrier Internet sites.

The Internet can also be used to communicate between individuals as well as between companies. Companies can use the Internet for EDI transmissions as well as for internal and external communications. Companies are beginning to use Internet-based systems to share demand and production forecasts. This concept, called collaborative planning, forecasting, and replenishment (**CPFR**), was promoted by Wal*Mart and some other retailers as a way to communicate inventory forecast and point-of-sale (POS) data to its suppliers. Store-level product forecasts and POS data are sent to the manufacturer, who then determines if this demand is consistent with its production plan. If not, the two firms collaborate until some agreement is reached on forecasted sales. The retailer then uses this forecast for merchandising and promotion, and the manufacturer uses it for production scheduling. An outgrowth of this concept is called collaborative transportation management (**CTM**). A strength of CPFR is its ability to let a supplier and its customer manage and optimize capacity. A weakness was not including the carrier base on these capacity decisions. CTM now allows the carrier base between a shipper and its customers to collaborate on available vehicle capacity to meet the forecasted demand.

Some shippers and carriers use the Internet in lieu of a broker. Available shipments are posted on an Internet site, and interested carriers can respond with a price quote for the move. A shipper can then either accept or reject the offer. If the offer is accepted, a confirmation message is generated and the transaction is completed. This concept is called a reverse auction.

Finally, the use of the Internet for cash transactions is growing. Because of the increased security offered by firms to protect credit card numbers and bank account numbers on the Internet, buyers and sellers can consummate sales through an Internet site, with cash flow occurring through a credit card or a bank. Although this use is minimal today, it is expected to grow tremendously in the future.

The growth of Internet users has been phenomenal. In 1996 there were approximately 10 to 20 million users in the United States alone. By the year 2010, it has been projected that the numbers of users on a worldwide basis will reach 1 billion.

Some challenges still remain with the use of the Internet for transportation transactions. First is the issue of capacity. Because no single entity owns the Internet, capacity decisions are not the responsibility of a central organization. An analogy would be if the interstate highway system had no single entity responsible for it. As traffic increases and capacity is constrained, the decision to add highway miles or add technology to manage traffic flow would be no one's responsibility. As usage on the Internet goes up, response times can go down. This is a major consideration for companies who have time-sensitive transmissions.

Second is the issue of security. Although protection of confidential information on the Internet has improved, no guarantee can be given that information transmitted will not be available to the public domain. In fact, many Internet sites provide a warning message before a transmission alerting the sender that the data could be accessed by unauthorized individuals.

The future of the Internet holds many applications for carriers and their customers. Carriers will be able to use the Internet as a sales interface. Information such as service offerings, routing guides, fleet availability, and pricing schedules would be easily accessible and maintained through the Internet. As some carriers have already proven, the Internet is effective as a customer service utility. Basic requests such as shipment status and arrival times can be accessed through the Internet, allowing carriers to utilize human customer service personnel more effectively. More and more companies could use the Internet for EDI transmissions. As security improves and capacity increases, firms with no need for dedicated links with their customers could use the Internet to provide a viable alternative to EDI.

One of the latest developments involving the use of the Internet has been growth and development of load-matching services. The firms serve the same purpose as a broker by linking the carrier and the shipper. One of the differences is that in some cases the shipper can post their loads and respond to offers by carriers directly without the use of a "middleman." Many of these firms charge a fee for their services and leave the negotiation of the transportation details to the shipper and carrier. Shippers can post loads with options ranging from simple faxes, which the operator will add to the site, up to sophisticated file transfer protocols. A few accept credit cards and some offer other services including truck stop directories, highway mileages, links to insurance companies, and e-mail service. One site even offers links to news and weather forecasting service as well as stock quotes.

The Internet could facilitate the sharing of information between carriers and their customers. This could include information regarding planned shipments, production schedules, fleet availability, and so on. The types of information that could be shared through the Internet are limited only by the restrictions placed on them by the firms involved.

Recent research has identified some trends in the use of the Internet to promote e-business to support transportation.[19]. Table 11.7 shows one of the results of this research. By far the largest use of the Internet is the use of e-mail to communicate with supply chain partners, followed by the generation of ASNs (advance shipment notices). This shows that the Internet is mainly being used for one-way communications given that two-way communications (collaboration) was only being used by 23 percent of the research respondents. Table 11.8 shows the importance to the firm by adopting e-business capabilities to transportation. Not surprisingly, customer service improvement was the most important impact. This would also include faster cycle times (a customer service output). Cost management was a close second in importance (reduced operating cost, improved employee productivity, and asset reduction). So, the use of e-business through the Internet is still in its development stage in transportation. Customer service improvement is obviously the most important priority in doing so.

STOP OFF

Technology to the Rescue

Now that shippers and carriers of hazardous materials are responsible for the security of both cargo and its associated shipment information, many are relying on technology to help them meet those obligations. And with some U.S. legislators proposing to make certain security technologies mandatory, products like satellite tracking systems, global positioning systems (GPS), and mapping software are likely to become an integral part of the written security plans that shippers and carriers must develop.

New security-enhancing products are being developed at a rapid pace. Here's a brief overview of some of these technologies:

Emergency alert systems confidentially send a distress signal to a dispatcher when the driver pushes a panic button or the vehicle or suddenly diverts from the scheduled route. Even cellular telephones may play a role in alerting dispatchers and deterring attacks on transportation.

Intelligent seals for containers, trailers, and rail cars transmit electronic signals regarding the integrity of the closure as well as the location and time of any attempt to enter a sealed unit. Electronically-operated release mechanisms remotely control locking and unlocking of doors. Some shippers also use seals that can only be removed with bolt cutters.

"Smart cards" with biometric identifiers and embedded data positively identify drivers picking up or delivering hazardous cargoes. They can even be used for controlling access to a vehicle. Drivers follow a "bio log-in" process that transmits a radio frequency signal to the dispatcher when they are at the wheel; unauthorized access triggers an ignition-system disconnect.

Electronic driver authorization systems are another means of preventing vehicle theft. One such system, marketed by Seneca Tank of Des Moines, Iowa, requires the operator to enter a preselected code before starting the engine or moving the vehicle left idling. The engine stalls if the driver releases the parking brake without entering a valid code.

Secure electronic shipping documents can only be accessed by authorized users. These "e-documents" can be included in a system that tracks shipment status and identifies anyone who has accessed the cargo from pickup to delivery.

Risk-management databases and software help shippers and carriers identify the safest routes for shipments of dangerous goods. One popular product is PC*Miller Hazmat routing software from ALK Associates of Princeton, N.J. Donald Stark, director of corporate safety for USF corporation, a nationwide motor carrier employing 16,000 drivers, uses a different type of resource for planning hazardous shipment routes. He relies on statistics provided by Exton, Pa.-based CAP Index Inc. to develop in-transit and site-specific security assessments for thousands of locations. These and similar products and services have often been cited in government reports on hazmat transportation security.

Source: *Logistics Management*, August 2003. Reprinted with permission.

Table 11.7 e-business Capabilities Adopted by Respondents To Support Transportation

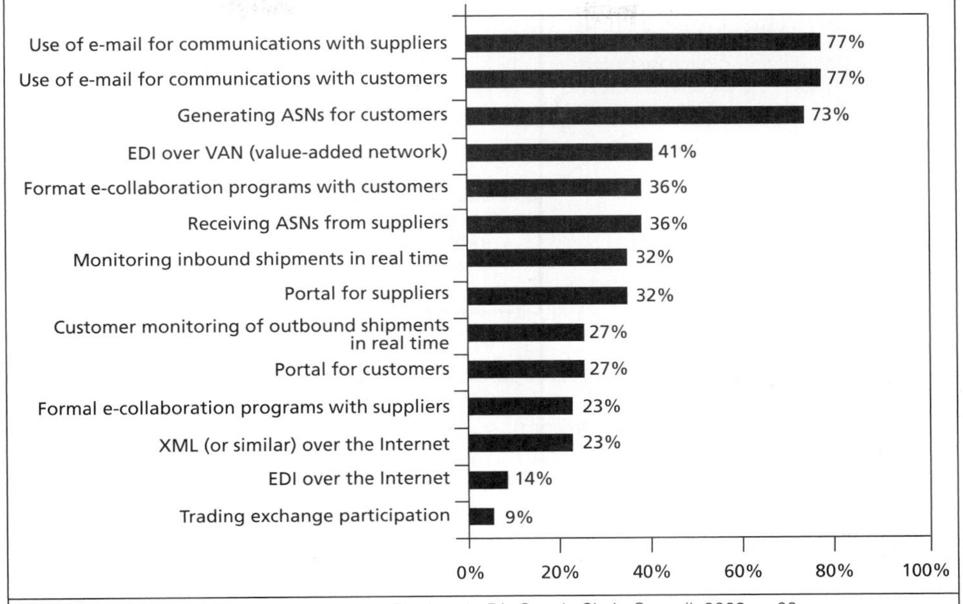

Source: *eBusiness and Supply Processes*, Pittsburgh, PA, Supply Chain Council, 2002, p. 90.

EMERGING: TRANSPORTATION REQUIREMENTS PLANNING

Transportation requirements planning (**TRP**) systems allow shippers and carriers to share information regarding transportation movements and to improve the efficiency and effectiveness of freight flows. TRP systems can be stand-alone systems or they can be connected to enterprise resource planning (ERP) systems. Figure 11.17 shows that the TRP system requires as inputs the freight movement information from the shipper as well as capacity and pricing information from the carrier. Once this information is received, the TRP system can provide optimal shipment planning, allowing truckload consolidation for the shipper and continuous moves for the carrier. The system also allows for real-time status reporting, if the carrier and

Table 11.8 Importance of the Adoption of e-business Capabilities to Specific Areas in Transportation

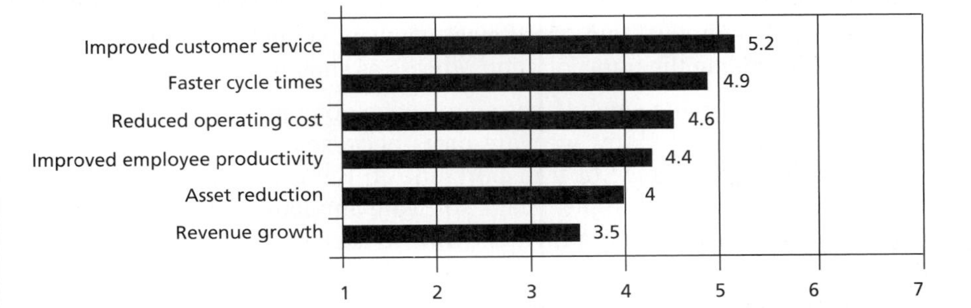

Source: *eBusiness and Supply Processes*, Pittsburgh, PA, Supply Chain Council, 2002, p. 91.

FIGURE 11.17 TRP Model

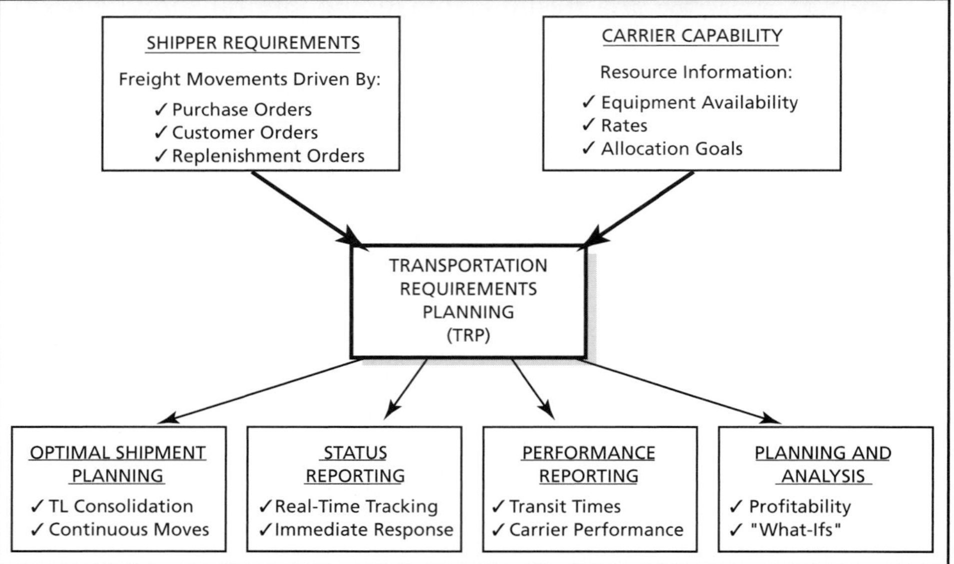

Source: W.L. Grenoble, Center for Supply Chain Research, Penn State University, 2003.

the shipper have the technology to capture real-time data. TRP systems can also provide performance reports as well as allow simulation analysis to answer "what if" types of questions.

A real-time application of a TRP system can be seen in Figure 11.18. This system, developed by Penske Logistics, is called a logistics management system (LMS). The LMS has interfaces with the warehouse, the carrier, and the customer. Electronic messages into and out of the system are shown with arrows. As customer orders are processed in the warehouse, the LMS is planning for the optimum shipment schedule, taking into consideration customer requirements as well as carrier equipment and driver requirements. Once the shipment schedule is made operational, the LMS communicates with the carriers via the Qualcomm network to update shipment status. After delivery, the LMS generates management reports as well as bills customers for the transportation service. As previously discussed, a system like this is successful only if the different systems and technologies can communicate with one another. Figure 11.18 shows how this communication takes place.

Figure 11.19 illustrates the types of information-systems relationships in a TRP system. Notice that this type of system allows the shipper to connect to suppliers, customers, and carriers. Again, this sharing of information is necessary to optimize freight movements. The TRP system also utilizes map and distance data (such as Rand McNally) as well as providing inputs to carrier freight payment systems. TRP systems are an application of managing the transportation process as shown in Figure 11.19.

Transportation management software development and implementation has become the focus of many software firms because of the growing use of ERP systems and the importance of transportation to the firm. Table 11.9 shows some of the firms involved in supply chain software implementation. Specifically, transportation software and its providers can be seen in the "Deliver" portion of the table. Many of these firms are also involved with ERP systems implementation as well as other types of logistics information system software. An important point to be made concerning emerging technologies is their flexibility and connectivity.

FIGURE 11.18 Logistics Management System

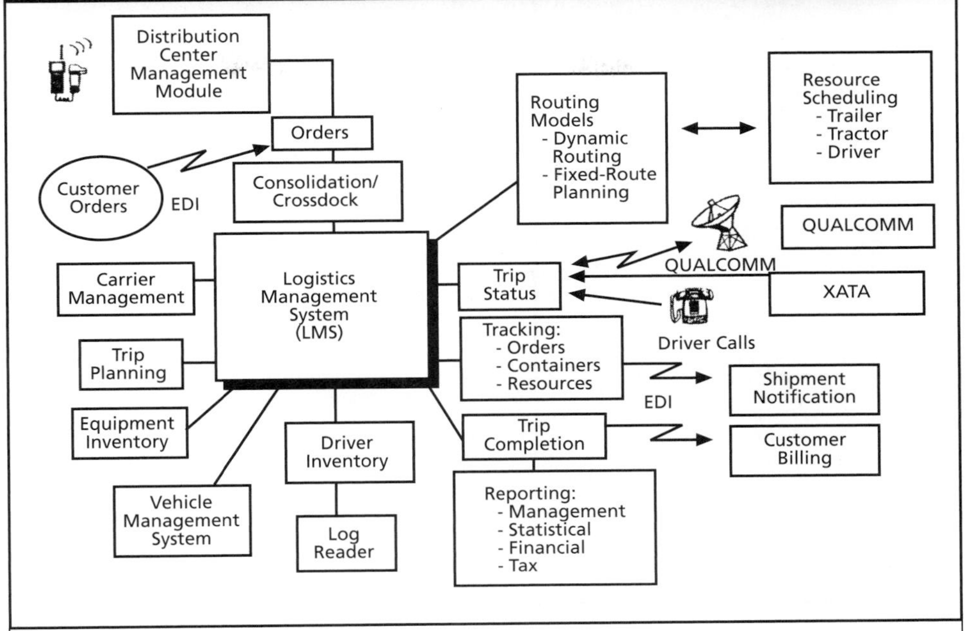

Source: Penske Logistics

FIGURE 11.19 TRP INFO Systems Relationships

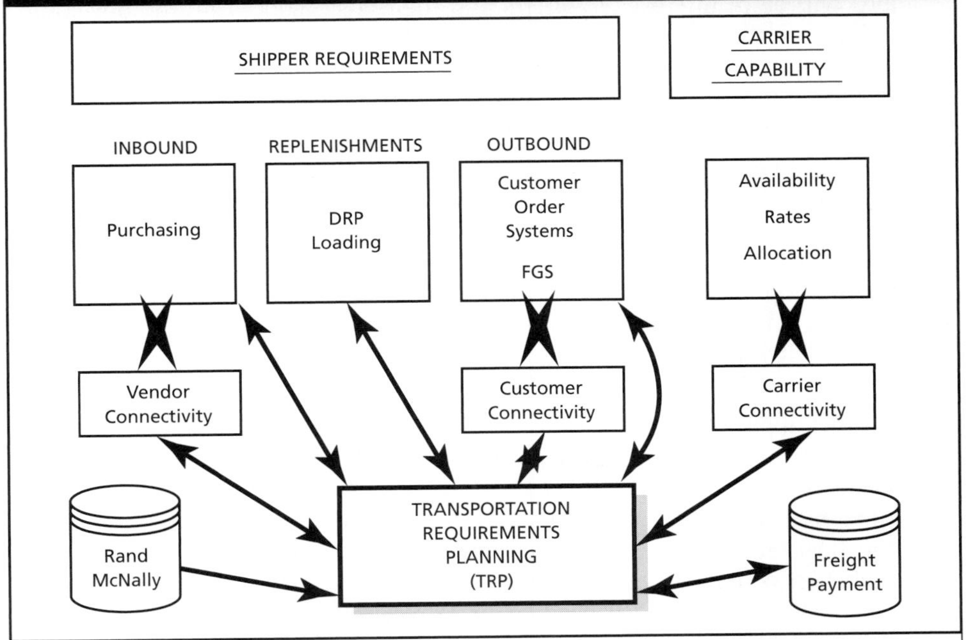

Source: W.L. Grenoble,Center for Supply Chain Research, Penn State University, 2003.

Table 11.9 Key Business-to-Business e-commerce (Internet) Tools

Supply Chain Processes	Web Tool Category	Example Providers
Plan	1. CPFR 2. CRP/VMI 3. Supply/Demand Planning 4. Supply Chain Event Management	1. Manugistics, i2, Logility, Syncra 2. Manugistics, IBM 3. Manugistics, i2, SAP, Adexa 4. Trilion, Vigilance
Source	1. Supplier Coordination 2. Source Searching 3. Bid/Auction Sales	1. Ariba, WebMethods, Exricity 2. TPNRegister, Procurenet 3. Fast Parts, FreeMarkets
Make	1. Share Production Needs 2. Component and Supplier Management	1. WebPlan 2. Aspect
Deliver	1. Customer Relationship Management 2. Order Management 3. WMS 4. Transportation Sourcing 5. Transportation Optimization 6. Track and Trace	1. Siebel, Onyx, SAP 2. IBM, Celarix, SAP 3. EXE, McHugh 4. NTE, Nistevo, Descartes 5. Manugistics, i2, Logistic.com 6. FedEx, UPS

Source: *eBusiness and Supply Processes*, Pittsburgh, PA, Supply Chain Council, 2002, p. 10.

Historically, information flowed vertically along functional lines within firms. These new technologies are allowing information flows to parallel the horizontal movements of product and cash. The management of these supply-chain flows is critical for being competitive in today's environment.

THE FUTURE: INTERNET-INTELLIGENT APPLICATIONS

Information technology has developed so quickly over the past few years that it is difficult to speculate what the future holds. However, some developing technologies will be of interest to carriers and their customers. The first developing technology is called **Internet-intelligent applications**. This technology would be very much like an Internet search engine. It could be programmed to search through the Internet until it finds what it needs, then it would initiate and consummate the transaction.

For example, a shipper using the Internet to post available loads today does so manually. The carrier also receives and analyzes these tenders and replies manually. The shipper then either accepts or rejects the carrier's offer manually. Internet-intelligent applications would allow the carrier and shipper to eliminate most of the manual interaction in the transportation process by determining heuristics for a carrier's pricing options and a shipper's acceptance options. The application could also acknowledge acceptance of the carrier's offer as well as determine pickup times and so on.

Another application is called Event Management. Both EDI and Internet communications can potentially transmit thousands of status messages between carriers and shippers. Although useful, this data usually becomes important when an exception to a requirement occurs. Event Management software is programmed to monitor these transmissions to detect these exceptions and then either notify the appropriate parties of this exception or actually initiate some type of action to address the software. Obviously, decision rules need to be introduced to the software. However, Event Management can be a very useful tool in managing the transportation process.

THE FUTURE: TRANSPARENT EDI

A second developing technology can be called **transparent EDI**. EDI transactions today are inflexible and require intensive set-up time because of the rigid standards necessary for both parties to communicate. Transparent EDI would make EDI transactions more user-friendly by allowing more flexibility in the standards (possibly using XML) and less investment in technology for firms to communicate. Radio frequency identification (RFID) could also be used in this application. RFID would allow the capture and transmission of data without the rigid standards and fixed infrastructure of traditional EDI networks.

THE FUTURE: DATA WAREHOUSING

Finally, the concept of **data warehousing** is growing among firms, especially those that have implemented ERP systems. Traditionally, firms held functional databases in computers that reflected the activities of a single functional activity, such as transportation. These databases were not relational; they were not connected, so communication among functional areas was not possible. Because ERP systems provide a common database, data warehouses are single-storage facilities for all functional data in a firm. Although sometimes very large, data warehouses allow a single access point for all data and all are connected by a common transaction base.

The advantage of a data warehouse is obvious: data connectivity. The disadvantage might not be as obvious. Data warehouses contain large amounts of data and require tremendous storage space. Because there is so much data, firms might become overwhelmed with trying to manage it. More data does not necessarily translate into more information. Carriers and their customers need to carefully examine their information needs to successfully manage the transportation process and access those data required to provide this information.

CONCLUSION

Information systems and information technology are critical to manage effectively the processes in the supply chain. Improvements in both of these areas over the past few years have allowed firms to significantly reduce assets and operating costs, as well as improve over logistics service. However, information technology is a means, rather than an end, to manage effectively the supply chain. Applying technology to a poorly designed process only allows mistakes to be made faster and possibly cheaper. The transportation management process is one of these. Carriers and their customers need to integrate transportation process requirements among all supply chain partners. Technology is then applied to make the process more visible and efficient.

Using information to replace assets and inventories has become a very successful strategy for today's leading firms.

Summary

- The use of technology in transportation is not new. What is new is the integration of this technology and its information among carriers, shippers, and receivers.
- Decisions are made at the transactional as well as at the strategic levels within firms. Information systems must capture the appropriate data and report them meaningfully to support these decisions.

- The four basic sources of information to manage the transportation process are the bill of lading, waybill, manifest, and freight bill.
- Firms are making significant investments in information technology applications to manage the supply chain and reduce pipeline inventories.
- Basic information technologies in transportation include EDI, bar coding, and track and trace.
- Emerging information technologies in transportation include the Internet, enterprise resource planning, and transportation requirements planning.
- The future of information technology applications in transportation include Internet-intelligent applications, transparent EDI, and data warehousing.

Key Terms

2-D bar code, 369
Bill of Lading, 355
Code 128, 369
Code 39, 368
CPFR, 376
CTM, 376
data warehousing, 383
electronic data interchange (EDI), 363
EPC tags, 375
freight bill, 358
GPS, 373
Internet, 376
Internet-intelligent applications, 382
license plate, 371
manifest, 357
matrix bar codes, 370
PDF 417 bar code, 369
radio frequency, 373
satellite technology, 362
transparent EDI, 383
TRP, 379
waybill, 357
XML, 367

Study Questions

1. What are the three types of information necessary to manage the transportation process? Give examples of the types of information classified in each.
2. What are the five purposes of a bill of lading?
3. What is the difference between a straight bill of lading and an order bill of lading?
4. What is the purpose of a waybill and a manifest? What information does each contain?
5. Describe how the freight payment process can be used to influence cash flows between a carrier and its customers.
6. What are the major reasons firms adopt EDI technology? What are some of the barriers to EDI implementation?
7. What is the difference between a Code 39 and Code 49 bar code?
8. What reasons have carriers used to rationalize their investments in satellite technology?
9. What are the advantages of using the Internet for transportation transactions? What are the disadvantages?
10. Discuss how a shipper's implementation of a TRP system will impact its carriers.

Notes

1. Alan J. Stenger, Steven C. Dunn, and Richard R.Young, "Commercially Available Software for Integrated Logistics Management," *The International Journal of Logistics Management*, Vol. 4, No. 2, 1993, p. 63.
2. This classification system is a modified version of one initially specified in Bernard J. LaLonde and Paul H. Zinszer's *Customer Service: Meaning and Measurement*, Chicago, IL: The National Council of Logistics Management, 1976, p. 281.
3. Stanley Scheff and David B. Livingston, *Computer Integrated Logistics: CIL Architecture in the Extended Enterprise*, Southbury, CT: IBM Corporation, U.S. Transportation Industry Marketing, 1991, p. 9.
4. Stephen Barr, "Putting It All Together," *CFO*, July 1995, p. 62.
5. See Lisa R. Williams, "Understanding Distribution Channels: An Interorganizational Study of EDI Adoption," *Journal of Business Logistics*, Vol. 15, No. 2, 1994, pp. 173–204.
6. For a detailed discussion of these barriers, see Robert A. Millen, "Utilization of EDI by Motor Carrier Firms: A Status Report," *Transportation Journal*, Vol. 32, No. 2, Winter 1992, pp. 5–13.
7. For a further detailed discussion of bar-coding technology, see Richard C. Norris,' "Bar Coding, Auto ID, and Data Carriers: Partners to EDI," *EDI Forum*, 1991.
8. Ibid.
9. Ibid.
10. Bob Trebilcock, "Beyond Linear Bar Codes," *Modern Materials Handling*, July 2003, pp. 34–35.
11. Ibid.
12. Chris Cummins, "Keeping On Track With Pallet 'License Plates'," *Food Logistics*, October/November 1997, pp. 68–71.
13. Ibid., p. 70.
14. Ibid, p. 71.
15. Robert Spiegal, "Bar Coding: An Extra Digit for Logistics," *Logistics Management*, June 2003, pp. 44–48.
16. "Smart Labels: They're (Almost) Here," *Parcel Shipping and Distribution*, May/June 1998, pp. 12–13.
17. Robert Spiegal, "Get 'Smart'", *Logistics Management*, July 2003, pp. 65–69.
18. Ibid.
19. Manugistics and Penn State University, *eBusiness and Supply Chain Processes*, Pittsburgh, PA: The Supply Chain Council, August 2003.

Suggested Readings

Angeles, Rebecca, and Ravi Nath. "Partner Congruence In Electronic Data Interchange (EDI) – Enabled Relationships," *Journal of Business Logistics*, Vol. 22, No. 2, 2001, pp. 109–128.

Bardi, Edward J., T.S. Raghunathan, and Prabir K. Bagchi. "Logistics Information Systems: The Strategic Role of Top Management," *Journal of Business Logistics*, Vol. 15, No. 1, 1994, pp. 71–85.

Binkow, Phil. "Electronic Freight Payables Processing Pays Off," *Parcel Shipping & Distribution*, May/June 1998, p. 28.

Bowersox, Donald J., and Patricia J. Daugherty. "Logistics Paradigms: The Impact of Information Technology," *Journal of Business Logistics*, Vol. 16, No. 1, 1995, pp. 65–80.

Critelli, Michael J. "Tilt," *Chief Executive*, July 1997, pp. 37–39.

Cummins, Chris. "Keeping On Track with Pallet 'License Plates'," *Food Logistics*, October/November 1997, pp. 68–71.

Donovan, R. Michael, "ERP Can Deliver Quantum Leap in Performance," *Inbound Logistics*, April 1, 1998, pp. 18–19.

Duff, Mike. "Satellite Tracking Provides More than Just Location," *Food Logistics*, August/September 1997, pp. 56–57.

Edwards, Peter, Melvyn Peters, and Graham Sharman. "The Effectiveness of Information Systems in Supporting the Extended Supply Chain," *Journal of Business Logistics*, Vol. 22, No. 1, 2001, pp. 1–28.

Gentry, Connie, "Logistics IT: Keystone to Integration," *Inbound Logistics,* April 1998, pp. 20–26.

Lewis, Ira, and Alexander Talalayevsky. "Logistics and Information Technology: A Coordination Perspective," *Journal of Business Logistics,* Vol. 18, No. 1, 1997, pp. 141–157.

Martin, Michael H. "Smart Managing," *Fortune,* February 2, 1998, pp. 149–151.

Narasimhan, Ram, and Soo Wook Kim. "Information System Utilization Strategy for Supply Chain Integration," *Journal of Business Logistics*, Vol. 22, No. 2, 2001, pp. 51–76.

Ramaswami, Rama. "Internet Customer Service," *Operations & Fulfillment,* January/February 1998, pp. 10–19.

Ruriani, Deborah Catalano. "Planning Efficient Loads: Software that Makes Cents," *Inbound Logistics,* April 1998, pp. 37–40.

Schwartz, Beth M. "Tracking Down Need," *Transportation & Distribution,* October 1997, pp. 50–55.

"Smart Labels: They're (Almost) Here," *Parcel Shipping & Distribution,* May/June 1998, pp. 12–13.

Spigel, Robert. "Get 'Smart'", *Logistics Management*, July 2003, pp. 65–69.

Walton, Lisa Williams. "Moving Toward LIS Theory Development: A Framework of Technology Adoption Within Channels," *Journal of Business Logistics,* Vol. 16, No. 2 1995, pp. 117–136.

Williams, Lisa, Auril Nibbs, Dimples Irby, and Terrence Finley. "Logistics Integration: The Effect of Information Technology, Team Composition, and Corporate Competitive Positioning," *Journal of Business Logistics,* Vol. 18, No. 2, 1997, pp. 31–42.

Williams, Lisa R., and Kant Rao. "Information Technology Adoption: Using Classical Adoption Models to Predict AEI Software Implementation," *Journal of Business Logistics,* Vol. 19, No. 1, 1998, pp. 5–16.

Case 11-1

Hardee Transportation

Hardee's line-haul tractors currently are equipped with the Qualcomm Satellite system. This allows Hardee to maintain real-time visibility of its tractors while they are either in motion or at rest. Trailer visibility is only available when it is hooked to a tractor. Hardee does not currently have electronic visibility of manifest/bill of lading (BOL) data in its trailers. In other words, Hardee's satellite system will tell it that tractor #3235 is currently hooked to trailer #13145. What the system does not tell it is who the driver is, what the vehicle weight is, or which BOLs are on the trailer. To this point, Hardee's system has served them well.

Hardee services many large manufacturers in the consumer goods industry whose main customers are large discount and specialty retailers. A current movement in this industry is the adoption of radio frequency identification (RFID) tags for full, real-time, visibility of inventory in the supply chain. Most of these efforts have taken place in manufacturing facilities, distribution centers, and retail stores. Some initiatives have placed RFID tags on pallets, cases, and individual consumer units. One of the disadvantages of these tags is the cost. Because of current low demand for these tags, each one can cost anywhere from \$0.50 to \$1.00. This cost could be prohibitive for large-volume customers.

One of Jim O'Brien's large customers (a manufacturer of consumer products) has begun a major initiative with one of its retailers to place RFID tags on their pallets. A future pilot program will start placing these tags on each individual shipping case. Jim's customer wants Hardee to become part of the pallet pilot because of the strategic role the carrier plays in this retail supply chain.

Jim knows little about RFID technology. What he does know is that the tags are expensive, require special receivers, and have a limited transmission distance (5 to 10 feet for passive tags). Hardee would need to develop the technology to track these pallets not only while sitting in Hardee's yard or on its dock but also while they are in transit. Jim is really not sure what this will mean for Hardee and how it will change its technology requirements.

Using the information in this chapter, what would you tell Jim about RFID? How will this technology impact his carrier's operations? How will he implement it while not incurring a huge expense? What will happen when the tags are placed on individual cases?

Case 11-2

Braxton Stores, Inc. (A)

Braxton Stores was established in 1924 as one of the first general merchandise retail establishments that offered a wide array of merchandise at prices attractive to the average consumer. Braxton started with one store in Emporia, Kansas, and has grown to over 1,500 locations today. The original store started as a stand-alone location. Most of Braxton's stores today are located in enclosed malls as anchor stores. The strengths of Braxton's product line were in tools and appliances. Although these lines are still strong today, Braxton has attempted to establish a very strong presence in clothing and electronics, especially personal computers.

Braxton's original competitors were other types of stores that were similar in product line and location. However, new competition has quickly emerged from discount stores that are either stand-alone or act as an anchor in strip malls. These new stores were quickly able to deteriorate Braxton's and their competitors' market shares by offering comparable quality goods at lower prices. This low-price strategy by the discount stores was enabled by the lower retail rents of their locations as well as by the efficiencies of their logistics operations.

Braxton was able to respond to this price pressure by initiating several new logistics initiatives. First, Braxton rationalized its warehouse network down to 15 from 35. This quickly reduced warehousing costs as well as inventory costs. Transportation to and from these larger warehouses was handled by truckload carriers, drastically reducing transportation costs. New materials-handling procedures, especially for garments on hangers, were introduced in both the warehouses and trailers to further increase logistics efficiency as well as to increase product availability at the store level. With these initiatives, Braxton was able to become price-competitive with the discount chains while maintaining its reputation for high-quality merchandise.

At a meeting of the top executives at Braxton, Alex Johns, vice president of marketing, indicated that a new type of competitor was starting to erode Braxton's market share in its core product lines. These competitors used the Internet to post their catalogues on websites so consumers could shop in the comfort of their own homes. "These new competitors are beginning to eat us alive in both clothing and electronics," Alex complained. "They're able to custom-embroider clothing or custom-build personal computers for consumers and guarantee delivery to the home within days. They do this while maintaining very little finished goods inventory. Granted, their transportation costs to consumers are higher, but these are passed on to them and they don't seem to mind. Our format forces us to have higher inventories, but our transportation costs are lower. We need to consider putting our clothing and electronics lines on our website to allow consumers to order in smaller quantities so we can compete in this new market."

Judith Noe, vice president of logistics, was well aware of the new competition but was quite uneasy about changing how Braxton traditionally went to market with these items. "Alex, I understand your concerns, but remember that we just streamlined our supply chain to gain volume efficiencies in our transportation network. Fewer warehouses and larger shipments made us competitive with the discount chains. Now you want to undo this and compete with the Internet firms. Taking these volumes out of our supply chain will increase the costs on the remaining product lines. Also, our warehouse-to-consumer shipments will need to be handled by small package carriers, driving our transportation costs through the roof. I don't see how we can compete in both markets. We will have to choose one market and stick with it."

Listening to this conversation was the CEO of Braxton, Samuel E. Braxton III. Having grown up in the retail business, Sam knew that competitors came and went and that Braxton was usually able to withstand new competition. However, Internet competitors were a totally new brand of retailer. "Consumers' buying habits and sophistication have changed since 1924," he stated. "Braxton has always been able to compete with brick and mortar retailers. We have always been able to find a way to compete in that channel. However, consumers are changing and telling us that brick and mortar stores are not always required in the purchase transaction. If we are trying to establish ourselves in the clothing and electronics lines, I see no alternative but to offer the Internet as an option for our consumers. Alex and Judith, I want both of you to develop a plan that will allow us, over the next 2 years, to be the leading retailer of clothing and electronics over the Internet."

Case Questions

1. What would be the strategy Braxton could use to introduce its retailing on the Internet? Would both product lines be introduced at once? Would items be home-delivered or would consumers be required to pick them up at the store?
2. How could you minimize the impacts on Braxton's supply-chain costs and service? What would the new transportation network look like? Are there shipper/ carrier network strategies that Braxton could use to manage the transportation in this new supply chain?
3. What would be the next logical use of the Internet for Braxton?
4. How would they integrate this with their carrier base?

Case 11-3

Braxton Stores, Inc. (B)

With all of the changes the Internet is bringing to Braxton, other types of technology have also evolved to present opportunities. Braxton operates its distribution centers (DCs) using traditional bar code technology with radio frequency bar code scanners. This has allowed Braxton to maintain real-time visibility of their inventory in the DCs. Braxton also uses bar code scanners in its retail outlets at checkout to monitor sales activity. Braxton uses this point-of-sale (POS) data for ordering replenishment shipments from its DCs.

Because of the sheer volume of shipment activity between its DCs and stores and the high inventory turns in the stores, Braxton doesn't check in inventory at the back door of its stores. Nor does it update inventory status when it replenishes the store shelves. The labor cost involved would more than offset the value of the inventory status information. However, Braxton has become increasingly concerned about this lack of visibility from DC to checkout. Inventory shortages and theft have become a serious concern for Braxton Management. To address this concern, Braxton is beginning a pilot program with one of its major suppliers to place RFID tags on both cases and individual products. Braxton is expecting its suppliers to absorb the cost of the tags, whereas Braxton would invest in the scanner technology needed at the DCs and stores.

A core carrier servicing Braxton's DCs is Hardee Transportation. Braxton realizes that if the cases have tags on them from the manufacturer to the DC, then the carriers should be involved in providing visibility in transit in these freight lanes. Jim O'Brien of Hardee Transportation was invited to a meeting between Braxton and its supplier partner in this project. His role was to provide information on how Hardee was going to become a partner in this project. Jim knew that this was a critical meeting for the future success for Hardee. If these customers were going to implement RFID, many more would follow.

Case Questions

1. If you were Jim, what would you tell Braxton management?
2. How could Hardee participate in this experiment? What would it need to do to provide visibility between manufacturers and Braxton's DC's?
3. How could Hardee justify the investment in the scanner technology for just this customer?
4. How would Hardee need to change its internal operations and information systems to implement this technology?

Appendix 11-A

Transportation Sites on the Internet

Many organizations have found the use of the Internet to be extremely beneficial in promoting their businesses. Transportation firms are no exception. This appendix contains only a sample of the transportation firms that have developed websites for potential and current customers.

Notice that many of the sites provide more than just information about the company. They allow customers to find rates as well as track shipments.

The flexibility and opportunities the Internet offers to these firms and their customers are quite broad. This can be seen on the Web pages to follow.

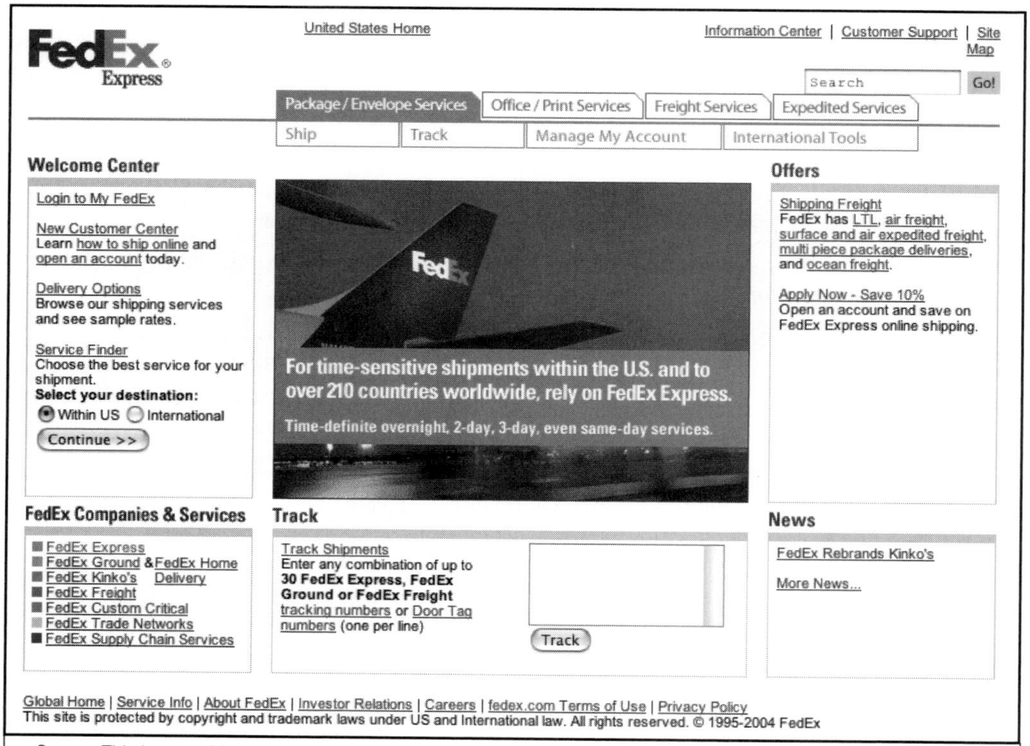

Source: This image of fedex.com homepage was reproduced on October 18, 2004. Information and services on fedex.com are subject to change.

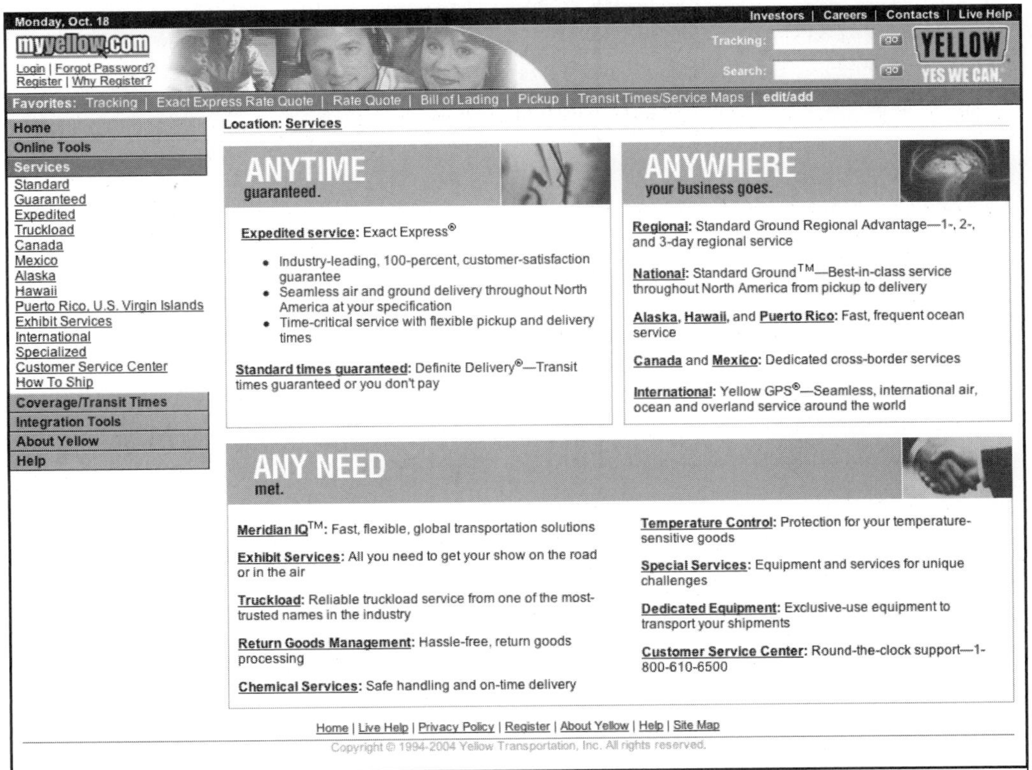

Source: Yellow Transportation, Inc. Reprinted with permission.

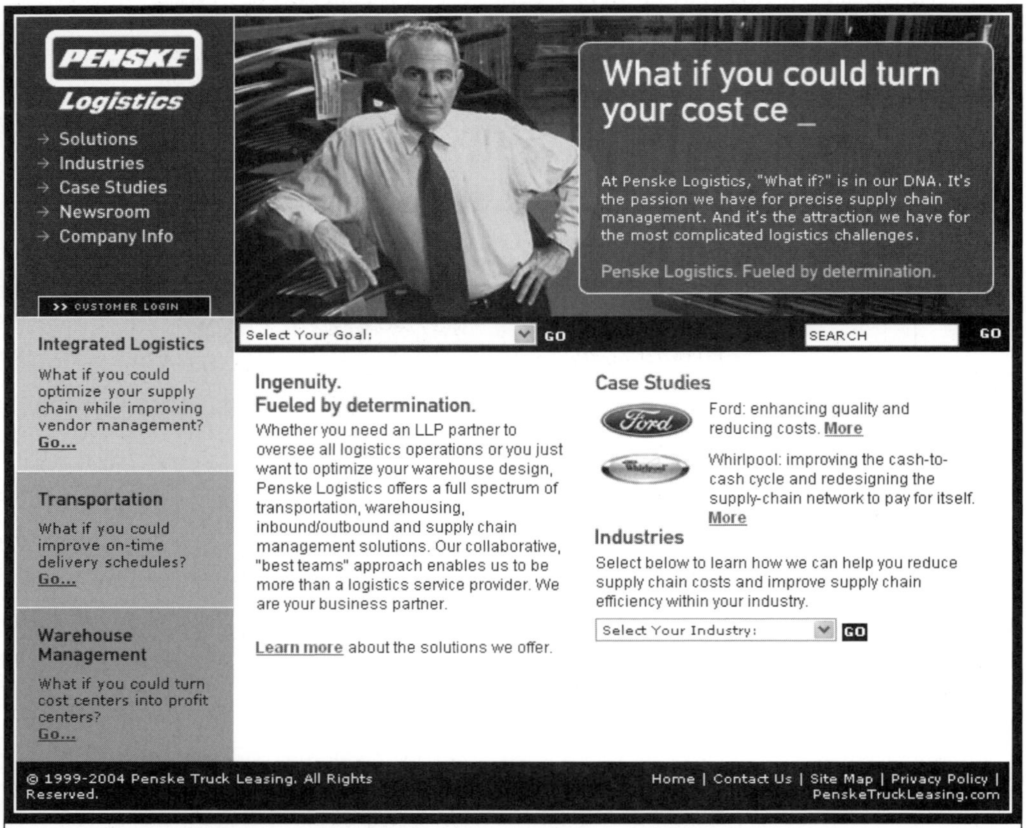

Source: Penske Logistics

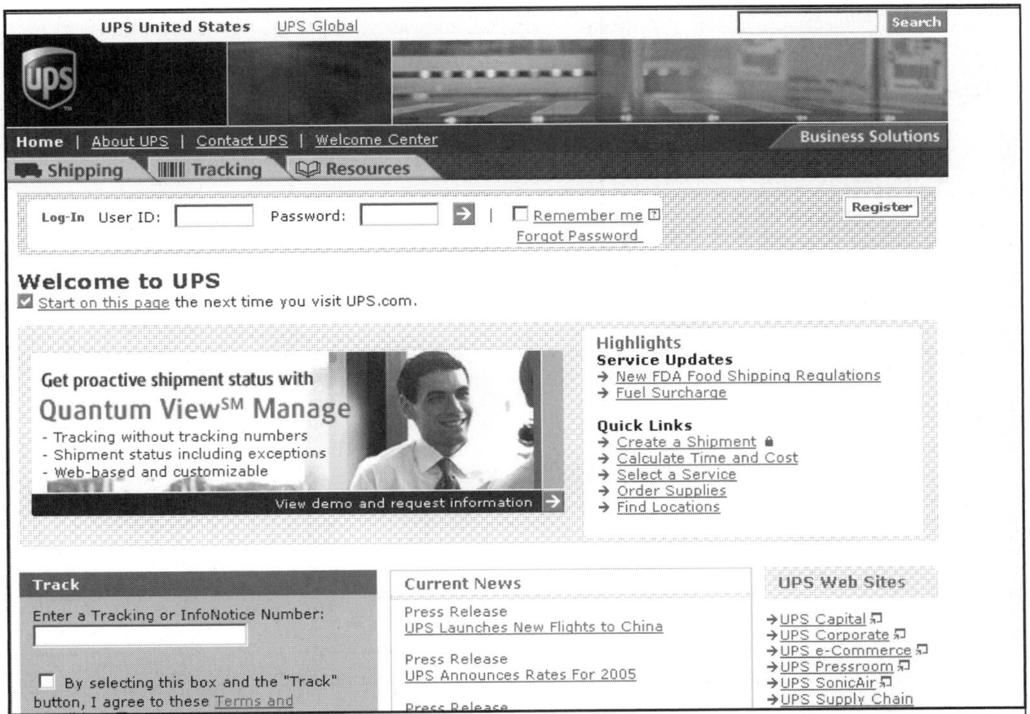

Source: This image is reproduced with permission of United Parcel Service of America, Inc. © Copyright 2004 United Parcel Service of America, Inc. UPS, the UPS brandmark and the color brown are trademarks that are used with permission by its owner, United Parcel Service of America, Inc. All rights reserved.

Source: BNSF Logistics, LLC.

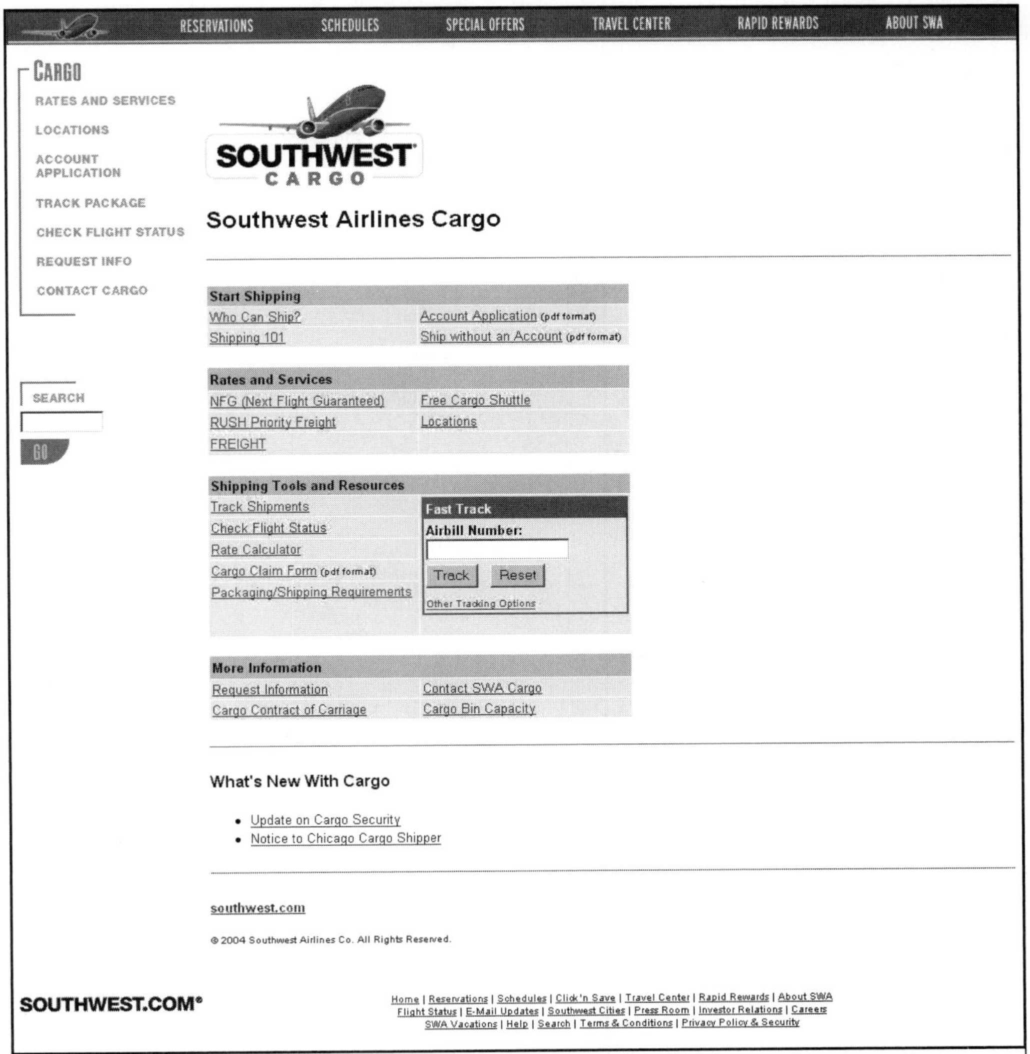

Source: Courtesy of Southwest Airlines Co.

Chapter 12

Shipper Strategies

Both shippers and carriers utilize strategies to manage their respective networks. The shipper strategy is focused on purchasing and managing transportation services to meet the needs of their external and internal customers. Carrier strategy is focused on the efficient use of resources to provide the economical and efficient service the shipping public desires. Carriers also try to maximize return on deployed assets.

In most shipper organizations, *transportation management* is the term used to describe the functional area dedicated to shipper network strategy. The transportation manager develops strategies to address the procurement of transportation in general, as well as small, bulk, and inbound shipments

This chapter presents many of the techniques used by shippers to effectively manage their transportation networks. The first part of the chapter deals with shipper strategies and transportation management, while the latter part is concerned with the development of relationships between shippers and third-party logistics providers (3PLs).

TRANSPORTATION MANAGEMENT

Traditionally, **traffic management** was the term used for the tasks of obtaining and controlling transportation services for shippers or consignees or both. It was a term applied to a position or an entire department in almost any extractive, raw material, manufacturing, assembling, or distribution firm. The term *transportation management* has generally replaced *traffic management*, and *transportation management* is currently the term applied to the purchase and control of transportation services in some organizations.

Transportation Management as a Procurement Function

Transportation management is a special form of procurement and purchasing. **Procurement** is a term that applies to a wide range of activities that basically consists of obtaining goods and services for the firm. Procurement includes analysis and activities in the following areas: 1) quality, 2) pricing, 3) specifications, 4) supply source, 5) negotiations, 6) inspection and assurance of quality, 7) timing, 8) conducting value analysis of alternative methods and sources, 9) capital analysis, 10) make or buy decisions, 11) legal and regulatory constraints, and 12) general management. All of these factors provide the firm with a system to obtain the physical goods and special services it requires.

Transportation management performs all of these specific activities in its acquisition and control of transportation *services* for the firm. Traditionally, a minimum transportation cost goal was employed for this function. In most firms, this was replaced by a goal of minimum total logistics expense. Today many companies first establish a customer service goal and then evaluate transportation and logistics in terms of minimized total logistics costs while attaining the service goal. This, in a way, is similar to the balanced-value approach.

Part of this change is the manner by which the performance of the transportation manager is evaluated. Historically, transportation managers were judged by their cost-control efforts. They were required to spend as little as possible for transportation. Because they were evaluated on this criterion, transportation managers would choose the lowest cost method consistent with the minimum service requirements. Under current management requirements, transportation managers are evaluated by how well they participate in the overall optimization and achievement of the logistics goals. This might include using premium transportation or other more expensive techniques, the cost of which is offset elsewhere in the logistics system.

In many firms, transportation managers have evolved from purely an operational role to a more strategic one. Because transportation is usually the single largest variable cost in logistics and because cycle times to customers are being reduced, transportation managers are having a greater impact on the strategic goals of the organization. The next section will examine some of the general types of strategies used by shippers to manage their transportation networks.

SHIPPER TRANSPORTATION STRATEGIES[1]

The transportation function is one element of the total logistics process. The strategies and operating decisions used in **transportation management** must support the strategies and objectives of the logistics process, the organization as a whole, and the members of the supply chain. Transportation decisions must be made to benefit the total logistics process and the firm, not merely the transportation department.

Current management strategy focuses on optimization between the various elements within the logistics system. Transportation is often one of the largest cost elements, and decisions in this area can favorably or negatively impact the total distribution performance. As an example, slow but low-cost transportation can have an adverse impact on customer service and inventory levels. Although such methods might minimize transportation cost, inventory levels might need to be much higher to accommodate longer transit times. These higher stocking levels, with the resultant increase in inventory-carrying costs, might be more than any saving in freight charges.

As Figure 12.1 indicates, transportation strategy is concerned with the purchase and control of transportation services. Transportation purchasing decisions include modal selection, consolidation, private transportation, intermediaries, and contracting. The resources, organization, and trade-terms decisions are concerned with controlling transportation. The strategies in guiding the transportation decision maker are discussed below.

General Strategy

As Figure 12.1 indicates, transportation strategies have been separated into those that apply to all types of shipments, including small and bulk shipments. Passage of the transportation deregulation acts dramatically changed general transportation management strategy. Before that time, transportation managers primarily were concerned with tariff rates and regulations.

Proactive Management

With the elimination of economic regulations to control transportation rates and services, the transportation manager is able to develop innovative approaches to a company's transportation problems. The "you cannot do that because of regulation" approach has given way to a proactive management philosophy that emphasizes finding solutions to company transportation problems. The transportation manager relies on basic management techniques to seek innovative transportation systems that will provide the company with a competitive price or service advantage in the marketplace.

The thrust of the proactive management strategy is problem solving. Before deregulation, transportation management was concerned with developing expertise in regulatory manipulation to gain a competitive edge in the market. Today the transportation

FIGURE 12.1 Transportation Strategy

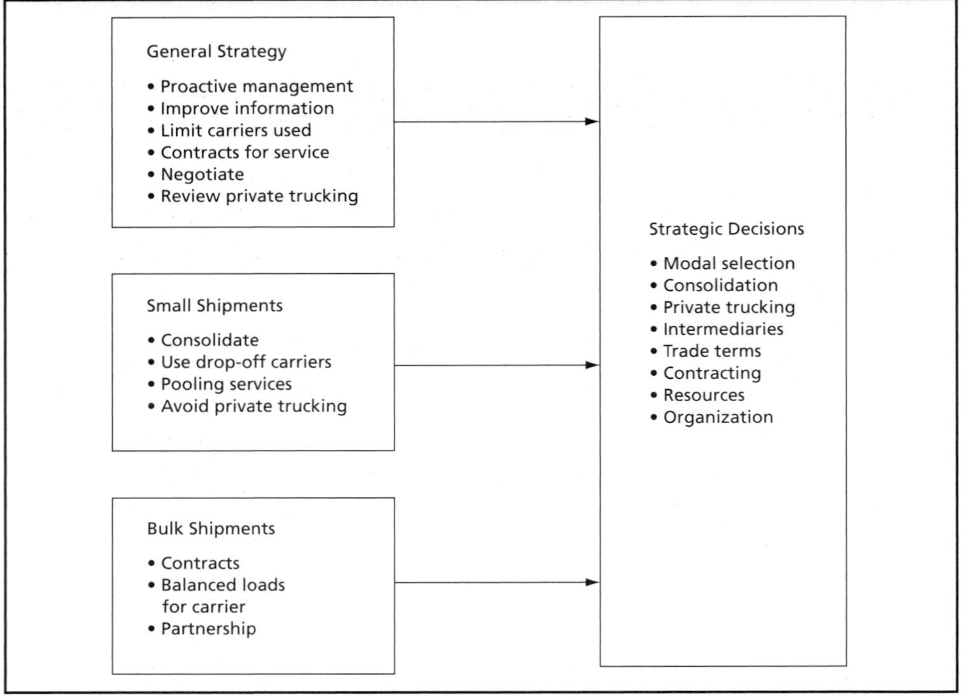

manager must rely on his or her ability and creativity to design a transportation system that permits product differentiation and a competitive advantage.

The current competitive environment requires that the transportation manager focus on customer service and competitive strategies. Successful logistics strategies are seen as a true competitive advantage, requiring transportation support that can respond to ever-increasing demands for smaller inventory levels combined with immediate delivery.[2]

Part of the success of major retailers such as Wal*Mart has been attributed to its success in increasing inventory turns while reducing distribution costs. Contributing to this success is their ability to control transit times and reliability between their suppliers, distribution centers, and stores. Often suppliers are expected to become "partners" with their customers, with transportation being one of the more critical elements. The ability of such techniques as JIT (just-in-time), ECR (efficient consumer response), CPFR (collaborative planning, forecasting, and replenishment), and VMI (vendor-managed inventories) relies on cost-efficient and sophisticated transportation methods.[3]

Improve Information

To effectively manage the transportation function, accurate and current information is a necessity. Without information, the manager is unable to plan and control the transportation activities or make sound decisions. Transportation costs, shipment volume, and carrier performance are the typical data collected. These data are essential to carrier negotiation, freight consolidation, contracting, and private motor carrier decisions.

A major source of transportation information is the bill of lading (discussed in Chapters 11 and 13). The bill of lading indicates the customer and shipper, the shipment volume, origin and destination, date, and carrier. The carrier's freight bill (invoice) provides similar data as well as the transportation cost for the shipment. Other sources include the purchase order, order entry system, invoice, and internal studies. Some companies use a third-party provider, such as a bank or freight payment company, to pay freight bills, and most of these freight payment firms have the computer capabilities to provide transportation data reports in the format required by management. Chapter 11 provides a more detailed discussion of information requirements for logistics and transportation.

Limit Number of Carriers Used

By reducing the number of carriers it uses, a shipper increases its market power and therefore its ability to effectively negotiate with its carriers. Each carrier has a larger share of the shipper's volume, making each carrier more important to the shipper. This also reduces the number of relationships that have to be managed. This usually results in more effective collaboration between the shipper and its carrier base that eliminates costs, thereby reducing the shipper's expense and increasing the carriers' operating margin.

It is quite common for a shipper to use fewer than 50 carriers to ship the majority of its freight, concentrating 75 to 80 percent of its total freight dollars with 25 or fewer motor carriers. Rail shippers commonly use just one or, at best, two carriers because usually only one rail carrier can provide service to the shipper's plant or warehouse.

A common practice has been the use of **"core" carriers** (discussed in Chapter 13). These firms are chosen from the existing carrier base, usually after an intensive bidding process. The "core" carriers usually divide the business, and their share might be as much as 25 percent of the total. It is not unusual for a shipper to go from nearly 100 carriers to fewer than 10. The risk is that should one of the core carriers exit the business, the remaining carriers might not be able to handle the business. Replacement carriers might be difficult to obtain in times of tight equipment or high demand.

The disadvantage of limiting the number of carriers used is the increased dependency on the carriers that are used. If one of the major carriers ceases operation, the service disruption results in a reduced customer service level, increased managerial costs, and greater transportation costs. The greater cost and lower customer service level exist until a replacement carrier is selected and is efficiently operating.

Carrier Negotiation

Negotiating with for-hire carriers is standard operating procedure today. Before deregulation, carrier negotiation was almost nonexistent, given the rate bureau influence in common carrier rate making. With the marketplace free of economic regulation, all carrier rates and services are matters for negotiation.

Market power determines the shipper's ability to negotiate acceptable rates and services. To increase market power as discussed above, shippers use the strategy of limiting the number of carriers, thereby concentrating more of its economic power with a carrier and increasing the carrier's dependence on the shipper.

A shipper's market power and negotiating strength also are determined by the characteristics of its freight. Freight that has low density, is hard to handle, is easily damaged, and moves in small volumes irregularly is undesirable freight for the carrier. Conversely, products that have high density and high value, are difficult to damage, and move in large volumes regularly are more economical for the carrier to move. Given the problems motor carriers have experienced in recruiting and retaining drivers, some firms have adopted new policies when responding to negotiation requests from shippers. Carriers are now seeking "driver-friendly" freight, which generally means that the driver does not have to assist with either the loading or unloading. One Fortune 500 shipper has responded by working with its retail customers to provide incentives for rapid unloading and relieving drivers of tasks other than driving. Finally, the shipper's negotiating position is improved if the freight moves in the direction of the carrier's empty backhaul.

Contracting

Deregulation has permitted increased contracting with for-hire carriers. The contracts allow the shipper to realize the lower rates and necessary service levels that are not attainable from a regulated carrier. During the term of the contract, the shipper is guaranteed the contracted rate and service (most contracts are for 1 year, but other time periods might apply). If properly written, the provisions of the contract take precedence over the bill of lading and transportation regulations. The transportation manager must take precautions to ensure that the contract provides desired terms such as rates, services, equipment, and liability.

Rail contracting is common today. Rail shippers usually have two or more rail contracts in effect to govern a given commodity move over a given origin–destination, and contracts generally are rate oriented. Motor carrier contracts usually cover 1 to 3 years with stipulations for tailored service. Negotiations and contracting will be discussed in more detail later in this chapter.

Review Private Motor Carrier Transportation

The decision to use or discontinue the use of private motor carriage is a continual strategic issue for the transportation manager. In today's dynamic transportation market, competitive pressures have forced for-hire motor carrier rates below the cost of many private fleet operations. Through the use of contracting, the service level of for-hire carriers is equivalent to that provided by private motor carriage. However, many shippers still desire to provide strict control over their freight movement because of customer requirements. Also, some shippers manage their private fleets as profit centers, arranging backhauls as common or contract carriers for other shippers or to pick up inbound materials to their facilities. With all of these factors to consider, the review of private motor carriage is a prevalent transportation strategy.

Small Shipment Strategy

As Figure 12.1 indicates, the small shipment strategies consist of freight consolidation, using drop-off carriers and pooling services, and avoiding the use of private motor carriage. The strategic thrust for small shipments is to reduce the inherently high transportation costs associated with small-sized shipments. By increasing the size of the shipments, the shipper can take advantage of the carrier's low rates for heavier shipments. Rate discounts from 30 percent to 50 percent or more are possible for heavier loads.

A shipper consolidates its freight by using its order entry system. As customer orders arrive, a computer uses a three-digit zip code to match shipments going to the same general area (this is also called transportation requirements planning, discussed in Chapter 11). As discussed above, the need for information is critical to any freight consolidation program. The transportation manager must know the shipments that are shipped to a given area on a given date, as well as delivery requirements.

If the consolidated load consists of many shipments going to different consignees in a general area, the shipper might use the **pooling** service offered by for-hire carriers. The pooling service charges the shipper the lower volume rate from one origin to one destination. Because the consolidated load contains shipments for many consignees at different destinations, a warehouse or drayage firm is used to separate and deliver the individual shipments, and an added cost is incurred for this additional break-bulk and delivery service.

Table 12.1 provides an example of the cost-saving potential from freight pooling. In this example, six small (LTL) shipments are destined for locales around Toledo, Ohio. The cost of shipping each shipment separately to the consignees is $2,948.43. (See the two columns labeled Direct LTL in Table 12.1.) By consolidating the six shipments into one 31,000-pound truckload shipment and shipping it to a warehouse in Toledo for reshipment to the individual consignee, the total cost is $2,340.50, a savings of $607.93 (20.6 percent). The pooled shipment rate of $7.55 per hundredweight (cwt) combines the line-haul rate to Toledo ($5.45) with the warehousing handling cost ($0.75) and local delivery rate ($1.35).

Another small shipment strategy is the use of **stopping-in-transit (SIT) service** provided by motor carriers. SIT permits the shipper to load a number of shipments on a vehicle and stop along the way to unload the individual shipments. Conversely, SIT can be used for inbound shipments by having the carrier stop along the way to load additional shipments and deliver a consolidated raw material shipment to the plant, warehouse, or retail store.

Figure 12.2 is an example of SIT. The shipper has two shipments departing from the origin (O), one destined for C1 (10,000 pounds) and one for D (20,000 pounds). The cost to ship the two shipments without SIT is $745.00, compared with $615.00 with the SIT, a savings of $130.00 (17 percent). SIT rules require the shipper to use the highest truckload (TL) rate ($1.90/cwt) and the highest weight in the vehicle at any time (30,000 pounds) and to pay for the intermediate stop(s) ($45.00).

Table 12.1 Freight Pooling Example

		Direct LTL		Pool Truck Service to Toledo			
Customer	Shipment Weight (lb)	Rate $/cwt	Total Cost	Line-Haul	Handling	Local	Total
Toledo	8,250	9.25	$763.13	$449.63	$61.88	$111.38	$622.88
Findlay	4,350	9.85	$428.48	$237.08	$32.63	$58.73	$328.43
Lima	3,600	9.95	$358.20	$196.20	$27.00	$48.60	$271.80
Sandusky	5,350	8.85	$473.48	$291.58	$40.13	$72.23	$403.93
Monroe	3,780	9.55	$360.99	$206.01	$28.35	$51.03	$285.39
Defiance	5,670	9.95	$564.17	$309.02	$42.53	$76.55	$428.09
Totals	31,000		**$2948.43**	$1,689.50	$232.50	$418.50	**$2,340.50**
				Saving with Pool Truck Service =			$607.93

Pooling Rates

Linehaul to Toledo	=	$5.45/cwt
Handling Cost	=	$0.75/cwt
Local Delivery Rate	=	$1.35/cwt
Total Rate	=	$7.55/cwt

FIGURE 12.2 Stopping-in-Transit Example

O ———— C_1 ———— D

Shipment Weight (lb)		Rates ($/cwt) LTL	TL	Minimum Weight (lb)	
O–C_1	10,000	$2.25	$1.70	30,000	Stopoff Charge = $45.00/stop
O–D	20,000	$2.60	$1.90	30,000	
	30,000				

Cost with SIT

300 cwt @ $1.90	=	$570.00
Stopoff Charge	=	$45.00
Total	=	**$615.00**

Cost without SIT

O–C_1	100 cwt @ $2.25	=	$225.00
O–D	200 cwt @ $2.60	=	$520.00
	Total	=	**$745.00**

Finally, the use of private motor carriage for small shipments is normally not cost effective. The small shipment size precludes full use of the private motor carrier equipment, with the result that costs are higher than the charges assessed by for-hire carriers. For-hire carriers are in a position to consolidate small shipments from many shippers to make the operation economical. One major exception to this strategy is the driver/salesperson operation in which the driver performs sales service functions (customer order filling and stock rotation, for example) in addition to driving.

Bulk Shipment Strategy

The primary strategy used in the transportation of bulk commodities is contracting. Most bulk raw materials are moved under long-term contracts with rail, water, and motor carriers. The large volume of product moved gives the shipper the requisite negotiating and market power to realize lower rates and guaranteed service levels.

The sheer volume of transportation involved has caused both shippers and carriers to realize their mutual dependency. If the carrier ceases operation, the shipper experiences serious disruptions in service, higher costs, and possibly a short-run closing of production because alternative transportation is not available. Likewise, the carrier is aware of the large percentage of its business that is accounted for by one shipper.

Given this mutual dependency, a shipper attempts to provide the carrier with a **balanced load**, that is, a load into the facility and one out of the facility. A balanced load eliminates the empty backhaul costs that the carrier must account for in the initial loaded move and enables the carrier to spread this round-trip cost over two commodity moves instead of one. To accomplish the balanced load strategy, cooperation is required between outbound and inbound (purchasing) transportation and might necessitate sourcing material purchases from areas where the carrier experiences empty backhauls. Recently, a major manufacturer contacted other shippers in an attempt to generate freight for its contract carrier to haul over an otherwise empty backhaul. This can be difficult if the commodity being transported requires dedicated or specialized trailers.

Inbound Transportation Strategy

Today companies are giving considerable attention to inbound logistics and inbound transportation. They are recognizing that the **terms of sale** used by purchasing do not provide them with sufficient control over inbound transportation costs. In the past, the purchase order items would stipulate "FOB, Delivered" or "ship the best way." These terms of sale give the supplier control over the purchaser's inbound transportation and assume that the supplier has the ability and desire to use the transportation carrier that minimizes the purchaser's costs.

By modifying the shipping terms to "FOB, Origin," the buyer takes on the inbound transportation responsibility and authority and can apply the transportation strategies identified above to achieve lower rates and improved service. Limiting the number of inbound carriers used builds market power, provides balanced loads to carriers, and results in lower inbound transportation costs.

Another approach is to use the "FOB, Delivered" term in the purchase order but request that the supplier use one of the carriers from a list of carriers approved by the buyer. This strategy concentrates the purchaser's inbound freight into a limited number of carriers but permits the supplier to select an acceptable carrier from the approved list. A more detailed discussion of FOB terms is found in Chapter 13.

In addition to increased attention to inbound shipments, **reverse logistics** is a new area requiring significant transportation activity and, in some cases, extreme control. Reverse logistics can cover everything from the return of repairable items and parts for rebuilding to the recall of food or pharmaceuticals. In some cases, this is really a continuous cycle. An example would be the return of an expended copier toner cartridge after it is replaced with a new one. Often, such items come in packaging materials that allow the round trip. The packaging might even contain a preaddressed label and prepaid shipping. In another situation, pallets, totes, and baskets are returned from a retail store to the distribution center for reuse or recycling.

Some firms, like GENCO, specialize in reverse logistics. GENCO has partnered with a major retailer to return its product to manufacturers. Some of the returns are moved by the retailers' private fleet, whereas others are transported by contract carriers. Other firms, including a computer manufacturer and a consumer goods electronics firm, have put reverse logistics programs into place.[4]

The strategies discussed above provide the guidelines for the transportation manager to follow in carrying out the transportation function. The next section examines some of the typical functions assigned to a transportation manager.

LINE ASPECTS OF TRANSPORTATION MANAGEMENT

The daily activities of transportation management are numerous. Although the management of individual transportation managers might vary, the typical transportation management process is as follows:

- Shipment planning
- Carrier selection
- Ordering service
- Expediting/tracing
- Pre-auditing/rating
- Auditing/paying the freight bill
- Detention/demurrage processes

- Claims, if any
- Other—private car or motor carrier fleet management, transportation budget management

Shipment Planning

Transportation management continually monitors inbound and outbound shipping schedules, which should be coordinated with purchasing and distribution or production. A continuous flow of product should be maintained, unhindered by the unavailability of transportation (no equipment or service). Further, physical loading and unloading must be planned according to the efficient use of docks and labor. Management must ensure that transportation is not scheduled too early or in excess of actual needs because dock and track congestion, as well as equipment detention and demurrage charges, will result.

Carrier Selection

This task involves selecting the actual carrier that will move the shipment. In the case of rail, this might be largely confined to the carrier that has a siding into the plant. But even here, the transportation manager might have some latitude in route selection through use of intermediate or alternative route carriers. In connection with motor carriers, transportation managers often will give shipment preference to the firm's own private carriage vehicles or use a contract carrier before considering common carriers. Within both rail or motor selection, transportation managers evaluate a number of factors to select a specific carrier.

Ordering Service

To order transportation service, the transportation manager might contact a railroad car distributor who will arrange empty car delivery or call a motor carrier's local **dispatcher**. Electronic methods are becoming more common, and the use of the Internet is accelerating this trend. In other cases, long-term arrangements for equipment supply include trailer pools and scheduled rotation. The transportation manager needs to inform the carrier personnel of the shipper's name and pickup point, weight, commodity, destination, and sometimes the cube measurement of the shipment. Upon vehicle arrival, the equipment is loaded according to plans established in the first step (shipment planning). They include crew assignment, loading arrangement, bracing, dunnage, documentation, and any other special needs.

Expediting/Tracing

The transportation manager keeps track of shipment progress and alerts the carrier of any in-route changes that might be necessary. Some shippers have direct computer links with carrier shipment systems. These provide daily position reports of all the shipper's railcars or shipments. Some carriers provide tracing services via the Internet. Other carriers place information on a secure website that only a particular shipper can access. This information is updated on a scheduled basis. Expediting/tracing is a valuable control tool for the shipper and consignee because they can plan production and assembly around shipment progress or problems.

Pre-auditing/Rating

Pre-auditing is the process of determining what the proper freight charges for a shipment should be. Often shippers pre-audit shipments before billing by the carrier so that freight bill overcharges and undercharges can be reduced or avoided. Computer rating systems have greatly assisted with this task.

Auditing/Paying the Freight Bill

Auditing entails checking the accuracy of the freight bill after it is presented by the carrier or after it has been paid. Some firms do this in house, whereas others hire outside consultants to perform this job after the bill has actually been paid. The transportation department generally confirms the freight bill and passes it along to the office responsible for payment.

Deregulation has largely been responsible for price simplification. Contract rates and services, the diminished importance of rate bureaus and their complex tariffs, and the growth of computers enable pre-auditing and post-auditing to take place with fewer resources than in the past. Many carriers offer their rates on computer floppy disks or will update a shipper's file via an electronic data exchange (EDI) link automatically. Rate checking and auditing can also be performed by many computer-based firms such as Cass Information Systems.

Detention/Demurrage Processes

Detention is a charge assessed by a motor carrier against a shipper or consignee for keeping equipment for loading or unloading beyond a specified period. **Demurrage** is the same concept in the rail industry. The transportation manager is usually responsible for monitoring, managing, and paying for detention and demurrage obligations. The manager must trade off the loading, unloading, and personnel costs against the cost of holding carrier equipment.

Claims

Loss and damage sometimes occur to shipments while in the possession of carriers. Transportation managers will then file **claims** to recoup part or all of these damaged amounts. They also handle overcharges on the freight bills.

Common carrier motor carrier companies and railroads are liable for all loss, damage, and delay to a shipment with limited exceptions as provided under the Carmack Amendment. These exceptions include the following:

- An act of God—an unavoidable catastrophe
- An act of a public enemy—armed aggression against our country
- An act of public authority—through due process of law, a government agency causes damage, loss, or delay
- An act of the shipper—actions by the shipper contribute to the damage, such as improper packaging
- The inherent nature of the goods—natural deterioration

To recover damages from a regulated motor carrier or railroad, the shipper must file a claim in writing within 9 months of the date of shipment. The carrier must acknowledge the receipt of the claim within 30 days and must inform the claimant within 120 days whether it will pay or refuse to pay the claim. If the carrier does not dispose of the claim within 120 days, the carrier must inform the claimant of the claim's status every 60 days. If the carrier refuses to pay the claim, the claimant has 2 years from the date of disallowance to bring legal action against the carrier.

The carrier is normally liable for the full value of the product at destination. However, carriers, especially motor carriers, can limit their liability by use of the released value rate. In return for a lower rate, the shipper agrees to hold the carrier liability to something less than the full value of the product. Some carriers have inserted automatic released value rules in their tariffs and terms of sale. The automatic released value rules reduce the value of the product to that stipulated in the tariff unless the shipper states otherwise on the bill of lading at the time of shipment. Until recently, motor carriers had to provide a full value rate for every shipment, allowing them to then provide released value rates for the shipper to choose. Today, however, motor carriers are not obliged to provide a full value rate for a shipment, allowing them the opportunity to provide only released value rates.

For other carriers (air and exempt motor carriage), liability for loss and damage is based on negligence. That is, the carrier is held liable if it did not provide the ordinary care a reasonable person would provide in protecting his or her goods. This is also the standard to which a warehouse is held. Claims are discussed in more detail in Chapter 13.

Private Car and Motor Carrier Fleet Management

In some firms, the transportation manager is also responsible for private railcar and motor carrier fleet management. This entails coordination and control tasks with the goal of minimizing fleet costs and providing quality service. For some shippers, especially those in the chemical and petroleum industries, this could involve the management of thousands of specialized rail or trailer fleets.

Transportation Budget Management

The transportation budget is the major overriding financial control in all these tasks. The transportation manager must keep track of current and future activities and expenditures and relate them to the original plan. Cost escalators, such as fuel and insurance, have created major problems for most transportation managers who attempt to operate within planned budgets. Escalation will no doubt continue to be a complicating cost and budget problem in the future.

Staff and Administrative Aspects of Transportation Management

Transportation management has grown over the years to become more than a mere line activity. Many planning tasks or staff activities have developed as support functions. These other activities increase the cost efficiency or customer service capability of the line activities.

Mode Selection

The transportation manager selects the mode for specific classes of shipments or products, market areas, or each plant or warehouse. Each mode offers specific inherent service and cost advantages. Usually, the selection is made infrequently so that routing and carrier selection personnel can operate within the modal choice.

Monitoring Service Quality

The quality of the transportation provided can differentiate a company's product, thereby providing a competitive advantage in the marketplace. If the transportation manager can get the products to the customer on a timely, consistent, and undamaged basis, the buyer's inventory and stockout costs are lowered, making it advantageous for the buyer to do business with the seller.

The key to monitoring transportation service quality is information. The transportation manager must have information regarding the customer's demands for transportation service and the service level provided by current carriers. This information is critical to making rational modal and carrier selection decisions and to meeting corporate service and cost goals.

Figure 12.3 is a sample **carrier evaluation** report. Usually on a quarterly basis, the transportation manager evaluates the current carriers based on actual performance versus targeted goals. The carrier evaluation report is used to assure that carriers are providing the service quality that is demanded by the customers or specified by agreement. Carriers not providing the expected level of service are asked to take corrective actions or the transportation manager will replace the carrier.

Examination of Figure 12.3 reveals the criteria used to evaluate carrier performance, which are the same as those used to select the carrier. Typically, the most important evaluation criteria are meeting pickup and delivery schedules and transit time. Normal transportation documentation—bill of lading, freight bill, and so on—does not contain this information. The transportation manager must obtain these data directly from the shipping and receiving areas.

FIGURE 12.3 Carrier Evaluation Report

CARRIER:________________ TIME PERIOD:__________

MAXIMUM SCORE	EVALUATION CRITERIA	CARRIER SCORE		COMMENTS
13	Meets Pickup Schedules	13		
13	Meets Delivery	10		
9	Transit Time	9		
10	Transit Time Consistency	7		
7	Rates	5		
3	Accessoral Charges	1		High residential delivery
5	Operating Ratio	3		96.5%, rising
4	Profitability	3		
3	Claims Frequency	3		
3	Claims Settlement	3		
10	Billing Errors	7		
9	Tracing Capabilities	7		
11	Equipment Availability	1		No flatbeds
100	TOTAL SCORE	72		

Evaluator: ________________ Date: __________

Best Score = 100; Worst Score = 0

Procedure:

1. Assign maximum score for each evaluation criteria; total maximum score = 100.
2. Give carrier score for each criteria, up to maximum score for criteria.
3. Add all criteria scores for carrier.
4. Carrier with highest score is "best."

Service/Supply Assurance

During the late 1990s, strikes in the motor carrier industry caused several periods of carrier supply disruption. Also, seasonality of demand many times puts pressures on equipment availability. As a reaction to those events, many firms have prepared for such future occurrences by planning for alternative and backup forms of transportation. This is a contingency type of management that heretofore was not necessary, nor was it employed until recently.

Negotiations

This activity is increasing in importance because of 1980s regulatory changes and the ICC Termination Act of 1995, which allowed great pricing flexibility. Rate negotiations are now a commonplace activity. Negotiations require a large degree of preparation, analysis, and proper approach and conduct. A negotiation that attains a rate that the carrier eventually finds unprofitable and incapable of serving effectively is to be avoided. In this instance, both the shipper and carrier lose.

Rail and motor contract services are increasing in use, and many negotiations take place for specific services, rather than lower rates. These include specific car supply or transit time performance. Here, too, a sound analysis and approach is necessary.

Regulatory Matters

Transportation managers and staffs traditionally had been involved in routine regulatory processes before federal and state agencies. These regulatory processes included rate protests, rail abandonment petitions, or carrier merger applications. Deregulation has almost eliminated the transportation manager's attention to regulatory matters. Safety issues such as hazardous materials transportation require expertise and skill to avoid serious problems. Safety issues, along with security issues, today takes up a larger portion of the transportation manager's time.

Policy Matters

Transportation managers often will become involved in presenting their firms' policy positions in proposed legislative or regulatory proceedings. These policy areas relate to carrier credit regulations, rail rate regulation standards, exempt transportation, or any other proposed change in the field. When involved in these areas, the transportation manager will conduct analyses, prepare position statements, be active in industry associations representing the firm, and often submit testimony on the firm's behalf.

Planning Annual Transportation Requirements

Another staff-related task is interpreting the firm's purchasing, production, and marketing plans for future periods and translating the plans into specific shipping needs. This list represents the specific type of equipment needed and the quantities and timing of its use. Automobile manufacturers often must work with railroads several years in advance so that railcars exist when new automobile models of specific sizes and shapes roll off assembly lines. In shorter-term contexts, this planning often entails leasing rail equipment, arranging for contract carriage, or merely determining whether the existing carriers will be capable of handling the forecasted shipments.

Budgeting

Transportation managers play the key role in establishing transportation budgets for future periods. The budget usually integrates volumes, expected modal mixes, specific shipping patterns, and expected inflationary impacts. Capital budgets are prepared for analyzing the technical and financial feasibility of proposed major asset acquisitions such as private fleets, railcars, new docks, expanded rail sidings, computer systems, or warehouse and dock space. The activity brings the transportation manager into contact with engineering and finance personnel, as well as top management.

Information Systems

The astute transportation manager will always seek ways to attain and report information relating to the carrier's services and individual manager performance. Many firms monitor and report cost and transit time performance for all movements, including the private fleet. They also might record cost recoveries and claims progress. In all, performance reevaluation and decision-making information systems are a prime necessity. The transportation manager can make recommendations about the design of these systems.

Systems Analysis

The combinations of transportation services and rates offered by carriers number in the hundreds. There is no one best way of always transporting a firm's goods. Where motor might be a proper choice in normal periods, air freight might be necessary occasionally. What is a good choice one day might be a poor one the next. Within transportation management, continuous analyses must be conducted to put together the best service and total cost configuration.

Transportation management must be integrated within the overall materials management and distribution scheme of the firm. In this context, transportation management often is forced to make less-than-optimal decisions in light of overriding system factors for the total cost and service pattern of the firm.

Management and Executive Development

Transportation is changing at a fast pace in a manner not experienced in the past. It is imperative that all personnel keep track of changes in the field, analyze them, and provide for positive action by the firm. They also must update their personal technical knowledge and management skills by reading about all aspects of transportation and management, keeping in contact with others through professional associations, taking advantage of educational opportunities, and keeping a perspective on how a present task and position fit into an overall business strategy scheme.

Transportation Department Human Resources Management

Another major area of managerial analysis with which transportation managers are concerned is the use of human resources within the department. Typically, a key area of discretion for the transportation manager is in assigning rate and analytical personnel either to pre-audit and post-audit freight bills or to create analytical projects that seek varied transportation and distribution methods. These decisions are being forced in many firms because many departments are required to show a profit or return to the company from employee wage dollars spent. In this regard, transportation managers often must determine whether human resource hours will return more for the firm if allocated to auditing freight bills or to analyzing new transportation processes. Because freight bills can be audited by outside auditing firms (the fees of which are based upon a percentage of the overcharges recovered), these human resource hours can often be applied more productively to transportation analysis.

In the next section, a more detailed discussion of mode and carrier selection is presented.

MODE SELECTION PROCESS

Purchasing transportation service is one of the primary transportation manager functions. The transportation manager's decisions have a direct impact upon the company's total logistics costs and quality of service provided to the customer.

The transportation selection decision is a two-part decision. The initial decision involves the selection of the mode and the second decision relates to the selection of the specific carrier within the mode. That is, the transportation manager examines the cost and service characteristics of the different modes, including the combination of two or more modes (intermodal or multimodal service), and selects the mode that matches the company's cost and service goals. Next, the transportation manager examines the cost and service characteristics of the individual carriers within the selected mode and selects the specific carrier to provide the desired transportation service.

The transportation decision begins with an identification of the cost and the service goals of the transportation service to be provided. From these goals the pertinent mode, service, and cost measures are identified and examined in the selection of the appropriate mode. The five modes of choice are air, motor, pipe, rail, and water. These are discussed in Chapters 3 through 6.

The relevant mode selection factors include transportation cost, transit time, transit time reliability, accessibility, capability, and security. These factors impact the total logistics costs of movement and storage and are used in both the selection of the mode and specific carrier.

Transportation Cost

The transportation cost factor includes the rate charged by the carriers in a particular mode. In addition, this factor examines the charges assessed by the carriers in a mode for ancillary services such as residential delivery, controlled-temperature vehicles, and stops in transit. The transportation cost varies from mode to mode because of the different cost structures of the modes, whereas the cost variation among carriers within a mode is less because the carriers have similar cost structures. Thus, transportation cost is somewhat more important in the modal selection decision than in the specific carrier selection decision.

Transit Time and Transit Time Reliability

As noted earlier in this section, the total-cost implication of the mode selection decision considers not only the direct transportation cost incurred but also the indirect costs associated with the quality of the service provided. **Transit time** and reliability of transit time are two transportation service qualities that affect both shipper and receiver inventory costs and stockout costs. Transit time impacts the level of inventory held and the consequent inventory-carrying costs. The longer the transit time, the higher the inventory levels and the higher the inventory-carrying costs. Therefore, the total cost impact of using a mode with a longer transit time is higher inventory-carrying costs.

Likewise, the reliability of transit time affects the level of safety stock inventory required. Unreliable transit time requires an increase in the level of inventory to guard against stockout conditions and the resultant cost of lost profit or lost productivity associated with not having the product available to meet the demand. Viewed from a marketing perspective, reliable transit time affords the buyer the opportunity to reduce or control both inventory and stockout costs. Thus, using a mode that provides reliable transit time provides the seller with a marketplace advantage.

Accessibility

The **accessibility** factor considers the ability of the mode to provide the transportation service between a specific origin and destination. The modes differ in their ability to provide direct service to specific locations. Physical limitations associated with roadways and terminals prohibit certain modes from providing direct services to a specific site. To overcome the accessibility of a mode, the services of another more accessible mode must be purchased. The additional expense to surmount a mode's inability to service a particular location is the accessibility cost.

For example, the motor carrier is the most accessible of the modes. It can go virtually anywhere there is a road. Conversely, water carriers are restrained to providing service to users located adjacent to waterways. Likewise, the railroads, except for intermodal service, have limited accessibility to shippers located along rail tracks with sidetracks, air carriers to freight shippers located at airports, and pipelines to servicing freight customers adjacent to the pipeline. Thus, the motor carrier is often used, at an additional transportation (accessibility) expense, to enable users of the other modes to gain direct transportation service to specific sites not adjacent to the mode's physical facilities.

Capability

The **capability** factor refers to the ability of the mode to provide the unique transportation services and equipment required by the user. The transportation manager will use the mode that has the ability to provide the unique services or equipment required. Examples of special equipment requirements include controlled-temperature vehicles for the movement of frozen foods, high-cube-capacity vehicles for the movement of low-density products (plastic bottles, for example), and tank vehicles for the movement of bulk liquids. Unique transportation service needs include specified pickup or delivery times, carrier information systems to locate and expedite shipments, and electronic data interchange capabilities.

Security

The final factor, security, considers the indirect transportation service cost if the shipment is damaged or lost in transit. A damaged shipment has the same impact on inventory costs and stockout costs as unreliable transit time. A product damaged or lost in transit is not available for use when demanded, and the user incurs the cost of processing a damage claim or legal action against the carrier to secure reimbursement, incurs the loss if reimbursement is not received from the carrier, or pays for insurance to provide protection against the in-transit damage.

The mode decision is made before the carrier decision because it carries more strategic and long-term implications for the transportation manager. In some cases, choosing a certain mode might require an investment by the shipper. For example, a shipper who decides to ship by rail might have to invest in infrastructure to provide a rail siding at a plant or distribution center. Also, each mode has its own cost and service characteristics. Shippers needing quick market response might use air or motor carriage to provide their transportation needs. If low cost is a strategic advantage, a shipper might use rail or water as its preferred mode. However, once the mode decision is made, a specific carrier or carriers from that mode must be chosen to provide the transportation service.

CARRIER SELECTION PROCESS

As previously mentioned, the five mode selection factors can come into play when selecting a particular carrier. In practice, each of these mode selection factors is broken down into a number of more specific measures of the cost and service characteristics. Usually, accessibility and capability for carriers within a mode are not issues. So, carrier selection factors focus on cost, transit time and reliability, and security. Table 12.2 shows an expanded list of carrier selection factors and the relative importance of each in selecting motor carriers. Reliability of transit time is the most important carrier selection factor, followed by transportation rate, total transit time, willingness to negotiate, and financial stability of the carrier. Less important selection factors may include special equipment, quality of carrier salesmanship, claims processing, and line-haul services. Once the carrier or carriers are selected, the transportation manager must establish the appropriate types of relationships with these service providers. This will be the topic of the next section.

RELATIONSHIP MANAGEMENT

By its very nature, logistics is a boundary-spanning discipline; that is, it relies on establishing relationships with organizations outside its own in order to meet its service and cost goals. This is especially true because logistics encompasses many activities, and an organization must decide which it will provide itself and which it will buy from the market. Once an organization decides to approach the market for a particular service, it must develop the proper relationship with the selected supplier(s) to assure quality and continuity of service at the lowest total cost to the buying organization. This is especially true with the transportation requirements of an organization.

Buyers and sellers of transportation services realize the importance of this activity to a tangible product. In many organizations, transportation is the single largest logistics variable cost expenditure. In some industries, transportation speed and reliability provide a significant competitive advantage. In most firms, transportation is the last link between a shipper and its customers. It has the opportunity to create positive or negative customer perceptions based on how well the delivery process is performed.

Table 12.2 Importance of Motor Carrier Selection Factors

Transit time reliability or consistency	Shipment expediting
Door-to-door transportation rates or costs	Quality of operating personnel
Total door-to-door transit time	Shipment tracing
Willingness of carrier to negotiate rate changes	Willingness of carrier to negotiate service changes
Financial stability of the carrier	Scheduling flexibility
Equipment availability	Line-haul services
Frequency of service	Claims processing
Pickup and delivery service	Quality of carrier salesmanship
Freight loss and damage	Special equipment

Source: Adapted from Edward J. Bardi, Prabir Bagchi, and T. S. Raghunathan, "Motor Carrier Selection in a Deregulated Environment," *Transportation Journal*, Vol. 29, No. 1, Fall 1989, pp. 4–11.

Taking these facts into consideration, it is easy to see that managing relationships between buyers and sellers of transportation services is a process that is critical to successfully meeting the transportation requirements of an organization. This section will discuss the different types of relationships that firms can be involved in, with special attention given to contracts and partnerships. Also discussed will be the concepts of outsourcing and third parties.

TYPES OF BUYER/SELLER RELATIONSHIPS

Buyers and sellers in a market achieve their mutual goals by establishing and managing a relationship between their respective organizations. The type of relationship that is necessary in each situation is determined by many factors. In general, however, three types of relationships exist: arm's length, contract, and partnership. These three are not as distinct as they might seem. Some research has proposed that relationship styles are positioned on a continuum, with one end anchored by arm's-length relationships and the other end anchored by a true partnership.[5] This makes sense because an arm's-length relationship between a carrier and a shipper can be implemented with a contract (such as a trip lease) or without one (such as common carriage, although this relationship is managed by the bill of lading contract rules), whereas a partnership can have a formalized document managing that relationship or can be consummated by a "handshake." Even though it might be difficult to determine a distinct difference among relationship types, specific types of relationships are better in some situations than they are in others.

Other efforts have been made to offer some insights to specific types of relationships and which ones are appropriate in different situations.[6] Six specific types of relationships have been identified: arm's length, Type I partnership, Type II partnership, Type III partnership, joint ventures, and vertical integration. Recognizing these different types is also important in determining the method used to establish relationships. The role these different types of relationships play in establishing relationships can be seen in Figure 12.4, which will be discussed later in this chapter.

Arm's-Length Relationships

These types of relationships last for a single transaction between two parties, and no commitments are made for future transactions. Normally, the single deciding

FIGURE 12.4 Third-Party Product Offerings and Relationship Type

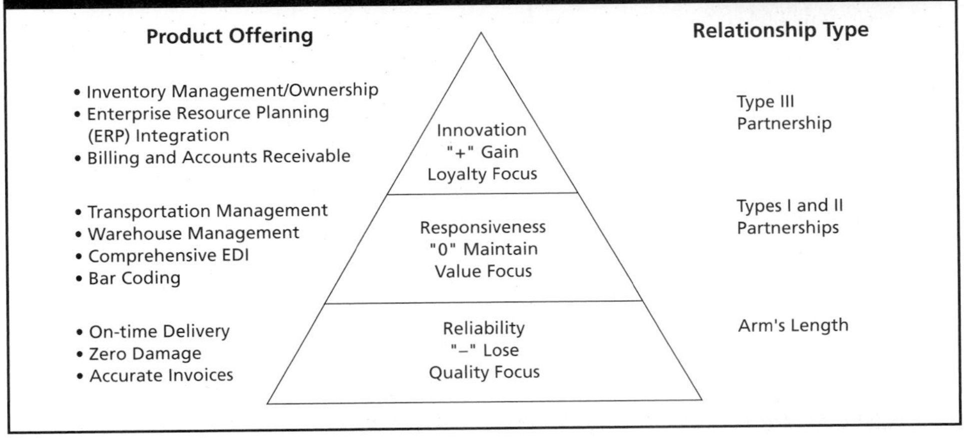

factor in these relationships is price. For example, a shipper who has a low-value commodity that is not time-sensitive might decide to offer that load to a broker (defined in Chapter 7, "Intermodal and Special Carriers"). The **standard service** required is the movement of one shipment between two points, a service any carrier should be able to provide. If the shipment is time-sensitive, a different type of relationship between the shipper and the carrier might be necessary.

Another example would be a shipper who has daily small packages to ship over a wide geographic area. Some days the shipments are tendered to UPS, some days to FedEx Ground, and some days to the United States Postal Service. Over the course of the year, each carrier receives multiple shipments. However, there is no commitment on the part of the shipper to guarantee volume to any one carrier on any given day. As such, each shipment is transactual. In both examples here, no commitment exists on the part of either the shipper or carrier to continue to do business together. Both examples also show relationships that are very short term in nature, (i.e., each shipment represents the length of the relationship). This type of relationship can minimize the risk to both the carrier and the shipper because neither has to commit volume or capacity to the relationship. However, the transaction might not result in the lowest price to the shipper because the carrier would not have had an opportunity to reduce its operating costs. Thus, arm's-length relationships are appropriate in certain situations. Carriers and shippers must assess the risks and rewards associated with these types of transactions. Many organizations consider an arm's-length, or transactual, relationship to be inefficient. This feeling is based on the notion that the carrier and shipper have little opportunity to interact, to get to know one another, to leverage volume, or to decrease transaction costs. However, these notions are more indicative of a contractual or partnership relationship than they are of an arm's-length relationship. An arm's-length relationship is appropriate when a carrier's service offerings are considered a commodity or are standard.[7, 8] Often these types of transactions are completed using mechanisms such as reverse auctions on the Internet.

Type I Partnerships[9]

Many definitions have been offered for the concept of a partnership. Some authors have even made the analogy between a partnership and a marriage.[10] The definition used here will be that offered by Ellram and Hendrick: A partnership is an ongoing relationship between two firms that involves a commitment over an extended time period and a mutual sharing of information and the risks and rewards of the relationship.[11] A Type I partnership can be described as a **short-term** contractual relationship that requires little investment on the part of either party and which has a limited scope of activities.

For example, a 1-year contract for truckload transportation service between Chicago and Dallas would be a Type I partnership. The service offered is not much different than what would be offered to the market in general. The only difference might be guaranteed delivery times and a minimum dedicated fleet on the part of the carrier and a guaranteed minimum volume on the part of the shipper. More than likely, the price for this service will be based primarily on volume. This type of relationship is very common in the transportation industry.

Type II Partnerships

These relationships can also be described as contractual in nature. However, these contracts are longer term in nature, might require investment from either party, and have a larger scope of activities. A good example of this type of relationship can be found in many carrier certification programs and core carrier programs.

Those carriers that have gained the status of "core carrier" enjoy a more integrated relationship with the shipper than other carriers. These carriers usually participate in guaranteed annual volume or dedicated freight lanes, are given incentives for cost-reduction efforts, perform more than basic transportation service, and are involved in a longer-term relationship with the shipper. This type of partnership takes longer to develop simply because of the trust and commitment that are necessary for this relationship to work. For some shippers, carrier certification can be a 3- to 5-year process. Although this type of time frame can **increase** the **risk** because of the potential loss of investment by either the carrier or shipper, the rewards of success can be substantial.

Type III Partnerships

A Type III partnership is not governed by a typical contract mechanism. Although a document might exist between the two parties, its purpose is to outline general operations and management philosophy. The relationship has **no formal endpoint**. These can also be referred to as **evergreen contracts**. Assets in the relationship can be jointly owned, and the scope of activities that is shared is substantial. Type III partnerships can be seen, in some instances, between carriers and firms in the automobile industry. In fact, these carriers are often referred to as "third parties" because of the scope of their responsibilities for the shipper. (Third parties will be discussed later in this chapter.) These carriers perform pickup at supplier locations for assembly-line delivery, provide break-bulk and consolidation, provide light manufacturing and assembly, handle returns of materials and storage media to suppliers, and, in some cases, provide inventory management for the automobile manufacturer. Planning and control of this relationship is done at a high executive level because of the significant economic impact that the success or failure of this relationship would have. Obviously, this type of relationship has a high risk and high investment on the part of both parties. This is why very few true Type III partnerships exist in the transportation industry. However, the success of this type of relationship can create a significant competitive advantage for both firms, the type of competitive advantage that neither firm could generate on its own.

Joint Ventures

Joint ventures represent a different type of relationship between two firms because the result of the relationship is usually the creation of another firm. This relationship obviously requires investments from both parties. The focus of a joint venture is for each party to benefit from the other party's expertise. For example, Encompass was the result of a joint venture between AMR (American Airlines) and CSX Railroad. Encompass was created to develop a global booking and tracking information system for freight movements. CSX brought its multimodal expertise to the joint venture because of its operation of a railroad, SeaLand Container Lines, and a motor carrier concern. AMR brought its system design expertise to the firm because of its experience with the development of SABRE, the booking system used by all the major airlines. These types of relationships, by definition, are long term in nature because of the need to generate a return on initial and continuing investments made by each firm.

Vertical Integration

Every firm requires some type of transportation support. To fill this need, a decision is made to either provide the transportation internally (make) or acquire it from the market (buy). If the decision is made to provide it internally, then the firm is vertically integrating transportation. The most common usage of vertical integration in transportation is the use of **private fleets**. Many cost and service reasons are used to justify the investment in vertical integration. For example, Harley-Davidson Motorcycles uses a private fleet to transport motorcycles to dealers and pick up parts and raw materials on the backhaul to be used in the manufacturing process. Their decision to utilize a fleet for a major portion of their transportation needs is based on both cost and service criteria. Wal*Mart uses its fleet to make deliveries to stores and pick up merchandise from suppliers on the backhaul to be delivered to its distribution centers. These round-trip operations provide high levels of service as well as reduced operating costs because of minimum empty miles.

Conclusion

Every type of business relationship has its appropriate business application. Relationships fail because the parties attempt to implement the wrong type of relationship to fit the situation or one party exercises their dominance in a detrimental manner over the other party. The first step, then, to a successful relationship might be to determine what type of relationship is appropriate based on what each party brings to and wants from that relationship.[12] Fitting the right relationship model to the situation can result in a successful endeavor.

WHY ENTER RELATIONSHIPS?

As previously mentioned, logistics and transportation are conducive to establishing relationships with external organizations because of their boundary-spanning responsibilities. The nature of the relationship will depend on what each party needs from the exchange, what each party offers, and how each treats the other. However, several general reasons can be offered as to why an organization would enter into a relationship with another organization. These relationships are many times called "third-party" relationships. Before beginning the discussion concerning why to enter a relationship with a third party, a short discussion on third parties is necessary.

The concept of third parties in logistics has existed for many years. When farmers moved their grain on railcars they were utilizing third parties. The first time the owner of goods put them in a public or contract warehouse, a third party was used. The term "third party" today has developed many definitions and is many times misused. Although this term can be used to represent a relationship between a carrier and a shipper, it is more appropriately used to represent a relationship between a shipper and a firm where more than a single function (such as transportation) is performed. This discussion will adopt the following definition of a third party: A third party logistics provider is a company that supplies/coordinates logistics functions across multiple links in the logistics supply chain. The company thus acts as a third-party facilitator between seller/manufacturer (the first party) and the buyer/user (the second party).[13] Many third-party relationships begin with carriers assuming responsibility for a firm's private fleet operations. This relationship could grow with the carrier assuming coordination for all freight activities and possibly freight payment and claims. Because of this close relationship between asset-based carriers and third parties, the term *third party* will be used for the remainder of the chapter to represent any type of firm that has a relationship with a shipper. This will include asset-based carriers as well as nonasset-based firms (fourth-party logistics providers) that provide both transportation and logistics services.

The **third party** industry has enjoyed a tremendous **growth** over the past several years. One source estimates that its size in the United States in 2001 was $60.1 billion.[14]

Regardless of the actual size of the market, one statement is true: Third-party use by shippers is substantial.

As previously mentioned, transportation is the most commonly outsourced activity to third parties. Research has identified various services provided by third parties and their current and future use by shippers. Table 12.3 shows the results of this research.[15] As this table shows, outbound transportation is the most common logistics activity given to third parties to manage. Other activities include warehousing, inbound transportation, freight bill auditing/payment, and customs.

Many third-party firms have also begun to offer consulting services for shippers because of the expertise third parties have developed in these various areas.

Having defined a third party and identified the nature of its markets, the remaining discussion will focus on the reasons shippers enter into relationships with third parties.

Availability of External Suppliers

An obvious reason for shippers to enter into a relationship with a third party is simply because of the large number of third parties that already exist. In many instances, no reason exists for a shipper to operate its own fleet of transportation vehicles. As such, relationships with third parties currently in the market are sufficient to meet a

Table 12.3 Outsourced Logistics Services

Logistics Activity	North America
Outbound Transportation	68%
Warehousing	65
Inbound Transportation	52
Freight Bill Auditing/Payment	48
Customs Brokerage	44
Freight Forwarding	43
Customs Clearance	41
Cross-Docking	31
Shipment Consolidation/Distribution	30
Selected Manufacturing Activities	24
Product Marketing/Labeling	24
Consulting Services	24
Order Fulfillment	23
Product Returns and Repair	17
Information Technology	17
Procurement of Logistics	15
Carrier Selection	14
Rate Negotiation	14
Inventory Management	12
Product Assembly/Installation	11
Fleet Management	11
Distribution Control	6
Supply Chain Manager/Integrator	5
Lead Logistics Provider	5
Customer service	4
Order Entry/Order Processing	2
Factoring (Trade Financing)	1

Source: 2004 Ninth Annual Third Party Logistics Study, Georgia Tech, Capgemini LLC, and FedEx Supply Chain Services, 2004.

shipper's needs. This is especially true because many of the activities transferred to a third party involve assets and a given level of expertise in their management. Little incentive exists for a shipper to duplicate assets or expertise when they exist in the marketplace.

Cost Efficiencies

Many third-party providers are asset-based organizations; in other words, they own vehicles, warehouses, or both. With the ownership of these assets come some **economies of scale** and **economies of scope**. The fixed costs associated with these assets can be allocated across various shippers, thus reducing fully allocated costs per unit. Shippers who own assets (vehicles or warehouses) to provide logistics service cannot generate similar economies. Many organizations have shed private fleets in exchange for a dedicated fleet operation run by a third party. For example, PPG Automotive Products Division, as well as Kimberly-Clark Corporation, have given the operation of their private fleets over to Schneider Logistics. Because Schneider is an asset-based third party, it is able to operate these fleets at a very competitive cost.

In fact, the results of a study published by Georgia Tech University showed that the respondent firms experienced a 7-percent reduction in logistics costs by using a third party.[16] Many times the costs that are reduced are operating costs (like fuel and wages) and overhead costs (salaries and administration).

In some instances, corporate profitability issues force an organization to shed assets to **improve financial performance**. Private fleets and warehouses are prime targets for this asset reduction. However, because there is a high availability of third-party suppliers in these markets, the final impact on the firm from a service and cost perspective can be minimized.

The financial impact of using a third party to shed assets needs to be given adequate attention by the shipper organization. Assets, like fleets or warehouses, impact assets and liabilities on a shipper's balance sheet. The shipper gets the advantage of the asset as collateral for future market funding as well as the use of depreciation to reduce taxes. Along with advantages comes the liability associated with the asset. This would involve the fact that the shipper has an obligation to repay the debt associated with the asset, as well as the fact that as assets increase, without a resulting increase in profits, return on investment will decrease. Eliminating the asset from the balance sheet should have an immediate impact on the shipper's balance sheet. However, the operating expenses of providing transportation will still be present and will impact the expense portion of the income statement. Along with this expense comes the management fee charged by the third party. This will also be a variable expense captured by the income statement. This increase in variable expenses might very well decrease short-term profitability. The use of a third party by a shipper to reduce assets is a trade-off between balance sheet impacts (and ROI) and income statement impacts (and profitability). Asset reduction might not be in the best interest of the shipper from a financial perspective. This aspect of the third-party relationship must be analyzed carefully.[17]

Third-Party Expertise

Many organizations believe that some of their activities are better performed by outside providers. The rationale for this decision is based on the principle of **core competency**, that is, do what you do best and let someone else do the rest. Although it sounds simple, it is obviously not. Very few arguments would be made by any organization that transportation is not important to their success. However, for many firms (like manufacturers) transportation is not an area of expertise. Some firms decide to develop the expertise by owning their own fleet. Other firms decide to let the experts provide the transportation: third-party providers. These firms are in the business of providing transportation; it is their core competency. Also, these firms bring a tremendous amount of expertise to a shipper from having done business with other shippers in similar industries. This expertise in transportation also allows these third parties to better manage the costs of transportation by utilizing their equipment and personnel in a more efficient manner.

Customer Service

Some research has identified service as being a problem when using third parties.[18] Other research has shown that relationships with third parties can actually improve service.[19] What makes the difference between whether service improves or not when using a third party is how the shipper and third party develop and manage the relationship. Many times the cause of service reductions when using a third party has been attributed to a loss of control over that service by the shipper. Control is lost only if the shipper allows it to be lost. A carefully managed and phased-in relationship between the third party and the shipper can actually improve service. L.L. Bean is in a very close relationship with Federal Express for the delivery of its merchandise. FedEx employees work in the L.L. Bean warehouse to facilitate the processing of shipments. This relationship is a strategic decision on the part of L.L. Bean to improve the speed and reliability of its delivery service.[20] The service experienced by PPG and Kimberly-Clark has been very acceptable since Schneider Logistics has taken over their fleets. In all of these operations, care was taken to build customer service into the relationship and to make it a critical element in the performance evaluation of the third party.

Over time, customers develop expectations for logistics service from a supplier. Changing the provider of this service can have a negative impact on the relationships a supplier has with its customers. Care must be taken to maintain and/or strengthen customer relationships when transferring transportation or logistics service to a third party.

Conclusion

The reasons used for entering third-party relationships also end up providing the largest benefits. One of the most significant benefits of using third-party relationships is lower cost.[21] The other most frequently cited benefits of third-party relationships can be seen in Table 12.4.

The use of third-party organizations is a viable way for a shipping firm to supplement or provide its logistics services. When these operations are transferred to a third-party, the management of the relationship between the shipper and the third party provider magnifies in importance. This is why relationship management has become so important for logistics managers today.

The word *logistics* as it is used for the balance of this chapter is meant to include transportation within its meaning. Logistics is so closely linked to transportation that one management area cannot be considered without the other. Most logistics strategies rely on transportation for the execution of the plan, and transportation is generally the largest single variable-cost component of logistics. Transportation managers must "think outside the transportation box" if they are to be fully successful in a logistics environment.

Table 12.4 Quantifiable Measures of 3PL Success

	North America
Logistics Cost Reduction	7%
Fixed Logistics Asset Reduction	16%
Average Order Cycle Length Changed	From 6.5 days to 4.3 days
Overall Inventories Reduced By	9%
Cash-To-Cash Cycle Reduced	From 20.4 days to 16.4 days
Service Improvement	63% Yes

Source: 2004 Ninth Annual Third Party Logistics Study, Georgia Tech, Capgemini LLC, and FedEx Supply Chain Services, 2004.

THIRD-PARTY RELATIONSHIP CHARACTERISTICS

The relationship between a third party and a shipper is usually different than traditional relationships. These relationships are often called partnerships, although many times they are not the same as they were defined earlier in this discussion. Regardless of what they are called, these relationships have certain characteristics that differentiate them from others. Previous research has found many common characteristics of third-party relationships.[22] In some instances, these characteristics have even been found to be instrumental to the success of the relationship (i.e., for a relationship to be successful it must include these characteristics).

Planning

Planning can be done at multiple levels within both organizations, from the operational to the strategic. In a third-party relationship, joint planning becomes effective at all levels. **Joint planning** requires input from both parties as well as "buy-in" from them. Once this occurs, both parties are in agreement on how the relationship is to be managed and how it is to grow. Penske Logistics and Whirlpool share in the planning process as it relates to volumes, product mix, and supplier selection. Allowing a third party into this type of process allows Whirlpool to treat Penske Logistics as more of a partner in their business, rather than just a supplier to their business.

Communications

As probably one of the most important aspects of a successful relationship, communications is also one of the most difficult to design and implement. However, successful communications between the appropriate individuals in a relationship are critical to making it work. As with planning, these communications take place at all levels within both organizations. Daily orders, weekly staffing requirements, monthly forecasts, and yearly long-range plans are all examples of communications. Also critical, however, is identifying who has the information and who needs it so the communication process can take place. For example, Schneider National can determine if a trailer is going to be late for a delivery by using data from its Qualcomm satellite system (this was discussed in Chapter 11, "Information Management and Technology"). This information is communicated to the fleet manager, who is responsible for notifying the consignee of the potential delivery delay. This allows the receiving location to take measures to minimize the resulting problems from the late shipment. The two critical questions in these relationships are *what* information, and for *whom?* These need to be identified in the planning stages of the relationship, rather than developed on an *ad hoc* basis.

Risk/Reward Sharing

A characteristic of a successful relationship is a true sharing of benefits and burdens. This can be very difficult because each organization in this relationship has its own financial goals to achieve. Sharing successes and losses can prevent one or both firms from achieving these goals. Another difficult decision is how much to share. Should the third party bear a majority of the burden and a minority of the success? This type of decision needs to be clarified very early in the negotiating stages of the relationship. Many agreements between third parties and shippers include sliding goal and management fee structures. For example, a service level of 98 percent provided by the third party will net the third party a management fee of $1 million, whereas a 96-percent level will net $750,000 and a 99-percent level a $1,250,000 fee. An increasing service level will benefit the shipper, and the resulting fee increase will benefit the third party. This type of sharing also allows both organizations to meet their financial goals without penalizing either party unfairly. Cost reduction efforts by the third party must also be addressed. If the third party can eliminate $1 million of cost from the shipper's process without affecting service levels, does the third party get to keep part of the savings? Providing incentives to the third party to reduce costs benefits both parties. Again, this needs to be addressed in the planning and negotiating process.

STOP OFF

Shippers, Unite!

In the transportation business, it's been several decades since strong profits were commonplace. Now an already difficult situation is getting uglier. Fuel prices are rising dramatically, giving carriers no choice but to raise prices. As a result, customers are facing an increase in rates without a concomitant increase in service. And the tenuous relationships that already exist between carriers and shippers are becoming more frazzled.

Fuel prices may currently be the largest fly in the transportation ointment, but they're hardly the only irritant. Tighter hours-of-service regulations, driver shortages, and higher tolls in both the United States and Europe are also straining truck capacity.

In addition to these complicating factors, companies are moving fewer goods more frequently. This means that more trucks are traveling partly loaded or empty. Meanwhile, customers are demanding faster response and tighter delivery windows from their carriers even as they build more centralized warehouses (which increases transportation times and costs) and do more global sourcing (which reduces item costs but increases transportation distances). Small wonder that carrier profitability—and consequently, carrier choice—is weak and getting weaker.

Share the Burden

The solution to most of these problems is increased collaboration. With modern technology, collaboration has become more feasible. Consider Ágoratrans, the European Web marketplace that helps match loads and trucks. Structured around partnerships between shippers and carriers, Ágoratrans hosts private forums that execute end-to-end processes, such as load planning, tendering, and delivery confirmation. The system includes a transportation management tool, closed transport communities, and a public exchange.

...Ágoratrans offers carriers a package of services designed to reduce costs and encourage use by shippers. For example, e-procurement capabilities can cut overall costs while making participation feasible for smaller carriers. Carrier-specific financial services are another benefit, with collective buying power potentially creating savings on insurance. Over time, members also are expected to reduce empty miles by 25 percent. And prompt electronic payment, another part of the package, is a considerable incentive for carriers accustomed to waiting 120 days or more for payment.

There also are opportunities for technologically sophisticated collaboration between shippers.

For example, Kimberly-Clark, a paper products manufacturer, and Lever Fabergé, a maker of home- and personal-care products, recently built a shared consolidation center. The two companies have 93 percent of their customers in common, so sharing their logistics and technology networks has the potential to reduce their logistics costs by up to 16 percent.

A Model for Managing Transportation

No universal procedure exists for shippers seeking to build a collaborative transportation relationship. However, the business-proven techniques of sourcing transportation, optimizing loads and routes, and sharing tracking and transaction information can help put companies on the right track. Consider the following template for developing a working collaboration:

1. *Lay the groundwork.* Sharing information and resources requires a high degree of standardization and consistency. For this reason, adjustments such as the following should precede a collaborative undertaking:
   - Improving the quality of volume and scheduling forecasts.
   - Developing new or enhanced communications links with carriers via EDI or the Internet.
   - Optimizing mode-mixing and mode-shifting opportunities.
2. *Find opportunities.* The potential for shippers to collaborate exists whenever two companies ship to and/or from the same location. Rationalizing transport providers, leveraging a common rate structure, and sharing savings can be tricky, but the basic inaugural process requires the following:
   - Identifying companies with similar or compensating traffic flows.
   - Calculating transport demand and the critical supply mass needed for a specific transport.
   - Maximizing visibility across regional organizations.
3. *Make it happen.* The next step is to develop workable routings and align contracts. This stage often requires advanced tools, methodologies, and third parties to achieve the following:
   - Re-evaluate intercompany transportation vendors and contracts.
   - Streamline and possibly centralize transportation operations.
   - Rationalize costs without undermining service or maintenance.
4. *Keep it going.* To maintain their competitive edge, partner companies must continually improve their collaborative arrangements. The greatest needs include:
   - Consistently improving management of real-time data.
   - Regularly analyzing alternative transport modes and technology-support opportunities.

Sometime in the future fuel prices may recede. But in the short term, transport costs will continue to consume 50 percent or more of a typical manufacturer's logistics budget, with shippers and carriers everywhere feeling the squeeze. For both sides, achieving greater efficiency through tight collaboration is the only viable response.

Patrick M. Byrne is managing partner of the Accenture *Supply Chain Management* service line, which provides consulting and outsourcing services for strategic sourcing, procurement, product design, manufacturing, logistics, fulfillment, inventory management, and supply chain planning and collaboration. Based in Reston, Va., he can be reached at pat.byrne@accenture.com.

Source: *Logistics Management,* July 2004, p. 25. Reprinted with permission of *Logistics Management.*

Trust and Commitment

In many relationships, third parties are placing their employees on site at their customer's location to manage some transportation or logistics activity. However, third-party relationships can often be distant relationships; in other words, the third party is managing a part of the shipper's business without having the shipper physically present. A certain level of trust needs to be in place for this situation to work. The shipper must have trust that the third party will act in the best interest of the shipper, whether it involves contact with a customer or a major cost reduction initiative.

The third party must have trust that the shipper will act in the best interest of the third party (i.e., treat the relationship with integrity and a long-term focus). Trust needs to be one of the critical factors assessed at the beginning of the relationship. However, trust really develops over the life of the relationship. Commitment and trust are not mutually exclusive. The commitment of both parties to the success of the relationship is necessary. Commitment to the relationship means a long-term focus, a willingness to tolerate failures, an encouragement for innovation and growth, and a respect for each firm's expertise and contribution to the relationship.

Scope of the Relationship

As previously mentioned, today's third-party relationships are characterized by the performance of more than just a basic logistics service. The larger the scope of activities performed by the third party, the stronger the relationship. For example, Penske Logistics manages the inbound logistics process for a General Motors plant. This involves inbound consolidation of parts and sub-assemblies, staging for production delivery, cart return, quality control, and even some light manufacturing. As the scope of activities increases, the ability to determine where one firm begins and the other one ends decreases.

Figure 12.4 shows the relationship between the nature of a third party's product offering, or the scope of activity with a shipper, and the type of relationship that will probably exist.[23, 24] This discussion will provide some general guidelines that exist in shipper/third-party arrangements. It must be remembered that exceptions to these guidelines will exist. Joint ventures and vertical integration are not included because they do not involve a traditional shipper/third-party service provider type of relationship. At the bottom of the triangle is what can be called "reliability" services. Third parties that interact with shippers at this level compete by offering such services as on-time delivery, zero damage, and accurate invoicing. These are called reliability services because the only measure of success is 100-percent accurate performance. This focus on 100-percent performance by a shipper indicates that these services are evaluated based on quality (for example, did the third party perform as promised?). A third party cannot gain market share by performing these services well but can lose market share by doing them poorly. In the logistics arena, these services are commodities and the relationship a shipper will have with a third party providing only these services will probably be arm's length. If a third party cannot provide basic on-time delivery on a consistent basis, another third party will. Consistently meeting shipper expectations for these services, however, will allow the third party an opportunity to elevate to the next level with the shipper.

"Responsiveness" services are evaluated by shippers as value-adding. A value-adding service can increase market share if done well and lose market share if done poorly. Examples of value-adding services would be transportation management, custom-tailored delivery systems, bar coding, EDI, warehouse management, and so on. They all build on basic transportation service but provide more value to the shipper because they integrate more logistics activities. Type I or Type II partnerships would probably be used here because of the longer-term nature of the relationship and the existence of a contract. Performing these services well over time can allow the third party the opportunity to advance to the next level in the triangle with a shipper.

Finally, the top-level product offering/relationship combination can be called "innovation." These services are meant to fully integrate a shipper's product, cash, and information flows. Third parties that reach this level with a shipper can gain significant market share by performing these services well but would probably not lose market share by not offering these service or doing them poorly. Service at this level might include inventory management/ownership, information system integration through an ERP system, billing and collections, and so on. These services build on those offered in the second level and are a result of and a cause of loyalty between the shipper and third party. This loyalty is developed between the shipper and third party by consistent performance by the third party at the reliability and responsiveness levels. A Type III partnership would more than likely exist at this level. An example of this relationship in the automotive industry is called the lead logistics provider, or LLP. An LLP is a third party that is responsible for contracting all logistics services from other third parties on behalf of the automobile manufacturer. This LLP manages the logistics process for the manufacturer.

Third parties must be able to identify and market their product offerings so the scope of the relationship can be defined at the very beginning of the relationship. Many relationships begin between shippers and third parties at the very bottom of the triangle and develop over time to move into each succeeding level. Trying to enter a new relationship at the responsiveness or innovation levels can be difficult, but it can be done.

Financial Investment

Firms that share investments in assets, people, or information systems tend to have a stronger commitment to the success of the relationship. Obviously, financial rewards are a result of this success. However, trust in the relationship is a requirement for this type of financial investment. Profitable firms invest in relationships that will further their profitability. This involves a certain trust in the other firm that it will make the right decisions concerning this investment so both parties can benefit. Many third-party relationships will jointly develop information systems to manage logistics activities. With many manufacturers implementing ERP systems, like SAP, third-party firms are developing and implementing compatible logistics information systems. Although a significant investment, these information systems provide a high level of synergy for the third-party firm across logistics activities within a single firm and across many firms.

Future Orientation

This characteristic is related to trust and commitment. A future orientation in a relationship focuses on what can be, not on what is or was. This is also related to planning. As previously stated, many third-party relationships start out simple in order to allow them to develop and mature. For example, a third party might enter into a relationship with a shipper to manage its private fleet, rather than undertake all of the shipper's transportation needs, thus beginning with reliability services. This allows the third party to focus its attention on one aspect of the logistics of the shipper. Once it masters the fleet management aspect, the third party can begin to grow into other areas within transportation. This is where the future orientation enters. Both parties agree that the long-term goal is to have the third party take on not only all transportation activities but also all warehousing activities, evolving into responsiveness services. However, the relationship starts with a single activity. This gives both parties agreement on what the future will look like and how the relationship will possibly develop into an innovative type of relationship.

Organization/Culture Change

For many firms, third-party management of logistics represents an organizational culture shock. This occurs because of the fear of losing control over logistics cost and service and the fear of losing jobs. Also, the mentality of "we can do it better" is difficult to shed. Managing relationships can be more difficult than managing operations. For some shipper logistics managers, this shift in management focus represents a tremendous challenge. However, successful third-party relationships have occurred because these logistics managers have changed the way they view their business and the roles they play in it. Many organizations have accepted the fact that logistics is not their area of expertise and have decided to turn over the execution of this process to organizations that possess that expertise. Logistics can never be totally eliminated from an organization; someone will always need to be present in the shipper organization to manage the relationship and assure that shipper financial and service goals are attained. However, the operations of logistics can be transferred to a third party. Doing this successfully and managing the resulting relationships can be problematic to some shippers because their organization structure and culture are not conducive to using third parties. However, successful third-party relationships are characterized by shippers that have recognized the need to change the way they do business and have begun the process to adapt both their organizations and culture.

RELATIONSHIP CHALLENGES

With an understanding of the characteristics inherent in a strong third-party relationship, it is possible to better understand the challenges faced by organizations as they decide to enter into a relationship with a third party. Suppliers and buyers alike need to develop new methods for managing the logistics process in these types of relationships. Too often, firms tend to continue utilizing traditional methods of doing business in a changing environment. The decision to use a third party is not necessarily an easy one. This section will discuss some of the challenges faced by buyers and suppliers of third-party services when entering into a relationship.[25]

Buyer Challenges

Buyers (shippers) are often not sure what they are buying or why. In most organizations, logistics cuts across functional boundaries. The decision to transfer a logistics activity to a third party then must include all of the parties impacted. This can make the decision process long and complex. For example, the decision to transfer the operation of the inbound warehouse that services the plant would possibly involve materials management (responsible for the inbound warehouse) and manufacturing (responsible for the plant).

Another challenge faced by potential buyers can be caused by who in the organization makes the decision to use a third party. In some instances, these decisions are not made in the logistics group but in finance or information systems.[26] Financial decisions are usually made to reduce assets and/or costs in logistics. When this occurs, the logistics manager might not be convinced which logistics activity should be given to a third party and what implications it might have on logistics cost and service.

Buyers do not perceive synergies from single-sourcing logistics. When the use of third parties began with buyers using common and contract carriers, the strategy was to spread risk among many suppliers. In this way, no single third party had a significant portion of the shipper's business and could not exert influence over the shipper's decisions. Also, if a third party left, it could be easily replaced. This mentality exists today in many firms. Logistics executives are reluctant to allocate too much business with a single supplier. However, this strategy limits a third party's ability to efficiently consolidate shipments and effectively route its equipments to take advantage of continuous moves.

Buyers do not understand how to change boundary-spanning, internal processes. Many third-party decisions are made and implemented by **cross-functional teams** within buyer firms. Inexperience at managing the team concept makes this decision a lengthy one. Coupled with this can be disagreement within the team concerning cost and service requirements from the third-party provider. Managing these two aspects of the decision is critical to providing the third party with a clear understanding of the scope of the relationship as well as what measurements will be used to measure the performance of the third party.

Sometimes what appears to be a lack of organization on the buyer's part in implementing the relationship is actually a reluctance to use a third party in the first place. If the logistics function is responsible for implementing the third-party relationship but was not part of the initial decision, there could be a reluctance on the part of logistics group to make it work. Logistics could see the third party as a threat to job security. As such, the implementation will be difficult to complete. Successful implementations include the implementing department in the third-party decision.

Finally, transferring a logistics activity to a third party requires that the buyer maintain a level of expertise in that activity. Logistics executives manage assets and relationships. If the assets are outsourced, the need to manage relationships is strengthened. However, a knowledge of the activity given to a third party is necessary to communicate expectations to the third party, develop appropriate measurement systems, and continue to implement solutions to improve the activity. Also, this expertise is necessary in case the activity is brought back "in-house." For example, a food manufacturer recently transferred its private warehouse network to a third party-provider. To prevent losing warehousing expertise, the manufacturer retains managers in the warehouses as well as one of the third-party managers in the manufacturer's corporate logistics office. This is also extremely beneficial to communications between the two firms.

Supplier Challenges

Many suppliers (third parties) have not achieved a "clarity of offer." Many third parties refer to themselves as "logistics companies" without having expanded their basic transportation service. Some have added broker services to justify the new title. These suppliers approach potential buyers offering logistics when, in fact, they still are transportation companies. Another mistake made by third parties is not clearly defining what services they provide. For example, one shipper explained that when it asked a third party, "What services do you provide?," the reply was, "What would you like us to provide?" This gives the impression that the third party is not sure what its core competencies are and is not sure what a third-party provider really is. (Refer to Figure 12.4, which addressed the concept of clearly defining the product offerings of a third-party supplier.)

Some suppliers have no proven method of marketing their services. Third parties traditionally approached either transportation or purchasing managers when marketing and selling their services. Because the single service being marketed was transportation, the point of contact in the buyer firm was relatively easy to determine. However, since the scope of services offered by true third parties has expanded and, in many cases, has crossed functional lines within the buyer firm, the contact point has become difficult to determine. In some instances, the contact person is in finance; in other instances, it is in logistics. Determining how to approach a firm is difficult without knowing who to contact. Traditional contacts in transportation or logistics might not be effective if they perceive third parties as a threat to job security.

Suppliers must compete against entrenched internal groups. A private fleet department within a buyer firm represents a formidable barrier to the success of a third party. This department has developed a reputation for service, a network of alliances with other departments, and an accepted methodology for costing and pricing their services. In these instances, the burden of proof is on the third party to prove its superiority to the internal group. This can pose a challenging problem for the third party because it needs to change the buyer firm's culture toward the internal group.

Suppliers have not proven long-term profitability. Third-party providers sometimes approach buyers with estimated "quick hit" cost reductions through asset elimination or nonunion labor. Although this provides an immediate improvement in buyer profits, it disappears in a short period of time. Buyers also sometimes require continuous cost reductions from the third party. This can result in additional profits for the buyer but might result in reduced profits for the third party because of a necessity to lower price. Long-term profitability for a buyer and supplier in a third-party relationship might actually require additional investments by both parties. This "return on investment" mentality is superior to that of short-term improvements in profits. However, many third parties are either reluctant to or are not capable of communicating their efficiency to the buyer in financial terms.

Conclusion

Third-party providers will continue to successfully serve the logistics needs of the market. Many successful relationships have been implemented and continue to grow. However, caution must be used by both the buyers and sellers in this market to approach the relationship in a way that will guarantee its success. Poor planning on either part will result in failure. Relationship management by logistics executives will continue to be an important part of managing the logistics process.

THE NEGOTIATION PROCESS

The previous discussion focused on the types of relationships that exist between buyers and sellers and how to manage third-party relationships in logistics and transportation.

The next logical discussion is one describing how to establish relationships between shippers and third-party providers. One method used for establishing these relationships is negotiations. This technique can be used to eliminate or minimize differences between the requirements of the two parties. This section will attempt to provide an overview of the negotiation process and its role in third-party relationships. Figure 12.5 provides a framework of the shipper/third-party negotiation process and will be used as the basis for discussion in this section. Market power, negotiating philosophy, and goals/objectives are part of what can be called environmental analysis and planning. These activities are crucial to the negotiation process because they allow each party an opportunity to develop a comprehensive plan to use as the basis for bargaining. Bargaining is where the parties attempt to close the gaps on any differences they might have on the issues. This is where the plan is put into place and modified when necessary. The last section is outcome. Two outcomes will be discussed: agreement and breakdown.

Market Power

Many firms operate from multiple plants and warehouses, which might be included within one operating division or across several operating divisions. Regardless,

FIGURE 12.5 Shipper/Third-Party Negotiation Process

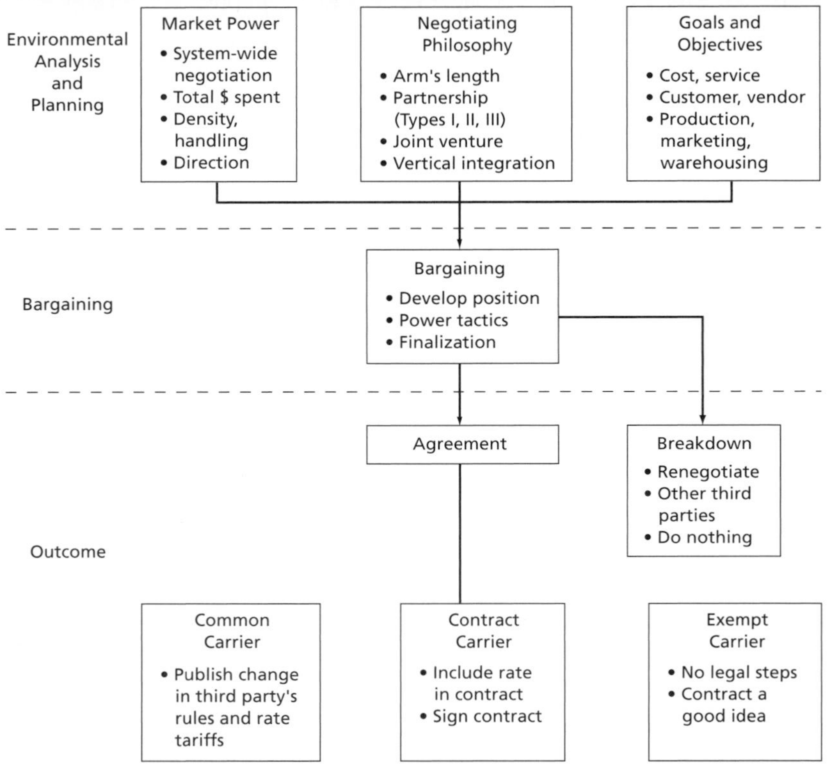

Source: Edward J. Bardi, 2003.

firms have discovered that volume can create leverage with third parties. Many firms have organized transportation councils, comprised of individuals representing the transportation function across several sites or operating divisions. These councils combine their freight to simplify the negotiation process with third parties as well as to attempt to lower freight costs. This **system-wide negotiation** has resulted in firms using fewer third parties and spending less on transportation.

Many other factors influence the market power that the buying firm might have in the negotiation process. These factors impact the third party's cost structure, and thereby influence prices. **Total dollars spent** by the buying firm represents the volume that is available to the third party from one firm or shipping location. As previously stated, the larger the volume or dollars spent, the more leverage the shipper has and the more volume the third party has over which to allocate its fixed costs. **Density and handling**, also used for freight classification, directly impact the third party's costs. Density influences the third party's ability to fully utilize weight and cube capacities of vehicles. The denser the freight, the more efficiently the equipment capacity is utilized. Handling is a variable cost that is passed on directly to the shipper in the freight price. The more often a product is handled by the third party, the more expensive it will be for the shipper. Pallets, consolidation programs, shipper load and count, and zone skipping are all methods to help reduce the number of times a third party needs to handle a product. These practices are discussed in more detail in Chapter 13, "Shipper Process." Finally, **direction** can create a forward haul or fill an empty backhaul. A third party's price will include a portion to cover the costs of system-wide empty miles. If a shipper's freight flow parallels a third party's empty backhauls, a significant cost reduction and price reduction can occur for both parties. However, if the freight flow is in the direction of major headhauls (and where third-party capacity is scarce), the value of service pricing is sure to be used.

Negotiating Philosophy

As discussed earlier in this chapter, many types of relationships exist between shippers and third parties. In developing a negotiating strategy, the shipper must identify the type of relationship desired with the third party. This will influence how both parties approach the negotiation.

Goals and Objectives

In any type of buying situation, the buyer will establish a set of **desires** (cost) and **demands** (service) to be obtained from the seller.[27] Buyers of transportation will usually pre-screen a third-party base using service requirements. This can also include a third party's information technology capabilities, which was discussed in Chapter 11. Only those third parties that can meet a certain minimum service level will move on to the second phase of the selection process. In most cases, these service requirements, or demands, are not negotiable. The second phase, dealing with desires or cost, is where much of the negotiation will take place. Service and cost objectives are set based on the requirements of the customer group to be satisfied: vendors, production, marketing, or warehousing. This underscores the importance of including customers in the development of the cost and service objectives. The transportation negotiator will then translate the objectives into terms that are understandable to and attainable by the prospective third parties.

Bargaining

Bargaining is the step in the negotiation process where the third party and shipper meet to develop their position and determine how close or far the parties are from agreement. If the parties are totally in agreement with their initial positions, bargaining is not needed. Normally, however, there will be some inconsistencies between the positions of the parties and bargaining is necessary. During this process, **power tactics** can be used to change the position of the other party so compromise can be reached. Market power analysis, discussed previously, will determine which party has power and which type of power it has for the bargaining process. Once the parties have reached agreement or compromise, **finalization** is performed. In this step, both parties "agree to agree" on each item discussed during the negotiation process. In other words, each agreement is revisited to make sure that what was agreed upon was what was intended. This step is necessary for contractual purposes. Once the parties leave the negotiation process with an agreement, an oral contract is in effect. This oral contract is subsequently put into writing by one of the parties. These two contracts should be one and the same. Once the contract is signed, either party has 10 days to invalidate the written contract. After the 10-day period, the contract becomes the governing document, even if it conflicts with the initial oral contract. This 10-day limit is a criterion in the "Statute of Frauds" clause in the Uniform Commercial Code. Thus, it is important to revisit the terms of the oral contract before it is put into writing, as well as to reexamine the written document to verify its accuracy.

Breakdown

If the initial positions of the parties are drastically different, bargaining might prove to be futile and breakdown might occur. Breakdown might also occur during bargaining when it becomes evident that one or both parties are no longer willing to compromise. Breakdown is also used as a power strategy. However, when breakdown occurs, three alternatives exist: renegotiate, explore other third parties, or do nothing. In many cases, a "cooling off" period is necessary for either one or both parties to rethink their positions. After this period, **renegotiation** is many times successful.

However, agreement between the parties still might appear to be impossible. In this situation, it is appropriate that both parties "agree to disagree"; both realize that agreement is futile and that the negotiation process has ended. At this point, the shipper can either investigate negotiating with other third parties or do nothing. The **"do nothing"** option is rarely used because customer needs do not disappear because of an unsuccessful negotiation process.

Agreement

An important step in the negotiation process is capturing the results in some type of document recognized by a regulatory, state, or federal government agency. The Overcharge Claim situation faced by shippers in the late 1980s and early 1990s was a result of this step not being properly managed. Carriers and shippers were quick to agree on rate reductions as an effective way to improve their business relationships. However, neither party bothered to make sure that these lower rates were published in a legal document, making them the rates that governed the relationship. Three options exist for formalizing the agreement. If the relationship is with a **common carrier**, the changes should be published in the carrier's rules and rate tariffs. (Tariff-filing requirements were discussed in Chapter 2, "Transportation Regulation and Public Policy.") If the relationship is with a **contract carrier**, the agreement must be formalized in a valid contract. The concept of a "valid" contract will be discussed in a following section. Finally, relationships with **exempt carriers** require no formalized legal steps. However, it is prudent to establish a written contract to govern long term and/or large volume relationships with exempt carriers.

THE BIDDING PROCESS

Negotiation is a process used when the services or costs requested by the shipper are not normal offerings made by third parties; in other words, a third party would have to alter its normal market offerings to satisfy the needs of the shipper. On the other hand, if the shipper only requires standard third-party services but desires a longer-term relationship, the bidding process is appropriate. Government agencies have used bidding in many of its supplier relationships. Bidding and negotiation are not mutually exclusive. Both processes can be used simultaneously to reach an agreement with a third party. What bidding allows is a standardization of the shipper's service demands. Negotiation then allows compromise on the shipper's price/cost desires. Figure 12.6 presents the framework for the bidding process to be discussed.

Qualifying Third Parties

The first step in the bidding process is to qualify third parties. This step is used to include only those third parties in the potential bid base that meet certain legal, financial, or operating requirements. Shippers will many times request proof of operating authority, copies of financial statements, equipment lists (number, age,

FIGURE 12.6 The Bidding Process

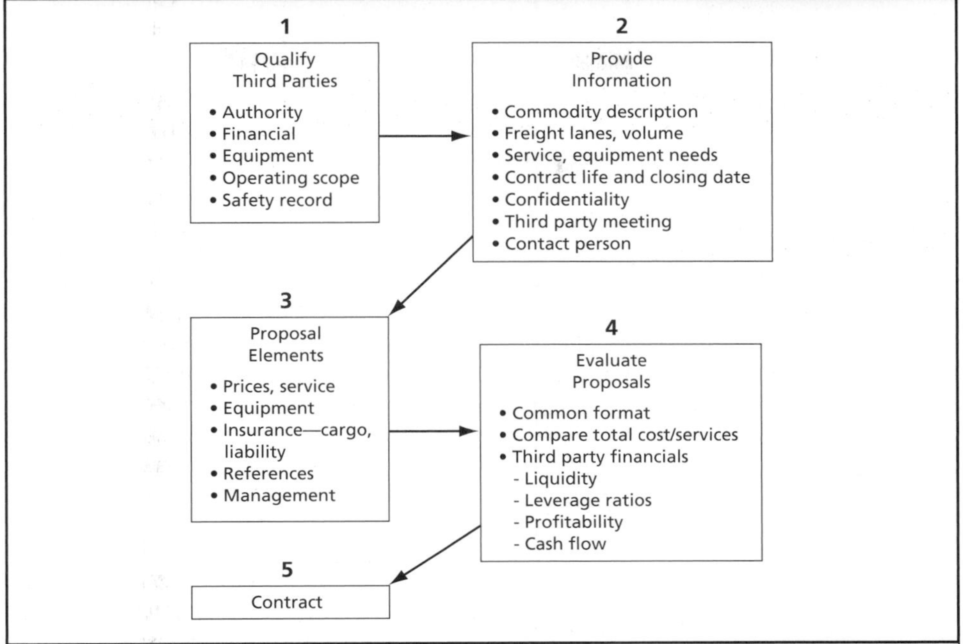

Source: Edward J. Bardi, 2003.

and ownership), operating scope, client references, and hazardous materials/safety qualifications from the third parties. This helps identify those third parties that the shipper desires to do business with as well as alleviate any fears the shipper might have about the third party's ability to provide the service needed in a fiscally responsible manner.

Providing Information

The shipper must carefully identify and communicate to the third-party base all data needed to describe the shipper's business and service requirements. Much of this data, such as freight flows, can be contained in a spreadsheet to be given to the third parties for analysis. Data must be accurate, complete, and timely because third parties will base their proposals on them. In some instances, shippers discover that their freight information systems do not capture all of the necessary data needed to develop a valid bid package. This would require either manual data generation or an investment in information system improvement. Shippers that use third-party freight payment firms can often gather all necessary bid data from the freight bill payment system. Other information provided to the third party would include contract length, delivery time requirements, payment/billing schedules, confidentiality clauses, and a requested third-party meeting.

Proposal Elements

To properly evaluate bids from several third parties, it is important that each contain the same type of data in the same format. Also important is that all data needs to be calculated in the same manner. This allows all bids to be directly compared to each other. The shipper then decides what elements should be contained in the proposal. Several types of proposal elements are identified in Figure 12.6. Unsolicited data from third parties should be avoided in the evaluation stage because this does not allow for unbiased analysis.

Evaluate Proposals

As previously mentioned, it is important that bids be presented in a common format. Oftentimes bids will also be in spreadsheet format to facilitate shipper analysis. As in the negotiation process, shippers must identify cost and service guidelines for evaluation proposals. Lowest price is slowly disappearing as the single criterion for bid evaluation, whereas lowest total cost is being used more and more as the final measure for bid evaluation. Lowest cost includes both third-party price and service in the analysis. For example, Federal Express partnered with National Semiconductor to operate a newly consolidated warehouse and provide expedited transportation service on a worldwide basis. Although the resulting transportation price increased in this relationship, National Semiconductor experienced tremendous overall savings in warehousing, planning, order processing, and inventory costs, more than compensating for the increased transportation price.[28] Thus, the cost implications of the third party's service must be included with the cost implications of the third party's prices.

Prudent shippers will also evaluate the financial implications of the third party's prices on the third party's financial position. Pricing strategies used by third parties in the early 1980s to price below variable cost to increase volume proved disastrous to their financial strength. Many third parties went out of business, leaving shippers without service and unpaid overcharge claims. If the relationship desired with third parties chosen with the bid process is to be long term, the shipper must assure that the third party's prices provide a suitable return to the third party to guarantee long-term financial success.

Contract

Like the negotiation process, a suitable outcome of the bidding process is a contractual relationship with the successful third party(s). The same logic applies to the bidding process as it did to the negotiation process when it comes to establishing relationships with common carrier-based third parties, contract carrier-based third parties, or exempt carrier-based third parties.

THIRD-PARTY CONTRACTS

Once a relationship between a shipper and a third party is established, it needs some type of document to make the arrangement legal and to be used as a guideline for implementation. The document that fills both roles is called a third-party contract. The Interstate Commerce Commission (ICC) initially identified guidelines to evaluate the validity of a third-party contract. (It must be remembered here that the ICC formerly and the STB currently regulate only rail transportation; this chapter is using the generic term "third party" to represent both transportation carriers and firms offering expanded logistics services.) These specific guidelines were necessary to complement the general contract guidelines offered by the Uniform Commercial Code. ICC guidelines were instrumental in the resolution of overcharge claims between shipper and third-party bankruptcy trustees. The latest version of the contract guidelines were specified in the Negotiated Rates Act of 1993 (NRA 1993) and adopted by the Trucking Industry Regulatory Reform Act of 1994. The ICC Termination Act of 1995 did not include

FIGURE 12.7 Guidelines for Third-Party Contracts

Suggested Minimum Content Requirements for a Motor Carrier Contract:

1. It must identify the parties.
2. It must commit the shipper to tender and the carrier to transport a *series of shipments* (emphasis added).
3. It must contain the contract rate or rates for the transportation service to be or being provided.
4. It must state that it provides for the assignment of motor vehicles for a continuing period of time for a shipper, or state that it provides that the service is designed to meet the distinct needs of the shipper.
5. It shall be retained by the carrier while in effect and for a minimum period of 3 years thereafter.

Source: Negotiated Rates Act of 1993, Section 6.

specific language regarding third-party contracts. (Chapter 2 discussed these Acts.) It replaced the term "contract carrier" with a "motor carrier that can enter into contracts." Figure 12.7 lists the third-party requirements as found in the NRA 1993. Although specific language is not required by current legislation, these guidelines should be used to help supplement those specified by the UCC.

Although all transportation contracts are unique, several topics are commonly addressed. Figure 12.8 contains a list of clauses, or sections, commonly contained in a third-party contract. The following is a brief discussion of these common sections.

Disclosure of Goods

The shipper has the duty to inform the third party of the nature of the product. This might include special handling requirements, temperature requirements, nature of hazard (if any), and value. Failure to inform the third party of the special characteristics of the shipment could preempt the shipper's ability to collect on damage claims. The third party could use the "Act of the Shipper" defense as the exemption from the claim action.

If the shipment is hazardous, the shipper is required by law to inform the third party of the type of hazard the shipment could pose in transit (contract liability) as well as the hazard it could pose to individuals and/or the environment if it was mishandled (strict liability). The Code of Federal Regulations (CFR), Title 49, contains severe penalties for shippers that attempt to ship a hazardous product without proper documentation, marking, labeling, and notification of the third party.

FIGURE 12.8 Common Sections Found in Third-Party Contracts

- Disclosure of Goods
- Responsibility for Goods
- Routing, Mode, and Method of Operation
- Term, Termination, and Modification
- Volume Requirements
- Scope of Operation
- Performance Standards
- Operational Standards—Indemnification
- Force Majeure
- Billing and Payment
- Applicable Law
- Assignability
- Breach of Contract
- Dispute Resolution
- Confidentiality

Responsibility for Goods

With all relationships between third parties and shippers, the basis for product liability must be defined. Under a contractual agreement, the value of the goods and the liability for the goods are determined by the parties of the contract. CFR Title 49 defines how product value is to be calculated and which party bears the liability for the goods. The **claims** filing **process** should also be defined. Unless otherwise stated, the claims process in a contract will be handled through the Uniform Commercial Code (UCC). Because the UCC is written for the transaction of products, many remedies allow for the product's replacement. The UCC defines several types of warranties a manufacturer makes about its product. If a warranty is breached, the UCC provides for the manufacturer to reimburse the buyer with either a replacement product or a refund of the purchase price. Many of these warranties do not apply to third parties because they do not manufacture or own the products they transport (unless it is private). As such, the UCC claims process is adequate but not effective for transportation claims. CFR Title 49 contains a detailed process for the filing and disposition of transportation claims, including overcharges, late delivery, and product damage. The updated provisions regarding motor carrier liability and claims filing can be found in Sections 14705 and 14706 of the ICC Termination Act of 1995. Many third-party contracts will reference the appropriate CFR sections for claims process governance.

Routing, Mode, and Method of Operation

The shipper and third party must agree on the equipment type and size to be used for the life of the contract. This is especially true for rail and motor carrier transportation because of the various types and sizes of railcars and trailers available. This section would also address special routing requirements the shipper might have. The growth of intermodal TOFC/COFC has prompted shippers to require notice from the third party if it intends to put the trailer on a rail flatcar. Trailer loading and product damage has influenced this decision by shippers. Some contracts have clauses preventing rail carriers from using hump yards to process a shipper's car. Again, this is caused by car loading and product damage concerns.

Term, Termination, and Modification

Legal contracts have beginning and end dates. End dates, however, can be fluid if the parties agree to extend the contract automatically unless either party objects. In either case, a contract is a document with a specific lifespan. This section also must address early termination by either party. The early termination process must be described, as well as who can initiate it and under what circumstances it can occur.

Contract modification is a very common practice. However, contracts normally do this process little justice. Items to be addressed include: 1) Under what circumstances can and should the contract be modified? 2) Who is responsible for contract modification? 3) Can the contract be modified automatically under certain circumstances? 4) Must every modification be handled as a renegotiation? Modification is especially important in longer-term contracts for transportation prices. Fuel price fluctuations, interest rate changes, and labor agreements can have dramatic impacts on a third party's operating costs. This section must identify if, when, and how a third party can increase or decrease prices. Special care must be taken when linking price changes to changes in an external index, such as the Consumer Price Index. The concern here is that the third party's cost change might have nothing to do with a change in the CPI. The resulting price changes then become random fluctuations without addressing the problem of the third party's cost changes. Because fuel and labor comprise the majority of every third party's variable costs, it might be prudent to develop an index (if one is to be used) based on these two cost drivers.

Volume Requirements

This is also called the **shipper's consideration** in a contractual relationship. Minimum volume commitments on the part of the shipper should be a requirement for a valid contract. In fact, CFR Title 49 was specific in requiring a "series of shipments" for a third party contract to be valid. Volume requirements can be stated in pounds, shipments, units, and so on. This volume requirement should be stated for a specific period of time, such as per week, month, or quarter.

This section can also be used to allow the third party to commit a minimum amount of capacity to the shipper's needs. Obviously, these capacity needs will be based on the shipper's volume commitment. This is especially helpful if the contract has a requirement for a drop lot at a shipper facility. For example, Schneider National and Corning Asahi (manufacturer of television picture tubes) had an agreement where Schneider maintains a minimum trailer pool at Corning Asahi's plant. This minimum trailer pool is based on minimum volume requirements, and the trailer pool is increased based on volume fluctuations.

Scope of Operation

This section describes exactly what is and what is not the responsibility of the third party. This section needs to be as detailed as possible. Activities such as vehicle spotting, loading, and unloading should be assigned as a responsibility of one of the parties. In the case of hazardous shipments, this section would identify who provides placards and who secures them to the vehicle. If the services provided include more than transportation, such as consolidation, order management, or total transportation management, this section should address all aspects of the third party's duties.

Performance Standards

This is part of the **third party's consideration** in a contractual relationship. Specific performance measures related to transit time, pickup/delivery reliability, damage rates, and billing accuracy are detailed in this section. In the case of expanded logistics services, KPIs (Key Performance Indicators) could be determined for each logistics activity performed by the third party. Care must be given to decide over what time period these measures are calculated. Are they to be weekly, monthly, or quarterly measures? For some of these measures, the third party might possess more accurate and timely data. This section must specify which party is responsible for collecting and compiling the data for measurement purposes.

Operational Standards—Indemnification

Many firms require certain indemnification clauses to be included with any contractual relationship with suppliers. The intent of these clauses is to protect the shipper from liability caused by the action or lack of action by the third party on issues not under the control of the shipper. For example, motor carriers are responsible to assure that their drivers are properly licensed to drive a particular class of vehicle. Assume that the shipper's goods are in a vehicle driven by an unlicensed driver and that vehicle is in an accident. An indemnification clause is designed to absolve the shipper of any liability for that accident or any damages it caused.

These clauses are intended to define the liability each party has in the relationship, unrelated to liability for the product (defined in Responsibility for the Goods).

Force Majeure

Conditions outside the responsibility of either party can occur that prevent the implementation of the contract. For common carriage, these are many times referred to as Acts of God. For example, natural disasters that destroy a third party's vehicles or facility or a shipper's facilities would prevent the movement of product as required by the contract. However, natural disasters are mostly unpredictable and uncontrollable. As such, the party affected should not be held in breach of the contract for nonperformance. This section should specify what occurrences are outside the responsibility of both parties that would prevent contract performance as well as the process used when such occurrences happen.

Billing and Payment

Most contracts are for large numbers of transactions across multiple facilities. Generating an invoice for each transaction can become tedious, confusing, and inefficient.

In many cases, a third party will generate one invoice per week for a shipper across all shipping points, with appropriate detail for each shipment attached. The shipper needs only to generate one check to satisfy payment. This is a very common practice for large customers of small package delivery services, such as UPS, FedEx, and FedEx Ground. It is important to identify who is responsible for receiving and paying the invoice.

Credit terms and payment cycle are important elements in this section. Will the third party offer a discount for early payment? A penalty for a late payment? How much time does the shipper have to pay the bill? What happens if the shipper does not pay? This section can also include requirements for the billing and payment cycle to be handled electronically. If this is the case, EDI transaction requirements would need to be detailed in this section.

Applicable Law

A contract can specify which state law will have jurisdiction over contract implementation or contract disputes. In the case of a dispute, the court system of the state specified would be used. If a state is not specified, intrastate contracts are under the jurisdiction of the state involved; interstate contracts are under the jurisdiction of the federal court system.

Assignability

If a third party cannot meet its vehicle requirements in terms of capacity for a given shipper's operation, three options exist. First, the shipper will not be able to move all of its product because of the third party's inability to supply the proper number of pieces of equipment. Second, the third party can assign the loads to another third party. Third, the shipper can find another third party to move the product. The difference between the second and third option is whose responsibility it is to find another third party. Option number one is not appropriate over the long term because of stock-out situations for the shipper's customers. Options two and three are the most common occurrences. However, some shippers do not want to allow a third party to assign a load to another third party. Lack of control over third-party quality is the single point of concern here. Some shippers do not have the capability on a short-term basis to find alternative third parties. Some contracts allow the contracted third party to assign missed loads to other third parties, but only if these alternative third parties are approved by the shipper. Many third parties operate brokerage services with other third parties in which a contract between the two parties is in effect. This allows for a better quality check on the assigned third party.

Breach of Contract

This section must specify what constitutes a breach for both parties. It must also describe the process used to rectify the breach and the process used to terminate the contract (this can be referred to in the Term, Termination, and Modification section). Also, any restitution to be paid by either party because of breach must be identified here.

Dispute Resolution

For product claims, CFR Title 49 can be used to describe the process to be used. However, this process does not recommend actions if and when the claim cannot be settled. In other words, if the claim is not resolved at the end of the process and a resolution is not imminent, Title 49 makes no recommendations on how to resolve the dispute. Other types of disagreements or disputes can occur in other areas of the contract. If not otherwise specified, these disputes are normally handled in the court system identified in Applicable Law. Although very effective, this method of resolution can be lengthy and expensive. An alternative method of dispute resolution is **arbitration**. Both parties must agree to arbitration because its decision is binding on both parties. If arbitration is chosen, then a decision needs to be made in this section as to how the arbitrator is to be chosen and paid.

Confidentiality

Almost every third party contract has a confidentiality clause. This clause protects proprietary data contained in the contract from reaching the public domain.

CONTRACTING HINTS

Contracts between third parties and shippers have been, and will continue to be, effective mechanisms for managing relationships. Many of these contracts, however, are written to satisfy the legal requirements rather than the operating requirements of the relationship. Although these legal requirements are necessary, they should not obscure the operating characteristics. Some contracting hints will be offered in this section that will allow the contract to be used more for operating purposes, rather than for legal purposes.

Indemnification Clauses

Most shipper legal departments will require that it be held blameless for any action the third party takes that might cause someone harm. These clauses, called indemnification clauses, are necessary for a contract to be approved by the shipper's legal department. One suggestion would be to include these clauses at the end of the document, rather than in front. A contract that immediately defers all blame to the third party might set a negative tone for the entire relationship.

Penalty Clauses

Contracts revolve around service/price commitments from third parties and volume commitments from the shipper. This *quid pro quo* provides the basis for the relationship. However, situations occur (not including force majeure) where one or both parties might fail to meet their obligations. Many contracts only "punish" the third party for failure, while leaving the shipper whole when it fails. Because contracts involve numerous transactions, it is inevitable that one or both parties will fail (even a six sigma philosophy will experience two failures per one billion occurrences). As such, "incentives to improve or comply" could be used in place of penalty clauses.

For example, a third party could be paid the agreed-upon price if it complies with a 96-percent service level, a lower price for a lower service, and a higher price for a higher service. Likewise, a shipper could be charged the agreed-upon price for meeting its agreed-upon volume commitments, a higher price for lower volume, and a lower price for a higher volume. The point of this philosophy is not to penalize either party for failure, but to include incentives for compliance and improvement.

Service Requirements

Special care must be taken to determine what the service requirements will be on the part of the third party, and additional care must be taken in defining these requirements. For example, is "on-time" defined as when the vehicle enters the consignee's location or when unloading/loading begins? This section of the contract needs to be very explicit. Delivery "windows" need to be identified as well as who is to collect the data for service performance measurement. Because of the increasing sophistication of third-party technology, some shippers have agreed to allow the third party to collect service performance data. Another consideration is the reporting period: Will it be weekly, monthly, or quarterly? Also, who is to receive these reports?

Finally, some contracts contain what is called a "balanced scorecard."[29] In a shipper/third-party environment, this would include various measures of service and financial performance on the part of the third party. Success is defined by the third party's achieving compliance with all measures, previously identified as KPIs, rather than achieving some and failing at others. These types of measurement systems provide incentive for the third party to reduce costs and provide exceptional service for the shipper. The incentive for the third party is in the form of higher financial compensation.

The "Living" Contract

Many contracts are written as very rigid documents; any changes negate the original document and require wholesale renegotiation. As a shipper/third-party relationship matures and grows, requirements will change. A "living" contract is written to allow these new requirements to be included effortlessly as part of the relationship. This type of contract will not work in every situation. However, in situations where both parties agree that the relationship will grow, it is quite appropriate. This is very evident in the movement from a "reliability" relationship to a "responsiveness" one, and on to an "innovation" relationship between the shipper and third party.

Prices

Always include the listing of prices and charges levied by the third party in the body of the contract. To refer to other documents or tariffs might not only be confusing but also might be illegal. This also allows the contract to become the comprehensive document governing the relationship.

CONCLUSION

The point of these contracting hints is to make the contract easy to understand, specific as to the duties of each party, and allow the contract to evolve into an operating document. Even though contracts are not necessary in Type III partnerships, the responsibilities of each party need to be defined in every relationship. Sometimes this definition is in writing; sometimes it is not. In either case, because success or failure by either party is assessed in the relationship, specific guidelines are needed to allow the relationship to grow and be successful.

Summary

- Transportation strategy is a key element of total logistics strategy and is used to guide the purchase and management of transportation services including bulk shipments and small shipments.
- When selecting a transportation carrier, the traffic/transportation manager will evaluate specific service characteristics, such as transit time, reliability, safety, capability, and accessibility in addition to the transportation rate.
- Traffic management in today's deregulated environment can be looked on as a special form of procurement emphasizing the purchase of transportation services.
- The scope of the traffic management function includes both line and staff responsibilities.
- Carrier and mode selection are critical shipper processes used in managing the transportation activity to meet the shipper's service and cost goals.
- Six different types of relationships are found to exist: arm's length, Type I, Type II, Type III, joint ventures, and vertical integration.
- Transportation and logistics are conducive to managing relationships because of their boundary-spanning responsibilities.
- Third-party organizations are used by shippers to provide not only transportation service, but also many other logistics services.
- The use of a third party to provide transportation and other logistics services has both risks and rewards. However, the risks can be minimized by incorporating certain concepts into the relationship.
- The negotiation process can be complex and time-consuming; it is most effective when used to establish relationships where the third party and shipper must alter their normal operating procedures to comply with each other's demands.
- The bidding process is also used to establish relationships; it is best used when the third party does not need to alter its basic service offerings to meet the demands of the shipper.
- Third-party contracts are documents that must meet both the legal and operating requirements of both parties.
- Third-party contracts can be written to elicit a positive working relationship between the third party and shipper while avoiding the negative connotations of "penalizing" failures.

Key Terms

arbitration, 439
accessibility, 413
auditing, 407
balanced load, 404
capability, 413
carrier evaluation, 409
claims, 407
claims process, 436
common carrier, 432
contract carrier, 432
core carriers, 401
core competency, 420
cross-functional teams, 428
demurrage, 407
density and handling, 430
desires and demands, 431
detention, 407
direction, 430
dispatcher, 406
"do nothing", 432
economies of scale, 420
economies of scope, 420
evergreen contracts, 417
exempt carriers, 432
finalization, 431
growth, 418
improve financial performance, 420
increase risk, 417
joint planning, 422
market power, 401
no formal endpoint, 417
pooling, 403
power tactics, 431
procurement, 398
renegotiation, 432
reverse logistics, 405
shipper's consideration, 437
short-term, 416
standard service, 416
stopping-in-transit, 403
system-wide negotiation, 430
terms of sale, 405
third party, 418
third-party's consideration, 437
total dollars spent, 430
traffic management, 398
transit time, 412
transportation management, 399

Study Questions

1. When a traffic/transportation manager evaluates potential carriers, what factors are taken into consideration in making a final decision?
2. Discuss the general strategies used by transportation managers for small shipments versus bulk shipments. Why are they different?
3. Traffic management is typically referred to as a special type of purchasing or procurement function. Why?
4. Describe the process used to monitor carrier service quality.
5. Distinguish between line and staff traffic-management responsibilities.
6. What are the six different types of third-party relationships? How are they different? In what types of situations would each relationship be most appropriate?
7. Why are relationships with third parties so prevalent in transportation today?
8. What are the characteristics of a successful relationship? What would prevent parties in a relationship from achieving these characteristics?
9. Identify the risks associated with outsourcing from the perspectives of both the buyer and the supplier.
10. What are the different elements of the negotiation process? The bidding process? When should each be used?
11. What are the legal requirements for a valid transportation contract?
12. Identify any five topics addressed in a transportation contract and explain their importance to the contract.
13. How would you prepare for a bid package? What information should be included? What information would you seek from the carrier? If you are the third party, what information do you want from the shipper?

Notes

1. Michael S. Galardi, "Transportation Strategies: A Review and Forecast," *Proceedings of the Council of Logistics Management,* Vol. 1, 1986, pp. 36–50.
2. Jeff Holmes, "Hot Spots of Supply Chain Management," *Inbound Logistics*, October 1997, pp. 40–44.
3. Helen Richardson, "Make Time an Ally," *Transportation & Distribution,* July 1995, pp. 46–50.
4. Toby Gooley, "There and Back Again," *Logistics Management,* April 1999, pp. 57–62.
5. John T. Gardner, Martha C. Cooper, and Tom Noordewier, "Understanding Shipper-Carrier and Shipper-Warehouser Relationships: Partnerships Revisited," *Journal of Business Logistics,* Vol. 15, No. 2, 1994, p. 123.
6. Douglas M. Lambert, Margaret A. Emmelhainz, and John T. Gardner, "Developing and Implementing Supply Chain Partnerships," *The International Journal of Logistics Management,* Vol. 7, No. 2, 1996, pp. 1–17.
7. Gardner, Cooper, and Noordewier, op.cit.
8. Lambert, Emmelhainz, and Gardner, op. cit., p. 2.
9. The discussion of the three types of partnerships is based on the framework developed by Lambert et. al.
10. James A. Tompkins, "Evaluating the Performance of Partnerships," *CLM Annual Conference Proceedings,* 1995, pp. 431–450.
11. Lisa M. Ellram, and Thomas E. Hendrick, "Partnering Characteristics: A Dyadic Perspective," *Journal of Business Logistics,* Vol. 16, No. 1, 1995, p. 41.
12. See, for example, the diagnostic tool developed by the research of Lambert et.al., op. cit.
13. Arnold B. Maltz, and Robert C. Lieb, "The Third Party Logistics Industry: Evolution, Drivers, and Prospects," *Proceedings of the Twenty-Fourth Annual Transportation and Logistics Educators' Conference,* Oak Brook, IL: Council of Logistics Management, 1995, pp. 45–75.
14. Armstrong & Associates, Inc., www.3plogistics.com, 2001.
15. C. John Langley, Jr., Gary R. Allen, and Gene R. Tyndall, *Third Party Logistics Study: Results and Findings of the 2002 Seventh Annual Study,* Georgia Tech University, 2003.
16. Ibid.
17. For a further discussion of the financial impacts of logistics on a firm's financial performance, see Thomas W. Speh and Robert A. Novack, "The Management of Financial Resources in Logistics," *The Journal of Business Logistics,* Vol. 16, No. 2, 1995, pp. 23–42.
18. Ibid.
19. Lambert, Emmelhainz, and Gardner, op.cit.
20. Robert A. Novack, C. John Langley, Jr., and Lloyd M. Rinehart, *Creating Logistics Value: Themes for the Future,* Chicago, IL: Council of Logistics Management, 1995, p. 197.
21. Robert C. Lieb, and Hugh L. Randall, "A Comparison of the Use of Third Party Logistics Services by Large American Manufacturers, 1991, 1994, and 1995," *Journal of Business Logistics,* Vol. 17, No. 1, 1996, pp. 305–320.
22. For example, see Lambert, et.al., op.cit.; Jakki Moore and Robert Spekman, "Characteristics of Partnership Success: Partnership Attributes, Communication Behavior, and Conflict Resolution Techniques," *Strategic Management Journal,* Vol. 15, 1994, pp. 135–152; Gardner, Cooper, and Noordewier, op.cit; Lisa. M. Ellram and Thomas E. Hendrick, "Partnering Characteristics: A Dyadic Perspective," *Journal of Business Logistics,* Vol. 16, No. 1, 1995, pp. 41–64.
23. This triangular concept was adapted from William C. Copacino's "Reliability is No Longer Enough," *Traffic Management,* August 1991, p. 65.
24. For a further discussion on the logistics product mix, see Robert A. Novack, C. John Langley, Jr., and Lloyd M. Rinehart's *Creating Logistics Value: Themes for the Future* Oak Brook, IL: Council of Logistics Management, 1995, pp. 112–114.
25. This discussion is based on research conducted by Arnold B. Maltz and Robert C. Lieb, "The Third Party Logistics Industry: Evolution, Drivers, and Prospects," *Proceedings of the Twenty-Fourth Annual Transportation and Logistics Educators' Conference* Oak Brook, IL: Council of Logistics Management, 1995, pp. 45–75.
26. Lieb and Randall, op.cit., p. 309.
27. Robert A. Novack, and Stephen W. Simco, "The Industrial Procurement Process: A Supply Chain Perspective," *Journal of Business Logistics,* Vol. 12, No. 1, 1991, pp. 145–168.
28. Novack, Langley, and Rinehart, op. cit., pp. 119–122.
29. Robert S. Kaplan, and David P. Norton, "The Balanced Scorecard—Measures that Drive Performance," *Harvard Business Review,* January-February 1992, pp. 71–79.

Suggested Readings

Con, Larry A. "Establishing Effective Transportation Controls in a Decentralized Company," *Council of Logistics Management Annual Conference Proceedings,* 1995, pp. 391–398.

Cooke, James A. "Blocking and Tackling and Beyond," *Logistics Management*, October 2003, pp. 24–27.

Foster, Thomas A., "Engineering the 3PL Selection Process," *Logistics Management*, June 2003, pp. e3–e17.

Gardner, John T., Martha C. Cooper, and Tom Noordewier. "Understanding Shipper-Carrier and Shipper-Warehouser Relationships: Partnerships Revisited," *Journal of Business Logistics,* Vol. 15, No. 2, 1994, pp. 121–143.

Greenfield, Mark. "Railroads Engineer Capacity Improvements," *Progressive Railroading,* March 1996, pp. 51–57.

Kling, James A., and Ken A. Smith. "Identifying Strategic Groups in the U.S. Airline Industry: An Application of the Porter Model," *Transportation Journal,* Vol. 35, No. 2, 1995, pp. 26–34.

Lambert, Douglas M., Margaret A. Emmelhainz, and John T. Gardner. "Developing and Implementing Supply Chain Partnerships," *The International Journal of Logistics Management,* Vol. 7, No. 2, 1996, pp. 1–17.

Lewis, Ira, and Alexander Talalayevsky. "Third Party Logistics: Leveraging Information Technology," *Journal of Business Logistics*, Vol. 21, No. 2, 2000, pp. 173–185.

Liberatore, Matthew J., and Ian Miller. "A Decision Support Approach for Transport Carrier and Mode Selection," *Journal of Business Logistics,* Vol. 16, No. 2, 1995, pp. 85–116.

Lieb, Robert C. and Hugh L. Randall. "A Comparison of the Use of Third Party Logistics Services by Large American Manufacturers, 1991, 1994, and 1995," *Journal of Business Logistics,* Vol. 17, No. 1, 1996, pp. 305–320.

Lu, Chin-Shan, "An Evaluation of Service Attributes in a Partnering Relationship Between Maritime Firms and Shippers in Taiwan," *Transportation Journal,* Vol. 42, No. 5, 2003, pp. 5–16.

Malone, Robert, "Cutting Costs on Urgent Shipments," *Inbound Logistics*, August 2003, pp. 18–20.

Malone, Robert, "Collaborating for Optimum Supply Chain Management," *Inbound Logistics*, December 2003, pp. 30–31.

Murphy, Paul R., and Richard F. Poist. "Third Party Logistics: Some User Versus Provider Perspectives," *Journal of Business Logistics*, Vol. 21, No. 1, 2000, pp. 121–133.

Novack, Robert A., and Stephen W. Simco. "The Industrial Procurement Process: A Supply Chain Perspective," *Journal of Business Logistics,* Vol. 12, No. 1, 1991, pp. 145–168.

O'Reilly, Joseph. "Making Cargo Count," *Inbound Logistics*, June 2003, pp. 36–40.

Rishel, Tracy D., J. Phillip Scott, and Alan J. Stenger. "A Preliminary Look at Using Satellite Communication for Collaboration in the Supply Chain," *Transportation Journal*, Vol. 42, No. 5, 2003, pp. 17–30.

Shanahan, John. "Dock Congestion: How Do You Spell Relief," *Logistics Management*, June 2003, pp. 29–32.

Sink, Harry L., and C. John Langley, Jr. "A Managerial Framework for the Acquisition of Third Party Logistics Services," *Journal of Business Logistics,* Vol. 18, No. 2, 1997, pp. 163–189.

Spiegel, Robert. "Truckload vs. LTL," *Logistics Management*, July 2003, pp. 54–57.

Stank, Theodore P., Scott B. Keller, and Patricia J. Daugherty. "Supply Chain Collaboration and Logistical Service Performance," *Journal of Business Logistics*, Vol. 22, No. 1, 2001, pp. 29–48.

Walton, Lisa Williams. "Partnership Satisfaction: Using the Underlying Dimensions of Supply Chain Partnerships to Measure Current and Expected Levels of Satisfaction," *Journal of Business Logistics,* Vol. 17, No. 2, 1996, pp. 57–76.

Weber, Charles A., John R. Current, and Anand Desai. "VENDOR: A Structured Approach to Vendor Selection and Negotiation," *Journal of Business Logistics*, Vol. 21, No. 1, 2000, pp. 135–167.

Case 12-1

Hardee Transportation, Inc.

Jim O'Brien was about to face a new challenge in his career: establishing a long-term relationship with one of his major customers. Although most of Hardee's business was locked up in contracts, the execution of these contracts was very informal. The contracts served as legal documents governing the relationship; how the services were performed was very loosely defined. Jim's philosophy was to do what the customer wanted, even if it wasn't defined in the contract.

Hardee was about to become a third-party provider (3PL). He had heard about this concept, but was not sure what it exactly entailed. His customers now wanted Hardee not only to provide transportation but also to provide some complex dock operations. In addition, his customers now also wanted Hardee to invest in new technology and significantly change their operations.

Jim knew that these new opportunities would require a relationship that Hardee had not experienced in the past. He also knew that if Hardee was not willing to undertake this new business model, his customers would find another 3PL to do the job. Jim also expected that customers would eventually begin to ask for more and more in the form of new services. How would Hardee continue to grow these relationships with these customers? How would he word the contract to specifically define the relationship? What are the risks and rewards of the new business model? Is this the market Hardee wants to be in? How will his role change in how he deals with these customers?

Using the information offered in this chapter, how would you answer Jim's questions?

Case 12-2

Commercial Gypsum

Founded in 1975, Commercial Gypsum (CG) manufactures several types of drywall products for the construction industry. Located in Jacksonville, Florida, CG has prided itself on high-quality products and timely and reliable delivery service. These are especially important to the construction industry because material and labor costs are significant in their overall cost structure. The industry is highly competitive because the product is considered a commodity by contractors and distributors. All of CG's sales are to these two customer groups. As such, price is really not a differentiating factor. This has driven CG to constantly look for programs to reduce its delivered cost. However, it cannot afford to sacrifice product quality and delivery reliability to achieve this cost reduction.

CG primarily services the major markets in the southeast United States. However, it does service some markets in the Southwest. CG manufactures 200 million pounds of drywall per year. The average value per pound across all types of drywall is $2. Of this total, approximately 60 percent of this is 1/2-half inch regular drywall, 20 percent in 5/8-inch regular drywall, and 20 percent in 5/8-inch "8-minute" drywall. This latter type of drywall is called such because it has a layer of fireproof material in each sheet that will contain a fire in a building for 8 minutes longer than regular drywall. The major markets for these products and their respective demands in percent are Atlanta, Georgia (30 percent);

Miami, Florida (15 percent); Charlotte, North Carolina (15 percent); Birmingham, Alabama (20 percent); and New Orleans, Louisiana (20 percent).

CG currently uses a mix of both truckload (TL) and rail shipments to each market. The TL rate is $1.25 per mile and the rail rate is $0.75 per hundredweight (cwt). Each TL shipment is 40,000 pounds (400 cwt) and each rail shipment is 100,000 pounds (1,000 cwt). Transit times and miles from Jacksonville to each market are as follows:

Destination	TL Time (days)	Rail Time (days)	Miles
Atlanta	1	2	354
Miami	1	2	369
Charlotte	1	3	399
Birmingham	2	3	500
New Orleans	2	4	582

CG's Jacksonville plant is on a rail siding serviced by the Lake City Short Line Railroad. It connects with the Southeast Express Railroad for the line-haul moves to the major markets. CG uses three different TL carriers: Carolina Express (CE) to Atlanta and Charlotte; Birmingham's Best (BB) to Birmingham and New Orleans; and Florida Central Trucking (FCT) to Miami. The following represents the service performance of the railroad to each market:

Destination	On-time (%)	Damage Rate (%)
Atlanta	85%	1.5%
Miami	90%	2.1%
Charlotte	80%	1.0%
Birmingham	75%	2.5%
New Orleans	70%	3.0%

TL service performance is as follows (the first number is on-time percent, the second is damage rate in percent):

Destination	CE	BB	FCT
Atlanta	92%, 1.0%	—	—
Miami	—	—	95%, 2.5%
Charlotte	85%, 1.8%	—	—
Birmingham	—	95%, 3.0%	—
New Orleans	—	85%, 2.5%	—

Each of the TL carriers has operations to all markets services by CG. However, CG is captive to its rail carriers.

Fred Macholz, director of transportation for CG, has been given the directive to reduce transportation costs to help improve margin. This is important because CG has no upward production flexibility. In other words, its maximum production capacity is 200 million pounds per year. It holds very little finished goods inventory. To improve profits, then, it does not have the option of increasing production. Fred is currently analyzing CG's mode and carrier mix to determine if he should shift volumes between modes and/or among his carriers to each market. He has 2 months in which to do his analysis and present the results to upper management.

Case Questions

1. How would you tell Fred to begin?
2. What criteria would you tell Fred to use in determining CG's mode and carrier mix?

3. How would you develop your analysis (criteria weightings, etc)?
4. How would you implement your new transportation system? Single transaction? Contracts?
5. How would you measure the performance of the new transportation system?

Case 12-3

Shipper—Carrier Negotiation Project

Shipper Situation

Boll Weevil, Inc. of Harrisburg is one of eight firms in Pennsylvania that harvest and sell raw "cumulus cotton" to textile manufacturers in the United States. The company has had previous problems gaining a competitive advantage in the market because of poor arrangements for transportation of the commodity between Harrisburg and textile mills in Knoxville, Tennessee; Greensboro, North Carolina; Atlanta, Georgia; Union, South Carolina; Elberton, Georgia; Lincolnton, North Carolina; and Pikeville, Tennessee. The former traffic manager, who perceived his job to be very similar to that of the Maytag repairman, has left you with the responsibility of arranging transportation for all future shipments of the commodity to these customers.

Cumulus cotton is a new product invention that allows the harvesting and transformation of clouds into a cotton-type product that can be used as a substitute for traditionally grown cotton. This product must be maintained at a temperature of between 5 and 38 degrees Fahrenheit at all times while in its raw state. Second, polypropho gas must be added to the product every 3 hours to allow the product to maintain its natural consistency. This gas is quite expensive ($5 for 20 pounds). Twenty pounds of gas will protect approximately 5,000 pounds of the cumulus cotton. Previous estimates of the density of the product indicate that 1,000 pounds of the cotton equals approximately 100 cubic feet of space.

Demand from these customers is anticipated to be a total of 10,500,000 pounds per year. Each individual customer's demand is expected to be as follows:

Knoxville	2,000,000 pounds
Pikeville	250,000 pounds
Atlanta	5,000,000 pounds
Elberton	250,000 pounds
Union	500,000 pounds
Lincolnton	500,000 pounds
Greensboro	2,000,000 pounds

The demand from each of these customers is expected to be fairly constant over the course of the year. Your landed production cost at the plant's shipping dock is $3 per pound; you can sell cumulus cotton to your customers at $5 per pound.

Production capacity has been listed at 20,000,000 pounds, which is within the needs of the anticipated market demands for all customers of the company. However, this capacity is not consistent over the course of the year. The following list indicates anticipated production capacity per month:

January	3,000,000 pounds
February	3,000,000 pounds
March	3,000,000 pounds
April	3,000,000 pounds
May	2,000,000 pounds
June	1,000,000 pounds
July	0 pounds
August	0 pounds
September	1,000,000 pounds
October	1,000,000 pounds
November	1,000,000 pounds
December	2,000,000 pounds

Your boss, who is the owner of the firm and one of the individuals who perfected the harvesting process, has recently learned that alternative transportation arrangements through contracts can save the company substantial sums of money and increase the service level from the carrier. Your responsibility is to create this type of benefit for the company.

Carrier Situation

The Baahd Company is a total transportation company that has a 48-state motor carrier operating authority to provide transportation service to shippers. A growing and highly competitive industry that requires transportation service is the "cumulus cotton" industry, which uses transportation service between points in Pennsylvania and southern markets that use the product in the manufacture of textile goods. Attached is a copy of the characteristics of this industry. The eight companies in this industry are identical in their characteristics and have similar points of origin.

Seven other transportation firms have also developed recent interest in this market and are pursuing business in this industry. All of these carriers have similar operating characteristics. For example, all pay their drivers $10 per hour. Fuel currently costs $1.50 per gallon, and the equipment of all carriers averages 6.5 miles per gallon on line-haul movements. All firms have relatively new equipment and estimate that their maintenance costs average $0.15 per mile. Administrative costs are anticipated to be 10 percent of the variable costs of the move.

Your boss, the marketing manager, has done some initial calculations that indicate you do not have the capacity to provide service to more than one of these shippers. However, she does want to establish your firm as a competitive transportation company in this market. You are therefore being saddled with the responsibility of securing business in this industry.

Destination Market	Miles from Harrisburg, Pennsylvania
Knoxville, Tennessee	455
Pikeville, Tennessee	532
Atlanta, Georgia	564
Elberton, Georgia	564
Union, South Carolina	320
Lincolnton, North Carolina	400
Greensboro, North Carolina	310

Your terminal in Harrisburg is located 15 miles from the shipper's location. Your terminal coverage in the Southeast allows each terminal to be located about 10 miles from each customer for his cotton.

Virgin Cumulus Cotton Industry

Eight firms in Pennsylvania harvest and sell raw "cumulus cotton" to textile manufacturers in the United States. The main markets for these firms are in Knoxville; Greensboro, North Carolina; Atlanta; Union, South Carolina; Elberton, Georgia; Lincolnton, North Carolina; and Pikeville, Tennessee.

As stated earlier, cumulus cotton is a new invention that can be used as a substitute for traditionally grown cotton. Total demand for virgin cumulus cotton production from each manufacturer in the southern markets is 10,500,000 pounds.

Case Questions

1. As transportation manager for Boll Weevill:
   - How would you prepare to negotiate with the Baahd Company for transportation service?
   - What price/service level combinations would you use as your starting points on concession points?
   - What type of relationship would you establish with Baahd? What would the contract look like?

Chapter 13

Shipper Process

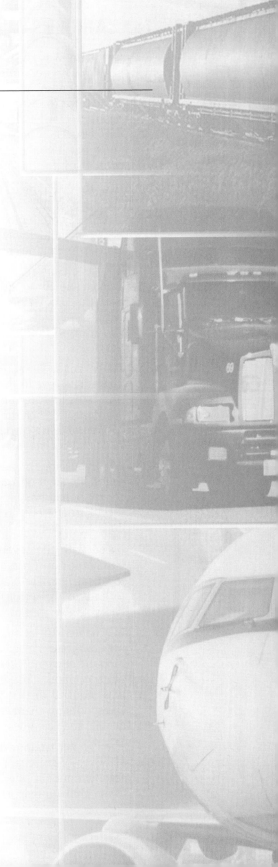

NO CARRIERS AVAILABLE

Tim Walsch, transportation team leader for the Vermont plant, reviewed the customer orders for Monday's pickups and came to the conclusion that Monday was going to be a bad day. There were 15 customer shipments scheduled for Monday, and as of Friday morning, Tim had carriers for only 8 of the loads. He called all of the carriers on his list, plus he had contacted three freight brokers. The answer was always the same: "We do not have equipment in your area, but if you are willing to pay two-way mile rates we could divert equipment to your plant for the move."

Tim has been the transportation team leader at Seaway Products' (SP) Vermont plant for the past 10 years. During this time he has experienced sporadic equipment shortages, but nothing like this. Part of the problem is the need for flatbed trailers to haul SP's cement highway barriers. SP is the leading manufacturer of highway construction barriers including cement highway dividers as well as the infamous orange barrels.

SP has a centralized transportation department housed in the Cleveland corporate office. The corporate transportation manager negotiates all contracts with carriers, and the plant transportation team leaders select carriers from those who have signed contracts with SP. This strategy enables SP to bring its full buying power to the transportation market, and has resulted in SP receiving favorable rates and services.

However, the Vermont plant has consistently experienced problems getting the contract carriers to serve its transportation needs. The contract carriers provide excellent service and rates to other SP plants but are often slow to respond to Vermont's request for equipment. When the corporate office pressures the contract carriers to provide service to Vermont, the carriers respond with a request for higher rates because of the empty backhaul posed by shipments to and from Vermont.

To fill the gap, Tim has reverted to using small, local carriers who charge SP round trip miles, rather than one-way miles, to make deliveries. The corporate transportation manager has criticized Tim for the higher delivery costs associated with using the local carriers, but no solution to the carrier availability problem has come from the corporate level.

Faced with the seven uncovered loads on Monday, Tim called the local trucking companies and arranged for pickup. Given the increased frequency of using the local carriers, Tim had to find a solution to the unwillingness of the contract carriers to haul loads out of the Vermont plant. As you read the chapter what suggestions can you give Tim to increase the availability of flatbed equipment?

In Chapter 12, attention was given to shipper transportation management strategy including carrier selection, contracting, negotiating, relationship management, and inbound strategy. The focus of this chapter is on implementation and execution of this transportation management strategy and, in particular, on the day-to-day shipper activities required to manage the domestic and global transportation process. Successful transportation management requires a solid grounding in the transportation process details, such as rate analysis, documentation, and claims.

The chapter begins with the domestic transportation process including the attendant activities of shipment source, shipment analysis, carrier scheduling, load tendering, shipment monitoring, and postdelivery maintenance. This is followed by a discussion of the global transportation process.

DOMESTIC TRANSPORTATION MANAGEMENT PROCESS

Figure 13.1 provides an overview of the domestic transportation management process that shippers utilize. The process begins with a customer order and/or purchase order. Next, the transportation manager analyzes the shipment, schedules the carrier, tenders the load, prepares the documentation, monitors the shipment while intransit, and performs postdelivery maintenance.

Shipment Source

The starting point in the transportation management process is either the customer order or purchase order, indicating a need for transportation services for either outbound or inbound transportation. The customer service, sales, or marketing departments are charged with the responsibility of receiving and processing the customer's order. The order may come into the seller's operation via mail, phone, fax, EDI, or the Internet. The most common order transmittal forms are phone and fax.

On the inbound side of the operations, the purchase order signals the need for transportation of materials from a vendor. The purchasing department is typically the initiator of the purchase order, telling the vendor that the company is authorizing the vendor to ship the product and the quantity indicated on the purchase order. Today, the phone and fax remain the dominant form of purchase order transmittal, but there is an increasing trend toward the use of the Internet.

Associated with the customer order and purchase order are the underlying terms of sale agreed to between the buyer and seller. For routine item sales, the seller's sales policy contains the terms of sale. For nonroutine item sales and most purchase orders, the terms of sale are negotiated.

The terms of sale place constraints on the transportation management process. The terms of sale indicate who has control over the selection of the carrier, who pays the transportation freight bill, and where title to the goods pass from the seller to the buyer. Essentially, the terms of sale define the buyer and seller transportation role in the sales transaction.

FIGURE 13.1 Domestic Transportation Management Process

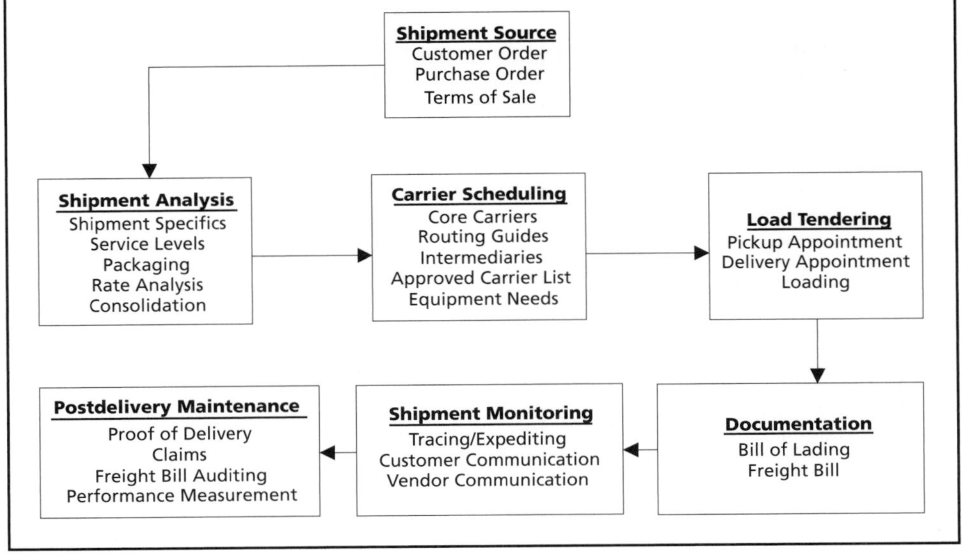

Figure 13.2 shows some typical domestic terms of sale. The free on board (FOB) domestic terms of sale have a named point that determines where title passes to the buyer, where responsibility for selecting and routing the shipment passes to the buyer, and where the buyer begins paying for the transportation charges. The four FOB terms included in Figure 13.2 are typical of those used in U.S. commerce today.

For example, the **FOB-delivered term of sale** states the seller pays the freight charges to the buyer's door, the seller selects the carrier and routes the shipment, and title passes to the buyer upon delivery to the buyer. The latter point means the seller has title to the goods during transit and bears the responsibility for filing claims for transportation loss and damage. (Claims will be discussed in a subsequent section of this chapter.)

The FOB-origin term of sale means the buyer incurs all transportation responsibility, cost, and claim responsibility. The seller is responsible for making the shipment available at the seller's door for the carrier that the buyer selects. The buyer selects the carrier, routes the shipment, pays the carrier, and assumes the responsibility for claims. The FOB-origin term of sale is used in purchasing of materials to enable the buyer to gain control over the cost and service of inbound transportation.

The FOB-Port of Entry term means the seller incurs all transportation responsibility up to the port of entry and the buyer assumes the responsibility from the Port of Entry to destination. For the FOB-Atlanta term, the buyer assumes all transportation responsibility from Atlanta to destination, whereas the seller is responsible for making the product available at Atlanta.

As you can see, the terms of sale used to sell and buy products determines the level of transportation control exercised by the buyer and the seller. If a firm buys all raw materials on an FOB-delivered basis and sells on an FOB-origin basis, the firm would have minimal transportation management responsibility. Today, many firms attempt to increase the amount of transportation management control by buying FOB-Origin and selling FOB-delivered. By using these two terms of sale, the firm can maximize its control over the cost of its products.

Shipment Analysis

The customer and purchase orders signal the need for transportation, but the transportation manager must have more information to complete the actual transportation aspect of the sales transaction. The shipment analysis function examines the specifics of the shipment, service levels required, packaging, rates, and consolidation.

FIGURE 13.2 Domestic Terms of Sale

	FOB-Origin	FOB-Delivered	FOB-Port of Entry	FOB-Atlanta
Carrier selected and shipment routed by	Buyer	Seller	Buyer from Port of Entry	Seller to Atlanta Buyer from Atlanta
Freight bill paid by	Buyer	Seller	Buyer from Port of Entry	Seller to Atlanta Buyer from Atlanta
Title to goods passes at	Origin	Buyer's door	Port of Entry	Atlanta
Freight claim filed by	Buyer	Seller	Buyer from Port of Entry	Seller to Atlanta Buyer from Atlanta

The shipment specifics come directly from the customer and purchase order, and define the product to be shipped, the quantity, the origin, the destination, the consignee, pickup and delivery dates, routing instructions, and delivery requirements. Figure 13.3 provides an example of the shipment specifics needed to effect the transportation of a customer or purchase order.

The information in Figure 13.3 provides all the information needed for the scheduling of a carrier. The transportation manager knows the origin, destination, product, quantity, and shipment date. In addition, the transportation manager knows that the carrier must call the consignee for a delivery appointment and the carrier selected for the move must be one listed in the buyer's routing guide issued 5/1/04. Implicitly identified in these shipment specifics is a 3-day service level; that is, delivery is to be made on the third day (5/17/04 to 5/20/04).

The service level requirement is often the company's stated delivery policy. Many Internet retailers state normal delivery as 5 business days and expedited delivery as the next day. If the buyer opts for expedited delivery, the transportation manager must select a carrier that will deliver the shipment the next day, typically an air or ground express carrier. Other sellers have a stated delivery policy indicating that 99 percent of the shipments will be delivered within 3 days. Both policies provide constraints on the transportation process to select carriers that are capable of meeting the delivery timeframes.

On the inbound side, many delivery requirements are very rigid and require the vendor to meet exacting specifications. For example, a manufacturer of overhead garage doors specified daily delivery of parts. A **blanket purchase order** was issued to the vendors for a specified annual quantity, but daily deliveries had to be made for the releases issued by the buyer from the blanket order. Another manufacturer required the vendor to use carriers that had satellite communication capabilities to permit direct contact with the driver. The direct carrier contact enabled the manufacturer to alter the destination of the shipment based on the raw material requirements at its different plants.

Packaging is typically the domain of engineering and production. The package must be strong enough to hold the product and pose minimal inefficiencies in the product-filling stage of the production process. The transportation manager must view packaging as to its ability to protect the shipment from damage while in transit. Also, many carriers specify in their rules tariffs the specific type of package to use for a product.

For example, the National Motor Carrier Classification contains fiberboard boxes specifications in Item 222. This item rule identifies the minimum combined weight

FIGURE 13.3 Shipment Specifics

CBN Manufacturing, Inc.
Outbound Shipment Specifications

Requested ship date: 5/17/04
Customer: XYZ Corporation
Delivery location:
1234 Main St.
Anywhere, US
12345-6789
Product: Reground plastic
Quantity: 20 skids, 44,000 pounds
Delivery instructions: Call for appointment
Routing instructions: Must use carrier listed in routing guide issued 5/1/04

Requested delivery date: 5/20/04
Phone: 123-456-7890, ext. 987
Contact: L. Waters

of facings, minimum bursting test of facings, and minimum puncture test of combined boards for various sizes of fiberboard boxes. Testing procedures for these specifications are described, as well as the box manufacturer's certificate that is to appear on the certified box.

Noncompliance with the box specifications can result in higher carrier rates and freight claim issues. Many LTL rates specify a particular type of box that is associated with a given rate. If the box of less durability is used, the carrier can charge a higher rate. Likewise, if the specified box is not used, the claim for damage can be denied because it resulted from an act of the shipper; that is, the shipper did not comply with the carrier's packaging requirement, which is an exception to carrier liability contained in the bill of lading contract or carriage.

Rate Analysis

Once the details of the shipment are known and the packaging issues are satisfied, the transportation process moves to the analysis of rates. More specifically, the transportation manager examines the cost of alternative shipment methods to accomplish the move with the desired service level. In the carrier costs and rates chapter (Chapter 9), attention is given to the various pricing bases carriers use in establishing rates and the resulting rates. In this section the freight cost is analyzed for alternative transportation methods and the accompanying rates.

It is often cheaper to use an express carrier rather than an LTL carrier for shipments weighing less than 400 pounds. Figure 13.4 contains the analysis for a 70-pound shipment from Alexandria, Virginia (zipcode, 22314), to Chicago, Illinois (zipcode, 60611). As the data in Figure 13.4 indicate, the cost of shipping a 70-pound package from Alexandria to Chicago ranges from \$20 to \$212. The LTL cost is based on the minimum charge without a shipper discount. The air express second-day delivery option is higher than the U.S. Postal Service charge, and the air express third-day delivery option is higher than the ground express service. The carrier selection decision will be based on the level of service required and the consistency of the carrier's service.

Another rate analysis that considers the size of the shipment examines the cost of shipping the product via LTL or using a TL carrier. Figure 13.5 contains an example of a 12,000-pound shipment of class 100 product from Atlanta to Chicago. The shipper

FIGURE 13.4 Small Shipment Rate Analysis Example

Shipment Specifics:
70 pounds in 24 x 112 x 12-inch box,
Value = \$50.00
Origin Zip = 22314; Destination Zip = 60611

Alternatives	Cost[a]
LTL[b]	**\$212**
Air Express:	
2nd -day Delivery	**\$75**
3rd -day Delivery	**\$65**
Ground Express[c]	**\$20**
U.S. Postal Service:	
2nd -day Delivery	**\$58**
4th -day Delivery	**\$21**

a) Average of different carriers.
b) Delivery time 3–4 days.
c) Delivery time 4–5 days.

FIGURE 13.5 Rate Analysis LTL vs. TL Carrier Example

Shipment Specifics:
Origin: Atlanta, GA — Destination: Chicago, IL
Weight: 12,000 pounds — Distance: 720 miles

Charges as LTL Shipment	Charges with Truckload Carrier
LTL Rate = $35.50/cwt.	Rate = $1.45/mile
Discount = 55%	Distance = 720 miles
Effective LTL Rate = $15.75	Charge = 720 miles @ $1.45
Charge = 120 cwt @ $15.75	= $1,044
= $1,890	

receives a 55-percent discount from the LTL carrier. The class 100 rate is $35.00 per cwt. and after the discount it is $15.75 per cwt. The TL rate is $1.45 per mile. The LTL charge is $1,890 and the TL carrier charge is $1,044. Even though the shipper does not have a full truckload, it is economical for the shipper to use a TL carrier and pay for the empty space. In addition, the transit time via the TL carrier may be less than that with the LTL carrier because the TL carrier will go directly to the destination, whereas the LTL carrier will bring the load to its terminal for consolidation.

The final function included in shipment analysis is **consolidation**. As noted in the preceding chapter, shippers follow a strategy of consolidating shipments so as to realize the lower freight rates associated with higher shipment quantities. This consolidation function can be performed for a single shipment or for multiple shipments. The pooling service offered by carriers permits the shipper to load multiple shipments going to the same general destination, where the carrier will break down and deliver the individual shipments to the respective consignees. Another multiple shipment consolidation practice is the stopping-in-transit service that permits the shipper to load two or more shipments into a trailer and the carrier stops along the way to drop off shipments to the respective consignees.

The consolidation of a single shipment is an application of the **weight break**. The weight break permits the shipper to be charged for more product than is being shipped, but at a lower rate than that applying to the actual quantity shipped. For example, if the rate for 2,000 to 4,999 pounds is $5.00 per cwt and for 5,000 to 10,000 pounds is $4.00 per cwt, the weight break is:

$$\$5.00\ (\text{WB cwt}) = \$4.00\ (50\ \text{cwt}),$$

where WB cwt is the cwt weight-break quantity

$$\text{WB cwt} = \$200/\$5.00/\text{cwt}$$

$$\text{WB cwt} = 40\ \text{cwt or } 4{,}000\ \text{pounds}$$

At 4,000 pounds, the charge for 4,000 pounds at $5.00 per cwt is $200, and the charge for 5,000 pounds at $4.00 per cwt is the same. For a 4,500-pound shipment, the shipper would be charged for 5,000 pounds at $4.00 per cwt ($200.00) and not for 4,500 pounds at $5.00 per cwt ($225.00). The shipper would save $25.00 or 11 percent.

Many sellers establish pricing discounts around the rate-break quantities. In the example above, a seller could establish one price for a 2,000-pound quantity and a lower one for a 5,000-pound quantity to correspond with the minimum quantities. Another pricing variation is to establish the price discount around the weight-break quantities, that is, a lower price exists for quantities above 4,000 pounds.

For shippers making numerous small package shipments via the postal service, a consolidation principle know as zone skipping can result in freight cost savings.

With **zone skipping**, the shipper, using a consolidator, bundles numerous shipments destined for an city, moves the bundled quantity to the postal system near the destination city, and the postal service delivers the packages to the respective consignees.

An example of zone skipping is in Figure 13.6. In this example the shipper would save $3,560, or 39.5 percent, by using zone skipping. The zone skipping cost is $5,440, which includes the consolidator and shipping cost from Atlanta to Chicago at $2.00 per mile and the postal delivery cost of $4.00 per package. The direct postal rate is $9.00 per package.

Carrier Scheduling

In the previous chapter, the various criteria used to select the mode and carrier were presented. In this section attention is given to the pragmatics of scheduling the carriers to handle the day-to-day shipments. The objective of carrier scheduling is to arrange

STOP OFF

Single-Shipment Pickups Will Cost Extra

If you are arranging to have a single LTL shipment picked up at one time and place, unaccompanied by any other shipment of any description from the same pickup site, more than likely the carrier making such a pickup will assess an additional charge.

Such additional charges range from a low of just under $10 to more than $20 per shipment. These extra fees vary considerably from motor carrier to motor carrier. You generally can find information about these additional charges in Item 885 of the LTL carrier's rules tariffs. They usually are titled something along the lines of "Single-Shipment Pickup Charge" or "Single-Shipment Payments."

Typically, these single-shipment pickup rules require the drivers to write or stamp such phrases or abbreviations as "Single Shipment," "Single," "One Shipment," "Only Shipment," "SS," or "S/S" on all copies of the bill of lading when such shipments are tendered to the motor carrier.

Some LTL carriers have instituted an additional provision stating that when the freight charges computed at the shipment's actual weight, using the applicable rate or rates plus the single-shipment pickup charge, exceed the freight charges computed at a weight of 500 pounds without the single-shipment charge, the latter rate basis will apply. Such provisions go on to state that in no case will the total freight bill be less than the applicable minimum charge plus the single-shipment pickup charge.

If you want to avoid paying single-shipment pickup charges, there are several ways you could do so. Hare some examples:

- A handful of LTL carriers do not assess a single-shipment pickup charge. One of these is Old Dominion Freight Line. Old Dominion only assesses such a charge when single shipments have been picked up by another carrier, as well as on Florida intrastate shipments.
- A motor carrier may not assess a single-shipment charge when shipments are tendered at the carrier's terminal by the consignor or the consignee's agent.
- Of course, if your shipments are picked up at the same time and place together with another shipment of any description originating from the same consignor, whether they are moving in interstate, intrastate, intracity, or foreign commerce to any destination within or beyond the territorial scope of the motor carrier' rules tariff, the single-shipment pickup charge would not apply.

And finally, don't overlook the fact that practically everything, including an additional charge like this one, can be negotiated. You might be able to get your LTL carrier to make an exception to its single-shipment rule for your account.

Source: Ray Bohman, "Single-shipment Pickups Will Cost Extra," *Logistics Management*, September 2003, p. 25. Reprinted with permission.

FIGURE 13.6 Zone Skipping Consolidation Example

Shipment Specifics:
Origin: Atlanta, GA Destination: Chicago, IL Distance: 720 miles
Shipment: 1,000 package weighing 10 pounds each

Direct Postal[a]	**Zone Skip**[a]
Rate = $9.00/package	Consolidator rate = $2.00/mile
Charge = 1,000 package @ $9.00	Consolidator Charge = $1,440
= $9,000	Local Postal rate = $4.00/package
	Postal Charge = 1,000 packages @ $4.00
	= $4,000
	Total Cost = $1,440 + $4,000
	= $5,440

[a] All rates assumed.

for a carrier to meet the shipper's transportation cost and service goals contained in the carrier selection decision. As indicated in Figure 13.1, the carrier scheduling techniques include core carriers, routing guides, approved carrier list, and intermediaries.

The **core carrier** concept is based on the principle of leveraging business volume to obtain desired cost and service. Shippers develop a cadre of core carriers, anywhere from 3 to 20 carriers, that are the prime providers of transportation service. These core carriers typically realize over 90 percent of the shipper's annual freight expenditure and are the first carriers the shipper contacts when there is a load to be moved.

The core carrier concept is ingrained with a degree of mutual dependency. The core carrier generally realizes a significant portion of its revenue from the shipper and is somewhat dependent on the shipper for its future viability. The shipper, likewise, focuses a large portion of its transportation requirements on a limited number of carriers, and is dependent on the core carriers to provide service. Both the core carrier and the shipper are dependent on the other: the shipper relies on the core carrier to move the loads and the core carrier relies on the shipper for a major source of its revenue.

Depending on the number of core carriers a shipper is using, the loss of one core carrier may result in a significant disruption of service to customers, plants, and warehouses. This is a common concern in the trucking industry which experiences thousands of bankruptcies per year. For example, many of the Internet and catalog retailers rely on FedEx, UPS, and USPS, with some retailers using a single carrier. For the single-source scenario, the loss of the carrier for any reason could spell disaster during a busy retailing season such as Christmas. If one of the three carriers discontinued service, a somewhat less disastrous impact would be felt by the retailer using all three.

The same dependency issues exist for a core carrier. The greater the portion of revenue coming from one shipper, the more dependent the carrier is on the shipper. For example, a small trucking company was a core carrier for a metal service center and realized over 95 percent of its revenue from the metal service center. After an analysis of its supply chain structure, the metal service center concluded it was switching to private trucking for delivery of its products. The metal service center's decision caused the small carrier to go into bankruptcy. Most larger transportation companies attempt to mitigate shipper revenue concentration by diversifying its shipper revenue base.

The core carrier concept provides some additional benefits to the shipper in the form of service compliance. The potential problems for the core carrier that does not provide the desired level of service is the loss of a significant portion of its revenue. This shipper leverage forces carrier compliance with the shipper's nonbasic service requests. For example, the establishment of EDI or Internet communication channels between the shipper and core carrier is much easier to obtain if the shipper has significant market power with the carrier. During the bid process, it is common for a shipper to stipulate that the core carrier will be required to maintain an Internet channel for load tendering, electronic load tracking, and satellite communication with the drivers. Because the volume of business is substantial, the core carriers are willing to comply.

To attain this carrier leverage across a large vendor base, companies utilize a **routing guide** that tells the vendor to use a carrier from a list of specified carriers. The routing guide is a matrix that tells the shipper which carrier to use for a given transportation link and focuses the inbound freight on a limited number of carriers. Figure 13.7 is an example of an LTL routing guide. From the carrier selection decision, four LTL core carriers, Yellow, Roadway, ABF and Con-Way, are the shipper's core LTL carriers. The routing guide is a quick reference to which carrier should be used for inbound and outbound moves between particular states. The carriers identified in the cell are the least-cost, best-service core carriers to use over the transportation link.

Figure 13.7 shows that for a movement from Ohio to New York the carrier of choice is Yellow Freight (YL). If Yellow Freight can not make the move, the next favorable carriers are Roadway Express (RD), Con-Way (CW) and Arkansas Best Freight (AB). In this example, the carriers are listed in order of priority based on cost and service. You will notice that from Indiana to New Jersey only two carrier are listed, Arkansas Best Freight and Roadway Express. The other two carriers either have unfavorable rates and/or service between Indiana and New York.

For inbound shipments the routing guide enables the buyer to control the inbound transportation and focus the inbound freight on its core carriers. The buyer instructs the vendor via the purchase order to utilize the routing guide and further informs the vendor that a penalty will be assessed for noncompliance. Many buyers have used the routing guide to concentrate inbound freight business on a limited number of carriers to gain lower freight costs and improved service.

The routing guide is useful for outbound shipments as well. Managers in charge of transportation at warehouses, distribution centers, and sales offices have a quick reference to which carrier to use for shipments to customers. The routing guide

FIGURE 13.7 LTL Routing Guide Example

	Origin State				
Destination State	IN	IL	KY	MI	OH
MD	CW YL	AB RD YL CW	RD YL CW	CW RD YL	RD YL CW AB
NJ	AB RD	AB RD YL CW	AB YL RD	CW RD AB	RD AB YL CW
NY	AB CW RD	AB CW RD YL	AB RD YL CW	CW YL AB RD	YL RD CW AB
PA	RD YL CW	CW YL RD	AB YL RD	CW RD YL AB	RD CW YL

AB = Arkansas Best Freight; CW = Con-Way; RD = Roadway Express;
YL = Yellow Freight.

helps corporate transportation managers gain control over decentralized operations by specifying acceptable carriers that the decentralized managers may schedule. This control helps leverage the corporate-wide freight spend to realize the desired transportation cost and services.

The approved carrier list is somewhat similar to the routing guide in that both provide a limited number of carriers from which to schedule the move. As indicated above, the routing guide provides a very limited number of carriers listed in order of priority; that is, the first carrier listed is the priority carrier, the second is next, and so on. The approved carrier list may have 8 to 10 carriers available for a given traffic lane, and the manager or vendor selects one of the listed carriers based on the carrier's performance at that facility.

For companies with numerous vendors, the approved carrier list allows the vendor to select the carrier that provides the best service at the vendor's location. At the same time, it enables the buyer to concentrate its inbound freight expenditure on 8 or 10 carriers, thereby increasing the buyer's transportation market power. Often times the buyer will include the approved carrier list as a condition in the purchase order.

Another carrier scheduling activity is the use of **intermediaries**. Intermediaries are noncarriers that are used by shippers to locate carriers to physically move the shipper's products. The classic intermediaries are the motor carrier freight broker and the railroad **intermodal marketing company (IMC)**. Shippers experiencing wide swings in demand for transportation find it difficult to establish long-term arrangements with carriers because there are periods throughout the year where there may be no demand for the carrier's service. The intermediary maintains contact with hundreds of carriers who have varying amounts of excess capacity and will bring together the shipper and a carrier that is available to haul the loads.

Hickory Farms, a producer and retailer of meat and cheese products in gift packages, experiences high demand during the Christmas season. From January to June, Hickory Farms' production and retail operations are very nominal, with production beginning in the summer for the Christmas season. With a very high concentration of sales in December, Hickory Farms may rely on freight brokers to get the necessary motor carriers to haul its products to its stores and mall kiosks. With such a concentrated demand period, the intermediary is a logical solution to scheduling carriers. Putting carriers under contract for only one or two months of the year would not be desirable to the carrier.

IMCs specialize in brokering piggyback service. The IMC buys large quantities of piggyback service from a railroad and sells it to shippers. Typically, the IMC buys the piggyback service from the railroad at a lower rate than that available to the shipper because the IMC buys large quantities, 50 to 60 piggyback cars per train. The IMC then acts in the capacity of a reseller of piggyback service and locates shippers needing the service.

The advantages of using an IMC are lower cost and better service. The IMC leverages its buying power to get a lower rate from the railroad and then passes some of the savings on to the shipper in the form of a lower rate than that charged by the railroad. Service benefits accrue to the shipper because the IMC is a one-stop operation, arranging for the pickup and delivery of the trailer to and from the railhead.

The final carrier scheduling activity is securing the type of equipment needed for the move. The type of equipment needed depends on the product's weight, length, width, height, temperature-control requirements, and customer service requirements. Heavy products requiring overhead cranes to load and unload, products such as the cement highway barriers, may dictate the use of flatbed or open top trailers or rail cars. Frozen foods necessitate the use of refrigerated equipment, whereas some products need equipment that can provide protection against cold or humidity. For low-density products, shippers request high cube equipment to maximize the amount of product the vehicle can transport. Finally, the customer may request a particular type of equipment because of physical or operational needs and the seller must comply.

Carrier scheduling difficulties arise from equipment needs, delivery location, and time of year. Not all carriers have unique equipment such as flatbed, refrigerated, tank, high-cube, and drop-frame equipment, thus placing a limitation on their availability compared to the standard van trailer. Certain regions of the country, such as the New York metropolitan area and South Florida, have heavier flow of product inbound than outbound, thereby creating excessive empty backhauls for the carriers. Carriers are reluctant to haul into a heavy inbound area because of the cost of returning the vehicle empty. Certain times of the year, such as the fall fruit harvest season, place great demands on refrigerated equipment and create equipment shortages. These and other operating constraints present daily challenges to the carrier scheduling function.

Load Tendering

Load tendering is the transportation management process that involves the offer and acceptance of the load, loading of the vehicle, and the attendant documentation. Figure 13.8 presents the different steps included in the load-tendering process. The process begins with the customer order or purchase order and ends with document preparation and vehicle loading.

From the customer or purchase order the transportation manager knows the load requirements and determines which carriers should be offered the load. The load offer can take the form of a phone call to the carrier, a fax, an e-mail, or an EDI transmission. The most common methods of offering the load are the phone and fax, but great strides are being made to utilize the electronic methods. The carrier accepting the offer will provide a formal acceptance via the transmission methods noted above and, depending on the shipper and carrier operating policies, may formally decline. The typical method of declining a load offer is no positive response; that is, if the carrier does not accept the load within a preset time limit the assumption is the carrier declines the load.

FIGURE 13.8 Load-Tendering Process

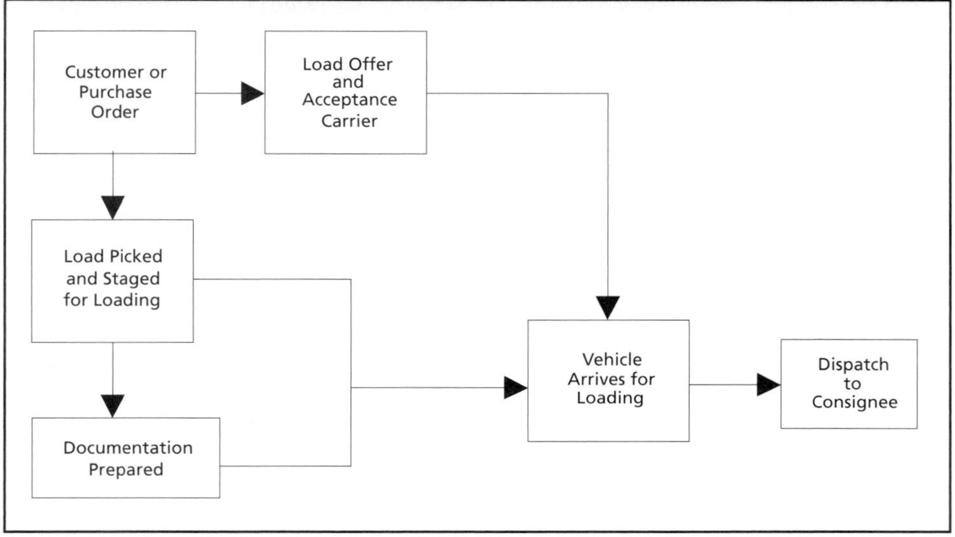

Once the carrier accepts the load, the shipper arranges a pickup appointment. The pickup appointment is becoming more critical today because revised driver hours-of-service rules count all waiting times as on-duty time. The pickup appointment also allows the shipper to level the workload at the warehouse and loading dock. The pickup schedule must provide sufficient time for the carrier to arrive at the pickup location and for the shipper to pick, pack, and stage the load.

Today, consignees are requiring the carrier to make a delivery appointment. This requirement and the consignee contact information are conveyed to the carrier at the time the load is accepted, giving the carrier sufficient time to contact the consignee and arrange a delivery time based on the scheduled loading time and driving time to destination.

The next step in the process is picking, packing, and staging the order. The order is picked from existing inventory or the items are produced for the order. In the Dell model, a product is produced after the customer places the order. When the order is picked, it is packed for shipment. In most operations, the items in an order are placed in a box or on a pallet along with packaging material to protect the shipment while in transit. The final step is to stage the load near the loading dock for quick loading when the truck arrives.

After the items are picked and staged, the final step in the process is the preparation of the shipping documentation. The documentation includes the **bill of lading** and packing or pick slip. These documents will be discussed in more detail below. After the vehicle is loaded and the documentation is prepared, the vehicle moves to the consignee's location for delivery.

Documentation

The most common domestic shipping document is the bill of lading. The bill of lading is the beginning of an interstate transportation shipment, unless the shipper and carrier have signed a long-term transportation contract that stipulates otherwise. It is the document that provides the carrier with the information necessary for the carrier to complete the move, and it governs the move. For interstate shipments, the carrier is responsible for completing the bill of lading, but the common practice is for the shipper to complete it. Because the shipper has all the information, it is more efficient for the shipper to prepare the document for the carrier's agent to sign at the time of pickup.

The bill of lading serves the following purposes:

- Receipt for the goods tendered to the carrier
- Provides shipment information
- Contract of carriage
- In the case of an order, bill of lading acts as certificate of title to the goods.

When the carrier's agent (driver) signs the bill of lading, the carrier has agreed that it has received the items itemized on the document. The signed bill of lading is the shipper's receipt that the carrier has taken possession of the goods named on it. If damage occurs to the shipment, the bill of lading provides proof of what was given to the carrier and the condition of the goods (assumed to be in good condition unless specified otherwise).

As noted in Figure 13.9, the bill of lading provides the carrier with the shipping information such as the name, address, and contact information for the shipper and consignee. In addition, the bill of lading may contain any special delivery instructions or directions.

The bill of lading contains the transportation contract terms (discussed below) governing the move. These terms are typically printed on the back of the bill of lading in rather fine print. It should be noted that the transportation contract terms of the bill of lading can be set aside by the terms contained in a long-term transportation contract signed by the shipper and carrier.

STRAIGHT BILL OF LADING

The bill of lading can be either a straight bill of lading or an order bill of lading. The straight bill of lading is a nonnegotiable instrument, which means title can not be transferred by endorsement. The terms of sale between the seller and buyer dictate where title to the goods passes to the buyer. The carrier delivers to the person named as consignee on the bill of lading and does not require presentation of the original copy of the straight bill of lading as a condition to delivery. The straight bill of lading does not act as certificate of title.

ORDER BILL OF LADING

The order bill of lading is a negotiable instrument and acts as a certificate of title to the goods named on it. Title to the goods remains with the seller until the goods are delivered to the person surrendering to the carrier the properly endorsed original copy of the order bill of lading. A sight draft is normally attached to the original copy of the order bill of lading and sent to the buyer's bank. Upon payment of the sight draft (the value of the shipment), the bank gives the buyer the properly endorsed, original copy of the order bill of lading and the buyer presents this to the carrier for delivery. The carrier is held liable for the goods if it delivers to someone other than the person who surrenders the original copy of the order bill of lading.

CONTRACT TERMS

The primary bill of lading contract-of-carriage terms govern carrier liability for loss and damage. These major liability terms are as follows:

1. ***Common carrier liability.*** The carrier is held liable for all loss, damage, or delay to the goods except for:
    a. Act of God—loss resulting from an unavoidable catastrophe. The catastrophe must be unavoidable for the carrier to claim an exception to liability. If the carrier could have avoided the catastrophe, then the carrier is liable for damage.
    b. Act of public enemy—loss resulting from armed aggression against the United States.
    c. Act of shipper—loss resulting from the actions of a shipper such as improper loading or packaging or concealment of the nature of the goods being shipped.
    d. Act of public authority—loss resulting from a public agency seizing and or destroying the goods by due process of law.
    e. Inherent nature of the goods—loss that is normal or expected such as evaporation.
2. *Reasonable dispatch.* The carrier is required to move the shipment with reasonable dispatch, and the shipper can hold the carrier liable for actual

FIGURE 13.9 Bill of Lading

7-30-4 ; 12:57PM ; :4194245222 # 1/ 1

Hancor

STRAIGHT BILL OF LADING--ORIGINAL--NOT NEGOTIABLE

NAME OF CARRIER	CARRIER'S NO.
J.B.HUNT TRANSPORT INC-	2040823
BILL OF LADING NO. 0 OC	ORDER NO. 63956
CUSTOMER PO	PICK SLIP NO. 0

FROM AT Ohio South Plant (09)
P.O. Box 1047
12370 Jackson TR 172
Findlay, OH 45839

DATE 11/19/03

the property described below, in apparent good order, except as noted (contents and condition of contents unknown), marked, consigned, and destined as indicated below, which said carrier (the word carrier being understood throughout the contract as meaning any person or corporation in possession of the property under the contract) agrees to carry to its usual place of delivery at said destination, if on its route, otherwise to deliver to another carrier on the route to said destination. It is mutally agreed, as to each carrier of all or any of said property over all or any portion of said route to destination, and as to each party at any time interested in all or any of said property that every service to performed hereunder shall be subject to all terms and conditions of the Uniform Straight Bill of Lading set forth (1) in Official, Southern, Western and Illinois Freight Classifications in effect on the date hereof, if this is a rail or rail-water shipment, or (2) in the applicable motor carrier classification or tariff if this is a motor carrier shipment.

Shipper hereby certifies that he is familiar with all the terms and conditions of the said bill of lading, including those on the back hereof set forth in the classification or tariff which governs the transportation of this shipment, and the said terms and conditions are hereby agreed to by the shipper and accepted for himself and his assigns.

(MAIL OR STREET ADDRESS OF CONSIGNEE--FOR PURPOSES OF NOTIFICATION ONLY)

CONSIGNED TO AND DESTINATION Hancor, Inc.
Hancor, Inc.
6001 Belmore Street, S.W.
P.O. Box 352
Olympia WA 98507

(*TO BE FILLED IN ONLY WHEN SHIPPER DESIRES AND GOVERNING TARIFFS PROVIDE FOR DELIVERY THERE AT)

ROUTE

Delivering Address *

DELIVERING CARRIER	CAR OR VEHICLE INITALS & NO.
J.B.HUNT TRANSPORT INC-	

No. Shipping Units	Haz. Mat.	Kind of Packaging, Description of Articles, Special Marks and Exceptions PLASTIC CORRUGATED PIPE AND/OR FITTINGS	*WEIGHT (SUBJECT TO CORR.)	CLASS OR RATE	CHECK COLUMN
63		04" SL F477 PERF 20	547 LB		
60		06" SL F477 PERF 20	1,193 LB		
1250		03" INTERNAL COUPLER 50BG	153 LB		
400		03" ELL 25BG	83 LB		
500		04" ELL 25BG	157 LB		
2800		04" TEE 25BG	1,061 LB		
100		06"X04" REDR 20BG	36 LB		
160		12" HI-Q COUPLER W/GSK 5BD	238 LB		
50		24" HI-Q COUPLER W/GSK 5BD	391 LB		
1200		02"X03"X03" DOWNSPOUT ADPT 50B	177 LB		

Subject to Section 7 of conditions of applicable bill of lading, if this shipment is to be delivered to the consignee without recourse on the consignor, the consignor shall sign the following statement.
The carrier shall not make delivery of this shipment without payment of freight and all other lawful charges.

Per

(Signature of Consignor)

If charges are to be prepaid, write or stamp here, "To be Prepaid."

Received $
to apply in prepayment of the charge on the property described hereon.

Agent or Cashier

Per
(The signature here acknowledges only the amount prepaid)

Charges Advanced
$

This is to certify that the above named articles are properly classified, described, packaged, marked and labeled and are in proper condition for transportation according to the applicable regulations of the Department of Transportation. If the shipment moves between two ports by a carrier by water, the law requires that the bill of lading shall state whether it is "carrier's or shipper's weight."
Shipper's imprints in lieu of stamp, not a part of Bill of Lading approved by the Department of Transportation.
NOTE--Where the rate is dependent on value, shippers are required to state specifically in writing the agreed or declared value of the property.
**The fibre containers used for the shipment conforms to the specifications set forth in the box maker's certificate, thereon, and all other requirements of Rule41 of the Uniform Freight Classification and Rule 5 of the National Motor Freight Classification.

THIS SHIPMENT IS CORRECTLY DESCRIBED. CORRECT WEIGHT IS LBS	The agreed or declared value of the property is hereby specifically stated by the shipper to be not exceeding per

Bill To:
Hancor, Inc.
Attention: Accounts Payable
P. O. Box 1047
Findlay, OH 45839-1047

Shipper Hancor, Inc. Agent JBHunt 11-19-03
Per
Customer Signature

Page 1

Source: Courtesy of Hancor, Inc., Findlay, Ohio.

loss or damage if the there is unreasonable delay in transit. There is no specific rule defining reasonable or unreasonable dispatch. The shipment specifics determine if the delay in transit was unreasonable under given circumstances.

3. *Articles of extraordinary value.* The carrier is not obligated to carry documents or articles of extraordinary value unless the carrier's tariff specifically rates such an item.
4. *No recourse.* If the shipper signs the no recourse clause, the carrier has no recourse back to the shipper for additional charges once delivery has been made. With the no recourse executed, the carrier's only recourse for additional freight charges after delivery is the consignee.

It should be noted that there are numerous rules contained in the carrier's rules tariff and in transportation contracts signed by a shipper and carrier. These rules may take precedence over the bill of lading terms, and the transportation manager must be aware of these additional terms and their impact on carrier liability.

For example, after enactment of the ICC Termination Act many motor carriers set limits on the maximum liability for damage. Some motor carriers implemented a maximum liability limit of $50,000 per shipment, even though the bill of lading stipulates the carrier is liable for the full value of the shipment. In addition, motor carriers have set limits on a per pound basis, one common example being $2.50 per pound. With these tariff limits in place, the shipper with a $100,000 shipment damage will receive a maximum of $50,000 and a shipper with a $3.00 per pound shipment damage will receive only $2.50 per pound. Freight claims are discussed in more detail in a subsequent section.

Shipment Monitoring

As noted in Figure 13.1 the shipment-monitoring function involves **tracing**/expediting, customer communication, and vendor communication. In essence, shipment monitoring is watching the progress of the shipment through the transportation system and communicating the status or problems to the customer or vendor. The widespread adoption of the Internet and GPS (Global Positioning System) has greatly enhanced the performance capabilities of carriers with regard to shipment monitoring.

Tracing involves determining where the shipment is at a given moment in time. With GPS, a carrier can determine within a few yards the exact location of a vehicle and the corresponding shipment. The trucking and air cargo industries have rapidly adopted these technologies. Water carriers, ports, and global intermediaries are quickly adopting these technologies at the insistence of the global shipper who wants to have product visibility throughout the global supply chain.

FedEx and UPS are prime examples of carriers with state-of-the-art electronic tracing capabilities. The shipper enters the airway bill number and the carrier's tracking system tells the shipper where the shipment is and gives some indication of when it will reach the consignee. The systems can tell the shipper when it was delivered and who signed for receipt of the shipment.

Once the shipment is traced and its location is noted, the **expediting** function attempts to hurry the shipment along to delivery. The steps include working with the carrier to attempt a correction in the normal movement process so the shipment can be delivered earlier. For example, a container was being moved through the port of Montreal to the UK. Using the carrier's tracking system, the shipper determined the container was at the port and was then able to have the carrier place the container on the next vessel sailing for UK instead of the scheduled sailing date in 6 days.

Customer and vendor communications are the next logical step in the shipment-monitoring process. If the shipment is going to be delayed, it is incumbent on the shipper to inform the consignee of the delay so the consignee can take appropriate actions. For example, by communicating to the buyer a delay in a shipment of raw materials, the buyer can place an expedited order (using expedited transportation) to guard against a stockout and plant shutdown. Likewise, retailers can place expedited orders to reduce lost sales resulting from a delayed shipment of a fast-selling item.

Some carriers have developed electronic notification of intransit delays and problems. A refrigerated motor carrier monitors the temperature in the trailer and notifies the shipper electronically if the temperature varies beyond the established tolerance limits. Other carriers have monitors that notify the shipper if the trailer doors are opened in transit. Lastly, GPS transponders attached to transport equipment can assist security officials to recover hijacked equipment because the GPS location of the stolen equipment and cargo is immediately known.

Postdelivery Maintenance

The postdelivery maintenance functions begin once the shipment is delivered, and are designed to make certain the shipment was delivered, cargo damage or loss is recovered, the correct freight charge is paid, and the carrier's performance is within acceptable limits. The specific functions include proof of delivery, claims, freight bill auditing, and performance measurement.

PROOF OF DELIVERY

The **proof of delivery** is verification provided by the carrier that the shipment was delivered. The verification is a delivery receipt signed by the consignee. Typically, the proof of delivery is the delivery copy of the bill of lading. Some carriers use a special delivery form.

There are two primary reasons for the proof of delivery receipt. First, the carrier must show that delivery was made and the consignee received the shipment to prevent a liability claim for nondelivery. Without this proof of delivery, the carrier could be held liable for the entire value of the shipment. The bill of lading indicates the items picked up by the carrier and the proof of delivery verifies the delivery of the items.

The second reason is for the seller to support or deny a buyer's credit request for missing items or nonreceipt of the shipment. By having a signed proof of delivery receipt, the seller can refute the buyer's request and indicate the person who received the shipment and the absence of a notation indicating missing items.

CLAIMS

When a shipment is delivered with items damaged or missing, the shipper or consignee files a claim with the carrier to recover the loss. Figure 13.10 provides an overview of the **freight claims process**. The FOB term of sale determines who is legally obligated to file the claim that is determined by the terms of sale. As noted above, the terms of sale indicates where the title passes to the buyer. Prior to the point where the title passes to the buyer, the seller is the owner and is required to file the claim. For example, under an FOB-Origin term of sale, the title passes to the buyer at the shipment

FIGURE 13.10 Freight Claim Process

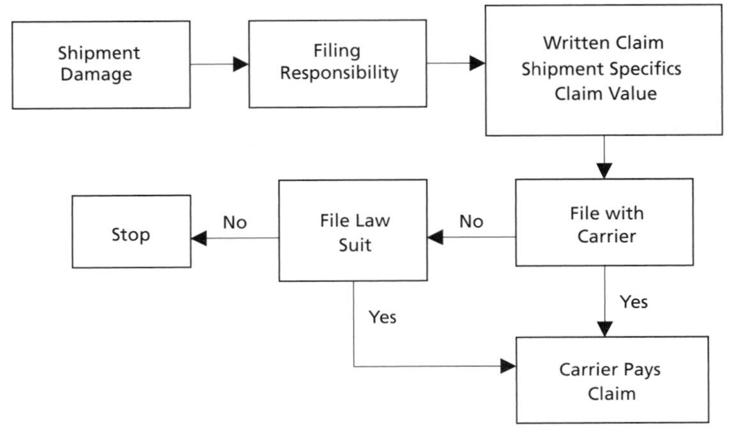

origin and the buyer would have responsibility to file the claim. The seller is responsible for claim filing with the FOB-Delivered term of sale.

In the documentation section above, it is noted the carrier is liable for all loss and damage to the shipment with the exceptions noted. Carrier tariff rules or shipper–carrier long-term transportation contracts may impact these liability rules. The most common variation is the motor carrier liability limitations on the total value of one loss or the liability value per pound.

Figure 13.11 shows the many different levels of liability coverage possible for a motor carrier. The range is from full-value liability with the bill of lading terms to zero liability with a shipper–carrier transportation contract. The other liability levels are associated with carrier tariff rules and rates. For example, the maximum liability and limited liability per-pound coverage is found in a carrier rule tariff, whereas the shipper released value level is found in the carrier's rate tariff. The limited package liability is an international water carrier regulation.

The freight claim is a written request the shipper files with the carrier requesting reimbursement for monetary losses resulting from loss, damage, or delay to the shipment or for payment overcharge. The claim can be filed with the originating, delivering, or intermediate carrier or with the carrier on whose line the damage occurred.

Damage may be either visible or concealed. Visible damage is discovered by the consignee usually at delivery and before opening the package. Concealed damage is detected after the package is opened. Concealed damage poses a unique problem in determining when the damage occurred—in the carrier's or consignee's possession. Some carriers require concealed damage claims to be filed within 15 days of delivery. This early filing deadline does not overrule the statutory filing deadline of 9 months for common carrier railroads and regulated motor carriers.

FIGURE 13.11 Motor Carrier Liability Coverage

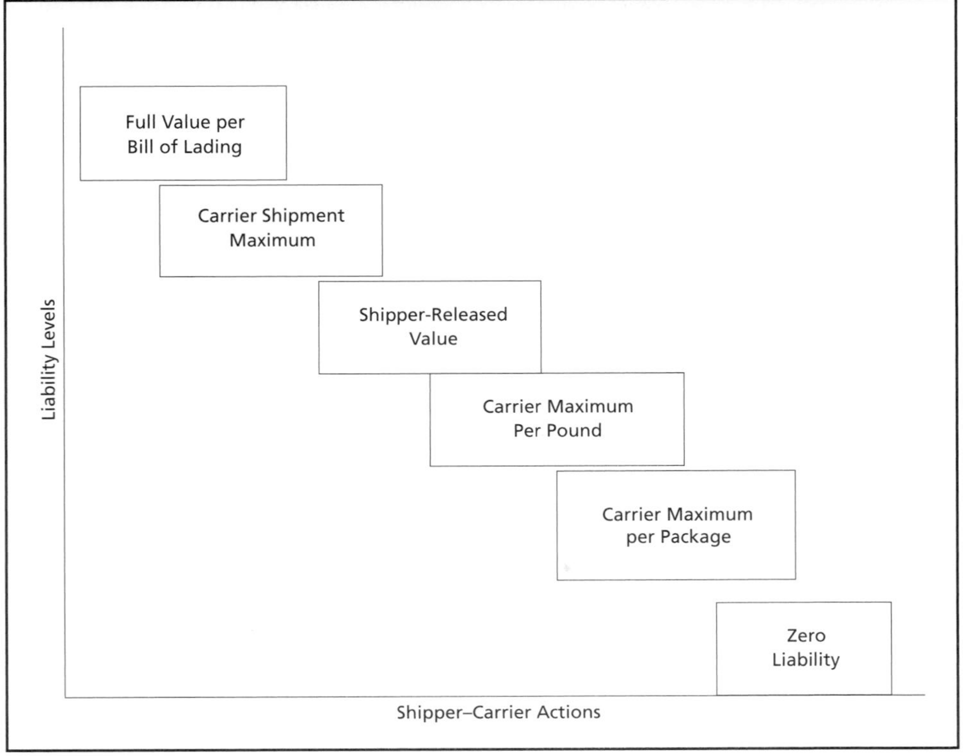

The claim must provide the shipment specifics including the shipper, consignee, date, and commodities. This information is the same as that included in the bill of lading governing the move. The claim should include a copy of the bill of lading to show the shipment was made and that the shipment was in good condition when picked up by the carrier (a clean bill of lading). The delivery copy of the bill of lading with damage noted should be included to indicate the shipment arrived in a damaged condition (a dirty bill of lading). A clean bill of lading at origin and a dirty bill of lading at destination are a *prima facia* case that the carrier damaged the goods and the burden of proof is on the carrier to prove that it is not liable for the damage.

The last piece of supporting documentation for the claim is an indication of value at destination. The principle in determining the value of the damaged shipment is to make the claimant whole again, that is, to place the claimant in the same position had the shipment arrived undamaged. An indication of value could be an invoice, catalog, or price list. For one-of-a-kind items not having a market value, the claimant may use cost accounting records. Some products have a wide variation in value, such as household goods, and an appraisal is required to show the value of the damaged items. If the shipper has opted for a released-value rate, the carrier's liability is limited to the released value selected by the shipper.

In the air transportation industry the liability limit for domestic shipments is a released value of 50¢ per pound per article. For international air shipments, the liability limit is $9.07 per pound. By specifying a higher value per pound and paying a fee, a shipper can obtain higher air carrier liability. International water carriers have a liability limit of $500 per package. If on the ocean bill of lading the shipment is described as one 40-foot container of computers and the shipment is destroyed, the water carrier is liable for $500 or one package (the container). To get full coverage for the computers, the bill of lading description should state the number of boxes of computers in the container.

The basic common carrier time frame for filing a motor carrier and railroad claim is 9 months from delivery. Air carriers have no industry-wide time limit for filing claims; each carrier has its own claim-filing time limit, ranging from 30 days to 9 months and 9 days. Some ocean carriers require the shipper to notify the carrier within a few days after delivery of the intent to file a claim. For air and water carriers, the shipper must consult the individual carriers rules tariffs regarding the time frame for filing a claim.

Once the claim is filed, the carrier can agree to pay the claim or deny the claim as indicated in Figure 13.10. If the carrier agrees to pay, the carrier will forward the appropriate amount to the claimant. It is not uncommon to find a carrier accepting liability for the damage but negotiating a payment value that is lower than the amount requested in the claim.

If the carrier denies the claim, the claimant must examine the rationale for the denial. All contested claims are ultimately resolved in court. To gain legal resolution to the denied claim, the claimant must file a lawsuit within 2 years from the date the claim is denied by the carrier. This is a costly endeavor, and the value of the claim must warrant the legal fees and time involved.

Another, less costly option to claim disputes is arbitration. The shipper and carrier agree to accept the arbitration decision based on written statements from each party. Agencies such as the American Arbitration Association and Better Business Bureau provide arbitration services.

Most companies analyze their freight claims in an attempt to prevent future claims. Such an analysis examines the carrier, shipper, receiver, product, shipment date, and packaging to determine a cause. It could be a carrier that has a poor freight-handling system or a package material that does not provide the needed protection. There could be a concentration of claims with a few buyers, indicating the need to educate the buyer on correct product-handling procedures. The goal of the claim analysis is to determine the cause of claims and to take corrective actions.

FREIGHT BILL AUDITING

Freight bill auditing is used to assess the correct amount to be paid to the carrier. This is typically done after payment; that is, the audit is performed after the original freight bill is paid. The postpayment audit process focuses on verification of the freight bill paid by confirming the following:

- The shipment was actually made.
- The freight bill was not paid previously.
- The shipment weight, freight rate, and calculation was noted.
- The ancillary services were requested and provided.
- The lowest tariff or contract rate was used.

The prepayment audit process audits the carrier's freight bill before payment. The steps are similar to those identified above for the postpayment, except the steps are performed before payment is made to the carrier. If the shipment volume is small, the prepayment audit can be performed manually. However, if the shipment volume is large, a manual prepayment audit may result in the shipper incurring a carrier's late payment fee. Large-volume shippers are using computers to calculate the freight charge for a shipment, compare the calculated freight charge with the freight bill submitted by the carrier, and resolve any discrepancies before payment.

A novel approach to freight bill auditing is to have the shipper calculate the freight charges, pay the carrier, and have the carrier perform the audit. This approach has been quite successful when combined with a long-term carrier contract that has a simplified rate base. For example, a shipper–carrier contract may specify the rate base in terms of cost per mile. Using mileage software, the distance between the shipping points is determined and the appropriate rate for the distance is calculated from the mileage rate table. The shipper calculates the charges and pays the carrier. The carrier then audits the shipper's payment for exceptions such as ancillary services provided or out-of-route miles caused by shipper diversion decisions.

PERFORMANCE MEASUREMENT

The final postdelivery maintenance function is measuring the carrier's performance. As shown in Table 13.1, carrier performance measurement considers both cost and service. The most widely used cost measurements are freight cost as a percentage of

Table 13.1 Transportation Performance Measurements

Transportation Cost	Transportation Service
Cost as percent total sales	Percent on-time pickup
Cost per unit	Percent on-time delivery
Cost per weight unit	Average transit time
Cost per order	Percent damaged shipments
Cost per ton-mile	Damage value per total sales
Cost per cube shipped	Percent Billing error
Cost per mile	

sales, cost per unit sold, cost per weight unit, and cost per order. These cost measurements match the base units used by top management, sales, and purchasing for control. For example, top management is interested in a quick measure of the portion of the sales dollar incurred for the transportation process. Sales is interested in the transportation cost per unit sold or per order to set the appropriate price for the product. Purchasing is concerned with the freight cost per weight unit, a common purchasing unit.

The cost per mile is widely used by firms that have private truck fleets to measure the performance of the private fleet against for-hire carriers. The cost per ton-mile is appropriate for shipping situations that have fluctuating shipping distances and weight. The cost per cube shipped is often used in water and air transportation situations in which the freight charges are based on the amount of cubic feet shipped. This latter cost measurement can be helpful in analyzing containers and private fleet equipment utilization.

The service performance measurements are based on the carrier selection criteria discussed in the previous chapter. On-time pickup and delivery and average transit time are the three most widely utilized service performance measures. Late pickups and deliveries impact the shipper and consignee warehouse-operating costs, as well as inventory and stockout costs. The average transit time also impacts inventory and stockout costs and the seller's level of customer service.

Shipment damage considers the percentage of shipments experiencing damage via a particular carrier and the damage value as a percentage of total sales. These two damage measurements provide an indication of the degree of poor service provided to the seller's customer and of the magnitude of the cargo loss and damage. Percentage of billing errors focuses on the amount of auditing that must be performed on the carrier's freight bills. If the percentage of error is high, the shipper must devote more resources to the freight bill auditing function.

The domestic transportation management process integrates a number of interrelated functions that are designed to implement the transportation strategy of a shipper. The next section examines the global transportation process.

GLOBAL TRANSPORTATION PROCESS

From the shipper's perspective, the management of international transportation involves the planning, implementation, and control of the procurement and use of freight transportation and related service providers to achieve company objectives. Managing the international transportation process is more complex than that of domestic transportation because of the many differences between the trading nations' transportation and customs regulations, infrastructure, exchange rates, culture, and language.

Figure 13.12 depicts the international transportation process. It begins with the buyer–seller agreement and the management areas of order preparation, transportation, and documentation. Each of these process elements is discussed below.

Buyer–Seller Agreement

The agreement between the buyer and seller determines the specific transportation criteria the seller must meet. These criteria include the product to be shipped, financial terms, delivery requirements (date and location), packing, the transportation method(s) to be used, and cargo insurance. In addition, the **INCOTERMS** agreed upon delineate the transportation responsibility between the buyer and seller.

FIGURE 13.12 Global Transportation Process

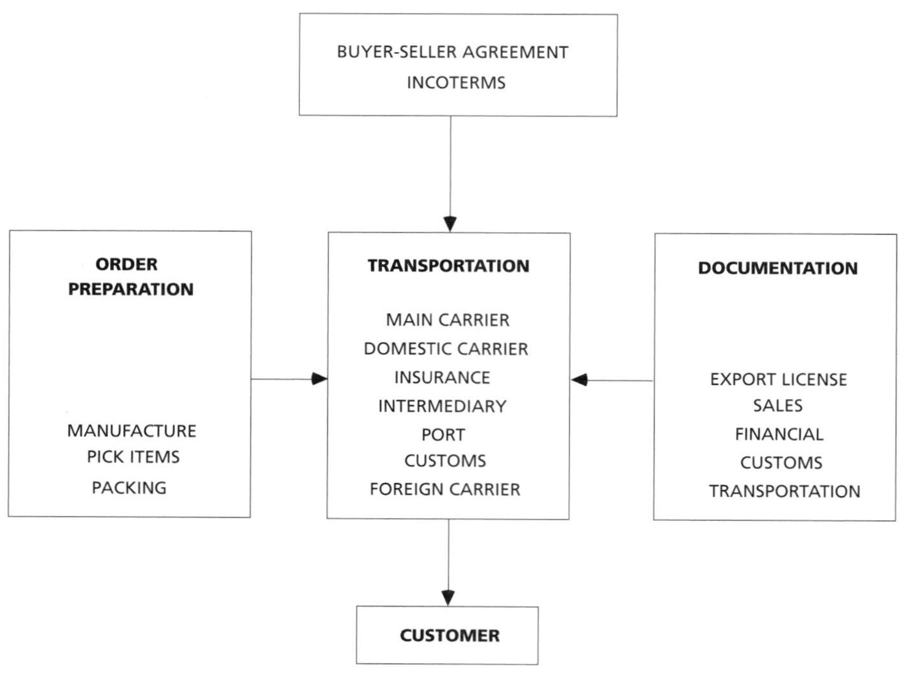

STOP OFF

When 'All Inclusive' Isn't Necessarily the Case

Have you ever been uneasy about importing costs? Do you always feel confident that your broker has supplied you with enough information so you cover every cost associated with receiving items from overseas?

You have a right to be concerned. There are more than 10 different potential costs associated with importing goods via ocean into the United States, and knowing them all is necessary for performing a proper cost/benefit analysis.

First, there are two distinct ways to quote an ocean shipment: all-water service (AWS) and mini-land bridge (MLB). An AWS quote is from the origin port to a port closest to the final destination. The primary benefit of AWS is that it tends to produce the lowest total transportation cost. The disadvantage of AWS is that transit time is longer than MLB by up to 10 days, depending on the final destination.

An MLB quote is from the origin port to the closest destination port. MLB offers the shortest total transit time because ocean transit time is minimized. The disadvantage is the total transportation cost is typically the higher of the two services. Obviously, the method that best fits your needs will depend on the demand and price you and your customers are willing to pay.

The responsibility for the costs associated with importing goods will shift between buyer and seller depending on the INCOTERMS agreed upon for the transaction. It is essential for the buyer/importer of record to be knowledgeable about all the related terms used in the transaction.

An apparent "all-inclusive price" my not be all inclusive. For instance, brokerage fees, merchandise processing fees, and harbor maintenance fees are likely not to be included in the quoted price. Be sure to ask whether or not these costs are included in the transportation quote. Other fees that should be questioned and discussed are crane charges (for loading and unloading of containers, separate from loading/unloading fees), bunker surcharges (fuel surcharge), and document-handling fees.

It is very easy to get overwhelmed by different fees that may apply to your import. Being well informed and asking your broker the right questions can prevent costly surprises.

Source: Meredith Bulkley and Gary LaPoint, "When 'All Inclusive' Isn't Necessarily The Case," *Inbound Logistics*, October 2003, p. 48.

INCOTERMS[1]

The international terms of sale are known as **INCOTERMS.** Unlike domestic terms of sale, in which the buyers and sellers primarily use FOB-origin and FOB-destination terms, there are 13 different INCOTERMS. Developed by the International Chamber of Commerce, these INCOTERMS are internationally accepted rules defining trade terms.

The INCOTERMS define responsibilities of both the buyer and seller in any international contract of sale. For exporting, the terms delineate buyer or seller responsibility for the following:

- Export packing cost
- Inland transportation (to the port of export)
- Export clearance
- Vessel or plane loading
- Main transportation cost
- Cargo insurance
- Customs duties
- Risk of loss or damage in transit

E TERMS

The E terms consist of one INCOTERM, Ex Works (EXW). This is a departure contract that gives the buyer total responsibility for the shipment. The seller's responsibility is to make the shipment available at its facility. The buyer agrees to take possession of the shipment at the point of origin and to bear all of the cost and risk of transporting the goods to the destination (see Figure 13.13 for additional responsibilities of the E Terms).

F TERMS

The three F terms obligate the seller to incur the cost of delivering the shipment cleared for export to the carrier designated by the buyer. The buyer selects and incurs the cost of main transportation, insurance, and customs clearance. **Free Carrier (FCA)** can be used with any mode of transportation. Risk of damage is transferred to the buyer when the seller delivers the goods to the carrier named by the buyer.

Free Alongside Ship (FAS) is used for water transportation shipments only. The risk of damage is transferred to the buyer when the goods are delivered alongside the ship. The buyer must pay the cost of "lifting" the cargo or container on board the vessel. **Free On Board (FOB)** is used for only water transportation shipments.

The risk of damage is transferred to the buyer when the shipment crosses the ship's rail (when the goods are actually loaded on the vessel). The seller pays the lifting charge (see Figure 13.13 for additional responsibilities on the F Terms).

FIGURE 13.13 Summary of INCOTERMS Cost Obligations

Cost or Activity	EXW	FCA	FAS	FOB	CFR	CIF	CPT	CIP	DAF	DES	DEQ	DDU	DDP
Export Packing	**B**	S	S	S	S	S	S	S	S	S	S	S	S
Export Clearance	**B**	S	S	S	S	S	S	S	S	S	S	S	S
Inland Transport (Domestic)	**B**	S	S	S	S	S	S	S	S	S	S	S	S
Vessel/Plane Loading	**B**	**B**	**B**	S	S	S	S	S	S	S	S	S	S
Main Transport	**B**	**B**	**B**	**B**	S	S	S	S	S	S	S	S	S
Cargo Insurance	**B**	**B**	**B**	**B**	**B**	S	**B**	S	S	S	S	S	S
Customs Duties	**B**	**B**	**B**	**B**	**B**	**B**	**B**	**B**	**B**	**B**	S	**B**	S
Inland Transport (Foreign)	**B**	**B**	**B**	**B**	**B**	**B**	**B**	**B**	**B**	**B**	**B**	**B**	S
Mode Applicability	X	X	W	W	W	W	X	X	X	W	W	X	X

B = **B**uyer; S = Seller; W = Water Carrier; X = Air, Motor, Rail, Intermodal.

C TERMS

The four C terms are shipment contracts that obligate the seller to obtain and pay for the main carriage and/or cargo insurance. **Cost and Freight (CFR)** and **Carriage Paid To (CPT)** are similar in that both obligate the seller to select and pay for the main carriage (ocean or air to the foreign country). CFR is only used for shipments by water transportation, whereas CPT is used for any mode. In both terms, the seller incurs all costs to the port of destination. Risk of damage passes to the buyer when the goods pass the ship's rail, CFR, or when delivered to the main carrier, CPT.

Cost, Insurance, Freight (CIF) and **Carriage and Insurance Paid To (CIP)** require the seller to pay for both main carriage and cargo insurance. The risk of damage is the same as that for CFR and CPT (see Figure 13.13 for additional responsibilities of the C Terms).

D TERMS

The D terms obligate the seller to incur all costs related to delivery of the shipment to the foreign destination. There are five D terms; two apply to water transportation only and three to any mode used. All five D terms require the seller to incur all costs and the risk of damage up to the destination port.

Delivered At Frontier (DAF) means the seller is responsible for transportation and incurs the risk of damage to the named point at the place of delivery at the frontier of the destination country. For example, DAF, Laredo, Texas, indicates the seller is responsible for making the goods available at Laredo, Texas. The buyer is responsible for customs duties and clearance into Mexico. DAF can be used with all modes.

Delivered Ex Ship (DES) and **Delivered Ex Quay (or wharf) (DEQ)** are used with shipments by water transportation. Both terms require the seller to pay for the main carriage. Under DES, risk of damage is transferred when the goods are made available to the buyer on board the ship uncleared for import at the port of destination.

The buyer is responsible for customs clearance. With DEQ, risk of damage is transferred to the buyer when the goods cleared for import are unloaded onto the quay (wharf) at the named port of destination.

Delivered Duty Unpaid (DDU) and **Delivered Duty Paid (DDP)** are available for all modes. DDU requires the seller to incur all cost, except import duties, to the named place in the country of importation. Risk of damage passes to the buyer when the goods are made available, duties unpaid, at the named place. (DDU is similar to DES.) DDP imposes the same obligations on the seller as DDU, plus the additional responsibility of clearing the goods for import and paying the customs duties. (DDP is similar to DEQ.) See Figure 13.13 for additional responsibilities of the D Terms.

Order Preparation

Order preparation involves either picking items ordered from inventory or manufacturing them. In either case, the seller must make sure the item prepared for shipping matches exactly what is ordered. Failure to comply with the product specifications contained in the buyer's purchase order indicates the buyer's refusal to accept the shipment or to pay the invoice.

Packing for international water shipments is usually more stringent than for domestic shipments because of the increased potential for damage. Shippers typically use an export packing company to pack the shipment for the rigors of frequent handling, lifting, and storage, as well as the rough ride of international water carriage.

For international air shipments, the domestic packing is usually sufficient.

Documentation

Global shipment movement is controlled by paper; without proper documentation the shipment does not move. A missing or incorrect document can delay a shipment and/or prevent the shipment from entering a country. These documents are governed by the customs regulations of the shipping and receiving nations.

Substantial improvements have been made to computerize the documentation process, but these automation improvements have not been made in all countries. In the United States, the Customs Service has developed the Automated Brokers Interface System and the Automated Export System. Canada has a computerized system called the Pre-Arrival Review Process for Canadian imports.

EXPORT LICENSE

No special authorization is needed to export, but the president of the United States is authorized to control exports for national security, foreign policy, and items in short supply. In addition, licensing by a federal agency having jurisdiction over a commodity can exercise licensing requirements for a given product, such as the Department of Agriculture having jurisdiction over grain.

The Department of Commerce issues two types of licenses: validated and general. The validated **export license** is required for commodities and destinations deemed important to national security, foreign policy, and items in short supply. A formal application for a license is required; after the authorized shipments are made, the license is returned to the Bureau of Export Administration.

If the commodities being exported do not require a validated license, the general license is needed. However, no actual general license is issued because U.S. law contains a blanket authorization for commodities and destinations not requiring a validated export license.

SALES DOCUMENTS

Three sales documents are generally used in international trade: a pro-forma invoice, a commercial invoice, and a consular invoice. All three contain essentially the same information: buyer, seller, product descriptions, payment terms, selling price, and other information requested by the buyer, bank, or importing country.

The **pro-forma invoice** is issued by the seller to acquaint the importer and import government authorities with details of the shipment. It may be required to obtain necessary foreign exchange information and/or an import license or permit. The **commercial invoice,** issued by the seller, is a bill of sale for the goods sold to the buyer, a basis for determining shipment value and importing duty assessment, and a requirement for clearing goods through customs. The **consular invoice** is the same as the commercial invoice, except it is a special form prescribed by the importing country and it must be completed in the language of the importing country.

FINANCIAL DOCUMENTS

In the buyer–seller agreement, the credit extended by the seller to the buyer is delineated and takes the form of either a letter of credit or draft. The **letter of credit**, issued by the buyer's bank, is a guarantee by the buyer's bank to the seller that payment will be made if certain terms and conditions are met. These conditions include, for example, documentation, shipping date, time limits, and so on. If these conditions are not met, payment will be withheld.

The **draft** is credit extended by the seller directly to the buyer. It is a written order for a sum of money to be paid by the buyer on a certain date. Upon presentation of the draft to the buyer's bank, the buyer's bank collects the money from the buyer, releases the shipment documentation to permit the buyer to receive the shipment, and remits the money to the seller.

CUSTOMS DOCUMENTS

As noted earlier, each nation has a unique set of customs regulations governing the global trade. In the United States, two common customs documents are the shipper's export declaration and the certificate of origin. To assist in identifying commodities throughout the world, an international commodity classification system, the Harmonized System, is used.

The **shipper's export declaration** is issued by the seller and acts to control the export of restricted goods (implements of war, high-level technology, etc.) and to provide statistics regarding exporting activity. The **certificate of origin** is used to certify the country of origin of the commodities and is particularly important for trade between countries that have special import duty treaties. For example, NAFTA provides lower import duties for commodities originating in the United States, Canada, or Mexico and destined for one of the respective countries.

TRANSPORTATION DOCUMENTS

As with domestic shipments, international shipments require a bill of lading. The **bill of lading** acts as a contract of carriage and a receipt for the goods, and provides carrier delivery instructions. For water shipments, an ocean bill of lading is used; an airway bill is used for air carrier shipments.

In addition to the bill of lading, most international shipments require a packing list that provides detailed information of the package contents, dimension, and weight. A dock receipt is issued by a water carrier when the goods arrive at the dock, but are not loaded onto the ship immediately; this transfers accountability, or liability, from the domestic carrier to the international carrier.

Transportation

The transportation elements include the selection of carriers, ports/gateways, intermediaries, and the acquisition of insurance. At least three carriers are involved in an international shipment: a domestic, an international, and a foreign carrier. The international transportation manager must select a domestic carrier to move the goods from the seller's door to the port or gateway, an international carrier to move it between countries, and a foreign carrier to move it to its final destination in the importing country. The responsibility for carrier selection is delineated by the INCOTERMS.

Selection of the port or gateway involves consideration of handling, carrier availability, handling equipment availability, convenience, frequency of damage, and freight rates. Cargo insurance is usually purchased for international shipments because of the complexity of international claim settlement associated with multinational laws. The buyer–seller agreement defines whether the buyer or seller is responsible for securing cargo liability insurance.

As can been seen from the above discussion of the global transportation process, it is much more complex than the domestic counterpart. The global process involves more documentation and regulations as well as terms of sale.

Summary

- The domestic transportation management process includes shipment source, shipment analysis, carrier scheduling, load tendering, documentation, shipment monitoring, and postdelivery maintenance.
- The shipment source considers the customer order, purchase order, and terms of sale.
- The domestic FOB term of sale delineates who has the responsibility for selecting and routing the carrier, who pays the carrier's freight bill, and where title to the goods passes.
- Shipment analysis examines the customer shipping requirements, service levels, and packaging needs.
- Rate analysis is the activity that compares alternative methods of shipping and the corresponding freight cost and service levels.
- Consolidation is the practice of combining smaller shipments into a larger shipment in order to realize lower freight rates. Zone skipping is an example of consolidation.
- Carriers are scheduled at the local level by using core carriers, routing guides, an approved carrier list, and intermediaries.
- Shippers use intermediaries such as brokers and intermodal marketing companies to obtain carriers when they experience spikes in demand for transportation or to realize lower freight costs.
- The load-tendering function involves contacting carriers to cover the load, arranging for pickup appointments, loading the vehicle, and preparation of the documentation.
- The bill of lading is a contract, receipt for the goods tendered to the carrier, and for an order bill of lading, a certificate of title to the goods.
- The bill of lading contract states the carrier is liable as a common carrier for all loss and damage with the exception of act of God, act of a public enemy, act of the shipper, act of public authority, and inherent nature of the goods.
- Shipment monitoring includes tracing and expediting a shipment and then the communication of this information to the customer and/or vendor.
- Postdelivery maintenance includes the proof of delivery, claims processing, freight bill auditing, and performance measurement.

- The INCOTERMS are the terms of sale for global business and define the responsibilities of the buyer and seller regarding packing, transportation, customs clearance, and insurance, and where title passes to the buyer.
- Global documentation includes export licenses and sales, financial, customs, and transportation documents.
- The global transportation decision includes the selection of carriers to perform the transportation within the seller's country, within the buyer's country, and between the two countries.

Key Terms

bill of lading, 463
blanket purchase order, 455
common carrier liability, 464
consolidation, 457
core carrier, 459
draft, 476
expediting, 466
export license, 475
FOB term of sale, 467
freight bill auditing, 470
freight claim, 467
INCOTERMS, 471
intermediaries, 461
intermodal marketing company, 461
letter of credit, 476
load tendering, 462
proof of delivery, 467
routing guide, 460
tracing, 466
weight break, 457
zone skipping, 458

Study Questions

1. Determine the buyer and seller responsibilities for carrier selection, freight bill payment, and filing of damage claims with the following domestic terms of sale: FOB-delivered; FOB-shipping dock; FOB-college book store.
2. The TieDie Shirt Company has a 12 × 12 × 12-inch box of college sweatshirts weighing 55 pounds going from State College, Pennsylvania (zip, 16802) to Toledo, Ohio (zip, 43615). The sweatshirts have a total value of $450.00 per box. Using the Internet, determine the cost of shipping this box via FedEx, UPS, and USPS for next-day and second-day delivery.
3. Determine the weight break for the following rate: LTL = $2.00 per cwt; TL = $1.25 per cwt, with a minimum weight of 30,000 pounds. What is the correct charge for a 19,000-pound shipment?
4. Explain zone-skipping consolidation.
5. Discuss the advantages and disadvantages of the core carrier, routing guide, and approved carrier list methods of carrier scheduling.
6. What is the role of the bill of lading in the transportation management process?
7. Discuss the different levels of carrier liability for shipment damage.
8. What are the cost and service criteria used to measure transportation performance and how do these criteria impact the shipper, customer, or vendor?
9. Explain the role of the INCOTERMS in the global transportation process and show the impact on a buyer of the ExWorks versus the Delivered Duty Paid INCOTERMS.
10. There are more documents required for a global shipment than a domestic shipment. Explain.

Notes

1. This section is based on the material found in John J. Coyle, Edward J. Bardi, and C. John Langley, *The Management of Business Logistics*, 7th ed., Mason, OH: South-Western, 2003, pp. 387–390.

Suggested Readings

Augello, William J. *Transportation, Logistic and the Law.* Huntington, NY: Transportation Consumer Protection Council, Inc., 2001.

Bradley, Peter. "How Far Can You See?" *Logistics Management*, September 2002, pp. 27–34.

Buckley, James J., and Lane C. Kendall. *The Business of Shipping*, 7th ed., Centerville, MD: Cornell Maritime Press, 2001.

Crum, Michael, and Paula C. Morrow. "The Influence of Carrier Scheduling Practices on Truck Driver Fatigue," *Transportation Journal*, Vol. 42, No. 1, 2002, pp. 20–41.

Forsyth, Gordon. "Zone-skippers," *American Shipper*, June 1999, pp. 77–79.

Giermanski, James R. "Dotting the i's and Crossing the Seas," *Logistics Management*, October 2000, pp. 101–106.

Gooley, Toby B. "8 Ways to Shrink Your Parcel Costs," *Logistics Management*, January 2003, pp. 43–46.

Kent, John L., R. Stephen Parker, and Robert H. Luke. "An Empirical Examination of Shipper Perceptions of Service-Selection Attributes in Five Truckload Industry Segments," *Transportation Journal*, Vol. 41, No. 1, 2001, pp. 27–36.

O'Reilly, Joseph. "Routing Guides: Inside the Matrix," *Inbound Logistics*, November 2002, pp. 57–58.

Wood, Donald F., and R. S. Nelson. "Industrial Transportation Management: What's New?" *Transportation Journal*, Vol. 39, No. 2, 2001, pp. 26–30.

Case 13-1

Rocket Electrical Parts, Inc.

Tom Grosserman, transportation manager of Rocket Electrical Parts, Inc. (RET), could not believe what he was reading. The CBC Freight Auditors' report of RET's 2004 freight bills uncovered overcharges of $1,000,000, or approximately 10 percent of the company's annual freight bill of $10,500,000. Tom had an idea that the carriers, mostly motor carriers, were overcharging RET, but the magnitude of the overcharge was beyond his expectations of human error.

RET is a wholesaler of electrical parts sold to industrial, commercial, and residential customers. In 2004 RET used 350 carriers, mostly LTL carriers because the shipments were generally small (under 1,000 pounds). RET's market area includes 20 Midwestern states. The company's annual sales increased an average of 10 percent from 2000 when it landed contracts with three national home-improvement retailers. Sales for 2004 were $20,000,000, and transportation expenditures were 5.25 percent of sales.

The rapid growth and the complexity of the sales to the individual retail outlets of the national home-improvement chains covered up some of the overcharge problems discovered by CBC Freight Auditors. For 2004 RET paid 50,000 freight bills and did a very cursory pre-audit of the freight bills before payment. Tom had relied on the postaudit to catch overcharges, but during 2004 the postaudit was not performed until January 2005, so the carriers had the free use of RET's money for the year.

The CBC report found that 25 percent of the freight bills had overcharged RET. The types of overcharges on these freight bills included the following:

- 10 percent were simple math errors
- 25 percent were duplicate bills (the original was paid twice)
- 50 percent did not apply the discounted LTL rate—RET paid the full LTL rate
- 15 percent charged for accessoral charges that were not requested

Given the magnitude of the freight overcharge issue, Tom was preparing, for top management, a plan to reduce paying the carrier more than is due. Tom has asked for your input in developing this plan.

Case Questions

1. What strategic steps would you recommend Tom implement to reduce the potential overcharges?
2. What pre-audit and postaudit recommendations would you make to Tom?
3. What should Tom do with the carriers who overcharged RET?

Case 13-2

Dollar Discounters

Dollar Discounters (DD) is a discount clothing retailer with stores located throughout the United States. DD sources the majority of its purchases from off-shore suppliers. During 2004 DD purchased 97 percent of its clothing from foreign suppliers. The vast majority of the suppliers are located in the Far East, and the clothing is shipped in containers via ocean carriers to the West Coast of the United States.

The transportation process for DD includes using a consolidator at the production location, truck or rail movement of the container to the foreign port, ocean carrier from the Far East to the West Coast, truck from the U.S. port to a distribution in Reno, Nevada, and truck and air from the Reno distribution center to the stores. Air transportation is used sparingly and only for hot-selling items that are seasonal or trendy.

During the past months DD has experienced delayed shipments. DD knows the shipment departed the supplier's dock, but it can not determine where the container is in the supply chain. On some occasions DD "found" the container sitting in the consolidators yard or at the foreign port. For seasonal and trendy items this delay means lost sales and nonsaleable merchandise.

DD's management has heard of global transportation providers that have state-of-the-art tracking systems that can provide shipment visibility throughout the supply chain. You have been asked to research these global tracking systems and report to top management.

Case Questions

1. Using the Internet, select three global transportation providers (ocean carriers, freight forwarders, or ports) and document the tracking systems available from each.

2. Compare the advantages and disadvantages of each company's system.
3. Make a recommendation along with your rationale for which company tracking system DD should use.

Appendix A

Selected Transportation Publications

Air Cargo World
(800) 717-0063

American Mover
703-683-7410

Air Force Journal of Logistics
(334) 416-4087

American Shipper
(800) 874-6422

Army Logistician
(804) 765-4761

Astralog
(404) 524-3555

Business Trucking
(888) 665-9887

Business Week
(212) 512-2511

Canadian Transportation & Logistics Magazine
(416) 442-2102

Commercial Carrier Journal
(610) 964-4514

Council of Logistics Management Annual Conference Proceedings
(630) 574-0985

Defense Transportation Journal
(703) 751-5011

Exporter Magazine
(212) 587-1340

Fleet Owner McGraw-Hill
(203) 358-9900

Food Logistics Magazine
(212) 979-4825

Global Logistics & Supply Chain Strategies
(516) 829-9210

Grocery Headquarters
(312) 654-2300

Harvard Business Review
(800) 274-3214

Heavy Duty Trucking
(949) 261-1636

Inbound Logistics
(212) 629-1560

Industrial Distribution
(617) 964-3030

Industry Week
(800) 326-4146

Intermodal Shipping
(770) 396-9676

International Journal of Physical Distribution and Logistics Management
(813) 974-6173

JOC Week
(800) 331-1341

Journal of Business Logistics
(630) 574-0985

Journal of Supply Chain Management
(480) 752-6276

Logistics Management and Distribution Report **(formerly *Traffic Management;* merged with *Distribution* magazine)**
(800) 662-7776

Logistics and Transportation Review
(888) 437-4636

Modern Bulk Transporter
(713) 523-8124

Parcel Shipping and Distribution
(608) 241-8777

Progressive Railroading
(414) 228-7701

Railway Age
(212) 620-7233

Refrigerated Transporter
(800) 441-0294

Traffic World
(800) 331-1341

Transport Topics
(800) 517-7370

Transportation Journal
(717) 748-8515

Wall Street Journal
(800) 221-1940

World Trade
(847) 291-5224

World Wide Shipping/WWS
(813) 920-4788

Appendix B

Transportation-Related Associations

Air Transport Association of America
1301 Pennsylvania Avenue, NW
Washington, DC 20004
(202) 626-4000

American Association of Port Authorities
1010 Duke Street
Alexandria, VA 22314
(703) 684-5700

American Institute for Shippers' Associations, Inc.
P.O. Box 33457
Washington, DC 20033
(202) 628-0933

American Society of Transportation & Logistics, Inc. (AST & L)
1700 N. Moore Street, Suite 1900
Arlington, VA 22209
(703) 524-5011

American Trucking Associations, Inc. (ATA)
2200 Mill Road
Alexandria, VA 22314
(703) 838-7935

Association of American Railroads
50 F Street, NW
Washington, DC 20001
(202) 639-2373

Canadian Industrial Transportation Association
75 Albert Street, Suite 1002
Ottawa, ON Canada M3C K1P 5E7
(613) 568-2482

Canadian Institute of Traffic & Transportation
10 King Street East, Suite 400
Toronto, ON Canada M5C 1C3
(416) 363-5698

Containerization & Intermodal Institute
195 Fairfield Avenue, Suite 4D
West Caldwell, NJ 07006
(973) 226-0460

Council of Supply Chain Management Professionals (formerly Council of Logistics Management (CLM))
2805 Butterfield Road, Suite 200
Oak Brook, IL 60523
(630) 574-0985

Delta Nu Alpha
530 Church Street, Suite 300
Nashville, TN 37219
(605) 251-0933

Eno Transportation Foundation, Inc.
44211 Statestone Court
Landsdowne, VA 22075
(703) 729-7200

Express Carriers Association
P.O. Box 4307
Bethlehem, PA 18048
(610) 740-5857

Inland Rivers, Ports, & Terminals, Inc.
P.O. Box 4363
Jackson, MS 39202
(601) 352-4778

The International Air Cargo Association
P.O. Box 661510
Miami, FL 33266
(786) 265-7011

Material Handling Industry of America
8720 Red Oak Boulevard, Suite 210
Charlotte, NC 28217
(704) 676-1190

National Air Transportation
Association, Inc.
4226 King Street
Alexandria, VA 22302
(703) 645-9000

National Customs Brokers and Forwarders
of America, Inc.
1200 18th Street, NW #901
Washington, DC 20036
(202) 466-0222

National Defense Transportation
Association (NDTA)
50 South Pickett Street, Suite 220
Alexandria, VA 22304-3008
(703) 751-5011

The National Industrial Transportation
League (NITL)
1700 N. Moore Street, Suite 1900
Arlington, VA 22209-1904
(703) 524-5011

National Private Truck Council (NPTC)
2200 Mill Road
Alexandria, VA 22314
(703) 683-1300

National Safety Council
1121 Spring Lake Drive
Itasca, IL 60143-3201
(630) 285-1121

National Small Shipments Traffic
Conference (NASSTRAC)
499 S. Capitol Street, SW
Washington, DC 20003
(202) 484-9188

Transportation Consumer Protection
Council, Inc.
120 Main Street
Huntington, NY 11743
(613) 549-8984

Transportation Intermediaries
Association (TIA)
3601 Eisenhower Avenue, Suite 110
Alexandria, VA 22304
(703) 317-2140

Transportation Research Board (TRB)
Transportation Research Board
2100 Constitution Avenue, NW
Washington, DC 20418
(202) 334-2934

Warehouse Educaton and Research
Council
1100 Jorie Boulevard, Suite 170
Oak Brook, IL 60523-4413
(630) 990-0256

Glossary

accessibility The ability of the carrier to provide service between the origin and destination. It also refers to the carrier's ability to serve the shipper or consignee's place of business. For example, in order to ship and receive a railcar, both the origin and destination must have a side track.

agency tariff A publication by a rate bureau that contains rates for many carriers. This publication is also called a "bureau tariff."

aggregate demand The total effective demand for the nation's output of goods and services. This can also refer to the sum of individual demands for a mode's or carrier's services.

air carrier A transportation firm that operates aircraft for the transportation of passengers or freight as a "common carrier."

air cargo Freight that is moved by air transportation.

air taxi An exempt for-hire air carrier that will fly anywhere on demand; air taxis are restricted to a maximum payload and passenger capacity per plane.

air traffic control system The method by which aircraft traffic is controlled in the air so that planes are separated by altitude and distance for safety. This system is administered by the Federal Aviation Agency.

Airport and Airway Trust Fund A federal fund that collects passenger ticket taxes and disburses those funds for airport facilities.

all-cargo carrier An air carrier that transports cargo only.

Amtrak A quasi-governmental agency that provides interstate rail passenger service.

any-quantity (AQ) rate A rate that applies to any size shipment tendered to a carrier; no discount rate is available for large shipments.

auditing A methodical examination of carrier freight bills to determine correct charges.

balance load This occurs when the shipper provides the carrier with round-trip loads to avoid an empty backhaul.

bareboat charter A long-term lease or charter where the lessee provides the crew, fuel, and supplies and operates the ship. The lessor provides only the ship.

barge The cargo-carrying vehicle that inland water carriers primarily use. Basic barges have open tops, but there are covered barges for both dry and liquid cargoes.

Bill of Lading A transportation document that is the contract of carriage between the shipper and the carrier; it provides a receipt for the goods tendered to the carrier, the "terms and conditions of sale" between the carrier and shipper, and the evidence of who has title to the goods while in transit.

blanket rate A rate that does not increase according to the distance a commodity is shipped.

boxcar An enclosed railcar, typically 40- to 50-feet long, used for packaged freight and some bulk commodities.

bracing Supports used to secure a shipment inside a carrier's vehicle to prevent damage.

break-bulk Ocean cargo that is not containerized but must be handled manually into and out of a ship.

broker An intermediary or "third party" who represents either the shipper or the carrier and seeks to match freight with empty trucks. The broker's fee can be included in the freight charges or collected separately. A broker is not considered a carrier for legal purposes.

bundle of services A grouping of services offered by a carrier that may be integrated into a total package. An example would be a carrier that offers line-haul, sorting, and segregating with local delivery to specific customers.

business logistics The process of planning, implementing, and controlling the efficient, effective flow and storage of goods, services, and related information from the point of origin to the point of consumption for the purpose of conforming to customer requirements. Note that this definition includes inbound, outbound, internal, and external movements.

cabotage A federal law that requires coastal and intercoastal traffic to be carried in U.S.-built and -registered ships.

capability The ability of a carrier to provide service or multiple services to the shipper to meet the specific requirements of that customer.

cargo preference A federal law requiring that at least 50 percent of certain U.S. government-owned or -sponsored cargo move on U.S. flag–registered vessels.

carload A full weight or size shipment placed into or on a railcar. This term also refers to rates that apply to a specific minimum weight for railcar shipments.

Carmack Act A law that defines the carrier's legal obligations to the owner of goods if they are lost or damaged while in the possession of a carrier. Recovery under the Carmack Act is subject to the terms contained in the bill of lading contract.

carriage and insurance paid to This term of sale defines the seller's obligations to pay transportation and insurance for a shipment to a specific location. At that location, the responsibility passes to the buyer.

carriage paid to This term of sale defines the seller's obligations to pay transportation for a shipment to a specific location. At that location, the responsibility passes to the buyer.

carrier A firm that transports goods or people.

carrier liability A common carrier is liable for all shipment loss, damage, and delay with the exception of that caused by act of God, act of a public enemy, act of a public authority, act of the shipper, and the goods' inherent nature.

carrying capacity The capability of a transport vehicle to carry or transport shipments of a particular weight or size in relation to the shipper's requirements. As an example, a 53-foot trailer could carry 48,000 pounds or a shipment of 3,392 cubic feet.

cash flow Funds or money as it passes from buyer to seller during a commercial transaction and is sometimes measured in a time relationship.

certificate of origin A legal document that verifies the country where a particular product originated. This certificate must often accompany the shipment so the importing country can determine if it complies with that country's laws.

certificate of public convenience and necessity The grant of operating authority that common carriers receive. A carrier must prove that a public need exists and that the carrier is fit, willing, and able to provide the needed service. The certificate may specify the commodities the carrier may haul, the area it may serve, and the routes it may use.

chock A wedge, usually made of hard rubber or steel, that is firmly placed under the wheel of a trailer, truck, or boxcar to stop it from rolling.

city driver A motor carrier driver who drives a local route as opposed to a long-distance, intercity route.

CL Carload rail service requiring shippers to meet minimum weight.

claim A demand for payment made to a carrier for loss or damage to a shipment or the refund of alleged overpayment of freight charges.

class I carrier A railroad with an annual income over $256 million or a motor carrier with an annual income over $10 million.

class II carrier A railroad with an annual income less than $256 million but more than $20.5 million, or a motor carrier with an annual income less than $10 million but more than $3 million.

class III carrier A motor carrier with an annual income less than $3 million.

class rate A rate constructed from a classification and a uniform distance system. A class rate is available for any product between any two points.

classification An alphabetical listing of commodities, the class or rating into which the commodity is placed, and the minimum weight necessary for the rate discount; used in the class rate structure.

classification yard A railroad terminal area where railcars are grouped together to form train units.

Clayton Act A law that strengthened the Sherman Anti-Trust Act and specifically described some business practices as violations of the law. This was done to counter some practices that were used to avoid the Sherman Anti-Trust Act.

Coast Guard A military unit attached to the Department of Transportation. The Coast Guard is charged with certain law enforcement tasks related to protecting the shores of the United States and the usage of waters both domestically and along the coasts. The Coast Guard is also tasked with safety standards for commercial users, search and rescue missions on inland and coastal waters, and small boat safety programs.

coastal carriers Water carriers that provide service along coasts serving ports on the Atlantic or Pacific Oceans or on the Gulf of Mexico.

COFC (container on flatcar) A type of rail shipment where only the container or "box" is loaded on the flatcar. The chassis with the wheels and landing gear is only used to carry the container to and from the railroad.

commercial invoice A specifically prepared invoice for the merchandise contained in a shipment. The document is often required for international shipments.

commercial zone The area surrounding a city or town to which rate carriers quote for the city or town also apply; the ICC defines the area.

commodities clause A clause that prohibits railroads from hauling commodities that they produced, mined, owned, or had an interest in.

commodity code A code describing a commodity or group of commodities pertaining to goods classification. This code can be a carrier tariff or regulating in nature.

commodity rate A rate for a specific commodity and its origin–destination.

common carrier A transportation company that provides freight and/or passenger service to any who seek its services.

common carriers' duties Common carriers must serve, deliver, charge reasonable rates, and not discriminate.

common cost A cost that a company cannot directly assign to particular segments of the business; a cost that the company incurs for the business as a whole.

common law A legal system based on court decisions and precedents that recognizes past decisions when deciding current legal questions. The legal system of the United States is based on common law along with civil or statuary law.

commuter air carrier An exempt for-hire air carrier that publishes a time schedule on specific routes; a special type of air taxi.

consignee The receiver of a freight shipment, usually the buyer.

consignment Goods shipped to an agent/customer when an actual purchase has not transpired until the consignee agrees to release the consigned goods for production and payment.

consignor The sender of a freight shipment, usually the seller.

consolidation Collecting smaller shipments to form a larger quantity in order to realize lower transportation rates.

consular invoice A specifically prepared invoice that is prescribed by the importing country for the merchandise contained in a shipment. The invoice will be written in the language of the importing country and may be required to be signed by an employee of the government of the nation to which the shipment is destined.

container A specific type of "box" into which freight is loaded before the shipment is given to the carrier. The container can be rectangular such as those used for rail and ocean shipments or can be shaped to fit the transport vehicle, such as an aircraft. The container avoids the need for the carrier to handle individual parts of the shipment.

container rate A rate that applies only when the shipment is placed into a container prior to tendering the shipment to the carrier. This rate recognizes that the shipment is much more easily handled by the carrier.

contract carrier A for-hire carrier that does not serve the general public but serves shippers with whom the carrier has a continuing contract.

contract logistics Third-party logistics relationship where a contract exists between a provider of third-party logistics service and client.

cooperative association A group of individuals or companies who band together to purchase goods or services jointly and achieve price incentives based on the combined purchasing power of the members. Typically, cooperatives are chartered as not-for-profit and require that the participant be members.

core competency The set of skills, technologies, and processes that provide the basics for what a company does well.

cost and freight A term of sale indicating that the price includes both the cost of the goods and the freight expense necessary to transport it to the buyer.

cost, insurance, and freight A term of sale indicating that the price includes the cost of the goods, insurance premiums necessary to protect the cargo, and the freight expense necessary to transport it to the buyer.

cost of lost sales The income that is lost when a customer chooses to purchase a product or service from another firm. This could be due to the product not being available when and where needed or the service did not meet the requirements of the buyer.

cost-of-service pricing A method used by carriers when they seek to only cover the actual expense of providing that specific service. Such pricing does not usually cover shared or overhead costs.

courier service A fast, door-to-door service for high-valued goods and documents; firms usually limit service to shipments weighing 50 pounds or less.

cross-docking The movement of goods directly from receiving dock to shipping dock to eliminate storage expense.

currency adjustment factor (CAF) An added charge assessed by water carriers for currency value changes.

customer attitude The customer's perception of the service or product provider.

customer filter The perception of the customer of the quality of the service that is "filtered" or influenced by more factors than just the quality of the specific offering.

customer perception The way in which the customer views or perceives the service offering that will influence their decision to buy or use the service. This view could be based on judgment or past experience.

customs broker A firm that represents importers/exporters in dealings with customs. Normally responsible for obtaining and submitting all documents for clearing merchandise through customs, arranging inland transport, and paying all charges related to these functions.

delivered at frontier A term of sale that indicates the title will pass from the buyer and seller. It also indicates to what extent freight and other expenses will be paid by the seller.

delivered duty paid A term of sale that indicates that the seller will pay any import duties or taxes levied by the importer's home country.

delivered duty unpaid A term of sale that indicates that the seller will not pay any import duties or taxes.

delivered ex quay A term of sale that indicates shipment will be delivered to the buyer at the seller's expense on the "quay" or pier alongside the ship. The seller will pay all expenses to that point including any cost associated with unloading the consignment from the ship.

delivered ex ship A term of sale that indicates shipment will be delivered to the buyer at the seller's expense alongside the ship. The seller will pay all expenses to that point, including any cost associated with unloading the consignment from the ship.

demand elasticity The amount that the demand for a product or service will change by the changes in price and the availability of substitutes.

demurrage The charge a railroad assesses for a shipper or receiver holding a car beyond the free time the railroad allows for loading (24 hours) or unloading (48 hours).

dedicated contract carriage A third-party service that dictates equipment (vehicles) and drivers to a single customer for its exclusive use on a contractual basis.

density A physical characteristic measuring a commodity's mass per unit volume or pounds per cubic foot; it is an important factor in rate making because density affects the utilization of a carrier's vehicle.

density rate A rate based upon the density and shipment weight.

Department of Transportation The cabinet-level branch of the U.S. government responsible for various aspects of transportation policy, safety, and, in some cases, economic regulation for all carriers and modes.

derived demand The demand for a product's transportation is derived from the product's demand at some location.

detention The charge a motor carrier assesses when a shipper or receiver holds a truck or trailer beyond the free time the carrier allows for loading or unloading.

dispatching The carrier activities involved with controlling equipment; it involves arranging for fuel, drivers, crews, equipment, and terminal space.

diversion A carrier service that permits a shipper to change the consignee and/or destination while the shipment is en route and to still pay the through rate from origin to final destination.

dock receipt A receipt that indicates a domestic carrier has delivered an export shipment to a steamship company.

domestic trunk line carrier A classification for air carriers that operate between major population centers. These carriers are now classified as major carriers.

double bottoms A motor carrier operation that involves one tractor pulling two trailers.

draft A type of bank transaction that insures payment for goods. It is a written order for a sum of money to be paid by the buyer to the seller upon presentation of the document to the buyer's bank.

drayage A motor carrier that operates locally, providing pickup and delivery service.

driving time regulations U.S. Department of Transportation rules that limit the maximum time a driver may drive in interstate commerce; the rules prescribe both daily and weekly maximums.

economic deregulation The removal of governmentally enforced price and entry controls in the transportation industry. The "free market" will provide the necessary competition to ensure competitive prices and services.

evergreen contract A contract that does not have a specified expiration date.

ex works The price that the seller quotes applies only at the point of origin. The buyer takes possession of the shipment at the point of origin and bears all costs and risks associated with transporting the goods to the final destination.

exception rate A deviation from the class rate; changes (exceptions) made to the classification.

exchange Electronic marketplace that facilitates buying and selling of products and services.

exclusive patronage agreements A shipper agrees to use only a conference member's liner firm in return for a 10- to 15-percent rate reduction.

exclusive use Vehicles that a carrier assigns to a specific shipper for its exclusive use.

exempt carrier A for-hire carrier that is exempt from economic regulations.

expediting Determining where an in-transit shipment is and attempting to speed up its delivery.

extent of market This relates to the extent of the size of a market that a firm may serve on a competitive basis. Cost of the product and freight will determine how far from its base a firm may compete effectively.

Federal Aviation Administration The federal agency within the Department of Transportaion that is responsible for regulating air safety, promoting development of air commerce, and controlling navigable air space.

Federal Energy Regulatory Commission The federal agency that oversees rates and practices of pipeline operators and is part of the Department of Energy.

Federal Highway Administration The federal agency that oversees motor carrier safety including hours of services, driver qualifications, and vehicle size and weight, as well as overall operation and development of the national highway system. This agency is part of the Department of Transportation.

Federal Highway Trust Fund A fund that receives federally collected fuel taxes used for highway construction and upkeep.

Federal Maritime Commission The federal agency that regulates international rates, practices, agreements, and services of common carrier water carriers.

Federal Railroad Administration The federal agency that oversees railroad safety by establishing and enforcing rules and regulations. This agency is part of the Department of Transportation.

Federal Trade Commission The federal agency that administers the Sherman Anti-Trust Act and the Clayton Act. This agency does not have direct control over transportation.

feu Forty-foot equivalent unit, a standard-size intermodal container.

fixed costs Costs that do not fluctuate with the business volume in the short run.

flatbed A trailer without sides used for hauling machinery or other bulky items.

flatcar A railcar without sides, used for hauling machinery.

FOB A term of sale defining who is to incur transportation charges for the shipment, who is to control the shipment movement, or where title to the goods passes to the buyer; it originally meant "free on board ship."

for-hire carrier A carrier that provides transportation service to the public on a fee basis.

foreign trade zone (FTZ) An area or zone set aside at or near a port or airport, under the control of the U.S. Customs Service, for the holding of goods duty-free, pending customs clearance.

free alongside ship A term of sale that indicates that the buyer will pay all freight and insurance charges necessary to bring the consignment to the side of ship but will not cover the cost of loading.

freight all kinds A pricing method where the carrier establishes a rate that will apply on any cargo loaded in the carrier's vehicle regardless of the nature of the freight.

freight bill The carrier's invoice for a freight shipment's transportation charges.

freight flows The geographic direction in which freight "flows" or moves from producing locations to areas of consumption.

freight forwarder A carrier that collects small shipments from shippers, consolidates the small shipments, and uses a basic mode to transport these consolidated shipments to a consignee destination.

freight transportation The movement of goods or products from the producer or manufacturer to the user or customer.

fronthaul The first half of a round-trip move from origin to destination. The opposite is "backhaul," which is the return of the equipment to its origin point.

fully allocated cost The variable cost associated with a particular output unit plus a common cost allocation.

gathering lines Oil pipelines that bring oil from the oil well to storage areas.

general cargo rate A pricing method where the carrier establishes a rate that will apply on any cargo loaded in the carrier's ship, regardless of the nature of the freight.

general-commodities carrier A common motor carrier that has operating authority to transport general commodities, or all commodities not listed as special commodities.

globalization Recognition that commercial activity now spans the world and that many firms buy and sell throughout the world.

gondola A railcar with a flat platform and sides 3- to 5-feet high, used for top-loading long, heavy items.

gross weight The total weight of the vehicle and the payload of freight or passengers.

harmonized commodity description and coding system (Harmonized Code) An international classification system that assigns identification numbers to specific products. The coding system ensures that all parties in international trade use a consistent classification for the purposes of documentation, statistical control, and duty assessment.

hazardous materials Materials that the Department of Transportation has determined to be a risk to health, safety, and property; includes items such as explosives, flammable liquids, poisons, corrosive liquids, and radioactive material.

headhaul The first half of a round-trip move from origin to destination. The opposite is "backhaul," which is the return of the equipment to its origin point.

Highway Trust Fund A fund into which highway users (carriers and automobile operators) pay; the fund pays for federal government's highway construction share.

highway use taxes Taxes that federal and state governments assess against highway users (the fuel tax is an example). The government uses the use tax money to pay for the construction, maintenance, and policing of highways.

home-flag airline An airline owned or sponsored by the government of the country in which the carrier is based. Typically, only home-flag airlines are allowed to operate between airports within that country. This prevents foreign carriers from serving domestic locations.

hopper cars Railcars that permit top-loading and bottom-unloading of bulk commodities; some hopper cars have permanent tops with hatches to provide protection against the elements

hub A central location to which traffic from many cities is directed and from which traffic is fed to other areas.

hub airport An airport that serves as the focal point for the origin and termination of long-distance flights; flights from outlying areas meet connecting flights at the hub airport.

hump yard A railroad yard that uses an artificial hill or "hump" to assist in switching and classifying railcars. The cars are pushed up the hill by a switch engine, and at the top of the hill the railcar or group of railcars is uncoupled and rolls down hill to the correct track.

hundredweight (cwt) The pricing unit used in transportation; a hundredweight is equal to 100 pounds.

igloos Pallets and containers used in air transportation; the igloo shape fits the internal wall contours of a narrow-body airplane.

in-bond goods Goods held or transported in-bond under Customs control either until import duties or other charges are paid, or to avoid paying the duties or charges until a later date.

incentive rate A rate that induces the shipper to ship heavier volumes per shipment.

INCOTERMS International terms of sale developed by the International Chamber of Commerce to define sellers' and buyers' responsibilities.

independent action A carrier that is a rate bureau member may publish a rate that differs from the rate published by the rate bureau.

information flow The flow or movement of information or data between trading partners or companies that facilitates commerce or business.

inherent advantage The cost and service benefits of one mode compared with other modes.

integration The act of mixing various elements into a single group. An example would to combine transportation and warehousing to allow trade-offs between the two functions for the maximum benefit.

interchange The transfer of cargo and equipment from one carrier to another in a joint freight move.

intercoastal carriers Water carriers that transport freight between East and West Coast ports, usually by way of the Panama Canal.

interline Two or more motor carriers working together to haul a shipment to a destination. Carriers may interchange equipment, but usually they rehandle the shipment without transferring the equipment.

intermodal The combination of various modes to form a transportation movement. An example would be a truck picking up a trailer and taking it to a rail yard for movement by train to the destination city where another truck would take the trailer to the receiver's location. This term may also refer to competition between modes such as truck and rail.

intermodal marketing company (IMC) An intermediary that sells intermodal services to shippers.

internal water carriers Water carriers that operate over internal, navigable rivers such as the Mississippi, Ohio, and Missouri.

interstate commerce The transportation of persons or property between states; in the course of the movement, the shipment crosses a state boundary.

Interstate System The National System of Interstate and Defense Highways; limited-access roads connecting major population centers.

intramodal Movement within a modal- or carrier-type category. This could refer to shipments moved with more than one truck line. This term may also refer to competition within a mode, such as between trucking firms.

intrastate commerce The transportation of persons or property between points within a state. A shipment between two points within a state may be interstate if the shipment had a prior or subsequent move outside of the state and the shipper intended an interstate shipment at the time of shipment.

joint cost A common cost in cases where a company produces products in fixed proportions and the cost the company incurs to produce one product entails producing another; the backhaul is an example.

joint rate A rate over a route that requires two or more carriers to transport the shipment.

just-in-time (JIT) inventory system An inventory control system that attempts to reduce inventory levels by coordinating demand and supply to the point where the desired item arrives just in time for use.

Kanban system A just-in-time inventory system used by Japanese manufacturers.

lading The cargo carried in a transportation vehicle.

land bridge The movement of containers by ship-rail-ship on Japan-to-Europe moves; ships move containers to the U.S. Pacific Coast, rails move containers to an East Coast port, and ships deliver containers to Europe.

land grants Grants of land given to railroads to build tracks during their development stage.

landed cost The cost of the product at the source combined with the cost of transportation to the destination.

landed cost advantage The advantage one supplier has over another based on the lower transportation cost due to favorable proximity to the market.

Lardner's Law A finding by transportation economist Dionysius Lardner that when transportation cost is reduced, the area where the producer can compete is increased in a directly proportional basis.

LCL Less than carload rail service; less than container load.

letter of credit A document issued by the buyer's bank that guarantees payment to the seller if certain terms and conditions are met.

lighter-aboard ship A type of vessel that is capable of carrying barges or "lighters" onboard. This method of transportation allows a barge to be loaded on an inland waterway, transported to shipside, and taken to a harbor nearest destination, and the barge can then be taken to the destination by an inland waterway without having to rehandle any of the cargo.

line-haul shipment A shipment that moves between cities and over distances more than 100 to 150 miles in length.

liner service International water carriers that ply fixed routes on published schedules.

load factor A measure of operating efficiency used by air carriers to determine a plane's utilized capacity percentage or the number of passengers divided by the total number of seats.

loading allowance A reduced rate that carriers offer to shippers and/or consignees who load and/or unload LTL or AQ shipments.

local rate A rate published between two points served by one carrier.

local service carriers A classification of air carriers that operate between less-populated areas and major population centers. These carriers feed passengers into the major cities to connect with trunk (major) carriers. Local service carriers are now classified as national carriers.

logbook A daily record of the hours an interstate driver spends driving, off duty, sleeping in the berth, or on duty but not driving.

long ton 2,240 pounds.

loss and damage The risk to which goods are subjected during the transportation cycle. The shipment may be separated from its documentation and misdirected. Handling by the carrier as well as in-transit incidents can cause damage to or destruction of the shipment. This is a factor in mode and carrier selection as well as packaging and handling techniques. This risk factor also enters into the carrier's pricing decisions.

LTL shipment A less-than-truckload shipment, one weighing less than the minimum weight a company needs to use the lower truckload rate.

lumping The act of assisting a motor carrier owner–operator in the loading and unloading of property; quite commonly used in the food industry.

manifest A list of all cargoes that pertain to a specific shipment, grouping of shipments, or piece of equipment. Ocean carriers will prepare a manifest for each container.

maquiladora The name for a manufacturing facility established inside Mexico within close distance of the U.S. border. Materials are shipped from the United States, processed in the maquiladora plant, and returned to the United States. No customs duties or fees are accessed.

marginal cost The cost to produce one additional unit of output; the change in total variable cost resulting from a one-unit change in output.

marine insurance Insurance to protect against cargo loss and damage when shipping by water transportation.

marketing mix This consists of the four basic elements of marketing: product, price, place, and promotion. This is also known as the "four P's" of marketing.

measurement ton Forty cubic feet; used in water transportation rate making.

merger The combination of two or more carriers into one company that will own, manage, and operate the properties that previously operated separately.

micro-bridge A technique where ocean containers are transported to an interior destination, such as Chicago or St. Louis, on a through bill of lading and the cost of the inland move is included in the total price.

mileage allowance An allowance, based upon distance, that railroads give to shippers using private railcars.

mileage rate A rate or price based on the total mileage between the origin and destination including stop-offs, if any.

mini-bridge A technique where rail transportation is substituted for a portion of ocean transportation. As an example, a shipment from Japan to New York could move via the Panama Canal. The mini-bridge substitutes rail from a West Coast port to New York for the Panama Canal portion.

minimum level of safety A base requirement for all aspects of safe operation by a transportation firm, as prescribed by a government agency.

minimum weight The shipment weight the carrier's tariff specifies as the minimum weight required to use the TL or CL rate; the rate discount volume.

mobility The ease or difficulty with which people or goods are moved by the transportation network.

modal demand The request or demand made by users for service provided by a particular type of carrier or method of transport.

modal split The relative use that companies make of transportation modes; the statistics include ton-miles, passenger-miles, and revenue.

monopolistic The ability of very few suppliers to set a price well above cost by restricting supply or by limiting competition.

monopoly A market segment where there is only one supplier, such as public utilities.

multiple-car rate A railroad rate that is lower for shipping more than one carload at a time.

national carrier A for-hire certificated air carrier that has annual operating revenues of $75 million to $1 billion; the carrier usually operates between major population centers and areas of lesser population.

National Highway Traffic Safety Administration (NHTSA) This branch of the U.S. Department of Transportation is responsible for motor vehicle safety. In this role, NHTSA oversees design features, sets performance-related safety standards, and oversees governmental fuel economy standards.

National Motor Freight Classification (NMFC) A tariff that contains descriptions and classifications of commodities and rules for domestic movement by motor carriers in the United States.

National Transportation Safety Board This agency is responsible for investigating transportation-related accidents, regardless of whether or not the incident involved the private sector or a public carrier. They are responsible for recommending preventative measures to avoid future accidents.

nationalization Public ownership, financing, and operation of a business entity.

negotiations A set of discussions between two or more enterprises to determine the business relationship.

net weight The weight of the merchandise, unpacked, exclusive of any containers.

noncertificated carrier A for-hire air carrier that is exempt from economic regulation.

nonvessel-owning common carrier (NVOCC) A firm that consolidates and disperses international containers that originate at or are bound for inland ports.

North American Free Trade Agreement (NAFTA) An agreement signed by the United States, Canada, and Mexico to establish free trade between the three countries.

not-for-hire A carrier who does not hold itself to the general public to provide transportation service but rather transports for the owner firm exclusively.

oligopoly A shared monopoly where there are few suppliers and, in the case of transportation, entry barriers and cost are significant. Examples would be railroads and airlines.

operating expense The cost of providing a service by a carrier. This can include such factors as taxes, interest, and depreciation but not necessarily profit.

operating ratio A measure of operating efficiency defined as operating expenses/operating revenues $\times$ 100.

out-of-pocket cost The cost directly assignable to a particular unit of traffic, which a company would not have incurred if it had not performed the movement.

outsourcing Purchasing a logistics service from an outside firm, as opposed to performing it in-house.

over-the-road A motor carrier operation that reflects long-distance, intercity moves; the opposite of local operations.

owner–operator A trucking operation in which the truck's owner is also the driver.

pallet A platform device (about 4-feet square) used for moving and storing goods. A forklift truck is used to lift and move the loaded pallet.

passenger-mile A measure of output for passenger transportation that reflects the number of passengers transported and the distance traveled; a multiplication of passengers hauled and distance traveled.

peak demand The time period during which customers demand the greatest quantity.

peddle run A truck operation where many pickups or deliveries are made while the vehicle travels over a preset route.

peddle time This is the time that the driver is actively involved in either pickup or delivery.

penetration price A pricing strategy that sets a price designed to allow the supplier to enter a market where there is already established competition by slightly underpricing the existing firms.

per diem A payment rate one railroad makes to use another's cars.

per se violations A violation of the law that is, on its own, deemed to be harmful, regardless of its effect on the market or competitors.

pickup and delivery (PUD) The act of collecting freight from shippers or delivering freight to consignees.

piggyback A rail-truck service. A shipper loads a highway trailer, and a carrier drives it to a rail terminal and loads it on a rail flatcar; the railroad moves the trailer-on-flatcar combination to the destination terminal, where the carrier offloads the trailer and delivers it to the consignee.

police powers The United States' constitutionally granted right for the states to establish regulations to protect their citizens' health and welfare; truck weight and speed, length, and height laws are examples.

port authority A state or local government that owns, operates, or otherwise provides wharf, dock, and other terminal investments at ports.

prepaid A freight term that indicates that charges are to be paid by the shipper.

price elasticity The measurement factor by which the change in demand for a product or service is affected by the price.

price inelasticity An economic condition where the change or increase in the price of a product or service does not produce a proportional change in demand.

price-sensitive The relationship between prices and the demand for products or services.

primary trip markets The geographic area of interest where a carrier focuses its sales and operational effort.

private carrier A carrier that provides transportation service to the firm that owns or leases the vehicles and does not charge a fee. Private motor carriers may haul at a fee for wholly owned subsidiaries.

procurement Another term for purchasing that represents more than just the buying of a product or service.

product flows The course where goods move between the point of origin to the point of consumption.

pro-forma A document issued by the seller to acquaint the importer/buyer and the importing country's government authorities with the details of the shipment.

profit ratio The percentage of profit to sales—that is, profit divided by sales.

proof of delivery (POD) Information supplied by the carrier containing the name of the person who signed for the shipment, the time and date of delivery, and other shipment delivery-related information.

pure competition A condition in which there is a large number of sellers, the product or service is standardized and interchangeable, and no one seller can control the price or output. An example would be the LTL sector.

quality gap The difference in perception of a product or service between the buyer and seller.

rate basis number This number is an expression of the relative distance between an origin and destination. The number may be given in miles or another factor and will form one of the required inputs to develop a rate between the two points.

rate basis point The major shipping point in a local area; carriers consider all points in the local area to be the rate basis point.

rate bureau A carrier group that assembles to establish joint rates, to divide joint revenues and claim liabilities, and to publish tariffs. Rate bureaus have published single line rates, which were prohibited in 1984.

reasonable rate A rate that is high enough to cover the carrier's cost but not high enough to enable the carrier to realize monopolistic profits.

reefer A refrigerated vehicle.

regional carrier A for-hire air carrier, usually certificated, that has annual operating revenues of less than $75 million; the carrier usually operates within a particular region of the country.

Regional Rail Reorganization Act of 1973 A law passed by Congress in response to the bankruptcies of the Penn Central and other railroads. Conrail, which has since been purchased by the Norfolk Southern Railroad and CSX, was created from this law to operate the lines of six northeastern U.S. railroads.

regular-route carrier A motor carrier that is authorized to provide service over designated routes.

relative use A fee placed on the users of a service or facility to cover the cost of providing that service or facility.

relay terminal A motor carrier terminal that facilitates the substitution of one driver for another who has driven the maximum hours permitted.

released-value rates Rates based upon the shipment's value. The maximum carrier liability for damage is less than the full value, and in return the carrier offers a lower rate.

reliability A carrier selection criterion that considers the carrier transit time variation; the consistency of the transit time the carrier provides.

return on investment The amount of money realized or generated on an investment that flows back to the lenders. This is often used to gauge the worthiness of an investment by measuring the potential profits and the source of the capital.

roll-on roll-off ship A type of vessel that has ramps upon which vehicles can be driven directly into the hold of the ship. This type of vessel is often used to transport buses, trucks, construction machinery on wheels, and other types of wheeled shipments.

Rule of Efficiency The "Rule" refers to the fact that the most efficient transportation is in a continuous, straight line. There should be little circuitry or out-of-route operations with as few stops and starts as possible.

Rule of Reason An alleged violation of an anti-trust law where economic harm to competitors must be proved.

security The actions of a carrier to protect the goods entrusted to their care from loss or damage.

service The furnishing of an operation that fulfills the needs of the customer. This could be transporting a product or person to the desired location.

service contract A contract between a shipper and an ocean carrier or conference, in which the shipper makes a commitment to provide a minimum quantity of cargo over a fixed time period. The ocean carrier or conference also commits to a rate or rate schedule as well as a defined service level, such as space, transit item, port rotation, or other features.

service elasticity Assuming no significant price differential, the mode or carrier providing the best level of service as perceived by the user will be the first choice.

service inelasticity Price, rather than service, is the controlling factor. The customer's choice of supplier will be made on price, assuming the service offered also meets the requirements as perceived by the user.

Sherman Anti-Trust Act A body of law that restricts businesses' ability to dominate a market by engaging in certain practices. This includes price fixing and other free-market–constricting activities.

ship agent A liner company or tramp ship operator representative who facilitates ship arrival, clearance, loading and unloading, and fee payment while at a specific port.

ship broker A firm that serves as a go-between for the tramp ship owner and the chartering consignor or consignee.

shipper The party that tenders goods for transportation.

Shipping Act of 1984 A body of law that governs the pricing and services of ocean carriers operating between the United States and foreign countries.

shipper's agent A firm that primarily matches up small shipments, especially single-traffic piggyback loads, to permit shippers to use twin-trailer piggyback rates.

shipper's export declaration A document filed by the shipper/exporter or its agent with the government of the country in which the shipper/exporter resides. This form supplies the government with information about the shipment for statistical and control purposes.

shippers association A nonprofit, cooperative consolidator and distributor of shipments that member firms own or ship; acts in much the same way as a for-profit freight forwarder.

shipping instructions A document detailing the cargo and the requirements of its physical movement.

short-haul discrimination Charging more for a shorter haul than for a longer haul over the same route, in the same direction, and for the same commodity.

short ton Two thousand pounds.

side-by-side merger A merger of railroads whose lines operate in proximity of each other, rather than end to end.

skimming price A price set by a provider who seeks to attract a market that is more interested in quality, uniqueness, or status and is relatively unconcerned with price.

sleeper team Two drivers who operate a truck equipped with a sleeper berth; while one driver sleeps in the berth to accumulate mandatory off-duty time, the other driver operates the vehicle.

slip seat operation A motor carrier relay terminal operation in which a carrier substitutes one driver for another who has accumulated the maximum driving time hours.

special commodities carrier A common carrier trucking company that has authority to haul a special commodity; the 16 special commodities include household goods, petroleum products, and hazardous materials.

spot To move a trailer or boxcar into place for loading or unloading.

spur track A railroad track that connects a company's plant or warehouse with the railroad's track; the user bears the cost of the spur track and its maintenance.

statutory law This is based on the Roman legal system and refers to a body of law passed by legislative bodies.

steamship conferences Collective rate-making bodies for liner water carriers.

stem time The time consumed by a truck to reach its first delivery after leaving the terminal and the time consumed by the truck to return to the terminal after making its last pickup.

stockout A situation in which the items a customer orders are currently unavailable.

stockout cost The opportunity cost that companies associate with not having supply sufficient to meet demand.

stowability and handling The ease or difficulty experienced in loading, handling, and unloading freight. This factor influences the carrier's cost of providing a service and will be reflected in the price charged for the shipment. This is also two of the four factors considered when classifying freight.

strategic alliance Relationship in which two or more business organizations cooperate and willingly modify their business objectives and practices to achieve long-term objectives.

strategy A course of action, a scheme, or a principal idea through which an organization or individual hopes to accomplish a specific objective or goal. In other words, a strategy is designed to determine how someone is going to achieve something that has been identified as being important to future success.

sunk costs Costs that cannot be easily retrieved or may not be retrieved at all when liquidating a business. This includes investments in specific machinery or buildings.

supplemental carrier A for-hire air carrier having no time schedule or designated route; the carrier provides service under a charter or contract per plane per trip.

surcharge An add-on charge to the applicable charges; motor carriers have a fuel surcharge, and railroads can apply a surcharge to any joint rate that does not yield 110 percent of variable cost.

Surface Transportation Board The agency created under the Interstate Commerce Commission Termination (ICC) to replace the ICC and exercise economic jurisdiction of the modes of transportation.

switch engine A railroad engine that is used to move railcars short distances within a terminal and plant.

switching company A railroad that moves railcars short distances; switching companies connect two mainline railroads to facilitate through movement of a shipment's rail car for longhaul movement.

tactic Refers to an operational aspect that is necessary to support strategy. Tactics are more likely to involve daily short-run operations that help achieve the strategy that has been identified or agreed upon in the organization.

tandem A truck that has two drive axles or a trailer that has two axles.

tank cars Railcars designed to haul bulk liquid or gas commodities.

tank farm A large group of storage tanks, usually at the end of a pipeline, where liquid products are stored pending transfer to a tank truck or tankcars for further shipment.

tapering rate A rate that increases with distance but not in direct proportion to the distance the commodity is shipped.

tare weight The weight of the vehicle when it is empty.

tariff A publication that contains a carrier's rates, accessorial charges, and rules.

technology The systematic knowledge of a particular discipline or science.

tenders An offer to provide a minimum shipment size or volume in exchange for a price proposal from the carrier. This may also represent the minimum volume a carrier will accept or the least amount of money the carrier will accept for transportation of a specific shipment.

terminal delivery allowance A reduced rate that a carrier offers in return for the shipper or consignee tendering or picking up the freight at the carrier's terminal.

terms of sale The details or conditions of a transaction including details of the payment method, timing, legal obligations, freight terms, required documentation, insurance, responsibilities of the buyer and the seller, and when the buyer assumes risk for the shipment.

TEU Twenty-foot equivalent unit, a standard-size intermodal container.

…e price discrimination A situation …ller sets two or more different prices for …oups of buyers of essentially the same

… logistics provider (3PL) An external …t performs all or part of a company's …tions.

time charter A rental or long-term lease that includes both the vessel and crew and is for a specific length of time.

time-definite services Delivery is guaranteed on a specific day or at a certain time of day.

time/service rate A rail rate that is based upon transit time.

time utility A value created by having a good or service available for sale at the time there is demand for the good or service.

time value of money This relates to the value of money over the lifetime of a project. As inflation reduces the value or purchasing capability of a dollar over the life of a project, this must be taken into consideration when establishing an interest or discount rate for the borrowed funds.

TL (truckload) A shipment weighing the minimum weight or more. Carriers give a rate reduction for shipping a TL-size shipment.

TOFC (trailer on flatcar) A method where a highway trailer complete with wheels and chassis is loaded on a flatcar.

tracing Determining a shipment's location during the course of a move.

trade lane The combination of the origin and destination points.

traffic management The buying and controlling of transportation services for a shipper or consignee, or both.

tramp An international water carrier that has no fixed route or published schedule; a shipper charters a tramp ship for a particular voyage or a given time period.

transit privilege A carrier service that permits the shipper to stop the shipment in transit to perform a function that changes the commodity's physical characteristics, but to still pay the through rate.

transit time The total time that elapses between a shipment's pickup and its delivery.

transloading facility A facility where shipments can be transferred from one mode to another or within the same mode between carriers. This may be a rail-to-truck transfer or a situation where larger shipments are broken down for delivery to individual stores or consignees.

transportation The act of moving goods or people from an origin to a required destination. It also includes the creation of time and place utilities.

transportation interaction The relationship and business exchanges between the three primary groups involved in this area: the users, the providers, and the government.

transportation management system (TMS) Logistics tool used to improve management of a firm's transportation processes, both inbound and outbound. A TMS can help optimize the movements of freight into multiple facilities, assist in tracking the freight through the supply chain, and then manage the freight payment process to the user's carrier base.

travel agent A firm that provides passenger travel information; air, rail, and steamship ticketing; and hotel reservations. The carrier and hotel pay the travel agent a commission.

trunk lines Oil pipelines used for the long-distance movements of crude oil, refined oil, or other liquid products.

unit volume pricing This is a technique whereby the carrier sets its prices to utilize its capacity to the fullest. Multiple pickup discounts in the LTL area and multiple car rates in the railroad sector would be two examples.

unit train An entire, uninterrupted locomotive, car, and caboose movement between an origin and destination.

user charges Costs or fees that the user of a service or facility must pay to the party furnishing this service or facility. An example would be the landing fee an airline pays to an airport when one of its aircraft lands or takes off.

utility creation This refers to a form utility that results from production, time, and place utilities created by logistics.

value added The value added to the product or service through the utility created by the logistics function.

value creation Value is created when the performance quality meets or exceeds customer perceptions of logistics service.

value-of-service pricing Pricing according to the value of the product the company is transporting; third-degree price discrimination; demand-oriented pricing; charging what the traffic will bear.

variable cost A cost that fluctuates with the volume of business.

vehicle standards The requirements imposed by the National Highway Transportation Safety Administration for the design and manufacture of motor vehicles.

voyage charter A rental or term lease that includes both the vessel and crew and is for a specific trip.

waterway use tax A per-gallon tax assessed for barge carriers for waterway use.

weight break The shipment volume at which the LTL charges equal the TL charges at the minimum weight.

weight-losing raw material A raw material that loses weight in processing.

zone price The constant price of a product at all geographic locations within a zone.

Name Index

Subject Index

A

D

E

N

O

P

S

U

V